The Cambridge Handbook of Situated Cognition

Since its inception some fifty years ago, cognitive science has undergone a number of sea changes. Perhaps the best known is the development of connectionist models of cognition as alternatives to classical, symbol-based approaches. A more recent – and increasingly influential – trend is that of dynamical-systems-based, ecologically oriented models of the mind. Researchers suggest that a full understanding of the mind will require systematic study of the dynamics of interaction among mind, body, and world. Some argue that this new orientation calls for a revolutionary new metaphysics of mind, according to which mental states and processes, and even persons, literally extend into the environment.

The Cambridge Handbook of Situated Cognition is a state-of-the-art guide to this new movement in cognitive science. Each chapter tackles either a specific area of empirical research or a specific sector of the conceptual foundations underlying this research. The chapter authors are leading figures in the emerging interdisciplinary field of situated cognition, including representatives from philosophy, psychology, neuroscience, linguistics, and anthropology.

Philip Robbins received his A.B. from Harvard University and his Ph.D. from the University of Chicago. Before coming to the University of Missouri, he taught at the University of Vermont and Washington University in St. Louis.

Murat Aydede received his B.A. from Boğaziçi University in Istanbul and his Ph.D. from the University of Maryland at College Park. Before coming to the University of British Columbia, he taught at the University of Chicago and the University of Florida.

The Cambridge Handbook of
Situated Cognition

Edited by

PHILIP ROBBINS

University of Missouri–Columbia

MURAT AYDEDE

University of British Columbia

CAMBRIDGE
UNIVERSITY PRESS

CAMBRIDGE UNIVERSITY PRESS
Cambridge, New York, Melbourne, Madrid, Cape Town, Singapore, São Paulo, Delhi

Cambridge University Press
32 Avenue of the Americas, New York, NY 10013-2473, USA

www.cambridge.org
Information on this title: www.cambridge.org/9780521612869

First published 2009

Printed in the United States of America

A catalog record for this publication is available from the British Library.

Library of Congress Cataloging in Publication Data

The Cambridge handbook of situated cognition / edited by Philip Robbins,
Murat Aydede.
     p.   cm.
Includes bibliographical references and index.
ISBN 978-0-521-84832-9 (hardback) – ISBN 978-0-521-61286-9 (pbk.)   1. Cognition.
I. Robbins, Philip, 1963–   II. Aydede, Murat.   III. Title.
BF311.C19   2009
153–dc22   2008017805

ISBN   978-0-521-84832-9 hardback
ISBN   978-0-521-61286-9 paperback

Contents

Acknowledgments

This volume has been a long time in the making, and we have gotten a lot of help from a lot of people. Accordingly, we have a long list of people to thank.

At the top of the list are our contributors, every one of whom did top-notch work for us. Among them, the four members of our advisory board – Larry Barsalou, Bill Bechtel, David Kirsh, and Rob Wilson – also assisted us with recruitment and other editorial matters. A number of other people, including several contributors, extended our editorial reach still further by reviewing individual chapters: Pascal Boyer, Philippe Chuard, Bill Clancey, Carl Craver, Chris Eliasmith, Shaun Gallagher, Kent Johnson, Hilary Kornblith, Alan Lambert, Edouard Machery, Eric Margolis, Pascale Michelon, Michael Wheeler, Wayne Wright, and Jeff Zacks. In the final phase, Chris Kahn came to our rescue by agreeing to format the entire manuscript for production, a task that he performed with admirable skill and care.

On the business end, Phil Laughlin, formerly of Cambridge University Press, encouraged us to take on the project and supervised its initial development. His assistant, Armi Macaballug, provided solid support throughout. After Phil left the Press, Eric Schwartz and his assistant, April Potenciano, took over supervision of the project and saw it through the home stretch. During the production phase, Shana Meyer oversaw the project from start to finish, guiding us skillfully through the maze. Katherine Faydash copyedited the manuscript, and Kate Mertes made the index for the book. Both of them did fine work.

Finally, our nearest and dearest – Sara and Judah, and Sema and Derya – helped immeasurably by just being there.

Hearty thanks to all.

Philip Robbins
Murat Aydede

Contributors

FRED ADAMS
Department of Linguistics and Cognitive
  Science
University of Delaware
USA

KENNETH AIZAWA
Department of Philosophy
Centenary College of Louisiana
USA

VAROL AKMAN
Departments of Computer Engineering and
  Philosophy
Bilkent University
Turkey

MURAT AYDEDE
Department of Philosophy
University of British Columbia
Canada

LAWRENCE W. BARSALOU*
Department of Psychology
Emory University
USA

WILLIAM BECHTEL*
Department of Philosophy
University of California, San Diego
USA

HENRY BRIGHTON
Center for Adaptive Behavior and
  Cognition
Max Planck Institute for Human
  Development
Germany

JEROME R. BUSEMEYER
Department of Psychological and Brain
  Sciences
Indiana University
USA

WILLIAM J. CLANCEY
NASA/Ames Research Center
USA

ANDY CLARK
Department of Philosophy
University of Edinburgh
Scotland

*Member of the editorial advisory board.

FREDERICA R. CONREY
Department of Psychological and Brain
  Sciences
Indiana University
USA

ERIC DIMPERIO
Department of Psychological and Brain
  Sciences
Indiana University
USA

CHRIS ELIASMITH
Departments of Philosophy and Systems
  Design Engineering
University of Waterloo
Canada

SHAUN GALLAGHER
Department of Philosophy and Cognitive
  Sciences Program
University of Central Florida
USA

JAMES G. GREENO
School of Education
University of Pittsburgh
USA

PAUL GRIFFITHS
Department of Philosophy
University of Sydney
Australia

RYAN K. JESSUP
Department of Psychological and
  Brain Sciences
Indiana University
USA

MICHAEL P. KASCHAK
Department of Psychology
Florida State University
USA

DAVID KIRSH*
Department of Cognitive Science
University of California, San Diego
USA

MALCOLM A. MACIVER
Department of Biomedical Engineering
Northwestern University
USA

RUTH MILLIKAN
Department of Philosophy
University of Connecticut
USA

ERIK MYIN
Department of Philosophy
University of Antwerp
Belgium

J. KEVIN O'REGAN
Laboratory of Experimental Psychology
Centre National de la Recherche
  Scientifique (CNRS)
France

JESSE PRINZ
Department of Philosophy
University of North Carolina at
  Chapel Hill
USA

DANIEL RICHARDSON
Department of Psychology
University of Reading
England

PHILIP ROBBINS
Department of Philosophy
University of Missouri–Columbia
USA

MARK ROWLANDS
Department of Philosophy
University of Miami
USA

ROBERT RUPERT
Department of Philosophy
University of Colorado at Boulder
USA

R. KEITH SAWYER
Department of Education

Washington University in St. Louis
USA

ANDREA SCARANTINO
Department of Philosophy
Georgia State University
USA

ELIOT R. SMITH
Department of Psychological and Brain
    Sciences
Indiana University
USA

MICHAEL SPIVEY
Department of Psychology
Cornell University
USA

JOHN SUTTON
Macquarie Centre for Cognitive Science
Macquarie University
Australia

PETER M. TODD
Department of Psychological and Brain
    Sciences
Indiana University
USA

MICHAEL TOMASELLO
Department of Developmental and
    Comparative Psychology
Max Planck Institute for Evolutionary
    Anthropology
Germany

BARBARA TVERSKY
Department of Psychology
Stanford University
USA

FELIX WARNEKEN
Department of Developmental and
    Comparative Psychology
Max Planck Institute for Evolutionary
    Anthropology
Germany

ROBERT A. WILSON*
Department of Philosophy
University of Alberta
Canada

ROLF A. ZWAAN
Department of Biological and Cognitive
    Psychology
Erasmus University
The Netherlands

Part I

BACKDROP

CHAPTER 1

A Short Primer on Situated Cognition

Philip Robbins and Murat Aydede

In recent years there has been a lot of buzz about a new trend in cognitive science. The trend is associated with terms like *embodiment, enactivism, distributed cognition*, and *the extended mind*. The ideas expressed using these terms are a diverse and sundry lot, but three of them stand out as especially central. First, cognition depends not just on the brain but also on the body (the embodiment thesis). Second, cognitive activity routinely exploits structure in the natural and social environment (the embedding thesis). Third, the boundaries of cognition extend beyond the boundaries of individual organisms (the extension thesis). Each of these theses contributes to a picture of mental activity as dependent on the situation or context in which it occurs, whether that situation or context is relatively local (as in the case of embodiment) or relatively global (as in the case of embedding and extension). It is this picture of the mind that lies at the heart of research on situated cognition. According to our usage, then, situated cognition is the genus, and embodied, enactive, embedded, and distributed cognition and their ilk are species. This usage is not standard, though

it seems to us as good as any (for competing proposals, see Anderson, 2003; Clancey, 1997; Wilson, 2002).

In this brief introductory chapter, we present a bird's-eye view of the conceptual landscape of situated cognition as seen from each of the three angles noted previously: embodiment, embedding, and extension. Our aim is to orient the reader, if only in a rough and preliminary way, to the sprawling territory of this handbook.

1. The Embodied Mind

Interest in embodiment – in "how the body shapes the mind," as the title of Gallagher (2005) neatly puts it – has multiple sources. Chief among them is a concern about the basis of mental representation. From a foundational perspective, the concept of embodiment matters because it offers help with the notorious "symbol-grounding problem," that is, the problem of explaining how representations acquire meaning (Anderson, 2003; Harnad, 1990; Niedenthal, Barsalou, Winkielman, Krauth-Gruber, & Ric, 2005).

This is a pressing problem for cognitive science. Theories of cognition are awash in representations, and the explanatory value of those representations depends on their meaningfulness, in real-world terms, for the agents that deploy them. A natural way to underwrite that meaningfulness is by grounding representations in an agent's capacities for sensing the world and acting in it:

> Grounding the symbol for 'chair', for instance, involves both the reliable detection of chairs, and also the appropriate reactions to them. . . . The agent must know what sitting is and be able to systematically relate that knowledge to the perceived scene, and thereby see what things (even if non-standardly) afford sitting. In the normal course of things, such knowledge is gained by mastering the skill of sitting (not to mention the related skills of walking, standing up, and moving between sitting and standing), including refining one's perceptual judgments as to what objects invite or allow these behaviors; grounding 'chair', that is to say, involves a very specific set of physical skills and experiences. (Anderson, 2003, pp. 102–103)

This approach to the symbol-grounding problem makes it natural for us to attend to the role of the body in cognition. After all, our sensory and motor capacities depend on more than just the workings of the brain and spinal cord; they also depend on the workings of other parts of the body, such as the sensory organs, the musculoskeletal system, and relevant parts of the peripheral nervous system (e.g., sensory and motor nerves). Without the cooperation of the body, there can be no sensory inputs from the environment and no motor outputs from the agent – hence, no sensing or acting. And without sensing and acting to ground it, thought is empty.

This focus on the sensorimotor basis of cognition puts pressure on a traditional conception of cognitive architecture. According to what Hurley (1998) calls the "sandwich model," processing in the low-level peripheral systems responsible for sensing and acting is strictly segregated from processing in the high-level central systems responsible for thinking, and central processing operates over amodal representations. On the embodied view, the classical picture of the mind is fundamentally flawed. In particular, that view is belied by two important facts about the architecture of cognition: first, that modality-specific representations, not amodal representations, are the stuff out of which thoughts are made; second, that perception, thought, and action are co-constituted, that is, not just causally but also constitutively interdependent (more on this distinction follows).

Supposing, however, that the sandwich model is retired and replaced by a model in which cognition is sensorimotor to the core, it does not follow that cognition is embodied in the sense of requiring a body for its realization. For it could be that the sensorimotor basis of cognition resides solely at the central neural level, in sensory and motor areas of the brain. To see why, consider that sensorimotor skills can be exercised either on-line or off-line (Wilson, 2002). On-line sensorimotor processing occurs when we actively engage with the current task environment, taking in sensory input and producing motor output. Off-line processing occurs when we disengage from the environment to plan, reminisce, speculate, daydream, or otherwise think beyond the confines of the here and now. The distinction is important, because only in the on-line case is it plausible that sensorimotor capacities are body dependent. For off-line functioning, presumably all one needs is a working brain.

Accordingly, we should distinguish two ways in which cognition can be embodied: on-line and off-line (Niedenthal et al., 2005; Wilson, 2002). The idea of on-line embodiment refers to the dependence of cognition – that is, not just perceiving and acting but also thinking – on dynamic interactions between the sensorimotor brain and relevant parts of the body: sense organs, limbs, sensory and motor nerves, and the like. This is embodiment in a strict and literal sense, as it implicates the body directly. Off-line embodiment refers to the dependence of cognitive function on sensorimotor areas of the brain even in the absence of sensory input and motor output. This type of embodiment implicates the body only indirectly, by way of brain areas that process body-specific information (e.g., sensory and motor representations).

To illustrate this distinction, let us consider a couple of examples of embodiment effects in social psychology (Niedenthal et al., 2005). First, it appears that bodily postures and motor behavior influence evaluative attitudes toward novel objects. In one study, monolingual English speakers were asked to rate the attractiveness of Chinese ideographs after viewing the latter while performing different attitude-relevant motor behaviors (Cacioppo, Priester, & Bernston, 1993). Subjects rated those ideographs they saw while performing a positively valenced action (pushing upward on a table from below) more positively than ideographs they saw either while performing a negatively valenced action (pushing downward on the tabletop) or while performing no action at all. This looks to be an effect of on-line embodiment, as it suggests that actual motor behaviors, not just activity in motor areas of the brain, can influence attitude formation.

Contrast this case with another study of attitude processing. Subjects were presented with positively and negatively valenced words, such as *love* and *hate*, and asked to indicate when a word appeared either by pulling a lever toward themselves or by pushing it away (Chen & Bargh, 1999). In each trial, the subject's reaction time was recorded. As predicted, subjects responded more quickly when the valence of word and response behavior matched, pulling the lever more quickly in response to positive words and pushing the lever away more quickly in response to negative words. Embodiment theorists cite this finding as evidence that just thinking about something – that is, thinking about something in the absence of the thing itself – involves activity in motor areas of the brain. In particular, thinking about something positive, like love, involves positive motor imagery

(approach), and thinking about something negative, like hate, involves negative motor imagery (avoidance). This result exemplifies off-line embodiment, insofar as it suggests that ostensibly extramotor capacities like lexical comprehension depend to some extent on motor brain function – a mainstay of embodied approaches to concepts and categorization (Glenberg & Kaschak, 2002; Lakoff & Johnson, 1999).

The distinction between on-line and off-line embodiment effects makes clear that not all forms of embodiment involve bodily dependence in a strict and literal sense. Indeed, most current research on embodiment focuses on the idea that cognition depends on the sensorimotor brain, with or without direct bodily involvement. (In that sense, *embodied cognition* is something of a misnomer, at least as far as the bulk of research that falls under this heading is concerned.) Relatively few researchers in the area highlight the bodily component of embodied cognition. A notable exception is Gallagher's (2005) account of the distinction between body image and body schema. In Gallagher's account, a body image is a "system of perceptions, attitudes, and beliefs pertaining to one's own body" (p. 24), a complex representational capacity that is realized by structures in the brain. A body schema, on the other hand, involves "motor capacities, abilities, and habits that both enable and constrain movement and the maintenance of posture" (p. 24), much of which is neither representational in character nor reducible to brain function. A body schema, unlike a body image, is "a dynamic, operative performance of the body, rather than a consciousness, image, or conceptual model of it" (p. 32). As such, only the body schema resides in the body proper; the body image is wholly a product of the brain. But if Gallagher is right, both body image and body schema have a shaping influence on cognitive performance in a variety of domains, from object perception to language to social cognition.

So far, in speaking of the dependence of cognition on the sensorimotor brain and body, we have been speaking of the idea that certain cognitive capacities depend on the structure of either the sensorimotor brain or the body, or both, for their physical realization. But dependence of this strong constitutive sort is a metaphysically demanding relation. It should not be confused with causal dependence, a weaker relation that is easier to satisfy (Adams & Aizawa, 2008; Block, 2005). Correlatively, we can distinguish between two grades of bodily involvement in mental affairs: one that requires the constitutive dependence of cognition on the sensorimotor brain and body, and one that requires only causal dependence. This distinction crosscuts the one mooted earlier, between on-line and off-line embodiment. Although the causal/constitutive distinction is less entrenched than the on-line/off-line distinction, especially outside of philosophy circles, it seems no less fundamental to an adequate understanding of the concept of embodiment. To see why, note that the studies described previously do not show that cognition constitutively depends on either the motor brain or the body. The most these studies show is some sort of causal dependence, in one or both directions. But causal dependencies are relatively cheap, metaphysically speaking. For this reason, among others, it may turn out that the import of embodiment for foundational debates in cognitive science is less revolutionary than is sometimes advertised (Adams & Aizawa, 2008).

2. The Embedded Mind

It seems natural to think of cognition as an interaction effect: the result, at least in part, of causal processes that span the boundary separating the individual organism from the natural, social, and cultural environment. To understand how cognitive work gets done, then, it is not enough to look at what goes on within individual organisms; we need to consider also the complex transactions between embodied minds and the embedding world. One type of such a transaction is the use of strategies for off-loading cognitive work onto the environment, a useful way to boost efficiency and extend one's epistemic reach.

One of the best articulations of the idea of cognitive off-loading involves the concept of epistemic action (Kirsh & Maglio, 1994). An epistemic action is an action designed to advance the problem solver's cause by revealing information about the task that is difficult to compute mentally. The best-known example of epistemic action involves the computer game Tetris, the goal of which is to orient falling blocks (called "zoids") so they form a maximally compact layer at the bottom of the screen. As the rate of fall accelerates, the player has less and less time to decide how to orient each block before it reaches the bottom. To cope better with this constraint, skilled players use actual physical movements on the keyboard to manipulate the blocks on the screen – a more efficient strategy than the "in-the-head" alternative of mentally rotating the blocks prior to orienting them on the screen with keystrokes. A roughly analogous strategy of cognitive off-loading facilitates more mundane tasks like grocery packing (Kirsh, 1995). The problem here is to arrange things so that heavy items go on the bottom, fragile items on top, and intermediate items in between. As the groceries continue to move along the conveyor belt, decisions about which items go where need to be made swiftly, to avoid pile-ups and clutter. As items come off the conveyor belt and enter the work space, skilled grocery packers often rapidly sort them by category (heavy, fragile, intermediate) into distinct spatial zones prior to placing each item in a bag. This procedure significantly decreases load on working memory relative to the alternative of mentally calculating the optimal placement of each item as it enters the work space, without the benefit of external spatial cues.

Both of these examples of epistemic action point to the importance of minimizing load on internal memory, on working memory in particular. This echoes the twin themes of Brooks's (1991) "world as its own model" (p. 140) and O'Regan's (1992) "world as an outside memory" (p. 461). The common idea here is that, instead of building up detailed internal models of the world that require continuous and costly updating, it pays to look up relevant information from the world on an as-needed basis. In other words, "rather than attempt to mentally store and manipulate all the relevant details about a situation, we physically store and manipulate those details out in the world, in the very situation itself" (Wilson, 2002, p. 629). The suggestion that intelligent agents do best when they travel informationally light, keeping internal representation and processing to a minimum, informs a wide spectrum of research on cognition in the situated tradition (Clark, 1997). Vision science affords a nice example of this trend in the form of research on change blindness. This is a phenomenon in which viewers fail to register dramatic changes in a visual scene – a phenomenon that some interpret as evidence that the visual system creates only sparse models of the world, giving rise to representational blind spots (O'Regan, 1992).

The embedding thesis, then, goes hand in hand with what Clark (1989) calls the "007 principle."

In general, evolved creatures will neither store nor process information in costly ways when they can use the structure of the environment and their operations upon it as a convenient stand-in for the information-processing operations concerned. That is, know only as much as you need to know to get the job done. (p. 64)

Embedding, in turn, goes hand in hand with embodiment, as off-loading cognitive work depends heavily on sensorimotor capacities such as visual lookup, pattern recognition, and object manipulation. Epistemic actions, for instance, typically require embodiment in a strict and literal sense, as they involve real-time dynamic interaction with the local physical environment.

The theoretical and methodological import of embedding, however, is much wider. It points to the importance, in general, of studying cognition "in the wild," with careful attention to the complex interplay of processes spanning mind, body, and world (Hutchins, 1995). The scope of this ecological perspective on the mind is very broad indeed. Having expanded far beyond Gibson's (1979) work on vision, it informs research programs in virtually every area of psychology, from spatial navigation to language acquisition to social cognition. It is nicely illustrated by theories of social rationality, which try to explain human judgment and decision making in terms of the structure of the social environment (Gigerenzer, 2000). Somewhat further afield, the ecological view has begun to show up with increasing frequency in the literature on phenomenal consciousness, that is, consciousness in the "what-it's-like" sense popularized by Nagel (1974). It is implicit, for example, in the enactivist idea that the felt quality of visual awareness is a by-product of ongoing agent-environment interaction (Noë, 2004). It also informs constructivist conceptions of consciousness, such as the idea that an individual's conscious mental life tends to mirror that of socially salient others (Robbins, 2008). Both of these suggestions about the nature of phenomenal consciousness – arguably the last bastion of Cartesian internalism – reflect a newly invigorated ecological perspective on the mind.

3. The Extended Mind

Assigning an important explanatory role to brain-body and agent-environment interactions does not constitute a sharp break from classical cognitive science. Both the embodiment thesis and the embedding thesis can be seen as relatively modest proposals, given that they can be accommodated by relatively minor adjustments to the classical picture, such as the acknowledgment that "not all representations are enduring, not all are symbolic, not all are amodal, and not all are independent of the sensory and effector systems of the agent" (Markman & Dietrich, 2000, p. 474; see also Vera & Simon, 1993). The same cannot be so easily said, however, of the claim that cognition is *extended* – the claim that the boundaries of cognitive systems lie outside the envelope of individual organisms, encompassing features of the physical and social environment (Clark & Chalmers, 1998; Wilson, 2004). In this view, the mind leaks out into the world, and cognitive activity is distributed across individuals and situations. This is not your grandmother's metaphysics of mind; this is a brave new world. Why should anyone believe in it?

One part of the answer lies in the promise of dynamical systems theory – the intellectual offspring of classical control theory, or cybernetics (Ashby, 1956; Wiener, 1948; Young, 1964) – as an approach to modeling cognition (Beer, 1995; Thelen & Smith, 1994; van Gelder, 1995). Using the tools of dynamical systems theory, one can describe in a mathematically precise way how various states of a cognitive system change in relation to one another over time. Because those state changes depend as much on changes in the external environment as on changes in the internal one, it becomes as important for cognitive modeling to track causal processes that cross the boundary of the individual organism as it is to track those that lie within that boundary. In short, insofar as the mind is a dynamical system, it is natural to think of it as extending not just into the body but also into the world. The result is a radical challenge to traditional ways of thinking about the mind, Cartesian internalism in particular:

> The Cartesian tradition is mistaken in supposing that the mind is an inner entity of any kind, whether mind-stuff, brain states, or whatever. Ontologically, mind is much more a matter of what we do within environmental and social possibilities and bounds. Twentieth-century anti-Cartesianism thus draws much of mind out, and in particular outside the skull. (van Gelder, 1995, p. 380)

Implicit in this passage is a kind of slippery slope argument premised on a broad theoretical assumption. Grant that cognition is embodied and embedded – something that the dynamical systems approach takes more or less as a given – and it is a short distance

to the conclusion that cognition is extended as well. Or so the reasoning goes.

Another part of the motivation behind the extension thesis traces back to a fictional (but realistic) scenario that Clark and Chalmers (1998) describe. They introduce a pair of characters named Otto and Inga. Otto is an Alzheimer's patient who supplements his deteriorating memory by carrying around a notebook stocked with useful information. Unable to recall the address of a museum he wishes to visit, Otto pulls out his trusty notebook, flips to the relevant page, looks up the address, and proceeds on his way. Neurotypical Inga, in contrast, has an intact memory and no need for such contrivances. When she decides to visit the museum, she simply recalls the address and sets off. Now, there are clear differences between the case of Otto and the case of Inga; Otto stores the information externally (on paper), whereas Inga stores it internally (in neurons); Otto retrieves the information by visual lookup, whereas Inga uses something like introspective recall; and so on. But according to Clark and Chalmers, these differences are relatively superficial. What is most salient about the cases of Otto and of Inga, viewed through a functionalist lens, are the similarities. Once these similarities are given their due, the moral of the story becomes clear: "When it comes to belief, there is nothing sacred about skull and skin. What makes some information count as a belief is the role it plays, and there is no reason why the relevant role can be played only from inside the body" (Clark & Chalmers, 1998, p. 14). As for the fact that this conception of mind runs afoul of folk intuitions, well, so much the worse for those intuitions.

This conclusion is not forced on us, however, and a number of theorists have urged that we resist it. For example, Rupert (2004) argues that generalizing memory to include cases like Otto's would have the untoward effect of voiding the most basic lawlike generalizations uncovered by traditional memory research, such as primacy, recency, and interference effects – and without furnishing anything comparably robust to substitute in their place. In short, insofar as the goal of scientific inquiry is to carve nature at its joints, and lawlike regularities are the best guide to the location of those joints, it is not clear that a fruitful science of extended memory is possible, even in principle. More generally, Adams and Aizawa (2008) contend that the standard argument for pushing the boundary of cognition beyond the individual organism rests on conflating the metaphysically important distinction between causation and constitution. As they point out, it is one thing to say that cognitive activity involves systematic causal interaction with things outside the head, and it is quite another to say that those things instantiate cognitive properties or undergo cognitive processes. Bridging this conceptual gap remains a major challenge for defenders of the extended mind.

4. Coda

Situated cognition is a many-splendored enterprise, spanning a wide range of projects in philosophy, psychology, neuroscience, anthropology, robotics, and other fields. In this chapter we have touched on a few of the themes running through this research, in an effort to convey some sense of what situated cognition is and what the excitement is about. The twenty-five chapters that follow it develop these themes, and other themes in the vicinity, in depth. Both individually and collectively, these chapters reveal what "getting situated" means to cognitive science, and why it matters.

References

Adams, F., & Aizawa, K. (2008). *The bounds of cognition*. Oxford: Blackwell.

Anderson, M. L. (2003). Embodied cognition: A field guide. *Artificial Intelligence, 149*, 91–130.

Ashby, W. R. (1956). *Introduction to cybernetics*. New York: Wiley.

Beer, R. D. (1995). A dynamical systems perspective on agent-environment interaction. *Artificial Intelligence, 72*, 173–215.

Block, N. (2005). Review of Alva Noë's *Action in Perception. Journal of Philosophy, 102*, 259–272.

Brooks, R. (1991). Intelligence without representation. *Artificial Intelligence, 47*, 139–159.

Cacioppo, J. T., Priester, J. R., & Bernston, G. G. (1993). Rudimentary determination of attitudes: II. Arm flexion and extension have differential effects on attitudes. *Journal of Personality and Social Psychology, 65*, 5–17.

Chen, S., & Bargh, J. A. (1999). Consequences of automatic evaluation: Immediate behavior dispositions to approach or avoid the stimulus. *Personality and Social Psychology Bulletin, 25*, 215–224.

Clancey, W. J. (1997). *Situated cognition*. Cambridge: Cambridge University Press.

Clark, A. (1989). *Microcognition*. Cambridge, MA: MIT Press.

Clark, A. (1997). *Being there*. Cambridge, MA: MIT Press.

Clark, A., & Chalmers, D. (1998). The extended mind. *Analysis, 58*, 10–23.

Gallagher, S. (2005). *How the body shapes the mind*. Oxford: Oxford University Press.

Gibson, J. J. (1979). *The ecological approach to visual perception*. Boston: Houghton Mifflin.

Gigerenzer, G. (2000). *Adaptive thinking*. Oxford: Oxford University Press.

Glenberg, A. M., & Kaschak, M. P. (2002). Grounding language in action. *Psychonomic Bulletin and Review, 9*, 558–565.

Harnad, S. (1990). The symbol grounding problem. *Physica D, 42*, 335–346.

Hurley, S. L. (1998). *Consciousness in action*. Cambridge, MA: Harvard University Press.

Hutchins, E. (1995). *Cognition in the wild*. Cambridge, MA: MIT Press.

Kirsh, D. (1995). The intelligent use of space. *Artificial Intelligence, 7*, 31–68.

Kirsh, D., & Maglio, P. (1994). On distinguishing epistemic from pragmatic action. *Cognitive Science, 18*, 513–549.

Lakoff, G., & Johnson, M. (1999). *Philosophy in the flesh*. New York: Basic Books.

Markman, A. B., & Dietrich, E. (2000). Extending the classical view of representation. *Trends in Cognitive Sciences, 4*, 470–475.

Nagel, T. (1974). What is it like to be a bat? *Philosophical Review, 82*, 435–450.

Niedenthal, P. M., Barsalou, L. W., Winkielman, P., Krauth-Gruber, S., & Ric, F. (2005). Embodiment in attitudes, social perception, and emotion. *Personality and Social Psychology Review, 9*, 184–211.

Noë, A. (2004). *Action in perception*. Cambridge, MA: MIT Press.

O'Regan, J. K. (1992). Solving the "real" mysteries of visual perception: The world as an outside memory. *Canadian Journal of Psychology*, 46, 461–488.

Robbins, P. (2008). Consciousness and the social mind. *Cognitive Systems Research*, 9, 15–23.

Rupert, R. (2004). Challenging the hypothesis of extended cognition. *Journal of Philosophy*, 101, 389–428.

Thelen, E., & Smith, L. B. (1994). *A dynamic systems approach to the development of cognition and action*. Cambridge, MA: MIT Press.

van Gelder, T. (1995). What might cognition be, if not computation? *Journal of Philosophy*, 91, 345–381.

Vera, A. H., & Simon, H. A. (1993). Situated action: A symbolic interpretation. *Cognitive Science*, 17, 7–48.

Wiener, N. (1948). *Cybernetics; or, Control and communication in the animal and the machine*. New York: Wiley.

Wilson, M. (2002). Six views of embodied cognition. *Psychonomic Bulletin and Review*, 9, 625–636.

Wilson, R. A. (2004). *Boundaries of the mind*. Cambridge: Cambridge University Press.

Young, J. Z. (1964). *A model of the brain*. Oxford: Oxford University Press.

CHAPTER 2

Scientific Antecedents of Situated Cognition

William J. Clancey

Introduction

In the late 1980s, an artificial intelligence (AI) researcher trying to untangle controversies about the nature of knowledge, memory, and behavior would have been surrounded by perplexed computer science and psychology colleagues who viewed situated cognition ideas as fool's gold – or even suggested that those ideas threatened the foundations of science itself. But scholars knew the concepts and methods of situated cognition from a much broader and deeper background, one that embraced Dewey's (1896) early objections to stimulus-response theory, Wittgenstein's (1953/1958) notions of family resemblances and language games, Gibson's (1966) affordances, Bateson's (1972) ecology of mind, Polanyi's (1966) tacit knowledge, von Bertalanffy's (1968) general systems theory, and so on, in the work of dozens of well-known figures in philosophy, psychology, linguistics, ethology, biology, and anthropology. Indeed, throughout science, including AI itself during the 1960s and 1970s, one finds at least the seeds for a situated theory of cognition. This chapter provides a broad historical review of the scientific antecedents of situated cognition; Gallagher (this volume) details philosophical aspects.[1]

What idea could be so general that it applies to every scientific discipline? And why was this idea so controversial in the AI community? What aspect of cognition relates the social sciences, linguistics, pedagogy, animal cognition, and evolutionary biology to neural theories of perception, learning, and memory? What problematic aspects of cognition in AI research foreshadowed the development of a situated epistemology? These are the topics I discuss in this chapter. In large part, the story centers on particular scientists, but I present the central ideas as crosscutting themes. These themes reveal that human cognitive processes are inherently social, interactive, personal, biological, and neurological, which is to say that a variety of systems develop and depend on one another in complex ways. Many stories can be told about these interrelations. The concepts, perspectives, and theoretical frameworks that influenced the situated cognition of the 1980s are still alive in potential for thoughtful reconsideration in tomorrow's cognitive research.

The key concept across the sciences that in the realm of AI and cognitive science manifested as situated cognition is today often called "systems thinking" (von Bertalanffy, 1968). This idea is manifested in different forms as general systems theory, complex systems theory (or simply "complexity"; Gell-Mann, 1995; Waldrop, 1992), system dynamics, chaos theory (Gleick, 1987; Prigogine, 1984), complex adaptive systems (Holland, 1995), and so on. These are modeling approaches with a broadly shared perspective on how causality operates in many natural systems and in some designed systems (Altman & Rogoff, 1987). For example, systems thinking views human expertise as occurring within and developing as a system involving an economic market, a community of practice, facilities, representational tools, reasoning, and perceptual-motor coordination (Lave, 1988).

The following section provides an introduction to systems thinking and its application in systems theory. The section is followed by a review of the historical context in which a non-systems-thinking perspective developed in the study of intelligence, particularly in AI research. I then briefly review how systems thinking relates to and is manifested in the study of cognition. The core of this chapter then summarizes crosscutting themes that constitute the scientific antecedents of situated cognition. Finally, I consider recent and continuing dilemmas that foreshadowed the acceptance of situated cognition in the fields of AI and psychology and suggest prospects for the next scientific advances.

Overview of Systems Thinking

Systems thinking involves studying things in a holistic way – understanding the causal dependencies and emergent processes among the elements that comprise the whole system, whether it be artificial (e.g., a computer program), naturally occurring (e.g., living systems), cultural, conceptual,

and so on.[2] A system is viewed as a dynamic and complex whole, an organization (e.g., a cell, a community) located within an environment. We look at the inputs, processes, outputs, feedback, and controls to identify bidirectional relationships that affect and constitute a system.

In identifying parts and wholes, systems thinking does not reject the value of reductionist compartmentalization and componential analysis; rather, systems thinking strives for a "both-and" perspective (Wilden, 1987) that shows how the whole makes the parts what they are and vice versa. For example, in conceptual systems, metonymic relations (tropes or figures of speech) may have a both-and meaning. Consider how the Sydney Opera House, derided at first as "a pack of French nuns playing football" (Godwin, 1988, p. 75), became a symbol for Australia – and thus changed the national identity, what *Australia* meant to the Australians and the world. The radical and captivating architecture, built for a high-culture purpose, marked Australia as a modern, preeminent society, occupying a unique position in the world (as does the building on the harbor's edge) and representing a force for change. Thus, the meaning of the nation (the whole) and the meaning of the building (a part) reaffirmed each other. The building is both contained in the country and a symbol for the country as a whole.

In situated cognition, one of the fundamental concepts is that cognitive processes are causally both social and neural. A person is obviously part of society, but causal effects in learning processes may be understood as bidirectional (Roschelle & Clancey, 1992).

Systems thinking also views the parts from different disciplinary viewpoints. For example, when building a highway, one can consider it within a broader transportation system, an economic system, a city and regional plan, the environmental ecology, and so on (Schön, 1987). Thus, different categories and relationships from different viewpoints frame the design of the highway system, producing different ontologies of parts and causal processes; the constraints between these perspectives are the basis for defining trade-offs of costs and benefits.

Such a multidisciplinary view of problem solving both extends and challenges the disciplinary notion of expertise that assumed an objective ontology (i.e., truth about the world), which was inherent in most knowledge-acquisition theories and methods (Hayes-Roth, Lenat, & Waterman, 1983). For example, in the 1970s, it was common to build a medical expert system for a clinic by working only with physicians in a particular subject area, omitting the nurses, hospital managers, computer system administrators, insurance companies, family doctors, and others.

By adopting a systems perspective, new insights may be gained into what problems actually occur in a given setting and why; what opportunities technology may offer; and how changes in tools, processes, roles, and facilities may interact in unexpected ways (Greenbaum & Kyng, 1991). These ideas were becoming current in business management (e.g., Jaworski & Flowers, 1996; Senge, 1990) just as situated cognition came onto the scene in AI and cognitive science.

Systems Theory

Systems theory is an application of systems thinking, closely related to cybernetics (Wiener, 1948) and what is now called "complex systems."[3] Systems theory was founded by von Bertalanffy (1968), Ashby (1956), and others between the 1940s and the 1970s on principles from physics, biology, and engineering. Systems theory was especially influential in social and behavioral sciences, including organizational theory, family psychotherapy, and economics. Systems theory emphasizes dynamics involving circular, interdependent, and sometimes time-delayed relationships.

Early systems theorists aimed for a general systems theory that could explain all systems in all fields of science. Wolfram (2002) argued that a computational approach based on cellular automata begins to provide an appropriate formulation of systemic structures and processes. However, computer scientists and psychologists who found situated cognition perplexing around 1990 did not recognize its roots in the work of von Neumann and Burks (1966), cybernetics (von Foerster, 1970), or parallel developments in general semantics (Korzybski, 1934/1994). Each of these theoretical developments contradicted the tenets of knowledge-base theories of intelligence (Clancey, 1997). These tenets include a temporally linear process model relating perception, conception, and action; stored propositional memory; identification of scientific models and knowledge; and a single-disciplinary view of problem formulation.

In contrast, the development of connectionism in AI (McClelland, Rumelhart, & PDP Research Group, 1986) promoted theories and models characterized as complex adaptive systems (Gell-Mann, 1995; Morowitz, 2002; Holland, 1995; van Gelder, 1991). This distributed-processing, emergent organization approach is also manifest in multi-agent systems modeling, which brings the ideas of cellular automata and systems theory back to the computational modeling of human behavior (Clancey, Sachs, Sierhuis, & van Hoof, 1998; Hewitt, 1977).

Features of Complex Systems

In systems theory, the term *complex system* (Center for the Study of Complex Systems, n.d.; Gallagher & Appenzeller, 1999; New England Complex Systems Institute, n.d.; Waldrop, 1992) refers to a system whose properties are not fully explained by linear interactions of component parts.[4] Although this idea was well known by the mid-1980s to many AI scientists in the technical areas of artificial life and genetic algorithms, its applicability to the study of cognition proper (e.g., the nature of conceptual systems, how memory directly relates perception and action) was not generally recognized. In particular, applications to education (situated learning; Lave & Wenger, 1991) and expert system design (communities of practice; Wenger, 1998) were difficult for proponents to articulate – and for others to understand – because the epistemological foundation of knowledge-based systems was at question.

The following features of complex systems are useful to consider when analyzing human behavior, a social system, an organizational design, and so on:

Emergence: In a complex system (versus a complicated one), some behaviors and patterns result from interactions among elements, and the effects are nonlinear.

Feedback loops: Both negative (damping) and positive (amplifying) feedback relations are found in complex systems. For example, in cognition, causal couplings occur subconsciously within processes of conceptualization and perception, consciously as the person reflects on alternative interpretations and actions, and serially as the physical world and other people are changed by and respond to the person's action. Situated cognition reveals nonconceptual and nonlinguistic aspects of these feedback relations while highlighting conceptual aspects that pertain to identity and hence social relations.

Open, observer-defined boundaries: What constitutes the system being studied depends on the questions at issue and the purposes of knowing. For example, is the boundary of a person his or her body? Are clothes part of the person? If you stand uncomfortably close to someone, have you crossed an emotional boundary?

Complex systems have a history: How the parts have interacted in the past has changed the parts and what constitutes their system environment (i.e., "the response function depends on a history of transactions" [Clancey, 1997, p. 280]; Shaw & Todd, 1980).

Compositional networks: The components of the system are often themselves complex adaptive systems. For example, an economy is made up of organizations, which are made up of people.

Historical Context of the Stored-Program Theory of Mind

Having now presented the seeds of the reformation (systems thinking and complex systems), I now return to the context of the reactionary – the cognitive theories that conflict with situated cognition. This brief synopsis provides a background for recognizing the novelty and usefulness of the crosscutting themes of sociology, language, biology, and others, which are presented subsequently.

First, one must recognize that the founders of AI in the 1950s were themselves reforming psychology and even the nature of science. Newell and Simon (1972, p. 9) explicitly contrast their reductionist process theory with behaviorism, which sought to explain behavior without reference to unobservable internal states. Minsky (1985) refers to gestalt theories as halting the analysis of cognition into interacting components. Thus, the founders of AI were biased to view cognition as fully explained by inputs and internal processes that could be broken down into structure states and functional transformations. Consequently, situated cognition claims that aspects of the mechanism of cognition were outside the head can be interpreted as a fruitless return to "the great debates about the empty organism, behaviorism, intervening variables, and hypothetical constructs" (Newell & Simon, 1972, pp. 9–10; cf. Vera & Simon, 1993).

Artificial intelligence research was strongly shaped by the stored-program von Neumann computer architecture, consisting of a processor that executes instructions separated from a memory containing data and programs (Agrawala & Noh, 1992). The derivative information-processing metaphor of the mind tended to equate data (i.e., inputs) with information, models (represented in the stored programs) with knowledge, logical deduction with reasoning, word networks with conceptual systems, and problem solving with all human activity (Clancey, 1997, 2002).

The success of the computational metaphor led to the view that a cognitive theory is not well formed or useful unless it is implemented as a computer program (Vera & Simon, 1993): "the model captures the theory-relevant properties of a domain of study" (Kosslyn, 1980, p. 119). Thus, in the study of intelligence, most researchers assumed that having a useful, functional understanding (i.e., knowledge) required a model (derived from theoretical understanding). Questioning this relation threatened the notion that progress in psychology (and hence AI) depended on explicating knowledge as propositions, rules, and functional procedures (e.g., the idea that commonsense knowledge should be exhaustively captured in a knowledge base; Lenat & Guha, 1990).

During the three decades starting in the mid-1950s, AI was largely separated from sociology and anthropology, and the seeds of situated cognition in ethology were largely ignored.[5] During this time, the knowledge-based paradigm took hold, and AI research shifted dramatically from "blocks world" games (specifically, stacking children's playing blocks, but also chess, cryptarithmetic puzzles, and so on) to the specialized expertise of professionals in medicine, science, and engineering. With the focus on individual experts (reinforced by the professional view of textbook knowledge; Schön, 1987), the idea of distributed cognition was not in vogue until the late 1980s, and, if considered at all, culture was viewed as a collection of common knowledge (rather than as a complex system of diverse artifacts, skills, and practices; Lave, 1988).

In trying to identify persistent internal structures that cause intelligent behavior, AI was philosophically grounded in objectivism (e.g., scientifically defined universal ontologies). Failing to recognize different disciplinary frameworks for modeling reality for different purposes (e.g., the road design example cited previously), AI explicitly embraced a reductionist theory that

knowledge consists of enumerable discrete elements (e.g., propositions, terms, relations, procedures). The folk distinction between skills and factual knowledge was well known, but the computational metaphor suggested that skills were simply compiled from previously known facts and rules (e.g., Anderson, 1983), which reinforced the stored-program memory metaphor. Systems thinking may have seemed incompatible or irrelevant to AI researchers because it threatened the grammar-based theories (see, e.g., Winston & Shellard, 1990) that had been so successful in facilitating the understanding of aspects of speech recognition, text comprehension, scene and object recognition, and problem solving.

As in other fields, the seeds of situated cognition were probably always present in the AI community. Connectionism might be viewed as the clearest outgrowth of systems thinking in AI, suggesting a theory of memory compatible with situated cognition (e.g., Clancey, 1997, pp. 69–75, chaps. 4 and 7; Clancey, 1999). Connectionism has direct origins in early neural network modeling (e.g., the work of Warren McCulloch) that inspired the founders of AI. Indeed, by 1950, Minsky had begun developing "a multiagent learning machine." However, "low-level distributed-connection learning machines" were too limited (Minsky, 1985, p. 323; Minsky & Papert, 1969), so Minsky focused instead on commonsense reasoning. Minsky (1998) expressed this continuing theoretical concern with examples such as knowing that "you can push things with a straight stick but not pull them."

Minsky's (1985) encompassing *Society of Mind* combined the original notion of a network of agents with nearly three decades of work on vision and simple problem solving, arguing (to paraphrase Winston & Shellard, 1990, p. 244) that intelligence emerges from contributions of a heterogeneous organization of agents. *Society of Mind* does not mention systems theory, but it does credit cybernetics with enabling psychology to use the concept of goal (p. 318). Minsky includes internal regulation and feedback in his framework, which is clearly based on biological theory.

But like Newell and Simon (1972), having conceived cognitivism as antibehaviorist, Minsky (1985) had difficulty relating his theories of agent interaction to systems thinking. He stated that emergence was a "pseudo-explanation" (p. 328), merely labeling phenomena that could be explained by taking into account the interactions of parts. In defining *gestalt*, for example, he says, "'holistic' views tend to become scientific handicaps," and that "there do not appear to be any important principles common to the phenomena that have been considered, from time to time, to be 'emergent'" (p. 328). Although Minsky was right to press for the study of parts and interactions, he appeared to deny the distinction between complex and complicated systems.

In contrast, at this time, Papert, Minsky's *Perceptrons* collaborator, pursued systems-thinking ideas in the realm of education, building on the work of Piaget to explicitly teach "administrative ways to use what one already knows" ("Papert's Principle," Minsky, 1985, p. 102), which Papert realized as a form of constructivism (see section "Constructivism$_1$: Philosophy + Cognition").

Also at the same time, Hewitt (1977), a student of Papert and Minsky, had promoted a decentralized procedural model of knowledge. His ideas were picked up in the blackboard architecture of AI programs, which harkened back to 1940s neurobiological models. The blackboard approach was successful in the 1970s because it provided an efficient functional decomposition of a complex process: heterogeneous knowledge sources (also called "actors," "beings," or "demons") operate in parallel to access and modify a symbolic construction (e.g., an interpretation of a speech utterance) represented at different levels of abstraction (e.g., phonemes, words). The relation of this computational architecture to complex, open systems in nature and society was not generally acknowledged until the 1990s (but see Hewitt, 1985).

We must recognize that every field has its own controversies and antinomies, with some individuals questioning what the majority of their colleagues take for granted. Even for well-established areas of study, the book is never entirely closed. For example, Kamin's (1969) research on simple animal cognition questioned whether even classical conditioning could be explained without delving into cognitive theory. *Society of Mind* is indeed a broad exploration that goes well beyond what could be implemented in a computer model when it was formalized from about 1975 to 1985. The formation of the Cognitive Science Society in 1980 can itself be viewed as a recognition of the need to regroup and identify the perspectives to be reconciled. Nevertheless, the strong reaction to situated cognition research from about 1985 to the mid-1990s demonstrates that something new and conceptually difficult to assimilate was being introduced. The next section outlines the leap to systems thinking that an understanding of situated cognition requires.

Manifestation of Systems Thinking in Situated Cognition

For psychologists in particular, systems thinking reveals contextual effects that cannot be viewed simply as environmental or as input. Thus, one studies authentic, naturally occurring behaviors, with the awareness that inputs and outputs defined by an experimenter (e.g., lists of words to be sorted) may set up situations unrelated to the person's problematic situations and problem-solving methods in practice (Lave, 1988). In particular, determining what constitutes information ("the difference that makes a difference"; Bateson, 1972, p. 453) is part of the cognitive process itself (versus being predefined by the experimenter) and often involves causal feedback with physical transformations of materials, such that looking, perceiving, conceiving, reasoning, and changing the world are in dynamic relation (Dewey, 1938).

One way to understand a dynamic process is that the system that is operating – the processes being studied, modeled, controlled, and/or designed – cannot be understood in its development or function as strictly localized within one level of analysis (e.g., Gould, 1987). That is, cognitive processes are not strictly attributable (reducible) to neurological mechanisms, nor are they purely conceptual (e.g., driven by knowledge), characteristics of a person, or properties of the physical world. But rather, what a person experiences and what an observer views – for example, of organisms, mental performance, individuals, organizations, populations, ecologies – is the ongoing product of a coupled causal relation, such that the entity being studied and its context (whether neurological, conceptual, physical-artifactual, interpersonal, or ecological) shape each other in a complex system. Thus, scientific insights of systems thinking (read "situated thinking") in areas of study ranging from neurology to environmentalism are often framed as blended disciplines: genetic epistemology, the biology of cognition, the sociology of knowledge, neuropsychology, evolutionary biology, social cognition, and so on.

Claims, Challenges, and Contributions

In summary, *situated* can be understood as emphasizing the contextual, dynamic, systemic, nonlocalized aspects of the mind, mental operations, identity, organizational behavior, and so on. Across the sciences of psychology, anthropology, sociology, ethology, biology, and neurology, and their specialized investigations of knowledge, language, and learning, the systemic, holistic view strives to explain behavior within a developmental and evolutionary framework. Specifically, situated cognition views human knowledge not as final objective facts but as (1) arising conceptually (e.g., dynamically constructed, remembered, reinterpreted) and articulated within a social context (i.e., a context conceived with respect to social roles and norms); (2) varying within a population in specialized niches (areas of expertise); (3) socially reproduced (e.g., learning in communities of practice; Lave & Wenger, 1991); and (4) transformed by

individuals and groups in processes of assimilation that are inevitably adapted and interpreted from unique perspectives (improvised in action, not simply transferred and applied).

Articulating the situated view of knowledge has been and remains difficult because, to some people, it has suggested the cultural relativism of science (Bruner, 1990; Slezak, 1989). Indeed, the debate appears on the public scene in the issue of how U.S. Supreme Court judges are to interpret the U.S. Constitution.[6] But ironically, fears of arbitrariness (stemming from the view that if an understanding is not objective it must be arbitrary) assume that either scientific or legal activities might occur in a vacuum, apart from a complex system of social-historical-physical constraints – as if, for example, a science that ignored physical realities of how sensors operate could accomplish anything at all, or that checks and balances in the legal system would allow a judge's ruling that ignored precedent to stand. Wilden (1987) refers to these confused debates (e.g., objective versus arbitrary) as "a switch between imaginary opposites" (p. 125). Thus, some objections to situated cognition arose because of a reactionary concern that open systems could be arbitrary, and that control must be imposed from outside to keep complex systems organized (see Clancey, 2005; Lakoff, 2002 [analysis of political metaphors]).

In summary, situated cognition developed not as a discipline (or a movement) within AI or psychology or educational technology but as a way of thinking proclaimed by some of the best-known scientists of the twentieth century in psychology, biology, ethology, sociology, psychiatry, and philosophy. Granting that the threads of the argument were known since Dewey (1896) at least, what did the proponents of situated cognition of the 1980s and 1990s add to our understanding of systems, causality, and mental operations? The contributions include:

- Better scientific models and modeling techniques (e.g., models of memory and learning, such as Edelman's 1987 neuronal group selection)

- Relating explanatory models on different levels (e.g., symbolic and neural models; Clancey, 1999)
- Improved theories and practices in learning and instruction (e.g., Koschmann, in press), as well as in software engineering (e.g., Clancey, 2006; Greenbaum & Kyng, 1991), arising through extensive multidisciplinary collaborations between social and computer scientists
- The extension of cognitive theory beyond games and expert problem solving to include the nature of consciousness and emotion (e.g., autism, dreaming, dysfunctions).

But perhaps most visibly and germane to the original objectives of AI, situated robotics flourished as dynamic cognition theories – based on feedback, interaction, and emergence – inspired new approaches to navigation, perceptual categorization, and language learning (Clancey, 1997, chap. 5).

Disciplinary Perspectives

In relating cognitive studies to other sciences, it is apparent that no single discipline has all the answers. All have had parallel developments that were contrary to situated cognition and even within their own discipline were viewed as lacking an appropriate contextual aspect. For example, some anthropologists might be critical of ethnoscience (a development within cognitive anthropology) because the study of how people perceive their environment through their use of language may use phonemic analysis too narrowly, thereby reifying linguistic categories as if they had a reality apart from their existence within conceptual and cultural systems.

Arguably, epistemology underlies all of situated cognition, and thus one might say that all cognitive research in sociology, anthropology, education, psychology, and even neurology is aimed at developing an appropriate epistemology and articulating

its manifestations in different settings. From a psychological perspective, the fundamental issues often boil down to how we should properly relate memory, perception, problem solving, and learning. For many AI researchers and cognitive psychologists, such a theory must be inherently expressed as a mechanism, in particular a computer program that implements the theory of memory and mental processing. But systems thinkers argued that cognitive processes are not like conventional computer programs. Wilden (1987), a communication theorist, contrasted a mechanism (meaning something like a clock made of gears, a "machineism") with an organicism (essentially an open system). Further, Bateson (1972), an anthropologist-philosopher, explored whether "mental" was a phenomenon that could be localized as a process inside the brain (as opposed to being a person-environment interactive process).

Telling this multidimensional, historical development is challenging, for it was never known to anyone at any time in all of its threads and perspectives. Moreover, because of its complex form, we cannot find a viewpoint for grasping it, as if it were a landscape, from a single, all-encompassing perspective. Post hoc we can trace themes, such as epistemology and the theory of memory, and make causal links among individuals, publications, institutions, and even pivotal academic meetings. Even a litany of concepts or issues is perspectival, articulated, and exploited within a particular community's interests and problems. It helps to recognize the many dimensions of analysis at play and to attempt to identify issues that pertain to different concerns, such as the examples that follow:

Academic disciplines: Philosophy, psychology, sociology, education, management, anthropology, biology, computer science, neural science
Cross-disciplines: Philosophy of mind/science, cybernetics, social psychology, cognitive anthropology, cognitive science, AI, neuropsychology,

evolutionary/genetic epistemology, evolutionary biology

Applications: Robotics, instruction and training, process control automation

Methodologies: Sociotechnical systems, ethnomethodology, knowledge acquisition, cognitive task analysis

Modeling/representational frameworks: Theory of computation, cybernetics, semantic networks, heuristic classification, qualitative causal modeling, neural networks (connectionist models), genetic programming

Cognitive functions: Representation, memory, knowledge, learning

Cognitive elements: Percepts, concepts, relations, procedures, beliefs, goals, desires, theories, activities, motives, skills

Cognitive behavior: Language, classification, problem solving, navigation

Systemic concepts: Dynamics, feedback, self-regulation, emergence, chaos, interactionism, constructivism, contextualism, ecology, ethnomethodology, self/identity

In teaching a course about situated cognition from a historical perspective, the pivotal scientific areas of study are the nature of learning (e.g., as social, psychological, neurological), animal cognition, and neurology (i.e., how the brain accomplishes cognitive functions). Indeed, although symbolic AI and problem-solving research in cognitive science fell behind the systems thinking developed in other sciences in the 1970s, it is apparent that systems thinking itself was changing dramatically, as it was rearticulated in a communication theory that combined physics and philosophy by cyberneticists (von Foerster, 1970, 2003), and then developed into chaos and complexity theory in the 1980s (Prigogine, 1984; Waldrop, 1992) and into what Wolfram (2002) calls "a new kind of science" based on cellular automata (pp. 12–14).

Is it a coincidence that the term *situated learning* was introduced in the 1980s not long after animal cognition became a mainstream topic for ethology, or at the same time the neural sciences adapted an AI computational modeling method to formulate the theory of connectionism? Strikingly, each 1980s thread relating to learning, animal cognition, and neurology was firmly grounded in well-known (including Nobel Prize–winning) research forty to one hundred years earlier. Indeed, one would have to view the development of scientific ideas relating to situated cognition as a complex system itself – nonlinear, historical, emergent, nested, networked, with open boundaries and feedback loops, and so on.

In particular, and crucially, no discipline or focus of study is more fundamental or "inside" another: a computational theory will not "explain" psychology any more than situated learning can explain culture. Also, insights do not accumulate monotonically; insights from Dewey or 1950s cybernetics might be stomped on by today's communication theory (Radford, 1994).

Not only the history of situated cognition but also the systems comprising cognition are in principle complexly related. Physiological, conceptual, and organizational systems are mutually constraining – not causally nested – in what Wilden (1987, p. 74) calls a "dependent hierarchy" of environmental contexts. Culture is the most diverse and complex system, but it lies at the bottom of the dependent hierarchy. Like any open system, culture depends for its existence on the systems that contain it environmentally – society, organic (biological), and inorganic nature (at the top). Diversity and complexity increase descending the dependent hierarchy; constraints become more general ascending. An individual organism is a complex of the two higher orders of complexity (organic plus inorganic), and "a person . . . is a complex of 'both-and' relationships between all four orders of complexity" (culture, society, organic, and inorganic), and so cannot be logically fitted within this hierarchy (Wilden 1987, p. 74).

At best, in writing a scientific history one can hope to mention most of the names and ideas that other stakeholders (e.g., researchers in education, psychology, anthropology) would cite, providing not as much a chronological tale but a coherent relation of people and concepts that fit to tell a coherent, useful story. Especially, the best motivation might be the question, What should any student know about the work that came before, particularly, what might be fruitfully read again, in the original, for inspiration? This is my criterion for selecting the scientific ideas that follow; I emphasize primary sources that future researchers should read and interpret for themselves.

Crosscutting Themes of Cognition

I organize scientific work related to situated cognition according to what discipline or field of study the advocates were grounded in – philosophy, education, sociology, linguistics, biology, neurology, anthropology – and then group related work by themes that were developed by studying cognition from the given perspective. This is different from a cognitive-element perspective, insofar as research on memory, for example, appears both in the "language + cognition" category as well as in the "neurology + cognition" category. My aim is to show fundamental relations between ideas, not what aspects of mind were derived from the studies. The themes are research topics embodying a situated perspective. Space allows for only a brief mention of each person's work – for elaboration, please see the references cited.

Constructivism₁: Philosophy + Cognition

Constructivism is a theory of learning according to which people create knowledge from the interaction between their existing knowledge or beliefs and the new ideas or situations they encounter.[7] Constructivist pedagogy tends to stress the importance of both teacher/environmental guidance and learner activity. One thread of constructivist thinking developed in the philosophy of psychology, in the late-nineteenth-century American pragmatism (Konvitz & Kennedy, 1960) of Charles Peirce, William

James, and John Dewey (see Gallagher, this volume). This perspective emphasized that knowledge was not merely transferred but that a transformation developed within and through the person's action. Most simply, this means that people can be instructed and are not simply learning habits (rote learning). Importantly, "being instructed" means that what is learned is subjectively interpreted and assimilated. The subjective aspect emphasizes both that knowledge cannot be identified with the curriculum – which Dewey (1902/1981) called a "map for learning" – and that the learner is consciously reflecting on and making sense of instructive situations and materials in actively looking and touching while doing things. Two constructivist principles suggested by von Glasersfeld (1984, 1989) build on Piaget's work and philosophical realism (Berkeley, 1710/1963; Vico, 1710/1858): (1) knowledge is not passively received but actively built up by the cognizing subject, and (2) the function of cognition is adaptive and serves the organization of the experiential world, not the discovery of ontological reality.

Constructivism₂: Education + Cognition

Constructivist epistemology combined with developmental psychology to greatly influence pedagogical designs in the twentieth century (Dewey, 1902/1981, 1934, 1938; Piaget, 1932, 1970, 1970/1971). Research emphasizes the development of individuals to understand the learner's active cognitive operations (e.g., Dewey's [1938] notion of inquiry) strategies, stages of conceptual development, and the nature of experiential processes of assimilation and accommodation. Learning interactions can be analyzed in many dimensions, including perception, conception, representation, skills, actions, material interaction, and transformation (e.g., interpreting instructions, arranging objects into a design). Perception-conception and action are understood to mutually interact (which Dewey [1896] called "coordination").

Constructivism₃: Sociology + Cognition

More broadly, a social perspective emphasizes that the environment includes (often physically but always conceptually) other people with whom the learner participates in activity systems (Leont'ev, 1979; Vygotsky, 1978; Wertsch, 1979, 1985, 1991). The individual and society are mutually interacting: "culture . . . is the capacity for constantly expanding the range and accuracy of one's perception of meanings" (Dewey, 1916, p. 123). A social-cognitive analysis emphasizes interpersonal communication; mutual, dependent action in a group (e.g., as in playing hide-and-seek); action by a group (e.g., involving specialized and coordinate roles, as in a team playing soccer); and identity (the conscious concept of self as a person engaging in normative, participatory activity).

Dewey and Bentley (1949) describe this system in which learning occurs as "transactional," emphasizing mutual, historical development across levels; between individuals; and through comprehending and doing (Clancey, in press). Cole (1996) and Cole and Wertsch (1996, p. 251) emphasize this co-construction aspect: both the child and the environment are active, and culture is "the medium within which the two active parties to development interact."

Both the social and perceptual-motor coordination perspectives suggest that the phenomenon of knowing (or mind) cannot be localized as a system existing wholly within a person's brain. As explained, this was seriously at odds with arguments against behaviorism and gestalt theory, and thus appeared to turn away again from decomposing the brain's structures and processes. Constructivism was not denying the role of the brain but emphasizing that it was not the locus of control in determining behavior – nor was the individual the locus of control – and in no case was human behavior simply a linear process of logical transformation from stimulus to decision to action.

Although not often cited in situated cognition research by psychologists, Mead (1934), a sociologist, developed a theory of the emergence of mind and self out of the social process of significant communication, which become the foundation of the symbolic-interactionist school of sociology and social psychology (Cronk, 2005). Symbolic interaction focuses on the construction of personal identity through interactions of individuals, especially through linguistic communication (i.e., symbolic interaction). Meanings are thus socially constructed and interrelate with actions. Other noted symbolic interactionists are Blumer (1969) and Goffman (1959). Polanyi (1966) developed these antipositivist theories further in his elucidation of the nature of tacit knowledge.

By the 1970s, sociology ideas stemming from turn of the century were reformulated in the sociology of knowledge (Berger & Luckmann, 1966), a constructivist theory that emphasized the learning of individuals in their social lives, as actively making sense of and thus forming a social reality (e.g., Shibutani, 1966). The anthropologist Hall's *The Silent Language* (1959/1973) provides a virtuoso exposition of the nature of culture, in a theory of communication that relates formal, informal (e.g., spatial-temporal layout, gestures), and technical conceptual systems. Latour (1999) has applied the social construction perspective to science itself, leading to the side debate that situated cognition was undermining the integrity of science (Slezak, 1989). Stemming from the early work by Durkheim (1912/1947), the philosophy of science here intersects with the epistemological study of common sense, namely that scientists and ordinary folk use different tools to develop theories of their world but are still constrained by (and actively changing) a social-historical environment of language, instruments, and values.

Remembering, Storytelling, Theorizing: Language + Cognition

Philosophy, pedagogy, and sociology defined broad constraints for a complex system theory of mind, but it remained for more specific studies of cognitive processes to elucidate what the processes were and how they were distributed and temporally developed. In particular, a focus on language in its manifestations of remembering, storytelling (narrative), and theorizing revealed a dynamic, constructive aspect that fit the pragmatists' and interactionists' views that behavior itself was transformative and not merely an applicative result (an output) from the "real" cognitive workings of information input, matching, retrieval, deduction, and action-plan configuration. Instead, we have the notions of dynamic memory, reconstructive memory, representing as an observable behavior (e.g., speaking as representing), and thinking as including nonverbal conceptualizing (versus purely linguistic deduction). In this shift – from information as stimuli extracted from the environment and responses as stored programs to a theory of remembering-in-action (a process memory) – situated cognition more radically turns from behaviorism than information processing was able.

The language-related foundations of situated cognition were well established before AI research on comprehension and discourse by the pragmatists (see especially Dewey's [1939/1989, p. 534] response to Russell, Wittgenstein's [1953/1958] break with positivism in his analysis of the language game, Ryle's [1949] distinction between "knowing how" and "knowing that," Langer's [1942/1958] distinction between discursive and presentational representation, Austin's [1962] view of language as speech acts, and the general semantics of Korzybski [1934/1994]).

Remembering

A situated theory of human memory is like an arch keystone that relates neural, symbolic information processing and social views of cognition. Bartlett's (1932/1977) notion of schemata was of course influential in qualitative modeling applications, ranging from visual processing (e.g., Minsky's [1985] frames) to expert (knowledge-based) problem solving and case-based reasoning

(see Shapiro, 1992, pp. 1427–1443). Ironically, Bartlett's theory of memory is based not on storage of schemata but rather on active processes that are always adaptively constructed within action, biased through previous ways of working together, and when engaged "actively doing something all the time" (Bartlett, 1932/1977, p. 201). Thus, he argued for a process memory, not a descriptive memory of processes or a preconfigured memory of stored procedures (see Clancey, 1997, chap. 3).

Bartlett developed his theory by analyzing story recollection, showing how details, fragmentary ideas, and narrative were remembered and reconstructed. Loftus (1979/1996) applied these ideas to reveal the improvisational aspects of memory in legal testimony. Bransford et al. (1977) and Jenkins (1974) demonstrated in experimental settings how linguistic-narrative memory blended phrases, roles, and themes in ways people did not realize. All of this suggested that remembering was not merely retrieving but actively reconstructing and reactivating ways of thinking – and seeing, hearing, doing.

Schank's (1982) *Dynamic Memory* highlighted how past experience, such as previous encounters in a restaurant, shapes how we interpret and act in situations we conceive to be similar. He suggested that failure of expectation was particularly important in constructing new concepts. Although formalized by Schank's research group in a network of stored descriptions, this work emphasized the historical nature of knowledge. Learning and behaving are inseparable, with learning occurring in behavior itself, in contrast with the view that learning occurs only in reflective reconstruction after a problem-solving episode is complete. Furthermore, normative (social) behavior can be described by scripts (Schank & Abelson, 1977), which are learned patterns of behavior based on the sequence of experience, not compiled from theoretical models about restaurants, and so on (for further relation of scripts to situated cognition, see Clancey, 2002).

Conceptual Structure

Focusing on aspects of storytelling, metaphor, and comprehension, researchers explored how concepts are related in human understanding, how these relations develop, and how they are manifest in linguistic behavior. This work tended to underscore that knowledge is more than conceptual networks with nodes and links representing words and their attributes. Instead, conceptual understanding is not separate from sensory and gestural (embodied) experience (Lakoff, 1987); relations can be mutually defining (e.g., Wilden's [1987] exposition of dialectics); and a linguist's reduction of speaking to grammatical form and definitions "alienates language from the self" (Tyler, 1978, p. 17). Similarly, Bruner (1990) highlighted the role of narrative in the construction of the self. Narrative is a representational form that transcends individual concepts through "tropes" of agents, scenes, goals, and so on, that have interpretive value, but not logical "truth conditions" (pp. 59–60). Thus understanding the genre, development, and function of narrative requires systems thinking.

These theoretical perspectives each sought in their own way to avoid the pitfalls of a narrow structuralism, which tended to localize behavior, knowledge, or meaning in one box of a mental process (e.g., conceptual memory, grammar) while ignoring the dynamic relations between systems (e.g., perception-conception-action, experience-self-participation).

Structuralism, attributed to Titchener (Plucker, 2003), sought to explain behavior through the interaction of component mental structures, in the manner of a chemist explaining reactions in terms of atomic and molecular interactions. In his core-context theory of meaning, Titchener suggested a complex system, by which "a new mental process (the core) acquired its meaning from the context of other mental processes within which it occurs" (Plucker, 2003). However, in most models of language until the mid-1980s (predating neural network models),

these relationships were viewed as enumerable, definable, and in some respects admitting to further decomposition. Such descriptions ignore the dynamic relations across perception and motor systems, the conceptual organization of physical skills (especially in the dynamics of and among gesture, sound, and vision), and how social norms (e.g., conceptualization of activity) develop through interactions. In particular, cues and timing (as in a dance or complex group conversation) cannot be easily pre-described or linearly sequenced as frames or schemata in a knowledge base. Rather, the mental constructs are behavior patterns that are activated and adaptively improvised through ongoing tacit reflection (e.g., Schön's [1987] knowing-in-action). This is not to say that the grammatical descriptions of observable patterns are not accurate or useful theoretical tools but to question whether such models can be identified with the neural structures that participate in the described behavior (see Clancey, 1997, chap. 1).

Learning by Doing and Inquiry

As previously noted, the philosophical, psychological, and social development of the systems view of cognition was often based on or directly influenced educational theory and designs. This is most obvious in the work of Dewey (who started his own school), Piaget, Bruner, and Papert, and then manifest in the analyses by Bamberger and Schön (1983) of learning in the arts, such as music (Bamberger, 1991) and architectural design (Schön, 1987). Each explored an aspect of constructionism (Papert & Harel, 1991), which claimed that making and experimenting with physical objects (including drawings and notations) facilitates the learning of abstract concepts, as well as the generation of new insights that promote abstract thinking. The theoretical claims were based on constructivism, but can be read as responding to AI's models of knowledge acquisition: (1) learning is an active, willful process, not a passive comprehension and storage of facts and procedures to be later applied, (2) understanding requires experience, whether physical or in the imagination, such that multiple modalities of thought are coordinated, and (3) conceptual understanding relies on perceptual-motor experience and simpler ideas, such that learning can be viewed and usefully guided in stages, which themselves require time and exploration to develop. Most important, this dynamic systems perspective does not deny the central role of formal representations (e.g., musical notation) but rather seeks to explain how representations are created and acquire meaning in practice.

Schön (1979, 1987) combined these ideas quite practically in his reinterpretation of Dewey's (1938) theory of inquiry (Clancey, 1997, pp. 207–213). For example, his analysis of architectural design revealed how conceiving, articulating, drawing, perceiving, and interpreting/reflecting were dynamically influencing one another in nested and parallel processes. Within the AI community, these ideas were first developed most visibly in the idea of cognitive apprenticeship (Brown, Collins, & Duguid, 1989; Collins, Brown, & Newman, 1989), which produced a lively debate (Bredo, 1994; Greeno, 1997; see also Clancey's [1992] response to Sandberg & Wielinga, 1991).

In related naturalistic studies, Gardner (1985) examined the varieties of intelligence, emphasizing skills in different modalities that people exhibited or combined in different ways. This work had the dual effect of highlighting what schoolwork and tests ignored and how the verbal emphasis of problem-solving research over the previous two decades had ignored physical, visual, and even interpersonal forms of knowledge.

Animal Cognition, Evolution, and Ecology Feedback: Biology + Cognition

In many respects, the application of systems thinking that was so confusing and indeed threatening to psychologists and AI researchers in the 1970s and 1980s was already well established in biology, as scientists came to realize that neither the cell nor the organism could be isolated for understanding the sustenance, development, or evolution of life. Systems thinking, involving notions of dynamic and emergent interactions, was necessary to relate the interactions of inherited phenotype, environmental factors, and the effect of learning. Indeed, in reviewing the literature, one is struck by how ethologists (studying natural behavior of animals), neurologists (focusing on neural and cell assemblies), and cyberneticists (forming cross-disciplinary theories of systems and information) were meeting and writing about similar aspects of life and cognition. Yet, with a more narrow focus on intelligence, and then expertise, the relevance of these broad theories to AI and cognitive science was not recognized for several decades. Thus, even though one can easily see cybernetics as kin to situated cognition, cybernetics was not presented in AI textbooks as a necessary background for studying the nature of intelligence.

Cybernetics

The intersection of neurology, electronic network theory, and logic modeling around World War II was popularized by Norbert Wiener (1948), who defined cybernetics as the study of teleological mechanisms, exemplified by the feedback mechanisms in biological and social systems. As we have seen throughout, the notions of memory and localization were central. Von Foerster (1973) wrote: "The response of a nerve cell does *not* encode the physical nature of the agents that caused its response. Encoded is only 'how much' at this point on my body, but not 'what'" (pp. 214–215). That is, the observer's described world of objects, properties, and events is not represented at this level in the nervous system; rather, what is registered or encoded is a difference or change as the body interacts with its environment.

Similarly, Maturana and Varela's notion of organizational closure views information ("in-formation") as a dynamic relation and not something that flows into the organism as instructions or objectively meaningful packets. Maturana and Varela's (Maturana, 1975, 1978, 1983; Maturana & Varela, 1980, 1987) theoretical framework of the biology of cognition also formalizes the complex-systems concepts of structural coupling (mutual causal relations between organism and environment) and autopoiesis (self-creating) (see Capra, 1996; Clancey, 1997, pp. 85–92). Von Glasersfeld (1974) called this "radical constructivism" (see also Riegler, 2001).

Bateson (1972, 1988, 1991) was a central figure in the inquiry relating cybernetics, biology, and cognition. His reach was especially broad, including cultural anthropology, ethology, and family therapy. For example, his theory of the double bind in schizophrenia claimed that contradictory messages (e.g., a verbal command and an incommensurate gesture) could disrupt conceptual coordination. Thus, in understanding schizophrenia as not only an internal mental-biological dysfunction but also a confused interpersonal dynamic – a disorganized relation between person and environment – Bateson brought a dialectic, ecological notion of information and communication to understanding development in biology and social science.

Ecological Psychology

Gibson (1979), a psychologist, developed a systems theory of cognition that explained behavior as a relation that develops in located action. For example, rather than saying that a person can jump over a stream, one might say that a given stream affords jumping when a person is running as he or she approaches (Turvey & Shaw, 1995). Such an affordance is a dynamic relation between a moving person and the environment, not located in the person or in the stream. Turvey and Shaw further developed this theory relating perception and motion, characterizing the organism-in-environment as a reciprocal relation, seeking a biologically relevant information theory (see Clancey, 1997, chap. 11). They explicitly argued against the

cognitivist perspective (see especially Shaw & Todd, 1980; elucidated by Clancey, 1997, pp. 280–283). In psychology this alternative view was also called "contextualism" (Hoffman & Nead, 1983).

Ethology

From a historical perspective, perhaps the oddest disconnection in the science of cognition is the study of intelligence by early AI and cognitive scientists without reference to animal research. In part, this could reflect perhaps a resistance to attribute cognition per se to animals, as animal cognition only flourished on the scientific scene in the 1980s (e.g., Gould, 1986; Griffin, 1992; Roitblat, Bever, & Terrace, 1984). And certainly the Skinnerian behaviorist psychology of the 1950s and 1960s appeared to be more about rote animal training than about problem solving. Nevertheless, the work of Konrad Lorenz, Karl von Frisch, and Nikolaas Tinbergen, winners of the Nobel Prize in 1973, was well known through the 1950s. In the autobiography accompanying his Nobel lecture, Lorenz (1973) says he early on believed that his responsibility ("chief life task") was to develop an evolutionary theory of animal psychology, based on the comparative study of behavior. He was influenced by Karl Bühler and Egon Brunswick to consider a psychology of perception tied to epistemology; similarly, he found in Erich von Holst "a biologically oriented psychologist who was, at the same time, interested in theory of knowledge."

Frisch's analysis of the "waggle dance" of honeybees, *The Bee's Language* (published in German in 1923), is an exemplary study of situated animal behavior in groups (compare this study over time and across locations with feeding pellets to pigeons in a cage apparatus). Tinbergen's (1953) *The Herring Gull's World* teased apart the stimuli organizing social behavior patterns.

The study of animal navigation and social behavior is especially profound for AI and cognitive science because it reveals what simpler mechanisms – fixed programs with perhaps limited learning during maturation – can accomplish. Studying animals forces the scientist to acknowledge that an observer's descriptive world maps and principled rule descriptions of behavior (as might be found in an expert system), though useful to model animal behavior, could not be the generative mechanism in creatures lacking a language for modeling the world and behavior. This realization, pioneered by Brooks (1991), produced in the late 1980s a wide variety of animal-inspired mechanisms in the field of situated robotics (Clancey, 1997, Part 2). The formulation of a theory of dynamic (complex) systems (termed *chaos systems*) by Prigogine (1984) helped explain, for example, ant organization around a food source. In particular, the complex systems concept of dissipative structures (in which decreased energy becomes a source of increased order) inspired Steels's (1990) designs of self-organizing robotic systems.

Related work in artificial life (Resnick, 1997) in the 1980s sought to explain the development of systemic organization and emergent properties through the same cellular automata mechanisms that inspired Minsky in 1950. Kaufmann (1993) moved this investigation to molecular biology, interestingly combining the strings-of-symbols idea from information processing with the notion of self-organizing feedback systems. He suggested the applicability of this approach to understanding economics, conceptual systems, and cultural organization – hence "the new kind of science" (Wolfram, 2002).

Neurology and Neuropsychology: Neurology + Cognition

Neuroscience, inspired by mechanisms of computational connectionism and grounded in magnetic resonance imaging and related methods for inspecting brain processes, raced ahead in the 1990s with new models of categorization learning, visual processing, sensory memory, and theories relating emotion to cognition (Damasio, 1994).

As previously related, connectionism derived from early work in neural network modeling (e.g., Head, 1920; Hebb, 1949; Lashley, 1951) and predated computational modeling of problem solving. Rosenfield (1988, 2000), Edelman (1987), and Freeman (1991) directly addressed and often critiqued cognitive theories, showing that they were incoherent from the perspective of complex systems theory and were biologically implausible.

Similarly, Sacks (1987), a neurologist, used case studies of how patients survive and adapt to reveal how neural processes, the environment, and issues such as selfhood interact to inhibit or enable mental experience. Sacks was especially adept at showing how conventional neurology's tests and dysfunctional categories veritably "decomposed" the patient by an inventory of deficits, while instead the patient's experience developed as a compensatory reorganizing process of preserving and reestablishing identity (persona). Notice how the idea of a person – involving personal projects (Sacks, 1995), temperament, friendships, cherished experiences, and so on – is very different from the typical antiseptic reference to humans as subjects of study, in which it becomes all too easy to then ignore issues of identity and consciousness.

Contemporary Theories of Knowledge and Learning: Anthropology + Cognition

At this point in the story, the history of science by the late 1980s becomes the contemporary development of situated cognition in AI and cognitive science (Clancey, 1997). Some social scientists were shifting from third-world sites to business and school settings in the United States, Europe, and South America, focusing especially on learning (e.g., Lave & Wenger, 1991). These researchers were especially influenced by Dewey, Vygotsky, Piaget (e.g., Cole & Wertsch, 1996), Bateson, Gibson, Hall, and Mead (e.g., Suchman, 1987). Often anthropology provided an organizing theoretical and methodological perspective (Greenbaum & Kyng, 1991). Studies of learning and instructional design were transformed to relate information and participatory processes in activity systems (Greeno, 2006).

Drawn in perhaps by the formation of the Cognitive Science Society in 1980, some social scientists and psychologists reacted especially to the theory that all problem-solving behavior was generated from a preformulated plan derived from verbally defined goals and deductive inference about problem-solving methods (Agre, 1997; Schön, 1987). For example, Lave (1988) questioned whether human expertise could be inventoried and indeed stored in a knowledge base. Situated action and situated learning sought to expose how people actually behaved, what they knew, and how they learned during work. Some of the earliest proponents were Scribner and Cole (1973), Rogoff and Lave (1984), and Suchman (1987). The previously mentioned ideas of cognitive apprenticeship developed in this academic community of practice, which resided predominantly at the University of California's Irvine and San Diego campuses, Xerox-PARC, Pittsburgh's Learning Research and Development Center (LRDC), the Massachusetts Institute of Technology's Media Lab, and the Institute for Research on Learning.

Foreshadowed Dilemmas in Cognitive Psychology and AI

Artificial intelligence and cognitive scientists were aware of gaps and oddities in mainstream theories of intelligence through the 1960s and 1970s. However, any science must exclude certain phenomena (one is tempted to say, "certain complexities"). Thus, it is no surprise that although engaging invited talks and textbook final chapters (e.g., Neisser, 1976) might mention autism, dreaming, and emotion, there was no coherent theory of consciousness. (Indeed, the new reputability of the topic of consciousness in cognitive science during the 1990s was somewhat like the admission of cognition into talk about animals in the 1980s.) Psychiatric disorders, for example, were difficult to make sensible from the perspective of a single seman-

tic network of concepts and relations – supposedly modified in long-term memory and processed by a central processing unit that was by assumption identical in every human brain.

Nevertheless, some cognitive phenomena stood out as requiring consideration: commonsense knowledge (nobody needs physics calculations to know whether a spilled liquid is likely to reach the end of a table), the relation of imagery and discursive thought (Langer, 1942/1958), the subjective nature of meaning versus the idea that knowledge consisted of stored proposition models of facts and rules (highlighted by the philosophical analysis of Winograd & Flores, 1986), language learning (how does a child learn so much grammar from so few examples?), ill-structured problems (Simon, 1973), musical creation and performance (e.g., Smoliar, 1973), how symbols in a cognitive system are grounded (Harnad, 1990), and so on.

Reflecting on the problems scientists had in bringing a complex-systems perspective to AI and cognitive science, Clancey (1997, pp. 345–364) formulated a set of heuristics for scientists: Beware an either-or mentality (e.g., knowledge is either objective or arbitrary). Try both narrow and broad interpretations of terms. Given a dichotomy, ask what both positions assume. Beware imposing spatial metaphors. Beware locating relations. Try viewing independent levels as codetermined. Don't equate a descriptive model with the causal process being described. Recognize that first approximations may be overstatements. Be aware that words sometimes mean their opposites. Enduring dilemmas are possibly important clues. Periodically revisit what you have chosen to ignore. Beware of building your theory into the data. Locate your work within historical debates and trends. "It's not new" does not refute a hypothesis. Beware of errors of logical typing. Recognize conceptual barriers to change. To understand an incomprehensible position, start with what the person is against. Recognize that the born-again mentality conceives sharp contrasts. Recognize how other disciplines study and use as tools different aspects of intelligence. Recognize the different mental styles of your colleagues.

Can we summarize the meaning of situated cognition itself, as seen through all the scientific disciplines over the past century? As stated, an all-encompassing generalization is the perspective of complex systems. From an investigative standpoint, the one essential theoretical move is contextualization (perhaps stated as "antilocalization," in terms of what must be rooted out): we cannot locate meaning in the text, life in the cell, the person in the body, knowledge in the brain, a memory in a neuron. Rather, these are all active, dynamic processes, existing only in interactive behaviors of cultural, social, biological, and physical environment systems. Meaning, life, people, knowledge, and so on, are not arbitrary, wholly subjective, culturally relative, or totally improvised. Rather, behaviors, conceptions, and emotional experiences are constrained by historically developed structural relations among parts and subprocesses in different kinds of memories – neural, artifactual, representational, and organizational – and are dynamically constrained in action across system levels.

Many difficult problems remain in understanding learning, language, creativity, and consciousness. From a computer scientist's standpoint, looking out over the vast landscape of more than a century of exploration, the nature of memory and development still appears pivotal. Almost certainly, elucidating the emergent structures and regulatory processes of genetic biology (Carroll, 2005) will inspire more complex computational theories and machines with perhaps reconstructive procedures and hierarchies. The nature of conceptualization and hence consciousness will gradually be articulated, comprising a complex order of molecular, physiological, neural, coordination memory, and activity systems. The nature of the self – unfolding, self-organized, and willfully determined – will be revealed as the essential cognitive dialectic: controlling, yet biased by ideas; open to change, yet inconsistent and inhibited; prone to ennui and powerless anxiety, yet in joy of nature and companionship always situated.

Acknowledgments

My understanding of situated cognition has been strongly influenced by courses at Rice University in 1971–1973 taught by Fred Gamst (Sociocultural Anthropology); Konstantin Kolenda (Philosophy of Knowledge; Philosophy of Literature); Ken Leiter, then visiting from University of California, Irvine (Ethnomethodology: The Radical Sociology of Knowledge); and Stephen Tyler (Language, Thought, and Culture). Conversations with my colleagues at IRL (1987–1997), particularly John Seely Brown, Jim Greeno, Gitti Jordan, Jean Lave, Charlotte Linde, Jeremy Roschelle, Susan Stucky, and Etienne Wenger, provided insights and motivation for putting these ideas together. I am grateful to Alex Riegler, Mike Shafto, Jim Greeno, and an anonymous reviewer for their comments on this chapter. My writing has been supported in part by NASA's Computing, Communications, and Information Technology Program.

Notes

1 This is a story about the conceptual foundations of situated cognition; for how the particular theories of situativity and learning in the 1980s and 1990s developed, see Sawyer and Greeno (this volume).

2 Definitions in this section are adapted from the Wikipedia discussion (retrieved June 7, 2005, from http://en.wikipedia.org/wiki/Systems_Thinking). For an introduction, see also New England Complex Systems Institute (n.d.).

3 Definitions in this section are adapted from the Wikipedia discussion (retrieved June 7, 2005, from http://en.wikipedia.org/wiki/Systems_theory).

4 Definitions in this section are adapted from the Wikipedia discussion (retrieved June 7, 2005, from http://en.wikipedia.org/wiki/Complex_system).

5 As a graduate student in the 1970s, I read a *Natural History* article about the dance of the bees and wondered, How did insect navigation relate to expert reasoning? Could we

model the bee's knowledge as rules? Brooks (1991) provided an alternative theory.

6 For a discussion of the dichotomy between the living constitution (arbitrariness) and strict interpretation (objectivity) – indeed an argument against either-or thinking – see Antonin Scalia's remarks at the Woodrow Wilson International Center for Scholars in Washington, DC, on March 14, 2005 (retrieved July 20, 2005, from http://www.cfif.org/htdocs/freedomline/current/guest_commentary/scalia-constitutional-speech.htm).

7 "Constructivism." In *Webster's Third New International Dictionary, Unabridged* (retrieved July 26, 2005, from http://unabridged.merriam-webster.com).

References

Agrawala, A. K., & Noh, S. H. (1992). Computer systems. In S. C. Shapiro (Ed.), *Encyclopedia of artificial intelligence* (pp. 241–248). New York: John Wiley & Sons.

Agre, P. E. (1997). *Computation and human experience*. Cambridge: Cambridge University Press.

Altman, I., & Rogoff, B. (1987). World views in psychology: Trait, interactional, organismic, and transactional perspectives. In D. Stokols & I. Altman (Eds.), *Handbook of environmental psychology* (pp. 7–40). New York: John Wiley & Sons.

Anderson, J. R. (1983). *The architecture of cognition*. Cambridge, MA: Harvard University Press.

Ashby, W. R. (1956). *An introduction to cybernetics*. London: Chapman & Hall.

Austin, J. L. (1962). *How to do things with words*. Oxford: Oxford University Press.

Bamberger, J. (1991). *The mind behind the musical ear*. Cambridge, MA: Harvard University Press.

Bamberger, J., & Schön, D. A. (1983). Learning as reflective conversation with materials: Notes from work in progress. *Art Education, 36*, 68–73.

Barker, R. G. (1968). *Ecological psychology*. Stanford, CA: Stanford University Press.

Bartlett, F. C. (1977). *Remembering: A study in experimental and social psychology*. Cambridge: Cambridge University Press. (Original work published 1932)

Bateson, G. (1972). *Steps to an ecology of mind*. New York: Ballantine Books.

Bateson, G. (1988). *Mind and nature: A necessary unity*. New York: Bantam Books.

Bateson, G. (1991). *Sacred unity*. New York: Cornelia & Michael Bessie.

Berger, P., & Luckmann, T. (1966). *The social construction of reality: A treatise in the sociology of knowledge*. New York: Anchor Books.

Berkeley, G. (1963). *A treatise concerning the principles of human knowledge*. La Salle, IL: Open Court. (Originally published 1710)

Blumer, H. (1969). *Symbolic interactionism: Perspective and method*. Englewood Cliffs, NJ: Prentice Hall.

Bransford, J. D., McCarrell, N. S., Franks, J. J., & Nitsch, K. E. (1977). Toward unexplaining memory. In R. E. Shaw & J. D. Bransford (Eds.), *Perceiving, acting, and knowing: Toward an ecological psychology* (pp. 431–466). Hillsdale, NJ: Lawrence Erlbaum.

Bredo, E. (1994). Reconstructing educational psychology: Situated cognition and Deweyan pragmatism. *Educational Psychologist, 29*(1), 23–35.

Brooks, R. A. (1991). How to build complete creatures rather than isolated cognitive simulators. In K. VanLehn (Ed.), *Architectures for intelligence: The 22nd Carnegie Mellon Symposium on Cognition* (pp. 225–240). Hillsdale, NJ: Lawrence Erlbaum.

Brown, J. S., Collins, A., & Duguid, P. (1989). Situated cognition and the culture of learning. *Educational Researcher, 18*(1), 32–42.

Bruner, J. (1990). *Acts of meaning*. Cambridge, MA: Harvard University Press.

Capra, F. (1996). *The web of life*. New York: Anchor Books.

Carroll, S. B. (2005). *Endless forms most beautiful: The new science of Evo Devo and the making of the animal kingdom*. New York: W. W. Norton.

Center for the Study of Complex Systems. (n.d.). Retrieved June 7, 2006, from http://www.cscs.umich.edu/

Clancey, W. J. (1992). Representations of knowing: In defense of cognitive apprenticeship. *Journal of AI Education, 3*(2), 139–168.

Clancey, W. J. (1993). Situated action: A neuropsychological interpretation (Response to Vera and Simon). *Cognitive Science, 17*(1), 87–116.

Clancey, W. J. (1997). *Situated cognition: On human knowledge and computer representations.* New York: Cambridge University Press.

Clancey, W. J. (1999). *Conceptual coordination: How the mind orders experience in time.* Hillsdale, NJ: Lawrence Erlbaum.

Clancey, W. J. (2002). Simulating activities: Relating motives, deliberation, and attentive coordination. *Cognitive Systems Research, 3*(3), 471–499.

Clancey, W. J. (2005). Folk theory of the social mind: Policies, principles, and foundational metaphors. In *Proceedings of the 27th Annual Meeting of the Cognitive Science Society.* Retrieved May 14, 2008, from http://www.cogsci.rpi.edu/CSJarchive/Proceedings/2005/docs/p465.pdf

Clancey, W. J. (2006). Observation of work practices in natural settings. In A. Ericsson, N. Charness, P. Feltovich, & R. Hoffman (Eds.), *The Cambridge handbook on expertise and expert performance* (pp. 127–145). New York: Cambridge University Press.

Clancey, W. J. (in press). A transactional perspective on the practice-based science of teaching and learning. In T. Koschmann (Ed.), *Theorizing learning practice.* Mahwah, NJ: Lawrence Erlbaum.

Clancey, W. J., Sachs, P., Sierhuis, M., & van Hoof, R. (1998). Brahms: Simulating practice for work systems design. *International Journal of Human-Computer Studies, 49,* 831–865.

Cole, M. (1996). *Culture in mind.* Cambridge, MA: Harvard University Press.

Cole, M., & Wertsch, J. V. (1996). Beyond the individual-social antimony in discussions of Piaget and Vygotsky. *Human Development, 39,* 250–256.

Collins, A., Brown, J. S., & Newman, S. (1989). Cognitive apprenticeship: Teaching the craft of reading, writing, and mathematics. In L. Resnick (Ed.), *Knowing, learning, and instruction: Essays in honor of Robert Glaser* (pp. 453–494). Hillsdale, NJ: Lawrence Erlbaum.

Cronk, G. (2005). Mead. *The Internet encyclopedia of philosophy.* Retrieved July 1, 2005, from http://www.iep.utm.edu/m/mead.htm

Damasio, A. (1994). *Descartes' error: Emotion, reason, and the human brain.* New York: Putnam.

Dewey, J. (1896). The reflex arc concept in psychology. *Psychological Review, 3*(4), 357–370.

Dewey, J. (1916). *Democracy and education: An introduction to the philosophy of education.* New York: Macmillan.

Dewey, J. (1934). *Art as experience.* New York: Minton, Balch.

Dewey, J. (1938). *Logic: The theory of inquiry.* New York: Henry Holt.

Dewey, J. (1981). *The child and the curriculum.* Chicago: University of Chicago Press. (Original work published 1902)

Dewey, J. (1989). Experience, knowledge and value: A rejoinder. In P. A. Schilpp, & L. E. Hahn (Eds.), *Philosophy of John Dewey* (3rd ed.). La Salle, IL: Open Court. (Original work published 1939)

Dewey, J., & Bentley, A. F. (1949). *Knowing and the known.* Boston: Beacon Press.

Durkheim, E. (1947). *The elementary forms of religious experience.* Glencoe, IL: Free Press. (Original work published 1912)

Edelman, G. M. (1987). *Neural Darwinism: The theory of neuronal group selection.* New York: Basic Books.

Freeman, W. J. (1991). The physiology of perception. *Scientific American, 264*(2), 78–87.

Gallagher, R., & Appenzeller, T. (1999, April 2). Complex systems [Special issue]. *Science, 79.*

Gardner, H. (1985). *Frames of mind: The theory of multiple intelligences.* New York: Basic Books.

Gell-Mann, M. (1995). *The quark and the jaguar: Adventures in the simple and complex.* New York: W. H. Freeman.

Gibson, J. J. (1966). *The senses considered as perceptual systems.* Boston: Houghton Mifflin.

Gibson, J. J. (1979). *The ecological approach to visual perception.* Boston: Houghton Mifflin.

Gleick, J. (1987). *Chaos: Making a new science.* New York: Viking.

Glenberg, A. M. (1997). What memory is for. *Behavioral and Brain Sciences, 20*(1), 1–55.

Godwin, J. (1988). *Australia on $25 a day.* Upper Saddle River, NJ: Prentice Hall.

Goffman, E. (1959). *The presentation of self in everyday life.* Garden City, NY: Doubleday/Anchor.

Gould, J. L. (1986). The locale map of honey bees: Do insects have cognitive maps? *Science, 232*(4752), 861–863.

Gould, S. J. (1987). *An urchin in the storm.* New York: W. W. Norton.

Greenbaum, J., & Kyng, M. (Eds.). (1991). *Design at work: Cooperative design of computer systems.* Hillsdale, NJ: Lawrence Erlbaum.

Greeno, J. G. (1997). On claims that answer the wrong questions. *Educational Researcher, 26,* 5–17.

Greeno, J. G. (2006). Learning in activity. In R. Keith Sawyer (Ed.), *The Cambridge handbook of the learning sciences* (pp. 79–96). Cambridge: Cambridge University Press.

Griffin, D. R. (1992). *Animal minds*. Chicago: University of Chicago Press.

Hall, E. T. (1973). *Silent language*. New York: Anchor Press. (Original work published 1959)

Harnad, S. (1990). The symbol grounding problem. *Physica D, 42*, 335–346.

Hayes-Roth, F., Lenat, D. B., & Waterman, D. A. (1983). *Building expert systems*. Reading, MA: Addison-Wesley.

Head, H. (1920). *Studies in neurology*. London: Oxford University Press.

Hebb, D. O. (1949). *The organization of behavior*. New York: Wiley.

Hewitt, C. (1977). Viewing control structures as patterns of passing messages. *Artificial Intelligence, 8*(3), 323–364.

Hewitt, C. (1985). The challenge of open systems. *Byte Magazine, 10*(4), 223–244.

Hoffman, R., & Nead, J. (1983). General contextualism, ecological science and cognitive research. *Journal of Mind and Behavior, 4*(4), 507–560.

Holland, J. H. (1995). *Hidden order: How adaptation builds complexity*. Reading, MA: Addison-Wesley.

Jaworski, J., & Flowers, B. (1996). *Synchronicity: The inner path of leadership*. San Francisco: Berrett-Koehler.

Jenkins, J. J. (1974). Remember that old theory of memory? Well, forget it! *American Psychologist, 29*(11), 785–795.

Kamin, L. J. (1969). Predictability, surprise, attention, and conditioning. In R. Church & B. Campbell (Eds.), *Punishment and aversive behavior* (pp. 279–296). New York: Appleton-Century-Crofts.

Kauffman, S. A. (1993). *The origins of order: Self-organization and selection in evolution*. New York: Oxford University Press.

Konvitz, M. R., & Kennedy, G. (Eds.). (1960). *The American pragmatists*. New York: World.

Korzybski, A. (1994). *Science and sanity: An introduction to non-Aristotelian systems and general semantics* (5th ed.). Englewood, NJ: Institute of General Semantics. (Original work published 1934)

Koschmann, T. (Ed.). (In press). *Theorizing learning practice*. Mahwah, NJ: Lawrence Erlbaum.

Kosslyn, S. M. (1980). *Image and mind*. Cambridge, MA: Harvard University Press.

Lakoff, G. (1987). *Women, fire, and dangerous things: What categories reveal about the mind*. Chicago: University of Chicago Press.

Lakoff, G. (2002). *Moral politics: How liberals and conservatives think* (2nd ed.). Chicago: University of Chicago Press.

Langer, S. (1958). *Philosophy in a new key: A study in the symbolism of reason, rite, and art*. New York: Mentor Books. (Original work published 1942)

Lashley, K. S. (1951). The problem of serial order in behavior. In L. A. Jeffress (Ed.), *Cerebral mechanisms in behavior* (pp. 112–136). New York: Wiley.

Latour, B. (1999). *Pandora's hope: Essays on the reality of science studies*. Cambridge, MA: Harvard University Press.

Lave, J. (1988). *Cognition in practice*. Cambridge, MA: Cambridge University Press.

Lave, J., & Wenger, E. (1991). *Situated learning: Legitimate peripheral participation*. Cambridge, MA: Cambridge University Press.

Leiter, K. (1980). *A primer on ethnomethodology*. New York: Oxford University Press.

Lenat, D. B., & Guha, R. V. (1990). *Building large knowledge-based systems*. Reading, MA: Addison-Wesley.

Leont'ev, A. N. (1979). The problem of activity in psychology. In J. V. Wertsch (Ed.), *The concept of activity in Soviet psychology* (pp. 37–71). Armonk, NY: M. E. Sharpe.

Loftus, E. (1996). *Eyewitness testimony*. Cambridge, MA: Harvard University Press. (Original work published 1979)

Lorenz, K. (1973). *Autobiography*. Retrieved July 1, 2005, from http://nobelprize.org/medicine/laureates/1973/lorenz-autobio.html

Luria, A. R. (1928). The problem of the cultural development of the child. *Journal of Genetic Psychology, 35*, 493–506.

Luria, A. R. (1979). *The making of mind*. Cambridge, MA: Harvard University Press.

Maturana, H. (1975). The organization of the living: A theory of the living organization. *International Journal of Man-Machine Studies, 7*, 313–332.

Maturana, H. (1978). Biology of language: The epistemology of reality. In G. A. Miller & E. Lenneberg (Eds.), *Psychology and biology of language and thought: Essays in honor of Eric Lenneberg* (pp. 27–64). New York: Academic Press.

Maturana, H. R. (1983). What is it to see? Qué es ver? *Archivos de Biología y Medicina Experimentales, 16*, 255–269.

Maturana, H. R., & Varela, F. J. (1980). *Auto-poiesis and cognition: The realization of the living*. Dordrecht: Reidel.

Maturana, H., & Varela, F. J. (1987). *The tree of knowledge: The biological roots of human understanding*. Boston: New Science Library.

McClelland, J. L., Rumelhart D. E., & PDP Research Group. (1986). *Parallel distributed processing: Explorations in the microstructure of cognition*. Cambridge, MA: MIT Press.

Mead, G. H. (1934). *Mind, self, and society*. Chicago: University of Chicago Press.

Minsky, M. (1985). *The society of mind*. New York: Simon & Schuster.

Minsky, M. (1998). "The mind, artificial intelligence and emotions: Interview with Marvin Minsky," conducted by Renato M. E. Sabbatini (Associate Editor, *Brain & Mind Magazine*). Retrieved July 1, 2005, from http://www.cerebromente.org.br/n07/opiniao/minsky/minsky_i.htm

Minsky, M., & Papert, S. A. (1969). *Perceptrons: An introduction to computational geometry*. Cambridge, MA: MIT Press.

Morowitz, H. J. (2002). *The emergence of everything: How the world became complex*. Oxford: Oxford University Press.

Neisser, U. (1976). *Cognition and reality: Principles and implications of cognitive psychology*. New York: W. H. Freeman.

Newell, A., & Simon, H. A. (1972). *Human problem solving*. Englewood Cliffs, NJ: Prentice Hall.

New England Complex Systems Institute. (n.d.). *Home page*. Retrieved June 7, 2006, from http://www.necsi.org/

Papert, S., & Harel, I. (1991). *Constructionism*. Norwood, NJ: Ablex.

Piaget, J. (1932). *The moral judgment of the child*. London: Routledge & Kegan Paul.

Piaget, J. (1970). *Structuralism*. New York: Basic Books.

Piaget, J. (1971). *Genetic epistemology*. New York: W. W. Norton. (Original work published 1970)

Plucker, J. A. (Ed.). (2003). *Human intelligence: Historical influences, controversies, teaching resources*. Retrieved July 1, 2005, from http://www.indiana.edu/~intell/titchener.shtml

Polyani, M. (1966). *The tacit dimension*. New York: Doubleday/Anchor Books.

Prigogine, I. (1984). *Order out of chaos*. New York: Bantam Books.

Radford, G. P. (1994). Overcoming Dewey's "false psychology": Reclaiming communication for communication studies. Presented at the 80th Annual Meeting of the Speech Communication Association, New Orleans, November 19–22. Retrieved August 5, 2005, from http://alpha.fdu.edu/~gradford/dewey.html

Resnick, M. (1997). *Turtles, termites, and traffic jams: Explorations in massively parallel microworlds*. Cambridge, MA: MIT Press.

Riegler, A. (2001). Towards a radical constructivist understanding of science. *Foundations of Science*, 6(1–3), 1–30.

Rogoff, B., & Lave, J. (Eds.). (1984). *Everyday cognition: Its development in social context*. Cambridge, MA: Harvard University Press.

Roitblat, H. L., Bever, T. G., & Terrace, H. S. (Eds.). (1984). *Animal cognition*. Hillsdale, NJ: Lawrence Erlbaum.

Roschelle, J., & Clancey, W. J. (1992). Learning as social and neural. *Educational Psychologist*, 27(4), 435–453.

Rosenfield, I. (1988). *The invention of memory: A new view of the brain*. New York: Basic Books.

Rosenfield, I. (2000). *Freud's megalomania*. New York: W. W. Norton.

Ryle, G. (1949). *The concept of mind*. New York: Barnes & Noble.

Sacks, O. (1987). *The man who mistook his wife for a hat*. New York: Harper & Row.

Sacks, O. (1995). *An anthropologist on Mars: Seven paradoxical tales*. New York: Knopf.

Sandberg, J. A. C., & Wielinga, B. J. (1991). How situated is cognition? In *Proceedings of the 12th International Conference on Artificial Intelligence* (pp. 341–346). San Mateo, CA: Morgan Kaufmann.

Schank, R. C. (1982). *Dynamic memory: A theory of reminding and learning in computers and people*. Hillsdale, NJ: Lawrence Erlbaum.

Schank, R., & Abelson, R. P. (1977). *Scripts, plans, goals, and understanding*. Hillsdale, NJ: Lawrence Erlbaum.

Schön, D. A. (1979). Generative metaphor: A perspective on problem-setting in social polity. In A. Ortony (Ed.), *Metaphor and thought* (pp. 254–283). Cambridge: Cambridge University Press.

Schön, D. A. (1987). *Educating the reflective practitioner*. San Francisco: Jossey-Bass.

Scribner, S., & Cole, M. (1973). Cognitive consequences of formal and informal education. *Science*, 182(4112), 553–559.

Senge, P. M. (1990). *The fifth discipline: The art and practice of the learning organization.* New York: Doubleday/Currency.

Shapiro, S. C. (Ed.). (1992). *Encyclopedia of artificial intelligence* (2nd ed.). New York: Wiley-Interscience.

Shaw, R. E., & Todd, J. (1980). Abstract machine theory and direct perception [Commentary on "Against Direct Perception" by Shimon Ullman]. *Behavioral and Brain Sciences, 3,* 400–401.

Shibutani, T. (1966). *Improvised news: A sociological study of rumor.* Indianapolis: Bobbs-Merrill.

Simon, H. A. (1973). The structure of ill-structured problems. *Artificial Intelligence, 4*(3), 181–202.

Slezak, P. (1989). Scientific discovery by computer as refutation of the strong programme. *Social Studies of Science, 19*(4), 563–600.

Smoliar, S. (1971). *A parallel processing model of musical structures* (Tech. Rep. No. AI TR-242). Cambridge, MA: Artificial Intelligence Laboratory, MIT.

Steels, L. (1990). Cooperation between distributed agents through self-organisation. In Y. Demazeau & J. P. Muller (Eds.), *Decentralized AI* (pp. 175–196). Amsterdam: North-Holland.

Suchman, L. A. (1987). *Plans and situated actions: The problem of human-machine communication.* Cambridge: Cambridge University Press.

Tinbergen, N. (1953). *The herring gull's world.* London: Collins.

Turvey, M. T., & Shaw, R. E. (1995). Toward an ecological physics and a physical psychology. In R. L. Solso & D. W. Massaro (Eds.), *The science of the mind* (pp. 144–172). New York: Oxford University Press.

Tyler, S. (1978). *The said and the unsaid: Mind, meaning and culture.* New York: Academic Press.

van Gelder, T. (1991). Connectionism and dynamical explanation. In *Proceedings of the 13th Annual Conference of the Cognitive Science Society* (pp. 499–503). Hillsdale, NJ: Lawrence Erlbaum.

Vera, A., & Simon, H. (1993). Situated action: Reply to William Clancey. *Cognitive Science, 17*(1), 117–135.

Vico, G. (1858). *De antiquissima Italorum sapientia.* Translated by F. S. Pomodoro, Naples: Stamperia de' Classici Latini. (Originally published 1710)

von Bertalanffy, L. (1968). *General system theory: Foundations, development, applications.* New York: George Braziller.

von Foerster, H. (1970). Thoughts and notes on cognition. In P. L. Garvin (Ed.), *Cognition: A multiple view* (pp. 25–48). New York: Spartan Books.

von Foerster, H. (2003). *Understanding understanding.* New York: Springer-Verlag.

von Glasersfeld, E. (1974). Piaget and the radical constructivist epistemology. In C. D. Smock & E. von Glasersfeld (Eds.), *Epistemology and education* (pp. 1–24). Athens, GA: Follow Through Publications.

von Glasersfeld, E. (1984). An introduction to radical constructivism. In P. Watzlawick (Ed.), *The invented reality* (pp. 17–40). New York: W. W. Norton.

von Glasersfeld, E. (1989). Facts and the self from a constructivist point of view. *Poetics, 18*(4–5), 435–448.

von Neumann, J., & Burks, A. W. (1966). *Theory of self-reproducing automata.* Urbana: University of Illinois Press.

Vygotsky, L. S. (1962). *Thought and language.* Cambridge, MA: MIT Press. (Original work published 1934)

Vygotsky, L. S. (1978). *Mind in society: The development of higher psychological processes.* Cambridge, MA: Harvard University Press.

Waldrop, M. M. (1992). *Complexity: The emerging science at the edge of order and chaos.* New York: Simon & Schuster.

Wenger, E. (1998). *Communities of practice: Learning, meaning, and identity.* New York: Cambridge University Press.

Wertsch, J. V. (Ed.). (1979). *The concept of activity in Soviet psychology.* Armonk, NY: M. E. Sharpe.

Wertsch, J. V. (1985). *Vygotsky and the social formation of mind.* Cambridge, MA: Harvard University Press.

Wertsch, J. V. (1991). *Voices of the mind: A sociocultural approach to mediated action.* Cambridge, MA: Harvard University Press.

Wiener, N. (1948). *Cybernetics: Or control and communication in the animal and the machine.* Cambridge, MA: MIT Press.

Wilden, A. (1987). *The rules are no game: The strategy of communication.* London: Routledge & Kegan Paul.

Winograd, T., & Flores, F. (1986). *Understanding computers and cognition: A new foundation for design.* Norwood, NJ: Ablex.

Winston, P. H., with Shellard, S. A. (Eds.). (1990). *Artificial intelligence at MIT: Expanding frontiers* (Vol. 1). Cambridge, MA: MIT Press.

Wittgenstein, L. (1958). *Philosophical investigations.* New York: Macmillan. (Original work published 1953)

Wolfram, S. (2002). *A new kind of science.* Champaign, IL: Wolfram Media.

CHAPTER 3

Philosophical Antecedents of Situated Cognition

Shaun Gallagher

In this chapter I plan to situate the concept of situated cognition within the framework of antecedent philosophical work. My intention, however, is not to provide a simple historical guide but to suggest that there are still some untapped resources in these past philosophers that may serve to enrich current accounts of situated cognition.

I will include embodied cognition as part of the concept of situated cognition. One often encounters these terms used together – *embodied cognition* and *situated cognition* – and it is clear that situated cognition cannot be disembodied, although some authors emphasize one over the other or provide principled distinctions between them.[1] Philosophical thought experiments notwithstanding, however, the often-encountered brain in a vat is, to say the least, in a very odd and artificial situation. Given what seems to be an essential connection between embodiment and situation, I will take the more inclusive and holistic route and view them accordingly.

The large landscape of sources for the concept of situated cognition is populated with important psychologists (from Vygot-sky to Gibson) and biologists (from von Uexküll to Varela), many of whom have had a significant impact on how we think of cognition as complexly embodied and situated.[2] I think that it is right to say that most contemporary philosophers who champion the idea of situated cognition have been positively influenced by this work in psychology and neurobiology. For the philosophers with whom we will be concerned, however, the psychology and biology of their time had less of a positive effect, and in some cases defined precisely what these philosophers were reacting against. What is even clearer is that these philosophers were reacting against a long philosophical tradition that simply ignored the importance of body and situation in favor of the isolated mind. This tradition included, of course, Descartes, but also Locke, Hume, and Kant, and almost every other modern philosopher one can name. To ignore embodiment and situation was the overwhelming tendency of the philosophical tradition up to and including many twentieth-century philosophers.

Before the twentieth century it is difficult, though not impossible, to find philosophers who could count as proponents of situated cognition. There is, however, a long tradition that emphasized practical reason, especially in discussions of ethics and politics, and in these discourses the idea of situated reasoning is not absent. One could mention here Aristotle's notion of *phronesis* (practical wisdom), which is a form of knowing or epistemic capacity that is highly dependent on the particular and practical (moral) situation in which it must be practiced. In the case of *phronesis*, one does not know in general, or by appeal to a set of rules, so much as one decides case by case – with special attention to the details of each case – what one must do. The Stoics also regarded the situation, defined in its most determined and concrete terms, as an important factor in knowing what one can and cannot do. These traditions, however, were not carried over into the realm of theoretical knowledge, or what philosophy has considered cognition per se (something closer to mathematics than to *phronesis*), which was most frequently thought to be independent of situation. Even moral deliberation was frequently modeled on context-free or mathematical thinking (think of Kant's categorical imperative or Bentham's utilitarian calculus). There may be a number of exceptions to this general view (I think Nietzsche would count as an exception, for example),[3] but nothing like a fully developed concept of situated cognition is to be found prior to the twentieth century.

In general, then, if the roots of the idea of situated cognition extend back into the history of philosophy, they remained undeveloped and well covered by the ground from which the Enlightenment grew, not even to be unearthed in all the digging for epistemological foundations. But in the twentieth century this idea did break the surface, and it started to grow in certain philosophers who were reacting critically against the modern philosophies of Descartes, Kant, and numerous others. I focus on four such philosophers: Dewey, Heidegger, Merleau-Ponty, and Wittgenstein. These are four philosophers among a list that could include

many others, such as William James, George Herbert Mead, Hans-Georg Gadamer, Aron Gurwitsch, Hans Jonas, Hubert Dreyfus, or more recently, Andy Clark, Mark Johnson (writing with George Lakoff), and Evan Thompson (writing with Francisco Varela).

Organism-Environment

Situated cognition has become an important concept in educational theory, and one of the most frequently cited philosophers in this context is John Dewey (see, e.g., Bredo, 1994; Brown, Collins, & Duguid, 1989; Clancey, 1997; Lave, 1988; Lave & Wenger, 1991). Curiously, just as much as Dewey is cited in discussions of situated learning, he is almost entirely ignored in the philosophy-of-mind discussion of situated cognition.[4] But Dewey was clearly the Dennett of his time, at least in terms of his enthusiasm for the science of mind and his rejection of Cartesianism. As early as 1884 Dewey reviewed the significance of the new physiological psychology, and he points to the importance of certain biological concepts of organism and environment:

> The influence of biological science in general upon psychology has been very great. . . . To biology is due the conception of organism. . . . In psychology this conception has led to the recognition of mental life as an organic unitary process developing according to the laws of all life, and not a theatre for the exhibition of independent autonomous faculties, or a rendezvous in which isolated, atomic sensations and ideas may gather, hold external converse, and then forever part. Along with this recognition of the solidarity of mental life has come that of the relation in which it stands to other lives organized in society. The idea of environment is a necessity to the idea of organism, and with the conception of environment comes the impossibility of considering psychical life as an individual, isolated thing developing in a vacuum. (Dewey, 1884, p. 280)

Dewey thus criticized conceptions of cognitive experience that construe it as narrowly individual, ideational, and passive. Experience is not something that happens in an isolated mind; rather, experience is biological, insofar as it involves an organism in an environment, and social, insofar as that environment is intersubjective. Cognition, then, emerges in the transactional relations that characterize organisms and the physical and social environment with which they engage. Experience is thus situated. "In actual experience, there is never any such isolated singular object or event; *an* object or event is always a special part, phase, or aspect, of an environing experienced world – a situation" (Dewey, 1938a, p. 67).

Dewey uses the notion of a problematic situation to describe how cognition involves coping with unfamiliar circumstances. Situations are problematic if there is some element of confusion, disturbance, uncertainty, or incompleteness that needs to be resolved and there is no clear direction that would lead to resolution. In such cases, cognition is a form of inquiry, and this is understood as a hands-on practical activity through which we transform the situation into one that is less confused and more comprehensible, and in which ideas for successful action start to emerge. An idea is not primarily an intellectual entity in the head but "an organic anticipation of what will happen when certain operations are executed under and with respect to observed conditions" (Dewey, 1938a, p. 109). Cognitive inquiry is not a purely mental phenomenon but involves an interaction between organism and environment to produce real changes in the causal couplings that characterize the situation. We should add the important point that the situation should be defined as inclusive of the inquirer. It is not I as cognitive inquirer confronting a situation; the situation surrounds and includes me.

Dewey was influenced by Peirce in his thinking that, in the process of coping with a problematic situation, we use not only ideas but also tools – physical ones like hammers with which we can physically reshape the environment, but also linguistic ones, which in communicative contexts may do just as well in reshaping the dynamics of the situation.[5] For Dewey, ideas, as well as gestures and speech acts, are themselves tools for this kind of interaction. Furthermore, whether we are moving things about or reconstructing meaning, cognition is primarily a social event and is often accomplished in a joint effort. Cognition and such communicative processes are measurable in terms of their pragmatic success. A good idea consists of a set of practices that resolves the problem.

Dewey was thus criticizing a strict Cartesian division of labor between mind and body – a division of labor that was not simply theoretical and a problem for philosophers but that was finding its way into the pragmatics of everyday life. Consider the following description of management practices from Taylor's 1911 textbook *Scientific Management*:

> *Thus all of the planning which under the old system was done by the workman, as a result of his personal experience, must of necessity under the new system be done by the management in accordance with the laws of the science.... It is also clear that in most cases one type of man is needed to plan ahead and an entirely different type to execute the work. The man in the planning room, whose specialty under scientific management is planning ahead, invariably finds that the work can be done better and more economically by a subdivision of the labour; each act of each mechanic, for example, should be preceded by various preparatory acts done by other men. (Taylor, 1911/1967, p. 37)*

The separation of mental experience from hands-on physical manipulation of the environment was, for Dewey, both a philosophical and a social problem.[6] For him, cognition is a form of action and not a relation between a thinking that goes on in the mind and a behavior that goes on in the world. The basic unit of experience is the organism-environment rather than a Cartesian cogito or Kantian pure ego:

> *We see that man is somewhat more than a neatly dovetailed psychical machine who may be taken as an isolated individual.... We know that his life is bound up with*

*the life of society . . . we know that he is
closely connected with all the past by the
lines of education, tradition, and hered-
ity. . . . We know that our mental life is
not a syllogistic sorites, but an enthymeme
most of whose members are suppressed;
that large tracts never come into consciousness; that those which do get into consciousness, are vague and transitory, with
a meaning hard to catch and read; . . . that
mind is no compartment box nor bureau
of departmental powers. (Dewey, 1884,
p. 278)*

Dewey's concept of cognition is not far
removed from what today is called "enactive
cognition," which is the idea that perception
and thinking are fully integrated with motor
action. Yet one thing that Dewey clearly
emphasizes and that is all but missing in
some discussions of the enactive approach
(e.g., Noë, 2004; Noë & O'Regan, 2002;
O'Regan & Noë, 2001) is the fact that cognition is always socially situated. Throughout Noë's (2004) analysis of enactive perception, for example, we find elements like
central nervous systems, sensory organs,
skin, muscles, limbs, movements, actions,
and plenty of physical and pragmatic situations to deal with. But there is no consideration given to the role that others (and our
social or intersubjective interactions with
them) play in the shaping of perceptual
processes. For Noë (2004), "the key to [the
enactive theory] is the idea that perception
depends on the possession and exercise of a
certain kind of practical knowledge" (p. 33).
The mind is "shaped by a complicated hierarchy of practical skills" (p. 31). If we ask,
How do we get this practical know-how?
his answer is embodied practice and action.
Dewey would not deny this, but he would
certainly proffer the idea that we also get
it from others – watching them act, communicating with them, and learning from
them through processes like imitation, and
indeed from the very start of life when we
are completely dependent on others.[7] What
is important in this context is to recognize
not simply that others populate our environment, or even that we interact with them

and perceive their intentions, but that such
interaction helps to shape our perception
and understanding of things.

Being in the World

Dewey's pragmatism acknowledges the
importance of situation for the biological organism, and as such, his position is
deep in the traditions of naturalism and
psychologism.[8] These views contend, for
example, that the rules of logic are not absolute or independent of the biological or psychological makeup of the organism. One
reaction to the relativism implied in such
views is to make the Fregean move to the
logic of pure concepts and to understand
conceptual meaning and truth to be independent of context. Another involves the
Husserlian move to a transcendental consciousness that is distinct from the particularities of any individual's psychological constitution. Both moves are clearly away from
the situatedness of experience and constitute a seeming retreat into a Cartesian, if
not Platonic, mind. Heidegger recognized
the ontological limitations of pursuing these
lines of thought. In his questioning about
the nature of the kind of entity that would
be capable of such decontextualized thinking, he implies that human existence is specifically not that kind of entity. He finds an
important clue to the nature of human existence and cognition in the notion of intentionality as it is developed in the work of
Brentano and Husserl. Intentionality, the
idea that all consciousness is consciousness
of something or about something, signifies
an unavoidable connection with the world.
For Heidegger (1968), the kind of being that
is capable of having an intentional relation
to the world is a being that is already in the
world in a more basic, ontological way. This
is what he sets out to show in *Being and
Time*, published in 1927.

From Heidegger's existential-phenome-
nological perspective, claims made by
Dewey about the organism's embeddedness
in the environment are claims informed by

common sense (what Husserl called the "natural attitude") and natural science, and are thus made from an objective (external or observational) perspective. Heidegger's project is to dig deeper into a question that still has the ring of a certain kind of transcendentalism about it: what kind of existence does the human being have such that it is necessarily situated or embedded in the world? His response can be put into Dewey's language[9]: the organism does not simply find itself deeply situated in an environment as one possibility rather than another. Rather, it is part of the very nature of human existence that being in the environment and being with others are necessary, existential characteristics. Dewey comes very close to saying precisely this:

> The statement that individuals live in a world means, in the concrete, that they live in a series of situations. The meaning of the word "in" is different from its meaning when it is said that pennies are "in" a pocket or paint is "in" a can. It means . . . that interaction is going on between individuals and objects and other persons. The conceptions of situation and of interaction are inseparable from each other. (Dewey, 1938b, p. 43)

In Heidegger's words, *Dasein* (human existence) is in the world, not in the sense that we are simply geographically placed in the environment, but in the sense that a meaningful world constitutes part of our existence. To be situated, for Heidegger, is not simply something that happens to the human being, but it is part of the being-structure of being human, and as such permeates every aspect of our cognitive and pragmatic activities and our social relations.

The world, in this sense, is not a collection of objects to be observed or contemplated by the mind. Rather, in a primary way, we have our hands in it. The world is "at hand" in an almost-literal sense (Heidegger uses the term *Zuhandensein* – being-to-hand). Things are not only available for our manipulation – we find ourselves already immersed in such manipulations or dealings, and the possibilities of such dealings shape our perceptions and actions. "The kind of dealing which is closest to us is . . . not a bare perceptual cognition, but rather that kind of concern which manipulates things and puts them to use; and this has its own kind of 'knowledge'" (Heidegger, 1968, p. 95). If, for example, I walk into my office, my primary relation to this setting is not as a collection of objects – desk, chairs, bookcases, computer, and so on. I do not *think* about the office door – I open it. I do not contemplate my desk or chair, I sit, absentmindedly, and start to work, with my attention on a problem to solve or a piece of correspondence to write. To use Gibson's term, the *affordances* offered by door, desk, chair, computer, and so on, are implicit in the way that I interact with them – they are ready-to-hand, as Heidegger (1968) says:

> The kind of Being which belongs to these entities is readiness-to-hand. But this characteristic is not to be understood as merely a way of [perceptually or cognitively] taking them, as if we were talking such 'aspects' into the 'entities' which we proximally encounter. (p. 101)

That is, in the majority of our everyday dealings, we do not first encounter objects cognitively, and then decide what they are and what they can be used for. Cognition is "a founded mode" of Being-in-the-world that depends on our primary, pragmatic interaction with things (Heidegger, 1968, p. 86). By the time we think about things, or explicitly perceive them as what they are, we have already been immersed in their pragmatic meaning.

To be pragmatically immersed in worldly contexts is to have a certain knowing relation to the world, which Heidegger calls "circumspection" (*Umsicht*) and distinguishes from theoretical knowledge. The latter takes things in the world as mere objects that we encounter in an observer mode (Heidegger refers to such objects as having a *Vorhanden* [present-to-hand] mode of being):

> "Practical" behaviour is not "atheoretical" in the sense of "sightlessness." The way it differs from theoretical behaviour does not

*lie simply in the fact that in theoretical
behaviour one observes, while in practical
behaviour one* acts, *and that action must
employ theoretical cognition if it is not to
remain blind; for the fact that observation
is a kind of concern is just as primordial
as the fact that action has its own kind of
sight. Theoretical behaviour is just looking,
without circumspection. (Heidegger, 1968,
p. 99)*

Heidegger points out that Cartesian philosophy and philosophical conceptions of science tend to overlook this basic ontological situatedness of the cognitive agent.[10] Science begins as something that is already a cognitive, theoretical project. Nature "itself can be discovered and defined simply in its pure presence-at-hand. But when this happens, the Nature which 'stirs and strives', which assails us and enthralls us as landscape, remains hidden" (1968, p. 100). Heidegger claims that something poetic that is tied to our situatedness is lost in the third-person objective observations of science. Of course it is important to point out that even our most theoretical contemplations are situated as well, and it is questionable whether it is ever possible to capture something in its pure presence-at-hand. Theoretical behavior is never just looking without circumspection, even if it is sometimes conceived as such.

Heidegger's analysis raises important questions about the very nature of the situatedness of cognition as we try to understand it in the varied contexts of education, psychiatry, artificial intelligence, and so on. Can situatedness be properly characterized in third-person accounts, or does it require an existential analysis of the sort provided by Heidegger? In this sort of analysis, we catch sight of what it means to be situated in an environment, what readiness-to-hand itself means, primarily when readiness-to-hand breaks down – for example, when something we intend to use is discovered to be unusable, or when something we need is missing, or when something we need to get around stands obstinately in the way. In such cases, things are no longer there ready-to-hand, and just in that instance we

catch sight of the very situatedness that normally characterizes our existence. In such instances, we do not escape being situated; rather, the situation simply shifts around us as different things become ready-to-hand for purposes of addressing the problem. But in this process the situation of always being in a situation announces itself and tells us something not simply about the world (or what Heidegger calls the "worldhood of the world") but about our own existence (i.e., that we are always situated, that we are in the world in such a radical way that we are never able to step outside of it). One can never get a "view from nowhere," as Nagel (1986) puts it. The situated view (which in other terms Heidegger calls the "hermeneutic situation") is something that qualifies all theoretical knowledge and all third-person scientific accounts. Moreover, being situated is something that in its inconspicuousness tends to escape our attention, but not simply because we overlook it, in the way that we might overlook something in the environment. Rather, it is part of what it means to be situated that the fact of being situated commonly goes unnoticed.

This inconspicuousness of being situated leads Heidegger to a number of interesting existential observations, for example, the idea that we are thrown into the world, that our familiarity and fascination with the world generally leads to our being lost to ourselves, a form of inauthenticity. To the extent that being situated commonly goes unnoticed, our sense of our own existence is curiously incomplete and likely misguided – something that gets cashed out in terms of the problems encountered by classical cognitive science and strong artificial intelligence (see Wheeler, 2005). At the same time, such incompleteness is part of what our existence means and is tied to the finitude of our understanding. Heidegger also suggests some caution about any philosophy of the world that starts with an understanding of the world as a *res extensa* – Descartes' notion of an extended, spatial thing – or any philosophy of mind that starts with an understanding of the mind as a *res cogitans*, the idea that the mind is a substance or thing that thinks. What the Cartesian ontology overlooks is exactly the kind of situatedness that Heidegger describes. For Descartes, a thing (whether extended or thinking) is a substance, which, Heidegger explains, is a form of being that is present at hand and precisely not that form of being through which we are always situated (the ready-to-hand). Indeed, for Descartes, as for metaphysics generally and for natural science, the kind of being attributed to things, including the entity of the human being, is the kind of being that we access in an explicit (third-person) observational attitude and the kind of being that is open to analysis by cognition, "*intellectio* in the sense of the kind of knowledge we get in mathematics and physics" (Heidegger, 1968, p. 128). Heidegger's existential analysis is meant to show that human existence is precisely not something present-at-hand, an object among other objects, but is in-the-world, that is, always situated in a way that the world is primarily ready-to-hand.

Within our everyday situated projects, we also encounter entities with a being that is different from the things that are simply ready-to-hand. These are other humans, that is, other entities who are in-the-world in the way that we are in-the-world. For Heidegger, others appear within the pragmatic contexts that characterize our life. Along with the activities that we are engaged in, "we encounter not only entities ready-to-hand but also entities with *Dasein*'s kind of Being – entities for which, in their concern, the product [e.g., that we may be engaged in producing] becomes ready-to-hand" (1968, p. 100). Likely as not, our own activities often require others to play some role. I am never an isolated I without others (1968, pp. 147–163). Moreover, I do not encounter others primarily as those who are in opposition to me but as those from whom I do not distinguish myself. That is, in regard to other persons, I do not first or in a primary way encounter strangers; rather, I find myself already included with others. According to Heidegger, this *with* is to be understood as part of the very structure of human existence. That is, being-in-the-world already

includes being-with; being situated already involves being situated with others.[11]

Heidegger also presents an analysis of spatiality that is tied to our situated condition. Space is objective only derivatively; it is first of all related to the kinds of activities in which we are engaged. Thus, "a pathway which is long 'Objectively' can be much shorter than one which is 'Objectively' shorter still but which is perhaps 'hard going' and comes before us as interminably long" (1968, p. 141). Far and close are determined by our pragmatic relations. Five miles is a long distance to go to buy a newspaper but not so long if you intend to purchase a new home. Far and close also become metaphors that inform our evaluation of situations. I may feel closer to a person who lives a thousand miles away than to the person standing next to me (1968, p. 141).

Heidegger's discussion of embodiment is minimal and is found mostly in the context of his analysis of spatiality. Closeness, he maintains, is not definable as an objective distance from one's body. Even the "here" is not defined in terms of bodily location, but relative to a "there" that is defined pragmatically. How do I reach the thing that is there; how do I move myself over there? Only in relation to such concerns do I start to consider my "here." In this sense, in my situation, I am always "there," or at least directed to the "there," and in that light my "here" is defined as too far (from the "there" where I need to be), or too awkwardly positioned, and so on. Heidegger even suggests that right and left emerge in such pragmatic relations, and that our spatialization "in its 'bodily nature' is likewise marked out in accordance with these directions" (1968, p. 143). According to Heidegger, however, our embodied sense of right and left play no role in these determinations.

Heidegger's accounts of both intersubjectivity and spatiality remain closely tied to his analysis of the pragmatic or instrumental situation. Our encounters with others are always situated in pragmatic contexts – he often uses the example of work-related projects. As such, we encounter others not directly but across our dealings with things.

Others "show themselves in the world in their special environmental Being, and do so in terms of what is ready-to-hand in that world" (1968, p. 160). That is, others appear as engaged in pragmatic contexts similar to (or different from) our own. This analysis leaves little room for more direct and personal relations such as those based on emotional or even biological attraction. Without doubt, such personal relations may also be situated in instrumental contexts, but it is also possible to find such relations in what are closer to purely social or communicative contexts. Likewise, spatiality is cast in purely instrumental terms with little role for embodied processes. Heidegger does not deny that our existence is embodied, but he does not say very much about it.

Embodiment and Beyond

Merleau-Ponty, working in the same phenomenological tradition, takes both embodiment and intersubjectivity as more central to the way that experience works. His anti-Cartesian view of the active body derives from his study of Bergson and what were Husserl's unpublished manuscripts (especially Husserl, 1952). Husserl had outlined a concept of embodiment that distinguished Descartes' concept of the objective body (the body as an object extended in space, or as studied by biological science) and the lived body (*Leib*), which is the body that I experience and with which I act. It is the lived body that gears into the affordances of the world, and that, according to Husserl, is lived as an "I can." I approach the world with all of the possibilities for movement and action that are of my body. I experience the world in an egocentric spatial framework that is determined by my body. In this regard, "my body appears to me as an attitude directed towards a certain existing or possible task. And indeed its spatiality is not, like that of external objects or like that of 'spatial sensations', a *spatiality of position*, but a *spatiality of situation*" (Merleau-Ponty, 1962, p. 100).

Bergson, too, had provided a rich concept of embodied cognition. In *Matter and Memory* (1911), he understands memory to accumulate in the body as a set of responses to a complex set of solicitations from the world. The body retains

> *from the past only the intelligently coordinated movements which represent the accumulated efforts of the past; and it recovers those past efforts, not in the memory-images which recall them, but in the definite order and systematic character with which the actual movements take place. In truth, it no longer* represents *our pasts to us, it acts it; and if it still deserves the name memory, it is not because it conserves bygone images, but because it prolongs their useful effect into the present moment. (Bergson, 1911, p. 93)*

Merleau-Ponty supplements these philosophical sources with his own study of psychology and neurology. He borrows the concept of body schema from Head and Holmes (1911–1912). Consistent with Bergson's concept of embodied memory, Head's (1920) body schema dynamically organizes sensorimotor feedback in such a way that the final sensation of position is "charged with a relation to something that has happened before" (p. 606). Head uses the metaphor of a taximeter, which computes and registers movement as it goes. Merleau-Ponty relates this metaphor to Husserl's analysis of time-consciousness, which shows that we should think of experience not as momentary but as a temporally extended yet cohesive flow structured to enable retentions (of the just past) and protentions (of the just about to be). For Merleau-Ponty (1968), action is also temporally extended and organized according to the "time of the body, taximeter time of the corporeal schema" (p. 173). And this includes a retentional component, as well as anticipatory aspects: "At each successive instant of a movement, the preceding instant is not lost sight of. It is, as it were, dovetailed into the present. . . . [Movement draws] together, on the basis of one's present position, the succession of previous positions, which envelop each other" (Merleau-Ponty, 1962, p. 140).

This temporality is essential to the structure of our situated experiences and actions. We are situated not only spatially but also in time, and more generally in history. Indeed, Merleau-Ponty suggests that the experience of meaning or our ability to make sense of things within the space of the environment is only possible if our experience is structured in this temporal (retentional-protentional) way. Imagine if every experience we had completely fell away into a past that remained inaccessible to us. If our perception or thought were a strictly synchronic experience, there could be no meaningful structure to it; it would lack context and connection with anything else that we experience. But, Merleau-Ponty warns, we should not think that the problem is solved on a purely physiological or purely psychological level. That is, as Bergson had shown, the temporality of experience that is a necessary condition for us to be in a situation is not explainable as a physical trace within an objective body or brain, as such traces would be purely present and not sufficient to explain the past. But, Merleau-Ponty suggests, for the same reason neither is some unconscious or psychical trace sufficient. A present representation of the past or any present content of consciousness remains present; it cannot explain why we might take it as representing the past. Rather, he proposes that we have a direct but incompletely constituted "contact with the past in its own domain" (1962, p. 413), but not in the form of an object of knowledge. Temporality is in some way a "dimension of our being" (p. 415). More specifically, it is a dimension of our situated existence. Merleau-Ponty explains this along the lines of the Heideggerian analysis of being-in-the-world. It is in my everyday dealings with things that the horizon of the day gets defined: it is in "this moment I spend working, with, behind it, the horizon of the day that has elapsed, and in front of it, the evening and night – that I make contact with time, and learn to know its course" (pp. 415–416). It is not

that I represent the day as measurable by the clock;

> *I do not form a mental picture of my day, it weighs upon me with all its weight, it is still there, and though I may not recall any detail of it, I have the impending power to do so, I still 'have it in hand.'... Our future is not made up exclusively of guess-work and daydreams. Ahead of what I see and perceive... my world is carried forward by lines of intentionality which trace out in advance at least the style of what is to come. (1962, p. 416)*

Thus, Merleau-Ponty suggests, I feel time on my shoulders and in my fatigued muscles; I get physically tired from my work; I see how much more I have to do. Time is measured out first of all in my embodied actions as I "reckon with an environment" in which "I seek support in my tools, and am at my task rather than confronting it" (p. 416). Accordingly, my sense of time emerges out of my situated actions: "What, in fact, do we mean when we say that there is no world without a being in the world? Not indeed that the world is constituted by consciousness, but on the contrary that consciousness always finds itself already at work in the world" (p. 432).

What finds itself already at work in the world is not the Cartesian *cogito*, which, Merleau-Ponty suggests, thought has to strain to discover. Rather, "my body, in a familiar surrounding, finds its orientation and makes its way among objects without my needing to have them expressly in mind" (1962, p. 369). It is not a matter of an "I" standing back as an observer of the things around me; "rather it is that my consciousness takes flight from itself and, in them, is unaware of itself" (p. 369), and it does this in perception as in action. Merleau-Ponty means that there is no explicit or conceptual or reflective awareness of myself, or of my body, when I am engaged in my everyday projects. It is not that, as if by some inner power, I conceive of a space through which I need to guide my hand as it reaches to grasp something; the shape of my grasp is not a representation of the object that I intend to grasp. How could anything like this be possible, Merleau-Ponty asks, if my hand was "not already situated on a path" of action (p. 370)? The situation, then, is not laid out before me, as an object of consciousness; it is *a tergo* – I am in it and it is affecting me before I know it. Merleau-Ponty brings this affectivity into focus as an important component of situated cognition in a way that the theorists of enactive perception sometimes lose sight of.

In agreement with such theorists, Merleau-Ponty would say that vision or, more generally, perception is a form of action (1962, p. 377).[12] Merleau-Ponty, however, would balance this claim with the idea that the world, the situation we find ourselves in, also shapes our vision, and there is an element of passivity, or more properly affectivity, that is built into our way of being in the world. Moreover, this is not simply the case for perception but extends to the full cognitive-emotional-linguistic life of an individual and can easily have a normative significance:

> Children and many grown people are under the sway of 'situational values', which conceal from them their actual feelings – they are pleased because they have been given a present, sad because they are at a funeral, gay or sad according to the countryside around them, and, on the hither side of any such emotions, indifferent and neutral.... Our natural attitude is not to experience our own feelings or to adhere to our own pleasures, but to live in accordance with the emotional categories of the environment. (1962, pp. 379–380)

This kind of affectivity is obviously involved in intersubjectivity, which Merleau-Ponty analyzes in terms of what he calls "intercorporeality." Although Merleau-Ponty acknowledges the kind of analysis that Heidegger provided (i.e., that we encounter others across the various instrumental contexts involved in everyday life; see Merleau-Ponty, 1962, pp. 347–348), this is not a sufficient account because it does not answer precisely how we come to recognize

them, in the first place, as other persons rather than as, for example, other, albeit peculiar, instruments, or how we escape a kind of philosophical autism. Rather, one needs to understand this problem in terms of embodiment and to recognize that "the very first of all cultural objects, and the one by which all the rest exist, is the body of the other person as the vehicle of a form of behavior" (1962, p. 348). My access to the other is not by way of inference or analogy, using the other's body as a means to project myself into his or her mind. Rather, there is a direct interrelation between my body and the other's body at the level of perception (see Gallagher, 2001, 2005, chap. 9). Merleau-Ponty suggests what developmental psychology has only recently shown; namely, even young infants are capable of perceiving the intentions of others (1962, p. 352; see, e.g., Baldwin & Baird, 2001; Baldwin, Baird, Saylor, & Clark, 2001; Meltzoff, 1995). But, more than this, there is a direct resonance between my bodily behavior and the bodily behavior of the other.

This concept of intercorporeality finds good support in recent research on mirror neurons and neuronal resonance systems (e.g., Decety & Sommerville, 2003; Jeannerod, 2001; Rizzolatti, Fadiga, Gallese, & Fogassi, 1996; Rizzolatti, Fadiga, Matelli, et al., 1996), although these phenomena would not have led Merleau-Ponty in the direction of simulation theory, as we find in many authors (e.g., Gallese & Goldman, 1998; Jeannerod & Pacherie, 2004). If by *simulation* one means the use of a model to understand something that cannot be understood directly (e.g., the other's mind), a routine in which I manipulate a set of first-person as-if intentions – and this is the concept of simulation as it is defined by simulation theory – then this is clearly not what is going on in the activation of mirror neurons. The activation of resonance systems is automatic and subpersonal; that is, it is not I who do it but rather a process in the perceiver's brain that is elicited by the perception of the other's action. It is not something the subject decides to do, or does actively, and therefore it is not a simulation in that sense. If activation of the mirror system looks like a first-person pretense, it does so only to an external observer, not to the subject or system itself. Neurons do not fire as if they were generating action; they just fire.[13] If intercorporeality is about action, it is not entirely about my action in response to others but must include the effect that the other's action has on my system. It is not that I simulate the action of the other; it is rather that the other's action elicits the resonant responses in my system. In this affectivity we find ourselves pulled into a situation that is already intersubjective. Just as Merleau-Ponty (1962) suggests that "the theory of the body is already a theory of perception" (p. 203), we could suggest that the theory of the body is already a theory of inter-subjectivity.

A similar affectivity can be found in language, which in some sense may be a tool that we use for communicative action with others – "I learn [language] as I learn to use a tool, by seeing it used in the context of a certain situation" (Merleau-Ponty, 1962, p. 403) – but in another sense is not something that we totally control in our speech acts; rather, it is something that contributes to the constitution of the situation in which we find ourselves immersed. Thus,

> language takes on a meaning for the child when it establishes a situation for him. . . . The power possessed by language of bringing the thing expressed into existence, of opening up to thought new ways, new dimensions and new landscapes, is, in the last analysis, as obscure for the adult as for the child. (Merleau-Ponty, 1962, p. 401)

For Merleau-Ponty, language has this effect on us; in the speech act, the subject does not first represent the words to him- or herself; the subject "plunges into speech," and in so doing "reveals a motor presence of the word which is not the knowledge of the word" (1962, p. 403). My speech involves both my action and a passive affectivity: it is "a certain use made of my phonatory equipment, a certain modulation of my body as a being in the world" (1962, p. 403) that is

simultaneously and ambiguously my action and something that language does to me.

Language in the Context of Everyday Life

It is also the case that language use is a socially constrained practice. According to Wittgenstein (1953), our use of language is similar to playing a game that has a particular set of rules. Each use of language, however, involves a different language game, where the various games are run according to different sets of rules, and there are no universal rules. The games are played, we might say, in the world, and linguistic meaning is determined by the circumstances in which any particular game is played. On this view, a private language – a language spoken by a person who somehow grasps a conceptual truth about the world and then simply expresses that truth in words that receive their meaning from what goes on in his or her isolated mind – is not intelligible to, or learnable by, anyone other than the speaker, because a language consists of a communicative system that exists only between agents who are in social interaction. Linguistic meaning is generated in that kind of contextualized communication:

> Language games are the forms of language with which a child begins to make use of words. . . . When we look at the simple forms of language the mental mist which seems to enshroud our ordinary use of language disappears. We see activities, reactions, which are clear-cut and transparent. (Wittgenstein, 1969, p. 17)

Language is grounded on acting in particular contexts, and in the immediate reactions we have to others. The meanings of words are not the products of the linguistic system nor derived from a one-to-one correspondence to items in the world; rather, they are generated in the activities in which they are used. In this sense the use of a term does not presuppose having a concept stored in one's head. Rather, language is generated in the experience of the various contexts, practices, and activities that generate meaning. I do not think first in abstraction and then put a word to the concept (see, e.g., Gauker, 2003, 2005; Travis, 1989). There are no abstract principles or universal rules that would allow me to do that. I am first involved in some project in a specific setting – for example, a science lab, an operating room, an airport – and in a specific kind of discourse or conceptual practice that others share just in such settings, in the same way that they share certain instruments and technologies.

Wittgenstein is thus committed to some form of externalism, the idea that the meaning of a word or statement depends on the linguistic community in which the word is used or on what exists or happens in the environment (for a discussion, see Overgaard, 2004). To know what something means is not equivalent to simply being in a certain psychological state (Putnam, 1975). Following a rule in a language game does not involve a metacognitive interpretation of a rule that we somehow hold in our head. It is rather an ability that consists in nothing more or less than a practice, the mastery of which has been fine-tuned in particular settings (Wittgenstein, 1953, §201). If the notion of situated cognition emphasizes the contextual dimensions of such practices, where the meaning of a concept and the significance of verbal and gestural actions are inseparable from the setting of action, or from a form of life, then Wittgenstein is clearly describing situated cognition. In a well-defined situation, a practice can be well defined not by the existence of a rule book that is consulted, or by an explicit understanding of the rules, but by the physical and socially defined situation itself. The meaning of a concept is not fixed or universal, as it is dependent on its use in specific contexts, which are subject to temporal and historical change. What determines our concepts, Wittgenstein asserts, is "the whole hurly-burly of human actions, the background against which we see any action" (1967, §567).

Wittgenstein (1953, §§2–21) describes the practices of a builder and his assistant cooperating on a project in which meanings are created by ostensive reference precisely because the context is narrowly circumscribed so as to define a shared communicative situation. The tasks that compose this project are context specific and require skills that are not only about material construction but also about conceptual construction. A language and a set of concepts are created by the particular purposes involved in the situation. The vocabulary involved in this context consists of four words – *block, pillar, slab, beam* – names of the four items that the builders use to build. Grammatically, the utterance of one word is, in this context, a sentence. Moreover, when the builder utters the word *slab*, something gets accomplished – the assistant passes on a slab. Thus, in contrast to traditional approaches that make concept use a matter of detached and deliberative judgment, Wittgenstein maintains that concept use is more like a practical skill.

Proponents of situated cognition have argued both for and against the idea that this kind of skill is nonrepresentational, an issue that is taken up in other chapters of this volume.[14] Here it may be helpful to mention how Wittgenstein fits into this debate. A radical situationist can argue that because we are already in the world, we do not need to replicate the world in our head; an internal representation would be no better than the access we have to the world itself (see, e.g., Noë, 2004, p. 219). That is, we do not need a representation of the world if, in fact, the world is there for our having. When the builder says "slab," the assistant does not need to form a mental image of a slab; the slab is perceptually and handily available.[15] His concept of slab – its meaning – is equivalent to what he can do with it. At the very least we can say that a representation in the form of a mental image is not necessary for the successful use of language. Rowlands (2007), however, argues that the Wittgensteinian appeal to practice, understood as a form of intentional action, is not sufficient to rid cognitive systems of representations.

Wittgenstein, famously, developed a paradox concerning the possibility of rule following. Many commentators have thought that the key to solving this paradox lies in Wittgenstein's (1953) appeal to practice: "And hence also 'obeying a rule' is a practice. And to *think* one is obeying a rule is not to obey a rule. Hence it is not possible to obey a rule 'privately': otherwise thinking one was obeying a rule would be the same thing as obeying" (§202; see also Rowlands, 2007).

That is, in our ordinary practice in everyday contexts, we do not explicitly consult a set of rules to guide our practice; indeed, consulting the rules would itself be a practice different from the worldly practice that we are trying to guide. But Rowlands argues that the appeal to practice cannot explain away representations because, at least in the traditional view, practice involves intentional action, and this presupposes some form of representational content. "A practice is *what we do*. However, doing, it seems, is a form of acting and, as such, is essentially connected to intentional states. But intentional states are individuated by their content. . . . And content arises through representation" (Rowlands, 2007). To defeat representationalism once and for all, Rowlands argues, one needs a different concept of action than the one Wittgenstein was working with.[16]

It is not clear, however, that Wittgenstein was working with one concept of action or one concept of representation. It would seem to be a Wittgensteinian principle that there is no one correct answer to the question of whether a representational concept of skill, or action, or mind is better than a nonrepresentational one. In the cognitive sciences, for example, there are in fact many different meanings to the term *representation* (sometimes the term is used in discussing mental images, sometimes in discussing reference, and other times in describing neuronal firing patterns), and whether we are willing to accept the implications carried by the term may depend on the particular theoretical context in which it is used. Likewise, in regard to the question of everyday practice, it may be the case that some practices are representational and some are not, depending on how the term might be descriptive of the different pragmatic contexts. The argument between representationalists and nonrepresentationalists, the Wittgensteinian might suggest, is complicated by the use of multiple language games that differ from one discourse to another, from phenomenology and philosophy to psychology and neuroscience. The term *representation* does not have a meaning outside of its particular uses in these different language games. Is it better to use the word *representation* than to not use it? Better for what? Assuming that in certain contexts we agree on the concepts of intentional state and intentional content, Rowlands's insistence on the notion of representation may be correct for those contexts.

This brings us to the possibility that theories of situated cognition are themselves differently situated, within different disciplines or discourses, shaped by specific debates and specialized vocabularies. In any case, it is generally understood that Wittgenstein offers significant resources in support of the notion of situated cognition and against both Cartesian dualist metaphysics and more recent computationalist views.[17] For Wittgenstein, cognition cannot be reduced to propositional knowledge tightly organized in a well-formed mind; cognition is really a collection of skills and practices that rely on commonsense know-how and context-specific knowledge. The contexts of cognitive practices are also always social, so that what we call our beliefs have meaning only in virtue of their role in the social contexts in which we participate (see, e.g., Brandom, 1994).

Conclusion

Dewey, Heidegger, Merleau-Ponty, and Wittgenstein provide continuing resources for approaches to cognition that recognize its situated nature. I have suggested that these thinkers are not just part of the historical background, but that we can learn by thinking further about their contributions. They remind us that cognition is not only pragmatically situated but also always socially situated, not simply in the sense that the world is populated with others with whom we communicate but also in the sense that this communication and inter-action shape our cognitive abilities from the very beginning. They push us to real-ize that cognition not only is enactive but also elicited by our physical and social envi-ronment; that it not only involves a deeply embodied and temporally structured action but also is formed in an affective resonance generated by our surroundings and by others with whom we interact. These thinkers also challenge us to consider what it means to think of cognition as situated, what it means to do the science of situated cognition, and what it means if we end up with more than one conception of what situated cognition means.

Notes

1   Clark (1997) provides one of the best analyses of embodied and situated cognition. Ander-son (2003), for example, provides the follow-ing principled distinction:

> In my view, it is the centrality of the physical grounding project that differ-entiates research in embodied cogni-tion from research in situated cognition, although it is obvious that these two research programs are complementary and closely related.... Although related to and continuous with situated cog-nition, [embodied cognition] takes the physical grounding project as its cen-tral research focus. This project calls for detailing the myriad ways in which cogni-tion depends upon – is grounded in – the physical characteristics, inherited abili-ties, practical activity, and environment of thinking agents. (pp. 92, 126)

For further discussion of this distinction, see Prinz (this volume).

2   For a review of the psychological sources, see Clancey (this volume).

3   If I say, "The mind thinks," Nietzsche (1967) responds in the following way:

> If I say 'lightning flashes,' I have posited the flash once as an activity and a sec-ond time as a subject, and thus added to the event a being that is not one with the event but is rather fixed, is, and does not 'become.' – To regard an event as an 'effecting,' and this as being, that is the double error, of interpretation, of which we are guilty. (p. 289)

To conceive of the mind as a Cartesian think-ing thing is to posit something over and above the situation in which thinking occurs. Think-ing is not something that happens in a mind, as an attribute or quality that belongs to a subject who is isolated from the world; it is an activity or event in the world.

4   One clear exception to this is Johnson (2007), who borrows extensively from Dewey to sup-port his conception of embodied, situated cognition.

5   David Kirsh (2004) summarizes Peirce's view that "thought is not just *expressed* in work, it is *executed* in work":

> C. S. Peirce, in his prescient way, was fond of saying that a chemist as much thinks with test tube and beaker as with his brain. His insight was that the activ-ity of manipulating tools – in Peirce's case, manipulating representation rich tools and structures such as measuring devices, controllable flames, the lines in diagrams, written words – this activity is part of the overall process of thought. There is not the inner component, the true locus of thought, and its outer expres-sion. The outer activity is a constituent of the thought process, though for Peirce it had to be continually re-interpreted to be meaningful. (Kirsh, 2004, p. 206)

6   We cannot help but be reminded of Marx's thoughts along this same line. He maintains that there is a close connection between con-sciousness, which is a social product, and labor – a connection that is ruined in alienated forms of labor (Marx, 1974; Marx & Engels, 1964).

7   In this regard, the work of Hurley (2006), who considers the importance of imitation, has a closer affinity to Dewey. Thompson and Varela (2001) also emphasize the impor-tance of "cycles of intersubjective interaction,

involving the recognition of the intentional meaning of actions and linguistic communication (in humans)" (p. 424). These authors never mention Dewey, however.

8 On Dewey's naturalism, see Santayana (1939).

9 Notably, in the early 1930s, Dewey expressed interest in Heidegger's project, "particularly in his conception of the human situation" (Spiegelberg, 1976, p. 272).

10 For an extended discussion of Heidegger in contrast to Cartesian psychology, see Wheeler (2005).

11 Heidegger points out that this is the case even if one is alone. The claim that our existence is characterized as being-with "must be understood as an existential statement as to its essence. Even if the particular factical Dasein does *not* turn to Others, and supposes that it has no need of them or manages to get along without them, it *is* in the way of Being-with" (1968, p. 160).

12 See Noë (2004, pp. 1, 73), who cites Merleau-Ponty in this context: "You aren't given the visual world all at once. You are *in* the world, and through skillful visual probing – what Merleau-Ponty called 'palpation with the eyes' – you bring yourself into contact with it.... Like touch, vision is *active*" (Noë, 2004, p. 73). The idea of enactive perception recently put forward by Varela, Thompson, and Rosch (1991), Hurley (1999), O'Regan and Noë (2001), and others, often with references to Merleau-Ponty, has been discussed at least since the end of the nineteenth century. Noë could just as easily have cited Dewey's statement from his 1896 essay "The Reflex Arc Concept in Psychology":

> not with a sensory stimulus, but with a sensori-motor coordination... it is the movement which is primary, and the sensation which is secondary, the movement of body, head and eye muscles determining the quality of what is experienced.... [In audition] the sound is not a mere stimulus, or mere sensation; it again is an act.... It is just as true to say that the sensation of sound arises from a motor response as that the running away is a response to the sound. (p. 358)

13 See Gallagher (2007) for a critique of implicit simulation theory. I thank Philip Robbins for alerting me to an article by Goldman and Sripada (2005). They define a minimal sense of simulation that does not involve subjective control or the generation of pretend states. How a minimal concept of simulation differs from perception on an enactive model is not clear, however.

14 See chapters in this volume by Adams and Aizawa, Clark, Eliasmith, Millikan, and Rowlands. See also Anderson (2003), Brooks (1999), Clancey (1997), Hutto (2005), Kirsh (2004), Noë (2004), Rowlands (2007), and the special issue of *Phenomenology and the Cognitive Sciences* (vol. 1, no. 4, 2002) on Dreyfus's antirepresentationalism.

15 This may run against situated approaches to language comprehension and concept use that emphasize the role of simulation. For discussion, see chapters in this volume by Zwaan and Kaschak, and by Barsalou.

16 For a discussion of content and practice in Wittgenstein, see Hurley (1998, chap. 6).

17 Even if some philosophers still think that Turing wins out over Wittgenstein, current theorists of artificial intelligence and robotics are not so sure. Dennett (2003, p. 3) writes: "What Turing saw, and Wittgenstein did not, was the importance of the fact that a computer doesn't need to understand rules to follow them. Who 'won'? Turing comes off as somewhat flatfooted and naive, but he left us the computer, while Wittgenstein left us... Wittgenstein." Rodney Brooks (1999), in his work on robotics, clearly takes Turing's gift but works with it in a Wittgensteinian situated framework.

References

Anderson, M. L. (2003). Embodied cognition: A field guide. *Artificial Intelligence*, 149, 91–130.

Baldwin, D. A., & Baird, J. A. (2001). Discerning intentions in dynamic human action. *Trends in Cognitive Sciences*, 5, 171–178.

Baldwin, D. A., Baird, J. A., Saylor, M. M., & Clark, M. A. (2001). Infants parse dynamic action. *Child Development*, 72, 708–717.

Bergson, H. (1911). *Matter and memory* (N. M. Paul & W. S. Palmer, Trans.). London: George Allen & Unwin.

Brandom, R. (1994). *Making it explicit: Reasoning, representing, and discursive commitment.* Cambridge, MA: Harvard University Press.

Bredo, E. (1994). Reconstructing educational psychology: Situated cognition and Deweyan pragmatism. *Educational Psychologist, 29,* 23–35.

Brooks, R. (1999). *Cambrian intelligence: The early history of the new AI.* Cambridge, MA: MIT Press.

Brown, J. S., Collins, A., & Duguid, P. (1989). Situated cognition and the culture of learning. *Educational Researcher, 18,* 32–42.

Clancey, W. J. (1997). *Situated cognition: On human knowledge and computer representation.* Cambridge: Cambridge University Press.

Clark, A. (1997). *Being there: Putting brain, body, and world together again.* Cambridge, MA: MIT Press.

Decety, J., & Sommerville, J. A. (2003). Shared representations between self and other: A social cognitive neuroscience view. *Trends in Cognitive Sciences, 7*(12), 527–533.

Dennett, D. (2003). Ludwig Wittgenstein. *The Time 100.* Retrieved May 9, 2008, from http://www.time.com/time/time100/scientist/profile/wittgenstein.html.

Dewey, J. (1884). The new psychology. *Andover Review, 2,* 278–289. Retrieved May 9, 2008, from http://psychclassics.yorku.ca/Dewey/newpsych.htm.

Dewey, J. (1896). The reflex arc concept in psychology. *Psychological Review, 3,* 357–370. Retrieved May 9, 2008, from http://psychclassics.yorku.ca/Dewey/reflex.htm.

Dewey, J. (1938a). *Logic: The theory of inquiry.* New York: Holt, Rinehart & Winston.

Dewey, J. (1938b). *Experience and education.* New York: Macmillan.

Gallagher, S. (2001). The practice of mind. *Journal of Consciousness Studies, 8*(5–7), 83–107.

Gallagher, S. (2005). *How the body shapes the mind.* Oxford: Oxford University Press.

Gallagher, S. (2007). Logical and phenomenological arguments against simulation theory. In D. Hutto & M. Ratcliffe (Eds.), *Minding our practice: Folk psychology re-assessed* (pp. 63–78). Dordrecht, the Netherlands: Springer.

Gallese, V. L., & Goldman, A. (1998). Mirror neurons and the simulation theory of mind-reading. *Trends in Cognitive Sciences, 2,* 493–501.

Gauker, C. (2003). *Words without meaning.* Cambridge, MA: MIT Press.

Gauker, C. (2005). On the evidence for prelinguistic concepts. *Theoria, 54,* 287–297.

Goldman, A. I., & Sripada, C. S. (2005). Simulationist models of face-based emotion recognition. *Cognition, 94,* 193–213.

Head, H. (1920). *Studies in neurology* (Vol. 2). London: Oxford University Press.

Head, H., & Holmes, G. (1911–1912). Sensory disturbances from cerebral lesions. *Brain, 34,* 102–245.

Heidegger, M. (1968). *Being and time* (J. Macquarrie & E. Robinson, Trans.). New York: Harper & Row.

Hurley, S. (1998). *Consciousness in action.* Cambridge, MA: Harvard University Press.

Hurley, S. (2006). Active perception and perceiving action: The shared circuits hypothesis. In T. Gendler & J. Hawthorne (Eds.), *Perceptual experience* (pp. 205–259). New York: Oxford University Press.

Husserl, E. (1952). *Ideen zu einer reinen phänomenologie und phänomenologischen philosophie.* Zweites Buch. (M. Biemel, Ed.), Husserliana IV. The Hague: Martinus Nijhoff.

Hutto, D. (2005). Knowing *what?* Radical versus conservative enactivism. *Phenomenology and the Cognitive Sciences, 4*(4), 389–405.

Jeannerod, M. (2001). Neural simulation of action: A unifying mechanism for motor cognition. *NeuroImage, 14,* 103–109.

Jeannerod, M., & Pacherie, E. (2004). Agency, simulation, and self-identification. *Mind & Language, 19*(2), 113–146.

Johnson, M. (2007). *The meaning of the body.* Chicago: University of Chicago Press.

Kirsh, D. (2004). Metacognition, distributed cognition and visual design. In P. Gärdenfors & P. Johansson (Eds.), *Cognition, education, and communication technology* (pp. 147–180). Mahwah, NJ: Lawrence Erlbaum.

Lave, J. (1988). *Cognition in practice: Mind, mathematics, and culture in everyday life.* Cambridge: Cambridge University Press.

Lave, J., & Wenger, E. (1991). *Situated learning: Legitimate peripheral participation.* Cambridge: Cambridge University Press.

Marx, K. (1974). *Economic and philosophical manuscripts of 1844.* Moscow: Progress.

Marx, K., & Engels, F. (1964). *The German ideology* (S. Ryazanskaya, Trans.). Moscow: Progress.

Meltzoff, A. N. (1995). Understanding the intentions of others: Re-enactment of intended acts by 18-month-old children. *Developmental Psychology, 31,* 838–850.

Merleau-Ponty, M. (1962). *Phenomenology of perception* (C. Smith, Trans.). London: Routledge & Kegan Paul.

Merleau-Ponty, M. (1968). *The visible and the invisible* (A. Lingis, Trans.). Evanston, IL: Northwestern University Press.

Nagel, T. (1986). *The view from nowhere*. Oxford: Oxford University Press.

Nietzsche, F. W. (1967). *The will to power* (R. Hollingdale & W. Kaufmann, Trans.). New York: Random House.

Noë, A. (2004). *Action in perception*. Cambridge, MA: MIT Press.

Noë, A., & O'Regan, J. K. (2002). On the brain basis of perceptual consciousness. In A. Noë & E. Thompson (Eds.), *Vision and mind: Selected readings in the philosophy of perception* (pp. 567–598). Cambridge, MA: MIT Press.

O'Regan, J. K., & Noë, A. (2001). A sensorimotor approach to vision and visual consciousness. *Behavioral and Brain Sciences, 24*(5), 939–973.

Overgaard, S. (2004). The private language argument and externalism. *Danish Yearbook of Philosophy, 39,* 17–48.

Putnam, H. (1975). *Mind, language, and reality: Philosophical papers* (Vol. 2). Cambridge: Cambridge University Press.

Rizzolatti, G., Fadiga, L., Gallese, V., & Fogassi, L. (1996). Premotor cortex and the recognition of motor actions. *Cognitive Brain Research, 3,* 131–141.

Rizzolatti, G., Fadiga, L., Matelli, M., Bettinardi, V., Paulesu, E., Perani, D., & Fazio, G. (1996). Localization of grasp representations in humans by PET: 1. Observation compared with imagination. *Experimental Brain Research, 111,* 246–252.

Rowlands, M. (2007). Understanding the 'active' in 'enactive.' *Phenomenology and the Cognitive Sciences, 6*(4), 427–443.

Santayana, G. (1939). Dewey's naturalistic metaphysics. In P. A. Schilpp (Ed.), *The philosophy of John Dewey* (pp. 245–261). Evanston, IL: Northwestern University Press.

Spiegelberg, H. (1976). *The phenomenological tradition*. The Hague: Martinus Nijhoff.

Taylor, F. W. (1967). *The principles of scientific management*. New York: Harper & Brothers, W. W. Norton & Company. (Original work published 1911)

Thompson, E., & Varela, F. (2001). Radical embodiment: Neural dynamics and consciousness. *Trends in Cognitive Sciences, 5*(10), 418–425.

Travis, C. (1989). *The uses of sense: Wittgenstein's philosophy of language*. Oxford, UK: Clarendon.

Varela, F., Thompson, E., & Rosch, E. (1991). *The embodied mind*. Cambridge, MA: MIT Press.

Wheeler, M. (2005). *Reconstructing the cognitive world*. Cambridge, MA: MIT Press.

Wittgenstein, L. (1953). *Philosophical investigations* (G. E. M. Anscombe, Trans.). Oxford, UK: Blackwell.

Wittgenstein, L. (1967). *Zettel*. Oxford, UK: Blackwell.

Wittgenstein, L. (1969). *On certainty*. New York: Harper & Row.

Part II

CONCEPTUAL FOUNDATIONS

CHAPTER 4

How to Situate Cognition

Letting Nature Take Its Course

Robert A. Wilson and Andy Clark

1. The Situation in Cognition

The situated cognition movement in the cognitive sciences, like those sciences themselves, is a loose-knit family of approaches to understanding the mind and cognition. Although it has both philosophical and psychological antecedents in thought stretching back over the past century (see Clancey, this volume; Gallagher, this volume), it has developed primarily since the late 1970s as an alternative to, or a modification of, the then-predominant paradigms for exploring the mind in the cognitive sciences. For this reason it has been common to characterize situated cognition in terms of what it is not – a cluster of anti-isms. Situated cognition has thus been described as opposed to Platonism, Cartesianism, individualism, representationalism, and even computationalism about the mind. A cluster of positive characterizations of the situated cognition movement has also been given, both in terms of adjectival descriptions based on the approach of one or more figures of influence (e.g., Gibsonian, Heideggerian) and in terms of a medley of

related but underexplicated notions, such as embodiment, embeddedness, and externalism. Importantly, researchers who self-identify with the situated movement in the cognitive sciences have not been paralyzed by a relative lack of attention to the conceptual articulation of their paradigm. They have instead gotten on with the task of showing how the situated perspective leads to interesting and novel approaches to understanding particular cognitive abilities.

In this chapter we do some conceptual stocktaking. We propose a way of thinking of situated cognition that captures at least one important historical strand to the situated cognition movement but, more important, also provides the field with some normative direction. In a nutshell, the basic idea is that we should think of situated cognition as a form of cognitive extension, or rather as a variety of forms that such cognitive extension can take. Our aim is not to specify the essence of situated cognition (a misplaced goal here, as in many places in philosophical theorizing) nor to do justice to all of the work that has, at various times, been referred to under the heading "situated cognition" (or one of its many noms de plume; see section 2). Rather, it is to provide a way of conceptualizing situated cognition that helps both to focus and to reorient the study of cognition as a situated phenomenon.

The chief innovation of the chapter thus lies in a preliminary articulation of the variety of forms that cognitive extension can take. This articulation involves two main dimensions, one tracking the nature of the augmentative resource and the other tracking the durability and reliability of the augmentation. The resulting matrix captures many forms of cognitive extension that seem almost trivial and that most parties to the debate over the nature of cognition can take for granted. But it also accommodates a variety of forms that cognitive extension can take that challenge us to reassess what cognition is, who we (as cognizers) are, and what the future holds for the study of cognition. In addition, once we provide such a nuanced framework for thinking about the varieties of cognitive extension, we are better able to respond to several important recent objections to the conception of situated cognition as cognitive extension.

To set the scene, we begin with some potted history, in the form of a brief tour through some of the anti-isms and positive characterizations of situated cognition. One caveat, however, before we get going. An important strand to the situated cognition movement that we are unable to discuss here directly concerns the ways in which cognition is embodied. There is a range of discussion of this idea elsewhere in the volume, as well as in our own previous work (Clark, 1997, 2003; Wilson, 2004a), but it remains a separate project to relate the embodiment of cognition to the idea of cognitive extension that we are concentrating on here (but see MacIver, this volume; see also Gallagher, 2005). Suffice it to say that we think that taking seriously the embodiment of cognition will reinforce the perspective that we are developing, primarily because many forms of embodied cognition, properly understood, will turn out to involve

just the kinds of cognitive extension that we articulate here.

2. Situated Cognition: A Potted Recent History

Cognition, it is widely agreed, both stems from and generates the activities of physical individuals located in particular kinds of environments. But despite this general consensus, the views of cognition and the mind that constituted a kind of status quo in the field by the end of the 1970s took a particular view of the relationship among cognition (or the mind), individuals, and environments – a view that was typically understood to have fairly direct implications for how to study cognition and the mind. According to this view, the cognitive sciences were to embrace what Jerry Fodor (following Hilary Putnam) called "methodological solipsism" and were, in effect, to bracket off the world beyond the individual in characterizing and individuating cognitive states and structures. We will follow common practice and refer to this as the individualistic conception of the mind and cognition (Wilson, 1995, 2003, 2004a, 2004b).

On one of the strongest such individualistic conceptions, cognition takes place inside the head, wedged between perception (on the input side) and action (on the output side), constituting what Susan Hurley (1998) has called a kind of cognitive sandwich. It involves the computational processing of mental representations, where these are language-like both in their constituents (concepts as words) and in their structural composition (mental representations as generated by, and decomposable in terms of, an underlying mental syntax). Such processing relies purely on formal or syntactic features of the symbols themselves and the rules by which they are manipulated, rather than on broader features of the individuals who instantiate them and the environments in which they operate. On the version of this view most influential among philosophers of mind, much of this cognitive architecture is universal across the species and innately specified. The task of developmental and cognitive psychologists is to uncover these innate structures and to understand how it is that they eventually gave rise to the diversity that we appear to see in everyday cognitive activity.

Even though cognition takes place inside the head, on this view, cognition is not simply to be given a neural description. For cognition is taken to be, in an important sense, substrate neutral: it is not what you are made of but how you are functionally organized that matters for cognition. This view, functionalism, has sometimes been presented as reflecting the old blues adage that "it ain't the meat, it's the motion" that matters (e.g., Clark, 1989, p. 21) – in this case, for mind. In truth, however, within the individualistic paradigm for the study of cognition that we are sketching there was not so much attention to motion as to relatively static functional structure and organization. That is why researchers constructing computer programs (and sometimes program-driven robots) could view themselves as contributing not simply to the study of cognition through simulation but also to the enterprise of creating genuinely cognitive beasts, with creating artificial intelligence. And that is at least one reason why the neurosciences were often viewed, at least until the 1980s, as a kind of junior partner in the venture to understand and explain cognition. Thus, although the neurosciences could tell us much about the realization of cognitive processes and structures in certain kinds of cognizers, their findings were explanatorily secondary to the investigations of psychologists, linguists, and computer scientists who were exploring the functional structure of the mind as such.

Fodor's *The Language of Thought* (1975) and *The Modularity of Mind* (1983) are particularly striking expressions of this kind of view in philosophy, with Fodor taking much of his cue from Noam Chomsky's work in linguistics. But this view of cognition was manifest across the cognitive sciences more generally, including in psychology

and artificial intelligence. Exemplars include Zenon Pylyshyn's *Computation and Cognition* (1984), and Allen Newell and Herb Simon's physical symbol system hypothesis (see Newell, 1980; Newell & Simon, 1976) according to which cognition is the algorithmic manipulation of symbol structures. Perhaps the best-known large-scale project in artificial intelligence that steadfastly adopts a classic, individualistic perspective is the CYC project, an ongoing, twenty-year project to create a general-purpose, commonsense reasoner (see http://www.cyc.com).

Philosophical doubts about individualism were first raised in the now-classic arguments of Hilary Putnam (1975) and Tyler Burge (1979), both turning on the question of whether individualistic views of the mind and cognition could adequately account for meaning or mental content. These original challenges to individualism were cast in terms of whether psychological states, particularly intentional states, should be individuated or taxonomized in accord with the constraint of individualism. For this reason one of us has elsewhere called the resulting forms of externalism *taxonomic externalism* (Wilson, 2000, 2004a); it has also been called "traditional externalism" and "philosophical externalism." The general idea was to continue to view intentional or content-laden mental states as some kind of internal state of the individual but to argue that, nonetheless, because of their content, they did not supervene on, or were not metaphysically determined by, what fell within the physical boundary of that individual. Hence the debates over whether folk psychology was individualistic (Burge, 1979; Fodor, 1982; Loar, 1988), over whether the notion of content used in David Marr's celebrated computational theory of vision is internalist or externalist (Burge, 1986a; Egan, 1992; Segal, 1989; Shapiro, 1997), and over the relationship between individualism and the normativity of the mental (Burge, 1986b; Ebbs, 1998; Pettit, 1993).

More radical forms of externalism about the mind abound and go by a variety of labels. These include *locational externalism*

(Wilson, 2000, 2004a), *environmentalism* (Rowlands, 1999), *vehicle externalism* (Hurley, 1998), and *the extended mind* (Clark & Chalmers, 1998). One way or another, all these locutions aim to suggest that the mind and the cognitive processes that constitute it extend beyond the boundary of the skin of the individual agent. The extended mind thesis very explicitly identifies cognitive systems themselves as reaching beyond individuals into their physical and social environments. Such theses challenge individualism directly by implying that an individualistic psychology, at best, can tell only part of the story about cognitive processing: the inside story. An early gesture at such a view was *wide computationalism* (Wilson, 1994), the view that the computational systems that make up the mind can extend into, and include as parts of themselves, aspects of an organism's environment, a view that we will discuss further herein.

Locational externalism, environmentalism, and the extended mind thesis are radical forms of externalism that do not rest on claims and intuitions about whether the content of a pair of states of two individuals in different environments (or one individual in two such environments over time) is the same or different, or on questions about how particular intentional states are taxonomized, or on questions concerning the role of the physical or social environments in individuating such states. Instead, they appeal to the nature of psychological processing, to the arbitrariness of the head (or the skin) for bounding cognitive systems, and to the structure of real-life, online cognitive activity in the world. Thus, if the extended mind thesis is true, it is true in virtue of something implementationally deep about cognition, rather than following directly from any traditionally externalist view of mental content.

We thus arrive at the basic idea of this chapter: work in situated cognition is best viewed as an ongoing series of investigations into cognitive extensions, extensions of the mind into the physical and social world.

3. Extensions in Biology, Computation, and Cognition

Cognitive extensions, like house extensions, come in a surprising variety of forms. Some are truly, massively, staggeringly transformative, and others are content to project a previously existing theme. Some are seamless and elegant, and others expose a barely connected hodgepodge of warring materials. Some are visibly permanent, built to persist as long as the main structure does, and others are more temporary, apt for rapid dissolution or replacement. Some appear homely, and others can seem alien (some find them monstrous). And the very idea of cognitive extension, just like its bricks-and-mortar cousin, can be apt to provoke objection and outcry. In this section and the next we present what seem to us to be the main varieties of possible cognitive extension. Distinguishing these varieties is, we believe, the crucial first step toward revealing the attractions of externalism, allaying the fears of critics, and generally restoring peace to the neighborhood that proponents and critics of externalism share.

We should go further, however, and not simply think of cognitive and house extensions as alike but as instances of the very same kind of activity: the activity of modifying one's environment from the situation in which one find's oneself in ways that meliorate that situation. Thinking is a kind of building, a kind of intellectual niche construction that appropriates and integrates material resources around one into preexisting cognitive structures. In cognition, agents modify or augment the capacities that those preexisting structures enable. Part of the point of suggesting that we move beyond the "minds are like houses" metaphor and view cognition itself as a kind of building activity is to introduce a deeper analogy for understanding the idea of cognitive extension, one anchored in recent thinking about genetics, development, and evolution. Several recent paradigms in the biological sciences – in particular, niche construction theory, developmental systems theory, and the idea of an extended physiology – advocate a move beyond the boundary of the organism and an accompanying reconceptualization of some of the processes at the core of biology. The idea of cognitive extension can be fruitfully approached by means of these examples (see also Wilson, 2004b, 2005).

Niche construction theory has been articulated by John Odling-Smee and his colleagues over the past twenty years and receives its most elaborate, synthetic exposition in Odling-Smee, Laland, and Feldman's *Niche Construction: The Neglected Process in Evolution* (2003). Niche construction, they say, "occurs when an organism modifies the . . . relationship between itself and its environment by actively changing one or more of the factors in its environment" (2003, p. 41). Niche construction (see also discussion in Clark, 2005b) is a widespread process in the natural world, encompassing not only the construction of nests and burrows in mammals, birds, and insects, but also the manipulation of existing social structures, the off-loading of physiological functions to environmental resources, and the appropriation and adaptation of environmental resources as biological and cultural tools. But although niche construction has long been recognized as an important process in certain contexts, Odling-Smee et al. place it center stage in the biological sciences, viewing it as introducing a missing dynamic aspect to the theory of evolution that has radical implications for the biological sciences. Niche construction, on this view, provides the key to integrating ecology and genetics via an extended notion of inheritance – ecological inheritance (inheritance via genetic and nongenetic – e.g., cultural, artifactual – means). And, they have argued, the pervasive character of niche construction and its contrast with natural selection make it "nothing less than a second selective process in evolution" (2003, p. 178).

Developmental systems theory (DST) derives from Susan Oyama's *The Ontogeny of Information* (1985) and has its flagship presentation in Oyama, Griffiths, and Gray's collection *Cycles of Contingency* (2001). De-velopmental systems theory is rooted in skepticism about the emphasis placed on the role of genes in accounts of development and evolution that arose in the wake of Richard Dawkins's *The Selfish Gene* (1976) and the development of sociobiology in the mid-1970s. Proponents of DST argue that genes are but one (albeit important) developmental resource, and that the basic unit of development is the developmental system that (typically) contains genes as components. Genetic systems thus do not exhaust the kinds of developmental systems there are with other developmental systems, such as the chromatin-marking system, being epigenetic, whereas others, such as those for the transmission of behavior and culture, stretch not simply beyond the boundary of the nucleus of the cell but beyond the organism into the environment (see Jablonka & Lamb, 2005). These wide or extended developmental systems have previously (and problematically) been conceptualized quite independently from individualistic developmental systems, separated by the divide between culture and biology, or that between learning and inheritance, or between environment and genes.

Finally, the ecological physiologist J. Scott Turner has recently presented a range of examples, including coral reefs (consisting of polyps, calcite deposits, and protozoan flagellates), termite mounds (complete with their own interspecies communities), and mole-cricket burrows in which, as Turner (2000) says of the first of these examples, an "important component of the physiological process takes place outside the animal" (p. 24). Turner aims to show, by a series of detailed examples, that the notion of physiological organ, given its role in biological and evolutionary explanation, ought to be understood so as to include key nonbiological structures such as the "singing burrow" that amplifies the song of the mole cricket (for discussion of this example, see Clark, 2005a). Turner takes his inspiration from Richard Dawkins's (1982) idea of the extended phenotype, according to which key survival-relevant genetic effects should not always be sought solely within the organismic skin bag. In a similar vein, Turner argues that physiological processes, such as metabolism, energy transfer, and homeostasis, extend beyond the boundary of the organism, and that this provides grounds for thinking of the physiology of organisms themselves as extending beyond their own outer membranes, whether it be skin, shell, or soft tissue.

These recent emphases on niche construction, developmental systems, and extended physiology in the biological sciences suggest blind spots in past biological thought and fruitful directions for future research. And the new suggestions all share a premise central to our idea of situated cognition as cognitive extension: the individual organism is an arbitrary stopping point for the scientific study of at least a range of relevant processes in the corresponding domain. In the domain of cognition, no one is an island.

Time, then, to get a little closer to cognition itself. Central to much cognitive science is the assumption that cognition is computational, an assumption manifest in general appeals to the metaphor of the mind as computer, in the construction of computational models for particular problem-solving processes, and in the claims of so-called strong artificial intelligence that appropriately programmed machines are (or would be, if we could only construct them) cognizers. At the start of this chapter we mentioned computationalism in the list of isms that have sometimes been thought to be challenged by the idea of situated cognition. We think, however, that any such inference is mistaken. It is mistaken because computation itself can be an extended process in just the sense in which we are suggesting that cognition can be an extended process.

This is the view that one of us has called "wide computationalism" (Wilson, 1994, 1995, chap. 3), and the basic idea behind it is simple. Traditionally, the sorts of computation that govern cognition have been thought to begin and end at the skull. Computationalism has thus been viewed as entailing an individualistic view of cognition.

But (see Hurley, 1998, pp. 335–336) why think that the skull constitutes a magic boundary beyond which cognitively relevant computation ends and mere causation begins? We are creatures embedded in informationally rich and complex environments. The computations that occur inside the head are an important but nonexhaustive part of the corresponding computational systems. A wide or extended computational perspective opens up the possibility of exploring computational units that include the brain together with aspects of the brain's beyond-the-head environment. Wide computational systems thus literally extend beyond the confines of the skull into the world.

The first point we want to make is that the idea of extended computation is entirely noncontroversial in noncognitive contexts. Indeed, it is presumed in a large variety of contexts in which computational techniques are brought to bear on understanding causal mechanisms and processes. Computational processes occur within discrete entities – whether they be biological cells, computer chips, or larger entities comprised of these units – but they can also occur between such units. Typically, such extended computational processes constitute a larger computational system, but that should not obscure the fact that, with respect to those discrete, metal-shell bounded units, genuine computational processes physically extend beyond the boundaries of those same units. There is nothing ersatz, for example, about the computations that flow across a grid system or a local area network.

The second point is that there are at least some cognitive contexts in which the idea of extended computation should be just as uncontroversial. As an example, and to illustrate how extended computationalism modifies the traditional view of cognition as computation, consider Figures 4.1 and 4.2, which depict two ways in which one might multiply two three-digit numbers.

On the traditional computationalist view, the first step in the process of multiplication is to code some form of input (e.g., visual or auditory input) from the world into internal symbols. The computations involved

Figure 4.1. Traditional computationalism: Multiplying with only internal symbols. Computational system ends at the skull. Computation must be entirely in the head: (1) code external world, (2) model computations between internal representations only, (3) explain behavior on the basis of outputs from step 2.

in multiplication then take place entirely between these internal symbols; computation ends at the skull. Contrast this with an extended computational view of multiplication, which involves some kind of internal symbol manipulation or computation, but which also involves the active manipulation of symbols – such as those on a piece of paper – that are not in the head, as depicted in Figure 4.2.

On the extended computationalist view, multiplication begins as a causal process between external and internal symbols, but that initial relationship is then incorporated as part of the computational process itself. The resultant computational system itself is not restricted to what is inside the head but includes both internal and external symbols. This allows one to understand the entire activity of multiplication as it is typically performed as a dynamic series of perception-action cycles that are computational in nature.

It is this conception of extended computation, we claim, that is invoked in much of the recent work in situated robotics (e.g., Brooks, 1991a, 1991b, 1999), animate vision

(e.g., Ballard et al., 1997), and cognitive anthropology (e.g., Hutchins, 1995). It is not a distinct, novel, or ersatz kind of computation but simply an extension of the standard view of computationalism, just as the three examples that we began this section with – that of niche construction, developmental systems, and extended physiology – are extensions of quite standard corresponding views in the biological sciences.

Wide computationalism (or extended computation) thus provides the basis for one direct argument for extended cognition. Suppose that we grant the assumption of computationalism that has structured much of the work in cognitive science. If the kinds of computation that at least parts of cognition involve are extended, then those parts of or aspects to cognition will also be extended. This is to reject the traditional individualistic understanding of computationalism, of course, but we have suggested that doing so does not require a novel or nonstandard view of computation itself. Rather, it is to sift the wheat of computation from the chaff of individualism. Thus, far from being incompatible with

Figure 4.2. Extended computationalism: Multiplying with internal and external symbols. Computational systems can extend beyond the skin into the world. Computation may not be entirely in the head: (1) identify representational or informational forms – whether in the head or not – that constitute the relevant computational system, (2) model computations between these representations, (3) behavior itself may be part of the wide computational system.

computationalism, situated cognition as extended cognition follows rather directly from it.

But whether or not one accepts computationalism, and the claims we have made about it here, there remain a variety of forms that extended cognition can take. We turn now to examine two major dimensions that structure much of this variety.

4. Articulating the Idea of Cognitive Extension

The first dimension concerns the nature of the nonneural resources that are incorporated into extended cognitive behaviors, dispositions, and activities. Such resources may be natural, technological, or sociocultural in nature, and each of these determines distinct kinds of cognitive systems. The second dimension concerns the durability and reliability of the larger (extended) system. The system may be a temporary and one-off construct, a temporary but repeatable one, or something more permanent. Let's take the two dimensions in turn.

Natural extended cognitive systems are those cognitive systems containing natural resources from the cognizer's environment that have been functionally integrated into the cognitive repertoire of that cognizer. A natural resource for a creature is any feature of its natural world that it draws on for some aspect of its continued functioning. Oxygen is a natural resource for respiration, and fruit (for humans and other primates) is a natural resource for nutrition. But some organisms also require cognitive resources, and many of these form part of the natural world of those organisms. Natural resources, including cognitive resources, can simply be used by organisms, but sometimes this use does not merely fuel a preexisting system – as in the previously mentioned cases of the respiratory and digestive systems – but also augments the system itself and the capacities that it possesses.

To take a noncognitive example, empty shells are a resource that hermit crabs use for protection. Because this use both physically and functionally changes the relevant capacities of hermit crabs, it is plausible and relatively uncontroversial to see the crab together with its appropriated shell as a unified entity, one with capacities and abilities due in part to the shell that a shell-less crab alone does not possess.

As in this example, one should expect to find natural extended systems for cognitive functions just when there has been sufficient world-mind constancy for organisms to reliably exploit that constancy to lighten their internal cognitive load. Such exploitation manifests what one of us (Clark, 1989) has dubbed the 007 principle: know only as much as you need to know to get the job done. As Clark said in articulating this principle, in general, "evolved creatures will neither store nor process information in costly ways when they can use the structure of the environment and their operations upon it as a convenient stand-in for the information-processing operations concerned" (1989, p. 64). Perception is one prima facie likely domain in which this is true. One of us has previously argued (Wilson, 1994, 1995, chap. 3) that it is here that some of the best candidates for wide computational systems can be found and (Wilson, 2004a, chap. 7) that Dana Ballard's animate-vision paradigm also exemplifies the 007 principle and posits natural extended cognitive systems for perception.

A second kind of extended cognitive system appropriates not natural but technological resources. In contrast with natural resources, technological resources are artificial in the sense of being made or developed by human agents. But like natural resources, they encompass a diverse range of resources, from those that are used in a novel, one-off manner, such as a book that you use on the spur of the moment to jam open a window, to those that represent permanent features of our everyday life, such as prosthetic limbs. In the cognitive domain, technological resources include dedicated cognitive artifacts, such as instruments for the measurement and recording of data, and those that extend our sensory abilities; make-do procedures, such as scribbling sticky notes as reminders and guiding one's immediate behavior by reference to improvised lists; and devices with more general functions, such as cell phones and other telecommunications equipment that can be used for cognitive augmentation (see Clark, 2003). Like natural extended cognitive resources, such technological resources can serve merely as inputs to a skin-bound cognitive system, but there is a range of cases in which they do more than this and become functionally integrated into a larger cognitive system.

An electronics engineer usually has a pretty clear sense of what is mere input to a system and what is an integrated addition that alters the system itself. The distinction here is intuitive enough, even if it is one that has been surprisingly hard to pin down (for a classic attempt, see Haugeland, 1995/1998; for a slightly different treatment, see Clark, 2007). Much obviously turns on degree and complexity of integration. But much also turns on how one conceives the goal or purpose of the system at hand. The purpose of the radio being to receive, decode, and play contents borne by radio signals, anything locally added that helps it do so (e.g., a better transistor at some key point, a signal amplifier) looks like an augmentation of the system rather than a mere input. This is so whether the additional transistor or amplifier falls inside the preexisting boundaries of the radio or lies beyond them.

In most cases when we are tempted to speak of cognitive augmentation, the same rule of thumb seems to apply: we find cognitive augmentation where new resources help accomplish a recognizable cognitive task in an intuitively appropriate manner, such as by enabling the faster or more reliable processing of information that some goal or project requires. The new resource need not bear any close mechanical or functional similarity to the rest of the system. Rather, it needs to achieve functional integrity when operating together with the rest of some cognitive system that serves the kinds of purposes that that cognitive system has served: to perceive, to decide, to remember, to behave. More radical cases of cognitive augmentation may be possible – such as those

in which the resulting system serves radically different purposes – but as with well-crafted devices generally, we think that cognitive extension tends to be stepwise, building on the solid achievements of systems that have already earned their keep in some particular domain.

A third kind of extended cognitive system is also worth distinguishing, though it might be thought subsumable under either the natural or the technological (or both). These are sociocultural systems, which are formed when there is stable reliance by an individual in his or her cognitive activity on social structures, other individuals, and their cultural products. These structures and products serve as resources for a range of cognitive activities. Perhaps the most striking examples of sociocultural cognitive resources involve writing systems, broadly construed, which have constituted a relatively durable, public cognitive resource crucial to education, training, regimentation, commerce, and military conquest in the Western world for millennia. But there are many others, including those that derive from practices of distributing cognitive labor between individuals, from the parental transmission of information to children to the establishment of ritual, musical, and ceremonial orderings.

For many individuals, such sociocultural resources are like natural cognitive resources in that they can be taken for granted as part of the normal conditions under which their cognitive abilities develop, they acquire specific skills, and they learn particular facts. Sociocultural resources are a kind of cognitive oxygen, simply given as part of the natural world in which at least much cognition takes place. On the other hand, sociocultural resources and the cognitive systems that they partially constitute are not biologically – genetically, physically, or evolutionarily – givens, as they have been created and modified by the activities of past generations of people. So sociocultural resources are distinguished by their origin. But they are worth highlighting in reflecting on extended cognition because, we claim, they constitute a crucial part of some of those cognitive abilities and activities that distinguish human cognition from its nearest neighbors. There may be animal cultures, but it is only in *Homo sapiens* that we find diverse cultures of cognition, social structures, and products that, whatever their own origins, now significantly augment the cognitive capacities of individuals who are embedded in them.

As we saw with extended cognitive systems that are either natural or technological, sociocultural extended cognitive systems exist when the appropriate type of resource is not simply used by an agent but becomes functionally integrated into the cognitive functioning of that agent (see also Clark, 2007). We think that the kinds of sociocultural resources that we have mentioned often meet this additional criterion. Writing systems, for example, are not simply used by agents with given cognitive abilities but significantly augment the cognitive abilities that those agents possess, such as the capacity for short- and long-term memory, the ability to keep track of the relationship between abstract propositions as is often required in reasoning, and the ability to systematically fix and then critique our own ideas (see Clark, 1998; cf. Goody, 1977). Similarly, mathematical notation does not simply feed existing mathematical abilities – although it does that, to be sure – but also builds on those abilities to produce an agent with significantly greater mathematical capacities. The difference between the ability to multiply using Arabic numerals versus that using Roman numerals serves as a reminder of how much specific forms of writing can contribute to particular abilities here.

So much for the first dimension to extended cognition, whether the cognitive resources it incorporates are natural, technological, or sociocultural. The second dimension concerns the durability and reliability of the extended cognitive system that results from the functional integration of such resources. Extended cognition, we have so far proposed, occurs when internal and external resources become fluently tuned and integrated so as to enable the larger system – the biological agent plus specific items of cognitive scaffolding – to engage

in new forms of intelligent problem solving. Sometimes these larger problem-solving ensembles are transient creations, geared toward a specific purpose (e.g., doing the accounts, writing a play, locating a star in the night sky), and combine core neural resources with temporary add-ons (e.g., pen, paper, diagrams, instruments). At other times, they involve more stable and permanent relationships between biological agents and extended cognitive resources. We first consider the more transient varieties.

Consider, by way of a staging analogy, the idea of a task-specific device (TSD) discussed by Bingham (1988). The notion of a TSD was introduced as a theoretical tool to help tackle the problem of understanding the organization of human action. In brief, a TSD is a temporary but highly integrated assembly created to accomplish some kind of goal. In the motor arena, a TSD is a soft-assembled (i.e., temporary and easily dissoluble) whole that meshes the dynamics that are inherent in the human action system and the so-called incidental dynamics contributed by various extraorganismic factors and forces. That is to say, TSDs are "assembled over properties of both the organism and the environment" (Bingham, 1988, p. 250). In each specific case, the biological action-system will need to recruit some complex, nonlinear combination of contributions from its four chief subsystems – the link-segment system, the musculoskeletal system, the circulatory system, and the nervous system – and do so in a way expressly tailored to accommodate and exploit the incidental task dynamics introduced by, for example, a handle on a paint pot, a bouncing ball, or a windsurfing rig out on the open sea. These examples span the three main kinds of incidental task dynamics identified by Bingham – namely, those tasks that simply introduce inertial and dissipative properties or mechanical constraints (as when we carry the paint pot by the handle); those that involve absorbing, storing, and/or returning energy (as when bouncing a ball); and those that involve coupling with systems that have their own independent energy sources (the windsurfing rig powered by the wind and waves of the open sea).

Why study such TSDs? One reason, the most obvious one, is that it is these very ensembles that are locally at work in many of the most distinctive cases of human action. We alone on the planet seem capable of creating and exploiting such a wide variety of action amplifiers, ranging from hammers and screwdrivers to archery bows and bagpipes, to planes, trains, and automobiles. But a second reason, far less obvious, is that working backward from the analysis of these complex wholes may itself contribute important insights concerning the contributions and functioning of the biological human action system itself. Although a natural first thought would be to try to understand each of the four main biological subsystems in isolation, then perhaps to look at their coupled interactions, then finally to add in the incidental dynamics, it turns out that this simple stepwise approach may be doomed to failure. The reason is that the potential behaviors of the whole biological action system are determined by staggeringly complex nonlinear interactions between the four main subsystems and the incidental dynamics. The good news, though, is that in a typical TSD the degrees of freedom of this large and unwieldy system are dramatically reduced. The whole point, in fact, of soft-assembling a TSD is to reduce the initially high-dimensional available dynamics to a much lower dimensional structure and thus to establish an effectively controllable resource (see, e.g., Fowler & Turvey, 1978; Salzman & Kelso, 1987). As a result:

> *The challenge is to work backwards from a description of the reduced dynamics to an understanding of the manner in which subsystem dynamics couple and co-constrain one another to produce the observed dynamical system. Because information about both task-specific dynamics and the individuated resource dynamics is required, the strategy unites the efforts of behavioral scientists and physiologists in an integrated and coherent effort. (Bingham, 1988, p. 237)*

We have described this strategy in a little detail because many of the key ideas apply directly, it seems to us, to the case of those extended systems that involve temporary, transient forms of cognitive augmentation. Let us label these "transient extended cognitive systems" (TECS).

A TECS is a soft-assembled whole that meshes the problem-solving contributions of the human brain and central nervous system with those of the (rest of the) body and various elements of local cognitive scaffolding. To further probe the structure of the space of possible TECS, we might distinguish cases according to the durability and reliability of the relationship between agent and resource. Thus we might want to distinguish temporary, one-off relationships from those that, though transient, are regularly repeated. To solve a new brainteaser, an agent may generate a brand-new, one-off kind of TECS. A practiced crossword-puzzle solver, by contrast, when confronted with a new puzzle (and as usual armed with pen and paper), may rapidly generate a well-understood, often-repeated form of TECS. An intermediate case, for many, might be when working on the popular and strangely satisfying Sudoku puzzles that have cropped up in newspapers all over the world. We could repeat this kind of exercise in filling out the details of many other examples of TECS. A seasoned journalist, armed with a word processor and a bunch of notes, may rapidly cycle through a whole range of TECS, some one-off and others repeated; ditto for the mountaineer equipped with compass, map, and altimeter, and so on.

Now, there is no doubt that, in each specific case involving a TECS, the biological brain is (currently) an especially active player, recruiting some complex, nonlinear combination of contributions from various types of onboard neural circuit and resources, and doing so in a way expressly tailored to accommodate and exploit the additional representational and computational potentials introduced by, for example, the compass, the pen and paper, or the word-processing package. These examples are, incidentally, the rough cognitive equivalents of the three main kinds of incidental task dynamics identified by Bingham – namely, those that simply introduce useful information or constraints (the compass), those that support the off-loading and returning of information (the pen and paper), and those that introduce new active sources of information processing and representation-transformation (the word-processing software). But despite this crucial role for the biological brain, there is much to be gained from the complementary study of TECS in their own right.

As before, the most obvious, and highly motivating, reason to do so is that it is these very ensembles that are locally at work in many of the most distinctive cases of human reasoning and problem solving. Here too, we alone on the planet seem capable of creating and exploiting such a wide variety of cognition amplifiers, ranging from maps and compasses to pen and paper, to software packages and digital music laboratories. But once again, a second and perhaps less obvious motivation is that working backward from the analysis of these complex wholes may itself contribute important insights into the contributions and functioning of the biological brain itself. For here, too, the various internal neural contributions interact in a complex, nonlinear fashion, and here, too, we may hope to gain valuable leverage on this forbidding internal complexity by analyzing cases in which some of the many degrees of freedom are deliberately (and profitably, relative to some specific goal) reduced by the use of external props and aids. For example, work on diagrammatic reasoning is beginning to track the various ways in which different kinds of diagram impose constraints on reasoning and action that (when the diagram is effective) echo those of some target domain (Stenning & Oberlander, 1995; see also Zhang & Norman, 1994).

The more general project known as external cognition explicitly aims to track and understand the complex and often unobvious relationship between internal and external forms of representation. Its guiding idea is that cognition is a function of both the internal and the external (Scaife & Rogers, 1996; Rogers & Scaife, 1997; see also Norman, 1993), and its practice involves seeking to understand the different properties of the internal and external structures and the way they fit together in specific problem-solving contexts. Sustained attention to the properties of, and varieties of, TECS may thus yield a good deal of indirect information concerning what the biological subsystems are and are not good at, and the forms of representation and computation on which they most likely depend. One key advantage is, of course, that in the case of the external props and aids themselves, we are able (as Hutchins [1995] nicely notes) to inspect directly the various forms of representation, and to observe directly many of the key information-processing moves and representational transformations.

Much more contentious sounding to some than the notion of a TECS is the notion of an extended mind (Clark & Chalmers, 1998). Yet in terms of our two-dimensional taxonomy, the notion of an extended mind is nothing more than the notion of a cognitive extension, of any one of our three kinds, that scores rather higher on the second dimension of durability and reliability. The extended-mind idea thus simply takes the kinds of observation that already motivate interest in TECS and asks what would happen if some such organization were made more permanently available. Thus, Clark and Chalmers (1998) imagined an agent, Otto, so thoroughly fluent in the use of a relatively permanent cognitive augmentation – a notebook, containing addresses and other such information – that the resource was deployed without conscious thought or intention, its operation and contents typically trusted, and the information it made available poised to affect conscious reason and deliberate action in very broadly the same way as might the same information were it stored in biological memory. In such a case, they argued, we should treat the nonbiological augmentation as part of the material supervenience base for some of Otto's long-term, nonoccurrent, dispositional beliefs (e.g., about the location of an art museum). The notebook and the physical traces therein should be treated as the physical vehicles of some of Otto's own nonconscious mental states.

Or consider, very briefly, another example that one of us has discussed previously in presenting the idea of extended cognition (Wilson, 2004a, chap. 8). Kanzi is a human-raised bonobo (pygmy chimpanzee) who has been thoroughly embedded from an early age in human-centered environments located in the research laboratories and grounds of Sue Savage-Rumbaugh (see Savage-Rumbaugh & Lewin, 1994; Savage-Rumbaugh, Shanker, & Taylor, 1998). As part of that enculturation process, Kanzi has learned how to use a 256-symbol, portable keyboard to communicate with people around him. Kanzi's actual developmental trajectory has taken him from using a technological resource designed by human agents, initially in temporary interactions then in repeated cycles of interaction, to becoming a distinctive agent whose persisting cognitive system has come to functionally integrate a much richer set of sociocultural resources into its purview. The system that Kanzi plus his keyboard constitute forms a cognitive system with memory and other cognitive capacities that seem qualitatively distinctive from that of other, unaugmented bonobos, capacities that are somewhere between those of humans and other apes. It is not simply that Kanzi's enriched learning environment has restructured his neural wiring (although it has almost certainly done that, too), but that his cognitive restructuring has proceeded through a potent cognitive extension involving these stable symbolic structures in his environment. Otto and keyboard-Kanzi are thus both cases where a relatively enduring augmentation, suggesting deep functional integration, plausibly results in a cognitively reconfigured agent, an agent with an extended mind.

There has been much recent debate over such radical-sounding claims, and we do not plan to repeat very much of it here. Instead, we simply note that the step from TECS to the extended mind is not really as large

as it may initially appear, especially once one recognizes the many grades along the continuum from the fleeting to the permanent, and further articulates the trichotomy among one-off, repeated, and permanent relationships uniting individuals and cognitive resources, as introduced previously. As we see it, an extended mind is what you get, given the more basic acceptance of the possibility of temporary, soft-assembled extended cognitive systems, if and when certain additional coupling conditions are met (for much further discussion, see Clark, in press). Such coupling conditions are meant to ensure that the capacities of the hybrid system – the biological organism plus augmentation – are plausibly seen as the capacities of a specific individual (e.g., Otto). We properly expect our individual agents to be mobile, more or less reliable, bundles of stored knowledge and computational, emotional, and inferential capacities. So we need to be persuaded that the new capacities enabled by the addition of the notebook are likewise sufficiently robust and enduring as to contribute to the persisting cognitive profile we identify as Otto the agent. The bulk of Clark and Chalmers' (1998) work was an attempt to isolate and defend a specific account of the conditions under which we would be justified in identifying such an extended mind. These amounted, in the end, to a set of conditions that (1) established the reliable presence of the new capacities as and when needed, and then (2) made sure that the mode of deployment of the resource (automatic, trusted) made it more like a proper part of the agent and less like a perceptually consulted independent oracle.

These conditions turned out to be fairly stringent, and it is unlikely that any actual notebook currently carried by a human agent will meet the demands. In the context of near-future technologies, however, it may be that reliable, more permanent forms of personal cognitive augmentation will become relatively commonplace. Two interlocking key developments (see Clark, 2003) likely to support such a transition are, first, the increasing use of portable (perhaps, though not necessarily, implanted) electronics, and second, the spread of ubiquitous and pervasive computing, infusing much of the routinely available material world with accessible information and added computational potential.

The point of choosing the simple, technologically unsophisticated notebook, however, was both to dramatize the importance of the reliability and coupling conditions and to highlight the relative unimportance of the intrinsic nature of the resource itself. For a simple notebook, plainly, is quite unlike biological memory in its representational format, computational activity, and (for what it is worth) material structure. Indeed, as critics seldom tire of pointing out, such differences obtain between most of our external props and aids and the inner biological engine whose cognitive capacities they augment in significant ways. But such disparities, far from being a problem, are (we will now argue) the source of much of the power and interest of cognitive extension.

5. Are Some Resources Intrinsically Noncognitive?

We said at the outset that our articulation of the very idea of cognitive extension would help to reveal shortcomings with some of the most prominent objections to the view of situated cognition as extended cognition. In this section and the next we concentrate on two recent critiques that we regard as posing some of the most challenging objections to this view of situated cognition, those of Adams and Aizawa (2001, 2008, in press, this volume) and Rupert (2004, in press). In both cases, we aim to respond to their critiques in part by pointing to the diverse forms that extended cognition can take, and in part (and perhaps more interestingly) by uncovering some deeper assumptions on which their critiques turn. We think that such assumptions are thrown into doubt by the framework that we have introduced here.

Adams and Aizawa have argued for what they term *contingent intracranialism*, according to which, as a matter of empirical fact, earthbound cognitive processes are currently (at least as far as we know) restricted to the head – better, the neural circuitry and central nervous system – of biological organisms. They thus reject the extended-mind thesis as described previously and assert instead that nothing that is, properly speaking, cognitive goes on outside the bounds of skin and skull.

One key failure of the arguments supporting the extended-mind story, they suggest (this volume), is the failure of those arguments to distinguish mere causal influence from constitution. Now merely coupling a resource to an agent does not, of course, make it part of the agent. But this does not show the nature and degree of intercomponential coupling to be irrelevant to the question of constitution. What makes my hippocampus part of my cognitive system, it seems fair to say, has a great deal to do with how it is informationally integrated with the rest of my cognitive system. We can imagine a case in which, despite being firmly located in my head, there is zero integration and hence the onboard hippocampus fails to form part of my active cognitive system. Contrariwise, we can imagine a hippocampus in a distant vat whose activity is so well integrated as to unproblematically count as part of my cognitive apparatus (see, e.g., Dennett, 1978 – a classic treatment titled "Where Am I?"). Coupling, we conclude, does not in and of itself render a tool or resource part of the agent's cognitive apparatus. But the right kind of coupling (one resulting in deep functional integration) is a major part of what determines the scope and bounds of an agent's cognitive apparatus. As one of us (Clark, in press) has addressed these issues at some length, we shall not repeat the exercise here.

In addition to the worry about coupling, Adams and Aizawa (2001, this volume) worry that certain kinds of nonbiological structures may be in some sense fundamentally inappropriate as elements in extended cognitive wholes. Thus at one point they write, "If the fact that an object or process X is coupled to a cognitive agent does not entail that X is part of the cognitive agent's cognitive apparatus, what does? *The nature of X of course*" (Adams & Aizawa, in press, 3; our italics). We find this revealing. It allows us to draw attention to what seems to be a crucial underlying belief or dogma without which Adams and Aizawa's larger vision would not go through. We shall call this the "dogma of intrinsic unsuitability."

The Dogma of Intrinsic Unsuitability

Certain kinds of encoding or processing are intrinsically unsuitable to act as parts of the material/computational substrate of any genuinely cognitive state or process.

In the work of Adams and Aizawa (2001), the dogma emerges as the claim that certain neural states, and no extraneural ones, exhibit "intrinsic intentionality," conjoined with the assertion that no proper part of a truly cognitive process can trade solely in representations lacking such intrinsic content, such as the conventionally couched encodings in Otto's notebook (on intentionality and extended cognition, see Wilson, unpublished). The upshot of this is that the notebook (or Kanzi's keyboard) is deemed unsuitable as an element in any putatively cognitive process (see, e.g., Adams & Aizawa, 2001, p. 53). The dogma is also at work in their later suggestion that cognitive psychology, in discovering pervasive features of human biological systems of memory and perception, is discovering features that may be the signatures of the kinds of causal process essentially required to support cognition. As a result, the absence of these signatures in the case of certain augmentations and add-ons is presented as a reason to doubt that the augmentations and add-ons contribute to cognitive processing properly understood (see, e.g., Adams & Aizawa, 2001, pp. 52, 61).

The biggest flaw in both of these arguments concerns the relations between putatively essential properties of a whole and essential properties of the parts. For even if we grant that every cognitive system needs to trade in intrinsic contents, it does not follow that each part of every such system needs do so (see Clark, in press). Something can be part of the supervenience base of something's having property P without itself having property P. To take a simple parallel suggested by David Chalmers, someone can be a leader by virtue of his or her relation to other people, without those other people being leaders or having intrinsic leadership.

The dogma of intrinsic unsuitability is just that: a dogma. Moreover, it is one that, we suggest, ultimately stands in some tension with a robust faith in one of the central tenets of computationally inspired cognitive science. This is the idea that pretty much anything, including any kind of processing or encoding, provided that it is properly located in some ongoing web of computational activity, can contribute to the nature and unfolding of the cognitively relevant computations, and hence emerge as a proper part of the material substrate of some target cognitive process or activity. Call this the "tenet of computational promiscuity." Given that we have defended the idea that cognition can be extended because the computations it involves are extended, this tenet leads directly to the view of situated cognition as extended cognition that we have been defending. When computational promiscuity meets intrinsic unsuitability, something surely has to give. We think what has to give is clearly the notion of intrinsic unsuitability.

The pressure on the dogma of intrinsic unsuitability here, however, does not stem solely from accepting the idea of extended computation. This is because the tenet of computational promiscuity is an instance of the broader functionalist insight that causal or functional networks of certain kinds are what are crucial to cognitive capacities, rather than anything about the particular stuff in which those networks are realized. To be sure, we should require that functional networks provide more than a shallow behavioral mimicry of indisputably cognitive creatures (see Block, 1978; Searle, 1980). But the kind of view that we have developed here, which begins with indisputably cognitive creatures and then argues that their cognitive systems are, in fact, extended, avoids this kind of problem at the outset.

Computational promiscuity is, it is important to note, fully compatible with the thought that certain kinds of computational structure may be necessary for fluid, real-world intelligence. It is even compatible with the thought that such necessary computational structures (if such there be) may all be located, at present at least, inside the heads of biological agents. It asserts only that once any such necessary structuring conditions have been met, there is then no limit on the kinds of additional resource that may then be co-opted as proper parts of an extended cognitive process.

Once any such core systems are in place, many other kinds of representational and computational resource may come to act either temporarily or permanently as proper parts of more complex, hybrid, distributed, cognitive wholes. In such cases, it is often the very fact that these additional elements trade in modes of representation and processing that are different from those of the cognitive core that makes the hybrid organization worthwhile. We think that tracing and understanding such deep complementarity is the single most important task confronting the study of situated cognition. The previously mentioned example of Kanzi is a case in point. There can be little doubt that, were it not for a wealth of pattern-recognizing know-how, Kanzi would not have been able to learn to use and deploy the symbol board. Yet there can also be little doubt that keyboard-Kanzi – the larger cognitive whole that results from the fluent coupling between bio-Kanzi and the new resource – is a fundamentally different kind of cognizing entity from his unaugmented cousins. Keyboard-Kanzi is not simply a cognitive core with an add-on symbol board. He is a new kind of hybrid thinking device.

6. Is Cognition Extended or Only Embedded?

Perhaps, though, we can carry out this project without buying into the idea of literal cognitive extensions. Perhaps it is enough, indeed, to speak merely of complementary processes, some cognitive, some not. Robert Rupert (2004, in press) offers just such a challenge for the kind of approach we have been describing. The challenge comes in two parts. The first concerns what Rupert sees as the severe costs of seriously adopting an extended cognitive systems perspective. The second concerns what Rupert depicts as the lack of added value provided by the adoption of an extended perspective. To offset the severe costs, he argues, the added value would have to be very great indeed. But in fact, the combined effect, he fears, is just the opposite. The large costs are offset by no correspondingly large gains, and so the project of studying cognition as an extended phenomenon is one that both philosophy and cognitive science would be wise to reject.

Rupert distinguishes two projects that he sees as competing proposals for understanding situated cognition. The first is the one we defend here. It embraces a vision of cognitive processing itself as (sometimes) quite literally extending into the extra-organismic environment. Rupert dubs this the hypothesis of extended cognition (HEC) and depicts it as a radical hypothesis apt, if true, to transform cognitive scientific theory and practice and to affect our conceptions of agency and persons. But it needs to be assessed, he argues, alongside a more conservative (though still interesting and important) competitor perspective. This is the perspective dubbed the hypothesis of embedded cognition (HEMC), according to which: "Cognitive processes depend *very* heavily, in hitherto unexpected ways, on organismically external props and devices and on the structure of the external environment in which cognition takes place" (Rupert, 2004, p. 393).

Why prefer HEMC over HEC? Rupert starts with an appeal to common sense. Common sense, he suggests, rebels at the vision of extended cognition, so we need sound theoretical reasons to endorse it. By contrast, HEMC is much more compatible with common sense.

Two main worries are then raised for HEC. The first worry, similar to one raised by Adams and Aizawa, concerns the profound differences that appear to distinguish the inner and outer contributions. Thus, for example, we read that "the external portions of extended 'memory' states (processes) differ so greatly from internal memories (the process of remembering) that they should be treated as distinct kinds" (Rupert, 2004, p. 407). Given these differences, there is no immediate pressure to conceive the internal and the external contribution in the same terms. But worse still, there is (allegedly) a significant cost. The cost is one that appears briefly in Rupert (2004) and is greatly expanded in Rupert (in press). For taking all kinds of external props and aids as proper parts of human cognitive processing robs us, he fears, of the standard object of cognitive scientific theorizing, namely, the stable persisting individual. Even in cases of developmental theorizing, where what is at issue is not so much stability as change, Rupert argues, one still needs to find an identifiable, though developing, core. Treating the temporary coupled wholes comprising organism and props as our target cognitive systems is thus a recipe for chaos:

> The radical approach offers developmental psychologists no more reason to be interested in, for example, the series of temporal segments we normally associate with Sally from ages two-to-six rather than to be interested in, say, Sally, aged two, together with a ball she was bouncing on some particular day, Johnny, aged five, together with the book he was reading on some particular afternoon, and Terry, aged seven, plus the stimulus item he has just been shown by the experimenter. (Rupert, in press, p. 9)

More generally then, Rupert worries that cognitive science and cognitive psychology would lose their grip on their subject matter, and with it whatever progress has been made so far, were they to identify human cognitive processing with the activity of these "short-lived coupled systems" (in press, p. 7). Given this very high cost, and given that all the genuine insights of HEC, so Rupert claims, can be accommodated in the more conservative

framework of HEMC, there can be no compelling reason to adopt HEC.

These are good questions to raise, and we find Rupert a thoughtful and engaging critic. Nonetheless, we think that Rupert's worries, including the very idea of a stark, all-or-nothing contrast between HEC and HEMC, are misplaced, and for two quite deep reasons.

The first is that no part of the arguments for extended cognition turn on, or otherwise require, the similarity of the inner and outer contributions. This point also deflects a related concern that Adams and Aizawa express. They say that, because the causal arrangements whereby external stuff contributes to action seem very different from those in place when internal stuff does so, there can be no unified science of the extended mind. Thus, they note (Adams & Aizawa, 2001, p. 61) that biological memory systems display a number of effects (e.g., recency, priming) that are not currently features of external modes of storage, such as Otto's notebook. True enough. Such differences, however, in no way compromise the case for extended cognition. For that case depends not on fine-grained functional identity but on the deep complementarity of inner and outer contributions whose joint effect (e.g., effective remembering) seems apt for the solution of a cognitive task, intuitively identified.

In the case of Adams and Aizawa, part of the confusion hereabouts may be due to a persistent misreading (one unfortunately invited by certain phrasings elsewhere in the original text) of what is sometimes now known as the "parity claim," originally introduced by Clark and Chalmers (1998). This was the claim that if, as we confront some task, a part of the world functions as a process that, were it to go on in the head, we would have no hesitation in accepting as part of the cognitive process, then that part of the world is (for that time) part of the cognitive process. Far from requiring any deep similarity between inner and outer processes, the parity claim was specifically meant to undermine any tendency to think that the shape of the (present-day, human) inner processes sets some bar (as, e.g., Adams & Aizawa, 2001, suggest) on what ought to count as part of a genuinely cognitive process. (For the same kind of move, see Hurley, 1998, pp. 190–193.)

The parity probe is thus meant to act as a kind of veil of metabolic ignorance, inviting us to ask what our attitude would be if currently external means of storage and transformation were, contrary to the presumed facts, found in biology. Thus were Martian biomemory systems found not to involve priming or recency effects, no one would (we suppose) treat that as a reason for not treating them as part of the Martian cognitive apparatus. Likewise, were such novel systems found inside human heads, no one would demur at their forming part of the human cognitive apparatus. This means that such systems pass the parity test (merely a rule of thumb or heuristic) as Clark and Chalmers intended it to be deployed. Notice then that the parity is not about the outer performing just like the (human-specific) inner. Rather, it is about avoiding a rush to judgment based on spatial location alone. (This, by the way, is very much how Turner approaches the idea of an extended physiology, which we discussed in section 3.) The parity principle thus appeals to our rough sense of what we might intuitively judge to belong to the domain of cognition – rather than, say, that of digestion – but attempts to do so without the pervasive distractions of skin and skull.

Rupert's worry, though closely related, turns not on the misplaced requirement of fine-grained functional identity of contribution but on the issue (also raised by Adams and Aizawa) of natural or explanatory kinds. Rupert thus seeks to question the idea, certainly present in Clark and Chalmers's original treatment, that treating the organism-notebook system as the supervenience base for some of Otto's dispositional beliefs was to be recommended on grounds of explanatory unity and power. The argument (and thanks to Rob Rupert for clarifying input here) took as a premise the idea that a kind is natural if it is adverted to by the laws or explanations of a successful science.

Biomemory thus meets the requirement as it falls under the laws and explanatory frameworks of a successful science – cognitive psychology or cognitive science more generally. But (the argument continues) extended memory does not fit the profile of memory as described by successful science and hence should not be subsumed under the heading of "memory" at all.

Our response to this is twofold. First, it is by no means clear that acceptable forms of unification require that all the systemic elements behave according to the same laws. For example, human biomemory systems may, as Rupert notes, themselves form a kind of family resemblance grouping that tolerates substantial variation in fine-grained nature. But second, and most important, the study of extended cognitive systems is just beginning, and it is no wonder that our best current unified understandings target the inner elements alone; that is where science has been looking, after all. It is the empirical bet of the extended systems theorist that the larger wholes, comprising biological and nonbiological elements, will indeed prove to be the proper objects of sustained scientific study, exhibiting features and answering to constraints characteristic of (different kinds of) extended problem-solving wholes. Examples of the payoff of that bet include Zhang and Norman's 1994 work on representations in distributed cognitive tasks, and Gray and Fu's 2004 systematic studies targeting the principles that govern the rapid recruitment of least-effort problem-solving packages that sometimes, but not always, incorporate neural, bodily, and environmental resources.

Contrary to any requirement of fine-grained similarity, then, what the friends of extended cognition actually expect, and (as we saw in section 4) study, are hybrid processes in which the inner and the outer contributions are typically highly distinct in nature, yet deeply integrated and complementary. As an epistemic aside, this complementarity is probably most evident if your vision of the inner realm departs fundamentally from that of classical cognitive science, as the stability, compactness, and arbitrariness of linguistic symbols and encodings contrasts dramatically with the fluid, distributed, context-sensitive representations developed by a connectionist or dynamical engine.

A second reason to resist the easy assimilation of HEC into HEMC concerns the nature of the interactions between the internal and the external resources themselves. Such interactions, it is important to note, may be highly complex, nested, and nonlinear. As a result, there may be no viable means of understanding the behavior and potential of the extended cognitive ensembles by piecemeal decomposition and additive reassembly. To understand the integrated operation of the extended-thinking system created, for example, by combining pen, paper, graphics programs, and a trained mathematical brain, it may be quite insufficient to attempt to understand and then combine (!) the properties of pens, graphics programs, paper, and brains. This may be insufficient for just the same kinds of reasons advanced by Bingham in the case of the human action system, or, within neuroscience itself, as reasons to study not just the various major neural substructures and their capacities but also the complex (often-transient) larger-scale activities in which they combine.

The larger explanatory targets here are whole processing cycles, involving soft-assembled coalitions of neural resources recruited for some specific problem-solving purpose. Such soft-assembled neural packages involve the temporally evolving, often highly reentrant activity of multiple populations of neurons spanning a variety of brain areas. Why, then, suppose that the soft assemblies most relevant to human cognitive achievements are essentially bounded by skin and skull? Why shouldn't the process of recruitment, and the skills of dovetailing the various contributions, yield, at least in our artifact-rich world, a succession of similarly complex hybrid ensembles spanning brain, body, and world?

What, finally, of the allegedly intolerable costs of such an enlarged perspective? In one sense, the worry is simply misplaced and results from a failure to appreciate the two independent dimensions that jointly construct the space of cognitive extensions. With this framework in mind, we see that there is no need, in taking cognitive extensions perfectly seriously, to lose our grip on the more or less stable, more or less persisting biological bundle that lies at the heart of each episode of soft assembly leading to a TECS. Occasionally, of course, we may confront genuine (permanent, reliable) extensions of that more or less persisting core. Otto's notebook and Kanzi's symbol board are, we think, gestures at examples of this kind: cases in which the persisting, mobile resource bundle is augmented in a robustly reliable manner. But in most other cases, we confront the cognitive equivalent of Bingham's TSDs: soft-assembled, temporary medleys of information-processing resources comprising a dovetailed subset of neural activity and environmentally routed augmentations. The costs of not accepting HEC are thus great indeed. For as cognitive extensions these are, quite literally, the soft-assembled circuitry of a great deal of practical human thought and reason. We ignore or downplay the importance of these ensembles, treating them as merely ersatz cognitive circuitry, at our theoretical peril. For the bulk of real-world problem solving, especially of the kinds apparently unique to our species, may be nothing but the play of representation and computation across these spectacularly transformative mixes of organismic and extraorganismic resources.

Overall, Rupert's strategy of argument rests on the claim that any benefits accruing to the expanded perspective can be as easily accommodated by the more conservative reading, according to which all the cognizing goes on in the biological elements, with the rest just a temporarily recruited set of input devices, props, and supports. In this respect, it is similar to the claims of behaviorists in the first half of the twentieth-century that they could account for all so-called cognitive phenomena solely in terms of behavior. Similarly, Griffiths and Scarantino (this volume) think the debate concerning the extended mind merely semantic and effectively opt for HEMC on grounds of minimal disruption.

But we should treat such conservative claims with great caution. Consider the following caricature:

> Look, there's all this new exciting talk about how the brain *is the causal basis for cognitive processing. Call this the hypothesis of in-brain cognition (HIC). Poppycock! For there is a more conservative hypothesis available, the hypothesis of in-neuron cognition (HINC): for any particular cognitive ability, there is a given neuron, N, that is* the real causal basis for that ability. *Cognitive processes depend very heavily, in hitherto unexpected ways, on the rest of the brain, but it is only a given individual neuron that is ever genuinely cognitive. Any useful accounts you may develop using HIC can, in any case, be fully accommodated by HINC, and HINC is significantly less radical than HIC in that it requires only that we take into account how* N *exploits information coming from the rest of the brain and how* N, *in turn, transmits other information to yet other parts of the brain. Hence, HINC is to be preferred to HIC.*

What makes this a caricature, of course, is the fact that as far as cognition goes, HINC lacks the explanatory successes of HIC. And this, presumably, is because the smallest systems that seem apt for the support of genuinely cognitive behavior have turned out to be larger than single neurons. Our best empirical research tells us that intuitively cognitive acts often involve lots of neurons spread throughout the brain. HIC is then a sort of shorthand that signals this. In fact, our best research has helped us to identify not the brain but specific (sometimes temporarily assembled) complexes of neural systems as the causal basis for particular cognitive acts and capacities.

If this kind of substantive justification (of our actual preference for HIC over HINC) is at all on track, then Rupert's claim that HEMC is preferable to HEC should seem suspect. For there is already much research that already fruitfully explores extended cognitive systems, and we have provided at least a preliminary sense of its diversity in the preceding sections. For some cognitive performances, it may very well be that the smallest systems that are apt for the support of the target behavior turn out to involve multiple looping processes that span brain, body, and aspects of the social or physical environment. The question, in each case, is where it is that we find functionally integrated systems that allow their bearers to perform cognitive tasks. We think that some of these are found solely in the head, and that some of them cross the cranial boundary and incorporate cognitive resources in an individual's environment. That is nature's way.

7. Conclusion: Letting Nature Take Its Course

Human agents exhibit both a metabolic and a cognitive organization. But whereas the former depends heavily on expensively maintained and policed organismic boundaries, the latter looks prone to repeated bouts of seepage in which cognitive processes productively loop through surrounding environmental structures. These structures may be natural, sociocultural, or technological, or any combination thereof. And the resultant wholes may be one-off, repeated, or relatively permanent. This two-dimensional matrix limns the space and structure of cognitive extensions. The study of situated cognition, we have argued, is the study of the many forms of cognitive extension that appear in this complex space. To study such systems is not perversely to focus on some strange mishmash of the cognitive and the noncognitive, study that pursues the mind into some place it is not. It is, rather, to corral cognition in its den: to track nature taking its cognitive course.

Acknowledgments

This project was completed thanks to teaching relief provided to Andy Clark under the AHRC Research Leave Scheme (Project: "On the Proper

Treatment of Embodiment"), and with the support of individual three-year grant 410-2005-1629 from the Social Sciences and Humanities Research Council of Canada to Robert A. Wilson. Thanks to Andrew Wilson for the pointer to Bingham's work on task-specific devices; and to Mark Rowlands, John Sutton, Michael Wheeler, Philip Robbins, Susan Hurley, Robert Rupert, Fred Adams, and Ken Aizawa for useful comments and discussions concerning many of the topics. The authors can be contacted at rob.wilson@ualberta.ca and andy.clark@ed.ac.uk.

References

Adams, F., & Aizawa, K. (2001). The bounds of cognition. *Philosophical Psychology*, 14, 43–64.

Adams, F., & Aizawa, K. (2008). *The bounds of cognition*. Oxford: Blackwell.

Adams, F., & Aizawa, K. (in press). Defending the bounds of cognition. In R. Menary (Ed.), *The extended mind*. Aldershot, UK: Ashgate.

Ballard, D., Hayhoe, M. M., Pook, P. K., & Rao, R. P. N. (1997). Deictic codes for the embodiment of cognition. *Behavioral and Brain Sciences*, 20, 723–767.

Bingham, G. (1988). Task-specific devices and the perceptual bottleneck. *Human Movement Science*, 7, 225–264.

Block, N. (1978). Troubles with functionalism. In N. Block (Ed.), *Readings in the philosophy of psychology* (Vol. 1, pp. 268–305). Cambridge, MA: Harvard University Press.

Brooks, R. A. (1991a). Intelligence without reason. In J. Myopoulos & R. Reiter (Eds.), *Proceedings of the 12th International Joint Conference on Artificial Intelligence (IJCAI-91)* (pp. 569–595). San Mateo, CA: Morgan Kaufmann.

Brooks, R. A. (1991b). Intelligence without representation. *Artificial Intelligence*, 47, 139–160. (Modified version reprinted in J. Haugeland [Ed.], *Mind design II: Philosophy, psychology, artificial intelligence* [pp. 395–420]. Cambridge, MA: MIT Press, 1997.)

Brooks, R. A. (1999). *Cambrian intelligence: The early history of the new AI*. Cambridge, MA: MIT Press.

Burge, T. (1979). Individualism and the mental. In P. French, T. Uehling Jr., & H. Wettstein (Eds.), *Midwest studies in philosophy* (Vol. 4, pp. 73–121). Minneapolis: University of Minnesota Press.

Burge, T. (1986a). Individualism and psychology. *Philosophical Review*, 95, 3–45.

Burge, T. (1986b). Intellectual norms and foundations of mind. *Journal of Philosophy*, 83, 697–720.

Clark, A. (1989). *Microcognition: Philosophy, cognitive science and parallel distributed processing*. Cambridge, MA: MIT Press.

Clark, A. (1997). *Being there: Putting brain, body, and world together again*. Cambridge, MA: MIT Press.

Clark, A. (1998). Magic words: How language augments human computation. In P. Carruthers & J. Boucher (Eds.), *Language and thought: Interdisciplinary themes* (pp. 162–183). New York: Cambridge University Press.

Clark, A. (2003). *Natural-born cyborgs: Minds, technologies, and the future of human intelligence*. New York: Oxford University Press.

Clark, A. (2005a). Beyond the flesh: Some lessons from a mole cricket. *Artificial Life*, 11, 233–244.

Clark, A. (2005b). Word, niche and super-niche: How language makes minds matter more. *Theoria*, 20, 255–268.

Clark, A. (2007). Re-inventing ourselves: The plasticity of embodiment, sensing, and mind. *Journal of Medicine and Philosophy*, 32(3), 263–282.

Clark, A. (in press). Coupling, constitution and the cognitive kind: A reply to Adams and Aizawa. In R. Menary (Ed.), *The extended mind*. Aldershot, UK: Ashgate.

Clark, A., & Chalmers, D. (1998). The extended mind. *Analysis*, 58, 10–23.

Dawkins, R. (1976). *The selfish gene*. Oxford: Oxford University Press.

Dawkins, R. (1982). *The extended phenotype*. Oxford: Oxford University Press.

Dennett, D. C. (1978). Where am I? In D. C. Dennett (Ed.), *Brainstorms* (pp. 311–323). Cambridge, MA: Bradford Books, MIT Press.

Ebbs, G. (1998). *Rule-following and realism*. Cambridge, MA: Harvard University Press.

Egan, F. (1992). Individualism, computation, and perceptual content. *Mind*, 101, 443–459.

Fodor, J. A. (1975). *The language of thought*. Cambridge, MA: Harvard University Press.

Fodor, J. A. (1982). Cognitive science and the twin-earth problem. *Notre Dame Journal of Formal Logic*, 23, 98–118.

Fodor, J. A. (1983). *The modularity of mind*. Cambridge, MA: MIT Press.

Fowler, C., & Turvey, M. T. (1978). Skill acquisition: An event approach with special reference to searching for the optimum of a function of several variables. In G. Stelmach (Ed.), *Information processing in motor control and learning* (pp. 1–40). New York: Academic Press.

Gallagher, S. (2005). *How the body shapes the mind*. New York: Oxford University Press.

Goody, J. (1977). *The domestication of the savage mind*. Cambridge: Cambridge University Press.

Gray, W. D., & Fu, W.-T. (2004). Soft constraints in interactive behavior: The case of ignoring perfect knowledge in-the-world for imperfect knowledge in-the-head. *Cognitive Science, 28*, 359–382.

Haugeland, J. (1998). Mind embodied and embedded. In J. Haugeland (Ed.), *Having thought: Essays in the metaphysics of mind*. Cambridge, MA: Harvard University Press. (Reprinted from *Acta Philosophica Fennica, 58*, [1995], 233–267.)

Hurley, S. (1998). *Consciousness in action*. Cambridge, MA: Harvard University Press.

Hutchins, E. (1995). *Cognition in the wild*. Cambridge, MA: MIT Press.

Jablonka, E., & Lamb, M. (2005). *Evolution in four dimensions*. Cambridge, MA: MIT Press.

Loar, B. (1988). Social content and psychological content. In R. Grimm & D. Merrill (Eds.), *Contents of thought* (pp. 99–110). Tucson: University of Arizona Press.

Newell, A. (1980). Physical symbol systems. *Cognitive Science, 4*, 135–183.

Newell, A., & Simon, H. (1976). Computer science as empirical enquiry. In J. Haugeland (Ed.), *Mind design* (pp. 35–66). Cambridge, MA: MIT Press.

Norman, D. (1993). Cognition in the head and in the world. *Cognitive Science, 17*, 1–6.

Odling-Smee, J., Laland, K., & Feldman, M. (2003). *Niche construction: The neglected process in evolution*. Princeton, NJ: Princeton University Press.

Oyama, S. (1985). *The ontogeny of information* (2nd ed.). Durham, NC: Duke University Press, 2000.

Oyama, S., Griffiths, P. E., & Gray, R. D. (Eds.). (2001). *Cycles of contingency: Developmental systems and evolution*. Cambridge, MA: MIT Press.

Pettit, P. (1993). *The common mind: An essay on psychology, society, and politics*. New York: Oxford University Press.

Putnam, H. (1975). The meaning of "meaning." In K. Gunderson (Ed.), *Language, mind and knowledge* (pp. 131–193). Minneapolis: University of Minnesota Press.

Pylyshyn, Z. (1984). *Computation and cognition*. Cambridge, MA: MIT Press.

Rogers, Y., & Scaife, M. (1997). Distributed cognition. Retrieved May 13, 2008, from http://www.irit.fr/ACTIVITES/GRIC/cotcos/pjs/TheoreticalApproaches/DistributedCog/DistCognitionpaperRogers.htm.

Rowlands, M. (1999). *The body in mind*. New York: Cambridge University Press.

Rupert, R. (2004). Challenges to the hypothesis of extended cognition. *Journal of Philosophy, 101*, 389–428.

Rupert, R. (in press). Representation in extended cognitive systems: Does the scaffolding of language extend the mind? In R. Menary (Ed.), *The extended mind*. Aldershot, UK: Ashgate.

Salzman, E., & Kelso, J. A. S. (1987). Skilled actions: A task dynamic approach. *Psychological Review, 94*, 84–106.

Savage-Rumbaugh, S., & Lewin, R. (1994). *Kanzi: The ape at the brink of the human mind*. New York: Wiley and Sons.

Savage-Rumbaugh, S., Shanker, S. G., & Taylor, T. J. (1998). *Apes, language, and the human mind*. New York: Oxford University Press.

Scaife, M., & Rogers, Y. (1996). External cognition: How do graphical representations work? *International Journal of Human-Computer Studies, 45*, 185–213.

Searle, J. (1980). Minds, brains, and programs. *Behavioral and Brain Sciences, 3*, 417–424.

Segal, G. (1989). Seeing what is not there. *Philosophical Review, 98*, 189–214.

Shapiro, L. (1997). A clearer vision. *Philosophy of Science, 64*, 131–153.

Stenning, K., & Oberlander, J. (1995). A cognitive theory of graphical and linguistic reasoning: Logic and implementation. *Cognitive Science, 19*, 97–140.

Turner, J. S. (2000). *The extended organism: The physiology of animal-built structures*. Cambridge, MA: Harvard University Press.

Wilson, R. A. (1994). Wide computationalism. *Mind, 101*, 351–372.

Wilson, R. A. (1995). *Cartesian psychology and physical minds: Individualism and the sciences of the mind*. New York: Cambridge University Press.

Wilson, R. A. (2000). The mind beyond itself. In D. Sperber (Ed.), *Misrepresentations: A multidisciplinary perspective* (pp. 31–52). New York: Oxford University Press.

Wilson, R. A. (2003). Individualism. In S. Stich & T. A. Warfield (Eds.), *The Blackwell companion to philosophy of mind* (pp. 256–287). New York: Blackwell.

Wilson, R. A. (2004a). *Boundaries of the mind: The individual in the fragile sciences: Cognition.* New York: Cambridge University Press.

Wilson, R. A. (2004b). Recent work in individualism in the social, behavioural and biological sciences. *Biology and Philosophy, 19,* 397–423.

Wilson, R. A. (2005). *Genes and the agents of life: The individual in the fragile sciences: Biology.* New York: Cambridge University Press.

Wilson, R. A. (unpublished). Meaning making and the mind of the externalist.

Zhang, J., & Norman, D. A. (1994). Representations in distributed cognitive tasks. *Cognitive Science, 18,* 87–122.

CHAPTER 5

Why the Mind Is Still in the Head

Fred Adams and Kenneth Aizawa

Philosophical interest in situated cognition has been focused most intensely on the claim that human cognitive processes extend from the brain into the tools humans use. As we see it, this radical hypothesis is sustained by two kinds of mistakes, the confusion of coupling relations with constitutive relations and an inattention to the mark of the cognitive. Here we wish to draw attention to these mistakes and show just how pervasive they are. That is, for all that the radical philosophers have said, the mind is still in the head.[1]

1. The Issue

In Adams and Aizawa (2001), we defended a commonsense and scientifically standard view of the locus of cognition we called "contingent intracranialism." According to this view, as a matter of contingent empirical fact, human tool use is typically a matter of intracranially localized cognitive processes interacting with extracranial biological, chemical, and physical processes. Current human use of pencils and paper,

computers, watches, telescopes, and hearing aids are all properly understood as cases in which cognitive processes interact with noncognitive processes. Although the tools we are familiar with are like this, not all tools are necessarily like this. Perhaps one day it will be possible to replace the rods and cones in the human retina with synthetic rods and cones. These synthetic cells – these microtools – might have the same size and shape as naturally occurring human rods and cones. They might have the same neurotransmitter-handling properties. They might have the same response properties to light. On the supposition that perceptual processes are cognitive and that they begin at the retina, it would turn out that in the future just described, there might well be individuals whose cognitive processes extend beyond their organismal boundaries, giving them transorganismal cognition.[2] Be the future what it may, our view is that these possible cases of tool use are unlike at least the vast majority of our contemporary cases of tool use.

In the face of both common sense and much contemporary science, an increasing number of philosophers and psychologists have found themselves attracted to contingent transcranialism.[3] This is the view that, in ordinary tool use, we have instances in which cognitive processes span the cranial boundary and extend into extracranial space. As Dennett (2000) puts it, *"minds are composed of tools for thinking that we not only obtain from the wider (social) world, but largely leave in the world, instead of cluttering up our brains with them"* (p. 21, italics in original). This is the view that when a student takes notes in class, the student literally commits information to memory. When someone uses pencil and paper to compute large sums, cognitive processes extend to the pencil and paper themselves. In these cases, the processes involving the pencil and paper constitute cognitive processes. Not all transcranialists make as sweeping a proposal as does Dennett. Some transcranialists think that only certain types of tool use bring about the extension of the cognitive into the extracranial world. Some transcranialists think that only special brain-tool couplings will let the cognitive enter the artifactual.[4] Be these refinements as they may, all transcranialists we know of have enthusiastically embraced what they recognize to be a radical departure from orthodoxy.

So described, intracranialists and transcranialists are concerned with the manner in which processes are subdivided. When a person uses pencil and paper to compute a sum, the intracranialist maintains that there is a natural kind of process (recognizably cognitive) that happens to occur within the brain, where the transcranialist maintains that there is a natural kind of process (recognizably cognitive) that extends from the brain to the pencil and paper. The radical transcranialist thesis that concerns us here must be distinguished from many less radical but related theses with which it might be confused. One thesis is that it is possible for cognitive processes to extend beyond the boundaries of the brain. Susan Hurley (1998), for example, and Andy Clark (2005, in press) are quite interested in this possibility.[5] We are not, because we think it is part of the standard functionalist view of cognition that a properly organized configuration of processes can simultaneously cross the boundaries of the brain and constitute cognition. Another thesis is Ron McClamrock's (1995) claim that "the information available to us in deciding what to do . . . is not so clearly circumscribed at the boundary of the physical organism" (p. 89). Although McClamrock appears to think this is controversial, it seems to us quite clear that information beyond the boundary of our bodies makes a difference to our decisions. Written material often contains useful information. That is why reading it is so often helpful in decision making. Another tangential issue is Clark and Chalmers's (1998) claim that

> *if, as we confront some task, a part of the world functions as a process which*, were it done in the head, *we would have no hesitation in recognizing as part of a cognitive process, then that part of the world is (so we claim) part of the cognitive process.* (p. 8)

We agree with this, because it seems to us to say nothing other than that the difference between being in the head and being outside of the head does not constitute a mark of the cognitive. Yet another tangential issue is the thesis that cognitive psychology should attend to the interactions between organisms and their environments, or between minds and their environments.[6] Insofar as this thesis requires only that one attend to the interactions of cognitive processes with noncognitive environmental processes, the intracranialist can accept it.[7] Finally, we are not concerned with whether the concept of cognition requires that cognition only be found in the brain.[8] We do not think it does, but we also do not think that this is all that interesting a question. It is no more interesting than whether our concept of water requires that it be found only on earth or whether our concept of a penguin requires that it be found only in the Antarctic. The transcranialist thesis we care about maintains that organism-environment interactions are to be understood as entirely cognitive processes rather than merely partially cognitive and partially noncognitive processes. Another way to put the matter is to say that the current issue is whether tool use is typically a matter of cognitive processes interacting with portions of the noncognitive environment (the contingent intracranialist view) or is typically a matter of cognitive processing throughout (the transcranialist view).

In this debate, a recurring worry for transcranialists is, or at least should be, that the reconceptualization they urge will degenerate into a mere terminological dispute over how to use the word *cognitive* and related descriptors.[9] It is not enough for transcranialists to argue that something extends beyond brain boundaries.[10] It is not enough that there be some scientific taxonomy that groups the intracranial and the transcranial under one set of kinds or processes. Physics, biology, and chemistry might well do that. The transcranialists need to maintain that cognition extends beyond the brain. So, they cannot simply propose to use *cognitive* and its kin to describe any old scientific kind. There must be some appropriate theoretical affinity between what they call "cognitive" and what has traditionally gone under the name *cognitive*. Clark and Chalmers (1998) try to address this problem by saying that

> *in seeing cognition as extended one is not merely making a terminological decision; it makes a significant difference to the methodology of scientific investigation. In effect, explanatory methods that might once have been thought appropriate only for the analysis of inner processes are now being adapted for the study of the outer, and there is promise that our understanding of cognition will become richer for it. (p. 10)*

This seems to us inadequate for two reasons. The first stems from the distinction made in the previous paragraph. Intracranialists can perfectly well accept the idea that brain-tool interactions and brain-world interactions are worthy of scientific investigation. The study of human factors – the way in which humans interact with products, tools, and procedures – is fine by the intracranialist. Vision science is also a perfectly legitimate area of scientific research.

What is at issue are the bounds of cognition. What regions of space-time contain cognitive processing? Clark and Chalmers's account is inadequate on another score. Grant, for the moment, their unsubstantiated claim that intracranialism and transcranialism lead to different scientific methodologies. This seems to us an insufficient basis to block the charge of this debate being a terminological dispute. Make up some terminological shift. Consider using *cognitive* to mean avian. Surely such a terminological shift will have dramatic methodological implications for the new cognitive science. So, as we said, there is reason to be dissatisfied with the solution that Clark and Chalmers propose.

It is not clear that the charge of terminological quibbling can be entirely avoided in favor of what all parties are interested in, namely, an understanding of brain-world interactions. Yet, here is our attempt. We maintain that there is something distinctive about the brain. There are natural kinds of processes that happen to occur only within the brain. These processes differ from neurophysiological processes insofar as they consist of (in general, poorly understood) causal operations on nonderived representations (representations whose content does not depend on other previously existing content). These processes also differ, we suppose, from typical processes that extend into the world from brains and from processes found in typical machines. In other words, we hypothesize that there are within the brain natural laws that are not identical to physical, chemical, biological, or neurophysiological covering laws spanning the cranium.[11] We are not offering a stipulative definition of the cognitive but some hypotheses about the nature of cognition. In taking this line, we suppose that it is recognition of the distinct type of information-processing capacities of the brain, rather than mere prejudice, that has inclined orthodox cognitive science to the view that cognitive processing is, in all actual cases, an intracranial affair.[12]

Reviewing the literature on this issue, one finds that there are two principal mistakes that sustain transcranialism. First, transcranialists are insensitive to the difference between cognitive processes being causally connected to environmental processes and cognitive processes being, in part, constituted by environmental processes. Second, transcranialists are insufficiently sensitive to the problem of distinguishing the cognitive from the noncognitive. In this chapter, we wish to show how these two mistakes run through much of the philosophical literature defending transcranialism.

2. The Coupling Arguments

Coupling arguments are far and away the primary sort of argument given in support of transcranialism. What is common to these arguments is a tacit move from the observation that process X is in some way causally connected (coupled) to a cognitive process Y to the conclusion that X is part of the cognitive process Y. The pattern of reasoning here involves moving from the observation that process X is in some way causally connected (coupled) to a process Y of type φ to the conclusion that X is part of a process of type φ. In attributing this pattern of reasoning to advocates of transcranialism, we do not mean that they consciously and deliberately draw a distinction between the coupling claim and the constitution claim, and then explicitly assert that coupling is sufficient for constitution. Far from it. What typically happens is that writers just casually slip between one and the other. When presented with this analysis, defenders of transcranialism typically deny that they reason in this way. What we are offering is a reconstruction of what appears to be going on in many cases. To make this analysis stick, while being as sympathetic as possible to transcranialists, we adopt the inelegant practice of quoting extensively from the transcranialists.

In our view, the coupling arguments are fallacious.[13] They commit what we call the "coupling-constitution fallacy." We can see that it is in fact a fallacy by considering some examples. Consider the bimetallic strip in an ordinary thermostat. The expansion and contraction of this strip is closely coupled to the ambient temperature of a room and the air-conditioning apparatus for that room. Nevertheless, this gives us no reason to say that the expansion and contraction of the strip extends beyond the limits of the strip and into the room or air conditioner. The Watt governor provides another example. The combustion of fuel in the governed engine is tightly coupled to the rotation of the weighted arms, yet the process of combustion does not extend beyond the bounds of the engine.[14] This is the generic form of a coupling argument, but we find a range of specific variations in the literature.

2.1. The Simple Coupling Argument

In what we call the "simple coupling argument," all that is invoked in arguing for an extended cognitive process is a causal connection or looping between the cognizing organism and its environment. The inference is most commonly made in the suggestion that in the use of pencil and paper to compute large sums one's cognitive processes include the pencil and paper. But other examples are invoked as well.

In chapter 8 of his book *Boundaries of the Mind*, Robert Wilson (2004) suggests that he plans to make a case for transcranialism (pp. 188–193). He then proceeds to describe a children's puzzle game, Rush Hour, wherein one moves wooden rectangles around in a wooden frame. Then following the presentation of the example, Wilson writes, "[when solving the puzzle] the mind extends itself beyond the purely internal capacities of the brain by engaging with, exploiting, and manipulating parts of its structured environment" (p. 195). In this context, it is plausible to read the inference from coupling to constitution into the following passage:

We solve the problem by continually looking back to the board and trying to figure out sequences of moves that will get us closer to our goal, all the time exploiting the structure of the environment through continual interaction with it. We look, we think, we move. But the thinking, the cognitive part of solving the problem, is not squirreled away inside us, wedged between the looking and the moving, but developed and made possible through these interactions with the board. (Wilson, 2004, p. 194)

What one might expect that Wilson means in the foregoing passage is that, in this case, cognitive processing is not squirreled away in the brain but extends into the interactions with the board. Now, if this is what he means, although he does not literally say it, then he appears to be guilty of the coupling-constitution fallacy. Of course, Wilson might not really mean this. He might mean only that, in this case, cognitive processing is developed and made possible by interactions with the board. But then the contrast implied in the first part of the final sentence comes out infelicitous and Wilson turns out not to be providing an argument for transcranialism after all. Wilson perhaps has enough wiggle room to avoid the charge of committing the coupling-constitution fallacy, but recognizing the fallacy is important in the recognition that Wilson is providing no argument for transcranial cognition.

Alva Noë (2004) provides a nice illustration of the casual shift between causation and constitution. He begins by describing perceptual experiences as external in the sense that they depend on causal interactions between the animal and the environment.[15] He then frames a slightly different question that might be taken to bear more closely on the constitution issue; namely, What is the causal substrate of an experience? As an answer, he writes, "perhaps the only way – or the only biological way – to produce just the flavor sensations one enjoys when one sips wine is by rolling a liquid across one's tongue. In that case, the liquid, the tongue, and the rolling action would be part of the physical substrate for the experience's occurrence" (Noë, 2004, p. 220). This could be a claim about constitution. Discussing the use of pencil and paper in complex calculations, Noë makes a similar move: "Indeed, for a great many calculations that we can perform, the pencil and paper are necessary. If the pencil and paper are necessary for the calculation, why not view them as part of the necessary substrate for the calculating activity?" (Noë, 2004, p. 220). This, too, might or might not be a claim about constitution. Perhaps Noë is not in these passages guilty of committing the coupling-constitution fallacy, because he does not specifically draw the constitution conclusion. Avoiding the fallacy by discussing only the substrate of cognition, however, becomes more difficult when Noë describes, with apparent approval, an idea he attributes to Clark and Chalmers (1998):

According to active externalism, the environment can drive and so partially constitute cognitive processes. Where does the mind stop and the rest of the world begin? If active externalism is right, then the boundary cannot be drawn at the skull. The mind reaches – or at least can reach, sometimes – beyond the limits of the body out into the world. (Noë, 2004, p. 221)

We think Noë's discussion here nicely illustrates our view that advocates of transcranialism are largely insensitive to the distinction between coupling and constitution and just casually slip between one and the other.[16]

Raymond Gibbs (2001) provides another case in point. He runs the simple coupling argument on intentions by appeal to what is involved in windsurfing:

The windsurfer continually affects and is affected by the set of the rig, so the behavioral intention to successfully windsurf emerges as a result of the interaction between the person and environment. Focusing on the agent alone, or on how the agent responds to the environment, fails to capture the complex nuances of windsurfing behavior. Just as it is important to understand the significance of paper and pencil when one does long division, where the cognition of doing long division is in part "offloaded" into the environment, the intentionality in windsurfing is best understood as a distributed cognitive behavior involving a person, a device, and the environment. (Gibbs, 2001, pp. 117–118)

In this passage, Gibbs urges two separate claims. One is the methodological thesis that we should not study intentions without keeping an eye on the interaction between the organism and the environment. Gibbs evidently refers to this issue when he describes the putative consequences of focusing on the agent alone. As indicated previously, we think the charge that cognitive science does not attend to environmental interactions is overblown but in any case should not be confused with the issue we care about here, namely, the boundary of the cognitive. The other claim in the foregoing passage is the ontological issue of the bounds on cognition, how the processes involved in windsurfing might be divided into the cognitive and the noncognitive. Gibbs at least comes close to the ontological issue when he claims that the intentionality in windsurfing is best understood as a distributed cognitive behavior involving a person, a device, and the environment. Unfortunately, he gives no reason to think this is so. In describing the windsurfer case, Gibbs apparently assumes that, in virtue of a causal coupling, the windsurfer and his or her environment should be analyzed as a single cognitive/intentional whole.

Clark (2001) gives us another example that is strikingly similar to the ones we have just seen, a case of writing an academic paper[17]:

> Confronted, at last, with the shiny finished product the good materialist may find herself congratulating her brain on its good work. But this is misleading. It is misleading not simply because (as usual) most of the ideas were not our own anyway, but because the structure, form and flow of the final product often depends heavily on the complex ways the brain cooperates with, and leans upon, various special features of the media and technologies with which it continually interacts. . . . The brain's role is crucial and special. But it is not the whole story. In fact, the true (fast and frugal!) power and beauty of the brain's role is that it acts as a mediating factor in a variety of complex and iterated processes which continually loop between brain, body and technological environment. And it is this larger system which solves the problem. . . . The intelligent process just is the spatially and temporally extended one which zig-zags between brain, body, and world. (Clark, 2001, p. 132; cf. Clark, 2002, pp. 23–24)

Here the intracranialist can agree with everything up until that last sentence. Here we find a familiar pattern, a long description of the causal connections between the brain and environment followed by the move to the view that these causal loops constitute part of the cognitive process. This is the simple coupling-constitution fallacy.[18] We can note as well that it is common ground that the brain and the tools are jointly responsible for the product, the journal article.[19] This, however, does not require that both the brain and tools constitute a single cognitive process. It is the interaction of the spinning bowling ball with the surface of the alley that leads to all the pins falling. Still, the process of the ball's spinning does not extend into the surface of the alley or the pins. There is no extended bowling ball that meshes with the alley, nor do we see any particular intimacy between a bowling ball and the alley.[20] Moreover, the contingent intracranialist has no objection to saying that operation of the tools and the brain provide the basis for hypothesizing a single causal process. The problem is that this provides no reason to think that the tools and the brain constitute a single "cognitive" process.

2.2. The System Version of the Coupling Argument

In an early presentation of this version of the argument, we find Tim van Gelder (1995) claiming the following:

> In this vision, the cognitive system is not just the encapsulated brain; rather, since the nervous system, body, and environment are all constantly changing and simultaneously influencing each other, the true cognitive system is a single unified system embracing all three. The cognitive system does not interact with the body and the external world by means of the occasional

static symbolic inputs and outputs; rather, interaction between the inner and the outer is best thought of as a matter of coupling, such that both sets of processes continually influencing [sic] each other's direction of change. (p. 373)

In this passage, van Gelder only claims that the brain, body, and environment constitute a cognitive system. Only later in the paper does he go further to claim that cognition extends outside the brain: "The Cartesian tradition is mistaken in supposing that mind is an inner entity of any kind, whether mind-stuff, brain states, or whatever. Ontologically, mind is much more a matter of what we *do* within environmental and social possibilities and bounds" (van Gelder, 1995, p. 380). Subsequently, Clark and Chalmers (1998) ran a version of the coupling argument inserting the idea that humans and their tools form a cognitive system.[21] They write:

> *In these cases [of external tool use], the human organism is linked with an external entity in a two-way interaction, creating a coupled system that can be seen as a cognitive system in its own right. All the components in the system play an active causal role, and they jointly govern behavior in the same sort of way that cognition usually does. If we remove the external components the system's behavioral competence will drop, just as it would if we removed part of its brain. Our thesis is that this sort of coupled process counts equally well as a cognitive process, whether or not it is wholly in the head.* (Clark & Chalmers, 1998, pp. 8–9)

More recently, Clark (2003) developed the system version of the argument by claiming that humans are hybrid artifact-organism systems, or cyborgs.[22] Robert Wilson also runs a system version of the coupling argument with a different example:

> *Consider Kanzi, the human-raised bonobo that has been central to both the life and research of the primatologist Sue Savage-Rumbaugh. Kanzi has been thoroughly enculturated, and engages in sophisticated linguistic communication through a 256-symbol keyboard that he can carry with him. Given Kanzi's actual developmental environment, Kanzi plus a 256-symbol keyboard forms a cognitive system with memory and other cognitive capacities that far exceed those of just Kanzi. (Much the same holds true of Alex, Irene Pepperberg's African grey parrot.) My point here is not the trivial one that enriched environments can causally produce smarter critters; rather, it is that what metaphysically determines the smartness of at least some critters is their being part of wide cognitive systems. (Wilson, 2004, p. 195; cf. Wilson & Clark, this volume)*

In the system version of the coupling-constitution fallacy, the argument begins with the observation of important causal connections (couplings) among the brain and body and the environment, then infers that these causal connections warrant the conclusion that the brain, body, and environment form a cognitive system. From there, there is the tacit move to the conclusion that cognition extends from the brain into the body and environment. The system version of the coupling-constitution fallacy, thus, differs from the simple version because of the intermediate inference concerning a system.

We can grant for the sake of argument that the combination of a human being with pencil and paper constitutes a system, that a person with a laptop computer constitutes a system, that a person with a notebook constitutes a system, and so forth. We can also concede that humans and their tools constitute cognitive systems. Still, this does not establish transcranialism. It does not follow from the fact that one has an X system that every component of the system does X. Obviously there are systems that consist of many types of components and involve a multiplicity of process types. An air-conditioning system, for example, can involve a thermostat, a compressor, an evaporation coil, a fan, and so forth. Perhaps we can say that the process of the air cooling as it passes over the evaporation coils is the process of conditioning the air, but surely the liquefaction of Freon and the electrical processes within the thermostat and the opening and closing of the circuit in the thermostat are not air-conditioning. Surely nothing forces us to lump all of these processes under a single descriptor, "air-conditioning." Another example is a personal computer, a computing system. Suppose, for the sake of argument, that we don't limit the notion of computing to what the central processing unit (CPU) does. Suppose that we understand computing broadly so as to cover many sorts of information processing. Thus, we might count the process of reading a floppy disk, reading a compact disc (CD), and turning the computer on as kinds of information processing, hence as kinds of computing. Even on this very broad understanding of computing, it is still not the case that every process in this computing system is a computing process. There is the production of heat by the CPU, the circulation of air caused by the fan, the transmission of electrons in the computer's cathode-ray tube, and the discharge of the computer's internal battery. Think of a sound system. Not every component produces sounds. The speakers do, but lasers in CD players, amplifiers, volume controls, and tone controls do not. Again, not every component of an X system does X. So, an appeal to the notion of a system does not help the transcranialist.

2.3. Gibbs's Interpersonal Coupling Argument

Gibbs (2001) claims that "intentions are, in many cases, emergent products of interactions between individuals, and between individuals and the environment, and that therefore they exist in a distributed manner across individuals" (p. 106). Clearly, Gibbs is a transcranialist about at least some intentions and, as we have seen, is prone to commit the simple coupling-constitution fallacy. In addition, however, he advances some more complicated versions of the fallacy. We will consider just one.

One of Gibbs's arguments is based on a dialogue he observed in a bar. The dialogue begins after John spills a beer:

> John: I wonder if there is a towel behind the bar.
> Nicole (goes over to the bar and grabs a towel): Here you go.
> John: Oh thanks! I wasn't actually asking you to get a towel for me. I just was thinking aloud about whether there might be a towel that I could get from the bartender. But thanks. (Gibbs, 2001, p. 109)

Gibbs begins his analysis of this dialogue by saying, "John intends his utterance with a particular meaning, but changes his mind and accepts Nicole's interpretation of what he said" (ibid.). We think that Gibbs's treatment of this case is flawed in many ways, so it will take a while to work through these problems before we can ultimately relate it to the other coupling arguments. So, first off, we think that Gibbs simply misunderstands John's comment. John is not changing his mind about anything. He is not adopting Nicole's interpretation of what he said; in fact, he is explicitly rejecting it. John says, "I wasn't actually asking you to get a towel for me," which is an explicit rejection of what he thinks Nicole thinks (or might think) he intends. When he says, "But thanks," he means that, even though he did not intend for Nicole to get him a towel, he is thankful that she did it anyway. It looks as though John's initial intention remains constant throughout the whole episode.

Not to rest our argument too much on what Gibbs might take to be our idiosyncratic understanding of the foregoing dialogue, we might try to develop an imaginary scenario in which John does change his initial intention. How would the scenario have to be different for John to have really changed his original intention? Let's say that at t_0 he had the intention merely to wonder out loud and so he proceeded to utter, "I wonder if there is a towel behind the bar." Nicole then goes and gets the towel and says, "Here you go." Now at t_1 let John say, "Thanks. I'm glad you discerned what I intended." Now at least Nicole's actions have provoked a kind of conflict between the intention John had at t_0 and the intention he implies (at t_1) he had at t_0. This, however, is still not an instance of the actions at t_1 changing John's intentions at t_0. Indeed, the mechanics of this exchange are that of a comic scene with Inspector Clouseau. Clouseau clearly intends one thing, has something unexpected arise, but then tries to play off the surprise as what he intended all along. What reason is there to think that John changed the intention he had at t_0 rather than that he changed his interpretation of the intention he had at t_0? It could be that John suffers from a failure of memory or self-deception. It must surely be admitted that self-deception or failures of memory can lead to distorted interpretations or assessments of the intentions one had in the past. So, why not in these types of cases? Gibbs provides no reason to prefer the view that John changed his intentions at t_0 to the view that John merely changed his assessment of his intentions at t_0. Worse, Gibbs appears to be insensitive to this distinction. Nowhere is this more evident than when he writes: "The fact that John altered *what he believed to be* his original intention shows that Nicole's interpretation of his intention actually shaped John's *own conception* of what that intention may be" (Gibbs, 2001, p. 110, emphasis added). What Gibbs says here can be conceded by the intracranialist. What Gibbs is hoping for, but has provided no argument for, is much stronger; namely, that John's intentions at t_0 were changed.

But suppose we set aside the infelicity of Gibbs's original example wherein John says, "I wasn't actually asking you to get a towel for me." Further suppose that at t_1 John really is able to do something to alter the intention he had at t_0. In particular, let us suppose that there are no problems with backward causation, that there is nothing wrong with events at t_1 causally influencing temporally prior events at t_0. (We think we are being especially generous here.) Still, Gibbs must come to grips with the funda-mental flaw in coupling arguments; namely, the fact that events at one time causally influence cognitive events at another time does not make it the case that those first events constitute part of a single cognitive process that includes the cognitive events. More concretely, the fact that Nicole's and John's actions made some cognitive difference to John's intention at t_0 is not enough to establish that Nicole's and John's actions are part of the same cognitive process or state as John's intention at t_0.

Further evidence that Gibbs is guilty of confusing constitution relations and causal relations in the analysis of this case is supported by his claims following another sample dialogue. He notes that "speakers' intentions also clearly shift as a result of conversation and may at times not be viewed as solely a product of an individual speaker's mind" (Gibbs, 2001, p. 111). It is surely common ground that intentions change over the course of a conversation. I ask you to pass the salt. That, against a backdrop of other factors, might cause you to form the intention to pass the salt. And, of course, in such a case, there is a perfectly good sense in which your intention is not solely a product of your mind; namely, your intention is not caused exclusively by events within your own mind. Yet such an admission does nothing to challenge the intracranialist position. For all that has been conceded, the intracranialist can still maintain that your intention to pass the salt is entirely constituted by events and processes within your cranium. So, even under quite generous concessions, Gibbs has not produced an argument for transcranialism.

Having surveyed a wide range of ways of committing the coupling-constitution fallacy, it should be clear how pervasive it is. What would help transcranialists at this point is a plausible theory that demarcates the cognitive from the noncognitive. Yet, as we will now argue, they do not have one.

3. The Mark of the Cognitive

When we claim that transcranialists have paid inadequate attention to the problem of the mark of the cognitive, we do not mean to imply that they have entirely ignored the issue. For example, Clark and Chalmers (1998) consider the idea that consciousness is the mark of the cognitive:

> Some find this sort of externalism unpalatable. One reason may be that many identify the cognitive with the conscious, and it seems far from plausible that consciousness extends outside the head in these cases. But not every cognitive process, at least on standard usage, is a conscious process. It is widely accepted that all sorts of processes beyond the borders of consciousness play a crucial role in cognitive processing: in the retrieval of memories, linguistic processes, and skill acquisition, for example. So, the mere fact that external processes are external where consciousness is internal is no reason to deny that those processes are cognitive. (Clark & Chalmers, 1998, p. 10)

Clark and Chalmers clearly deserve credit for broaching the issue. Further, they deserve credit for providing reasonable arguments against this theory of the cognitive. Yet their paper comes up short in its failure to specify what they believe does distinguish the cognitive from the noncognitive. Further, Clark and Chalmers, like all the other transcranialists we have read, do not address any version of the rules-and-representations conception of cognition – arguably the received view of the nature of cognition. Adams and Aizawa (2001) drew attention to this conception by venturing two hypotheses concerning how the cognitive would turn out to be different from the noncognitive. The first hypothesis was that cognitive processing involves nonderived content, that is, that cognitive states have the content they do in virtue of the satisfaction of certain naturalistic conditions that do not depend on the existence of other content-bearing, representational, or intentional states. The second was that cognitive processes are to be distinguished by certain sorts of principles that are found to operate in the brain but not elsewhere. As examples, we noted the existence of certain laws of memory formation and retention and certain psychophysical laws, such as Weber's law.

Because we have already twice defended our original articulation of this view, which is in any case a common view in cognitive science, we will not here belabor our positive account.[23]

Inattention to the mark of the cognitive figures into the debate over intracranialism and transcranialism as follows. If one views the world simply in terms of causal processes, then one will likely miss the difference between what goes on inside the brain and what goes on outside. After all, causal processes are transcranial. Alternatively, if one is only interested in a science of the artificial, rather than cognitive science, one is likely to be drawn to transcranialism. Alternatively, if one is only interested in finding systems, or cognitive systems, one is liable to miss the point at which cognitive processes leave off and noncognitive processes begin. Consider, now, some of the others more subtle ways in which theories of the mark of the cognitive abet transcranialism.

3.1. Cognition as Information Processing

Clark (in Wilson & Clark, this volume) and Rowlands (1999) suggest that cognition is information processing.[24] We have considerable sympathy for this as a part of a theory of the cognitive, but we think that cognitive processing is only a narrow subspecies of information processing. Not all information processing is cognitive processing. Compact disc players, DVD players, FM radios, digital computers, cell phones, and so forth, are all information processors, but none of them is a cognitive processor. Any theory of the cognitive that does not notice the difference is clearly missing something relevant to cognitive psychology. This difference is presumably part of the difference between a scientifically interesting cognitive psychology and a scientifically uninteresting consumer electronics.

3.2. The Cognitive as the Computational

Similar in spirit to the idea that cognition is information processing simpliciter, there is the idea that cognition is computation simpliciter. This appears to be how Edwin Hutchins motivates the view that, in the navigation of a ship by a team of sailors, cognition is extended throughout the team in a kind of supermind over and above the minds of the individual sailors:

> Having taken ship navigation as it is performed by a team on the bridge of a ship as the unit of cognitive analysis, I will attempt to apply the principal metaphor of cognitive science – cognition as computation – to the operation of this system. In so doing I do not make any special commitments to the nature of the computations that are going on inside individuals except to say that whatever happens there is part of a larger computational system. But I do believe that the computation observed in the activity of the larger system can be described in the way cognition has traditionally been described – that is, as computation realized through the creation, transformation, and propagation of representational states. (Hutchins, 1995, p. 49)

If cognition is just any sort of computation, then by this relatively broad theory of the mark of the cognitive, then it should not be so surprising that cognition is found in hitherto unsuspected places, such as spanning the boundary of brains, bodies, and environment of a group of sailors. But, then again, by this standard, we would have cognition in personal computers. As we understand it, the orthodox computational theory of the mind maintains not that any computation is a kind of cognition, but that only some specific forms of computation (yet to be discovered and characterized) constitute cognition.[25]

3.3. *The Cognitive as the Meaningful*

Haugeland (1998) urges another theory of the cognitive, or of human intelligence. Haugeland contrasts the representational and the meaningful. Representations are symbolic markers that denote things; they are the data structures of computational theories of mind. The meaningful, however, is a broader kind. Representations have one kind of meaning or significance, but the meaning-ful is more inclusive. As Haugeland (1998) tells it:

> A hammer, for instance, is significant beyond itself in terms of what it's for: driving nails into wood, by being wielded in a certain way, in order to build something, and so on. The nails, the wood, the project, and the carpenter him or herself, are likewise caught up in this "web of significance", in their respective ways. These are the meaningful objects that are the world itself; and none of them is a representation. (p. 233)

So, we may now ask, "What kind of significance constitutes the cognitive?"[26] Were we to review Haugeland's arguments in favor of using the broader notion of the meaningful in cognitive science, we would find that they are simply the system versions of the coupling argument, an argument form we have found inconclusive. Note as well, however, that even if there were a science of the meaningful, this would not necessarily constitute a cognitive psychology. Surely, the vast differences between hammers and saws, on the one hand, and cognition, on the other, are part of what interests cognitive psychologists.[27] Surely a cognitive psychology that ignores such differences is ignoring something important.

3.4. *Operationalizing the Cognitive*

Another way that transcranialists attempt to provide a mark of the cognitive is by a tacit operationalism. They may well reject this characterization of their project, but one can see it in their tacit assumption that whatever process or mechanism accomplishes a given task must be a cognitive process or mechanism. In the closing pages of his paper on embodied and embedded cognition, Haugeland invites us to consider the ability to go to San Jose. He observes that there are many ways one might accomplish this task, such as retaining a horse that is trained to go to San Jose or picking a road that leads to San Jose. And, of course, he is right that there are many ways of getting to San Jose. Further, he is right that not all of these ways involve representation of the sort postulated in the familiar rules-and-representations kind of cognitive science. But it also appears that not all of the ways to get to San Jose involve cognitive processing. A train on rails has the ability to go to San Jose from a point out of sight. A cloud can blow to San Jose from a point out of sight. An intercontinental ballistic missile has the ability to go to San Jose from a point out of sight. These abilities require no intelligence, no cognition. There are lots of combinations of cognitive abilities that one might deploy to get to San Jose, but not every way of getting to San Jose involves cognition. Once one abandons the idea that the ability to move to a point out of sight is a criterion for the cognitive, these possibilities should be clear.

In truth, a more famous case of tacitly operationalizing the cognitive is in Rodney Brooks's discussion of his robot Herbert. Brooks (1997) reports that Herbert has the task of finding soda cans in offices at MIT, picking them up, and bringing them back to a start point. Brooks tacitly presupposes that this task requires intelligence, that any device that can accomplish this task must be intelligent. So, if one adds to this the view that Herbert lacks representations of the sort postulated by rules-and-representations theories of cognition, one can infer that intelligence without representation is possible. Yet suppose we challenge the idea that any device that can collect soda cans in the offices at MIT must be intelligent or must be a cognitive agent. In that case, a different analysis becomes available. That is, one is free to suppose that, although the soda-can collection task can be accomplished in the way humans do it, namely, by deploying cognitive processes, other devices can also accomplish the task through chains of simple noncognitive mechanisms. To decide between these two analyses of what Herbert is doing, we need a substantive theory of what constitutes the cognitive.

The most extensive example of trans-cranialists operationalizing the cognitive is found in Rowlands (1999). When he begins his discussion of perception, he claims that he is not presupposing any controversial definition of cognition. He proposes that cognitive tasks involve the acquisition and employment of information, information in the sense of a nomological dependence between event types. Further, he suggests that a cognitive process is one that is essential to the accomplishment of some cognitive task and that involves operations on information-bearing structures.[28] As we see things, this is a species of operationalism and is fundamentally misguided.

Here is a task: make sure that when the electric garage-door opener lowers the door, the door does not close on anyone. This task apparently requires that the garage-door opener have some more or less reliable mechanism for detecting the presence of a person beneath the door. In other words, the opener must acquire and use information regarding the presence or absence of a person beneath the closing door. So, by Rowlands's account, this task is a cognitive task. The most common way electric garage-door openers gather this information these days is by passing a light beam from a source on one side of the entrance of the garage to a detector on the other side. If some object, such as a person, breaks the beam, the door opener will raise the door. The system is not perfectly reliable, however. A person positioned in just the right way beneath the door need not break the beam. It is also possible to have other sorts of objects break the beam, resulting in false-positives for the presence of a person. Presumably, the light source, detector, and accompanying wiring are essential to the accomplishment of the task and use information about the presence of objects in the light path. Thus, by Rowlands's account, the light source, detector, and its accompanying wiring constitute a cognitive processor.

Contrast the foregoing method of ensuring that the door does not close on anyone with a more old-fashioned way. Not so many years ago, whenever a garage door was to be closed, a person would position him- or herself so as to have a clear view of the space where the door will close, then start the garage-door opener when he or she could see that the path is clear.

Clearly there is some difference between the new way and the old way of operating an electric garage-door opener. A very reasonable empirical hypothesis is that the process by which the electric eye works to detect objects beneath the door is different from the process by which the human eye and visual system detects objects beneath the door. It also seems very reasonable to us to suppose that figuring out what is going on in the human eye and visual system is part of what has interested cognitive scientists who have studied vision in recent years. It is this difference that makes the study of the human eye and visual system intellectually challenging, where the electric eye is a boring piece of hardware you can buy at Sears. So, even if Rowlands were given the term *cognitive* to use as he pleases, there still appears to be a natural kind of process, at least reasonably construed as cognitive, that is worthy of scientific investigation.

Now Rowlands will say that both the new way and the old way of avoiding accidents with electric garage-door openers involves information processing, hence that both are cognitive. As we saw, however, the problem with Rowlands's approach is that even if we accept his conception of the cognitive as essentially information processing, there remains a scientific natural kind of processing that appears to be worthy of scientific investigation in its own right, a scientific, natural kind of processing that traditional intracranialist cognitive scientists have been investigating. Perhaps the human brain is an information processor in just the sense in which a CD player, a DVD player, a television, a cash register, and an automobile gas gauge are information processors. But it is presumably the specific differences between the brain and these other devices that have engaged intracranialists. What interests cognitive psychologists, in part, are the specific ways in which the brain processes information.

3.5. *Rowlands's Evolutionary Argument*

Although Rowlands has a theory of the mark of the cognitive, he seems to lose sight of it during the course of an evolutionary argument for transcranialism. At the least detailed level, Rowlands's evolutionary argument might be viewed as having the form of modus ponens:

1. Development of our cognitive capacities has followed the most efficient evolutionary path.
2. If development of our cognitive capacities has followed the most efficient evolutionary path, then cognitive processes are an essentially hybrid combination of internal and external processes (cf. Rowlands, 1999, p. 25).
3. Therefore, cognitive processes are an essentially hybrid combination of internal and external processes.

Matters would have been simpler had Rowlands just presented this argument and stood by it. At least this argument has the virtue of having a conclusion that is inconsistent with intracranialism. Unfortunately, various reasons move Rowlands to depart from this. In running the argument, Rowlands wants to mark the conclusion as a defeasible inference. Thus, in his version of the consequent and the conclusion, we are told that we should expect our cognitive processes to be an essentially hybrid combination of internal and external processes. Yet the conclusion of this argument is logically consistent with intracranialism, and so technically irrelevant. So, we should probably interpret what Rowlands writes to make its relevance clearer, namely, in the way presented previously. Second, in a desire not to rely too heavily on empirical assumptions about evolutionary history, Rowlands wants to assert only something like the second premise. Yet premise 2 is logically consistent with intracranialism, and so not particularly germane to the debate. Third, it should be noted that essentially all of Rowlands's discussion in chapter 4 of his book is directed toward the exposition and defense of something like premise 1, where nothing at all is said in defense of premise 2. Reading Rowlands as interested only in premise 2 is, in this regard, a distortion of the argumentation of his book. We propose not to be a part of it and instead hold Rowlands to the preceding argument.

So, what are we to make of the foregoing argument? Aside from the fact that Rowlands provides no evidence or argument for premise 2, we think this premise is clearly false.[29] In general, an inference of this form is no good, because the second premise is false:

1. Development of our capacities for X has followed the most efficient evolutionary path.
2. If development of our capacities for X has followed the most efficient evolutionary path, then processes for X are an essentially hybrid combination of internal and external processes (cf. Rowlands, 1999, p. 25).
3. Therefore, processes for X are an essentially hybrid combination of internal and external processes.

Consider human spermatogenesis. Even if this were a capacity that had followed the most efficient evolutionary path, it is evidently not a process that extends into the external world. Consider the phosphorylation of ADP to form ATP. Even if the phylogenetic development of this capacity had followed the most efficient evolutionary pathway, it is pretty clearly an intracellular process if anything is. Consider the transcription of DNA into RNA, meiosis, the phases of mitosis (prophase, metaphase, anaphase, and telophase), the secretion of bile, filtration of the blood in the kidneys, and pumping of blood. All are intraorganismal processes. What does it matter how efficiently they evolved?

Nor are counterexamples to the preceding form of argument limited to processes that are clearly internal to the body's functions. Even processes that have presumably been selected for their role in aiding an organism in responding to its environment have their easily recognized internal subprocesses.[30] Presumably the patellar reflex was selected for to prevent injury to the patellar tendon. Still, we recognize

that the process of extending the lower leg involves subprocesses of distinct kinds internal to the leg. There is the stretching of the proprioceptive cells in the tendon, the firing of the proprioceptive cells, the propagation of the action potentials to the spinal cord, the release of neurotransmitters in the spinal cord, the firing of motor neurons in the spinal cord, the propagation of the action potentials to the sundry muscles of the thigh, the release of neurotransmitters at the neuromuscular junction, and the contractions of the muscles, just to name a few. None of these processes extends into the environment, despite their interaction with the environment. Take the isomerization of rhodopsin in the retina on absorption of light. Presumably this chemical change has been selected for, but there is no temptation to suppose that the chemical change extends into the environment. Consider dilation of the pupil in response to low light. The process of dilation is causally linked to environmental stimuli and the explanation of why a pupil dilates on a given occasion may make some reference to the level of ambient lighting, but, all the same, the process of dilation takes place within the eye.

Rowlands may well wish to say that these counterexamples merely clarify what he had already conceded, namely, that the inference he is making is defeasible. His idea is really that, if the development of a capacity has followed the most efficient evolutionary path, then this gives us some defeasible reason to think that the process is a hybrid combination of internal and external processes. This, however, misses what should be the moral of the counterexamples. The point is that there is no reason to link the property of being a product of natural selection with the property of extending into the environment. They appear to be entirely orthogonal concerns.

Here is another way to make the foregoing point. Rowlands spends the bulk of chapter 4 of The Body in Mind making a kind of plausibility argument for the view that using tools makes for greater fitness than not using tools. We concede, just for the sake of running another argument more simply, that this is so. Our objection to Rowlands's evolutionary argument is that, even if organisms that use tools are more fit than organisms that do not, this has nothing to do with how we discriminate among types of processes and their subcomponents. Surely, the most reasonable thing to expect evolutionary theory to do is provide a theoretical taxonomy of processes based on evolutionary theory, not a theoretical taxonomy of processes based on cognitive theory. Evolutionary theory parses the world up into units that are significant in terms of evolution, not in terms of cognition. So, one should expect that appeals to evolutionary theory are entirely orthogonal to the intracranial-transcranial debate. Here again, we think that, were consideration of the mark of the cognitive brought to the fore, this sort of misdirected argument might be avoided.

4. Conclusion

In this chapter we have drawn attention to what appear to us to be the two principal weaknesses in current developments of transcranialism. They are that transcranialism is regularly backed by some form of coupling-constitution fallacy and that it does not have an adequate account of the difference between the cognitive and the noncognitive. A more nagging worry, however, is the motivation for transcranialism. What reason is there to make this proposed conceptual shift? Why parse up causal processes in the transcranialist way rather than in the intracranialist way? We have tried to motivate the intracranialist approach by drawing attention to the existence of distinctive causal processes that take place intracranially. For example, the human visual system appears to have information-processing channels for such things as color, motion, and form, where digital camcorders do not. Further, human memory appears to show primacy and recency effects unlike those that occur in computer hard drives or pen and paper. We think that greater attention to cognitive psychology textbooks helps to highlight these differences, where greater attention to ordinary language tends to efface these differences. We also think that the existence of these processes, rather than mere prejudice or tradition, explains why the orthodox position in cognitive science is intracranial.[31] Finally, we think that these differences explain why even transcranialists maintain that cognition extends from brains into the extraorganismal world rather than from the extraorganismal world into brains.

Notes

1 Ideas in this chapter are precursors to those we have developed in more detail in our recent book (Adams & Aizawa, 2008).
2 Although there is a difference between the intracranial and the intraorganismal, it is not a difference we propose to trouble about here.
3 Among philosophers we count van Gelder (1995); Dennett (1996); Clark and Chalmers (1998); Haugeland (1998); perhaps Hurley (1998); Rowlands (1999, 2003); Noë (2004); and Sutton (2005). Among psychologists we count Donald (1991); O'Regan (1992); Thelen and Smith (1994); Hutchins (1995); and Gibbs (2001). An interesting early advocate of extended cognition is the anthropologist Bateson (1972). Following this rising tide in support of extended cognition are voices of resistance. These include Adams and Aizawa (2001, in press); Wilson (2002); Susi, Lindblom, and Ziemke (2003); Rupert (2004); Sterelny (2004); Block (2005); Rupert (in press, this volume); and Aizawa (2007).

   Actually, some extracranialists sometimes wish to maintain that cognitive processes are essentially extended into the external world. Insofar as we are successful in arguing that cognitive processes are typically not extended, it will follow that they are not essentially extended. We do not, however, maintain that cognitive processes are essentially internal.
4 Haugeland (1998), Clark and Chalmers (1998), and Clark (in press), for example, are fairly explicit about the kinds of couplings they have in mind.
5 Cf. Hurley (1998, pp. 2–4); Clark (2005, p. 1); and Clark (in press).
6 Cf., e.g., McClamrock (1995, pp. 3–4); Haugeland (1998, pp. 209–210); Rowlands (1999, pp. 106–113); and Gibbs (2001, pp. 117–118).

7   In fact, contemporary intracranialist cognitive science appears to do this already. The interaction between organism and environment is at the heart of the lively empiricist-nativist debates. Insofar as contemporary ethology is intracranialist, it too studies organism-environment interactions, namely, the interactions of organisms with their natural environments. And where would the study of sensation and perception be if it did not study the interaction between organism and environment?

8   In correspondence, Dan Dennett indicated that what he was concerned to point out is that our concept of cognition does not require that it be found in the brain.

9   Cf., e.g., Clark and Chalmers (1998, p. 10) and Rowlands (1999, pp. 115–116). Rowlands (1999, pp. 115–116) tries to put the burden of avoiding a terminological dispute on the intracranialist. Susi, Lindblom, and Ziemke (2003) also raise this concern.

10 Clark (in press) sometimes appears not to appreciate this.

11 One might make the case that psychology should be understood in terms of mechanisms, rather than ceteris paribus laws, something along the lines suggested by Machamer, Darden, and Craver (2000). Perhaps this is so, but we do not see that debate between intracranialists and transcranialists depends on this. In addition, one might make the case that psychological explanations should be understood in terms of functional analysis (cf. Cummins, 1983). Perhaps so, in which case we might reformulate our approach within this framework. For the sake of simplicity of exposition, however, we forbear here.

12 Here we find ourselves at odds with Haugeland (1998); Rowlands (1999, 2003); Clark and Chalmers (1998); and Clark (2005), who suggest that it is mere prejudice that sustains the orthodox intracranialist position in cognitive science.

13 This is a line of criticism we broached in Adams and Aizawa (2001). The same kind of argument has recently been applied by Block (2005) in a critique of Noë's (2004) theory of enactive perception. See also Rupert (in press).

14 For other examples, see Adams and Aizawa (2001, in press).

15 Who since about Leibniz has doubted this?

16 Chapter 1 of Noë (2004) is much more explicit about the distinction between causation and constitution and can be viewed as a defense of the view that cognition is constituted, in part, by one's body. In his chapter 1, Noë defends the view that perceptual abilities are constituted, in part, by sensorimotor skills. Given the assumption that the exercise of perceptual abilities are cognitive processes and that sensorimotor skills are constituted in part by muscles and peripheral nerves, one has the view that cognitive processing is constituted, in part, by bodily processes. In this chapter, Noë is pretty explicit in favoring the constitutive claim over the causal claim. Aizawa (2007) provides a detailed critique of this case for extended cognition.

17 Actually, the example first appears in the work of Clark (1997), but its use to support extracranialism is less marked there.

18 This jointly responsible idea figures more prominently in the version presented in Clark (1997). Haugeland (1998) runs the same "jointly responsible" line about navigating to San Jose. By driving the interstate, one relies on the structure of the interstate and on one's cognitive abilities in dealing with roads. Thus, the road and the brain are between them responsible for successfully navigating to San Jose and they constitute a single causal process. Still, that does not make the interactions between the road and the brain a single *cognitive* process. Establishing the latter stronger claim is what the extracranialist needs.

19 This jointly responsible idea figures more prominently in the version presented in Clark (1997). Haugeland (1998) runs the same jointly responsible line about navigating to San Jose. By driving the interstate, one relies on the structure of the interstate and on one's cognitive abilities in dealing with roads. Thus, the road and the brain are between them responsible for successfully navigating to San Jose and they constitute a single causal process. Still, that does not make the interactions between the road and the brain a single cognitive process. Establishing the latter stronger claim is what the extracranialist needs.

20 Cf. Haugeland (1998): "If . . . there is a constant close coupling between the ant and the details of the beach surface, and if this coupling is crucial in determining the actual path, then, for purposes of understanding the path, the ant and beach must be regarded more as an integrated unit than as a pair of distinct components. This is the simplest archetype of what I mean by *intimacy*" (p. 217). Substitute

bowling ball for *ant* and *alley* for *beach* and you are well on your way to committing Haugeland to something rather wild.

21 In fact, one can pick up a reference to a system in the passage from Clark (2001), cited previously. Much of Haugeland (1998) can be viewed as an elaborate case of the system version of the coupling-constitution fallacy: "The strategy will be to bring some well-known principles of systems analysis to bear on the mind-body-world 'system' in a way that refocuses questions of division and unity" (pp. 208–209).

22 Doesn't the cyborg example play into the intracranialist's hand? After all, cyborgs are hybrids of organism and artifact rather than simply organisms. So, shouldn't humans with tools be hybrids of cognizers and artifacts rather than simply cognizers?

23 Aizawa and Adams (2005) and Adams and Aizawa (in press).

24 Clark (in press); Wilson and Clark (this volume); and Rowlands (1999, pp. 26, 115, 119, 122).

25 Incidently, if one hypothesized that cognitive processing is just the evolution of a dynamical system, then it will of course turn out that cognitive processing extends into the body and environment. Of course, on such a lax theory of the mark of the cognitive, there will be cognition in Watt governors, the pendulums in grandfather clocks, and so on.

26 Haugeland (1998, p. 233) puts the matter this way: "The real question is: Which sense matters in the context of understanding human intelligence?" This way of formulating the issue risks inserting controversy over exactly what constitutes "understanding human intelligence." We wish to avoid this tangential issue here.

27 Adams and Aizawa (2001) provide reason to be skeptical of the possibility of a science of the artificial.

28 This seems to be Rowlands's "official" theory of the mark of the cognitive, where the idea that cognition is simply information processing is merely a view suggested by stylistic variations in Rowlands's writing. Cf., e.g., Rowlands (1999, pp. 102–103, 116, 137).

29 Clearly the truth value of premise 2 is a primary concern whether Rowlands wants to assert just premise 2 or run the whole modus ponens sketched previously.

30 Rowlands (1999) adds another small wrinkle to his argument:

> If we have adopted the most efficient strategy for accomplishing tasks, then the cognitive mechanisms we have evolved should be designed to function in conjunction with environmental structures. Then, the cognitive processes realized by these mechanisms would have to be understood as straddling both internal processes and those external processes whereby the organism interacts with these environmental structures. (p. 25)

The consequent in the second sentence motivates the present paragraph. Note as well that it is the move from the second sentence to the third in this passage that constitutes for us the non sequitur.

31 Rupert (2004) provides a nice elaboration of this kind of consideration, which we broached in Adams and Aizawa (2001).

References

Adams, F., & Aizawa, K. (2001). The bounds of cognition. *Philosophical Psychology, 14,* 43–64.

Adams, F., & Aizawa, K. (2008). *The bounds of cognition.* Oxford: Blackwell.

Adams, F., & Aizawa, K. (in press). Defending the bounds of cognition. In R. Menary (Ed.), *The extended mind.* Aldershot, UK: Ashgate.

Aizawa, K. (2007). Understanding the embodiment of perception. *Journal of Philosophy, 104,* 5–25.

Aizawa, K., & Adams, F. (2005). Defending non-derived content. *Philosophical Psychology, 18,* 661–669.

Bateson, G. (1972). *Steps to an ecology of mind.* New York: Ballantine Books.

Block, N. (2005). Review of Alva Noë's *Action in perception. Journal of Philosophy, 102,* 259–272.

Brooks, R. (1997). Intelligence without representation. In J. Haugeland (Ed.), *Mind design II* (pp. 121–145). Cambridge, MA: MIT Press.

Clark, A. (1997). *Being there: Putting brain, body, and world together again.* Cambridge, MA: MIT Press.

Clark, A. (2001). Reasons, robots, and the extended mind. *Mind & Language, 16,* 121–145.

Clark, A. (2002). Towards a science of the bio-technological mind. *International Journal of Cognition and Technology, 1,* 21–33.

Clark, A. (2003). *Natural-born cyborgs*. Oxford: Oxford University Press.

Clark, A. (2005). Intrinsic content, active memory and the extended mind. *Analysis, 65*, 1–11.

Clark, A. (in press). Memento's revenge: The extended mind, extended. In R. Menary (Ed.), *The extended mind*. Aldershot, UK: Ashgate.

Clark, A., & Chalmers, D. (1998). The extended mind. *Analysis, 58*, 7–19.

Cummins, R. (1983). *The nature of psychological explanation*. Cambridge, MA: MIT Press.

Dennett, D. C. (1996). *Kinds of minds*. New York: Basic Books.

Dennett, D. C. (2000). Making tools for thinking. In D. Sperber (Ed.), *Metarepresentations: A multidisciplinary perspective* (pp. 17–29). Oxford: Oxford University Press.

Donald, M. (1991). *Origins of the modern mind*. Cambridge, MA: Harvard University Press.

Gibbs, R. J. (2001). Intentions as emergent products of social interactions. In B. F. Malle, L. J. Moses, & D. A. Baldwin (Eds.), *Intentions and intentionality* (pp. 105–122). Cambridge, MA: MIT Press.

Haugeland, J. (1998). Mind embodied and embedded. In J. Haugeland (Ed.), *Having thought* (pp. 207–237). Cambridge, MA: Harvard University Press.

Hurley, S. L. (1998). Vehicles, contents, conceptual structure, and externalism. *Analysis, 58*, 1–6.

Hutchins, E. (1995). *Cognition in the wild*. Cambridge, MA: MIT Press.

Machamer, P., Darden, L., & Craver, C. (2000). Thinking about mechanisms. *Philosophy of Science, 67*, 1–25.

McClamrock, R. (1995). *Existential cognition*. Chicago: University of Chicago Press.

Noë, A. (2004). *Action in perception*. Cambridge, MA: MIT Press.

O'Regan, J. K. (1992). Solving the "real" mysteries of visual perception: The world as an outside memory. *Canadian Journal of Psychology, 46*, 461–488.

Rowlands, M. (1999). *The body in mind*. Cambridge: Cambridge University Press.

Rowlands, M. (2003). *Externalism: Putting mind and world back together again*. Montreal: McGill-Queen's University Press.

Rupert, R. (2004). Challenges to the hypothesis of extended cognition. *Journal of Philosophy, 101*, 389–428.

Rupert, R. (in press). Representation in extended cognitive systems: Does the scaffolding of language extend the mind? In R. Menary (Ed.), *The extended mind*. Aldershot, UK: Ashgate.

Schlatter, M., & Aizawa, K. (2008). Walter Pitts and "A logical calculus." *Synthese, 162*, 232–250.

Sterelny, K. (2004). Externalism, epistemic artifacts, and the extended mind (pp. 239–254). In R. Schantz (Ed.), *The externalist challenge*. Berlin: Walter de Gruyter.

Susi, T., Lindblom, J., & Ziemke, T. (2003). Beyond the bounds of cognition. In K. Forbus, D. Gentner, & T. Regier (Eds.), *Proceedings of the 25th Annual Conference of the Cognitive Science Society* (pp. 1305–1310). Mahwah, NJ: Lawrence Erlbaum.

Sutton, J. (2005). Memory and the extended mind: Embodiment, cognition, and culture. *Cognitive Processing, 6*(4), 223–226.

Thelen, E., & Smith, L. (1994). *A dynamical systems approach to the development of cognition and action*. Cambridge, MA: MIT Press.

van Gelder, T. (1995). What might cognition be, if not computation? *Journal of Philosophy, 91*, 345–381.

Wilson, M. (2002). Six views of embodied cognition. *Psychonomic Bulletin and Review, 9*, 625–636.

Wilson, R. (2004). *Boundaries of the mind: The individual in the fragile sciences*. Cambridge: Cambridge University Press.

CHAPTER 6

Innateness and the Situated Mind

Robert Rupert

Many advocates of situated approaches to the study of cognition (e.g., Griffiths & Stotz, 2000; Thelen & Smith, 1994) explicitly take exception to cognitive science's pronounced nativist turn.[1] Other proponents of situated models seek to mitigate strong nativist claims by, for example, finding ways to acknowledge innate contributions to cognitive processing while at the same time downplaying those contributions (Wilson, 2004, chap. 3). Still others leave implicit their apparent opposition to nativism: they emphasize the environment's contribution to cognition so strongly as to suggest antinativist views but do not take up the issue explicitly (Clark, 1997; Varela, Thompson, & Rosch, 1991).[2] Thus, situated theorists have reached something approximating an antinativist consensus. In this chapter, I argue that they should not embrace the antinativist view so readily. To this end, I divide the situated approach into two species, extended and embedded views of cognition, arguing that each version of the situated view admits of a plausible nativist interpretation with respect to at least some important cognitive phenomena. In contrast, I

also argue for the nonnativist interpretation of certain cognitive phenomena; nevertheless, these antinativist recommendations come heavily hedged – in some cases, at the expense of a robust reading of the situated program or one of its subdivisions.

1. Extended Cognition and Nativism

Consider first the view that cognitive processes extend beyond the boundary of the organism. The intimacy of the human organism's interaction with its environment during cognitive processing suggests that those cognitive processes literally comprise elements of the environment beyond the boundary of the human organism (Clark & Chalmers, 1998). I shall refer to this view as the "hypothesis of extended cognition," or HEC. As I understand it, HEC entails that the human mind is extended. Accordingly, the subject matter of HEC (i.e., the kind of cognition at issue) had better be the sort that bears on the location of the mind. This seems fair enough. The explananda of cognitive science are various mental capacities broadly pertaining to belief formation, such as the capacities to reason, perceive, remember, construct theories, and use language. Thus, whatever model of cognition we ultimately adopt will be a model of the mind's activities or capacities; and if the activities of a mind take place at a particular spatiotemporal location, that mind is at least partly at that location.[3] On this view, a given mind has a location in space-time and, according to HEC, this location includes points outside the skin bag, as Andy Clark (2003) has colorfully dubbed the boundary of the human organism. Thus we arrive at the division mentioned previously. A view is extended if it holds that, in some cases, a system composed of a human organism together with material (possibly including other organisms) existing beyond that organism's boundaries instantiates cognitive properties relevant to the location of a mind; views that merely emphasize the human organism's heavy dependence on, and frequent interaction with, the environment during cognitive processing are embedded views, discussion of which is deferred to subsequent sections.

If extended systems are the proper objects of study in cognitive science, antinativism seems to follow, particularly if one accepts the common notion that a trait is innate if and only if it is specified by the genome (Block, 1981, pp. 280–281; Elman et al., 1996, p. 22). The advocate of extended cognition urges us to focus on the traits of extended systems, and it is difficult to see how genes could encode such traits, for genes would seem to affect directly only the organism itself. Extended theorists typically hold that cognitive systems include such external components as hard drives; notebooks; text messages; and, in the case of vision, whatever the subject happens to be visually engaged with. How, one might wonder, could genes specify anything about such external resources? These extended elements are disconnected from the organic milieu of the genome and thus beyond the genome's direct causal or informational purview. Given the great variability in the external resources alleged to become part of

extended cognitive systems, it would seem that not even the entire set of biological resources internal to the organism can specify what will become part of the resultant extended cognitive system.

This antinativist argument from HEC seems quite powerful. What, in contrast, might motivate a nativist reading of HEC? Consider two widely discussed measures of a trait's or a capacity's innate status: canalization (Ariew, 1999) and generative entrenchment (Wimsatt, 1999). The canalization-based approach to nativism holds that a trait is innate to the extent that it resists perturbation across changes in the environment. As an account of innateness, this allows a trait to be more or less innate, depending on the breadth of environments in which the trait appears.

Now consider some systems typically claimed to involve extended cognition: a human together with a map (Hutchins, 1995); a human together with a pencil and paper on which she performs mathematical calculations (Clark, 1997); a human together with auditory patterns of spoken language (Clark, 1997; Rowlands, 1999); a human together with the visible objects in his immediate environment (O'Regan, 1992); and a human together with gross physical structures in her environment, for instance, a human and a roadway that he is following (Haugeland, 1995).

At least some traits of such systems exhibit a high degree of canalization. Take, for example, a human using external symbols – say, self-directed speech – to guide herself through a complicated task (Clark, 1997, 1998). Humans typically live in groups and use language, and thus the typical human subject is likely to engage in some kind of self-directed symbol use across a wide range of environments. Furthermore, even in the absence of a clear channel of learning from conspecifics, humans tend to create linguistic or quasi-linguistic symbol systems (Bloom, 2000, chap. 10; Goldin-Meadow & Zheng, 1998). To the extent that subjects developing in abnormal environments use partly externalized, self-devised systems to guide their own thought and behavior, the self-directed use of a symbolic system passes the deprivation test for canalization (Ariew, 1999): deprived of a species-typical environment, the trait emerges nonetheless. The use of the environment as visual memory is, perhaps, even more broadly canalized; this trait appears in all but the most extreme environments, such as those involving physical damage to the visual system or restriction to dark environments. Once we have placed extended cognitive systems on par with organismic systems, the canalization theory of innateness delivers a nativist vision of many of the former systems' traits.[4]

Move now to William Wimsatt's (1999) theory of generative entrenchment.[5] According to this view, a cognitive capacity or trait is innate to the extent that its appearance is a prerequisite for the appearance of traits emerging later in development. Some important and prima facie cognitive characteristics of extended systems seem to satisfy the criterion of generative entrenchment. Consider, for example, the human organism's spoken-out, rote learning of times tables. This is a prerequisite for the acquisition of many later-emerging traits of the extended cognitive system. Typically, when learning the times tables, subjects intentionally create external sound (or print) structures to facilitate learning. For many subjects, either the continued vocalization of basic facts about multiplication or the internal representation of such verbalization proves invaluable in the solving of more complex problems (compare the intentionally created, linguistic means of external control discussed by Clark, 1997, pp. 195–196, 1998, pp. 173, 181). At the very least, one would think that, for any given subject, there must have been a time when the extended trait appeared; it is difficult to learn the times tables without verbalizing them (or writing them out – another extended process). The ability to solve problems involving the multiplication of large numbers depends on the memorization of the times tables, and the ability to solve problems involving the multiplication of large numbers grounds many further abilities, for example,

those underlying feats of engineering and commerce (cf. Wimsatt's [1999, p. 143] discussion of generative entrenchment and cultural evolution).

The antinativist advocate of HEC might respond directly, attempting to show that when properly applied, considerations of canalization and generative entrenchment do not support a nativist reading of HEC's favored examples. It is, however, difficult to execute this strategy without relegating external resources to second-class status, which crosses purposes with HEC; for the most promising antinativist response invokes asymmetries in the contribution of the organism to the apparent canalization and generative entrenchment. It is not a trait of the extended system that is, for example, canalized, so much as the ability of the human organism to enter into certain relations with external resources (cf. Clark, 2003); the appearance of alleged extended systems depends on the latter ability. Furthermore, this dependence is asymmetric: the intentions, desires, and purposes of the organism provide impetus missing from external resources (I discuss this point in more detail herein). This asymmetry implies that the organismic portions of extended systems are deeply privileged, to an extent that should unsettle the advocate of HEC (cf. Rupert, 2004). The antinativist HEC theorist might do better, then, to advocate a distinct biological perspective on innateness. Of most promise would seem to be developmental systems theory, or DST, which appears not only to preserve HEC's antinativist credentials but also to support directly the HEC-style individuation of cognitive systems.

Developmental systems theory is often seen as an antidote to twentieth-century biology's overemphasis on the gene. For many years, textbook presentations characterized genes as the codes for and the determinants of phenotypic traits of living things; these encodings were selected for because they determined the presence of phenotypic traits that confer reproductive advantage on their bearers. In contrast, the advocates of DST point to the wide range of contextual factors affecting gene expression and, more generally, the development of phenotypic traits. The most uncontroversial of these contextual factors reside in the organism itself. Developmental systems theorists go one further, however, to argue that determination involves the entire host of factors shaping the phenotype (i.e., the entire host of factors that create a life cycle), which, in many cases, includes factors in the environment beyond the organism's boundary (Griffiths & Gray, 2004).

Developmental systems theory emphasizes the ways in which organismic resources contribute to the shaping of environments (e.g., in niche construction) that confer reproductive advantage on the very organismic resources that help to create those environments. As a result, those environments are more likely to be re-created or maintained. Thus, environmental factors can themselves exhibit the dynamics of selection as it is thought to operate on genetic resources: the environmental resources exhibit traits that, given the context, increase their own fitness. In fact, the environments are selected for along with the selection for organisms that create those environments. Because reproduction of the two systems – organismic resources and external ones – rely on each other for success, selection is for the composite package of resources, internal and external: the entire developmental system, organism-and-environment, is selected for.[6]

Developmental systems theory thus appears to support HEC in a fairly straightforward way. According to DST, evolutionary forces often operate on transorganismic, or extended, systems. Assuming that cognitive traits were selected for, it is no surprise that transorganismic systems should exhibit such traits. The HEC theorist simply takes the systems instantiating cognitive properties to be, or to at least be similar in scope to, the systems of fundamental importance with respect to the biological processes that give rise to cognitive phenomena.

What is more, DST seems to ground a nonnativist account of the cognitive traits of extended systems. Traditional notions of innateness presuppose an important distinction between the organism (or the mind) and its environment; nativists claim that, in some substantive sense, internal structures (beliefs, theories, concepts) arise independently of the environment (or of what is external to the mind) and are innate for just that reason. According to DST, evolutionary processes select for traits determined by more than the organism itself. On the traditional view of innateness, then, where there is extraorganismic determination of phenotypic traits, the traits in question are not innate. Similarly, in the case of cognitive systems: if a cognitive system includes the environment in nontrivial ways – ways that pertain directly to the cognitive capacities or structures in question – this precludes a nativist account of those structures; for surely the cognitive capacities in question are not sufficiently independent of the environment to be innate.[7]

Both appeals to DST fail the HEC theorist. Take first the nonnativist interpretation of DST and, derived from it, the nonnativist interpretation of HEC. If there is any single overarching idea driving nativist thought throughout the centuries, it is the equation of innateness with what follows from the internal properties or states of a system. If, however, the relevant system is extended, the internal-external boundary shifts accordingly: it separates what is internal to that extended system, including its organismic and extraorganismic parts, from what falls outside that extended system. It follows from HEC, then, that traits arising exclusively or largely from what is internal to the entire developmental system are innate to that system: they are determined by the resources internal to it. Both Wilson (1999, pp. 363–364) and Wimsatt (1999, p. 160) entertain this view, or something close to it, though neither embraces it. It is a challenge, though, to see where precisely it goes wrong.

It might fall to eliminativism. The advocate of HEC might argue either that innateness, in general, is too fractured a concept to be of any use (Griffiths, 2002) or that the particular conception of innateness currently at issue floats too far from the traditional one to merit the title. Such qualms miss the mark, though, by failing to appreciate the fundamental role of the internalist view in historical and contemporary thinking about innateness. According to Plato, knowledge is innate because it is already in the mind, as a result of the soul's experiences prior to earthly embodiment. On Leibniz's view, knowledge is present in the mind like veins in marble and thus is innate – similarly for most contemporary views. The idea that what is innate is what is genetically determined expresses the internalist view: genes constitute the relevant material internal to the system; therefore, whatever they create is innate. Various other views, for example, that what is innate is canalized, universal, or typical to the species, arguably constitute diagnostic measures of the organism's internal contribution – the contribution of what is internal to all members of a given species and in virtue of which they are members of that species. At the very least, the internalist conception constrains theories of innateness: any conception of innateness that rules a trait to be noninnate when the system's internal properties are primarily responsible for that trait's appearance thereby faces a serious objection. It is not credible, then, to dismiss the internalist concept of innateness as unprincipled, fractured, or deviant. Thus, DST does not secure a nonnativist reading of HEC.

Moreover, closer examination of DST's implications regarding systems individuation undermines HEC's appeal to DST as a general source of support. One of the primary problems currently faced by DST is the problem of systems individuation in the theory of selection (Griffiths & Gray, 2004, pp. 423–424). Advocates of DST have made a strong case that external resources contribute significantly to the traits on which selection operates. Nevertheless, this does not settle the issue of what are, properly speaking, biological individuals; if we were to accept that anything causally relevant to the development of a trait becomes part of a biological individual, we would saddle ourselves with a profligate metaphysics for

biology. There are alternatives, however. If one focuses on selection for individual traits, one can, in many cases, interpret the selection process in either of two ways: as the selection for extended biological systems or as selection for traits of individual organisms that occurs within a particular environment (which might, for example, include the presence of other organisms with the same or a complementary trait; Sterelny & Griffiths, 1999, pp. 166–172).

To distinguish cases, Sterelny and Griffiths propose a common-fate criterion (1999, pp. 161, 172–177). Say that we encounter what appears to be an extended system, one that includes something more than a single organism. We can ask to what degree the various components of that system are subject to the same selection pressure, that is, to what extent the reproductive fate of the components is shared. In the extreme case, every part of a system reproduces together or not at all; there is no independent reproduction or survival of parts.[8] In such cases, a trait exhibited by the entire system is possessed by that system as a biological individual. In other cases, though, the organism interacts with its environment in reproduction-enhancing ways, without shared fate. In these cases, traits are selected for because of their bearers' interactions with components of some larger system; it is only in the context of those interactions that the trait confers its selectional advantage. Still, the bearers in question can and sometimes do go it alone: they can survive and reproduce in the absence of the other components on which the utility of some of their own individual traits depends. In such cases, although an extended system might seem to exhibit a single trait, the components of that system are reproductively independent; and thus the traits on which selectional forces operate are traits of the components. In these cases, componential explanation – that is, explanation given in terms of selection pressures operating on the traits of the components as biological individuals – is to be preferred; and in this way, we avoid profligate metaphysics. Many selection-based explanations depend on distinguishing parts of the system. Once such smaller individuals have been admitted into our ontology, there is no reason to add an extended system; analysis in terms of the smaller individuals situated in their environments suffices to explain whatever effects the trait in question has, including effects that change how selectional forces operate on the trait.[9]

Thus, although DST might lay firm biological ground for some extended cognitive systems, significant limitations apply: extended systems exist only where the parts of the extended system share a common fate; only in those cases do facts about extended trait selection bear on cognitive systems individuation because only in those cases do facts about extended trait selection bear on the individuation of biological systems. The problem is that most of the systems of interest to HEC theorists do not satisfy the shared-fate criterion; these systems exhibit significant asymmetries among their components, analogous to asymmetries resulting in reproductive independence in the biological context. In lieu of some other more convincing criterion for the individuation of biological systems, these asymmetries undermine the DST-based case for HEC.

Consider the genesis of extended cognitive systems. The volition of the organism, its intention to take up tools, and its abilities to do so are asymmetrically responsible for the creation of extended cognitive systems.[10] For example, an organism with no need to solve complex mathematical problems does not create a system of written numerals, the manipulation of which facilitates the solving of those problems. I would like to pursue this concern about asymmetry, but in the interest of variety, I shall do so in the context of a different example, one presented by Clark (2003, pp. 76–77): the artist using a sketch pad who creates drawings via a feedback loop. The artist begins a sketch by making preliminary figures. The results of these early strokes impinge on the organism, causing her to "see" the artistic possibilities in a new light and thus to make different, often more sophisticated sets of new strokes; the cycle repeats, with the final art object taking a form that the artist would not have envisioned without the use of the sketch pad as a tool. Nevertheless, if the organismic subject had not been interested in drawing, the organism would not have taken up a sketch pad; that is, the extended system in question would never have come into existence. Asymmetrically, the sketch pad's interests, goals, or other internal processes provide little impetus for the creation of the system in question. (Artists might describe their sketch pads as calling to them, but they would, I take it, be speaking figuratively of their internal states.)

Admittedly, there is some bare counterfactual sense in which the sketch pad causes the existence of the extended system: in the nearest possible world in which the sketch pad does not exist, the particular extended system in question does not come into existence. Despite this causal contribution on the part of the sketch pad, the asymmetry is genuine. Keep in mind how lopsided are the relative contributions of the organismic and extraorganismic portions of the extended system. Consider what happens if a particular sketch pad or a particular artist is deleted from history. The human, wishing to draw, is likely to find or make a different sketch pad if the particular one she would otherwise have gotten is destroyed. The sketch pad seems less likely to find or make a different human if her user has been removed. This may be partly a contingent statistical factor – at any given time, the proportion of artists who want to sketch who find sketch pads is much greater than the proportion of sketch pads ready for use that in fact get used – but behind it lies the point about impetus made previously: the human who wants to sketch will go out of her way to find or make a sketch pad; the sketch pad instantiates no internal processes that home in on or actively create users. Now consider a slightly different kind of counterfactual variation: type-level obliteration. Wipe the sketch pads from history and human organisms still exist. Wipe the humans from history, and there will be no sketch pads. Finally, take a special case of the preceding point, a world in which no sketch pads exist or ever have existed. It is likely that human organisms will create sketch pads, but the converse will not happen: no sketch pad will bring a human into being. So, there appears to be an asymmetric relation between the causal processes responsible for the existence of the components of the extended system.[11]

Return now to the question of whether DST, qualified by the shared-fate criterion, supports HEC. In light of the preceding discussion of asymmetries, it seems clear that the human organism is reproductively independent of the sketch pad and thus that the composite system of sketch pad plus human does not satisfy the shared-fate criterion. Does this concern carry over to other examples? It would appear that the standard examples of extended systems – those involving language, mathematics, external memory storage, and nautical artifacts – manifest most or all of the asymmetries discussed previously. Furthermore, although the development of these tools surely affected humans' rate of reproduction, human organisms are reproductively independent of all such resources (having reproduced without them for millennia).

In the end, then, two systems-based concerns threaten the marriage of DST and HEC. First, a plausible DST validates only a narrow range of genuinely extended biological individuals; the shared-fate criterion severely limits the number of such extended systems. Second, no matter how things turn out with respect to biology, we cannot ignore the potential for mismatch between the extended individuals established by DST and those systems claimed by HEC to be extended cognitive systems. Clearly these two worries operate together: given the broad range of extended cognitive systems, the narrowness of the range of extended biological systems dims the prospects for cross-disciplinary fit. It may well be that natural forces sometimes select for extended systems, but such systems might not be the ones of interest to psychology (Rupert, 2004, n22; Wilson, 1999, p. 363).[12] If, for example, extended selection requires a stable environmental contribution, yet cognitive

science is interested in abilities that can be exercised flexibly across a wide range of environments, danger of mismatch looms large. These concerns about mismatch, together with the nativist results of combining DST and HEC, suggest that the anti-nativist HEC theorist should try a different tack: to set aside entirely the appeal to biology – DST and all the rest – and look instead to psychological criteria of innateness.

2. Extended Systems, Nativism, and Psychology

Before turning to psychological criteria of innateness, we should address the prior question: are there extended systems that might plausibly serve as bearers of innate psychological capacities or traits? If there are no such systems, it is moot whether psychological criteria would pronounce their cognitive traits to be innate. To prosecute this question, it is helpful to take up more general issues pertaining to the explananda of cognitive psychology, its investigative methods, and the relation of both to HEC.

Humans categorize, perceive, remember, use language, reason, and make sense of the actions of others – these and more are abilities of persisting systems. In contrast, most actual extended systems are short-lived: they involve the human organism's short-term use of or interaction with some kind of external resource. The importance of systems that persist and cohere, even through change, is especially clear in developmental psychology: we want to know how that system – a single developing human – came to be the way it is and how a similar course of development happens, on average, for the relatively homogeneous multitude of such persisting human systems. We want to understand how and why the capacities and abilities of individual persisting systems change over time and eventually take a stable form. If the systems to be investigated were relatively short-lived systems – the organism together with its immediate linguistic environment, for example – developmental inquiry would seem incoherent. We want to be able to explain why, for example, the child categorizes on the basis of appearance at age two but pays more attention to insides at age five (Carey, 1995; Keil, 1989; Markman, 1989). How can this question be sensibly posed – and in such a way that it might motivate a research program – if all that exists are ephemeral systems, lacking in the continuity that makes the child at five the same system as the child at two?[13]

In response, the advocate of HEC might remind us of the aim to reconceptualize cognitive systems. Such reconceptualization founders on a dilemma, however: either we pursue genuine reconceptualization of cognitive systems as relatively short-lived systems, at great cost to cognitive psychology, or we can jury-rig a method of cognitive-systems individuation that preserves the successes of cognitive psychology and is consistent with a viable investigative method – but unmotivated and unnecessarily complex.

Consider what is lost if the HEC theorist pursues the former tack. The typical experiment in cognitive psychology yields useful and coherent results by assuming such privileged grouping of various short-lived systems (i.e., the typical experiment presupposes that subjects are persisting, organismically bound cognitive systems).[14] Think of the multitude of within-subject analyses of results on short series of experiments, all data lost, absent privileged groupings. Radical reconceptualization, however, offers developmental psychologists no more reason to be interested in, for example, the series of temporal segments we normally associate with Sally from ages two to six than it offers to be interested in, say, Sally, at age two, together with a ball she was bouncing on some particular day; Johnny, age five, together with the book he was reading on some particular afternoon; and Terry, age seven, plus the stimulus item he has just been shown by an experimenter. It is simply not clear how one should proceed after giving up the traditional method of systems individuation.

These problems are not limited to developmental psychology. Investigations of adult capacities, for memory and language use, for example, normally presuppose that the subjects of investigation are individual persisting systems. Some such studies are explicitly longitudinal (Bahrick, 1979, 1984) and thus much like developmental psychology in the relevant respects. Beyond these cases, psychologists and linguists frequently study contextual effects. It is striking that the same person behaves in one way in one context – say, when not primed – and behaves differently in another slightly different context, when, in contrast, he or she has been primed. There is an enormous body of fascinating literature filled with experiments interpreted in just this way; their explananda are taken to be persisting individuals with various capacities or abilities that they exercise in different ways in different contexts.

A focus on the persisting individual is also evident in research on perception. We would like to know why, for example, the subject perceives certain features under some conditions – say, against a particular background – but does not perceive those same features under other conditions (see, e.g., various results surveyed in Treisman, 1998). The experimenter asks a single system to perform various visual tasks, and the outcome sheds light on the process by which that system sees. Perhaps, as is sometimes emphasized, the subject does something as a way to get information visually (Churchland, Ramachandran, & Sejnowski, 1994). Still, such results reveal something about the ability of a single persisting system: they reveal how that system gets visual information.[15]

The preceding argument against extended individuation might seem to have ignored an important aspect of standard methodology: researchers frequently assign experimental subjects to different groups; in a typical experiment, these consist of a control group and an experimental group. In such experiments, researchers do not appear to be investigating the capacities of individually persisting systems as they change over time or as they exercise their capacities in varying circumstances. This rejoinder misinterprets standard methodology, however.

Researchers assign subjects to different groups on the assumption that the set of members of each group represents a standard distribution of cognitive skills and capacities across a population of members of the same kind. By statistical analysis of the results, we think we discover something about the way the standard persisting human system reacts under different conditions.

The HEC theorist might, in response, point out that data is sometimes analyzed simply by condition or by question. This rejoinder, however, takes too narrow a view of the ways in which analysis by question is used. Normally, researchers compare the results of analysis by condition to the results of a similar analysis of results in conditions – the point being to see how systems of the same kind behave under different conditions. Such comparative analysis presupposes that the individuals involved in both (or the many) conditions are representative of the human population; thus, we are, once again, comparing the responses of a single (kind of) system under different conditions.

Of course, sometimes we naturally and legitimately group together temporally disjoint systems. Consider the practice of medical doctors, who talk about the same patient over time, even though, at the biological level, that patient changes his or her constitution (cells die; new ones form). This, however, only emphasizes the need for a principle of organization to ground the groupings. Organismic integrity and the way it physically grounds health and disease recommend treating a person over time as a single patient returning for visits. Insofar as an organizing principle motivates the groupings of alleged cognitive systems into privileged sets (and legitimates the chosen groupings), this principle is similarly organism based – which is, of course, just how traditional cognitive science identifies its systems of interest. This moderate position – the second horn of the dilemma mentioned previously – is not worth its price. The HEC theorist buys a highly counterintuitive claim about minds (that they are extended beyond the organismic boundary) for the cost of unnecessary complications, without any substantive departure from standard individuating practice.

We should not pronounce in advance what a completed cognitive psychology will bring. Nevertheless, insofar as we can make out a genuinely extended-systems-based alternative to existing methodology, it faces deep problems. It introduces a profligate set of distinct cognitive systems the richness of which confounds standard methodology, with no productive replacement in sight. In contrast, it is open to the HEC theorist to partition extended systems into useful subgroups, but this amounts to little more than a co-opting of the success of standard methodology. On measures of simplicity and conservatism, then, this strategy clearly loses out to the traditional approach (and to an embedded approach). Of course, costly revisions in theoretical frameworks are justified when they offer sufficient gains along other dimensions (e.g., in explanatory power or accuracy). The shift under consideration does not, however, do so. The range of provocative and fruitful results in contemporary cognitive science can reasonably and manageably be cast in terms of organismically bounded cognitive systems that frequently interact intimately with their environments.

Where does this leave us with respect to HEC and nativism? Previously I recommended that HEC abandon biology-based theorizing about innateness and draw instead from sciences closer in subject matter to HEC's own domain. Before concluding this section, let us briefly consider a pair of widely discussed psychological criteria of innateness. First, take the primitivist view (Cowie, 1999; Fodor, 1981; Samuels, 2002). According to this view, a psychological trait is primitive if and only if there is no psychological account of its appearance.[16] The asymmetries discussed herein suggest that, in most cases, the appearance of an extended cognitive trait has a psychological explanation: extended systems, and thus their traits, originate in the psychology of the organism and thus would not count as innate by the primitivist criterion.[17] Application of a second commonly used psychological measure of innateness, domain specificity (Cowie, 1999; Keil, 1990), yields similar results. The basic idea is that if a cognitive capacity can be exercised only with respect to a proprietary set of inputs or tasks, it is innately dedicated to those inputs or to that task domain, and the capacity in question is thus innate. Many of the relevant capacities of extended systems are not domain specific. Pen and paper are used to draw diagrams, to solve math problems, and to make sketches, and thus, they are not categorized as innate by this criterion. Surprisingly, this might even hold in the case of extended visual systems. Keep in mind that the organism together with what it visually perceives constitutes the relevant system; so, even if the organism's visual system is domain dedicated, it is not clear what the domain-specific restrictions are relative to the entire extended system (i.e., the visual apparatus taken together with what is seen).

Thus, the antinativist HEC theorist wins a Pyrrhic victory. The psychological criteria of primitiveness and domain specificity plausibly categorize at least some of the relevant cognitive capacities in a way consistent with the nonnativist leanings of many situated theorists. Consequently, if extended systems were the right sort of thing to which to attribute psychological properties, the advocate of HEC would have found antinativist support in the application of these psychological criteria for innateness. Cognitive science, however, takes as its explananda cognitive capacities of persisting systems; it is wrongheaded to attribute innate capacities to systems that are short-lived relative to the capacities in question, largely because the capacities of the short-lived systems are not the proper objects of inquiry in cognitive science. Thus, I conclude that there are few or no innate capacities of extended systems – but for reasons HEC theorists cannot embrace.

3. Embedded Cognition and Context-Specific Representations

Many embedded views appeal to context-specific representations, the contents of which seem best understood in nonnativist terms. These context-specific representations amount to little more than mental demonstratives, internal placeholders that take ephemeral values relative to the task being performed (Ballard, Hayhoe, Pook, & Rao, 1997); as such, their contents depend heavily on the contribution of the environment. The embedded view's deep reliance on context-specific representation promises to provide the situated program with an importantly nonnativist aspect, for representations play a central role in many embedded models, and questions about representation, concepts, and content stand at the center of many debates about nativism (Cowie, 1999; Fodor, 1981; Rupert, 2001). If embedded cognition avoids nativism along this dimension of the debate, embedded cognition is nonnativist in at least one substantive respect. Nevertheless, although there is a fairly robust sense in which the content of context-specific representations is not innately determined, the theory of content best suited to such representations entails a significant nativist contribution to their content – or so I argue in this section.

Generally speaking, the embedded approach aims to minimize the amount of internal representation used to model the human performance of cognitive tasks (Ballard et al., 1997; Clark, 1997, chap. 8; McClamrock, 1995, chap. 6).[18] To appreciate the kind of minimization at issue, let us first consider a contrasting approach. On a more traditional understanding of cognition, the subject performs a complex analysis of a problem before acting: in the case of action or inference based on visual perception, such complex analysis involves the construction of a detailed internal representation of the immediate environment; in the case of abstract planning (e.g., the choice of which college to attend), the subject might explicitly represent the costs and benefits of each of a range of options, as well as the likelihood of success of each option and the maximum cost the subject is willing to pay to achieve his or her goal. On an embedded view of the former case, the subject uses context-specific correlations to act on the basis of visual perception in a way that requires substantially less in the way of representational resources than would be required to build a detailed internal representation of the relevant environment. To illustrate, consider Clark's (1995) example of finding the photo-development counter at a supermarket. Given the market dominance of Kodak, the area above or around the photo-development counter is normally splashed with yellow. This suggests a simple strategy to the consumer in search of the photo counter: enter the supermarket and swivel one's head about to look for a large patch of yellow.

At work in this example are three tactical principles by which embedded models minimize the subject's use of internal representational resources. First, the subject need not explicitly represent – in working memory or any other sort of cognitive work space – any very elaborate theory or conception of photo counters. She needs only to activate a routine that exploits the local, contingent correlation between patches of yellow and the location of photo counters. Second, the subject represents what might be called a "coarse-grained" property: the subject looks for a large patch of yellow, not one of any particular size. Third, the subject collects only the information she needs. Mind you, the requisite representational resources far exceed nil. The subject must, for example, represent in some way the project or plan she is engaged in: a person should not wander through life looking for yellow patches. Once the goal has been determined, though (e.g., to get one's photos developed) and the subject has found and entered the store, the amount of information needed, at that moment, is fairly small. The subject need not know the general layout of the building, the location of the restrooms, the number of cashiers on duty, or which cashier lines are open. The subject might need access to

some of these other facts at some time during the visit; but on entering the store and beginning to look for the photo counter, he can ignore these other matters.

A more general idea binds these three principles to the embedded theorist's minimalist approach to representation: as much as possible, let the environment do the cognitive work (Brooks, 1991; Clark, 1989, p. 64). Perhaps surprisingly, all of these principles – from the overarching idea of letting the world do the work to the more specific tactical principles particularly to do with representation – apply also to the case of decision making, in which many of the points about visual engagement with the world might seem to have little application. The general strategy of letting the world do the work could be applied in the following way: the agent sets a maximum acceptable cost of achieving her goal as well as a minimum probability of success, then accepts the first satisfactory option offered by the environment. This requires some internal calculation on the subject's part and thus some internal representation, but it is much less demanding than an optimizing comparison of a good number of options. Thus, this approach remains in step with the embedded emphasis on minimizing internal representational resources. Furthermore, the three principles listed in connection with the example of visual cognition are at work, at least to some extent. In many actual environments, there is a contingent correlation between *being an option that presents itself* and *being a satisfactory option*.[19] Of course, if there were only a weak correlation or none at all, the subject might spend a lot of time performing a series of quick and dirty analyses of the many possibilities that present themselves, determining serially that none will do. It is often observed, though, that humans structure their environments, institutions, and social interactions in such a way as to strengthen the kind of correlation at issue – so that, for example, if the subject decides on the first college she comes across that meets her minimum standards, she will probably achieve her related goals (e.g., to become reasonably well educated). Also, given that the subject makes no detailed comparison of options, she can represent coarse-grained properties – such as *being a fairly prestigious school* – in place of any attempt to make a fine-grained determination of, for example, relative degree of prestige of a range of alternatives. Imagine a case where two or more options fall in roughly the same ball park in terms of costs and benefits; if the subject's charge is to figure out which is better overall, she cannot coarse grain – coarse graining leads to a tie. Decision making under such conditions required fine-grained comparison. If, however, the subject considers the first opportunity that presents itself, sees that it offers sufficient promise of success while falling at or below the maximum acceptable cost, then she is off to the races. The discussion of coarse graining makes clear that embedded accounts of decision making embody the last of the three representation-minimizing principles discussed in connection with visual perception: collect only the information needed. The amount of information one needs to gather to determine that a single school is fairly prestigious falls far short of the amount the subject would need to gather to determine which of a number of fairly prestigious schools beats all the others in the group.

The drive to minimize the use of internal representational resources seems to recommend heavy reliance on ad hoc, context-specific representations. Such representations do not persist content intact, but rather depend for their content on the immediate and typically short-lived contribution of their environment. The embedded approach would thus seem to suggest a cognitive system that does as much as possible with only a standing collection of mental demonstratives (e.g., pointers instantiated in visual cortex) that take different values depending on their short-lived relationships to environmental factors; or perhaps in the extreme, the subject might construct new pointers in new situations, so that even individuated nonsemantically, the pointers have little integrity over time. On the embedded

view, then, representational content clearly depends on the contribution of the subject's immediate local environment, something that, having set aside HEC and DST, we can assume is not innate to the subject. Let us pursue this approach to representation, to see whether one can reasonably expect it to deliver a robustly nonnativist understanding of mental content.

It might be too demanding to insist that the embedded theorist have in pocket a fully worked-out theory of content for context-specific representations. Furthermore, limitations of space prevent a sustained attempt to determine here which, among the various leading theories of mental content, correctly characterizes the kind of content carried by context-specific representations.[20] Of extant theories, Robert Cummins's (1996) combination of intenders and isomorphism can be most naturally applied to the embedded approach. On Cummins's view, the cognitive system consists largely of functionally discrete components – intenders – each of which aims at a particular kind of target, for example, the spatial layout of the immediate environment. Each intender employs a set of representational primitives that can be activated in complex arrangements. The representational value of each arrangement is determined by isomorphism alone, leaving each arrangement wildly ambiguous. Nevertheless, a mental state – a belief, for example – can be determinately correct because the function of an intender in which the representation appears limits that representation's contribution to something from the appropriate range of targets (i.e., targets appropriate to the intender in which the representing structure is activated).[21]

How does any of this bear on the question of innateness? It depends partly on how we resolve a question that Cummins himself leaves open, the question of how the intenders acquire their functions. On the one hand, Cummins considers the approach he helped to found, that of homuncular or systemic decomposition. According to this view, the contribution of a component to the performance of its containing system determines that component's function. If intender I_1 contributes what – in the context of the system's overall behavior – is best construed as perceptual uptake, then I_1 has some particular aspect of the immediate environment as its target (which aspect depends on what kind of perceptual uptake I_1 is best understood as contributing to the overall performance of the system). Cummins also considers a Millikan-style teleofunctional view (Millikan, 1984). On this approach, evolutionary selection determines an intender's function (Cummins, 1996, chap. 8).

The former approach is problematic, for reasons parallel to those Cummins (1996, pp. 41–51) wields against functionalist (or conceptual role) theories of content. In conflict with a fundamental constraint on any theory of mental content, functionalist theories do not seem to allow for error. Take a case in which we think a subject has made a representation-based error. Recall that the functions at issue are computational-mathematical functions; thus, it will always be possible to locate some other function – that is, some function other than the one we thought the system was computing – relative to which the system's computation was accurate. Similarly, though, this strategy of alternative interpretation applies to any case of what we might think of as erroneous representation within an intender. If, for example, it seems that I_1 contributes information about spatial layout to the functioning of its containing system, but on some particular occasion its output causes the containing system to trip over a table, we can reinterpret I_1's function as representing the spatial layout of the room adjusted in such and such a way (e.g., I_1 is supposed to represent spatial layout excepting tables on Tuesdays, if that is when the trip occurred).

The teleofunctionalist view fares better because, presumably, it is a matter of fact what a particular functional component was selected for (assuming it was selected for the performance of a function!). If a component kept its owners alive longer because it conferred the ability to see berries, then this component had better have the function of accurate visual detection. There is no case to be made that accurate berry detection on Tuesdays led to reproductive advantage, partly because there is no relevant aspect of the organism's physiology connected nomically to the property *being eaten on a Tuesday*. But – and here is the punch line – if embedded cognition relies on the teleosemantic version of Cummins's theory of content, content is innate in one very important respect. Any given representing structure is isomorphic to a great number of external structures; the intender plays an essential disambiguating role by determining which of a representation's many values that representation contributes to the content of the mental state in question. The representational content of that mental state rests immediately and synchronically on the function of the intender in which the representation appears, and the function of that intender is determined innately.

One might think that causal contact with the environment minimizes nativist commitments: after all, in the typical embedded model, the subject causally interacts with the portion of the world to which his or her context-specific representations are bound. Even here, however, innate contributions play a prominent role. In one of Ballard et al.'s (1997) examples, a single pointer gets bound to the color of a block in a visual display, but that block has texture as well as shape and other visually detectable properties. What determines that the pointer is bound to the color of the block? Presumably, the pointer's content depends on the function of that pointer in a routine, which is partly determined by the intender(s) involved, in Cummins's view. This routine can have complex structure, for example, in terms of the way it uses the bound information, and this structure determines to what the pointer is bound.[22] To the extent that this complex structure of the routine arises from its teleofunction, its contribution to the content of the relevant cognitive state is innately determined to a significant extent.

Of course, there is also a significant sense in which embedded models remain empiricist: the world contributes specific content (e.g., *green* or *yellow*) to the pointer. Here Wilson's (2004) two-dimensional analysis of the nativism-empiricism debate may be useful. Put simply, there are two dimensions of complexity, the internal and the external. If the internal mechanisms driving some cognitive process are rich and complex and largely independent of environmental control, but the external contribution is minimal, we rightly label that process "innate." If, in contrast, the internal mechanism driving a cognitive process is simple in structure, but the external contribution is rich and complex, an empiricist conclusion is warranted. In mixed cases, such as the present one, the two-dimensional analysis fails to deliver a particular judgment – innate or not. Thus, Wilson's two-dimensional analysis explains our discomfort in issuing either a firmly nativist or firmly empiricist judgment about the content of context-specific representations.

4. Nativism and Persisting Representations

Theories of cognition must make some allowance for persisting, internal representations. Children employ amodal representations from early on; concepts are used in abstract thought, when one is, for example, alone in the study; theorists conceptualize, reason, design experiments, and write papers (about, for example, embedded cognition); and what is more, embedded models themselves appeal to standing routines, intentions, or programs in ways touched on previously. I do not offer this observation in argument against embedded models. Rather, the present section fleshes out a sense in which embedded models help to explain – in an empiricist way, no less – how the content of persisting representations is fixed.

Think of the human cognitive system as two layered; this is surely an oversimplification, but it allows us to focus on the relevant issues without, I think, distorting the conclusions reached. One layer consists of

perceptual systems or modules. Call the representations employed at this level "peripheral representations." These include such representations as the visual image of a tree currently in the subject's view; typically the context-specific representations posited by embedded models fall into this category. The second layer is what some theorists call "central processing" (Fodor, 1983). Let us dub the representations appearing at this level "central representations." Theoretical, abstract, and nonsensory concepts, such concepts as PROTON, JUSTICE, and CHAIR (as a general kind) fall into this category.

It might appear that central representations come into no special contact with the embedded program. I propose a contrasting view: peripheral representations mediate the causal relations that fix the content of many central representations; furthermore, one of the most commonly cited examples of embedded representational activity – the active use of language – contributes significantly to the fixation of the content of central representations, by helping to bring them into the causal relations that determine what they represent. This view does not require that central representations inherit their content directly from some selection of peripheral representations or from external symbols; nor does it require that peripheral representations or external symbols define central representations. Thus, the current proposal is not empiricist in the traditional sense: central representations can and typically do have content that outruns the content of the subject's sensory representations or logical constructions from those sensory representations.[23]

In what sense, then, is the current proposal empiricist? Because atomic central representations are stable, reappearing units, it seems likely that their content can be fixed without the contribution of an intender that determines the target of the representation on particular occasions of use. Moreover, application of the primitivist criterion suggests that the content of central representations is not innate; peripheral representations and external symbols mediate content fixation, which typically involves a fairly detailed psychological explanation of the fixation of the content of central representations (cf. Cowie, 1999). This nonnativist implication of the primitivist criterion follows from a central commitment of the embedded approach. A recurring theme in the embedded literature has been the extent to which humans simplify their cognitive tasks by structuring their external environment in ways that facilitate the performance of those tasks (Clark, 1997; Dennett, 1996; McClamrock, 1995). Some such simplification can be effected through the use of language and the assignment of a privileged role to certain observations. Straightforward examples involve the construction of written descriptions or visual diagrams meant to convey a new concept to others, that is, to get their central representations causally connected to the correct properties or kinds. In another sort of case, the individual formulates his or her own observation-based heuristic, for example, of the form, "When I see such and such, it means there is a C present," where C is a central representation. In all of these cases, a peripheral representation comes to mediate the activation of a newly created central representation or a central representation to which the peripheral representation had not previously been connected. In the initial case, where the subject coins a new central representation that representation might not carry any determinate content or at least not the content it will ultimately carry (Margolis, 1998; Rupert, 1996, chap. 4, 1998, 2001). As various peripheral representations become causally connected to the newly coined central representation, the latter can come into a content-determining causal relation to an external property, kind, or individual. Adverting to the human habit of actively structuring her environment so that she has certain sensory experiences constitutes a powerful psychological explanation of how a human comes into the right causal position to have a central representation with the content *electron*. (In fact, in the case of some kinds, for example, *electron*, this process seems the only plausible way for a human to get a repre-

sentation with that kind as its content – see Fodor, 1998.)

Granted, the contents of peripheral or organismically external representations do not exhaust the contents of the central representations in question, and thus the organism must make some internal contribution to the fixation of content for the latter representations. For Fodor (1975, 1981), this contribution – together with the absence of a hypothesis-testing explanation of the acquisition of central representations – secures the innateness of those representations. To a certain extent, I think Fodor is right. Even with a set of mediating mechanisms in place, including peripheral representations, the organism must at least be disposed to come into the appropriate content-fixing causal relation to one external kind or property rather than another. Thus, there is some innate contribution to the content of central representations. All the same, there is a rich and complex psychological explanation of how mediating mechanisms contribute to the fixation of content for central representations, while the nonpsychological story is very thin. Furthermore, both the nature of the environment and the causal properties of the material available to instantiate peripheral representations in the human brain substantially limit the innate, internal contribution. There is a limited number of genuine properties and kinds present in the subject's environment. Moreover, the mechanisms that mediate the tokening of the central representations in question themselves have limited causal properties: the visual cortex may be capable only of relaying reliable signals to central processing about certain available properties among that limited set present in the environment. Thus, it may be that the human mind develops a representation of, for example, *electron* in a given set of circumstances not because a central representation has *electron* as its innate content but rather because the contingent facts about the environment the human is thrown into and the physical substance its perceptual mechanisms are made of do not allow the central representation in question to be attached in the proper fashion to any kind other than *electron*. It is plausible that the physical mechanisms realizing sensations were selected because of the way they respond causally to certain physical features of the subject's environment. In contrast, the physical material that realizes central processing was selected for its relative flexibility, not its physical ability to carry information about any specific aspects of the environment. Thus, central processing contributes very little to the content of such concepts as ELECTRON that is innately keyed specifically to their content.

In the end, we might try grafting Wilson's two-dimensional view to the primitivist theory of innateness – the two dimensions becoming psychological and nonpsychological contributions to the development of the trait (acquisition of the concept) in question. In the present case, this approach yields a fairly strong judgment on the empiricist end of the spectrum. The psychological story of content fixation is quite rich, whereas the nonpsychological internal contribution consists only in a disposition to be causally connected in one way rather than another given a certain complex psychological and physical environment.[24]

5. Conclusion

Much of this chapter has been an exploration of possibilities, an attempt to show that the situated program does not reside squarely in either the empiricist or the nativist camp. Along the way, I have argued that, on various plausible assumptions, some situated models are subject to a clear nativist gloss, contrary to the leanings of many situated theorists. As development of situated program proceeds, we should keep in mind the wide range of theoretical possibilities open with respect to nativism and the situated modeling of cognition.

Acknowledgments

Work on this chapter was supported by a National Endowment for the Humanities Fellowship for College Teachers. My thanks to the NEH. I would also like to thank Edward Averill and Robert Wilson for comments on an earlier draft.

Notes

1 For a substantial list of references to influential nativist work, see Elman et al. (1996, pp. 107–108).

2 Although Clark (1997, chap. 2) discusses Thelen and Smith's (1994) developmental work in some detail, he avoids the question of nativism (but see Clark & Thornton, 1997, p. 63, where antinativist leanings are made a bit more explicit). Similarly, Varela, Thompson, and Rosch (1991, chap. 9) address biological issues of genetic determination – advocating positions that are often taken to support antinativist views – without addressing the question of nativism head on. Note that I use *antinativist*, *nonnativist*, and their cognates as umbrella terms to cover all manner of empiricist and eliminativist views, where an eliminativist view holds that the empiricist-nativist distinction is incoherent or for some other reason should be excluded from theoretical discourse (Griffiths, 2002).

3 For a contrasting view, see McGinn (1989, pp. 24–26, 46, 116, 210).

4 I do not wish to oversell this point, however. Kim Sterelny has rightly emphasized the prevalence of cases in which traits alleged to be exhibited by extended cognitive systems – mathematical abilities involving the use of external media, for example – emerge only with great difficulty and often do not appear at all in the extended systems in question, even after extensive tutelage (Sterelny, 2004). Note, though, that the HEC theorist incurs a cost by pursuing this response to the nativist charge. He must be prepared to assert that in cases where, for example, a student cannot seem to acquire the relevant mathematical skill, an extended cognitive system exists nonetheless, so that the system's failure to develop the ability in question counts against the canalization of that ability in the kind of system in question. This creates some tension when conjoined with the examples typically used to motivate HEC, for such examples almost invariably involve successful activity: showing that an extended system

successfully performs the tasks we associate with human cognitive capacities is meant to show that the extended system has cognitive capacities, that is, that it is an extended cognitive system. The organism's bare disposition to try to use pencil and paper to solve math problems does not sufficiently motivate HEC, although antinativist HEC theorists must count this system as an extended cognitive system to avail themselves of the antinativist defense bruited previously.

5   Keep in mind, however, that Wimsatt sometimes leans toward eliminativism, describing generative entrenchment as a successor concept to innateness (1999, p. 139; see also pp. 162–163 and n22).

6   Developmental systems theory has played an important role in discussions of group selection (Sterelny & Griffiths, 1999), where conspecifics or their traits constitute the relevant environment. Throughout the discussion of DST and HEC, I focus instead on systems that comprise individual organisms together with nonorganismic aspects of the environment.

7   Griffiths and Stotz (2000) present their account of extended inheritance in this way; see pp. 34–9 for a juxtaposition of the extended view of selection and their antinativist reading of it. See also Griffiths and Gray (2004, p. 425) for the view that extended inheritance is inimical to nativism. Griffiths and Stotz (Griffiths, 2002; Griffiths & Stotz, 2000) object to the association of innateness with human nature (or species nature), and this motivates some of their resistance to the nativist characterization of extended inheritance. In the present case, however, it seems that extended systems do have a nature: if there are mechanisms – both internal and external to the organism – in place to reliably reproduce extended systems, then the requirements for the entire system's being a natural kind seem to have been met. I am, however, getting ahead of myself.

8   The form of independence I have in mind is not full-blown probabilistic independence but rather the more intuitive idea of there being a nonnegligible probability of one thing's reproducing successfully when the other does not.

9   This point might be articulated in terms of trait groups. A trait group with respect to trait F is a collection of individuals such that instantiation of F by some sufficient number of the individuals enhances the fitness of each of the individuals in the group. (The idea is that sometimes the presence of a trait enhances the fitness of an individual, even where that individual does not possess the trait in question but rather benefits from other individuals' possession of it.) A given individual, however, can be a member of many trait groups, the members of which vary significantly. Thus, to avoid a Byzantine network of partially overlapping, composite biological individuals (and to ensure that our account of composite, biological individual tracks only the theoretically important individuals – see Griffiths & Gray, 2004, p. 423), we might lay down the following necessary condition: for two individuals to be members of the same composite biological organism, both should be members of all, or nearly all, of the same trait groups. A given person's brain and heart, for instance, are part of the same composite biological individual because the brain's and the heart's probabilities of contributing to the appearance of others of their own kind are enhanced by the same (or very nearly same) group of traits, establishing what is, extensionally, the same trait group relative to the many traits that affect the brain's and heart's fitness. Any composite biological individual satisfying this criterion is such that its component individuals have a very high probability of a shared fate; they will not reproduce independently of each other.

10 Cf. Wilson's locus-of-control argument for the privilege of the organismic system (2004, pp. 197–198; for a similar argument, see Butler, 1998).

11 Compare Clark's (2003) sustained argument that humans are, by their nature, tool users. Clark may well be correct about human nature, and there is at least a clear sense to his claim. It is a bit difficult to understand the converse claim – that it is the nature of external resources that they be used by humans; insofar as it does have clear meaning, it seems obviously false: it is not the nature of iron ore that it be wrought by humans into automobile parts or anything else. (Note that Clark sometimes wields his argument about human nature and tool use to a different end: to support HEC. So far as I can tell, the argument faces serious difficulties, partly because it highlights significant asymmetries between the contributions of various

portions of allegedly extended cognitive systems. Given the asymmetric contribution of human organisms to the formation of such systems, I take Clark's argument to support the embedded approach rather than HEC.) See also Sterelny (2004), where he argues for other substantial asymmetries, both epistemic and representational.

12 With regard to biology alone, different interests might lead to different principles of systems individuation (Griffiths & Gray, 2004, pp. 419–420), as well as to different standards of innateness: Ariew (1999, p. 120) argues that within biology itself, different research programs have made use of conflicting conceptions of innateness.

13 Clark and Chalmers's (1998, p. 10) discussion of portability as a criterion for cognitive states seems partly motivated by a concern for persisting systemic integrity. There is a gap, however, between the various hypothetical systems discussed by Clark and Chalmers – systems that may well qualify as cognitive systems with persisting abilities – and systems subject to cognitive scientific inquiry; I am concerned with the latter systems.

14 Even those researchers who focus on short-lived, extended dynamical systems must take the traditional approach in certain respects. For example, Thelen and Smith (1994, pp. 288–289) attempt to explain children's performance on specific A-not-B trials by adverting to characteristics of a short-lived dynamical system; but insofar as Thelen and Smith's dynamical approach can explain the child's developmental trajectory – how competency changes over time – they must appeal to changes in the capacities of the persisting organismic system; after all, the toys and the wells need not change at all. What changes is the cognitive capacity of the organism. In Thelen and Smith's terms, what changes is the child's ability to enter into dynamic relations with the environment; in which case, we should, for simplicity's sake, appeal to this organismically bounded cognitive capacity to explain the results of any specific trial.

15 Consider a further worry about perception and HEC. In perception and in action based on perception, humans often think about or perceive the same things with which they interact; if the cognitive system is individuated liberally, these things are part of the subjects' minds, because the subjects' perception depends heavily on them. But this leads to a kind of idealism that should give us pause: on this view, humans do not, on the basis of perception, interact with the objects perceived; rather, certain parts of the human mind interact with other parts of the human mind!

16 I do not claim that the primitivist view is without problems. Many authors reject Fodor's radical concept of nativism because it counts too many concepts among the innate – in Samuels's terms, it overgeneralizes (2002, pp. 256–259). Samuels responds to problems of this kind by adding the following condition to primitivism: a psychological ability, capacity, or state that is primitive, yet arises only in nonstandard environments, is not innate. But consider the case of cognitive deficits resulting from childhood lead poisoning. There was a time when exposure to lead threatened to become part of the developing child's normal environment – species wide – yet, even if the threat had been fully realized, having impaired cognitive functions of the relevant kind (e.g., lowered IQ) would not have been innate. And notice, this is not a far-out thought experiment; only by political action and policy changes was the problem mitigated in technologically developed countries. Even today, in many regions and cities of the world, exposure to unhealthy levels of lead is so common as to count, from a statistical standpoint, as a normal condition of childhood development.

17 But, as argued previously, such asymmetries also cut against HEC's plausibility; see note 11.

18 Note that embedded views minimize internal representation via a different strategy than the one often employed by HEC theorists: the extended approach lends itself to the external placement of the vehicles or bearers of representational content (Houghton, 1997; Hurley, 1998; Wilson, 2004), whereas the embedded view keeps the vehicles on the inside but, typically, binds them in a context-specific way to aspects of the immediate environment. Of course, the HEC theorist or the advocate of the embedded approach could take an eliminativist view of representation (Brooks, 1991), more plausibly at the subpersonal than at the personal level (Dennett, 1987). Note, however, that if HEC theorists commit to eliminativism about representation at the very level of the extended model, their talk about external vehicles is

misleading (what do the vehicles bear, if not content?) (cf. Clark, 2005, n1; Hurley 1998).

19 I adopt the following orthographic conventions: terms referring to properties or kinds, in the abstract, as well as terms that refer to mental contents, are set in italics; concepts, considered as mental particulars, are set in capital letters, where a given concept's label (HORSE, for instance) derives from the content we assume to be carried by that mental particular.

20 Note, though, that many of these theories are designed, in the first instance, to apply to representational structures that persist and are repeatedly activated (or tokened), carrying their standard meaning on each occasion of activation – which seems to remove these theories from the running in the present context. Consider Fred Dretske's (1988) influential account of representational content. Dretske's presentation relies in a substantive way on processes that extend through time. A structure that at one time merely indicates a state of the environment acquires, by a kind of reinforcement-based learning, a role in the cognitive system (e.g., the function of controlling a particular motor response). That structure thereby becomes a representation, its content being whatever property or state the structure indicated such that the structure's indication of that property or state explains why the structure acquired its motor-controlling role in the cognitive system. Granted, although Dretske's presentation typically suggests longer time scales, the relevant learning process could occur very quickly. Keep in mind, however, that Dretske also intends to solve the problem of misrepresentation: later tokenings of the structure in question misrepresent when the structure's tokening is caused by something other than what it indicated when it first acquired its function in the cognitive system and in virtue of the indication of which it acquired that function. Without working through the details, we cannot be sure whether Dretske's theory could be plausibly adapted to cover context-specific representations, that is, whether his story about learning could plausibly apply on very short time scales and in a way that handles the problem of misrepresentation. Instead of taking on this project, though, it seems better advised to look for a theory of content that applies in a straightforward way to context-specific representations.

21 Gallistel (1990) and Grush (1997) offer related views.

22 Cf. Cummins's discussion of indexicality and nested intenders (1996, pp. 118–120).

23 Rupert (1996, 1998, 1999, 2001) develops many of the details of such a view; see also the work of Fodor (1987, 1990, 1998), Margolis (1998), and Prinz (2000), for views that are amenable in one way or another to the sort of position outlined in the text. Note that the present question concerns primitive central representations, not structured central representations that somehow copy the structure of complex sensory representations; thus, the antiempiricist objections raised by Fodor (2003) do not apply.

24 If the human organism is innately endowed with the tendency to create or structure environments so as to lead to concept acquisition in the manner described in the text, then a further innately determined source contributes in a significant way to the content of central representations.

References

Ariew, A. (1999). Innateness is canalization. In V. Hardcastle (Ed.), *Biology meets psychology: Conjectures, connections, constraints* (pp. 117–138). Cambridge, MA: MIT Press.

Bahrick, H. P. (1979). Maintenance of knowledge: Questions about memory we forgot to ask. *Journal of Experimental Psychology: General, 108*, 296–308.

Bahrick, H. P. (1984). Semantic memory content in permastore: Fifty years of memory for Spanish learned in school. *Journal of Experimental Psychology: General, 113*, 1–29.

Ballard, D. H., Hayhoe, M. M., Pook, P. K., & Rao, R. P. N. (1997). Deictic codes for the embodiment of cognition. *Behavioral and Brain Sciences, 20*, 723–742.

Block, N. (1981). Introduction: What is innateness? In N. Block (Ed.), *Readings in the philosophy of psychology* (Vol. 2, pp. 279–281). Cambridge, MA: Harvard University Press.

Bloom, P. (2000). *How children learn the meanings of words*. Cambridge, MA: MIT Press.

Brooks, R. (1991). Intelligence without representation. *Artificial Intelligence, 47*, 139–159.

Butler, K. L. (1998). *Internal affairs: Making room for psychosemantic internalism*. Boston: Kluwer.

Carey, S. (1995). *Conceptual change in childhood*. Cambridge, MA: MIT Press.

Churchland, P. S., Ramachandran, V., & Sejnowski, T. (1994). A critique of pure vision. In C. Koch & J. Davis (Eds.), *Large-scale neuronal theories of the brain* (pp. 23–60). Cambridge, MA: MIT Press.

Clark, A. (1989). *Microcognition: Philosophy, cognitive science and parallel distributed processing*. Cambridge, MA: MIT Press.

Clark, A. (1995). Moving minds: Situating content in the service of real-time success. In J. Tomberlin (Ed.), *Philosophical perspectives: Vol. 9. AI, connectionism, and philosophical psychology* (pp. 89–104). Atascadero, CA: Ridgeview.

Clark, A. (1997). *Being there: Putting brain, body, and world together again*. Cambridge, MA: MIT Press.

Clark, A. (1998). Magic words: How language augments human computation. In P. Carruthers & J. Boucher (Eds.), *Language and thought: Interdisciplinary themes* (pp. 162–183). Cambridge: Cambridge University Press.

Clark, A. (2003). *Natural-born cyborgs*. Oxford: Oxford University Press.

Clark, A. (2005). Intrinsic content, active memory, and the extended mind. *Analysis, 65*, 1–11.

Clark, A., & Chalmers, D. (1998). The extended mind. *Analysis, 58*, 7–19.

Clark, A., & Thornton, C. (1997). Trading spaces: Computation, representation, and the limits of uninformed learning. *Behavioral and Brain Sciences, 20*, 57–66.

Cowie, F. (1999). *What's within? Nativism reconsidered*. Oxford: Oxford University Press.

Cummins, R. (1996). *Representations, targets, and attitudes*. Cambridge, MA: MIT Press.

Dennett, D. (1987). *The intentional stance*. Cambridge, MA: MIT Press.

Dennett, D. (1996). *Kinds of minds: Toward an understanding of consciousness*. New York: Basic Books.

Dretske, F. (1998). *Explaining behavior: Reasons in a world of causes*. Cambridge, MA: MIT Press.

Elman, J., Bates, E., Johnson, M., Karmiloff-Smith, A., Parisi, D., & Plunkett, K. (1996). *Rethinking innateness: A connectionist perspective on development*. Cambridge, MA: MIT Press.

Fodor, J. (1975). *The language of thought*. Cambridge, MA: Harvard University Press.

Fodor, J. (1981). The present status of the innateness controversy. In J. Fodor (Ed.), *Representations* (pp. 257–316). Cambridge, MA: MIT Press.

Fodor, J. (1983). *The modularity of mind*. Cambridge, MA: MIT Press.

Fodor, J. (1987). *Psychosemantics: The problem of meaning in the philosophy of mind*. Cambridge, MA: MIT Press.

Fodor, J. (1990). *A theory of content and other essays*. Cambridge, MA: MIT Press.

Fodor, J. (1998). *Concepts: Where cognitive science went wrong*. Oxford: Oxford University Press.

Fodor, J. (2003). *Hume variations*. Oxford: Oxford University Press.

Gallistel, C. R. (1990). *The organization of learning*. Cambridge, MA: MIT Press.

Goldin-Meadow, S., & Zheng, M. (1998). Thought before language: The expression of motion events prior to the impact of a conventional language model. In P. Carruthers & J. Boucher (Eds.), *Language and thought: Interdisciplinary themes* (pp. 26–54). Cambridge: Cambridge University Press.

Griffiths, P. (2002). What is innateness? *Monist, 85*, 70–85.

Griffiths, P., & Gray, R. (2004). The developmental systems perspective: Organism-environment systems as units of development and evolution. In K. Preston & M. Pigliucci (Eds.), *Phenotypic integration: Studying the ecology and evolution of complex phenotypes* (pp. 409–431). Oxford: Oxford University Press.

Griffiths, P., & Stotz, K. (2000). How the mind grows: A developmental perspective on the biology of cognition. *Synthese, 122*, 29–51.

Grush, R. (1997). The architecture of representation. *Philosophical Psychology, 10*, 5–23.

Haugeland, J. (1995). Mind embodied and embedded. In Y. Houng & J. Ho (Eds.), *Mind and cognition* (pp. 3–37). Taipei, Taiwan: Institute of European and American Studies, Academia Sinica.

Houghton, D. (1997). Mental content and external representations. *Philosophical Quarterly, 47*, 159–177.

Hurley, S. (1998). Vehicles, contents, conceptual structure, and externalism. *Analysis, 58*, 1–6.

Hutchins, E. (1995). *Cognition in the wild*. Cambridge, MA: MIT Press.

Keil, F. (1989). *Concepts, kinds, and cognitive development*. Cambridge, MA: MIT Press.

Keil, F. (1990). Constraints on constraints: Surveying the epigenetic landscape. *Cognitive Science*, 14, 135–168.

Margolis, E. (1998). How to acquire a concept. *Mind & Language*, 13, 347–369.

Markman, E. (1989). *Categorization and naming in children: Problems of induction*. Cambridge, MA: MIT Press.

McClamrock, R. (1995). *Existential cognition: Computational minds in the world*. Chicago: University of Chicago Press.

McGinn, C. (1989). *Mental content*. Oxford: Basil Blackwell.

Millikan, R. G. (1984). *Language, thought, and other biological categories: New foundations for realism*. Cambridge, MA: MIT Press.

O'Regan, J. K. (1992). Solving the "real" mysteries of visual perception: The world as an outside memory. *Canadian Journal of Psychology*, 46, 461–488.

Prinz, J. (2000). The duality of content. *Philosophical Studies*, 100, 1–34.

Rowlands, M. (1999). *The body in mind: Understanding cognitive processes*. Cambridge: Cambridge University Press.

Rupert, R. (1996). *The best test theory of extension*. Unpublished doctoral dissertation, University of Illinois at Chicago.

Rupert, R. (1998). On the relationship between naturalistic semantics and individuation criteria for terms in a language of thought. *Synthese*, 117, 95–131.

Rupert, R. (1999). The best test theory of extension: First principle(s). *Mind & Language*, 14, 321–355.

Rupert, R. (2001). Coining terms in the language of thought: Innateness, emergence, and the lot of Cummins's argument against the causal theory of mental content. *Journal of Philosophy*, 98, 499–530.

Rupert, R. (2004). Challenges to the hypothesis of extended cognition. *Journal of Philosophy*, 101, 389–428.

Samuels, R. (2002). Nativism in cognitive science. *Mind & Language*, 17, 233–265.

Sterelny, K. (2004). Externalism, epistemic artefacts and the extended mind. In R. Schantz (Ed.), *The externalist challenge: New studies on cognition and intentionality* (pp. 239–254). Berlin: de Gruyter.

Sterelny, K., & Griffiths, P. (1999). *Sex and death: An introduction to philosophy of biology*. Chicago: University of Chicago Press.

Thelen, E., & Smith, L. (1994). *A dynamic systems approach to the development of cognition and action*. Cambridge, MA: MIT Press.

Treisman, A. (1998). The perception of features and objects. In R. D. Wright (Ed.), *Visual attention* (pp. 26–54). Oxford: Oxford University Press.

Varela, F., Thompson, E., & Rosch, E. (1991). *The embodied mind: Cognitive science and human experience*. Cambridge, MA: MIT Press.

Wilson, R. (1999). The individual in biology and psychology. In V. G. Hardcastle (Ed.), *Where biology meets psychology: Philosophical essays* (pp. 357–374). Cambridge, MA: MIT Press.

Wilson, R. (2004). *Boundaries of the mind: The individual in the fragile sciences*. Cambridge: Cambridge University Press.

Wimsatt, W. (1999). Generativity, entrenchment, evolution, and innateness: Philosophy, evolutionary biology, and conceptual foundations of science. In V. G. Hardcastle (Ed.), *Where biology meets psychology: Philosophical essays* (pp. 139–179). Cambridge, MA: MIT Press.

CHAPTER 7

Situated Representation

Mark Rowlands

PART I: CRITERIA OF REPRESENTATION

In the voluminous literature on the subject, it is possible to identify six generally accepted criteria of representation: (1) the combinatorial constraint, (2) the informational constraint, (3) the teleological constraint, (4) the decouplability constraint, (5) the misrepresentation constraint, and (6) the causal constraint. The final constraint claims that in order for an item, r, to qualify as a representation, it must play an appropriate role in guiding a subject's behavior. The first five constraints can be regarded as constraints on what makes an item representational: that is, the sort of item that could be about something else. The final constraint provides an additional condition that an item must meet in order to be counted not only as representational but also as a representation. In this chapter, I shall have little to say about the causal constraint but a lot to say about the first five constraints on the list.

Even focusing only on the first five constraints, however, the logical status of each constraint is less than transparent. First, none of these "generally accepted" constraints on representation comes even close to univocal acceptance; and some constraints are more controversial than others. Second, on certain interpretations, some of the constraints are incompatible with others. Third, none of the conditions in itself is taken to be sufficient for representation. However – and this is why the constraints count as constraints – if we assume that a naturalistic account of representation is possible, there is general consensus that the conditions collectively provide a necessary and sufficient condition for representation. That is, if any item were to satisfy all five conditions, then it would count as a representation if anything does.[1]

This chapter divides fairly naturally into two halves. The first half surveys and explicates each of the first five constraints; that is, the constraints that delineate, given broadly naturalistic assumptions, which sorts of items might qualify as representational. The second half shows how the constraints apply in the specific context of situated models of cognition.

1. The Combinatorial Constraint

It is often claimed that for any item to count as representational, it must form part of a general representational scheme or framework (Haugeland, 1991, p. 62). That is, a representational stand-in must be part of a larger scheme of stands-ins. This allows the standing in to occur systematically and for a variety of related representational states. In other words, representational items are subject to a combinatorial constraint:

Combinatorial constraint: For any item r to qualify as representational, it must occur not in isolation but only as part of a more general representational framework.

The combinatorial requirement is controversial, but much of this controversy can be obviated by careful attention to two distinctions: (1) the distinction between semantic and iconic forms of representation and (2) the vehicle-content distinction.

Semantic and Iconic Representations

The most familiar example of a representational system that satisfies the combinatorial condition is human language. In virtue of its structure, linguistic forms are susceptible to certain sorts of transformation. This susceptibility is underwritten by semantic structure; specifically, which modes of combination are permitted and which are not are determined by their relation to semantic properties such as truth and reference. Thus, the paradigmatic combinatorial mechanisms are the logical connectives: *and, or, not, if and then, some, all*, and so on. The fact that the sentences of a language are truth evaluable entails that the language admits structuring by way of these connectives. Thus, when we talk about the truth of a sentence or proposition, we are talking about a property that bears this sort of relation to the logical connectives. Second, the concept of reference, as applied to constituents of propositions, is a function of the contribution these constituents make to the truth conditions of the propositions that contain them. Thus, any relation between a word and object that is to count as reference must potentially satisfy clauses of the form: if F refers to dogs and a refers to Nina, then Fa is true if, and only if, Nina is a dog. A relation that did not meet this requirement would not count as reference, at least not of the sort that can legitimately be applied to subsentential components. And the reason is, of course, that this relation would not be appropriately connected to the concept of truth.

However, it would be a mistake to suppose that all representational systems possess semantic structure. For example, a cognitive map (or mental model), like any map, mirrors (i.e., is geometrically isomorphic with) the region it maps, and it does so if it accurately replicates the region's geometric features. In doing so, a cognitive map is clearly a representational item. But the notions of truth and reference that underlie the representational features of propositions are not applicable to cognitive maps. Crucially, the concept of geometric isomorphism does not interact in the same way with the logical connectives. The negation of a sentence is another sentence. But the negation of a map is not a map. To the extent we can make sense of a negated map, the idea would be that a negated map is a different map. So, in this sense of negation, any map distinct from m would be a negation of m. Yet, it is not true that any sentence distinct from p is a negation of p. Similarly, what is the geometric analogue of disjunction? The disjunction of two maps is not itself a map – but the disjunction of two sentences is a sentence.

These sorts of points are familiar ones (see McGinn, 1989). They are rehearsals of the idea that the way a model represents the world is different from the way a sentence represents the world. Nevertheless, a mental model is certainly no less a representational device than a sentence of "mentalese." Thus, while we might accept that any representational item must be part of a general representational framework, we should reject the claim that the mode of combination involved in such a framework must be semantic. Mental models are what we might call "iconic representations." Correctness conditions for representations are not coextensive with truth conditions; and the domain of representation is broader than the domain of reference.[2]

Vehicles and Contents

Transformations of the sort characterized formally by way of the logical connectives are expressions of certain transitions that the content of representations may undergo. To use these to deduce claims about the structure of the representational vehicles of that content would be to fall victim to a vehicle-content confusion. Thus, we cannot, legitimately, use these sorts of transformations to argue for a language-of-thought hypothesis. The representational properties of representations may be intimately bound up with patterns of semantic combination, but this does not entail that the vehicles that carry these properties are similarly structured. All we can conclude, in fact, is this: in the case of some representations, the representational vehicles need to be such that the content they bear is susceptible to the sort of transformations licensed by the logical connectives. This does not entail that the vehicles themselves be structured in the same way as the content.

2. The Informational Constraint

Many people, though by no means all, claim that the idea of representation can be captured, in part, in terms of the concept of information:

Informational constraint: An item r qualifies as a representational item only if it carries information about some state of affairs s that is extrinsic to it.

Information is generally understood as consisting of relations of conditional probability. The most uncompromising account of information associates it with a conditional probability of 1 (Dretske, 1981). So, for r to carry the information that s, the probability of s given r must be 1. A weaker version of the informational constraint (e.g., Lloyd, 1989) associates an increase in conditional probability but not necessarily an increase to the value of 1. On this weaker view, r will carry information about s if the probability of s given r is greater than the probability of s given not r.

On either account of information, the concept of information can be further explicated in terms of the concept of law. On the more stringent conception of information that requires a conditional probability of 1, the laws in question must be strict. On the weaker conception of information, the laws in question need be only probabilistic rather than strict. But, in both cases, the idea of information can be further explained in terms of the concept of law. Therefore, if r consists of a mechanism M's going into state F, and s consists in the world W being in condition G, then r carries information about s if, and only if, it is a law that M is F only if W is G.

Informational approaches to representation are committed to regarding information as a perfectly objective commodity. The strategy is to explain the representational in terms of the informational. This strategy would be obviously circular if the informational were dependent on the representational. The objectivity of information is also evident in the response of informational approach to what is known as the "problem of the relativity of information." The information that r carries about s may, it seems, vary depending on what information, Q, is already available to the subject of r. Dretske (1981, pp. 78–81) provides what has become a well-known illustration. Consider four shells, beneath one of which is a peanut. Suppose person A has already turned shells 1 and 2 and found them empty. Person B has not. If so, then finding shell 3 empty does not supply A and B with the same information. Finding shell 3 empty informs A that the peanut is under shell 4, but informs B only that it is under shell 1, 2, or 4.

This relativity of information seems, prima facie, to provide a problem for the attempt to reduce the representational to the informational. The difference in information acquired by A and B derives from the fact that prior to the turning over of shell 3, A knew things that B did not or was aware of things of which B was not. But knowing is a representational state; and so the relativity of information seems to indicate that the attempt to reduce the representational to the informational is circular.

I think that Dretske's (1981) attempt to deal with this problem is exactly right. According to Dretske, we must clearly distinguish the idea that the information contained in a signal is relative, in general, from the idea that it is relative specifically to the representational states of a subject. In the case of the shells, the information is relative simply to further information – information contained in the configurations of the shells and their history – but not relative to representational states of these subjects.

Another important implication of the concept of information as nomic dependence is that information is ubiquitous. It exists wherever there are nomic dependencies of the required sort. Such dependencies may exist between an internal configuration and an external state of affairs. But, equally, they can exist in the relation between two external, and nonmental, states of affairs.

A persistent problem for purely informational approaches has been accommodating the normativity of representation. If r represents that s, then given the instantiation of r, the world should be s. To see the problem, consider a now-classic example from Fodor (1990). Let us refer to the representation of a horse by way of the capitalized HORSE. The representation HORSE, it seems, means "horse." And, at the very least, this means that the tokening of the representation makes a normative claim about the way the world should be. When HORSE is tokened, the environment should contain, in an appropriate way, a horse. However, it also seems possible, indeed likely, that HORSE can be caused by things that are not horses. Donkeys in the distance and cows on a dark night might, in certain circumstances, be equally efficacious in causing a token-

ing of HORSE. According to informational accounts, representation is to be explained in terms of nomic dependence. However, if the representation HORSE can be tokened in the absence of horses, then HORSE does not seem nomically dependent on horses. Rather, what HORSE does seem nomically dependent on is not the property of being a horse but the disjunctive property of being a horse or a donkey in the distance or a cow on a dark night. Thus, if information is a matter of nomic dependence, and if representation is purely a matter of information, then we seem forced to say that what HORSE represents is not the property of being a horse but the preceding disjunctive property.

It might be thought that we could avoid this problem simply by abandoning the stringent version of the concept of information – the version that associates information with a conditional probability of 1. Then, the fact that HORSE is not correlated in a strict exceptionless way with horses would not count against the former carrying information about the latter. However, this response fails to understand the real problem. This is a problem concerning the normativity of representation, and, as such, is indifferent to the character of the laws thought to underwrite the concept of information: for both strict and probabilistic laws fail to accommodate this normative dimension. Thus, it is true that the tokening of HORSE in a subject might increase the probability of there being a horse in the environment. However, the tokening of HORSE, we are supposing, can also be caused by donkeys in the distance and cows on a dark night but not, presumably, by other things. Therefore, the tokening of HORSE also increases the probability of there being a cow or donkey in the environment.

Even if we retreat to the more sophisticated idea of relative increases in conditional probability – the idea that HORSE means "horse" because the probability of the latter given the former is greater than the probability of the presence of cows or donkeys given the latter – the problem of normativity remains. In such cases, the problem can be made graphic by considering various twin- or inverted-Earth-type scenarios where malign or unfortunate environmental circumstances have conspired to remove horses from the environment while making subjects incapable of registering this fact. If HORSE is tokened, then the world should contain, in the relevant way, a horse. But nomic dependence – whether strict or probabilistic – is not normative in this way. The representation HORSE is nomically connected to whatever does, in fact, produce it and not to what should produce it. Thus, to arrive at an adequate account of representation, we need to inject an element of normativity that is lacking on the purely informational approach. This has led many to suppose that informational accounts need either supplementation with or replacement by a teleological account.

3. The Teleological Constraint

Many suppose that models of representation are subject to a teleological constraint. Roughly:

Teleological constraint: An item r qualifies as representational only if it has the proper function either of tracking the feature or state of affairs s that produces it, or of enabling an organism or other representational consumer to achieve some (beneficial) task in virtue of tracking s.[3]

Central to teleological approaches is the concept of proper function. The proper function of some mechanism, trait, state, or process is what it is supposed to do, what it has been designed to do, what it ought to do. Consider the following simplified version of Millikan's already-simplified version of her definition of proper function given in *Language, Thought, and Other Biological Categories* (1984).[4]

An item X has proper function F only if (1) X is a reproduction of some prior item that, because of the possession of certain reproduced properties, actually performed

F in the past, and X exists because of this performance; or (2) X is the product of a device that had the performance of F as a proper function and normally performs F by way of producing an item like X.

This definition, though simplified, takes some unpacking. The concept of a proper function is a normative concept. The proper function of an item is defined in terms of what an item should do, not what it generally does or is disposed to do. What something does, or is disposed to do, is not always what it is supposed to do. This is for three reasons. First, any mechanism, trait, or process will do many things, not all of which are part of its proper function. A heart pumps blood; it also makes a thumping noise and produces wiggly lines on an electrocardiogram. But only the first of these is its proper function, because only pumping blood is something performed by hearts in the past that explains the existence of hearts in the present. Second, a mechanism, trait, or process can have a proper function even if it never, or hardly ever, performs it. To use a flagship example of Millikan's, the proper function of the tail of a sperm cell is to propel the cell to the ovum. The vast majority of sperm cell tails, however, do not accomplish this task. Third, a mechanism, trait, or process may have a proper function and yet not be able to perform it properly. A person's heart may be malformed and thus not able to pump blood properly. Nevertheless, pumping blood is its proper function because ancestors of the person whose heart it is had hearts that pumped blood and this (in part) explains why they survived and proliferated and, thus, why the person in question possesses a heart.

Underlying the normativity of proper functions is their essentially historical character. The proper function of an item is determined not by the present characteristics or dispositions of that item but by its history. This is the import of (1) in Millikan's definition of proper function. Hearts have the proper function of pumping blood because hearts possessed by our ancestors succeeded in pumping blood, and we have hearts today because the hearts of our ancestors were successful in this regard. That (i) be satisfied is a necessary condition of an item possessing what Millikan calls a "direct proper function." Such possession is essentially a matter of history. There are no first-generation direct proper functions.

There is, however, an important distinction to be observed between (1) direct, (2) adapted, and (3) derived proper functions. For example, chameleons are able to camouflage themselves. They do this by way of a pigmentation mechanism that alters the distribution of pigment in the chameleon's skin.

1. The direct proper function of the pigmentation mechanism is to cause the chameleon's skin to match its immediate surroundings. The chameleon possesses this (token) mechanism because its ancestors possessed (token) mechanisms that performed this function. It is the performing of the function that explains why such mechanisms proliferated.
2. Suppose, now, that the chameleon is placed in a particular immediate environment. In fact, let's make the chameleon work hard and place it on a Jackson Pollock No. 4. The chameleon's skin, therefore, takes on a "Pollockian" arrangement. In these circumstances, the pigmentation mechanism has the adapted proper function of producing a Pollockian skin pattern. This is not a direct proper function of the device: the device has not proliferated as a result of producing, specifically, Pollockian skin patterns. Producing such a pattern is a proper function only adapted to a given context. Such a pattern is what Millikan calls an "adapted device."
3. Adapted devices possess derived proper functions. The derived proper function of the Pollockian arrangement of pigmentation in the chameleon's skin is to match the chameleon to the Jackson Pollock No. 4 on which the poor chameleon has been placed. In general, the proper functions of adapted devices are derived from the proper functions of the mechanisms that produce them.[5]

Like direct proper functions, both adapted and derived proper functions are normative in character. However, unlike direct proper functions, there can be first-generation adapted and derived proper functions. The pigmentation mechanism has the adapted proper function of producing a Pollockian skin pattern, and the pattern has the derived proper function of matching the chameleon to the Pollock No. 4, even if no chameleon has been placed on a Pollock No. 4 before – hence, even if the pattern has never been produced before.

The proper function – whether direct, adapted, or derived – of many evolved items is often relational in character. A device has a relational proper function if it is its function to produce something that bears a specific relation to something else – for example, the relation "same color as." More generally, many evolved devices have proliferated precisely because they enable the organism to cope with its environment: to locate food, evade predators, protect itself from heat and cold, and so on. This is what underwrites their relational character. All of the three types of proper function identified herein can be relational.

The core idea of the teleological approaches to representation is that the mechanisms responsible for mental representation are evolutionary products, and that we can therefore understand representation in terms of the apparatus of direct, adapted, derived, and relational proper functions. Suppose we have a mechanism M that is capable of going into a variety of states or configurations. The direct proper function of mechanism M is, let us suppose, to enable the organism to track various environmental contingencies. In the event that the environmental contingency is the world W's being G, M has, let us suppose, the adapted proper function of entering state or configuration F. And the state that consists in M's being F has, therefore, the derived proper function of occurring only when W is G. And it is this derived proper function that makes M's being F a representation of W's being G.

The normativity of proper functions is crucial to this story. M is supposed to enable organism O to track various environmental contingencies. To this end it is supposed to go into state F when and only when W is G. And M's being F is supposed to occur only when W is G. This elegant account of the normativity of representation is generally regarded as an important strength of the teleological approach to representation, particularly in comparison with a purely informational alternative. Thus, according to teleological approaches, HORSE represents the property of being a horse and not the disjunctive property (horse or donkey in the distance or cow on a dark night) because the direct proper function of the mechanism M is to adopt certain configurations contingent on the presence of certain environmental states of affairs. Therefore, M also has the adapted proper function of producing HORSE in the presence of horses. That is what (presumably among other things) the mechanism has been selected for. It does not have the adapted proper function of producing HORSE in the presence of donkeys or cows, whether in the distance or on a dark night. And, on a teleological account, the content of HORSE derives from the adapted proper function of M. Thus, HORSE is about horses and not about donkeys, cows, or disjunctions of the three. Providing a solution to the misrepresentation problem requires, in effect, detaching the content of a representation from the property with which it is maximally correlated. And this is precisely what the teleological account allows us to do.

4. Stimulus and Benefit in Teleosemantics

The preceding section slid over a crucial ambiguity in the concept of a proper function – whether direct, adapted, or derived. Consider an example, made famous by Dretske (1986). Some marine bacteria have internal magnets, magnetosomes, which function like compass needles: they align the bacteria parallel to the earth's magnetic field. The result is that bacteria in the Northern Hemisphere propel themselves in the direction of geomagnetic north. In the Southern Hemisphere, the magnetosomes are reversed, and southern bacteria propel themselves toward geomagnetic south. The survival value of these magnetosomes is that they allow the bacteria to avoid the oxygen-rich surface water that would be lethal to them. In the Northern Hemisphere, movement toward geomagnetic north will take the bacteria away from oxygen-rich surface water toward the comparatively oxygen-free water lower down.

What is the adapted proper function of the magnetosomes? Is it to indicate the direction of geomagnetic north? Or is it to indicate the direction of oxygen-free water? Geomagnetic north provides the stimulus that allows the magnetosomes to perform their proper function: the magnetosomes track geomagnetic north and track oxygen-free water only in so far as this is correlated with geomagnetic north. But it is oxygen-free water that provides the benefit to the organism of the magnetosomes tracking geomagnetic north. Is representation determined by stimulus or benefit? Dretske endorses a stimulus-based account:

When an indicator, C, indicates both F and G, and its indication of G is via its indication of F . . . then despite the fact that it is the existence of G that is most directly relevant to explaining C's recruitment as a cause of M (F is relevant only in so far as it indicates that G exists), C acquires the function of indicating that F. It is F – the (as it were) maximally indicated state – that C comes to represent. (Dretske, 1990, p. 826)

The magnetosomes, thus, represent geomagnetic north. This is the stimulus for the magnetosome, and representation tracks stimulus, not benefit. Millikan, on the other hand, endorses a benefit-based approach:

What the magnetosome represents is only what its consumers require that it correspond to in order to perform their tasks. Ignore, then, how the representation . . . is normally produced. Concentrate instead on how the systems that react to the representation work, on what these systems need in order to do their job. What they need is only that the pull be in the direction of oxygen-free water at the time. For example, they care not at all how it came that the pull is in that direction. . . . What the magnetosome represents, then, is univocal; it represents only the direction of oxygen-free water. (Millikan, 1989/1993, p. 93)

This disagreement is usually taken as a problem for teleosemantic accounts: the idea is that because such accounts cannot adjudicate between stimulus- and benefit-oriented interpretations means that they are committed to the claim that the content of such representational states is indeterminate. However, I think that there is, in fact, no incompatibility between stimulus- and benefit-based accounts of representation and no problem of indeterminacy.

The notion of a representational consumer is ambiguous between personal and subpersonal levels. Here is one of Millikan's examples. The beaver's tail splash indicates danger – typically, the presence of a predator. When a beaver splashes its tail, other beavers quickly return to the water. If we allow that the tail splash is a representation, what, in this case, is the consumer of the representation?[6] The most obvious answer is other beavers. The consumers of the representation are, thus, other organisms. The same is true of another example commonly employed by Millikan: the dance of the honeybee. Here, the consumers are other bees. In both examples, we have personal-level consumers.[7] The crucial idea is that the representational consumers are organisms, and not internal, subpersonal, mechanisms possessed by organisms.

However, beavers do not just jump into the water on hearing the tail splash. Their motor response is mediated by way of various mechanisms. The acoustic properties of the splash have to be registered and transmitted to the brain, and in the brain a link

has to be set up with the motor cortex. At this level, too, we have representational consumers. These are the mechanisms whose operation will eventually allow the beaver to dive into the lake. So, in addition to personal consumers – other beavers – we also have subpersonal consumers.

This ambiguity passes over and infects the notion of a consumer performing its allotted task and the related idea of what it needs to do its job. The allotted task of the beaver, in this case, is evading predators. So what it needs to do its job is that the splash be, within certain limits, reliably correlated with the presence of predators. So, in the case of personal consumers, one could plausibly argue that representation tracks benefit. And as we have seen, this is precisely Millikan's claim. However, when we switch to subpersonal consumers, an entirely different story emerges. What do the acoustic mechanisms responsible for registering the tail splash require to do their job? Basically, it seems, they require that the splash has certain appropriate acoustic properties. What do the motor mechanisms that produce the beaver's rapid motion into the lake require to do their job? Basically, they require that message of a certain type has been transmitted from the beaver's perceptual cortex. No part of their job requires sensitivity to the benefit associated with the splash. Personal-level consumers are sensitive to the benefit of a representational item; subpersonal consumers are not.

On the basis of the distinction between personal and subpersonal consumers of a representation, we can introduce a corresponding distinction between personal and subpersonal proper functions. This distinction allows us to reconcile stimulus- and benefit-based accounts of representation. Thus, suppose mechanism M of organism P goes into state S in the presence of environmental item E. Going into S in the presence of E is, let us suppose, an adapted proper function of M. Then, the orthodox teleosemantic story is that state S has the derived proper function of occurring in the presence of E, and thus represents, or is about, or means E. The distinction between personal and subpersonal proper functions applies to the derived proper functions of S; thus, (1) subpersonal derived proper function, tracking E, and (2) personal derived proper function, enabling P to φ in virtue of tracking E, where φ denotes a form of action or behavior.

Generally, a subpersonal derived proper function will be to track (i.e., occur in and only in the presence of) some or other feature of the environment. A personal derived proper function will be to enable an organism to accomplish some or other task in virtue of tracking that feature. Each distinct derived proper function will license the attribution of a distinct content. And, crucially, they will license the attribution of this distinct content to distinct individuals. Subpersonal derived proper functions license the attribution of content to subpersonal mechanisms. Personal derived proper functions license the attribution of (a distinct) content to the organism ("person") as a whole.

Suppose we have an organism O sensitive to some feature of the environment E. On the basis of this sensitivity, let us suppose, we can attribute a content C_O to the organism. However, O's sensitivity to this feature of the environment is underwritten by mechanism M, whose direct proper function is to track a certain range of environmental features and whose adapted proper function is to enter state S in the presence of E. Therefore, the derived proper function (see section 3) of S is to track E, and, on the basis of this, we can attribute the content C_M to S. It does not follow, however, and indeed is usually false, that $C_O = C_M$. This is true even though it is M's being S that allows O to be sensitive to its environment in a way that warrants the attribution of content C_O to it. That is, even though it is the adapted proper function of M that allows the attribution of C_M to S, and even though it is the fulfilling of M of its adapted proper function that allows the content C_O to be attributed to O, it does not follow, and indeed is almost always false, that $C_O = C_M$.

To see why, consider another well-known example. Rattlesnakes have certain cells that fire only if two conditions are satisfied. First, the snake's infrared detectors, situated in its nose, must be stimulated. Second, the visual system must get positive input. The former condition is satisfied when there is a localized source of warmth in its environment, the latter when there is a localized source of movement. When these two systems are simultaneously activated, the snake's hunting mechanisms are engaged. In the snake's ancestral home, there will indeed be food about, because the combined input is typically caused by a field mouse, the snake's usual prey. Of course, the rattlesnake can be easily fooled. An artificially warmed imitation mouse on the end of a stick would do the trick. So, what is the adapted proper function of the snake's prey-detection mechanism? What does it represent? Stimulus-based accounts would focus on what activates the mechanism (i.e., localized warmth and movement) and claim that the relevant state of the mechanism represents those features. Benefit-based accounts would focus on the benefit associated with the mechanism performing its proper function – the snake gets to eat – and claim that the relevant state of the mechanism represents food. However, the distinction between personal and subpersonal derived proper functions allows us to see that these answers are not incompatible.

First, there is the personal derived proper function of the state S of the rattlesnake's system (S is understood to be a conjunction of states, one in the infrared detection mechanism and one in the movement detection mechanism). The personal derived proper function of S is to enable the rattlesnake (the "person") to do something – namely, to detect a certain affordance of the environment. S enables the rattlesnake to detect that the environment affords eating. Thus, the personal derived proper function of S is sensitive to the benefit of the prey-detection mechanism fulfilling its adapted proper function.

Second, there is the subpersonal derived proper function of S. The prey-detection mechanism's fulfilling of its personal derived proper function is what enables the rattlesnake to detect that the environment affords eating. However, it does this by way of a certain method or algorithm: the detection of warmth and movement. The subpersonal derived proper function of the state S of M is to track warmth and movement. This latter proper function is, therefore, sensitive to the stimulus, rather than the benefit, of the mechanism fulfilling its adapted proper function.

Each proper function licenses the attribution of a distinct content to a distinct individual. The personal derived proper function warrants the attribution of the content "Eatability, there!" to the rattlesnake as a whole. The subpersonal derived proper function licenses the attribution of the content "Warmth/movement, there!" to the state S of mechanism M. So not only do we have attributions of distinct contents, but also those attributions are made to distinct things.

In such cases, we have neither indeterminacy of function nor indeterminacy of content. We have two individual things – one an organism, the other a mechanism – performing distinct but entirely determinate functions. Because the resultant contents are also attributed to distinct things, there is no basis for the worry that this is a case of the indeterminacy of content. Two distinct but entirely determinate contents do not add up to one indeterminate content.

Seen in this light, stimulus- and benefit-based accounts are not competing accounts of representation. They correspond to two distinct types of derived proper function. Both stimulus- and benefit-based accounts, therefore, have a legitimate role to play in a teleological account of representation.

5. The Decouplability Constraint

It is common to hold that, to be regarded as genuinely representational, a representation must be decouplable from the environment, in the sense of being able to occur in the absence of the feature whose function it is to track. That provides us with our fourth putative constraint on representation:

Decouplability Constraint: Item r qualifies as representing state of affairs s only if r is, in an appropriate sense, decouplable from s.

This is one (but, I think, not the only) way to give expression to the idea that representations are distinct from what they represent. A representation is decouplable when the representing organism is able to deploy it to guide its behavior in the absence of the environmental feature of which that representation is a representation. For something to count as a representation, it must be the sort of thing that is capable of deployment in off-line contexts. Or, as Haugeland puts it, to count as a genuinely representation-using system, that system must (1) be able to coordinate its behaviors with environmental features that are not always reliably present to it, and (2) do this by having something else stand in or go proxy for a signal directly received from the environment and use this to guide behavior in its stead (Haugeland, 1991).

Decouplability is a far more controversial condition on representation than the informational or teleological conditions, and it is far from clear that the constraint can be accepted as a general condition on representation. As Andy Clark (1997, pp. 144–145) points out, at least some cases of representation do not satisfy the decouplability requirement. For example, there is a population of neurons in the posterior parietal cortex of rats whose function is to carry, by way of an appropriate coding system, information about the direction in which the rat's head is facing. However, this population functions only in tandem with a continuous stream of proprioceptive information from the rat's body. Thus, it does not seem to satisfy the decouplability requirement. Nevertheless, the neuronal population's function is pretty clearly representational. Glossing states of the population as codings for specific head positions allows us to understand the flow of information within the system (e.g., when we find other neuronal groups that consume the information encoded in the target population). Thus, as Clark points out, treating the neuronal encodings as representations buys us genuine explanatory leverage, and it is, therefore, unclear why we should deny these encodings the status of representations. Decouplability is, almost certainly, a feature of many representations, perhaps most. But it is not clear that it is a feature of all representations. Still less is it clear that it is a necessary feature of representations.

6. The Misrepresentation Constraint

As we have seen, in connection with the informational constraint, the possibility of representation is closely tied to the possibility of misrepresentation.

Misrepresentation Constraint: Item r qualifies as representing state of affairs s only if it is capable of misrepresenting s.

The misrepresentation constraint is not controversial. Indeed, it is a relatively straightforward consequence of the normativity of representation. A representation makes a claim about the way the world should be, given that the representation is activated, and this must accommodate the possibility that the world is not, in fact, that way. In this sense, the misrepresentation constraint is derivative of the normativity constraint: any model that satisfies the latter automatically satisfies the former also. If you can satisfy the normativity constraint, the misrepresentation constraint comes for free.

PART II: REPRESENTATION AND SITUATED COGNITION

Much recent work on cognition is characterized by an augmentation of the role of action coupled with an attenuation of the role of representation. A general theoretical framework for this is provided by what has become known as "vehicle externalism" or the "extended mind."[8] The general contours of this position are given by way of the following claims:

1. The world is an external store of information relevant to cognitive processes such as perceiving, remembering, reasoning, and so on.

It is such a store because, as we have seen, information is ubiquitous. One item will carry information about another in virtue of appropriate relations of conditional probability between them. But such relations can be instantiated in the environment just as much as in the relation between an internal representation and its external correlate. In virtue of this, information exists in the environment, and there are certain environmental structures that carry information relevant to cognition.

2. Cognitive processes are essentially hybrid – they straddle both internal and external forms of information processing.
3. The external processes involve manipulation, exploration, exploitation, and transformation of environmental structures that carry information relevant to the accomplishing of the cognitive task at hand.
4. At least some of the internal processes involved are ones concerned with supplying the cognizing organism with the ability to appropriately use relevant structures in its environment.

The traditional construal of representations sees them as internal configurations of a subject, individuated by way of their higher-order physical or functional properties. Different versions of vehicle externalism have different conceptions of how much of the function of representations, thus construed, can be usurped by action. At one extreme are eliminativist treatments that see essentially no role left over for traditional

representations.[9] Other versions are less san-
guine and see the role of action as supple-
menting, rather than supplanting, that of
traditional representations.[10] However, all
forms of vehicle externalism agree that at
least some of the role of representations,
traditionally construed, can be taken over
by action. Accordingly, an appeal to action
is to be found at the core of any such
externalism.

7. Representation and the Extended Mind: Two Interpretations

One claim that unites all forms of vehicle externalism is that the role traditionally
assigned to representations can, at least to
some extent, be taken over by suitable action
on the part of the representing organism.
In interpreting the role of representation
within this framework, the first question
that must be addressed is, Can all of the roles
traditionally assigned to representations be
played by suitable action on the part of the
representing organism? If you answer yes
to this question, then you combine vehicle externalism with a form of eliminativism
about representation.

Certain interpretations of vehicle externalism do indeed go hand in hand with a
general antipathy toward the idea of representation. For example, many dynamicist
approaches staunchly reject the idea that
the concept of a representation will play
any genuine role in accounting for cognition.
Among dynamicists, such sentiments have
been expressed by Maturana and Varela
(1980), Skarda and Freeman (1987), Smithers
(1994), Thelen and Smith (1994), Wheeler
(1994), and van Gelder (1995). Nor are these
sentiments restricted to narrowly dynamicist approaches. In situated robotics, we find
Webb (1994) endorsing a similar rejection
of representations. And in the very different arena of visual perception, many of the
pronouncements of O'Regan and Noë (2001,
2002) seem to veer in this general eliminativist direction.

Some, however, answer no to the question. This typically drives them in the

direction of a dual-component account of
representation.[11] According to this interpretation, a case of representation can be fac-
tored into two components, one that is genuinely representational and one that is not.
What is involved in being a genuinely representational component of action is something that can be cashed out in terms of
one's preferred account of the representational relation. This genuinely representational component, on the dual component
interpretation of the extended model, functions in tandem with suitable acts of environmental action – worldly manipulation,
exploitation, and transformation, for example. The relation between these two components can be extremely intimate. It may
be, for example, that the genuinely representational component of at least some
representations has been designed to function in tandem with acts of environmental
activity, so that the former cannot fulfill its
function in the absence of the latter. However, what is crucial to the dual-component
interpretation is the claim that the action-
based component is (1) logically distinct
from the representational component and
(2) is not, therefore, itself representational.
The action-based component allows or facilitates the genuinely representational component, sometimes perhaps essentially, but it
does not itself represent anything.

For the purposes of this chapter, what
is important is not how eliminativist and
dual-component interpretations differ but
what they share. And what they share is
the idea that representation and action are
two logically distinct activities. Given this
assumption, it becomes a fundamentally
empirical question how much of each activity is involved in an organism's ability to
successfully negotiate its environment. The
eliminativist interpretation says (crudely),
"All action, no representation," and the
dual-component interpretation says, "Some
action, some representation." According
to the former, then, action supplants or
replaces representation; according to the latter, action supplements it.

In the rest of this chapter I shall
draw attention to the formidable difficulties

involved in the claim that action can either supplant or supplement representation. In either case, the appeal to action is in danger of being impaled on one or another horn of a dilemma.

8. The First Horn: Action as Presupposing Representation

Traditionally understood, action can neither supplant nor supplement representation for the simple reason that it presupposes representation. Specifically, both the status of an event as an action and its identity as the particular action it is depend on its connection to prior intentional, hence representational, states. The precise nature of this connection will depend on which theory of action you endorse, but all theories assert that there is some appropriate connection. For example, suppose you are patting your head while rubbing your stomach. What makes this an action? On any traditional philosophical account of action, its status as an action depends on its standing in some appropriate connection to intentional, hence representational, states. The term *appropriate* is defined only within a theory. On a causal theory of action, for example, *appropriate* is explained in terms of certain sorts of causal relations – the movement constitutes an action because it is caused by some prior intentional state or complex – an intention, volition, belief-desire coupling, and so on. Other theories give very different accounts of what an appropriate relation is, but all assert that bearing some relation to other intentional states is essentially involved in being an action (as opposed to bodily movement).

Second, consider the identity of actions. Is patting your head while rubbing your stomach one action, or two, or many? Again, on traditional accounts, the individuation of actions is essentially bound up with the individuation of other intentional states. Returning to the causal theory, for example, the idea would be that if the intention or volition that causes my action is a single state, then the action counts as one rather than many. Thus, if my intention is to pat my head while rubbing my stomach – a single intention – then the action counts as one action. If, on the other hand, I am the subject of two distinct intentions – to pat my head and to rub my stomach – which just happen to be contemporaneously activated, then the action counts as two, rather than one.

Traditional accounts of action make both the status of an event as an action and its identity as the particular action it is essentially dependent on its relation to other intentional states. But intentional states are individuated by their content. And content arises through representation. So, the appeal to action presupposes representation and therefore cannot be used either to supplant or supplement it.

9. The Second Horn: The Contribution of Action as Merely Causal

The most obvious response to the first horn of the dilemma is to recast the type of action involved in the elimination of representation as nonintentional activity of some sort. This response, however, is likely to lead to a distinct but equally serious problem: it means the appeal to action will fail to play the role required of it. In particular, action will be able to play no role in accounting for the normativity of representation.

The danger underlying the second horn of the dilemma is that the retreat from an intentional conception of action will leave us with something very much like bodily movement. And the contribution that bodily movement can make to representation is a purely causal one. This causal contribution may, at some level, be extremely useful in helping us represent the world. It may play a very important role in facilitating our ability to represent the world. However, this facilitatory role is restricted to causal impingements: it allows us to causally affect the world in new and expedient ways, but it has no normative dimension.

This interpretation entails that action can play no role in explaining the normative dimension of representation. But this dimension of representation derives from its content – it is because representations possess content that they make claims about the way the world should be. This means that if the action-based component of representation plays a purely causal, facilitatory role, then it can play no role in explaining representational content. To do so, it would have to be possible to factor off content into normative and nonnormative components. But normativity is an essential feature of content; anything that is to count as content must be normative. Therefore, it is not possible to factor off content in this way. Therefore, any purely causal component of representation could play no role in explaining representational content.

Given one further assumption, however, this failure of a purely causal conception of action to play a role in explaining representational content leads to serious trouble for the idea that action can be employed to either supplant or supplement representation. The assumption is this: the normatively constrained content of a representation exceeds that which can be provided by any internal, genuinely representational core. Most forms of vehicle externalism, if they have anything at all to say about representation, are committed to this claim.[12]

To take just one example, consider the enactive or sensorimotor model of visual perception developed by O'Regan and Noë (2001, 2002) and Noë (2004). They have shown that our sense of encountering in perception a complex, rich, and detailed world is something that cannot be explained purely by reference to what is going on inside the head – for what is going on there can, at most, provide us with the rough gist of the situation. Rather, our sense of encountering a complex, rich, and detailed world is underwritten, partly but essentially, by the fact that the world we encounter is visually complex, rich, and detailed, and we exploit this complexity, richness, and detail in the formation of our experiences. This complexity, richness, and detail is, accordingly, part of the content of our visual experience, but

it is a part not provided by any internal representational core.

It is characteristic of vehicle externalist approaches, to the extent they have anything to say about representation, to be committed to the claim that the content of representations exceeds that which can be provided by what is inside the head of the representing subject. But content, however it is constituted, is an essentially normative phenomenon. Therefore, if the conception of action we employ to explain or explain away this content is nonnormative – if, for example, we invoke a merely causal conception of action – then this conception of action cannot explain what it is required to explain. No addition of nonnormative material can ever provide us with an understanding of a phenomenon that is essentially normative. No number of exculpations can ever add up to a justification. This is not to deny, of course, that the action-based dimension of representation does provide us with additional means of causally affecting the world. There is a causal story to tell here. But if the normative dimension of representation exceeds that which can be provided by the internal, genuinely representational, component alone, and if action is to play a role in representation, there must be more than a causal story to tell about this role. In such circumstances, action must be infused with normativity if it is to play any role in helping us understand representation. The action-based dimension must itself be normative; it must be part of the space of reasons.

10. Representation in Action

We are now in a position to appreciate the problematic nature of an appeal to action in our attempt to understand – explain or explain away – representation. In the traditional sense of action, both the status of an item as an action and its identity as the particular action it is derive from its connection to antecedent intentional, hence representational, states. Therefore, to appeal to action in this sense is to presuppose representation rather than explain it.

Essentially the same problem would also arise if we were to appeal to a conception of action that inherits not full intentional status from antecedent representational states but merely some of the necessary features of representation. For example, if the actions to which we appeal were to possess a normative status that they have inherited from the normative character of antecedent intentional states, we would be presupposing one of the defining features of representation rather than explaining it. And, of course, in the project of understanding representation, this would be a Pyrrhic victory at best.

However, neither can we appeal to a concept of action that is not normative. We cannot understand action as merely providing us with additional means of causally impinging on or affecting the world. Representation is essentially normative, and the normatively constrained content of representation exceeds that which can be provided by some putative internal representational core. Therefore, if the conception of action to which we appeal is not normative, it can play no role in helping us understand representation.

Therefore, the appeal to action faces a dilemma. If representation is an essentially normative phenomenon, and this normative dimension exceeds that which can be provided by an internal representational core, then appeal to a nonnormative conception of action can in no way help us understand representation. If, on the other hand, we appeal to a concept of action that acquires its normative status from antecedent intentional – hence normative – states, then we have simply presupposed the most perplexing feature of representation and not explained it. So, it seems the concept of action to which we appeal in our goal of understanding representation must both be and yet cannot be a normatively constrained concept.

There is, however, a way out of this dilemma. The appeal to a normative conception of action will beg the question only if the action acquires its normative status from something else – for example, from a prior intentional state. But suppose, however, that the normative status of the action is not derived from anything else. Suppose actions can be normative for the same reason that intentional states are normative. For example, suppose the historical account of normativity defended in part 1 of this chapter were correct. Then suppose also that essentially the same story could be told of at least certain sorts of actions, and could be told quite independently of the connection these states bear to other intentional, hence representational, states. Then, whatever reasons we have for supposing representational states to be normative, we would also have precisely the same reasons for supposing that these sorts of actions were normative. In such circumstances, the appeal to this type of action would not beg the question. And in employing this concept of action, we would not be reiterating a purely causal, nonnormative, conception of the role played by action in representation.

Elsewhere, I argue that the requisite conception of action exists. Moreover, these are precisely the sorts of actions that are likely to be involved in our representing of the world (Rowlands, 2006). Moreover, as we have seen, normativity is likely to lie at the core of any account of representation. And this raises an even more intriguing possibility: that certain sorts of actions themselves satisfy the criteria of representation discussed in the first part of this chapter. If this were so, then there would be no possibility of separating off, as the dual-component interpretation would have it, the genuinely representational from the action-based component of representation. Therefore, a fortiori, there is no possibility of eliminating representation in favor of action. Actions and representations do not make even notionally separable contributions to the overall task of representing the world. Representation and action are, indeed, essentially connected – because acting can be a form of representing. Representation does not stop short of its objects: representation is representation all the way out.[13]

Acknowledgments

I am grateful to the Arts and Humanities Research Council for providing me with a research-leave grant. This chapter was written during the period of this grant. Thanks to Chris Eliasmith for comments on an earlier version of this chapter.

Notes

1   I do not, in fact, think that a complete account of representation can be given within a naturalistic framework. This chapter, therefore, is best viewed as an attempt to examine the implications of a naturalistic account of representation for situated models of cognition.

2   Thus, my interpretation of the combinatorial constraint is quite distinct from that made famous by Fodor. Fodor (1990) argues that the mode of combination invoked by the constraint must be semantic. I, for the reasons outlined previously, disagree.

3   One need not, in fact, regard the teleological constraint as a constraint at all. Rather, one might regard it as a theory introduced to meet other constraints – for example, the misrepresentation constraint. This complication will have little bearing on the discussion to follow, and one is accordingly free to read the teleological account as providing either a constraint or a theory.

4   This definition is taken from Millikan (1993, p. 123).

5   I am going to ignore Millikan's distinction between adapted derived proper functions and invariant derived proper functions. Although important in some contexts, the distinction will play no role in this chapter.

6   It is not, in fact, a full-blown representation, as it presumably fails to satisfy some of the criteria of representation (e.g., combinatorial constraint). It corresponds to what Millikan calls an "intentional icon" rather than a full-blown representation. This does not matter for our purposes. What does matter is that it has at least proto-representational status.

7   Here the content of the personal is given simply by its opposition to the concept of the subpersonal. So, there is no claim that bees, or even beavers, are persons. If you do not like the terminology, feel free to replace *personal* with *organismic* (the terminology I employed in earlier work).

8   This view of the mind has, in recent years, been defended by Donald (1991), Hutchins (1995), Clark (1997, 2004), Wilson (1995, 2004), Clark and Chalmers (1998), Hurley (1998), and Rowlands (1999, 2003).

9   Certain dynamicist accounts fit this profile. See, for example, van Gelder (1995).

10 See, for example, Clark (1997), Clark and Toribio (1994), and Rowlands (1999).

11 The label is intended to draw attention to the parallels with an interpretation of good old-fashioned content externalism. For a cogent defense of this interpretation of content externalism, see McGinn (1982).

12 For detailed defense of this claim, see Rowlands (2006).

13 I defend this conception of action in Rowlands (2006).

References

Clark, A. (1997). *Being there: Putting brain, body, and world together again.* Cambridge, MA: MIT Press.

Clark, A. (2003). *Natural-born cyborgs.* New York: Oxford University Press.

Clark, A., & Chalmers, D. (1998). The extended mind. *Analysis, 58,* 7–19.

Clark, A., & Toribio, J. (1994). Doing without representing. *Synthese, 101,* 401–431.

Donald, M. (1991). *Origins of the modern mind.* Cambridge, MA: Harvard University Press.

Dretske, F. (1981). *Knowledge and the flow of information.* Cambridge, MA: MIT Press.

Dretske, F. (1986). Misrepresentation. In R. Bogdan (Ed.), *Belief* (pp. 17–36). Oxford: Oxford University Press.

Dretske, F. (1990). Reply to reviewers. *Philosophy and Phenomenological Research, 1*(4), 819–839.

Fodor, J. (1990). *A theory of content and other essays.* Cambridge, MA: MIT Press.

Haugeland, J. (1991). Representational genera. In W. Ramsey, S. Stich, & J. Garron (Eds.), *Philosophy and connectionist theory* (pp. 61–89). Hillsdale, NJ: Lawrence Erlbaum.

Hurley, S. (1998). *Consciousness in action*. Cambridge, MA: Harvard University Press.

Hutchins, E. (1995). *Cognition in the wild*. Cambridge, MA: MIT Press.

Lloyd, D. (1989). *Simple minds*. Cambridge, MA: MIT Press.

Maturana, H., & Varela, F. (1980). *Autopoiesis and cognition*. Dordrecht, The Netherlands: Reidel.

McGinn, C. (1982). The structure of content. In A. Woodfield (Ed.), *Thought and object* (pp. 207–258). Oxford: Oxford University Press.

McGinn, C. (1989). *Mental content*. Oxford, UK: Blackwell.

Millikan, R. (1984). *Language, thought and other biological categories*. Cambridge, MA: MIT Press.

Millikan, R. (1989/1993). Biosemantics. In R. Millikan (Ed.), *White queen psychology and other essays for Alice* (pp. 83–101). Cambridge, MA: MIT Press. (Reprinted from *Journal of Philosophy*, 86, 281–297.)

Millikan, R. (1993). *White queen psychology and other essays for Alice*. Cambridge, MA: MIT Press.

Noë, A. (2004). *Action in perception*. Cambridge, MA: MIT Press.

O'Regan, J. K., & Noë, A. (2001). A sensorimotor account of vision and visual consciousness. *Behavioral and Brain Sciences*, 23, 939–973.

O'Regan, J. K., & Noë, A. (2002). What it is like to see: A sensorimotor theory of perceptual experience. *Synthese*, 79, 79–103.

Rowlands, M. (1999). *The body in mind: Understanding cognitive processes*. Cambridge: Cambridge University Press.

Rowlands, M. (2003). *Externalism: Putting mind and world back together again*. London: Acumen.

Rowlands, M. (2006). *Body language: Representation in action*. Cambridge, MA: MIT Press.

Skarda, C., & Freeman, W. (1987). How brains make chaos in order to make sense of the world. *Behavioral and Brain Sciences*, 10, 161–195.

Smithers, T. (1994). Why better robots make it harder. In D. Cliff, P. Husbands, J. Meyer, & S. Wilson (Eds.), *From animals to animats 3* (pp. 64–72). Cambridge, MA: MIT Press.

Thelen, E., & Smith, L. (1994). *A dynamic systems approach to the development of cognition and action*. Cambridge, MA: MIT Press.

van Gelder, T. (1995). What might cognition be, if not computation? *Journal of Philosophy*, 91, 345–381.

Webb, B. (1994). Robotic experiments in cricket phonotaxis. In D. Cliff, P. Husbands, J. Meyer, & S. Wilson (Eds.), *From animals to animats 3* (pp. 45–54). Cambridge, MA: MIT Press.

Wheeler, M. (1994). From activation to activity. *Artificial Intelligence and the Simulation of Behaviour Quarterly*, 87, 36–42.

Wilson, R. (1995). *Cartesian psychology and physical minds: Individualism and the sciences of the mind*. New York: Cambridge University Press.

Wilson, R. (2004). *Boundaries of the mind: The individual in the fragile sciences*. New York: Cambridge University Press.

CHAPTER 8

Dynamics, Control, and Cognition

Chris Eliasmith

1. Once upon Real Time

A dynamic object is an object whose properties change over time. A static object is an object whose properties do not change over time. Given such an idealization, the notion of "static" lies at an extreme end of the spectrum of temporal relations between objects and properties. Indeed, modern physics tells us that no objects are truly static. Nevertheless, many of our physical, computational, and metaphysical theories turn a blind eye to the role of time, often for practical reasons. So, perhaps it is not surprising that in the philosophy of mind – where physical, computational, and metaphysical theories meet – there has been a consistent tendency to articulate theories that consider function and time independently. As a result, contemporary theories in cognitive science consider time unsystematically (for specific examples, see the next section). In this chapter, I suggest that the problem with this "ad-hockery" is that the systems we are trying to characterize are real-time systems, whose real-time performance demands principled explanation (a point on

which many of these same contemporary theorists agree). After a discussion of the importance and roots of dynamics in cognitive theorizing, I describe the role of time in each of the three main approaches to cognitive science: symbolicism, connectionism, and dynamicism. Subsequently, I outline a recently proposed method, the neural engineering framework (NEF), that, unlike past approaches, permits a principled integration of dynamics into biologically realistic models of high-level cognition. After briefly presenting a model, BioSLIE, that demonstrates this integration using the NEF, I argue that this approach alone is in a position to properly integrate dynamics, biological realism, and high-level cognition.

Historically, many cognitive theories have not been particularly informed by our understanding of biological systems. Arguably, this is because our understanding of the mechanisms driving biological systems was in its infancy until very recently. This suggests that there was little opportunity for theories of mind to gain insight from our understanding of the kinds of systems that putatively have minds. So, there was little inspiration to be drawn from biology regarding mentality. However, recent decades have seen a radical change in this state of affairs. Neuroscience, the subdiscipline of biology most relevant to theories of mind, began to systematically explore neural mechanisms only quite recently (e.g., after the pioneering experiments of Hodgkin & Huxley, 1952; Hubel & Wiesel, 1962; Wiesel & Hubel, 1963).[1] Despite these relatively recent beginnings, the annual conference of the Society for Neuroscience features approximately thirty thousand attendees, most of whom are directly involved in exploring the mechanisms of the brain. I suspect that all of them, almost without exception, are acutely aware of the dynamics of the mechanisms they are studying.

The importance of the dynamics of neural mechanisms for understanding the brain can be gleaned from the kinds of vocabulary typically employed by neuroscientists. They inevitably speak of time constants; time courses; fluctuations; firing rates; spike-timing dependent plasticity; oscillations; molecular kinetics; membrane dynamics; protein dynamics; short and long-term plasticity; synchrony; temporal correlations; and so on. In other words, a careful examination of the mechanisms underlying mental phenomena have demanded temporally laden descriptions.

Of course, there is no obvious reason why it is necessary to learn about the brain before gleaning the importance of dynamics. Perhaps the traditional division between cognition and perception/action, reflected neatly in the notion of humans as rational animals, suggested to many early cognitive scientists that rationality, a reasonably outside-of-time kind of behavior, is their target of inquiry. Unfortunately, this view relegates many of the dynamical aspects of behavior to the status of an afterthought. No doubt this perspective was bolstered by the development of the von Neumann architecture for computers, which neatly distinguishes input and output functions from central processing, whose temporal properties are determined by a clock that can be sped up or slowed down with little functional conse-

quence. And it was clear to anyone studying computer systems that the central processor was the most important part of the system. This characterization is efficiently captured in the now-famous mind-as-computer metaphor that has so dominated the history of cognitive science.

Perhaps one way to move past this metaphor for mind is to learn more about the target of the metaphor. That is, it may be no coincidence that, as our understanding of the brain has improved, the standard conception of cognition has become more dynamical. In other words, I suspect that the broad dynamical shift of cognitive science is widely inspired by the "neuralizing" of the discipline.

Although our improved understanding of neural mechanisms has likely cemented the importance of dynamics for understanding cognition, another route to this view can be found in the history of psychology. In particular, the work of psychologist J. J. Gibson and his colleagues at Cornell University provides further impetus for taking dynamics seriously (Gibson, 1966; Gibson & Gibson, 1955). In fact, the focus of this research was not on dynamics per se but on the active role that a perceiver takes in exploiting its own motion to extract relevant information or to underwrite environmental interactions. Gibson described agents as resonating with certain information in their environment that is relevant for their potential actions. His well-known notion of an "affordance" captures this theoretical position. It is affordances, after all, that agents are specially tuned to pick up as environmental objects of interest to them (e.g., a tree stump affords living quarters for an insect but a seat for us).

This emphasis on the environment, and on the relation between agents and environments, has served as a theoretical predecessor to the contemporary concern for the situatedness and embodiedness of agents.[2] Such theories, including Gibson's original characterization, focus attention on movements of an agent within an environment. This necessarily highlights the importance of characterizing both environmental and agent-centered dynamics. For instance, an

approach to characterizing visual perception championed by Dana Ballard, animate
vision, focuses on determining what information agents actively extract from a visual
scene through rapid eye movements, rather
than taking the traditional Marrian approach
of trying to reconstruct the entire visual
scene in a three-dimensional internal representation (Ballard, 1991). It is the dynamics of the agent and the environment that
determine what information is available to
be acted on.

Despite the fact that traditional computational approaches to understanding
cognitive function often label themselves
"information-processing approaches," the
strongest arguments for the importance of
situatedness come from information theoretic considerations. Simply put, there is too
much information in an environment for
any known sensory organ to extract it all.
Sensory organs clearly have limited bandwidth; that is, a limited ability to extract
the various information available in natural environments. And although there is evidence that many such systems are near their
theoretical limits for extracting information
(Rieke, Warland, de Ruyter van Steveninick,
& Bialek, 1997), even reaching such limits
will not ameliorate the problem of dealing
with all the information in an environment.
Given such hard constraints, it is not surprising that biological systems have developed various means of targeting evolutionarily relevant information sources in their
environment. It is those sources, after all,
that determine whether they live or die. As
a result of these considerations it becomes
clear that how these systems target information is as important as how they pick up that
information once they are oriented toward
it. Furthermore, if those methods of targeting are highly sensitive to environmental
dynamics, as they clearly seem to be,[3] then
it is also essential to understand the dynamics of such an environment. As a result, the
dynamics of the agent, the dynamics of the
environment, and equally important, their
interaction, are what need to be understood
to properly characterize information processing in biological systems.

In short, experimental considerations of
neural mechanisms and theoretical considerations of agent-environment interactions
conspire to suggest that dynamics are an
inescapable feature of cognitive systems.
This is in contrast to the traditional view
that cognitive systems are best characterized through a firm theoretical grounding
in computational theory. The problem with
this traditional picture is that artificial intelligence and computer science researchers
are not especially interested in dynamical
systems. That is, although the design of
real-time systems is only one small part of
computer science, the only kind of systems
ever designed by Mother Nature are real-
time systems. At the moment, by far the
most impressive cognitive systems are natural ones.

2. Dynamic Duels: Dynamics and Cognitive Architectures

Having briefly argued for the importance
of dynamics to understanding cognition, I
turn to the issue of how dynamics have been
integrated into various theories of cognition.
After a brief historical discussion, I describe
the strengths and weaknesses of the three
main contenders in cognitive science, especially in relation to their incorporation of
time into their methods of model construction.

2.1. Behaving in Time

In the early part of the past century, the
dominant theory in psychology was behaviorism. Famously, behaviorism espoused the
view that the only scientifically respectable
"observables" that could underwrite a psychological theory were behavioral events.
They argued that only such external events
were objectively observable, and thus that
only they could be the subject of an objective scientific theory (Watson, 1913). It
is somewhat unclear from their collective
writings exactly how important dynamics
were, or were not, for supporting this understanding of psychological agents.[4] Whatever

the case, their behavioral standpoint was unarguably infused with dynamics in the hands of the cyberneticists.

Cybernetics is the study of feedback and control in both artificial and biological systems. It grew from a wartime interest in real-world, goal-directed systems – especially enemy-directed systems. Norbert Wiener (1948), who coined the term "cybernetics," was a mathematician with interests in communication theory who worked on gun controllers. It has been suggested that Wiener realized that the study of stability and control of the antiaircraft systems he was working on could be extended to the operator of the system as well (Freudenthal, 1970–1990). As a result, he had the insight that the same mathematical tools for understanding goal-directed artificial systems could be applied to goal-directed natural systems.

The mathematical tools that Wiener used are typically grouped under the heading of "classical control theory." Very briefly, classical control theory considers the system under study as implementing a temporal transfer function, which describes how inputs are converted into outputs over time. The point of classical control is to design a control system that can be used to alter the inputs of the system to achieve a desired output. In open-loop control, the controller simply provides inputs that should, under normal circumstances, achieve the desired outputs. However, because normal circumstances are often difficult to define in advance, and the circumstances themselves are likely to change over time, a more sophisticated form of control, closed-loop control or feedback control, is more commonly employed. In closed-loop control, the inputs provided to the system depend on its current outputs, which are often affected by the current circumstances (e.g., in automobile cruise control, road conditions, hills, and so on, greatly affect the effect of various accelerator inputs). The effectiveness of closed-loop controllers was demonstrated time and again during World War II, by their inclusion in target trackers, self-guided torpedoes, and various other servomechanisms (Mindell, 1995).

To this day, classical control methods are taught to engineers to provide them with strong intuitions about how simple control systems can be analyzed and designed. These methods play this role because they are largely graphical; are easily applicable to simple, single input–single output systems; and introduce a number of useful heuristics for control design. However, when trying to understand a complex control system like the brain, many of these pedagogical strengths become practical weaknesses. For instance, there is no reason to think that a biological system is a single input–single output system. As well, when dealing with complex controllers, graphical methods soon become limiting and clumsy because of their restricted dimensionality. Additional theoretical limitations on classical control include an inability to quantify optimal control, to characterize adaptive control, and to systematically include considerations of noise.

Despite these limitations, classical control successfully began a practical quantification of real-time systems. As well, the cyberneticist focus on temporal input-output relations (captured by the transfer functions) integrated well with the behaviorist psychology of the day. That is, both classical control theorists and behaviorists did not need to look inside the systems they were interested in understanding. What the control theorists added, of course, was an explicitly dynamical dimension to an otherwise static characterization of cognitive systems.

2.2. A Cognitive Resolution

The famous cognitive revolution that took place in the mid-1950s is often hailed as an essential turning point in the history of cognitive science, a turning point without which cognitive science would not have fruitfully developed (Bechtel & Graham, 1999; Thagard, 1996). This may be true in part, but there was also a significant price that was paid for the sweeping adoption of the cognitivist view. This is because the resolution of behaviorist difficulties came in two parts. One was a shift in focus from input-output relations to internal states of cognitive systems. The second was a shift from mathematical models of behavior to computational ones. With this second shift came a general acceptance that the relevant formal theory for characterizing cognitive systems was grounded in abstract entities that have no connection to time: Turing machines. For instance, Newell and Simon (1972) wrote in their historical epilogue:

> The formalization of logic showed that symbols can be copied, compared, rearranged, and concatenated with just as much definiteness of process as boards can be sawed, planed, measured, and glued.... Symbols became, for the first time, tangible – as tangible as wood or metal. The Turing machine was an all-purpose planar and lathe for symbols. (pp. 877–878)

A basic assumption of this kind of computational theory is that resources are infinite. So a computable function is one that can be accomplished regardless of temporal, memory, or other constraints. Unfortunately, despite the fact that considering internal states is independent of the formal theory for considering such states, it so happened that, by adopting computational theory, time was pushed aside by the cognitive sciences. In other words, it just so happened that the formal theory that informed this symbolicist characterization of cognition cleaved time from function – an assumption not reflected in natural cognitive systems.

As a result, it is not surprising that in their attack on the temporal deficiencies of these symbolic characterizations of cognitive systems, Port and van Gelder (1995) claim that the symbolicists *"leave time out of the picture"* (p. 2, italics original). But, on the face of it, this is untrue. Consider, for instance, Newell's (1990) paradigmatic symbolicist cognitive model SOAR. In his discussion of this model, and its theoretical underpinnings, Newell includes "operate in real time" as the third of thirteen constraints that shapes the mind (p. 19). Thus, it is simply not the case the symbolicists ignore time.

However, I believe it clearly is the case that they have great difficulty meeting this essential constraint.

Newell appeals to various neurological data to lend support to his assumption that any particular step (or "production") in a cognitive algorithm operates on the time scale of approximately 10 ms (Newell, 1990, p. 127). However, his application of this constraint seems rather contrived. For instance, in one application, SOAR employs a single production to encode whether or not a light is on (Newell, 1990, p. 275). But, in a second application, SOAR uses a single production to encode: "If the problem space is the base-level-space, and the state has a box with nothing on top, and the state has input that has not been examined, then make the comprehend operator acceptable, and note that the input has been examined" (Newell, 1990, p. 167). It seems highly unlikely that both of these productions should fire within the same time scale (i.e., approximately 10 ms). Time values, the number of productions per step, and the complexity of those productions have clearly been chosen to allow the total reaction time of the models to fall within human limits found through psychological experimentation. The claim that SOAR has somehow allowed rough predictions of human reaction time is thus very unconvincing, given this ad hoc methodology. It is rather more likely that the modeler's analysis, experience with psychological results, and chosen time values allowed such predictions (Newell, 1990, pp. 274–282). In summary, there is no mention of how to systematically relate productions to neural firings, and worse, the few examples provided are highly unsystematic.

Although it may not be completely futile for the symbolicist to attempt to incorporate realistic time constraints into his or her model, it is undeniably more natural for this constraint to be satisfied by intrinsically dynamic models – that is, models that, in virtue of their underlying formal theory, have time constraints included. In the end, symbolicists have not convincingly described how time in their model of cognitive processes (model time) systematically relates to time in a natural cognizer (real time). This is important because, as Newell (1990) himself notes, "minor changes in assumptions move the total time accounting in substantial ways that have strong consequences for which model fits the data" (p. 294). This comment reflects two important conclusions of this discussion. First, time is often included in symbolicist models – symbolicists clearly took time very seriously, contrary to some characterizations. Second, there is a massive slippage between a cognitive model and a real cognitive system for symbolicists. This is the high price symbolicists have paid for considering time independently of cognitive function.

2.3. *Dynamicism: Mind as Motion*

In the mid-1990s, a movement in cognitive science called "dynamicism" began to flourish by arguing that these kinds of temporal limitations of symbolism doomed it to failure (Abraham, Abraham, & Shaw, 1991; Busemeyer & Townsend, 1993; Port & van Gelder, 1995; Robertson, Cohen, & Mayer-Kress, 1993; Thelen & Smith, 1994; van Gelder, 1995, 1998). The dynamicists espoused what they characterized as a diametrically opposed view, which elevated time to be the single most important constraint on good cognitive models. In doing so, they embraced a different formal theory, dynamic systems theory, which is a branch of mathematics that describes time-varying behavior using sets of differential equations.

Often explicitly, the dynamicist movement was a theoretical transition back to the methods and commitments of the cyberneticists. Perhaps reflective of the cyberneticist relation to behaviorism, dynamicists tend to reject both computation and representation (Port & van Gelder, 1995; Thelen & Smith, 1994),[5] despite the fact that cyberneticists had remained largely silent on this point. As well, this concern with representation and computation may have seemed more pressing as a result of the dynamicist discontent with the symbolicist paradigm. In any case, it should be clear that the rejection of computation and representation does not follow

from the adoption of dynamic systems theory as a formal means of describing their models. So it may not be surprising that the antirepresentationalist stance of dynamicists is generally considered a poorly motivated aspect of dynamicism (Bechtel, 1998; Eliasmith, 2003).[6]

There have been a number of other concerns expressed with the dynamicist approach, including the following (Eliasmith, 1996, 2000, 2001):

1. The lumped parameters (i.e., parameters that somehow summarize the underlying neural complexity) and variables in the differential equations used by dynamicists are generally not mapped to physical states of the system (except inputs and outputs). As a result, it is difficult to gain independent empirical support for the models (e.g., there is no role for or relation to neural data).

2. The exemplar dynamical system, the Watt governor (van Gelder, 1995), is a typical classical control system. This means that the espoused methods are classical input-output analyses, which do not account for considerations of multiple inputs and outputs, noise, multiple loops, optimality, and so on.

3. From the preceding concern, another arises that dynamicism will have all of the same problems that behaviorism has had (e.g., difficulties explaining cognitive behaviors not obviously linked to input states; difficulties explaining recursive processing). This concern is strengthened by the dynamicist rejection of internal representation.

4. Dynamicists restrict themselves to low-dimensional dynamical systems (in an attempt to distinguish their models from connectionist ones; van Gelder, 1998).[7] This greatly reduces the flexibility of the system and opens the possibility that certain natural behaviors will fall outside of the dynamicist approach.

Perhaps the most important of these limitations for this discussion is expressed by the first concern. Ironically, from that concern it follows that there is no explicit link between dynamicist models and the temporal constraints imposed on real cognitive systems. This is because those temporal constraints are most obvious, and best understood, at the level of single neurons and small networks of neurons. Because there is no mapping between dynamicist model parameters and the physical substrate that these models are trying to explain, it is unclear to what extent the time in the models reflects the time in the real system. So, although dynamicists have inherently included time in their models, it is unclear whether it is the correct, biologically relevant (i.e., real) time. Because there is no commitment to an explicit mapping between model time and real time, it is up to each individual modeler to choose some mapping or other that will result in the appropriate outputs. This difficulty, of course, is reminiscent of the massive slippage between cognitive model and cognitive system that plagued the symbolicists. So, similarly, this degree of arbitrariness is damaging to the dynamicists' claim that they are trying to understand "cognitive phenomena, like so many other kinds of phenomena in the natural world" (Port & van Gelder, 1995, p. 6), given that they have provided no systematic relation between time in their explanations and real, natural, cognitive time.

As a result of the variety of difficulties mentioned previously, dynamicism, as a cognitive paradigm, has become somewhat marginalized in cognitive science. Nevertheless, dynamicism has left a valuable legacy of researchers no longer being able to simply ignore temporal constraints or assume that those constraints will somehow be taken care of after the fact.

2.4. Connectionism in Time

The place of time in connectionist modeling is much more complicated than for either symbolicism or dynamicism. This is largely because the label "connectionism" applies to a wide variety of modeling assumptions. In general, a model is considered connectionist if it consists of simple computational units (nodes) connected together in large, usually parallel, networks. The units produce a numerical output based on weighted numerical input from the other nodes to which they are connected. The interpretations of such models have ranged widely, both in terms of what each unit represents and in terms of the kinds of network topologies that are relevant for understanding the mind. The models range from atemporal localist models (e.g., Thagard, 1992), in which each node represents the strength of a concept or sentence, to atemporal distributed models (Elman, 1991), in which concepts are represented by the activity of several nodes combined, to (usually distributed) models whose dynamics are of central interest (Lockery, Fang, & Sejnowski, 1990). However, it is fair to say that the core of connectionism, represented by the best-known connectionist models, is atemporal (Gorman & Sejnowski, 1988; Rumelhart & McClelland, 1986; Sejnowski & Rosenberg, 1986). As a result, the case can be made that the spirit of connectionism is not essentially dynamical. This captures at least one concern of the dynamicists regarding the connectionist approach to understanding the mind (Port & van Gelder, 1995).

Nevertheless, the contrary case can be made as well, albeit for a subset of connectionist models: distributed recurrent networks. The timing of such networks is, as in any dynamical system, integral to the equations describing the system. Connectionists constructing such models do not need to contrive to include time in a model of cognition, as symbolicists do. Rather, such network models naturally incorporate time constraints. Hence, Churchland and Sejnowski (1992) claim: "A theme that will be sounded and resounded throughout this book concerns time and the necessity for network models to reflect the fundamental and essential temporal nature of actual nervous systems" (Churchland & Sejnowski, 1992, p. 117). I take this to be a supremely dynamicist sentiment.

As a result, some connectionist models clearly have the potential to be inherently temporal. A connectionist network can be, after all, "a dynamical system, meaning its inputs and internal states are varying with time; it is basically engaged in spatiotemporal vector coding and time-dependent matrix transformations" (Churchland & Sejnowski, 1992, p. 338). The main difficulty for connectionists is not whether they can include time but whether they can do so in a way that can be informative of the systems being studied. To better understand this challenge, consider the vast literature on attractor networks (see, e.g., Plaut & McClelland, 1993). Attractor networks are recurrent networks that, as their name suggests, evolve over time to exploit the existence of state space attractors (i.e., points or sets of points that are dynamically stable). However, the particular length of time it takes a connectionist attractor network to settle is seldom related to the time constraints imposed on real nervous systems. Rather, it is determined by how big the time step that is chosen by the modeler happens to be (where a time step is the length of time it takes to complete one stage in the recurrent processing). As a result, such networks are essentially temporal, but that temporality is not linked to real organisms (i.e., it is not linked to real time). This, of course, is the same problem that, as I have already argued, plagues dynamicists and symbolicists: how should model time and real time be systematically linked? Nevertheless, attractor networks are a useful advance over completely atemporal connectionist networks.

It is important to note that there is another subset of connectionist models that are directly constrained by observed temporal properties of organisms. These are the so-called low-level connectionist models, where the nodes are mapped one-to-one onto real neurons. However, these kinds of low-level models are considered distinct enough from core connectionism that there arc unique conferences (e.g., Computational Neuroscience [CNS], Computational and Systems Neuroscience [COSYNE]) and journals (e.g., *Journal of Computational Neuroscience, Biological Cybernetics*) that focus on these far more biologically plausible networks. Most researchers in this domain refer to themselves as computational neuroscientists or theoretical neuroscientists and consider what they do quite distinct from artificial neural networks or connectionism (although the historical and theoretical relations are clear). It is in these biologically plausible models where real-world dynamics become an inescapable feature of the models. It is here that there is a systematic relation between model time and real time. In particular, the empirically measurable time constants, voltage and current rate changes, and so on, of real neurons are explicitly included in the models. So, as modelers begin to map computational units in their model networks onto computational units in biological systems (i.e., neurons), and as these model units resemble the biological units more and more, dynamics, especially the particular dynamics of natural systems, become crucial for explaining network behavior. This is hardly surprising because these modelers are now directly addressing the same phenomena that gave rise to the dynamics-laden vocabulary of neuroscientists. One way to characterize this important and unique step in understanding cognitive systems is to realize that temporal assumptions regarding the model parameters are independently testable assumptions. That is, neuroscientists can go to the system being described and measure those parameters directly. This is not true for firing times of productions, time courses of lumped parameters, or time steps in recurrent networks.

Unfortunately, a new problem arises for these biologically plausible networks. If this biological connectionism, like dynamicism and symbolicism, is to be a paradigm for understanding cognitive systems, it is essential to describe how these low-level biological models relate to high-level cognition. Simply including the dynamics of neurons does not explain how or why those dynamics give rise to complex, higher-level cognitive dynamics. In general, it is fair to say that the extent to which most such models have included real time is proportional to the extent to which they are noncognitive. What is missing is a systematic method for growing extremely complex dynamical models from these well-grounded beginnings.

2.5. *Dynamic Difficulties*

Given the preceding discussion, it seems that the history of cognitive science teaches us three main lessons about dynamics. The first, noted most effectively by the dynamicists, is that cognitive systems are organisms embedded in natural environments to which they are dynamically coupled. As a result, it is highly unlikely that addressing the organism's cognitive behaviors independently of temporal constraints on those behaviors will result in explanatorily fruitful theories.

The second lesson is that model time and real time must be systematically related. It is one thing to write down a differential equation over the variable t, but it is another thing to say how that t relates to the real t observed by experimentalists. Because the mapping between nodes for connectionists, or parameters for dynamicists, and the underlying neural implementation is not systematized by either paradigm, it is a mistake to suppose that time will somehow take care of itself. Despite the switch in formal theories, this problem is closely related to the mistaken assumption of symbolicists that time is somehow independent of function. The difference is that for dynamicists and connectionists the independence is more subtle. Although they include time variables in their models, the lack of an explicit relation between model components and the physical system being modeled means that it may well not be the right time.

The third and final lesson is that, even once an explicit mapping has been made between model time and organism time, more work must be done to understand truly cognitive dynamics. This is simply a consequence of the fact that typically cognitive phenomena are the result of complex interactions between millions, if not billions, of neurons. Although an explicit, systematic relation between models and physical implementation may exist at the neuron level, to make such models cognitive requires methods for growing this mapping to an appropriate level of complexity.

In the remainder of this chapter, I describe a framework that shows how to resolve these remaining difficulties (see also Eliasmith, 2003).

3. Dynamics and the Neural Engineering Framework

The neural engineering framework (NEF) is a general theory of neurobiological systems proposed in Eliasmith and Anderson (2003). The theory consists of three quantified principles that characterize neural representation, computation, and dynamics. In this discussion, I focus on the third principle. It is stated in Eliasmith and Anderson (2003) as follows: "Neural dynamics are characterized by considering neural representations as control theoretic state variables. Thus, the dynamics of neurobiological systems can be analyzed using control theory" (p. 15).

Although succinct, this principle makes plain how the difficulties faced by symbolicism, connectionism, and dynamicism are addressed. In short, the systematic mapping between model time and real time is accomplished in virtue of the fact that the representations whose dynamics are expressed by control theoretic equations are precisely neural representations. This means that the various time constants of single neurons are mapped onto appropriate time constants in model neurons. In other words, there is a one-to-one mapping between model neurons and modeled neurons, just as for the computational neuroscientific subset of connectionism. However, the NEF goes beyond standard computational neuroscience methods by providing an additional suggestion for how to write modern control theoretic equations over these neural representations.

Because control theoretic equations simply are sets of differential equations, as in dynamicism, the NEF essentially integrates the biological connectionist view with the dynamicist view of cognitive systems. The benefit is that, unlike dynamicism, the NEF sets up a systematic mapping between model time and organism time, and unlike standard computational neuroscience, the NEF explicitly describes the relation between neuron activity and higher-level variables of the system. So, the NEF simultaneously suggests a method for building toward cognitive dynamics and remains responsible to single-cell dynamics.

In addition, the kind of control theory adopted by the NEF, modern control theory, suffers none of the limitations of the tools used by the cyberneticists. As suggested by the dynamics principle of the NEF, modern control theory considers the internal states of the system (i.e., the state variables) to understand the dynamics of the system's output given its input. As well, modern control theory provides for the analysis of multiple input–multiple output systems and multiple-loop systems, and incorporates noise, optimality constraints, and adaptive control. In short, modern control theory is an excellent formalism for analyzing and synthesizing real-world physical systems – including the brain.

To better understand how this principle, and modern control theory, is applied in the NEF, let us consider a simple example. One of the most basic and central properties of recurrent networks is their ability to extend network time constants far beyond the time constants of the individual cells that constitute the network (time constants, here, measure how long a signal takes to decay). So, for instance, if we expose a single cell to a brief pulse (e.g., 1 ms) of input current, there will be a more slowly decaying current in its cell body (e.g., that lasts, say, 5 ms). Although this intrinsic current will outlast the length of the actual input, in general it does not last much longer. However, if we take an ensemble of such cells and connect them appropriately, we can cause a similar injection of current to the population of neurons to be effectively sustained over a very long period of time (e.g., 10 s).

This property can be extremely computationally useful. For instance, it can cause a population of neurons to act like a memory, encoding information about an event that occurred in the past. As well, it can be

used to accumulate information over time, tracking long-term changes. More generally, such a network acts as one of the basic temporal transfer functions, integration. Integration is so important for understanding dynamical systems, that it is the basic transfer function for modern control theory. The ubiquity of recurrent connections in the brain, coupled with the ease of building integrators with recurrent networks, and the importance of integrators for implementing a wide variety of dynamical behaviors suggests that neural integration may be a fundamental neural function. Indeed, the integrator has been used in models of a wide variety of neural systems, including working memory (Miller, Brody, Romo, & Wang, 2003), head-direction tracking (Zhang, 1996), eye-position control (Seung, 1996), the vestibular-ocular reflex (Eliasmith, Westover, & Anderson, 2002), and allocentric position tracking in an environment (Conklin & Eliasmith, 2005).

Characterizing the precise relation between integration and any one of these specific models would take us too far afield, so let us consider a generic neural integrator. That is, let us assume that we wish to build a neural circuit that has the properties described previously: a circuit whose network time constant far exceeds the time constants of any of the constituents. Employing the NEF, we first take the computational units in our model to be single neurons whose temporal properties are matched to those of the neural system we are studying. This gives rise to a variety of single-cell models whose distribution of input-response functions reflects the experimentally observed distribution in the relevant part of the brain.[8] These constitute the computational elements of the model, and their dynamics are assumed to be carefully matched to the dynamics of the neural system.

Second, it is generally observed in the brain that many different cells carry information about a given set of internal or external states. As a result, we must determine how the cells in our circuit relate to the states of interest to them. Again, this information can be gathered experimentally. This is a typical step in single-cell physiology experiments, when neuroscientists construct what they often term "tuning curves." These curves determine which activity states of neurons carry information about which states of the world (e.g., a neuron in the nucleus prepositus hypoglossi is said to carry information about eye position as reflected by its tuning curve, which is a monotonically increasing firing rate as a function of eye position).[9] It is the population-wide neural representation of those states of the world that are considered state variables in our control theoretic description of the behavior of the circuit.

Third, we must express the dynamics of the circuit in control theoretic terms. Simply put, this means writing a set of differential equations that describe the overall circuit dynamics in terms of the state variables. In the case of a single variable neural integrator, we can write the integration as $x(t) = \int u(t)dt$, where x is the state variable, and u is the input to the circuit. As a simple control structure, this can be written as $\dot{x} = \frac{dx}{dt} = Ax(t) + Bu(t)$, where $A = 0$ and $B = 1$. However, because neurons have intrinsic dynamics dictated by their particular physical characteristics, we must adapt this standard control structure to a neurally relevant one. Fortunately, this can be done in the general case (Eliasmith & Anderson, 2003).

Finally, we must use our characterization of single-cell representation and circuit dynamics to determine the connection weights between neurons that exploit the single-cell properties to realize the defined control structure. The details of the analytical methods to determine the weights are found in Eliasmith and Anderson (2003). It is also demonstrated there that the preceding steps can be carried out in the general case; that is, for linear or nonlinear control structures, and for scalars, vectors, functions, or any combination of these under noise (for examples of each of these cases, see Eliasmith, 2005b). There is no reason to suppose that this degree of generality will, in any way, be limiting to constructing models of cognitive systems.

Even in the simple integrator circuit, we can see how the difficulties faced by past methods are resolved. First, the dynamics of natural systems are mapped directly onto the dynamics of constituents of the circuit. This solves the problem faced by both dynamicists and connectionists regarding adopting natural, realistic dynamic constraints in their models. Second, the description of our model necessarily includes time, as it is written as a set of differential equations. Third, unlike computational neuroscientists, we have an explicit method for relating the activities of individual cells in the circuit to higher-level behaviors of the group of cells (e.g., integration in this case). This simple circuit, of course, does not demonstrate that the method will help build traditionally cognitive models. For this reason, in the next section I briefly present an application of the NEF to a more typical cognitive phenomenon.

4. From Neurons to Cognition

Fodor and Pylyshyn (1988), and more recently Jackendoff (2002), have suggested that neurally plausible architectures do not naturally support structure-sensitive computation, and that such computation is essential for explaining cognition. Notably, Fodor and Pylyshyn (1988) in particular have further argued that, to the extent such architectures could be forced into performing this kind of computation, they would turn out to be merely implementations of symbolicist cognitive systems. For the purposes of this section, I accept that structure-sensitive processing is fundamental to understanding cognition but show how neurally plausible architectures can support such processing in a nonsymbolicist way. The specific model I present captures the context-sensitive linguistic inference exhibited by human subjects in the Wason card task (Wason, 1966). To do so, the model employs biologically realistic neurons to learn the relevant structural transformations appropriate for a given context, and it generalizes such transformations to novel contents with the same syntactic structure. Given the salient properties of the model, I refer to it as BioSLIE (BIOlogically plausible Structure-sensitive Learning Inference Engine).

In the Wason task, subjects are given a conditional rule of the form, "If P, then Q." They are then shown four cards. Each card expresses the satisfaction (or not) of condition P on one side and the satisfaction (or not) of condition Q on the other. The four visible card faces show representations of P, Q, not-P, and not-Q. Subjects are instructed to select all cards, which must be turned over to determine whether the conditional rule is true. A vast majority of subjects (greater than 90 percent) do not give the logically correct response (i.e., P and not-Q). Instead, the most common answer is to select the P and Q cards, or just the P card (Oaksford & Chater, 1994). However, it became apparent that performance on the task could be greatly facilitated by changing the content of the task to be more realistic or thematic, often by making the rule a permissive one (e.g., "If someone is drinking alcohol, then that person is over twenty-one"; Sperber, Cara, & Girotto, 1995). To distinguish these two versions of the task, I refer to them as the abstract and permissive versions of the task, respectively. Human performance on the Wason task is an ideal target for providing a neural model of cognition because it is considered a phenomenon that can be explained only by invoking structure-sensitive processing. As a result, the task allows BioSLIE to demonstrate its ability to generalize across structures – that is, to be systematic – an ability that many, including Fodor, Pylyshyn, and Jackendoff, take to be a hallmark of cognitive systems.

The model takes advantage of the NEF, recent advances in structured vector representations, and relevant physiological and anatomical data from frontal cortices. Since the early 1990s, there has been a series of suggestions as to how to incorporate structure-sensitive processing in models employing distributed, vector representations (including spatter codes, Kanerva, 1994; holographic reduced representations [HRRs], Plate, 1991;

and tensor products, Smolensky, 1990). Few of these approaches have been used to build models of cognitive phenomena (but see Eliasmith & Thagard, 2001). However, none of these methods has been employed in a biologically plausible computational setting. Fortunately, the NEF can be employed to implement the necessary nonlinear vector computations demanded by these solutions.

In particular, BioSLIE employs one-hundred-dimensional HRR vectors to encode linguistic structure. The details of implementing HRRs using the NEF can be found elsewhere (Eliasmith, 2004). In short, we can construct rules, like those needed to understand the Wason task, using vector multiplication and addition in a biologically plausible network. So, for instance, the rule "If a, then b," or Implies(a,b), can be encoded into a single vector:

$$R = relation \otimes implies \\ + antecedent \otimes a + consequent \otimes b,$$

where each variable in this equation is a one-hundred-dimensional vector, and each such vector is represented by neural spiking. It is here, in constructing our representation R in this manner, that we avoid merely implementing a symbolist system. This is because this representational format, being a compressed vector representation, does not explicitly include the constituents of the representation R in the representation itself. As a result, the representation is noncompositional, violating a basic constraint that Fodor and Pylyshyn (1988) place on symbolist cognitive systems (for further discussion, see Eliasmith, 2005a). Notably, the resultant representation, R, can be transformed in various ways to provide information about the contents of that vector representation. In particular, R can be transformed to report any of the constituents of the representation or transformations of those constituents as demanded by a given task. It is precisely such transformations that the system must learn in performing the Wason task. In short, BioSLIE must learn how to transform R in different

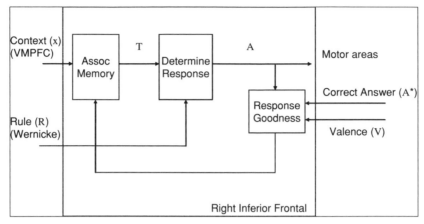

Figure 8.1. Functional decomposition and anatomical mapping of the model. The single letters indicate the vector signals in the model associated with the area.

contexts (i.e., the permissive and abstract contexts) to return the appropriate elements of the structure (e.g., a and not-b in the permissive case, and a and b in the abstract case).

Of course, to use this characterization of structure-sensitive processing in an explanatorily useful model, it is essential to suggest which anatomical structures may be performing the relevant functions. Only then is it possible to bring to bear the additional constraints of (and make predictions relating to) single-cell physiology and functional imaging data. Figure 8.1 shows how BioSLIE is mapped to functional anatomy. Specifically, the network consists of (a) input from ventromedial prefrontal cortex (VMPFC), which provides familiarity, or context, information that is used to select the appropriate transformation (Adolphs, Bechara, Tranel, Damasio, & Damasio, 1995), (b) left language areas, which provide representations of the rule to be examined (Parsons, Osherson, & Martinez, 1999), and (c) the anterior cingulate cortex (ACC), which gives an error signal consisting of either the correct answer or an indication that the response was correct or not (Holroyd & Coles, 2002). The neural populations that make up BioSLIE itself model the right inferior frontal cortex, where VMPFC and linguistic information is combined to select

and apply the appropriate transformation to solve the Wason task (Parsons & Osherson, 2001). It is during the application of the transformation that learning is also presumed to occur in an associative memory. Given this mapping to anatomy, we can appeal to work in frontal cortices that have characterized the kinds of tuning curves pyramidal cells in these areas display.

To perform the needed HRR vector operations, learning, and so on, BioSLIE further decomposes this high-level functional mapping into neural subsystems responsible for these tasks. The resulting set of subnetworks is shown in Figure 8.2, which is a model that consists of ten interconnected neural populations, for a total of approximately seventeen thousand neurons.

When run, the model is able to reproduce the typical results from the Wason task under both the abstract and permissive contexts (not shown). Simply put, this means that the model is taught and successfully reproduces the transformation, "If a then b → {b, a}" in the abstract context and the transformation "If a then b → {~b, a}" in the permissive context. So, when the context signal is switched, the model applies a different transformation, as expected. The point of mentioning these results is simply to emphasize that this is done using biologically plausible neurons in a complex neural

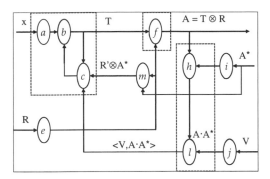

Figure 8.2. The complete network at the population level. The lowercase letters indicate populations of approximately two thousand neurons each. Uppercase letters indicate the signals being sent along the relevant projections. The dotted boxes indicate how this diagram relates to the functional decomposition of Figure 8.1, and hence the anatomical mapping discussed earlier.

network, not by having a computer perform these logical transformations directly. And, although simple, this model does show rudimentary structural transformations. This, however, is not enough to support the claim that the model is structure sensitive. The obvious concern is that the model is simply "memorizing" a mapping it has seen (i.e., it is constructing a lookup table). If this were true, the model would not truly be generalizing over the appropriate syntactic structures, as demanded by systematicity.

To demonstrate that the network is truly learning a languagelike transformation in a context, Figure 8.3 shows that it does in fact generalize learned, structure-sensitive transformations to unfamiliar contents (i.e., "If someone votes, then that person is over eighteen") in a familiar context (i.e., the permissive context). This demonstrates that the system has learned a systematic syntactic regularity. That is, it can transform novel structured representations based solely on the syntax of the representation.

Let us consider Figure 8.3 in more detail. In the simulation the permissive context signal is kept constant and there are three separate rules that are presented to BioSLIE. While learning is on, the rules Implies (drinking-alcohol, over-21) and Implies

(driving, over-16) along with their expected answers are presented to the network. The learning is then turned off, and it is presented with the novel rule Implies(voting, over-18). Notably, because the context is the same in the novel case as in the previous examples, the same transformation should be applied. Indeed, BioSLIE infers that "voting" and "not-over-18" are the expected answers (i.e., the cards that need to be checked to ensure the rule is not violated). In the last quarter of the simulation, no rule is presented and thus no answer is produced (i.e., all similarity measures are very low).

Figure 8.3 thus demonstrates that Bio-SLIE is systematically processing language-like structures with biologically realistic computational components. As a result, it not only provides an explicit counterexample to Fodor, Pylyshyn, and Jackendoff's claims but also demonstrates how the NEF can relate single-neuron dynamics to the dynamics of cognitive behavior. Admittedly, BioSLIE most directly addresses the issue of how the appropriate representations and transformations for accomplishing cognitive tasks can be understood in a neurally plausible way. It does not directly map onto the observed dynamics of human performance on the Wason task (the model is much faster, though it is appropriately constrained by single-neuron dynamics). This, no doubt, is because far more than the few brain areas modeled by BioSLIE are employed by human subjects to perform the task. Nevertheless, timing constraints on certain aspects of the task can be inferred from BioSLIE's performance (e.g., minimum transformation times). And, more importantly for this discussion, the methods provided are general enough to address a wide variety of cognitive tasks in a way that directly incorporates underlying neurodynamical constraints.

5. Embeddedness and the NEF

To this point I have discussed how the NEF relates low-level neural dynamics with higher-level circuit dynamics, and I have

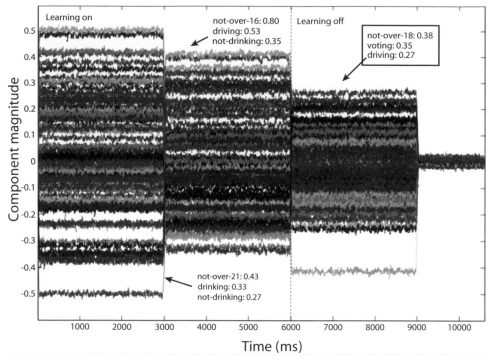

Figure 8.3. Generalization across different rules in the same context. Each line indicates the value of one dimension of the one-hundred-dimensional vector encoded in neural spiking in the *f* population from Figure 8.2. The top three similarity results of each transformation are shown to demonstrate that simple thresholding results in the correct answer. See text for further discussion.

demonstrated that it is possible to build rudimentary cognitive systems using the NEF. Earlier, I briefly touched on the shared inspiration for taking dynamics seriously and for being concerned with the embeddedness, or situatedness, of cognitive agents. Here I want to discuss what, if any, consequences the NEF has for our understanding of cognitive embeddedness.

Note that for some dynamicists, taking dynamics seriously means holding a fairly strong embedded view: "In this vision, the cognitive system is not just the encapsulated brain; rather, since the nervous system, body, and environment are all constantly changing and simultaneously influencing each other, the true cognitive system is a single unified system embracing all three" (van Gelder, 1995, p. 373). For dynamicists, then, a distinction between the sys-

tem and the system's environment becomes very difficult – system boundaries become obscure. Dynamicists often claim that this result is a unique strength of the dynamicist approach and an accurate reflection of the true state of cognitive systems (Port & van Gelder, 1995). Similarly, those focused on the situatedness of cognitive systems have argued that the traditional boundaries between an agent and its environment, provided by the skin, are unreasonably hegemonic and that, instead, "the mind extends into the world" (Clark & Chalmers, 1998/2002, p. 647).

I suspect that such conclusions are misguided, and we can turn to the NEF to see why. As discussed, the NEF adopts modern control theory as a means of specifying dynamics. Control theory, as opposed to dynamic systems theory, has a number of benefits for describing cognitive systems. First, control theory explicitly acknowledges system boundaries, in virtue of identifying state variables with subsystems of the overall system of interest. Second, control theory explicitly introduces the central notion of control and related notions such as controllability. These notions help underwrite distinctions between systems whose dynamics are fixed or otherwise independent of one another. And finally, control theory has its roots in engineering, a discipline concerned with implementational aspects of physical systems, including noise and other component limitations. These concerns contrast with dynamic systems theory, whose roots are in mathematics. This is not to say that either control theory or dynamic systems theory is somehow more mathematically powerful, but rather it is to point out that the methods have different emphases, one of which is more appropriate for understanding physically realized, natural cognitive systems.

Let us consider each of the first two benefits in more detail. The importance of acknowledging system boundaries cannot be overstated when pursuing system analysis. Decomposition of complex systems is essential for our understanding of such systems, whether they be biological, ecological, economic, meteorological, or what have you. As Bechtel and Richardson (1993) have argued at length, "a mechanistic explanation identifies these [system] parts and their organization, showing how the behavior of the machine is a consequence of the parts and organization. . . . A major part of developing a mechanistic explanation is simply to determine what the components of a system are and what they do" (pp. 17–18). Blurring, shifting, or removing system boundaries, as dynamicist and embedded agent theorists often advocate, is seriously detrimental to making progress in our explanations of such systems. This is especially true if there are no theoretical principles for determining which shifting or removing of boundaries is justified and which is not. As a result, considering a cognitive system (constituted by brain, body, and world) as

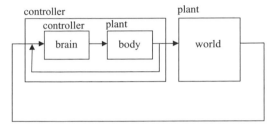

Figure 8.4. Brain, body, and world as controllers and plants. Drawing such system boundaries and making plant-controller distinctions make clear the differences between subsystems and their interactions.

a single unified system is both impractical and uninformative from a scientific point of view – it in no way helps determine what the components are. Notice that advocating the identity of system components does not imply that such decompositions should not be reassembled for explaining certain properties. Rather, it is the observation that to explain a large, complex system requires identification and explanation of both its subsystems and their interactions. And, to do that, those subsystems must themselves be identified and well understood.

This leads naturally to the second point: that the introduction of the notion of control helps to categorize different kinds of subsystems. A typical dynamical system in control theory consists of a plant and a controller. The plant is a physical system whose inputs we would like to change to result in particular outputs from that system. The controller plays the role of producing the necessary inputs to result in those particular outputs. This basic distinction is one that helps us understand the different roles brain, body, and world play in an overall explanation of a behaving agent in an environment. With this distinction, we can see what is special about the brain. We have fairly good physical theories that can be used to explain the kinetics and dynamics of bodies and of the world. However, we have little idea how to understand the more complex dynamics found in the brain. As a result, it is natural to consider the brain as the controller of the body as a plant, together acting as controller for the environment as a plant (see Figure 8.4).

Our goal in understanding a cognitive system is to elucidate the qualitatively different dynamics internal to the brain. The most obvious differences are the speed of information flow (i.e., bandwidth), and the degree and kind of coupling. Because bodies have mass, they tend to slow down the transfer of information to the world from the brain (i.e., they effectively act as a low-pass filter). However, no such impediment to information flow exists between brain areas. This results in a huge difference between the kinds of coupling that can be supported between brain subsystems and between the brain and the external environment. In short, interactions with the environment are slower than intrabrain interactions. I find it rather ironic, or perhaps surprising, that researchers who embrace the importance of dynamics for understanding cognitive function, and who argue that differences in dynamics are cognitive differences (when confronting symbolicists; van Gelder, 1998, p. 622), then suppose that differences in dynamics between brain-brain and brain-world interactions can be overlooked when arguing for embeddedness (Clark & Chalmers, 1998/2002, p. 648; van Gelder, 1995, p. 373). I think it is much better to consistently claim that differences in dynamics often result in distinct properties and behaviors. If we adopt that view, it becomes clear that the suggestion that "nothing [other than the presence of skin] seems different" between brain-brain and brain-world interactions (Clark & Chalmers, 1998/2002, p. 644) is plainly false.

I should note that I do not want to suggest that determining the appropriate system boundaries will be an easy task (nor that it stops at the skin). Indeed, it is unclear whether we will be able to identify general, consistent principles for identifying system boundaries. Nevertheless, it is essential to realize that this is a task worth pursuing, and that simply blurring systems over boundaries, or suggesting that such boundaries do not really exist, is bad for both practical (i.e., trying to do science) and theoretical (i.e., appropriate conceptual application) reasons.

6. Dynamics + Control = Cognition

It is important to take the critical considerations of this chapter in their appropriate context. Although I have expressed serious concerns with both dynamicism and embedded approaches to understanding cognitive systems, it should be clear that the positive view I have espoused is highly sensitive to the concerns that gave rise to these positions. The NEF undeniably draws inspiration from dynamicism, as it includes at its core an acknowledgment of the importance of time for understanding natural cognitive systems. Although the NEF rejects the non-computationalism and antirepresentationalism of dynamicism, it does so in a way that is consistent with dynamicist arguments against the symbolicist treatment of time.

As well, the fundamental insights of those interested in the embeddedness of cognitive systems is not lost in the NEF. Characterizing the brain as a control system means understanding the dynamics of its inputs and its coupling to the environment. However, I have suggested that this can be done in such a way that traditional distinctions among brain, body, and world are preserved. In other words, consideration of ecological (i.e., real) operating environments is imperative for trying to comprehensively understand a dynamical system interacting with that environment. This is true regardless of how that system might be broken into subsystems. In fact, there are good reasons, even dynamical reasons, for performing a decomposition consistent with traditional boundaries. It is evidently a mistake, then, to rule out decomposition merely because of dynamic coupling. Unfortunately, this seems to have been the tendency of those espousing the embodied, embedded, and extended views of cognition.

In summary, the intent of the NEF is to provide a suggestion as to how we might take seriously many of the important insights generated from cognitive science: insights from symbolicists, dynamicists, and connectionists. I have argued that it embraces realistic neural dynamics, can help us understand high-level cognition, and is consistent with traditional boundaries among brain, body, and world. I suspect it is far from a complete theory, but perhaps it is a useful start.

Notes

1   Of course, much of the groundwork was laid before this. But even as late as 1906, there was still public debate (at the Nobel Prize awards ceremony) regarding the existence of individual nerve cells. As well, intracellular recording techniques were not developed until the 1940s, and basic single-cell ion dynamics were not characterized until the 1950s. For an extended account of the early history of neurobiology, see Finger (2000).

2   Although it should be noted that some symbolicists also seem to have been sensitive to the importance of this interaction, "[a] proper understanding of the intimate interdependence between an adaptive organism and its environment is essential to a clear view of what a science of an adaptive species can be like" (Newell & Simon, 1972, p. 870).

3   This is just the observation that change is often an important environmental cue. Thus, visual features such as motion are often used to orient an animal toward potentially interesting or dangerous aspects of its environment.

4   Neither Skinner nor Watson, for instance, makes special mention of dynamics. However, Hull (1935), in his quest to write Newtonian-like laws for behavior, seems somewhat concerned with the effects of interstimulus delays during learning. However, none of the equations he explicitly writes have a time parameter.

5   Van Gelder (1995) is quite explicit in his rejection of representation, noting that "the notion of representation is just the wrong sort of conceptual tool to apply" (p. 353) in describing dynamical systems. Similarly, Port and van Gelder (1995) state that cognitive systems are not best understood as the result of computing over representations: "a cognitive system is not a discrete sequential manipulation of static representational structures" (p. 3).

6   In fact, more recent work by van Gelder (1999) and others also begins to backpedal on the earlier stricture against representa-

tion: "Dynamical models usually also incorporate representations, but reconceive them as dynamical entities (e.g., system states, or trajectories shaped by attractor landscapes). Representations tend to be seen as transient, context dependent stabilities in the midst of change, rather than as static, context-free, permanent units" (p. 244). Nevertheless, the original nonrepresentational ideal remains: "Interestingly, some dynamicists claim to have developed wholly representation free models, and they conjecture that representation will turn out to play much less of a role in cognition than has traditionally been supposed" (ibid.).

7   For instance, van Gelder (1998) states: "Another noteworthy fact about these models is that the variables they posit are not low-level (e.g., neural firing rates), but rather macroscopic quantities at roughly the level of the cognitive performance itself" (p. 619). Similarly, Port and van Gelder (1995) note that the purpose of a dynamicist model is to "provide a *low-dimensional* model that provides a scientifically tractable description of the same qualitative dynamics as is exhibited by the high-dimensional system (the brain)" (p. 28).

8   Input response functions are a plot of the input current versus the resultant firing rate. This is like an input-output response function for a cell. More precisely, these curves have a temporal dimension as well, given dynamic single-cell effects like adaptation. For simplicity, this will be ignored in the present example.

9   Again, this is a simplification, as many neurons carry information about internal states or act largely in a control capacity. This simplification serves a pedagogical purpose and does not speak to a limitation in the generality of the NEF.

References

Abraham, F. D., Abraham, R., & Shaw, C. D. (1991). *A visual introduction to dynamical systems for psychology.* Santa Cruz, CA: Aerial Press.

Adolphs, R., Bechara, A., Tranel, D., Damasio, H., & Damasio, A. R. (1995). Neuropsychological approaches to reasoning and decision-making. In A. R. Damasio, H. Damasio, &

Y. Christen (Eds.), *Neurobiology of decision-making* (pp. 157–80). New York: Springer-Verlag.

Ballard, D. H. (1991). Animate vision. *Artificial Intelligence, 48,* 57–86.

Bechtel, W. (1998). Representations and cognitive explanations: Assessing the dynamicist challenge in cognitive science. *Cognitive Science, 22,* 295–318.

Bechtel, W., & Graham, G. (Eds.). (1999). *A companion to cognitive science.* London: Blackwell.

Bechtel, W., & Richardson, R. C. (1993). *Discovering complexity: Decomposition and localization as strategies in scientific research.* Princeton, NJ: Princeton University Press.

Busemeyer, J. R., & Townsend, J. T. (1993). Decision field theory: A dynamic-cognitive approach to decision making in an uncertain environment. *Psychological Review, 100*(3), 432–459.

Churchland, P. S., & Sejnowski, T. (1992). *The computational brain.* Cambridge, MA: MIT Press.

Clark, A., & Chalmers, D. (2002). The extended mind. In D. Chalmers (Ed.), *Philosophy of mind: Classical and contemporary readings* (pp. 643–652). New York: Oxford University Press. (Reprinted from *Analysis, 58,* 10–23.)

Conklin, J., & Eliasmith, C. (2005). An attractor network model of path integration in the rat. *Journal of Computational Neuroscience, 18,* 183–203.

Eliasmith, C. (1996). The third contender: A critical examination of the dynamicist theory of cognition. *Philosophical Psychology, 9*(4), 441–463.

Eliasmith, C. (2000). Is the brain analog or digital? The solution and its consequences for cognitive science. *Cognitive Science Quarterly, 1*(2), 147–170.

Eliasmith, C. (2001). Attractive and in-discrete: A critique of two putative virtues of the dynamicist theory of mind. *Minds and Machines, 11,* 417–426.

Eliasmith, C. (2003). Moving beyond metaphors: Understanding the mind for what it is. *Journal of Philosophy, 100*(10), 493–520.

Eliasmith, C. (2004). Learning context sensitive logical inference in a neurobiological simulation. In S. Levy & R. Gayler (Eds.), *AAAI Fall Symposium: Compositional Connectionism in Cognitive Science* (pp. 17–20). Menlo Park, CA: Association for the Advancement of Artificial Intelligence Press.

Eliasmith, C. (2005a). Cognition with neurons: A large-scale, biologically realistic model of the Wason task. In G. Bara, L. Barsalou, & M. Bucciarelli (Eds.), *Proceedings of the 27th Annual Meeting of the Cognitive Science Society.* Mahwah, NJ: Lawrence Erlbaum.

Eliasmith, C. (2005b). A unified approach to building and controlling spiking attractor networks. *Neural Computation, 17*(6), 1276–1314.

Eliasmith, C., & Anderson, C. H. (2003). *Neural engineering: Computation, representation and dynamics in neurobiological systems.* Cambridge, MA: MIT Press.

Eliasmith, C., & Thagard, P. (2001). Integrating structure and meaning: A distributed model of analogical mapping. *Cognitive Science, 25*(2), 245–286.

Eliasmith, C., Westover, M. B., & Anderson, C. H. (2002). A general framework for neurobiological modeling: An application to the vestibular system. *Neurocomputing, 46,* 1071–1076.

Elman, J. L. (1991). Distributed representations, simple recurrent networks, and grammatical structure. In D. Touretzky (Ed.), *Connectionist approaches to language learning* (pp. 91–122). Dordrecht, The Netherlands: Kluwer.

Finger, S. (2000). *The minds behind the brain: A history of the pioneers and their discoveries.* Oxford: Oxford University Press.

Fodor, J., & Pylyshyn, Z. (1988). Connectionism and cognitive architecture: A critical analysis. *Cognition, 28,* 3–71.

Freudenthal, H. (1970–1990). Norbert Weiner. In C. C. Gillespie (Ed.), *Dictionary of scientific biography.* New York: Scribner's.

Gibson, J. J. (1966). *The senses considered as perceptual systems.* Boston: Houghton Mifflin.

Gibson, J. J., & Gibson, E. J. (1955). Perceptual learning: Differentiation or enrichment? *Psychological Review, 62,* 324–341.

Gorman, R. P., & Sejnowski, T. J. (1988). Analysis of hidden units in a layered network trained to classify sonar targets. *Neural Networks, 1,* 75–89.

Hodgkin, A. L., & Huxley, A. F. (1952). A quantitative description of membrane current and its application to conduction and excitation in nerve. *Journal of Physiology, 117,* 500–544.

Holroyd, C., & Coles, M. (2002). The neural basis of human error processing: Reinforcement learning, dopamine, and the error-related negativity. *Psychological Review, 109,* 679–709.

Hubel, D., & Wiesel, T. (1962). Receptive fields, binocular interaction and functional architecture in the cat's visual cortex. *Journal of Physiology* (London), *160,* 106–154.

Hull, C. (1935). The conflicting psychologies of learning – a way out. *Psychological Review, 42,* 491–516.

Jackendoff, R. (2002). *Foundations of language: Brain, meaning, grammar, evolution.* Oxford: Oxford University Press.

Kanerva, P. (1994). The spatter code for encoding concepts at many levels. In M. Marinaro & P. G. Morasso (Eds.), *Proceedings of the International Conference on Artificial Neural Networks* (Vol. 1, pp. 226–229). Sorrento, Italy: Springer-Verlag.

Lockery, S., Fang, Y., & Sejnowski, T. (1990). A dynamical neural network model of sensorimotor transformation in the leech. *Neural Computation, 2,* 274–282.

Miller, P., Brody, C. D., Romo, R., & Wang, X. J. (2003). A recurrent network model of somatosensory parametric working memory in the prefrontal cortex. *Cerebral Cortex, 13,* 1208–1218.

Mindell, D. (1995). Engineers, psychologists, and administrators: Wartime control systems research, 1941–1945. *IEEE Control Systems Magazine, 15*(4), 91–99.

Newell, A. (1990). *Unified theories of cognition.* Cambridge, MA: Harvard University Press.

Newell, A., & Simon, H. A. (1972). *Human problem solving.* Englewood Cliffs, NJ: Prentice Hall.

Oaksford, M., & Chater, N. (1994). A rational analysis of the selection task as optimal data selection. *Psychological Review, 101*(4), 608–631.

Parsons, L., & Osherson, D. (2001). New evidence for distinct right and left brain systems for deductive versus probabilistic reasoning. *Cerebral Cortex, 11,* 954–965.

Parsons, L., Osherson, D., & Martinez, M. (1999). *Distinct neural mechanisms for propositional logic and probabilistic reasoning.* Paper presented at the 40th Annual Meeting of the Psychonomic Society, Dallas, TX.

Plate, A. (1991). Holographic reduced representations: Convolution algebra for compositional distributed representations. In *Proceedings of the 12th International Joint Conference on Artificial Intelligence* (pp. 30–35). San Francisco, CA: Morgan Kaufmann.

Plaut, D. C., & McClelland, J. L. (1993). Generalization with componential attractors: Word and nonword reading in an attractor network. In *Proceedings of the 15th Annual Conference of the Cognitive Science Society* (pp. 824–829). Hillsdale, NJ: Erlbaum.

Port, R., & van Gelder, T. (Eds.). (1995). *Mind as motion: Explorations in the dynamics of cognition.* Cambridge, MA: MIT Press.

Rieke, F., Warland, D., de Ruyter van Steveninick, R., & Bialek, W. (1997). *Spikes: Exploring the neural code.* Cambridge, MA: MIT Press.

Robertson, S. S., Cohen, A. H., & Mayer-Kress, G. (1993). Behavioural chaos: Beyond the metaphor. In L. B. Smith & E. Thelen (Eds.), *A dynamic systems approach to development: Applications* (pp. 120–150). Cambridge, MA: MIT Press.

Rumelhart, D. E., & McClelland, J. L. (1986). On learning the past tenses of English verbs. In J. L. McClelland & D. E. Rumelhart (Eds.), *Parallel distributed processing: Explorations in the microstructure of cognition* (Vol. 2, pp. 216–271). Cambridge, MA: MIT Press.

Sejnowski, T. J., & Rosenberg, C. R. (1986). Nettalk: A parallel network that learns to read aloud. *Cognitive Science Quarterly, 14,* 179–211.

Seung, H. S. (1996). How the brain keeps the eyes still. In *Proceedings of the National Academy of Science, 93,* 13339–13344.

Smolensky, P. (1990). Tensor product variable binding and the representation of symbolic structures in connectionist systems. *Artificial Intelligence, 46,* 159–217.

Sperber, D., Cara, E., & Girotto, R. (1995). Relevance theory explains the selection task. *Cognition, 57,* 31–95.

Thagard, P. (1992). *Conceptual revolutions.* Princeton, NJ: Princeton University Press.

Thagard, P. (1996). *Mind: Introduction to cognitive science.* Cambridge, MA: MIT Press.

Thelen, E., & Smith, L. B. (1994). *A dynamic systems approach to the development of cognition and action.* Cambridge, MA: MIT Press.

van Gelder, T. (1995). What might cognition be, if not computation? *Journal of Philosophy, 91*(7), 345–381.

van Gelder, T. (1998). The dynamical hypothesis in cognitive science. *Behavioral and Brain Sciences, 21*(5), 615–665.

van Gelder, T. (1999) Dynamic approaches to cognition. In R. Wilson & F. Keil (Eds.), *The MIT encyclopedia of the cognitive sciences* (pp. 244–246). Cambridge, MA: MIT Press.

Wason, P. C. (1966). Reasoning. In B. M. Foss (Ed.), *New horizons in psychology* (pp. 131–151). Harmondsworth, UK: Penguin.

Watson, J. (1913). Psychology as the behaviorist views it. *Psychological Review, 20,* 158–177.

Wiener, N. (1948). *Cybernetics: Or the control and communication in the animal and the machine.* New York: John Wiley.

Wiesel, T. N., & Hubel, D. H. (1963). Effects of visual deprivation on morphology and physiology of cells in the cat's lateral geniculate body. *Journal of Neurophysiology, 26,* 978–993.

Zhang, K. (1996). Representation of spatial orientation by the intrinsic dynamics of the head-direction cell ensemble: A theory. *Journal of Neuroscience, 16,* 2112–2126.

CHAPTER 9

Explanation

Mechanism, Modularity, and Situated Cognition

William Bechtel

The situated cognition movement has emerged in recent decades (although it has roots in psychologists working earlier in the twentieth century including Vygotsky, Bartlett, and Dewey) largely in reaction to an approach to explaining cognition that tended to ignore the context in which cognitive activities typically occur. Fodor's (1980) account of the research strategy of methodological solipsism, according to which only representational states within the mind are viewed as playing causal roles in producing cognitive activity, is an extreme characterization of this approach. (As Keith Gunderson memorably commented when Fodor first presented this characterization, it amounts to reversing behaviorism by construing the mind as a white box in a black world.) Critics as far back as the 1970s and 1980s objected to many experimental paradigms in cognitive psychology as not being ecologically valid; that is, they maintained that the findings applied only to the artificial circumstances created in the laboratory and did not generalize to real-world settings (Neisser, 1976, 1987). The situated cognition movement, however, goes much further than demanding ecologically valid experiments – it insists that an agent's cognitive activities are inherently embedded and supported by dynamic interactions with the agent's body and features of its environment.

Sometimes advocates of a situated approach to cognition present their position in an extreme manner that sets the situated approach in opposition to attempts in cognitive science and cognitive neuroscience to understand the mechanisms within the mind/brain that underlie cognitive performance (Agre, 1995; Beer, 1995; Brooks, 1991; Suchman, 1987, 1993; Thelen & Smith, 1994). Advocates of the extended-mind perspective maintain that cognitive activities (perceiving, reasoning, problem solving, remembering) do not happen just in the head but extend out into the environment. These environmental factors become, in this view, part of the mind (Clark & Chalmers, 1998). Such challenges are sometimes presented as opposing the search for mechanisms inside the head to explain cognitive activity.

My contention is that an appropriate understanding of the situatedness of cognition does not require the denial that the proper locus of control (I will elaborate on this notion, developed in Bechtel & Richardson, 1993, further herein) for cognitive activity is the mind/brain. That is, for mental phenomena it is appropriate to treat the mind/brain as the locus of the responsible mechanism and to emphasize the boundary between the mind/brain and the rest of the body and between the cognitive agent and its environment. The phenomena for which such a strategy is not appropriate are ones in which the agent is so intertwined with entities outside itself that the responsible system includes one or more cognitive agents and their environment. These are prototypically social phenomena, not behavioral or psychological ones. There are explanatory principles that determine when it is appropriate to identify the mind-brain as the locus of control and when it is appropriate to identify a larger system as responsible. I will articulate a view that maintains that for most explanatory challenges addressed by cognitive science, the mind/brain is the appropriate locus of control even for activities that depend critically on how the agent is situated in an environment.

Reconciling the cognitive science project of identifying and describing the operations of mechanisms inside the head with the claims that cognition is situated requires an appropriate understanding of mechanisms. Mechanisms are bounded systems, but ones that are selectively open to their environment and that often interact with and depend on their environment in giving rise to the phenomenon for which they are responsible. Moreover, biological mechanisms operate in the context of active, self-maintaining organisms that are dependent on their environments and, yet are in an important sense autonomous from them. Developing this perspective, however, will require a bit of an excursion through theoretical biology. It will bear fruit as I consider later in the chapter how the mind and its cognitive mechanisms should be considered distinct systems while acting through and depending on the world external to them. Biological mechanisms, including cognitive

mechanisms, it will turn out, are always situated and dependent on their environments as well as in a critical sense distinct from them.

The same theoretical considerations that inform discussion of the situatedness of cognition also provide insight into a related controversial topic in cognitive science – the modularity of cognitive systems. In this case, however, the insights into the nature of mechanisms will lead to rejection of the extreme claims made on behalf of modularity. On the surface, advocates of modularity seem simply to be advancing the same claim as those identifying the mind/brain as the locus of control for mental activity, only this time at a finer level, identifying it not with the whole mind/brain but with a module within it. But this strategy of identifying the locus of control for a mental activity at a finer level in a mental module is, in general, poorly motivated. It fails to consider that explaining the mind/brain's performance of a cognitive task involves decomposing it into component operations, each of which contributes differentially to the performance of the task. Performance of most cognitive tasks requires the orchestrated contribution of many components of the cognitive system, not just one subsystem.

The tension in rejecting modularity and yet treating the mind/brain as the locus of control for cognitive activity should be apparent: modularity is rejected as failing to recognize the diverse components involved in performing a cognitive task, and advocates of situated cognition likewise maintain that many cognitive activities involve components outside the agent itself. Yet it is a consistent position to reject modularity within the mind/brain and yet maintain that the mind/brain is the locus of control for cognitive activities. Showing why this is consistent requires developing in more detail the project of explanation in terms of mechanism. To set the context for that, I will begin by exploring the reasoning that has guided advocates of modularity and contrast that with the mechanistic perspective.

1. Dividing Minds

Dividing the mind/brain into component systems or modules has been a common strategy in both philosophical and psychological theorizing. Plato's tripartite division of the soul into a reasoning, a spirited, and an appetitive element was an early exemplar. Faculty psychology, as developed in the eighteenth century by Christian von Wolff and Thomas Reid, appealed to separate mental faculties responsible for activities such as reasoning, remembering, judging, and willing. At the outset of the nineteenth century Franz Joseph Gall (1812) aligned the division of the mind into faculties with his differentiation of regions in the brain. Gall's characterization of brain regions in terms of cranial protrusions and indentations was problematic, but the project of localizing mental faculties in the brain obtained greater respectability when Paul Broca (1861) proposed the localization of articulate speech in the left prefrontal cortex on the basis of deficits in patients with brain lesions.

The localization projects of the nineteenth century were supplanted in the early twentieth century by more holistic views of the brain and the behaviorist tradition in psychology (both traditions are exemplified in the work of Karl Lashley, 1950). The behaviorist tradition emphasized general learning procedures and hence rejected the quest for discrete psychological mechanisms underlying different behaviors. One of the features of the development of cognitive psychology in the 1950s and beyond was the attempt to identify different mechanisms as responsible for different abilities (consider, for example, the different types of memory stores posited in Atkinson & Shiffrin's 1968 classical memory model, as well as the differentiation of memory systems by Tulving and his collaborators; see Schacter & Tulving, 1994).

In this context the term *module* began to be employed for the mechanisms responsible for different types of processing. The term has been used in a variety of ways

that emphasize more or less separation of the activities associated with modules. Perhaps the most extreme view of the segregation of modules is found in Fodor (1983). He identifies nine characteristics of modules: they (1) are domain specific, (2) are mandatory in their operation, (3) allow only limited access to the computations of other modules, (4) are fast, (5) are informationally encapsulated, (6) have shallow outputs, (7) are associated with fixed neural architectures, (8) exhibit characteristic and specific breakdown patterns, and (9) exhibit a characteristic pace and sequence in development. Of these, the fifth, informational encapsulation, is both the feature Fodor most emphasizes and the one that makes his account of modules especially strong. Informational encapsulation, for Fodor, entails that a module only employs information encoded within it in its processing; it cannot use information stored in another module, or in what he terms *central cognition*. Central cognition, in contrast, is holistic in that anything a person knows might be applied in revising one's beliefs or determining how well supported a belief is. As a result of being encapsulated, modules for Fodor do not exhibit much intelligence; accordingly, he views only input processing, language processing, and possibly motor-output processing as modular. He construes the modularity of input processing as in fact a virtue. Insofar as input modules cannot be influenced by one's knowledge and expectations, they can provide information about the world that is not theory laden and can hence provide a theory-neutral basis on which to evaluate competing scientific hypotheses (Fodor, 1984).

Evolutionary psychologists have adopted Fodor's conception of modules without limiting them to input systems. Instead, they "see cognition as modular right through from input to decision processes" (Shettleworth, 2000, p. 54). Although there are weaker notions of modularity available, there is a powerful, if ultimately mistaken, consideration that leads evolutionary psychologists to extend Fodor's conception of encapsulated modules. A major objective of evolutionary psychology is to show how human cognitive abilities such as reasoning about coalitions, detecting cheaters, making risk-aversive decisions, or understanding other minds could have emerged through evolution. For theorists such as Cosmides and Tooby (1994; see also Cosmides, Tooby, & Barkow, 1992), the evolution of new modules, especially in the relatively recent period since the Pleistocene, is possible only if the modules are encapsulated and able to be selected individually. Cummins and Allen (1998) succinctly capture the close affinity evolutionary psychologists identify between modularity and evolution:

> Taking an evolutionary approach to the explanation of cognitive function follows naturally from the growing body of neuroscientific evidence showing that the mind is divisible.... The Cartesian view of a seamless whole makes it hard to see how such a whole could have come into being, except perhaps by an act of divine creation. By recognizing the modularity of mind, however, it is possible to see how human mentality might be explained by the gradual accretion of numerous special function pieces of mind. (p. 3)

Not all theorists who invoke mental modules treat encapsulation as the central feature. Dan Sperber (1994, 2001, 2005), for example, construes as the defining mark of modules the fact that they operate on specific domains of inputs. On such an account, domains such as arithmetic, face recognition, and reading are viewed as processed by distinct dedicated modules. Even for Sperber, modules operate relatively independently of one another: a module is triggered by input within its specific domain and, "once it is performing its function, a module works on its own and is unable to take advantage of information that might be present in the system as a whole but that is found neither in the input nor in the proprietary data-base of the module" (Sperber, 2005, p. 56).

The opposition to dividing the mind into modules is usually portrayed as stemming from radical holists who emphasize the unity of mind. The rejection of the possibility of dividing minds was a central feature of Descartes' contention that the mind could not be a physical entity but must be immaterial. It also figured prominently in Flourens's (1824) criticisms of Gall's phrenology and in the early-twentieth-century rejection of neural localization by Lashley (1929) and others. A similar holist bent manifests in many contemporary dynamical systems theorists who reject the decomposition of the mind into component functions and the attempt to localize such functions in the brain either through lesion experiments or functional neuroimaging (Uttal, 2001; van Orden & Paap, 1997; van Orden, Pennington, & Stone, 2001).

Fodor's rejection of modules in central cognition ironically aligns him (an arch defender of symbolic accounts of cognition) with dynamical systems theorists. His construal of central cognition as using any information the agent possesses reflects a strong holistic perspective. But whereas Fodor sees the inability to differentiate central cognition into modules as undermining the possibility of scientific explanation (Fodor's first law of the nonexistence of cognitive science), dynamical systems theory advances a scientific program for explaining the activities of cognitive systems. The strategy is to develop differential equations relating variables that characterize the system being modeled. The nonlinear nature of these equations generates complex patterns of change that can be represented in diagrams showing, for example, the attractor landscape of such a system, but not easily characterized in terms of the behavior of individual system components.

Not only do some dynamical systems theorists resist any attempt to decompose the mind into separate modules (van Gelder, 1995, 1998), but also they reject drawing a sharp distinction between the mind/brain and the rest of the body and the environment in which the mind operates. Equations describing the relations between variables within the brain can be coupled with those characterizing variables external to it (Beer, 2000; Keijzer, 2001; Kelso, 1995). Because on such an approach there is no fundamental difference between variables characterizing the cognitive system and those characterizing features outside the system, the dynamical approach is readily able to integrate phenomena from the mind and the world and capture the embodied and situated nature of cognition.

Although much is often made of the opposition between modular and holistic approaches, I will argue that the dichotomy is actually a false one. This is best appreciated by considering the nature of mechanistic explanation. Whereas most philosophical accounts, including philosophical accounts of psychology, advert to laws as the vehicle of explanation, most explanations advanced in the life sciences make no reference to laws, and when laws do appear, they do so in an ancillary role. As Robert Cummins (2000) notes, in psychology laws are typically referred to as effects, and they typically characterize phenomena in need of explanation but do not themselves explain the phenomena. Rather, what serves to explain a phenomenon is an account of the mechanism responsible for producing it. As will be discussed herein, the parts of biological mechanisms are not totally isolated modules. Rather, the parts of a mechanism are often highly interactive in the production of any phenomenon. Yet they also have an identity of their own, and there are good explanatory reasons to differentiate them from their environmental context.

2. Mechanisms and Mechanistic Explanations

The conception of mechanism has its roots in the machines that humans build. Much of Greek philosophy viewed machines as operating in opposition to nature. For many natural philosophers of the scientific revolution, however, machines came to provide the model for understanding processes in the natural world (Garber, 2002). Descartes extended the idea of mechanism not only to the inorganic world but also to the animate world itself, construing the nervous systems of humans and animals as hydraulic systems in which the flow of animal spirits was altered by sensory experience and directed through the system so as to cause the motion of the limbs. Subsequent to Descartes, the strategy of explaining biological phenomena in terms of machines was pursued by many biologists, though contested by others who insisted that some features of living systems simply could not be explained in mechanical terms and required something extra. This was the basis of the long-enduring vitalist/ mechanist controversy in biology.

For Descartes and other early mechanists, a mechanism produced its behavior in virtue of the size, shape, and motion of its parts. Over time the repertoire of types of component parts expanded and these parts increasingly were conceived of as entities actively doing things. For example, after Berzelius (1836) introduced the notion of a catalyst as an entity that promoted a chemical reaction without being consumed in it, chemists commonly invoked catalysts to explain reactions that would not otherwise occur under the conditions realized (e.g., at the existing temperature). In the early nineteenth century many chemists construed yeast not as a living organism but simply as a chemical catalyst that promoted fermentation. Once it was determined to be a living organism in the middle of the century, chemists and subsequently biochemists sought catalysts, later termed *enzymes*, within yeast that could account for fermentation. This project finally bore fruit in the early decades of the twentieth century (Bechtel, 1986, 2006, chap. 3). Implicit in early accounts of mechanism was the fact that the parts of a mechanism had to be appropriately organized to perform their functions; the emphasis on organization became far more explicit after Bernard (1865) appealed to the organization in living systems in his attempt to explain how organisms could do the sorts of things vitalists had claimed would not be possible if the organisms were mere mechanisms.

Recently, a number of philosophers have advanced accounts of what counts as a mechanism in biology (Bechtel & Richardson, 1993; Glennan, 1996, 2002; Machamer,

Darden, & Craver, 2000). My preferred account is this one: "A mechanism is a structure performing a function in virtue of its component parts, component operations, and their organization. The orchestrated functioning of the mechanism is responsible for one or more phenomena" (Bechtel, 2006; Bechtel & Abrahamsen, 2005).

Mechanisms exist in nature, whereas mechanistic explanation involves an investigator presenting an account of the mechanism taken to be responsible for a given phenomenon. Typically, the explanation involves describing or depicting the component parts, operations, and their organization (diagrams are often far more useful than linguistic descriptions for this purpose). Understanding how the orchestrated operation of the parts produces the phenomenon of interest, investigators must simulate the operation of the mechanism, either mentally or by using model systems or computer simulations.

At the heart of the understanding of a mechanism is the idea that it consists of parts that perform different operations. Already here the conception of components of a mechanism departs from the conception of modules. Although advocates of modules do sometimes talk in terms of submodules, they do not focus on the decomposition of what the overall system does into contributing operations. Rather, a module is identified with a domain of performance – the module performs one of the tasks performed by the overall system. In fact, sometimes the discovery of a mechanism begins in this way (in Bechtel & Richardson, 1993, we spoke of this as *simple localization*). But over time investigators often learn that other parts are involved in producing the phenomenon and that the part in question only performs one of the required operations. The result is a model of an integrated system responsible for the phenomenon, not a single component.

Identifying the parts and their operations requires decomposing the mechanism. Different techniques enable investigators to decompose a mechanism into component operations (functional decomposition) or into component parts (structural decomposition). Ultimately, the goal is to line up the parts with the operations they perform, which Richardson and I refer to as "localization" (Bechtel & Richardson, 1993). Although the notion of levels has proved a vexed one (Craver, 2007), there is a clear sense in which the parts and operations within a mechanism are situated at a lower level of organization than is the mechanism itself. Mechanistic explanation is in this sense reductionist (Bechtel, 2007). The fact that the operations that parts of a mechanism perform are different from the phenomenon exhibited by the whole mechanism and individually do not realize the phenomenon makes the working parts of a mechanism different from domain-specific modules.

The parts of a mechanism need not be spatially contiguous but may be distributed throughout the mechanism. What is essential for something to count as a part is that it performs an operation for the mechanism that is different from the operations performed by other parts. The cardiovascular system of an organism and the glycolysis system of a cell each consists of distributed parts that perform different operations. Individual enzymes, for example, catalyze different reactions, whereas individual cofactors are reversibly oxidized in particular reactions. These are distributed through the cytoplasm of the cell, but their operations are so coordinated as to constitute the mechanism of fermentation. As I will develop in the next section, neither such mechanisms themselves nor their parts are encapsulated from each other in the manner of Fodorian modules.

3. Nearly Decomposable Mechanisms versus Encapsulated Modules

At first pass, mechanistic explanation may seem not to alter the modules/holism dichotomy but rather simply to take the side of modularity. A mechanism is differentiated from its environment and the mechanism is decomposed into parts that perform their own operations. In fact, taking mechanisms seriously and focusing especially on the sorts of mechanisms that arise in biology radically alters the picture. It is no longer appropriate to think in terms of a dichotomy between modular accounts and holistic ones, but of a continuum in which various designs of mechanisms occupy the middle. The differentiation of mechanisms from one another and the division of mechanisms into component parts and operations is partial. This is because the operations of the component parts of a mechanism are determined not just by their internal constitution (their subparts, the operations of these subparts, and the way they are organized) but also by both the conditions arising within the mechanism as a result of the operation of other components and the external factors impinging on the mechanism. The boundaries of the part partially isolate it from other parts but do not completely encapsulate it in Fodor's sense. Rather, each part is typically affected in a variety of ways by activity occurring elsewhere in the mechanism.

The assumption of decomposability in scientific investigations is a heuristic assumption that is only partially true of any given mechanism. Herbert Simon articulated the idea that natural systems would most likely be nearly decomposable, hierarchical systems and that our ability to understand them depends on this characteristic. By characterizing natural systems as hierarchical, Simon (1996) claims that they are "composed of interrelated subsystems, each of the latter being in turn hierarchic in structure until we reach some lowest level of elementary subsystems" (p. 184) and, moreover, that there is a "*small or moderate number*" of types of subsystem at any level in the hierarchy (p. 186). *Decomposability* refers to the independence of the subsystems at any given level. If the subsystems are completely independent, except for sending outputs from one subsystem to another, the system is fully decomposable. If the interactions are weak, but not negligible, according to Simon the system is nearly decomposable. Simon (1996) offers the following as the main theoretical consequences of near decomposability:

(1) in a nearly decomposable system the short-run behavior of each of the component subsystems is approximately independent of the short-run behavior of the other components; (2) in the long run the behavior of any one of the components depends in only an aggregative way on the behavior of the other components. (p. 198)

One factor making for nearly decomposable systems in the organic world is the fact that chemical bonds are of different strengths. Covalent bonds require much more energy to make or break than do ionic bonds, and these in turn are stronger than hydrogen bonds. Structures built with stronger bonds will remain stable despite the formation or breaking of weaker bonds, enabling higher-level structures to form without disrupting more basic structures. Thus, the system can be decomposed at one level, leaving intact structures at levels lower in the hierarchy.

Hierarchical, nearly decomposable systems are not the only possible complex systems. But Simon offers a powerful reason for thinking that natural systems, especially biological systems, will be such: nearly decomposable systems are much more likely to form, especially via processes such as natural selection. Simon illustrates this point through the parable of two watchmakers who make equally fine watches of one thousand parts. Tempus shuns hierarchical designs and makes watches in which all one thousand parts must be in the right configuration before the watch is stable. Hora, on the other hand, adopts the principle of hierarchical design in which the whole watch consists of ten stable subassemblies, each comprising ten parts that are in turn stable subassemblies made of ten parts. Allowing that there is a small probability (.01) of interruption per addition of a part (e.g., for phone calls to take orders), Simon establishes that it will take Tempus four thousand times as long to make a watch as Hora. Simon generalizes this point to evolution by arguing that stable subassemblies can be selected for even in the absence of the fully developed system that is responsible for a trait in modern organisms, whereas without stable subassemblies the emergence of complex systems would be virtually impossible because it would require a very unlikely constellation of independent events.

Simon (1996) thinks not only that systems in nature are nearly decomposable hierarchical ones but also that we may be able to understand only those systems in our world that are such:

> The fact then that many complex systems have a nearly decomposable, hierarchic structure is a major facilitating factor enabling us to understand, describe, and even "see" such systems and their parts. Or perhaps the proposition should be put the other way round. If there are important systems in the world that are complex without being hierarchic, they may to a considerable extent escape our observation and understanding. Analysis of their behavior would involve such detailed knowledge and calculation of the interactions of their elementary parts that it would be beyond our capacities of memory or computation. (p. 207)

Already in Simon's account of Tempus and Hora there is clearly a strong contrast between modular accounts in cognitive science and components of a system for Simon. The parts of a watch do not themselves keep time but perform operations that enable the watch to keep time. Likewise, it is not the tasks carried out by the whole cognitive system that are assigned to parts, but operations that work together to perform the task. Near decomposability allows that the components, to a first approximation, depend only on the overall operation of the other components, not on the individual steps in the operation of the other components. Operations within components, Simon maintains, will transpire on a shorter time scale than operations between components and can be averaged over. Moreover, modifications in one component that do not affect features on which other components depend can be made independently, allowing selection to promote variants in one component without sacrificing the success of other components.

Although Simon phrases his account in terms of near decomposability rather than strict decomposability, he does not advance reasons for thinking that living systems will be only nearly decomposable rather than strictly decomposable. But a brief glance at the genetics of modern organisms suggests a reason: most genes do not directly code for traits but rather regulate the expression of other genes. This suggests that evolution has not worked simply by promoting individual components but by modulating the behavior of already-existing components. Such modulation of one component by another is manifest not just in genetic regulation but also in the operation of components within organisms. The biochemical system in even relatively simple organisms involves a huge number of interactions among different chemical pathways, allowing different pathways to shunt products elsewhere or recruit materials from elsewhere. This quickly reduces the decomposability of the overall system, yet it does not yield complete holistic integration. Individual pathways operate semiautonomously even while coordinating and orchestrating their operation with other components. Scientists can isolate subsystems, either in their models or in their experiments, and render the operation of the whole system intelligible in terms of its parts, even while recognizing how different components can also modulate the operation of other components. In their understanding, the components are independent only to a first approximation. This first account can then be elaborated in a more refined account that recognizes the interaction of the components.

Simon provides one avenue for appreciating the sorts of differentiation of components that arise in biological systems and how such differentiation differs from that proposed in modular accounts of cognition. But a different perspective can be provided by considering some of the basic demands placed on living organisms, demands that make it important for them to segregate themselves from their environments and ultimately to segregate some of their mechanisms from one another. As a result of being highly organized, biological systems, like humanly constructed mechanisms, must be assembled and will dissipate over time. Unlike humanly constructed mechanisms, however, biological systems cannot rely on external agents either for their initial assembly (development) or for maintenance and repair. The living organism must perform these activities itself.

Performance of these activities requires that organisms exist in energy gradients from which they can extract and use free energy and raw materials. Any living system therefore requires metabolic processes that capture and render energy in usable forms. Metabolism is also required to process matter recruited from outside into a form from which its parts can be constructed or reconstructed, and additional mechanisms are required to carry out these constructions. Although it is conceivable that such processes could occur in an aqueous milieu that imposed no separation from the surrounding environment as long as the requisite metabolites and enzymes were in sufficiently high concentrations, such a set of metabolic and constructive processes would be extremely vulnerable. Biochemical reactions depend on concentrations of reactants, and most reactions are reversible and will run in the opposite direction when reactant concentrations are unfavorable. Thus, some means must be found to segregate these constituents of living systems from their environments and maintain them in high concentration if the reactions are to function properly. Living systems rely on biological membranes to segregate themselves, and component systems within them, from their environment. Following such a line of reasoning, Tibor Gánti (1975, 2003) incorporated a metabolic system and a membrane-construction system as two of the three constituents in his "chemoton" model of the simplest chemical system exhibiting the features of life. Gánti effectively demonstrated how such a system would exhibit many of the features we associate with life.

Biological membranes are semipermeable. Even passively they allow some metabolites to pass from the side in which they are in higher concentration to the side in which they are in lower concentration. Accordingly, while segregating many of their constituents from the external milieu, membranes do not cut them off completely. Membranes, moreover, are not limited to passive transport but can incorporate enzymes that actively transport selected substances across them, either to move substances across the membrane that are unable to pass through it on their own or to move substances in opposition to their concentration gradients. Through opportunistically designed transport mechanisms, living systems are able to admit selectively those substances they need to continue the process of constituting and reconstituting themselves and to remove substances, including the waste products of their metabolism, that will prove toxic to their internal operations. Of course these capacities of the membrane do not come for free – they must be paid for in the currency of energy and constructed through the mechanism of catabolism and synthesis. But the critical point is that a minimal living system such as I have characterized constitutes what Alvero Moreno, following Maturana and Varela (1980), calls an "autonomous system": "a far-from-equilibrium system that constitutes and maintains itself establishing an organizational identity of its own, a functionally integrated (homeostatic and active) unit based on a set of endergonic-exergonic couplings between internal self-constructing processes, as well as with other processes of interaction with its environment" (Ruiz-Mirazo, Peretó, & Moreno, 2004, p. 330). A critical feature of an autonomous system is that it is an active system that operates to maintain itself. As such, it imposes a demand on the subsystems (mechanisms) that constitute it – their operation is keyed to the survival of the system itself.[1]

Even in this minimal configuration, an autonomous system is operating on its environment by extracting nutrients from it and excreting waste products into it. If the environment is particularly hospitable and constant, such a simple organism may succeed in preserving itself by absorbing metabolites and expelling waste. Many marine invertebrates, such as jellyfish, are osmoconformers – they are isotonic with their saltwater environment and rely on that environment to provide the appropriate concentrations of salt and other essential solutes. Typically, however, such a hospitable environment cannot be counted on and an organism must be proactive and generate the right circumstances in its environment or navigate to suitable environments. But the principles already articulated can be extended to allow for a broader range of engagements with the environment, including operations that change conditions in the environment. For example, a cell might excrete chemical substances into the environment that alter the environment in ways advantageous to the organism. Once an organism develops mechanisms for locomotion (e.g., flagella in single-celled organisms), it is no longer dependent on the environment to bring nutrients to it and remove its waste, but it can move to secure nutrients and avoid the toxic effects of its waste products. These operations of the living system involve changes to the environment outside the organism, but the operations are performed by the organism (or mechanisms within it).

Focusing on the fact that biological systems are autonomous systems in the sense described, we can understand why, in theorizing about them, it is appropriate to construe them as differentiated from their environments. Their autonomy depends on their having component mechanisms that perform the necessary operations to maintain themselves and that these are organized so as to operate appropriately together. As such, living systems are appropriate objects of analysis. They are what Richardson and I termed *loci of control* for various vital phenomena. This does not mean that they are isolated and totally independent of their environment. Rather, as open systems, they are critically dependent on their environment for energy and raw materials and to remove their waste products. In more complex organisms, operations reach out into the environment so as to procure these resources. But there is also systemic closure – the parts and operations within the system operate to maintain themselves as a system even as environmental conditions change. Understanding how they do so is an important scientific challenge and justifies the strategy of conceptualizing them as independent.

So far I have focused only on segregating the whole living organism from its external environment. Simple living organisms such as bacteria have only a membrane surrounding their whole cytoplasm. This provides for extremely efficient exchange between different chemical constituents such as the metabolic pathways, the process of protein synthesis, and the information-storage system (DNA). But as more complex systems evolved, a new problem arose – the possibility that different mechanisms would interfere with one other. A particularly dramatic example is provided by the introduction of hydrolytic enzymes that serve to decompose cellular structures as they age or are no longer needed so that their constituents can be either reused by the cell or expelled. Such enzymes play an important role in enhancing the autonomy of these cells. Because such enzymes would clearly be dangerous if they were allowed to float free in the cytoplasm, internal membranes had to evolve to segregate them from the rest. In eukaryote cells several such sets of membranes have evolved to segregate sets of enzymes responsible for different cell operations into distinct organelles. As with the cell membrane itself, though, these membranes are semipermeable and, though they concentrate particular materials, provide them with a hospitable context to perform their operations and somewhat segregate them from other cell components, they do not impose absolute boundaries. In fact, impenetrable boundaries between component organelles would be extremely deleterious for a cell because coordinating the operations performed by the different organelles typically relies on complex messaging systems linking different mechanisms and parts of mechanisms.

4. Situated and Embodied Cognitive Mechanisms

Having argued that mechanistic explanation does not have to endorse either the strongly modular approach of Fodor and evolutionary psychologists or the extreme holism of dynamicist critics, but allows for identifying systems on a continuum between them, I turn now to the specific implications of thinking about cognition as embodied and situated. As we will see, the account I have offered supports an understanding of embodiment and situatedness without requiring that we extend the mind out into the world or deny the differentiation of the mind/brain from the rest of the organism and the external world.

We have already seen in the previous section that living organisms are differentiated from their environments as systems that construct and reconstruct themselves. Moreover, to understand how organisms accomplish this, scientists need to differentiate the organism from its environment while recognizing the various ways in which the organism engages its environment. In the account so far I have focused only on individual cells and single-celled organisms. The evolutionary route from single-celled organisms to multicellular organisms is far from clear, but it is evident that true multicellular organisms are more than an aggregation of single-celled organisms. Rather, they involve a differentiation of cell types that perform different operations. Once cells are differentiated and perform different functions, some means of integrating them into an operative whole is required. Such integration does not obviate the demand that individual cells maintain themselves but extends the resources for doing so by allowing for specialization of the functioning of individual cells so that each performs a different set of operations needed by the others. Accordingly, theorists such as Rudolf Virchow (1858), who played a major role in establishing that cells derived from pre-existing cells via cell division, conceived of multicellular organisms as cell republics.[2] Although each cell is a living unit, division of tasks becomes possible, making each dependent on the operations of the others. As a result, a cell republic (multicellular organism), like a political republic, is capable of doing things that an individual cell or person cannot. The whole organism now becomes an autonomous system, needing to construct and maintain itself in the face of environmental factors that would lead to its dissipation.

The division of labor and mutual dependency between parts of the system is especially clear with organisms composed of different organ systems. Individual organs perform different operations that are required by the whole organism – extracting nutrients and oxygen from the environment, distributing these through the organism, executing locomotion, and so on. Segregating these activities in different organs allows each to perform its operations without continual interference from the others. But it is also important that these systems remain open to one another so as to maintain the appropriate conditions for the operation of each component. In an early attempt to understand such coordinated operation, and thereby provide an answer to vitalists (e.g., Bichat, 1805) who thought maintaining life was beyond the capability of any mechanism, Claude Bernard (1865) introduced the idea of differentiating two environments – the environment in which the organism as a whole lives and the internal environment in which the different organ systems operate. By construing each organ as responsive to the conditions of the internal, not external, environment, Bernard proposed to show that their operations were causally determinate, which Bichat had denied. But more importantly, he viewed each organ as operating so as to maintain specific aspects of the internal environment in a constant condition, thereby making the whole organism stable against perturbations in the external environment. This idea was further developed by Walter Cannon (1929), who introduced the concept of homeostasis and described a number of mechanisms through which organs of the body helped maintain homeostasis. These mechanisms may involve behaviors of the whole organism that configure the environment in a manner that preserves the homeostasis of the individual (Richter, 1942–1943).[3]

Many of the control mechanisms Cannon identified involved the brain, specifically the autonomic nervous system. As important as the brain is as a regulator of what occurs elsewhere in the body, there is a risk of focusing exclusively on it. When we conceptualize control, we often think hierarchically and situate all decision making at the top of the hierarchy. This, however, works poorly in both biology and social institutions. As a result, biological systems usually have multiple layers of control arranged such that higher-level control systems can bias the functioning of lower-level ones (often by affecting the conditions under which more local control systems operate) but do not directly determine the behavior of the lower level systems. This can be appreciated by focusing on organisms in which cortical-level control systems have been removed – in such cases, many functions continue unimpaired but cannot be (directly) coordinated in the service of higher-level objectives (Stein & Smith, 1997). (They can sometimes be indirectly coordinated via their interaction with other components of the system that may still be under higher-level control. Thus, in patients in which a severed corpus callosum prevents direct communication between the two hemispheres of the brain, one hemisphere can still learn from observing the behavior resulting from the motor commands that the other hemisphere has issued.) The existence of multiple control systems all modulating the behavior of local components requires that these components not be encapsulated from other components of the system but open in appropriate ways to them.

The perspective of organisms as autonomous systems maintaining themselves through their activities, including activities that modify the world around them, provides a way to conceptualize the mind/brain both as an organ of a living organism and as embodied and situated in the world. As part of an organism, it is differentiated from the

world in which it operates but is nonetheless highly connected to that world. Even the simplest living organisms, as we have already noted, are distinct autonomous systems that extract energy and raw materials from their environment and put these to use to constitute and reconstitute themselves. But in more complex animals, this will involve performing a larger variety of behaviors (preying on other organisms or avoiding predators) and navigating the environment. These interactions with the environment alter it, often in ways that affect the organism itself. Accordingly, there is both isolation from the environment as the organism maintains its own identity and engagement with it.

The dependencies on the environment are particularly important in understanding higher cognitive tasks. There has been a tendency to think of these as occurring solely in the organism, but doing so runs the risk of assuming that the mind can do more than it in fact can. The symbolic tradition in cognitive science, for example, tends to assume that the mind itself has the power of a universal computer. It is useful in this regard to recall how Turing (1936; see also Post, 1936) himself was led to the conception of a Turing machine as an abstract model for a computer. Extant computers – humans whose profession was to carry out complex arithmetic calculations – provided the model for the Turing machine. These individuals learned and applied a finite number of procedures to problems that were written on paper. In turn they wrote the results of successive operations on the paper and used these as inputs for further operation. The human provided the model of the finite state device in the Turing machine, and the paper became the model for the tape (or memory in the computer). In thinking of the mind itself as a Turing machine or a computer, the operations that reached out into the environment are resituated inside the mind. But the mind/brain may not have such resources and, by thinking it does, cognitive scientists may set themselves up for failure.[4]

Nonetheless, while relying on environmental resources, it is still the cognitive agent that is performing these activities in pursuit of its ends. It is the cognitive agent that has an interest in performing the task and in recruiting components of its environment to enable such performance. Indeed, in the case of the human computer performing calculations, he or she typically did so for basic biological ends – securing a paycheck that would provide the food and other resources needed to maintain him- or herself. In this the cognitive agent is like autonomous biological systems that perform operations in their environment so as to secure matter and energy needed to build and repair themselves and dispose of wastes that are toxic to them.

Just as the move from individual cells to cell republics resulted in identifying a new locus of control at the level of the organism for the behaviors of the organism, so researchers may find the need to move to a more inclusive system for explaining some phenomena involving humans or other animals. Just as individual cells may specialize their operations and coordinate them so as to maintain a multicellular organism, so individual organisms may specialize their activities and coordinate them to maintain a larger system such as a social network. In these cases, the social network becomes the locus of control for certain phenomena – those that are carried out by the social network in the service of it. Such activity, however, takes us beyond situated cognition to social activity. Moreover, there is a principled reason for shifting the locus of control to the social network: it is the network itself that is being maintained by the operations performed (either between the constituents of the network or in the environment in which the social network is situated). Situated cognition, though, refers to the cognitive activities of agents situated in an environment, and the locus of control for these cognitive activities remains the individual cognitive agent.

5. Conclusions

By considering the kind of explanation appropriate to biological systems, mecha-

nistic explanation as applied to biological organisms, I have extracted some insights into both the modularity of the mind/brain and the situatedness of cognition. Biological systems are typically bounded, and there are good reasons for the mechanisms within them, including cognitive ones, to be segregated from one another. But the boundaries between the organism and its environment and between components and subcomponents within it are permeable. Accordingly, even when we identify a particular system as a locus of control of a particular function, we need not impute full responsibility to that component. Its operation may be dependent on features of its environment, whether an internal environment within the organism or an external environment in which the organism functions. It may act on and alter its environment in ways that facilitate maintaining itself as an individual system. Thus, we can demarcate the cognitive system while still examining how it is situated in and interactive with the rest of the organism and the environment in which the organism is situated.

Turning to organisms, I have identified reasons why it is useful to segregate different operations in different organs or parts of the system. Unlike in appeals to modularity, the focus in developing mechanistic explanations is on decomposing the overall activity into component activities. Segregating, however, does not mean isolating. In fact, living systems are typically highly integrated despite the differentiation of operations between different organs and cell types. The mind/brain seems to be no different on this score – it consists of component processing areas that perform different computations that are nonetheless highly integrated with one another. Such a mechanism does not typically include encapsulated modules, and one is not likely to find them in the mind/brain.

Turning to the whole organism, the traditional view, which treats the skin as the boundary of the organism and the mind as coterminous with the brain and central nervous system, is well motivated. The organism is the system that maintains itself as a result of the operations it performs, and the brain and central nervous system comprise the system within it that performs critical regulatory tasks. The mind/brain itself and the organism as a whole are open systems and dependent on the environment; hence, the quest to understand how a cognitive agent together with its various cognitive mechanisms is situated in its environment is also well motivated.

Acknowledgment

I thank Carl Craver both for very helpful comments on a draft of this chapter and for many productive discussions about mechanism and mechanistic explanation.

Notes

1   I will refer to the whole living organism as a system, not a mechanism per se. The question of whether an organism itself should count as a mechanism is complicated. Typically, one begins the analysis of a mechanism with an account of the phenomenon for which it is responsible. There are a host of different phenomena one might associate with an organism, and depending on which is selected, researchers will select different parts of the organism as the responsible mechanism and develop a different decomposition of it into parts (Kauffman, 1971).

2   Virchow's (1858) emphasis in developing this metaphor was to focus the study of living processes, especially those involved in pathology, on the individual cells. Cells were the most basic organized form: "the last constant link in the great chain of mutually subordinated formations that form tissues, organs, systems, the individual. Below them is nothing but change." Quoted in Coleman, 1977, p. 32.

3   I thank Carl Craver for pointing me to Richter's development of homeostasis to include behaviors that served to maintain internal homeostasis.

4   Turing's initial perspective was rekindled in Rumelhart, Smolensky, McClelland, and Hinton's (1986) account of human performance in multiplying large numbers. Such activity may rely not on internal symbols but on external ones on which a mind, operating like a connectionist network that has learned to associate one pattern with another, may operate. For further discussion, see Clark (1987) and Bechtel and Abrahamsen (2002).

References

Agre, P. E. (1995). Computational research on interaction and agency. *Artificial Intelligence*, 72, 1–52.

Atkinson, R. C., & Shiffrin, R. M. (1968). Human memory: A proposed system and its control processes. In K. W. Spence & J. T. Spence (Eds.), *The psychology of learning and motivation: Advances in research and theory* (Vol. 2, pp. 89–195). New York: Academic Press.

Bechtel, W. (1986). The nature of scientific integration. In W. Bechtel (Ed.), *Integrating scientific disciplines* (pp. 3–52). Dordrecht, The Netherlands: Martinus Nijhoff.

Bechtel, W. (2006). *Discovering cell mechanisms: The creation of modern cell biology*. Cambridge: Cambridge University Press.

Bechtel, W. (2007). Reducing psychology while maintaining its autonomy via mechanistic explanation. In M. Schouten & H. Looren de Jong (Eds.), *The matter of the mind: Philosophical essays on psychology, neuroscience and reduction* (pp. 172–198). Oxford, UK: Blackwell.

Bechtel, W., & Abrahamsen, A. (2002). *Connectionism and the mind: Parallel processing, dynamics, and evolution in networks* (2nd ed.). Oxford, UK: Blackwell.

Bechtel, W., & Abrahamsen, A. (2005). Explanation: A mechanist alternative. *Studies in History and Philosophy of Biological and Biomedical Sciences*, 36, 421–441.

Bechtel, W., & Richardson, R. C. (1993). *Discovering complexity: Decomposition and localization as strategies in scientific research*. Princeton, NJ: Princeton University Press.

Beer, R. D. (1995). A dynamical systems perspective on agent-environment interaction. *Artificial Intelligence*, 72, 173–215.

Beer, R. D. (2000). Dynamical approaches to cognitive science. *Trends in Cognitive Sciences*, 4, 91–99.

Bernard, C. (1865). *An introduction to the study of experimental medicine*. New York: Dover.

Berzelius, J. J. (1836). Einige Ideen über bei der Bildung organischer Verbindungen in der lebenden Naturwirksame, aber bisher nicht bemerke Kraft. *Jahres-Berkcht über die Fortschritte der Chemie*, 15, 237–245.

Bichat, X. (1805). *Recherches physiologiques sur la vie et la mort* (3rd ed.). Paris: Machant.

Broca, P. (1861). Remarques sur le siège de la faculté du langage articulé, suivies d'une observation d'aphemie (perte de la parole). *Bulletin de la Société Anatomique*, 6, 343–357.

Brooks, R. (1991). Intelligence without representation. *Artificial Intelligence*, 47, 139–159.

Cannon, W. B. (1929). Organization of physiological homeostasis. *Physiological Reviews*, 9, 399–431.

Clark, A. (1987). *Microcognition: Philosophy, cognitive science, and parallel distributed processing.* Cambridge, MA: MIT Press.

Clark, A., & Chalmers, D. (1998). The extended mind. *Analysis*, 58(1), 7–19.

Coleman, W. (1977). *Biology in the nineteenth century.* Cambridge: Cambridge University Press.

Cosmides, L., & Tooby, J. (1994). Origins of domain specificity: The evolution of functional organization. In L. S. Hirschfeld & S. A. Gelman (Eds.), *Mapping the mind* (pp. 85–116). Cambridge: Cambridge University Press.

Cosmides, L., Tooby, J., & Barkow, J. H. (1992). Introduction: Evolutionary psychology and conceptual integration. In J. H. Barkow, L. Cosmides, & J. Tooby (Eds.), *The adapted mind: Evolutionary psychology and the generation of culture* (pp. 3–18). New York: Oxford University Press.

Craver, C. (2007). *Explaining the brain: Mechanisms and the mosaic unity of neuroscience.* New York: Oxford University Press.

Cummins, D. D., & Allen, C. (1998). Introduction. In D. D. Cummins & C. Allen (Eds.), *The evolution of mind* (pp. 3–8). Oxford: Oxford University Press.

Cummins, R. (2000). "How does it work?" versus "What are the laws?": Two conceptions of psychological explanation. In F. Keil & R. Wilson (Eds.), *Explanation and cognition* (pp. 117–144). Cambridge, MA: MIT Press.

Flourens, J. P. M. (1824). *Researches expérimentales sur les propriétés et les fonctions du système nerveux dans les animaux vertébris.* Paris: Crevot.

Fodor, J. A. (1980). Methodological solipsism considered as a research strategy in cognitive psychology. *Behavioral and Brain Sciences*, 3, 63–109.

Fodor, J. A. (1983). *The modularity of mind.* Cambridge, MA: MIT Press.

Fodor, J. A. (1984). Observation reconsidered. *Philosophy of Science*, 51, 23–43.

Gall, F. J. (1812). *Anatomie et physiologie du système nerveaux et général, et du cerveau en particulier, avec des observations sur la possibilité de reconnoitre plusieurs dispositions intellectuelles et morales de l'homme et des animaux, par la configuration de leur têtes.* Paris: F. Schoell.

Gánti, T. (1975). Organization of chemical reactions into dividing and metabolizing units: The chemotons. *BioSystems*, 7, 15–21.

Gánti, T. (2003). *The principles of life.* New York: Oxford University Press.

Garber, D. (2002). Descartes, mechanics, and the mechanical philosophy. *Midwest Studies in Philosophy*, 26, 185–204.

Glennan, S. (1996). Mechanisms and the nature of causation. *Erkenntnis*, 44, 50–71.

Glennan, S. (2002). Rethinking mechanistic explanation. *Philosophy of Science*, 69, S342–S353.

Kauffman, S. (1971). Articulation of parts explanations in biology and the rational search for them. In R. C. Bluck & R. S. Cohen (Eds.), *PSA, 1970* (pp. 257–272). Dordrecht, The Netherlands: D. Reidel.

Keijzer, F. (2001). *Representation and behavior.* Cambridge, MA: MIT Press.

Kelso, J. A. S. (1995). *Dynamic patterns: The self-organization of brain and behavior.* Cambridge, MA: MIT Press.

Lashley, K. S. (1929). *Brain mechanisms and intelligence.* Chicago: University of Chicago Press.

Lashley, K. S. (1950). In search of the engram. *Symposia of the Society for Experimental Biology, IV: Physiological mechanisms in animal behaviour* (pp. 454–482). New York: Academic Press.

Machamer, P., Darden, L., & Craver, C. (2000). Thinking about mechanisms. *Philosophy of Science*, 67, 1–25.

Maturana, H. R., & Varela, F. J. (1980). Autopoiesis: The organization of the living. In H. R. Maturana & F. J. Varela (Eds.), *Autopoiesis and cognition: The realization of the living* (pp. 59–138). Dordrecht, The Netherlands: D. Reidel.

Neisser, U. (1976). *Cognition and reality: Principles and implications of cognitive psychology.* San Francisco: W. H. Freeman.

Neisser, U. (1987). Introduction: The ecological and intellectual bases of categorization. In U.

Neisser (Ed.), *Concepts and conceptual development: Ecological and intellectual factors in categorization* (pp. 1–10). Cambridge: Cambridge University Press.

Post, E. L. (1936). Finite combinatorial processes – formulation I. *Journal of Symbolic Logic, 1*, 103–105.

Richter, C. P. (1942–1943). Total self-regulatory functions in animals and human beings. *Harvey Lectures, 37*, 63–103.

Ruiz-Mirazo, K., Peretó, J., & Moreno, A. (2004). A universal definition of life: Autonomy and open-ended evolution. *Origins of Life and Evolution of the Biosphere, 34*, 323–346.

Rumelhart, D. E., Smolensky, P., McClelland, J. L., & Hinton, G. E. (1986). Schemas and sequential thought processes in PDP models. In J. L. McClelland, D. E. Rumelhart, & T. P. R. Group (Eds.), *Parallel distributed processing: Explorations in the microstructure of cognition* (Vol. 2, pp. 7–57). Cambridge, MA: MIT Press.

Schacter, D. L., & Tulving, E. (1994). What are the memory systems of 1994? In D. L. Schacter & E. Tulving (Eds.), *Memory systems, 1994* (pp. 1–38). Cambridge, MA: MIT Press.

Shettleworth, S. (2000). Modularity and the evolution of cognition. In C. Heyes & L. Huber (Eds.), *The evolution of cognition* (pp. 43–60). Cambridge, MA: MIT Press.

Simon, H. A. (1996). *The sciences of the artificial* (3rd ed.). Cambridge, MA: MIT Press.

Sperber, D. (1994). The modularity of thought and the epidemiology of representations. In L. Hirschfeld & S. Gelman (Eds.), *Mapping the mind: Domain specificity in cognition and culture* (pp. 39–67). Cambridge: Cambridge University Press.

Sperber, D. (2001). In defense of massive modularity. In E. Dupoux (Ed.), *Language, brain, and cognitive development: Essays in honor of Jacques Mehler* (pp. 47–57). Cambridge, MA: MIT Press.

Sperber, D. (2005). Modularity and relevance: How can a massively modular mind be flexible and context-sensitive? In P. Carruthers, S. Laurence, & S. Stich (Eds.), *The innate mind: Structure and content* (pp. 53–68). Oxford: Oxford University Press.

Stein, P. S. G., & Smith, J. L. (1997). Neural and biomechanical control strategies for different forms of vertebrate hindlimb motor tasks. In P. S. G. Stein, S. Grillner, A. I. Selverston, & D. G. Stuart (Eds.), *Neurons, networks, and motor behavior* (pp. 61–73). Cambridge, MA: MIT Press.

Suchman, L. (1987). *Plans and situated actions: The problem of human-machine communication.* Cambridge: Cambridge University Press.

Suchman, L. (1993). Response to Vera and Simon's situated action: A symbolic interpretation. *Cognitive Science, 17*, 71–75.

Thelen, E., & Smith, L. (1994). *A dynamic systems approach to the development of cognition and action.* Cambridge, MA: MIT Press.

Turing, A. (1936). On computable numbers, with an application to the Entscheidungs problem. *Proceedings of the London Mathematical Society*, 2nd ser., 42, 230–265.

Uttal, W. R. (2001). *The new phrenology: The limits of localizing cognitive processes in the brain.* Cambridge, MA: MIT Press.

van Gelder, T. (1995). What might cognition be, if not computation? *Journal of Philosophy, 91*, 345–381.

van Gelder, T. (1998). The dynamical hypothesis in cognitive science. *Behavioral and Brain Sciences, 21*, 615–628.

van Orden, G. C., & Paap, K. R. (1997). Functional neural images fail to discover the pieces of the mind in the parts of the brain. *Philosophy of Science, 64*(4), S85–S94.

van Orden, G. C., Pennington, B. F., & Stone, G. O. (2001). What do double dissociations prove? Inductive methods and isolable systems. *Cognitive Science, 25*, 111–172.

Virchow, R. (1858). *Die cellularpathologie in ihrer begründung auf physiologische und pathologische gewebelehre.* Berlin: August Hirschwald.

CHAPTER 10

Embedded Rationality

Ruth Millikan

Philosophers and laypeople alike have traditionally assumed that whether you can reason well, make valid inferences, avoid logical mistakes, and so forth, is entirely a matter of how well the cogs in your head are fashioned and oiled. Partner to this is the assumption that careful reflection is always the method by which we discover whether an inference or reasoning process is correct. In particular, further experience, observation, or experiment never bear on the question of whether an inference is valid. Validity is best checked with your eyes tightly closed so you can attend solely to the internal relations among your ideas.

There seems to be no need to defend these assumptions, nor, to my knowledge, has anyone ever tried. They are pure common sense. Occasionally, however, common sense is a repository for obdurate error. My claim is that that is so in this case. Rather than being an a priori matter, I will argue, good reasoning needs constant empirical support. Clear thinking is possible only as embedded in a cooperative external world. Because this claim flies rather rudely in the face of common sense, I will first introduce

it slowly in several different ways and then illustrate it with a variety of examples.

Among the most common informal fallacies in reasoning are fallacies of ambiguity. These are mistakes that hinge on a word or phrase that has one meaning in some or all of the premises of the argument but another meaning in other premises or in the conclusion. A traditional toy example runs as follows:

> The police enforce the laws.
> The law of gravity is a law.
> So the police enforce the law of gravity.

Real examples of this fallacy are not so blatant, of course. But according to tradition, if any such fallacy should occur in one's reasoning, it will always be detectable by careful enough reflection on the meanings of the terms in the premises and the conclusion. Terms in a language (words, phrases) are importantly unlike terms in one's thought (mental terms, thoughts of things) in that exactly the same word can denote different things in different contexts, but the same thought always denotes the same thing.

Thoughts are never ambiguous, never equivocal. By paying careful attention to the thoughts behind the words, refusing to let the words get in the way, a rational person can always avoid fallacies of ambiguity.

That is the first part of the view to be challenged. I will argue that one can fail to know that the denotation of a thought is unstable. It is possible to have an equivocal thought, to possess a single mental term that denotes more than one thing. You can have two people confused together in your mind, taking them for the same person, storing all the information you have about each of them in one and the same bin in your head. Or you can have two properties confused in your mind, as mass and weight were confused together in people's minds before Newton. Just like words, equivocal thoughts do not display their ambiguities on the surface. It is, in general, an a posteriori matter, a matter of experience, whether one's thoughts are equivocal. So it is possible to fall into fallacies of ambiguity that are not discernible by hard thinking alone.

The opposite of fallacies of ambiguity are inferences one fails to make because one is unaware that two words or phrases denote the same thing. For example:

Woodchucks are mammals.
Mammals are warm blooded.
Therefore groundhogs are warm blooded.

This is a perfectly rational inference if you happen to know that woodchucks are the same thing as groundhogs, but, of course, you might not know that. Although tradition says that the same thought is always a thought of the same thing, it also accepts, what is obvious, that different thoughts can be of the same thing and can be so without your knowing it. You can think of Mark Twain and then think of Samuel Clemens without knowing they are the same man, or think of woodchucks and then think of groundhogs without knowing they are the same species. The same mental term always denotes the same thing, but different mental terms can also denote the same thing, and this will not generally be known a priori.

But tradition then says that inferences like the preceding woodchuck-groundhog one are invalid, even if you do already happen to know that woodchucks are groundhogs. They are invalid, that is, unless you explicitly add into your premises that woodchucks are the same thing as groundhogs. The inference is invalid because one does not know of the identity of woodchucks and groundhogs by mere reflection, so one cannot know just by reflection that the conclusion of such an argument follows from the premises.

These doctrines both flow directly from the premise that what logically follows can always be known a priori. If you can always tell by reflection alone that an argument is valid and does not equivocate, then the same mental term must always denote the same thing. And if you cannot tell by reflection alone that different mental terms denote the same, then arguments that turn on different thoughts of the same (woodchuck and groundhog) are invalid. Both these conclusions follow from the premise that the world outside you, the world known through sensory experience, is in no way involved in your being rational. Being rational is something you do in your head.

But again, I will argue, this is a mistake. Whether a mental term is equivocal is an a posteriori matter, a matter of experience. So if any inferences at all are to count as valid, inferences that are valid in all other ways and that also do not commit fallacies of ambiguity should surely count as valid, even though the fact that they are not prey to ambiguities is known only a posteriori. Otherwise no mediate inferences at all (that contain empirical terms) will ever count as valid. That is, either we define valid inference such that all inferences that are valid must be known to be valid a priori but there are no valid inferences, or we define valid inference such that there are some valid inferences but they are not known to be valid a priori. The latter seems a more sensible way to speak. We do not want the term *valid inference* to be empty. But the way experience teaches us whether a mental term is equivocal or not is exactly the same way that it teaches us whether one term is equivalent to another.

So if one knows from experience that two terms denote the same thing, inferences in which one freely substitutes the one term for the other should be valid so long as no other fallacy is present.

Here is a third way of explaining the proposal I want to make. Closely related to the rationalist view of rationality described previously is the commonsense view that if you are genuinely thinking of something, you really cannot fail to know what it is you are thinking of. Bertrand Russell put the matter this way: "it is scarcely conceivable that we can make a judgment or entertain a supposition without knowing what it is we are judging or supposing about" (1912, p. 58).

So if you were thinking of two different things merged into one thought, of course you would know it. But Russell drew a more dramatic conclusion. The passage continues:

> We must attach some meaning to the words we use, if we are to speak significantly and not utter mere noise; and the meaning we attach to our words must be something with which we are acquainted . . . [but] Julius Caesar is not himself before our minds, since we are not acquainted with him. We have in mind some description of Julius Caesar . . . some description of him which is composed wholly of particulars and universals with which we are acquainted. (1912, pp. 58–59)

By "not acquainted with" Julius Caesar, Russell means not that we have never met Julius Caesar but that Julius Caesar is not a sense datum! For, Russell supposes, only sense data, sensory impressions, auditory or visual sensations, and so on, and their properties, can literally be directly before one's mind, and only if what one thinks of is, in this way, literally before or within one's conscious mind could one be sure what it was one was thinking of. The immediate result of this sort of Russellian move was the emergence of various versions of verificationism and phenomenalism, an era to which we have no wish, I imagine, to return.

A ubiquitous contemporary and parallel move is clearly illustrated by Michael Dummett (1978): "Meaning is transparent in the sense that, if someone attaches a meaning to each of two words, he must know whether these meanings are the same" (p. 131).

But, of course, you can fail to know that two words in your vocabulary stand for the same thing. You can fail to know that Mark Twain is Samuel Clemens; you can fail to know that woodchucks are groundhogs. You can have two thoughts of the same thing without knowing it. Still, according to Dummett you cannot attach the same meaning to two words without knowing it. It follows that the meaning you think of when you understand a word must be separable from the thing you think of when you hear the word. It must be separable from the word's referent or denotation. Although *Mark Twain* and *Samuel Clemens* refer to the same man, they must have different meanings or express different thoughts. Perhaps they express different descriptions, as Russell suggested, through which one thinks of the same man. Although *woodchuck* and *groundhog* denote the same species, they, too, must have different meanings or express different thoughts, perhaps expressing different descriptions of this species. Accordingly, numerous philosophers have distinguished what they call "reference" – what the thought is of – from something else, which has gone under various different names, such as *sense, mode of presentation, intension,* or sometimes just *meaning* or *thought.*

According to this view, valid arguments can be known to be valid a priori because instead of concerning what thoughts are about – reference, denotation – correct reasoning concerns only senses, modes of presentation, or whatever. It concerns only what is before the mind, but referents (e.g., Julius Caesar himself) are never directly before the mind, of course. Sense determines reference: there are no equivocal thoughts; the same thought always has the same referent. It is just that reference does not determine sense: the same referent is not always thought of in the same way. Thus it is that the previous toy argument about laws can be known to be invalid a priori and the one about woodchucks and groundhogs can be known to be invalid a priori as well.

That meaning is not the same thing as reference makes a lot of sense when one considers words like *moreover* and *hurrah* and *or* that clearly do have meanings yet do not seem to have any referents at all. Similar are words like *phlogiston* and *Santa Claus*. But to claim that words that do have referents and do have the same referents always have different meanings whenever someone might not know their referents were the same is peculiar. I have a daughter who collects nicknames the way fugitives collect aliases. Natasha gets called "Tasha," she gets called "Nat," sometimes "Ta" sometimes "Banana," often "Mouse" or "Mousie," and so forth. There may easily be folks who do not know, say, that Nat Millikan is Ta Millikan. Does it really follow that *Nat Millikan* and *Ta Millikan* have different meanings? Indeed, do *woodchuck* and *groundhog* really have different meanings?

Two different questions, often confused, should be distinguished here. The first is whether a name such as *Mark Twain* or *Tasha Millikan* or *woodchuck* corresponds to some one particular thought or sense or mode of presentation (or whatever) that every competent user of that name must have in mind when using that name, or whether, instead, different competent speakers may use different thoughts, different modes of presentation, when understanding a name of this kind. For example, is there a particular description or descriptions of Mark Twain that everyone who uses the name *Samuel Clemens* with comprehension must have in mind, or might different competent people associate entirely disjoint sets of descriptions with *Samuel Clemens*? Is there some definition of *woodchuck* that is different from the definition of *groundhog* that every competent user of *woodchuck* must have in mind? Or perhaps you are not a competent user of the word *woodchuck* unless you know that woodchucks are groundhogs (and vice versa)? The position that I would argue for (and have argued for

at some length in Millikan, 2000) is that, with few exceptions, words that denote do not correspond to any definition or mode of presentation that all competent users understand in common. But that will be only a secondary theme in this essay, for I want to talk mainly about thought rather than language.

The second question to be distinguished might count as the central theme of this essay. The question is whether when one thinks of a thing such as Mark Twain or woodchucks one does generally think of it under some mode of presentation or, as is often said, in some particular way. When I think to myself *Mark Twain was a writer* and when I think to myself *Samuel Clemens was a writer*, am I really thinking two different thoughts? When I think to myself *Woodchucks look like they have zippers down the front* and when I think to myself *Groundhogs look like they have zippers down the front* am I really thinking two different thoughts? Obviously, if I don't know that Mark Twain is Samuel Clemens or if I don't know that woodchucks are groundhogs then these are indeed different thoughts. They form, as it were, different patterns in my head. But does it follow that they remain different thoughts after I am thoroughly convinced of the relevant identities? Moving closer to home, I cannot really make out how my thoughts *Nat is gray eyed* and *Ta is gray eyed* differ in any way. Try it yourself with an old friend and the friend's nickname. Perhaps different associations may go with a person's formal name and his or her nickname, but a whole different way of thinking about them?

The mistake that has been made, I believe, is to confuse different ways of recognizing, or different keys to recognizing what it is that one is receiving information about, with different ways of thinking about that thing. How I recognize that it is my daughter that someone is talking about is not a way of thinking of her. I recognize who is being talked about when people say, "Ta," and when they say, "Nat," and when they say, "Mousie," and so forth, but surely I have only one way of thinking about this daughter. I have only one term in my mental vocabulary for her. There could be some people, of course, that I have different ways of recognizing without knowing it so that I keep in my mind more that one mental term for them. But surely for my very good friends, I generally have very many different ways of recognizing them, both in direct perception and through a variety of linguistic manifestations such as names and descriptions, but only one way of thinking of them, only one mental term for them. Indeed, the idea that every way that I have of recognizing a thing yields a different way of thinking of it, a different mode of presentation of it, drifts into incoherency as soon as we seriously try to count ways of recognizing. Ways of recognizing a thing typically are as uncountable as portions of water in a pond. *Ways of recognizing* is not a count noun – or so I will argue.

To have a concept of an individual, of an empirically evidenced natural property, or of a natural kind, typically involves a capacity to recognize that same thing, as such, in a great variety of ways. Speaking more exactly, typically it involves a keen, though fallible, ability to channel both natural information of numerous kinds that may affect one's sensory surfaces and much information contained in the language one hears so that it comes to a single focus in one's mind, being understood to concern one and the same thing. Knowing what you are thinking of is having this capacity with regard to the thing you are thinking of, and Russell was surely right that one cannot "make a judgment or entertain a supposition" about some thing without having this capacity at least to some degree. But Russell was wrong to suppose that knowing what you are thinking about is an all-or-nothing affair. Many forms of information may be recognized as concerning the same thing without all forms of information about that thing being recognized. And although it may not be usual, it certainly is possible to have two concepts, two focal points for information, two mental terms, for the same thing – "without knowing it" obviously goes without saying, for knowing it could be constituted only by merging these two mental terms into one,

putting all the incoming information into one folder (see Millikan, 2000, chaps. 8–11; Strawson, 1974). That is the thesis I will support, mostly by displaying a variety of illustrative examples.

Good examples with which to begin are thoughts of empirical properties. Many modern theories describe concepts of individuals or kinds as though these thoughts were reducible to thoughts or judgments about complexes of properties and then ignore the question of what it is to think of a property. Thoughts of individuals are analyzed in terms of definite descriptions (as in the previous quote from Russell) and thoughts of kinds in terms of properties supposed to define them. Soon I will argue against these classical analyses; but supposing they were right, then showing that thoughts of properties are discovered to be univocal only a posteriori would show that thoughts of individuals and kinds were so as well.

Thoughts of properties obviously cannot all be analyzed in terms of thoughts of complexes of more fundamental properties without regress. The objects (the content) of our most basic concepts of perceptual properties must be determined by our capacities to respond to these properties when they are made manifest to our senses through natural information (on natural information, see Millikan, 2004, chaps. 3–4). To have a concept of square, for example, involves the capacity to respond to natural information concerning the presence of square things as it impinges on one's senses – similarly for concepts of other perceptible shapes, of sizes, of colors, of textures, of softness and hardness, of heaviness and lightness, of lengths and distances. So let us consider how some of these properties are in fact recognized.

What is involved in being able to recognize, for example, shapes? Think of the variety of proximal visual stimulations to which a given shape may give rise when viewed from various angles, from different distances, under different lighting conditions, through various media such as mist or water, when colored in different ways, when partially occluded and so forth. How the visual system achieves shape constancy, the capacity to recognize the same shape as the same under a wide range of conditions, is a problem of nearly unimaginable complexity on which psychologists of perception are still hard at work. And shape is also perceived by the haptic system. You can feel the shape of a small object in your hand in a variety of ways, for example, with these fingers or with those, when the object is turned this way or that way in your hand, perhaps by using two hands, either merely by holding the object or by actively feeling or stroking it. You can perceive larger shapes (say, in the dark) by exploring with larger motions that involve your arms, body, and perhaps legs and by employing the touching surfaces of a wide variety of your body parts. This kind of perception of shape, involving the coordination of information about the exact positions of one's body parts with information about what touches these parts, is of such a complex nature that, to my knowledge, psychologists have not even attempted to study it.

Similarly, how color constancy, texture constancy, size constancy, distance constancy, and sound constancy are achieved are enormously complicated matters. (We are adept at identifying sounds, especially speech sounds, as the same sound at origin whether near or far, through air or through water, muffled or distorted, and so forth.) In each of these cases in which perceptual constancy is achieved, it is abundantly clear that no single rule is applied. Different clues are used by the perceptual systems in different circumstances, separately or together. For example, depth is perceived with the help at least of ocular disparity, tension in the focusing muscles, occlusion of one object by another, knowledge of the size of objects viewed, and atmospheric haze. We also recognize distances by touch and stretch using many different parts of the body, and by ear we recognize fairly well the distances from ourselves of things that make noises. The blind can often tell where nearby walls are located by reflected sound. Measuring distances with a ruler or a tape measure or just

a string, or measuring as a surveyor does by triangulation, or measuring with an odometer or a micrometer or by timing the return of light, are also ways of determining distances.

That all of these ways of determining a particular distance are ways of recording one and the same property obviously is not something determined by reflection alone. Coordination of these diverse ways of identifying one and the same property has been achieved through long experience, experience of the race during evolution, experience of the growing child resulting in perceptual tuning, experience in measuring and calculating with the use of a wide variety of instruments. Evidence that our concepts of distances are univocal concepts is deeply empirical.

Several more points deserve to be made here. First, none of these ways of telling distances is infallible, certainly none is known to be infallible a priori. Second, none of these ways of telling distances is any more definitional of our concepts of distances than any other. No one of them defines distance, the others being merely correlated, yet each adds something to our concepts of distances; nor could we have distance concepts at all were we not in command of at least some of these methods of recognition. Third, it should be clear that these various ways of telling distances do not correspond to a collection of prior concepts of properties that are then judged to concern one and the same property. If there were such a collection of prior concepts, with which we would make judgments about distance-as-perceived-thusly$_1$ versus distance-as-perceived-thusly$_2$, and so forth, presumably these concepts would be countable. But ways of perceiving a property are not countable, not just because they are too numerous but also because they are not the right kind of thing to count. Think, for example, of the myriad different perceptual data structures, in meandering continuous patterns merging into one another, any one of which might lead you to judge that you had perceived, by sight and/or by feel, something of a particular shape, say, the shape of a hammer. These could no more be counted than, say, the number of areas there are on a sheet of paper. That basic perceptual properties are thought of through myriad different modes of presentation that are then judged to be presentations of the same is a hopeless idea.

The situation is similar with thoughts of individuals. Traditionally it is supposed that to think of an individual is either to capture that individual in one's mind with some description that uniquely identifies it or to be able to recognize it perceptually. But uncountably many different descriptions will fit any individual uniquely and there are uncountably many ways that any individual might be recognized in perception, for example, (if it is a person) by family members or close friends. A family member might be recognized, say, from front, back, or side; by the stance of his or her body, by voice, by characteristic expressions or doings, under each of myriad different lighting- or sound-mediating conditions, and so forth. There are innumerable alternative methods that might result in thinking of the same individual. Different people can have quite different kinds of concepts of the same individual by using quite different descriptions or methods of recognition, and a single person may be in command of innumerable different ways of identifying the same individual. Surely the ways I have of recognizing each of my daughters are not countable. Nor do any of these methods constitute a definition of any of my daughters for me. Natasha, say, is not defined for me by the way I recognize her, by the look of her face (from this angle or that), by the sound of her voice (when she is happy or sad), and so forth. She does not have a definition, either an appearance or a set of properties, that makes her be who she is. None of the ways I can recognize her either in perception or by description is more important than any other in determining who my Natasha thought is a thought of.

Nor is it determined a priori that my Natasha thought is of any one definite person, that these various methods of recognition all converge on the same thing.

Indeed, for any single way of identifying Natasha it is not determined a priori even that this single method always captures the same person. Whatever appearances I go by, it is not determined a priori that I will never encounter someone else who has that appearance as well. It is similar for descriptions: descriptions are never known a priori to fit one and only one individual; they can be empty and they can fail to be unique. Thoughts apparently of individuals can be equivocal (Tweedledum mixed with Tweedledee) and they can be empty (Santa Claus) without one's knowing this a priori.

Thoughts of individuals can also be redundant without one's knowing it. You can have two different thoughts of Samuel Clemens without knowing it or fail to know that two people named *Dr. Jones* are in fact the same person. When this latter happens there will indeed be separate ways that you go about identifying Dr. Jones that feed into your separate mental terms for him, separate congeries of overlapping methods. But these will not be different ways of thinking of Dr. Jones, different modes of presentation of him, but only separate ways that thoughts of him are stimulated. If you discover that this is really one and the same man, then that will not result in a new belief taking up residence in your head, a special kind of belief called an "identity belief." The result will be that you merge your two concepts of Dr. Jones into one, now bringing all your methods to a single focus. The result will be that you now know somewhat better than you did before just who it is you are thinking of when you think of Dr. Jones.

Thoughts of biological kinds can be considered in somewhat the same light. This is what J. S. Mill said about them: "A hundred generations have not exhausted the common properties of animals or plants . . . nor do we suppose them to be exhaustible, but proceed to new observations and experiments, in the full confidence of discovering new properties which were by no means implied in those we previously knew" (from Hacking, 1991, p. 118).

We now know what Mill did not know; namely, why this is the case. Biological species are not mere classes. The members of a species are not bound into a unit by possessing certain defining properties in common. Members of the same species originate in the same gene pool, but gene pools typically contain alleles for all or most genes. Typically, there are no genes that every member of the species has in common with every other member. On the other hand, as Mill observed, the members of a species do tend to be like one another in an enormous number of respects. This is partly because they originate from genes that have been replicated from one another and like genes (in like genetic context) often produce like phenotypes. It is also because a variety of factors that tend to produce homeostasis in the gene pool so that novel genes entering the pool are unlikely to survive unless they produce extremely minor changes. Thus, the various individuals within a species mostly resemble one another in a great variety of ways, but they do not all resemble one another in any particular ways. What pulls them together as a group is not just that they have common or overlapping properties but that they have common and overlapping properties for a good reason. There is a good reason why one member of the species will probably be like the next in very numerous respects. This is why "a hundred generations have not exhausted the common properties of animals or plants."

Because biological species are not classed together merely by some set of common or overlapping properties, the extension of the concept of a species cannot be determined merely by a conjunctive or disjunctive set of properties represented in the mind. Moreover, just as no common way of identifying an individual or a property is required of all who think of that individual or property, there is no central set of properties that everyone must use to identify a given species. Typically there are very numerous properties that, taken either alone or in small sets, are each diagnostic of the kind. And just as with individuals and with properties, it is true that each person may have very many alternative ways of recognizing a species. Consider how many different ways

you have of recognizing the presence of a dog or a cat or a horse. For many familiar species, one's ability to recognize the species may be constantly improving, as one learns to recognize it by a wider and wider diversity of diagnostic signs and under a wider diversity of conditions.

Nor do any of the particular methods that a person uses for recognizing a species constitute some sort of final criterion of encounter with that species. None is more definitional than any other, even for that individual. So the same situation obtains here as with concepts of individuals and of empirical properties. There is no a priori guarantee that it is really the same species, the same glued-together unity, that one's various ways of identifying are reaching. Nor is there an a priori guarantee that any one way that one tries to identify a species always reaches the same kind. It is not known a priori that my ways of identifying dogs, say, do not lump two or more species together under one concept, making that concept equivocal. It is not even given a priori that they do not ever fail to reidentify anything objective at all, that they are not empty. That my ways of identifying reach an actual species is not a priori.

Because there is a reason why the members of a species are like one another, various kinds of inductions drawn over the members of a species will mostly yield true conclusions for a reason. That these conclusions turn out to be true is not accidental. Thus, again following Mill, species are what can be called "real kinds"; they are not merely nominal kinds. Elsewhere I have argued that there is a variety of different principles that can cement the members of real kinds together such that there is a reason why one member of the kind is likely to be like another (see Millikan, 2000). Some real kinds, such as the various biological species, are historical kinds, their members being alike because something like copying has been going on against the background of some relevant, ongoing historical environment. Copying from one another or from the same original plan is why the restaurants within a given restaurant chain tend to be alike, why various renditions of Beethoven's Fifth Symphony or of "The Irish Washerwoman" are much alike, why Greek salads tend to be similar, why Gothic cathedrals have similar plans, why American doctors have so many bits of knowledge and also so many attitudes in common, and so forth. A different but more familiar example of a principle that binds real kinds together binds natural kinds (in Putnam's sense) together. The members of natural kinds are alike because they possess a common inner nature of some sort, such as an inner molecular structure, from which the more superficial or easily observable properties of the kind's instances flow. The inner structure results in a certain selection of surface properties or in given selections of properties under given conditions.

I have argued that the majority of kinds that are recognized by natural language are real kinds (Millikan, 2000). This is because only real kinds can be genuine subjects of knowledge. It is only when individuals are banded together such that there is a reason why each individual should be like the others in various respects that we can obtain knowledge about this unit as such, unless, of course, by examining each member separately. Thoughts of units of this kind are the seeds from which all empirical knowledge is built, for all empirical knowledge is inductive.

But more important for our purposes here, it is always possible to have a concept of a real kind in any of a variety of different ways, using a variety of different techniques for recognizing its members, either separately or together. This is obvious, for example, in the case of Putnam-style natural kinds. There are, in general, many different techniques for detecting any particular chemical element or compound, many reliable tests for it. Of course the basic structure of the element or compound may be known as a result of scientific investigation (i.e., from experience), but one does not just look and see, say, that a substance is composed of atoms with sixteen protons! Historical kinds are less often talked about, so let me finish by giving some examples of ways of identifying members of historical kinds that will illustrate why they are never defined by just one method of recognition.

Consider again the various biological species. Aristotle thought that what bound individual organisms into the same species was that they had a single (Aristotelian) form in common. Roughly, he thought of species as being Putnam-style natural kinds. After the Darwinian/Mendelian revolution, we think we know better. We know that species are historical kinds: dogs are dogs because they partake not of the same form but of the same gene pool. Aristotle's mistake illustrates a very important point; namely, that you can have perfectly good concepts of real kinds without necessarily having an understanding of what holds these kinds together. Surely Aristotle was as capable of having thoughts of dogkind or humankind as we are. To think of a real kind you do not have to grasp its basic principle of unity. But suppose that you do grasp this principle. So you decide to use as your basic criterion for whether a creature is a dog that it was born of a dog (better, of two dogs). Now, how will you tell whether it was born of a dog? Well, first you have to be able to recognize whether its mother was a dog (and its father)! Knowing the principle of unity that binds the members of a historical kind into a unit takes you nowhere toward recognizing these members. We are back where we started then; there are many equally good ways of recognizing dogs, none of them definitional, and they converge on the same species as a matter only of empirical fact.

Now consider renditions of "The Irish Washerwoman." What makes a playing of "The Irish Washerwoman" into a playing of "The Irish Washerwoman" is that it is copied from an earlier rendition of "The Irish Washerwoman" or played from a score copied from earlier renditions and so forth. But that does not tell you how to recognize "The Irish Washerwoman." On the other hand, if you can recognize this tune, it is likely that no more than ten consecutive notes anywhere in it will be enough for you to identify it. A tune has no definition. It can be played badly or well, by this instrument or that, with missed notes and sour notes, with variations. But a tune, a ballad, a symphony, an opera, is a real kind, and despite having no definition, it can, of course, be thought of perfectly well.

Similarly, a Gothic cathedral is one because it has been copied from other Gothic cathedrals. Otherwise it is not actually Gothic. But knowing that does not tell you anything about the character of Gothic cathedrals. You have to see one or hear it described. Gothic cathedrals are pretty easily recognizable by any number of features, but Gothic cathedrals do not have a definition. That the various different patterns of features by which they might be reliably identified are diagnostic of a single architectural style is an a posteriori matter, a matter of causal-historical connections.

As a final and more sophisticated example, consider Western medical doctors. Children recognize doctors by their stethoscopes and tongue depressors, by the fact that they are taken to see doctors when they are hurt or ill, by the fact that people call them "doctor" and talk about having going to them when they were hurt or ill, and so forth. Adults know which are the doctors by where their names are listed in the Yellow Pages and by the signs on their office doors, because they say they are doctors, and because other people say they are, and so forth. But all of that is superficial, you will say; what really makes a doctor into a doctor, in the Western world anyway, is that he or she has been trained in an accredited medical school, passed certain examinations, and fulfilled various other requirements (e.g., residency), and been licensed to practice medicine by the appropriate legal authority in some country or state. In North America, for example, medical schools are accredited by the Liaison Committee on Medical Education (LCME), which is sponsored by the Association of American Medical Colleges and the American Medical Association. But first, note that children and probably many adults do not know that fact, nor would they, for the most part, even know there were such formal facts about doctors or even who to ask to find out the details of these facts (I found a medical student to ask, who did not know exactly but sent me to a Web site), yet this ignorance does not inhibit them from thinking thoughts of doctors. Second, consider what *accredited* means or what *licensed by a legal authority* means, and so forth. Well, that is complicated, and different things are entailed in different countries and states. But, in general, it will involve certain actions on the part of certain institutions that have been granted certain authorities by certain political bodies. In the abstract, that a certain person is a medical doctor will rest on the actions of certain social bodies. Take one of them, for example, the American Medical Association. Which social body is that? How are we to recognize it? Social bodies do not have definitions any more than people do. An individual social body is composed of a historically situated group of people who bear certain complex relations to one another. Identifying the American Medical Association is in many ways like identifying an individual person, or perhaps like identifying activities of the species *dog*. There are lots of ways to identify this organization or its activities, but none are definitional, and the fact that these various ways all connect with the same organization is an empirical matter, not something known a priori.

Then, do medical doctors, Western style, form a real kind? There is much knowledge and many skills that they mostly have in common, and many attitudes and practices, and these similarities obtain for a good reason. Doctors have learned from one another; from teachers who have learned from one another; from the same traditions, indeed, from many of the same textbooks and journals. Their techniques and attitudes have been passed from teacher to student and from colleague to colleague, across national lines and within them. There are good reasons why certain generalizations apply to most or many Western doctors and good empirical reasons why doctors can be identified – though fallibly, of course – in any number of ways. Modern Western medical doctors do not merely form a class. They form a real kind about which a good deal can be learned.

The case of Western doctors is a rather complicated case. But think back now to the earlier discussions of empirical properties, of individuals and of biological species. These paradigms guide us easily to the following general conclusions.

Abilities to identify and reidentify appearances of the same objective thing as appearances of the same constitute a substantial part of the possession of any empirical concept. Whether these concepts are of empirical properties, of individuals or of real kinds, the abilities to reidentify that underlie them rest on the natural laws that structure natural information. An ability to recognize something is, obviously, not contained in your head alone, any more than the ability to ride a bicycle is contained in your head. It depends on causal interactions between you and what you perceive, on the way channels of natural information are structured, and so forth. Perfecting the ability to collect this information accurately and efficiently – an ability originally derived through evolutionary history; then through perceptual learning; and finally through experience in making judgments based on perception, linguistic input, and inference – is at every stage an empirical matter. The tests by which we tune our abilities to recognize what is objectively the same as the same are empirical tests all the way down. (These tests are described in some detail in Millikan, 1984, chaps. 18–19; 2000, chap. 7; 2004, chap. 19.) Learning what is the same as what is at the base of all conceptual development, and conceptual development is a rich and structured interaction between the organism and its environment. To be thinking at all is already to be employing abilities that are deeply embedded in the world.

To discover that Mark Twain is Samuel Clemens or that woodchucks are groundhogs is just one further small step in conceptual development, one more small step in the fallible process of learning what information is carried through what media. Having made this step helps to perfect one's conceptual repertoire; it does not add a necessary step or a new premise in one's valid reasoning from knowledge of properties of Twain to properties of Clemens or from properties of woodchucks to properties of groundhogs. Learning to identify things in new ways is not storing away special beliefs called "identity beliefs" but improving one's concepts, improving one's basic abilities to think at all.

Like all other abilities that rest partly on the structure of the world outside the organism, of course these abilities are not infallible. It is always possible that an empirical concept binds together information about things that are not the same, hence becomes equivocal, the test for this being, in general, further experience. Ultimately, then, that an empirical concept is not prey to ambiguities is known to one only a posteriori; that one's mediate inferences are valid is known in the same way. One's rationality depends at every point on the complex causal and informational structure of the empirical world. Rationality is firmly embedded in the world outside the mind.

References

Dummett, M. (1978). *Truth and other enigmas.* London: Duckworth.

Hacking, I. (1991). A tradition of natural kinds. *Philosophical Studies*, 91, 109–126.

Millikan, R. G. (1984). *Language, thought and other biological categories.* Cambridge, MA: MIT Press.

Millikan, R. G. (2000). *On clear and confused ideas.* Cambridge: Cambridge University Press.

Millikan, R. G. (2004). *Varieties of meaning.* Cambridge, MA: MIT Press.

Russell, B. (1912). *The problems of philosophy.* New York: Henry Holt.

Strawson, P. F. (1974). *Subject and predicate in logic and grammar.* London: Methuen.

Part III

EMPIRICAL DEVELOPMENTS

CHAPTER 11

Situated Perception and Sensation in Vision and Other Modalities

A Sensorimotor Approach

Erik Myin and J. Kevin O'Regan

Voir un objet, c'est ou bien l'avoir en marge du champ visuel et pouvoir le fixer, ou bien répondre effectivement à cette sollicitation en le fixant. Quand je le fixe, je m'ancre en lui, mais cet 'arrêt' du regard n'est qu'une modalité de son mouvement: je continue à l'intérieur d'un objet l'exploration qui, tout à l'heure, les survolait tous.

Maurice Merleau-Ponty, 1945

1. Introduction

Seeing and perceiving are not achievements of an isolated head or brain, quietly humming along on its own. The organism moves its eyes, repositions its body to get a better perceptual grip on the objects that surround it, and thereby attempts to advance in the execution of the hierarchy of ongoing projects it is engaged in. The locus of perceptual processing includes the world rather than being just confined to the head. In the case of vision, at any moment, only the precise information that is needed at that moment is sought by moving the eye, the body, or by shifting attention to where in the world this information is to be found.

In this chapter, we will set out how an account of vision in which the world is considered to form an external memory allows for explanation of the experienced continuity of vision. We will show how the hypothesis of the world as an outside memory is supported by findings in the change and attentional blindness paradigms, as well as by the study of vision in action.

Then we turn to the sensorimotor contingency approach to sensation and perception in general. Here, as in the hypothesis of the world as an outside memory, the explanatory load for understanding the character of sensory experience is put on the precise ways in which an organism perceptually interacts with its environment. We present recent empirical research from the sensorimotor perspective, and end by pointing out how a sensorimotor account provides the possibility of explaining how perception differs from thought.

2. The Visual Field and the World as an Outside Memory

2.1. *Continuity in Experience*

What do you see when you see? Different things at different times, of course, but your visual experience almost always has the character of a seen scene. You see an expanse of objects and backgrounds, with their shapes, colors, and motions, which stretches out from a certain extent to your left, to a certain extent to your right, as well as up and down. It certainly appears to us as if what is often called our "visual field" is spatially continuous in the sense that everything in it is seen in roughly the same way. Things to the side of what you are most pointedly looking at, even if at the periphery, surely seem seen, and they have the same visual characters (e.g., shape, color, motion) as that which you directly look at.

Consider your current visual experience as you are reading this page. Don't you see the whole page, book, or even part of your hands or the desk that is supporting it – even if you are only reading part of the text at each moment? And aren't the pages sprayed with what is definitively text – in regular format?

Corollary to this spatial continuity, vision also seems temporally continuous. The contents of the visual field change frequently, but, unless we close our eyes, the field remains continually present.

Yet temporal continuity loses its aura of evidence when confronted with the mundane observation that we blink every few seconds. Why doesn't this lead to an interruption of visual experience – as happens when we are in a room in which the light goes out from time to time? Worse than blinks, eye movements create displacements of the retinal image at a rate of about three to five times a second all the waking day. One might think that we should see our world continually jumping around. Why don't we?

2.2. *Anatomical Discontinuity*

There not only would appear to be a problem in explaining the perceived temporal continuity of the world, but anatomical factors pose problems concerning the world's apparent spatial continuity.

First of all, the retina is not a uniform sensor: photoreceptors are arranged in a nonhomogeneous fashion, most closely spaced at the center of the fovea, with spacing increasing linearly all the way through the fovea and out to about ten to fifteen degrees in periphery. The type of receptor also changes as you move out into the periphery, with cones being in the majority up to about five degrees, and then rods taking over as the main receptor type further out in periphery. A second curious fact about the retina is the fact that it is inverted, with the axons and blood vessels that irrigate it placed on the anterior surface; that is, facing the light. This means that shadows of these structures obscure the light-sensitive surface. In one particular place on the retina, the axons and blood vessels come together to leave the eyeball where they form the optic nerve. At this location about ten to fifteen degrees on the nasal side of each eye there can be no photoreceptors and there is a scotoma, or blind spot, whose approximate six-degree projection in the visual field is sufficient to engulf an orange held at arm's length. And yet despite these defects of the eye's receptor surface, we do not see spatial nonhomogeneities in our visual fields.

Another curious fact concerns the optics of the eye. Compared to even a low-cost camera, the eye's lens lacks surprisingly in quality. Chromatic aberration creates a difference of about 1.6 diopters in the focal length for red and blue light – meaning that the eye cannot simultaneously focus features of different colors. Spatial distortions due to imperfections in the lens shape and to the sphericity of the eyeball are also significant outside the foveal zone.

It is striking, however, that none of these anatomical particularities are reflected in the experienced phenomenal field. If they were, we would experience our visual field not only as inverted but also as having a small central region in full color and detail and a blurred surround in drained colors.

But of course the visual field does not appear to us that way. Instead it looks smooth and roughly continuous: with things in it seen in roughly the same way all over. How is this possible? How can our experience have the continuity it has despite what seem like grave defects in the anatomy?

2.3. *The Hypothesis of the World as an Outside Memory*

To begin to answer this question, consider the light in a refrigerator (Thomas, 1999). Unless we knew better, we would believe that the refrigerator's light is always on. Indeed, whenever we open the door to look at it, it is on. It seems continuously on, not because it is always on, and certainly not because we continuously see it as being on, but because it is on whenever we look.

In a similar vein, we suggest, the scene we are confronted with seems to be detailed, not because we see all of the details all of the time but because we find the details whenever we look for them.

That is, the elements of the scene that are in peripheral vision or are currently not attended to are seen only in a secondary sense. The retina registers these elements, but we do not see them fully as we see something we attend to. Only when we turn to them and scrutinize them, do we actually see all the detail.

Our sense of seeing everything all at once is greatly enhanced by the property we call "grabbiness." Grabbiness refers to the fact that the visual system is so wired that visual transients – sudden changes in visual stimulation (e.g., those arising from a sudden motion or a sudden change in color) – generally trigger a jump of the eye so as to bring the fovea in line with it. This means that normally a significant visual change in the scene will be immediately recognized and scrutinized. Grabbiness supports our feeling of visually experiencing the whole scene because it, normally, ensures that no significant change in visual properties escapes our notice. What better evidence could one have that one is fully and continually seeing some-

thing than the fact that one notices whenever it changes?

In which sense is our pretheoretical understanding of seeing as continuous wrong and in which sense is it right? It is wrong to the extent that in a certain sense we do not really fully see all the detail at any moment; in fact, seeing is sequential rather than continuous.[1] It is right in that in some sense we still do actually see it!

The approach we propose can be called the hypothesis of the world as an outside memory, following O'Regan (1992), because of the emphasis on the fact that it is the world itself, rather than some internal memory store, that is continually interrogated and dealt with.

So, the apparent contradiction between the smoothness of experience and the apparent defects of our retinas can be avoided by understanding the active nature of vision, and by realizing that no internal replica of the world needs to be reconstructed inside the brain to account for every feature of awareness. For example, the very strong nonhomogeneity of retinal sampling, with resolution dropping off drastically for every degree we move out into peripheral vision, the poor optical quality of peripheral vision, and the lack of color-sensitive cones in periphery do not give us the phenomenal feel of a poor-quality, out-of-focus, monochrome world in our peripheral fields. Again, the reason is that we do not see the retina: we see the world, as probed by the retina, which we use as a tool. This is analogous to what happens when we feel a table through tactile exploration: we do not feel our hands and their imperfections – gaps, fingernails, differences in tactile resolution – rather, we feel the table by using our hand as a tool. We do not think there are gaps in the tabletop where there are gaps between our fingers. This is presumably not because we have a gap-filling-in mechanism to compensate the gaps but because feeling the table does not consist in exhaustively scanning the table to re-create inside the head a kind of internal model. Rather, feeling the table is an ongoing exploratory activity in which we can instantaneously access any information we require by displacing our hand. In the same way, in vision, eye movements and attention changes can instantaneously provide any information that may be necessary about objects in the visual field. As MacKay suggested (1962, 1967, 1973), the retina is like a giant hand that can be moved over the scene.

3. Change Blindness

An interesting empirical prediction follows from the hypothesis of the world as an outside memory. Under this view, the impression of seeing everything in the visual field in front of us derives not from all the detail actually being continuously represented in the brain, but from its immediate accessibility at the mere flick of the eye or of attention. If this is true, then large changes in an image should surely go unnoticed when these occur on parts of the image that are not currently part of what the viewer is visually exploring.

The problem is that this prediction cannot be tested under normal circumstances because of the grabbiness we have just described: usually changes in an image provoke rapid motion signals and contrast-change signals in the low-level visual system that immediately grab the viewer's attention. If it were possible to prevent such transients from occurring, or to somehow mask them, then, under the view of the world as an outside memory, the changes should not be noticed (unless by chance the viewer happened to be scrutinizing the very location that changed).

These ideas were the motivation for the paradigm of change blindness that O'Regan, Rensink, and Clark (1999) and Rensink, O'Regan, and Clark (1997, 2000) introduced. In this paradigm a large change in an image is made but a brief flicker or "mud splash" is simultaneously superimposed on the screen (see Figure 11.1). This produces transients all over the image that drown out the local transient that corresponds to the true image-change location. Another effective way to prevent the attention-grabbing action of

Figure 11.1. Example of the mud-splash phenomenon (O'Regan, Rensink, & Clark 1999). If the five patterned ellipses (mud splashes) appear very briefly and disappear at the same time as a large change in the picture (e.g., the solid white line in the street becomes a dashed line), this will often not be noticed. For other demonstrations of change blindness, see http://nivea.psycho.univ-paris5.fr.

local transients is to make them occur extremely slowly (see Auvray & O'Regan, 2003; Simons, Franconeri, & Reimer, 2000). The results of all these experiments confirm the following: unless observers happen to be scrutinizing the changing location as the change occurs, they tend to miss the change.

The change blindness paradigm has generated much research (cf. Simons & Rensink, 2005) and can be observed in a variety of other situations (when the image change occurs during eye saccades, eye blinks, cuts in a film sequence, or even in candid-camera type situations in everyday life; cf. Simons & Levin, 1997). It is a direct prediction of the idea of the world as an outside memory. It was discovered following elaboration of that idea, and it can be considered striking empirical support for the theory.

Further empirical confirmation of the idea that we do not continually represent the entire visual field in all its richness comes from the inattentional blindness paradigm (see Mack & Rock, 1998; Simons & Chabris, 1999). In this it is shown that when observers are intently engaged in a task like following a ball in a complex scene, they can fail to notice a totally obvious and striking event occurring right before their eyes, such as a person dressed in a gorilla outfit passing through the scene. Phenomena like this are, in fact, well known as "looked but failed to see" errors in ergonomics, where it has been observed that vehicle drivers frequently collide with obstacles that they are directly looking at (e.g., trains passing by at railway crossings, police cars stopped by the side of the road, bicycles passing directly in front of them, airplanes parked in the middle of the runway; see Herslund & Jorgensen, 2003; Hills, 1980; Langham, Hole, Edwards, & O'Neil, 2002). They show again the importance of attentive exploration of the scene for there to be awareness of its contents. This further bolsters the hypothesis of the world as an outside memory.

Figure 11.2. Example from Rensink, O'Regan, and Clark (1997) in which a change in the size of the glass of milk is generally noticed immediately because this is a central interest part of the picture.

4. Clarification Concerning Representations

It is important to point out exactly how the hypothesis of the world as an outside memory offers a different explanation of the experience of visual continuity from that of the more traditional representational account.

What the hypothesis denies is not the general claim that there are representations operative in one or various stages of visual processing but that the feeling of seeing all the detail at any moment is the result of a fully detailed, continuously present representation of all the detail.[2]

What change blindness highlights, according to the hypothesis of the world as an outside memory, is the falseness of the idea that you see all the detail at any moment. Regions that are seen peripherally, or that are not attended to, are not seen in detail. If they were, you would see the changes. Indeed, in the change blindness paradigm exposure, if you happen to be focusing on or attending to the elements to which the changes occur, you do see the changes. If the change occurs in the thematically central element of the scene, you

do not fail to notice it, despite an inserted blank screen (Rensink et al., 1997) or the presence of mud splashes (see Figure 11.2; O'Regan et al., 1999).

Because you do not fully see the peripheral or unattended details, it seems pointless to try to account for their being seen via a fully detailed representation. Rather, what should be given an explanation is the pretheoretical conviction that we nevertheless see everything continually. Such an explanation is precisely what is provided for in the approach of the world as an outside memory: you think you see all the detail at any moment not because you actually see it continuously but because you see detail whenever you care about detail – remember the refrigerator light.[3]

Thus, no detailed representation is necessary to account for visual awareness according to the world-as-an-outside-memory hypothesis, which provides a simpler account without such a detailed representation and is in accordance with data from visual anatomy. It leads to correct predictions for the phenomenon of change blindness. Further evidence for the hypothesis can be found in the study of vision in the context of activities such as reading, playing a ball game, and solving a visual problem, which will be reviewed in the next section.

5. Vision in Action

Data obtained by studying vision in natural conditions have highlighted features that are strongly supportive of the hypothesis of the world as an outside memory. In particular, such studies have indicated the large degree to which seeing is the following:

- Economical or sparse, in the sense that, at successive moments of visual activity, only a very small part of a scene is actually being processed
- Task dependent, or specifically adapted to the ongoing project, because what is looked at is that about which information is currently needed to support one's current activity
- On-line and on-demand, which means that visual processing happens at the moment the object or part of the scene of interest is attended to

For example, in reading, though eye movements follow a general reading-specific pattern, they are influenced by specifics of the text being read (cf., e.g., O'Regan, 1990; Rayner, 1998). General features of eye movements in reading are a sequence of forward-going saccades with length seven to nine letter spaces, to a certain extent independent of font size, with occasional backward-going regressions. Saccades are separated by eye fixations with durations of about 150 ms to 350 ms. Saccade lengths and fixation durations are determined by a number of factors, ranging from low level to high level. Thus, whereas there is clearly an ongoing reading rhythm or strategy (O'Regan, 1990; Vitu, 1999, 2003; Yang & McConkie, 2001, 2004), ongoing cognitive processing at the fixation location clearly affects the precise eye-movement scanning parameters, at least on a temporal scale extending over two or three fixations (Rayner, Sereno, & Raney, 1996). For example, more difficult words tend to require more numerous or longer-duration fixations, and word-skipping tactics may be influenced by local moment-to-moment lexical, syntactic, or semantic processing (Reichle, Rayner, & Pollatsek, 2003; Reilly & Radach, 2003). This suggests that text processing occurs to some extent in an on-line fashion, at the locus of fixation, instead of being carried out on the basis of information stored in a cumulative visual buffer. This is further evidenced by the fact that changes made to the text during a fixation affect both the duration of the current fixation and the size of the subsequent saccade (Rayner, 1998).

Although the seven- to nine-letter span covered by saccades is sampled by foveal vision, some general information (e.g., word-boundary information) in a span up to about fourteen letter spaces from the fixation point affects the reading process (Rayner, 1998). Interestingly, and very telling, changes outside the fourteen-letter span have virtually no effect on processing or on the reader's awareness. So subjectively there is no difference between a reader in front of a computer screen in which changes in peripheral text areas is synchronized with the reader's gaze changes and that same reader in front of a regular, static, text-filled screen. Thus, vision in reading is sparse: readers are, at any moment, only effectively visually in touch with a small part of the environment – in this case, essentially the seven- to nine-letter portion of the page or screen that is currently being processed. Note that, nevertheless, as emphasized earlier, the experienced visual field covers significantly more.

Studies of visual exploration during everyday activities such as making tea (Land, Mennie, & Rusted, 1999) or preparing a sandwich (Hayhoe, 2000) confirm this conception of vision as very much an on-line activity, which, through its task dependence, is sparse. Invariably such studies have found that the gaze is almost uniquely directed to the objects relevant to the task (e.g., the kettle, its lid, the tap, and the stove), and that objects are looked at in serial order, roughly as long as it takes to manually deal with the object. Several saccades (up to eleven for the initial visual manipulation of the kettle) can be made to (different parts of) the same object. In the tea-making study, the overall structure of gaze dynamics and the number of fixations to different objects were found to be similar across subjects. In the sandwich- and tea-making studies, the functionality and economy of looking is conspicuous. For example, it was found out that the number of task-irrelevant objects viewed was less than 19 percent, and often less than 5 percent (Land, 2004).

Investigations of seeing in steering (Land & Lee, 1994) and ball-game playing (Land & McLeod, 2000) have shown that subjects direct their gaze at the richest source of relevant information. In steering on a winding road, for example, a driver will look (i.e., fixate) ahead at the tangent point on the upcoming bend; the batsman in cricket will look at the place where the ball is expected to bounce. In both cases, these points are most informative with respect to the action the subject is about to undertake (turning the steering wheel, returning the ball). In the former case, this is so because the angle between the line of sight and the tangent point corresponds to the angle to which the steering wheel has to be turned to keep the car on the road; in the latter case, it is because knowing about the location where the bouncing ball hits the ground disambiguates a previously multiply interpretable input and allows thus for prediction of precisely where the ball will be at a point optimal for the returning shot (Land & Furneaux, 1997).

In driving, other relevant cues, especially the car's position relative to the nearer parts of the road (as opposed to the more distant tangent point) are continually monitored by peripheral vision. This is shown by the fact that tampering with this source of information results in the driver's holding the road position less accurately (for further data and discussion, see Land, 2004).

Similar findings were reported in a well-known study of eye movements in a manipulative task, described in Ballard, Hayhoe, Li, and Whitehead (1992) and Ballard, Hayhoe,

Pook, and Rao (1997). Here subjects were given the task of copying a pattern of colored blocks shown on a computer screen, using a resource of similar blocks in no particular order shown next to it. Using a mouse, subjects could pick up, drag, and drop blocks from the resource area to create the copy in a work space. Eye movements and mouse manipulations were continually monitored. A typical sequence of fixations and actions was as follows:

1. A fixation at a block in the model
2. A fixation at a block in the resource area that matches the color
3. Picking it up
4. A fixation at the block in the model (again)
5. A fixation at the corresponding place in the resource area
6. Dragging and dropping of the chosen block

This work of Ballard and colleagues once more testifies to the task-oriented, on-demand character of saccade dynamics. This comes out most clearly in the fact that the amount of visual information taken in appeared to be minimal, determined only by the current task demands. Thus, instead of remembering a block's color and location, most of the time subjects revisited a block to find out about its destination location after previously having been at the same block to check for its color. In other words, the world serves as an outside memory.[4]

6. The Sensorimotor Approach

We have described how the hypothesis of the world as an outside memory accounts for the continuity of vision by emphasizing a particular way a perceiver interacts with his or her environment. Indeed, relative to a traditional representational account, the explanatory load for the continuity of visual experience shifts from the internal (what is in the head) to the external: the temporally spread interaction of a perceiver with his or her environment.

In the sensorimotor contingency approach to sensation and perception, this shifting of the explanatory load is carried further and applied across the board. According to this approach, the perceived quality of sensory stimulation is determined by the particular way subjects interact with their surroundings rather than by the specific character of any intervening brain processes or representations.

In the sensorimotor contingency theory, the experienced quality of perceptual feelings is taken to arise from the precise ways in which one perceptually explores one's environment. Sensorimotor contingencies (a term borrowed from MacKay, 1962) are the ways in which, during such an exploration, perceptual input varies as a function of perceptual exploratory actions.[5]

Consider the tactile perception of the softness of a sponge (O'Regan, Myin, & Noë, 2005a, 2005b). According to the sensorimotor approach, perceiving the softness of the sponge derives from regularities such as the fact that if one presses, the sponge yields. If one manually explores an object and finds that such sensorimotor interactions hold, one perceives softness. If one would detect that on pressing there is strong resistance, one perceives hardness.

In the following sections, we will consider some consequences of this view, as concerns perception of space, position, color, as well as sensory modality.

6.1. *An Example: Felt Location*

When there is tactile stimulation of the body, the location where it is experienced is usually thought to be the result of activation of a cortical map in the brain corresponding to that location. Although the sensorimotor approach accepts that such cortical activation occurs and is necessary for the sensation of local touch to occur, the approach questions the explanatory weight that the activation itself carries. Under the sensorimotor approach, the sensation of location does not arise because of activation in a cortical map per se. Instead, it arises because, by this activation, a particular assembly of

potentialities for action becomes available; namely, the assembly of action potentialities that corresponds to the felt position. For example, if someone taps my leg, the sensation is perceived on my leg and not on my foot because moving my leg, but not my foot, can cause the sensation to change. The sensation is also perceived on my leg because I can touch my finger to that location and create a similar feeling to the one that I am currently feeling. Furthermore, I can move my eyes to the location on my leg and see the person tapping, whereas if I move my eyes to other parts of my body, I do not see the person tapping.

It is worth mentioning that as regards the notion of location, the conception of the sensorimotor approach is related to Poincaré's (1905) conception of space as intimately connected with action: the measure of the position of an object is constituted by the sequence of actions that I can potentially undertake to reach it. Philipona, O'Regan, and Nadal (2003) and Philipona, O'Regan, Nadal, and Coenen (2004) have indeed shown how an organism can infer the notion of three-dimensional space from sensorimotor contingencies. By studying the laws that determine how sensory input changes as a function of actions, an organism can discover which bodily actions produce the different types of translations and rotations in the world it inhabits, and thereby find out about spatial structure in general. It can do this without knowledge of the neural code that codes its sensory inputs or motor outputs – in fact, it can do this without knowing from what kind of sensors it is getting sensory input, and even without knowing which neural signals are sensory and which are motor.

6.2. *The Rubber Hand Experiment*

The rubber hand experiment of Botvinick and Cohen (1998) provides excellent confirmation of these ideas. Precursors of the experiment have been known since Aristotle, and more recently Tastevin (1937). The principle has been put to use by Ramachandran and Rogers-Ramachandran (2000) in the rehabilitation of chronic phantom-limb pains.

The subject sits with his or her hand lying on a table. The hand is hidden from the subject's view by an opaque screen. Instead of his own hand, the subject sees a rubber replica, also in front of him on the table. The experimenter taps, touches, and moves the fingers of the rubber hand while the subject watches. At the same time, the experimenter exactly replicates his or her actions on the subject's real hand behind the screen. He takes care to make the manipulation synchronous on the real and the rubber hand.

After about two minutes the rubber hand illusion occurs: subjects have the distinct feeling that the rubber hand is their own hand. This first result, already demonstrated by Botvinick and Cohen (1998), shows that the sense of ownership and felt position of a tactile stimulation is modified very rapidly by correlations between visual and tactile stimulations. This is expected from the sensorimotor theory, because by definition what is meant by the experience of location at a body position is, among other things, the fact that tactile stimulation at that location will be correlated with visual changes occurring when the eyes are directed at the location. A number of authors have confirmed that, when stimulation of rubber and real hand is asynchronous, the illusion does not occur, as expected from sensorimotor theory (e.g., Tsakiris & Haggard, 2005).

Cooke and O'Regan (2005) also examine what happens when the rubber hand is bigger or rather smaller than the subject's hand. After the illusion sets in, the experimenter asks the subject to close his eyes and to attempt to touch his thumb and index finger to two points that are marked on the table in front of him, in a sort of pincer motion. It is observed that in the synchronous condition, the size of the pincer motion is strongly affected. When the rubber hand is smaller than the subject's hand, the pincer motion is too large. When the rubber hand is larger than the subject's hand, the pincer is too small. This is consistent with the possibility, expected in the sensorimotor theory, that the subject's perceived hand size is modified by the visual-tactile correlations that he observes in the immediately preceding stimulation phase.

6.3. Sensory Quality and Sensory Substitution Experiments

An obvious experimental prediction of the sensorimotor theory is that it should be possible to create substitution of one sense modality by another. It should, for example, be possible to obtain a visual sensory experience through auditory input. This is predicted because the theory claims that a particular sensory experience does not derive directly from the neural channels that are involved in transmitting the information but from the sensorimotor laws that link input to output. A visual stimulation is one that obeys certain laws that are typical of the visual modality: the stimulation changes drastically when one blinks, it is modified in precise ways when one approaches or recedes from an object, information from objects can be interrupted by other objects occluding them, and so on. Auditory stimulation, for example, obeys other laws: the stimulation is not affected by blinks but by head movements. Sound sources do not occlude one another in the way visual sources occlude one another, and so on. If one were able, for example, to recreate the laws usually associated with seeing but in the auditory modality, then one should, according to the sensorimotor theory, be able to see through one's ears.

The idea of sensory substitution is not new, and it had been experimented with by Paul Bach-y-Rita and collaborators as early as the 1950s, with the tactile visual sensory substitution device (Bach-y-Rita, 1967, 1972; Bach-y-Rita, Collins, Saunders, White, & Scadden, 1969). This device converted a video image into a tactile stimulation on a twenty-by-twenty matrix of vibrators that a blind person, for example, could wear on his or her abdomen. For technical reasons, among others, the work is only gradually coming to fruition. Today a number of sensory substitution devices are being perfected and put to use to transform from one sensory modality to another (cf. Bach-y-Rita & Kercel, 2003). For reasons related to the feasibility of creating devices that can translate the very high spatial resolution of the human eye into another sense modality, visual substitution devices are only partly effective. Nevertheless, there are blind people who use them regularly and report that in some sense they see with these devices (Apkarian, 1983; Guarniero, 1974). Devices that convert between other modalities are also being developed. Some that convert vision into sound are moderately successful (Arno et al., 2001; Cronly-Dillon, Persaud, & Gregory, 1999; Cronly-Dillon, Persaud, & Blore, 2000; Meijer, 1992; see also an evaluation of this latter device in Auvray, Hanneton, & O'Regan, 2007). The question of whether observers can really experience the existence of an outside world with such devices has been investigated with varying results (Auvray, Hanneton, Lenay, & O'Regan, 2005; Epstein, Hughes, Schneider, & Bach-y-Rita, 1986). A particularly successful device is one that allows patients with vestibular lesions to regain their sense of balance. Here an accelerometer is coupled to a tongue-display unit that delivers stimulation to a twelve-by-twelve matrix of electrodes worn on the tongue (Tyler, Danilov, & Bach-y-Rita, 2003). The tongue-based device has also been used for vision (Bach-y-Rita, Kaczmarek, Tyler, & Garcia-Lara, 1998; Sampaio, Maris, & Bach-y-Rita, 2001).

6.4. *The Sensory Quality of Color*

A major challenge for a sensorimotor theory of sensation is the problem of color, as it is difficult at first to envisage how the experience of, say, a flash of red light, could in any way be conceived of as involving a sensorimotor interaction. There would appear to be no exploratory behavior in color perception that might be analogous to pressing the sponge.

Yet given the advantage of taking the sensorimotor approach, it is worthwhile to try to find some way to apply the approach to color. The fact that it is possible to do this has recently been demonstrated, with sur-

prising success, by Philipona and O'Regan (2006). The idea is to propose that color should not be conceived of as resulting from activation of color channels in the brain. Instead, perceiving color is a perceptual interaction that involves monitoring the way colored surfaces change incoming light into outgoing light. As one moves a red piece of paper around under different illuminations, the light reflected off the paper into one's eye is different, depending on whether the paper is mainly receiving bluish skylight, yellowish sunlight, or reddish lamplight. The idea is to suggest that perceiving the color red corresponds to the observer having implicit knowledge about the law that governs how the piece of paper affects the incoming light. The analogy with the sponge is now apparent: just as softness is a property of the sponge that can be tested by pressing on it, redness, it is claimed, is a property of the red paper that can be tested by moving the paper around under different light sources (or by moving oneself around the piece of paper).

Applying these ideas to the sensation of color allows for a surprisingly accurate account of color judgments, particularly the fact that certain colors – namely red, yellow, blue, and green – are in a very precise sense special: they affect incoming light in a simpler way than do all other colors. From this finding it is possible to deduce accurate predictions for well-established results from color science, in particular facts about color naming, unique hues, and hue cancellation (Philipona & O'Regan, 2006). The predictions are in fact more compatible with known empirical data than are predictions made from standard neurophysiologically based, opponent-channel models of color perception (see Figure 11.3).

6.5. *Experiments on Adaptation of Color Experience to Action*

If the quality of a sensory experience is determined by the sensorimotor interactions involved in that experience, it should be possible to change sensory quality by changing the interactions that are generally

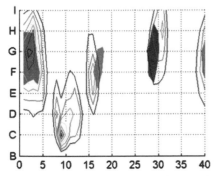

Figure 11.3. Comparison between observed and predicted salience of different surface colors. The coordinate system for a selection of Munsell color chips is the one used by Kay, Regier, and Cook (2003). For example F17 would be a particular green, G2 a particular red, C9 a particular yellow, and G28 a particular blue. The contour plots indicate the peaks where the theory proposed by Philipona and O'Regan (2006) predicts that surface colors should be singular. The patches near these peaks are taken from Berlin and Kay's (1969) world color survey (see also Kay, Regier, & Cook, 2003) and correspond to surface colors that, across a sample of 110 different languages, possessed a name for more than 20 percent of the maximum number of speakers. Thus, colors predicted to change light in a singular way are seen to correspond quite precisely with those given names across different languages.

associated with a stimulation. In an attempt to verify this prediction of the sensorimotor approach, Bompas and O'Regan (2006a, 2006b) performed a series of experiments in which a new, artificial dependency was created between a displayed color and eye movements. In one experiment, the subject wore spectacles tinted blue in one hemifield and yellow in the other. This situation has the effect that when the observer moves her eyes, say, to the left, the world is tinted with blue, and when she moves them to the right, the world is tinted with yellow. After approximately forty-five minutes of adaptation with such spectacles, the observer removes the spectacles and her perception of color is tested. It is found that when the subject looks to the left, a gray patch of color on a computer monitor now has to be tinted with yellow for it to be

perceived as gray, apparently to counterbalance an excess of perceived blue on the left. When the observer looks right, the patch has to be tinted with blue for it to be perceived as gray, apparently to cancel an excess of perceived yellow on the right. This confirms that the same retinal region can give rise to two different color percepts, depending on the eyes' direction of gaze.

The result is consistent with the idea, implied by the sensorimotor approach, that experience of color depends on potential associations with actions. Further experiments have confirmed that the effect can be obtained without tinted spectacles, by systematically linking particular color changes occurring on a computer monitor to particular eye-movement directions (Bompas & O'Regan, 2006b). In all cases, the effects are not explicable by peripheral adaptation phenomena, because the very same retinal cones are being stimulated in exactly the same way, and simply depending on gaze direction the color percept is different.

6.6. Situating Sensory Consciousness

O'Regan et al. (2004, 2005a, 2005b) have argued that the sensorimotor approach allows one to understand what is specifically sensory about perceptual consciousness by means of the concepts of bodiliness (also corporality) and grabbiness (also alerting capacity), introduced in O'Regan and Noë (2001a,b) and in Myin and O'Regan (2002). Basically, the concepts offer an analysis of the way in which conscious perception differs from thinking or imagining.

Consider what it is to actually stand in front of an elephant compared to what it is to think about an elephant or to imagine standing in front of an elephant. In the first case, the elephant is experienced as having a sensory presence. This presence, following philosophers such as David Hume and Edmund Husserl, can be taken as a defining characteristic of sensory and perceptual experience.[6]

O'Regan et al. (2004, 2005a, 2005b) suggest that there are several important characteristics of the perceptual interactions involved in sensation that in a natural way provide a plausible account of this perceptual presence.

First and foremost, sensation, considered a sensorimotor interaction, is in an essential way related to body movements. Whereas the processes of thinking, deciding, and remembering can occur without potential bodily motions, the sensory processes like seeing, hearing, and touching involve potential body action in a fundamental way. This is what O'Regan et al. (2004, 2005a, 2005b) call "bodiliness," or corporality: when one sees, the slightest movement of one's eyes, body, or the object in question necessarily immediately provokes changes in sensory input. The sensory input from the elephant changes drastically if one so much as slightly moves one's head. On the other hand, bodily actions do not in such a necessary fashion change the contents of our memories or our thoughts. One can keep on entertaining the same thought even while walking; and starting to walk does not automatically makes one think a different thought. When sensations are considered sensorimotor interactions it becomes possible to account for the difference between sensations and mental processes in terms of the effects bodily actions have on the former but not on the latter.

The already-introduced notion of grabbiness, or alerting capacity (O'Regan et al., 2004, 2005a, 2005b), refers to a complementary aspect of sensory systems. Grabbiness occurs because sensory systems in biological organisms are hardwired in such a way to detect sudden changes. When these occur, alerting mechanisms incontrovertibly notify the perceiver, so that his normal cognitive functioning is interrupted. When the elephant moves slightly, or when a bird flies by or a light flashes, one will automatically cast one's eye or attention on that sudden event.

This suggests that this potential alerting capacity of sensory channels is another constitutive difference that accounts in a natural way for the difference in presence between sensation and other mental processes like thoughts. Sensations impose themselves on you because they have the potential to surprise you and to divert your normal thought processes. In fact, even without the action of hardwired detectors of sudden change, sensory skills necessarily involve the organism trying to adapt to outside events that have a life of their own, escaping to some extent the control of the perceiver. Thoughts and memories on the other hand are (barring exceptional cases like obsessive thoughts) completely the product of the individual's mind, and so do not have the autonomy that characterizes sensory input. It is therefore natural that a perceiver will have quite a different feeling: less a feeling of control, more a feeling of imposition, when he or she is engaging in sensory interactions than when he or she is thinking or remembering.

Bodiliness and grabbiness are dynamic perceiver-environment relations that are typical and unique for sensation and perception, and absent in other mental phenomena such as thinking or desiring. The sensorimotor proposal, then, is that these unique features provide an account for the particular sensory or perceptual feel that differentiates awareness in sensation and perception from awareness in thoughts. So, focusing, through bodiliness and grabbiness, on the embodied and situated interaction with the environment leads – at the very least – to an interesting perspective on one of the most puzzling problems of the science of vision and perception in general, the question of consciousness and perceptual awareness. Because the sensorimotor account considers that the perceived quality of a sensation is not generated by some as-yet-unknown brain process but rather is constituted by the inherent nature of the exploratory interaction that is involved, the concepts of bodiliness and grabbiness take on an explanatory status. Now it is possible to explain, without appeal to further brain mechanisms, the differences within and between sensory modalities, and why sensations have the presence that thoughts lack. Whatever's one's opinion on whether this achieves the goal of fully bridging the explanatory gap (Levine, 1983) between perceptual consciousness and the physical world, it certainly seems to testify once more to the fruitfulness and the potential inherent in thinking of sensation and perception – in vision and other modalities – from a sensorimotor perspective.

Acknowledgments

Erik Myin is grateful for funding from the Research Foundation-Flanders (FWO).

Notes

1 As also stressed in Findlay and Gilchrist (2003).

2 These points are also noted and discussed by Noë (2004, chap. 2).

3 Nothing in our approach precludes that the not-fully-seen elements have effects on memory or behavior. There is plenty of evidence that is often interpreted in this way (for a recent overview and discussion, see Simons & Silverman, 2004). But none of the evidence seems to us to indicate that you fully see every detail of the whole scene at any time. In other words, none of this evidence disconfirms our account.

4 Note that subjects can also do the task in an internalist way, though less efficiently (Ballard et al., 1997). The externalist mode seems to be the preferred and most optimal way to operate (this primacy of the external mode is a leading theme in Findlay & Gilchrist [2003], which provides an excellent overview of the active vision field).

5 Note that *contingency* is not the normal philosophical use of the term: what is meant are the necessary laws linking potential actions and their sensory consequences.

6 Hume (1777/1975) talks about vivacity, Husserl (1907/1973) about *Leibhaftigkeit*. On the latter notion and its potential relevance for cognitive science, see Pacherie (1999).

References

Apkarian, P. (1983). Visual training after long-term deprivation: A case report. *International Journal of Neuroscience*, 19(1–4), 65–83.

Arno, P., Vanlierde, A., Streel, E., Wanet-Defalque, M.-C., Sanabria-Bohorquez, S., & Veraart, C. (2001). Auditory substitution of vision: Pattern recognition by the blind. *Applied Cognitive Psychology*, 15, 509–519.

Auvray, M., Hanneton, S., Lenay, C., & O'Regan, J. K. (2005). There is something out there: Distal attribution in sensory substitution, twenty years later. *Journal of Integrative Neuroscience*, 4(4), 505–521.

Auvray, M., Hanneton, S., & O'Regan, J. K. (2007). Learning to perceive with a visuo-auditory substitution system: Localization and object recognition with "The vOICe." *Perception*, 36(3), 416–430.

Auvray, M., & O'Regan, J. K. (2003). L'influence des facteurs sémantiques sur la cécité aux changements progressifs dans les scènes visuelles. *Année Psychologique*, 103, 9–32.

Bach-y-Rita, P. (1967). Sensory plasticity: Applications to a vision substitution system. *Acta Neurological Scandinavica*, 43(4), 417–426.

Bach-y-Rita, P. (1972). *Brain mechanisms in sensory substitution*. New York: Academic Press.

Bach-y-Rita, P., Collins, C. C., Saunders, F., White, B., & Scadden, L. (1969). Visual substitution by tactile image projection. *Nature*, 221, 963–964.

Bach-y-Rita, P., Kaczmarek, K., Tyler, M., & Garcia-Lara, J. (1998). Form perception with a 49-point electrotactile stimulus array of the tongue. *Journal of Rehabilitation Research and Development*, 35(4), 427–430.

Bach-y-Rita, P. W., & Kercel, S. (2003). Sensory substitution and the human-machine interface. *Trends in Cognitive Sciences*, 7(12), 541–546.

Ballard, D. H., Hayhoe, M. M., Li, F., & Whitehead, S. D. (1992). Hand-eye coordination during sequential tasks. *Philosophical Transactions of the Royal Society, Series B*, 337, 331–339.

Ballard, D. H., Hayhoe, M. M., Pook, P. K., & Rao, R. P. N. (1997). Deictic codes for the embodiment of cognition. *Behavioral and Brain Sciences*, 20, 723–767.

Berlin, B., & Kay, P. (1969). *Basic color terms: Their universality and evolution*. Berkeley: University of California Press.

Bompas, A., & O'Regan, J. K. (2006a). Evidence for a role of action in colour perception. *Perception*, 35(1), 65–78.

Bompas, A., & O'Regan, J. K. (2006b). More evidence for sensorimotor adaptation in color perception. *Journal of Vision*, 6(2), 145–153.

Botvinick, M., & Cohen, J. (1998). Rubber hands "feel" touch that eyes see [Letter]. *Nature*, 391(6669), 756.

Cooke, E., & O'Regan, J. K. (2005). *Manipulations of the body schema*. Masters thesis, Master de Sciences Cognitives, Ecole Normale Supérieure and Université Paris Descartes.

Cronly-Dillon, J., Persaud, K., & Blore, F. (2000). Blind subjects construct conscious mental images of visual scenes encoded in musical form. *Proceedings of the Royal Society London, Series B, 267, 2231–2238.*

Cronly-Dillon, J., Persaud, K., & Gregory, R. P. F. (1999). The perception of visual images encoded in musical form: A study in cross modality information transfer. *Proceedings of the Royal Society London, Series B, 266,* 2427–2433.

Epstein, W., Hughes, B., Schneider, S., & Bach-y-Rita, P. (1986). Is there anything out there? A study of distal attribution in response to vibrotactile stimulation. *Perception, 15,* 275–284.

Findlay, J. M., & Gilchrist, I. D. (2003). *Active vision: The psychology of looking and seeing.* Oxford: Oxford University Press.

Guarniero, G. (1974). Experience of tactile vision. *Perception, 3,* 101–104.

Hayhoe, M. (2000). Vision using routines: A functional account of vision. *Visual Cognition, 7,* 43–64.

Herslund, M. B., & Jorgensen, N. O. (2003). Looked-but-failed-to-see-errors in traffic. *Accident Analysis and Prevention, 35*(6), 885–891.

Hills, B. L. (1980). Vision, visibility, and perception in driving. *Perception, 9*(2), 183–216.

Hume, D. (1975). *Enquiries concerning human understanding and concerning the principles of morals.* Oxford: Oxford University Press. (Original work published 1777)

Husserl, E. (1973) Ding und Raum. Vorlesungen 1907. [Thing and space. Lectures 1907.] In U. Claesges (Ed.), *Hussserliana 16.* The Hague: M. Nijhoff. (Original work published 1907)

Kay, P., Regier, T., & Cook, R. S. (2003). Focal colors are universal after all. *Proceedings of the National Academy of Sciences, 102,* 8386–8391.

Land, M. F. (2004). Eye movements in daily life. In L. M. Chalupa & J. S. Werner (Eds.), *The visual neurosciences* (Vol. 2, pp. 1357–1368). Cambridge, MA: MIT Press.

Land, M. F., & Furneaux, S. (1997). The knowledge base of the oculomotor system. *Philosophical Transactions of the Royal Society, Series B, 352,* 1231–1239.

Land, M. F., & Lee, D. N. (1994). Where we look when we steer. *Nature, 369,* 742–744.

Land, M. F., & McLeod, P. M. (2000). From eye movements to actions: How batsmen hit the ball. *Nature Neuroscience, 3,* 1340–1345.

Land, M. F., Mennie, N., & Rusted, J. (1999). The roles of vision and eye movements in the control of activities of daily living. *Perception, 28,* 1311–1328.

Langham, M., Hole, G., Edwards, J., & O'Neil, C. (2002). An analysis of "looked but failed to see" accidents involving parked police vehicles. *Ergonomics, 45*(3), 167–185.

Levine, J. (1983). Materialism and qualia: The explanatory gap. *Pacific Philosophical Quarterly, 64,* 354–361.

Mack, A., & Rock, I. (1998). *Inattentional blindness.* Cambridge, MA: MIT Press.

MacKay, D. A. (1962). Theoretical models of space perception. In C. A. Muses (Ed.), *Aspects of the theory of artificial intelligence* (pp. 83–104). New York: Plenum.

MacKay, D. M. (1967). Ways of looking at perception. In W. Wathen-Dunn (Ed.), *Models for the perception of speech and visual form* (pp. 25–43). Cambridge, MA: MIT Press.

MacKay, D. M. (1973). Visual stability and voluntary eye movements. In R. Jung (Ed.), *Handbook of sensory physiology* (Vol. 7/3A, pp. 307–331). Berlin: Springer.

Meijer, P. B. L. (1992). An experimental system for auditory image representations. *IEEE Transactions on Biomedical Engineering, 39*(2), 112–121.

Merleau-Ponty, M. (1945). *Phénoménologie de la perception.* Paris: Gallimard.

Myin, E., & O'Regan, J. K. (2002). Perceptual consciousness, access to modality and skill theories. *Journal of Consciousness Studies, 9*(1), 27–46.

Noë, Alva (2004). *Action in perception.* Cambridge, MA: MIT Press.

O'Regan, J. K. (1990). Eye movements and reading. In E. Kowler (Ed.), *Eye movements and their role in visual and cognitive processes* (pp. 395–453). Amsterdam: Elsevier.

O'Regan, J. K. (1992). Solving the "real" mysteries of visual perception: The world as an outside memory. *Canadian Journal of Psychology, 46,* 461–488.

O'Regan, J. K., Myin, E., & Noë, A. (2004). Towards an analytic phenomenology: The concepts of "bodiliness" and "grabbiness." In A. Carsetti (Ed.), *Seeing, thinking and knowing* (pp. 103–114). Dordrecht, The Netherlands: Kluwer.

O'Regan, J. K., Myin, E., & Noë, A. (2005a). Sensory consciousness explained (better) in terms of "corporality" and "alerting capacity." *Phenomenology and the Cognitive Sciences*, 44(4), 369–387.

O'Regan, J. K., Myin, E., & Noë, A. (2005b). Skill, corporality and alerting capacity in an account of sensory consciousness. In S. Laureys (Ed.), *Progress in brain research* (Vol. 150, pp. 55–68). Amsterdam: Elsevier.

O'Regan, J. K., & Noë, A. (2001a). A sensorimotor account of vision and visual consciousness. *Behavioral and Brain Sciences*, 24(5), 883–917.

O'Regan, J. K., & Noë, A. (2001b). Acting out our sensory experience. *Behavioral and Brain Sciences*, 24(5), 955–975.

O'Regan, J. K., Rensink, R. A., & Clark, J. J. (1999). Change blindness as a result of "mudsplashes." *Nature*, 398, 34.

Pacherie, E. (1999), Leibhaftigkeit and representational theories of perception. In J. Petitot, F. Varela, B. Pachoud, & J.-M. Roy (Eds.), *Naturalizing phenomenology: Issues in contemporary phenomenology and cognitive science* (pp. 148–160). Stanford, CA: Stanford University Press.

Philipona, D., & O'Regan, J. K. (2006). Color naming, unique hues and hue cancellation predicted from singularities in reflection properties. *Visual Neuroscience*, 23(3–4), 331–339.

Philipona, D., O'Regan, J. K., & Nadal, J.-P. (2003). Is there something out there? Inferring space from sensorimotor dependencies. *Neural Computation*, 15(9), 2029–2050.

Philipona, D., O'Regan, J. K., Nadal, J.-P., & Coenen, O. J.-M. D. (2004). Perception of the structure of the physical world using unknown multimodal sensors and effectors. *Advances in Neural Information Processing Systems*, 15.

Poincaré, H. (1905). *La valeur de la science*. Paris: Flammarion.

Ramachandran, V. S., & Rogers-Ramachandran, D. (2000). Phantom limbs and neural plasticity. *Archives of Neurology*, 57(3), 317–320.

Rayner, K. (1998). Eye movements in reading and information processing: 20 years of research. *Psychological Bulletin*, 124(3), 372–422.

Rayner, K., Sereno, S. C., & Raney, G. E. (1996). Eye movement control in reading: A comparison of two types of models. *Journal of Experimental Psychology: Human Perception and Performance*, 22(5), 1188–1200.

Reichle, E. D., Rayner, K., & Pollatsek, A. (2003). The E-Z reader model of eye movement control in reading: Comparisons to other models. *Behavioral and Brain Sciences*, 26, 445–526.

Reilly, R., & Radach, R. (2003). Foundations of an interactive activation model of eye movement control in reading. In J. Hyönä, R. Radach, & H. Deubel (Eds.), *The mind's eye: Cognitive and applied aspects of eye movements* (pp. 429–455). Amsterdam: Elsevier.

Rensink R. A., O'Regan, J. K., & Clark, J. J. (1997). To see or not to see: The need for attention to perceive changes in scenes. *Psychological Science*, 8, 368–373.

Rensink, R. A., O'Regan, J. K., & Clark, J. J. (2000). On the failure to detect changes in scenes across brief interruptions. *Visual Cognition*, 7, 127–146.

Sampaio, E., Maris, S., & Bach-y-Rita, P. (2001). Brain plasticity: "Visual" acuity of blind persons via the tongue. *Brain Research*, 908, 204–207.

Simons, D. (2000). Current approaches to change blindness. *Visual Cognition*, 7, 1–16.

Simons, D. J., & Chabris, C. F. (1999). Gorillas in our midst: Sustained inattentional blindness for dynamic events. *Perception*, 28(9), 1059–1094.

Simons, D. J., Franconeri, S. L., & Reimer, R. L. (2000). Change blindness in the absence of visual disruption. *Perception*, 29, 1143–1154.

Simons, D. J., & Levin, D. T. (1997). Change blindness. *Trends in Cognitive Sciences*, 1, 261–267.

Simons, D. J., & Rensink, R. A. (2005). Change blindness: Past, present, and future. *Trends in Cognitive Sciences*, 9, 16–20.

Simons, D. J., & Silverman, M. (2004). Neural and behavioral measures of change detection. In L. M. Chalupa & J. S. Werner (Eds.), *The visual neurosciences* (Vol. 2, pp. 1524–1537). Cambridge, MA: MIT Press.

Tastevin, J. (1937). En partant de l'expérience d'Aristotle. *L'Encephale*, 1, 157–184.

Thomas, N. (1999). Are theories of imagery theories of imagination? An active perception approach to conscious mental content. *Cognitive Science*, 23, 207–245.

Tsakiris, M., & Haggard, P. (2005). The rubber hand illusion revisited: Visuotactile integration and self-attribution. *Journal of Experimental Psychology: Human Perception and Performance*, 31, 80–91.

Tyler, M., Danilov, Y., & Bach-y-Rita, P. (2003). Closing an open-loop control system: Vestibular substitution through the tongue.

Journal of Integrative Neuroscience, 2(2), 159–164.

Vitu, F. (1999). About saccade generation in reading. *Behavioral and Brain Sciences*, 22, 702–703.

Vitu, F. (2003). The basic assumptions of E-Z reader are not well-founded. *Behavioral and Brain Sciences*, 26(4), 506–507.

Yang, S.-N., & McConkie, G. W. (2001). Eye movements during reading: A theory of saccade initiation times. *Vision Research*, 41, 3567–3585.

Yang, S.-N., & McConkie, G. W. (2004). Saccade generation during reading: Are words necessary? *European Journal of Cognitive Psychology*, 16(1–2), 226–261.

CHAPTER 12

Spatial Cognition

Embodied and Situated

Barbara Tversky

What does it mean to say that cognition is situated? Like many interesting questions, this one has many answers, probably at least one for every chapter in this volume (for an early one, see Varela, Thompson, & Rosch, 1991). Cognition is inescapably affected by the immediate who, what, where, when, and perhaps why. Walking past a gift store is a reminder to buy a birthday present; leftovers in the fridge inspire a new recipe; fingers are handy for counting. The world serves not just our own minds but also our communications with other minds: a glance at the door tells a partner it is time to leave; the salt and pepper shakers on a dinner table act as props in a dramatic retelling; *here*, *that*, and *this way* can be understood efficiently but only in context. This kind of cognition can be called "on-line" situated cognition.

Less immediately, that is, off-line, cognition is situated by facts about our bodies and the world they inhabit. Bodies and the world have properties that afford, enable, and constrain perception and action. These affordances, enablings, and constraints have enduring, biasing effects on cognition. Here are some of them. We are upright creatures with three axes: an elongated, asymmetric head-to-feet axis that is aligned with gravity, which is a strong asymmetric axis of the world; and two axes that are not aligned with gravity, a front-back axis that is asymmetric, and a left-right axis that is for the most part symmetric (these ideas draw on and expand ideas articulated by Clark, 1973, and Shepard, 1984). We have four mobile appendages, two legs that can move us preferentially in one direction on the ground, the direction we call "forward," and two arms that are free to manipulate objects in the world, preferentially in the forward direction. We have a set of sense organs oriented in the direction of movement. Our actions in the world are for the most part goal directed and hierarchically so.

Based in part on collaborative work with, in order of mention: Julie Morrison, Nancy Franklin, David Bryant, Holly Taylor, Jeffrey M. Zacks, Bridgette Martin Hard, Paul Lee, Julie Heiser, and Angela Kessell. I am grateful for the opportunity to work with such a talented set of individuals.

Those actions as well as the structure and movement of the other things in the world are constrained by gravity and the other things in the world. Of primary importance among those other things are other beings like us. We are deeply social creatures, dependent on others to fulfill our needs and desires throughout our entire lives. Coordinating our needs and desires with those of others depends on communication, verbal and nonverbal, explicit and implicit.

These facts about the world, in constraining perception and behavior, bias and constrain mental representations of space and of action. The interactions of the body in the external world not only bias perception and action but also craft symbolic perception and action, and form the basis for abstract thought. This view follows from the ideas that the brain and the body evolved, among other things, to manage perception and action in the world, and that evolution builds new functions from old structures. Cognition is not just situated, it is also embodied, in ways that are hard to untangle.

These are heady ideas. To develop them, two questions will be addressed: How does the body in the world shape thought? How does the body in the world shape communication? The answers will come from research in our laboratory, neglecting many of the rich contributions of others, only some of whom are represented in these pages. We begin at the beginning: thinking about space.

Shaping Thought: Space and Action

Spaces for Thought

SPACE IS SPECIAL
Spatial thinking is essential for survival. Elementary to survival is knowing where to go to find food, water, and shelter and knowing how to return, as well as how to gather the food and water when they are located. Perhaps because of its centrality for survival, spatial thinking forms a foundation for other thought, amply illustrated in the ways we talk (e.g., Clark, 1973; Lakoff & Johnson, 1980; Talmy, 1983), the ways we depict (e.g., Tversky, 1993, 2001), and the ways we reason

(the previous, and too many to list, some herein and some in the companion chapters of this handbook). We say that our thoughts run in circles, we hope that the Dow Jones tops the charts, we give a thumbs-up to a performance. External representations as well as internal ones reflect spatial thinking: charts of social networks, like family trees or organizations; depictions of religious ideas, like mandalas or Kabbalah; diagrams of scientific theories, like the structure of an atom or the expression of a gene, are spatial whether in the mind or on paper.

Space for the mind is not like space for the physicist or surveyor, where the dimensions of space are primary and things in space are located with respect to those dimensions. For people, the things in space are primary and the reference frames are constructed out of them. Which things and which reference frames depends on which space, how it is perceived, and how it serves. Because spatial thinking is central in existence, all people become expert in it – which is far from saying that they are perfect at it; on the contrary, spatial memory and cognition have systematic biases (e.g., Tversky, 1981, 2000).

The thesis to be developed is that people's conceptions of space differ for different spaces and are a joint product of perception and action appropriate for those spaces. People act differently in different spaces: the space of the body, the space immediately around the body, and the space of navigation, the space too vast to be seen from a single viewpoint. Because perception and action in each space differ, so conceptions of these spaces differ. One reason the mind creates mental spaces is to understand perception and action; another reason is to enable perception and action. Correspondingly, the discussion will shift emphasis from space to action.

Space of the Body

The body is the first space encountered, even before birth. Experience of other spaces is channeled through the body, through perception and action. Like other objects, bodies have parts. Decomposing an object into parts is an important way to know an object, as different parts have different appearances and different functions, and the appearance of parts can serve as clues to their functions (Tversky & Hemenway, 1984). Prominent among body parts are those named frequently across many languages, including head, chest, back, arms, hands, legs, and feet (Andersen, 1978; Brown, 1976). They are prominent, in part, literally because they extend from the contour of the body; they literally stick out. They are the parts drawn by children all over the world, the familiar tadpole figures (e.g., Goodnow, 1977; Kellogg, 1969). For objects in general, the parts that are defined by discontinuities in object contour are perceptually salient (e.g., Hoffman & Richards, 1984), are frequently named, and are rated as good parts (Tversky & Hemenway, 1984). They are also parts with functional significance. Consider the legs of tables and jeans and horses, the handles of hammers and suitcases. It is noteworthy that the parts of objects that enjoy perceptual distinctiveness also enjoy functional significance. This supports inferences from perception to function (Hemenway & Tversky, 1984), a fact that children use in bootstrapping from categories based on perceptual similarity, like shape and color, to categories based on function, like clothing and tools (Tversky, 1989).

Viewed from the outside, bodies are like other objects. But bodies are also experienced from the inside. The body parts that extend from the body contour act on the world and sense the world. They are overrepresented for their size in the sensorimotor cortex, as depicted in the homunculus popular in textbooks. These correspondences are a striking contrast to physical measurement: the brain, naming across languages, and children's drawings across cultures converge to suggest that large parts are not the most significant for bodies. Other evidence indicates that bodies are perceived differently from objects. Detecting differences in body configurations is easier when participants move the relevant half of the body, top or bottom, but detecting differences in Lego figure configuration is

not facilitated by movement (Reed, 2002; Reed & Farah, 1995). For bodies, apparent motion follows biomechanical trajectories rather than the shortest path, as for other objects (Chatterjee, Freyd, & Shiffrar, 1996; Shiffrar & Freyd, 1993). Size, however, enjoys support in object cognition. In imagery, large parts of animals, such as the back of a rabbit, are verified faster than small distinctive parts, such as the ears of a rabbit (Kosslyn, 1980). Intuitively as well, large parts should be detected faster, just as finding a large person in a crowd is easier than finding a small person.

Does part distinctiveness and function or part size dominate the body schema? To address this, Morrison and Tversky (2005; see also Tversky, Morrison, & Zacks, 2002) investigated a body-part verification task, using the parts named across cultures: head, front, back, arm, hand, leg, and foot. In some experiments, the body-body task, participants saw pairs of realistic profiles of bodies in different orientations, each with a part highlighted by a white dot. In other experiments, the name-body task, participants saw the name of a body part followed by a picture of a body with a part highlighted. In both tasks, participants were to respond as quickly and accurately as possible whether the indicated parts were the same or different. The data of interest were the same reaction times to the different body parts.

In all experiments, size lost. The parts high in distinctiveness and function were verified faster than the large parts; for example, verifying head was faster than verifying back. The body-body task and the name-body task differed in a subtle way, corresponding to the differences between part distinctiveness and part significance. Although part distinctiveness and functional significance are correlated, the correlation is not perfect. In particular, the chest is regarded as a relatively significant body part even though it lacks perceptual distinctiveness. Its significance seems to derive from the fact that it is the forward part of the body, the direction of perception and action, and the fact that it encases important internal organs. In the body-body verification task, chest was relatively slow, reflecting the perceptual nature of the task. In the name-body verification task, however, chest was relatively fast. The compelling explanation for the advantage of functional significance is that language is abstract, so names are more likely to prime functional features than perceptual ones. This explanation is consonant with other situations, where naming calls attention to abstract features, notably function (Tversky, Zacks, Morrison, & Hard, in press).

The space of the body serves us to keep track of where body parts are relative to one another, either our own bodies, through proprioception, or other bodies, through vision. Where body parts are relative to one another affects and provides clues to what body actions are possible and likely. On the whole, though not always, the parts that are perceptually distinctive are also those that are functionally significant. Surprisingly, it is not the large parts but those that are salient and significant that people recognize most quickly and that appear to dominate the terrain of the space of the body.

Space around the Body

Now we venture outside the body, to the space immediately surrounding it. This is the space of actual or potential perception and action, the space in reach of hand or eye. Of course, not all things in view can be readily reached or acted on; Daedalus could not fly to the sun. People are remarkably adept at keeping track of the positions of things in the world as they move about, even when things are out of view, like the stores they have just passed while running errands. Storytellers rely on this ability by invoking imaginary characters moving in imaginary worlds. How do people keep track of locations of things as they move?

To study how people keep track of the things around them as they move, Franklin and Tversky (1990) devised constrained worlds, objects around the body in natural scenes, and constrained movements, rotating in place. We instilled these worlds with words, not with experience (though we later

replaced descriptions with scenes, described subsequently), simultaneously showing that worlds that are described rather than experienced could be imagined and updated. We proposed that people keep track of the relative positions of the objects around them as they move by constructing a spatial-mental framework out of the three axes of the body and appending objects to it, updating it as the situation changes. We reasoned that accessibility of objects should reflect characteristics of the body axes and the world relevant to perception and action. The head-feet axis has salient asymmetries both perceptually and behaviorally; moreover, for the canonically upright observer, it correlates with the only asymmetric axis in the world, the up-down axis of gravity. The front-back axis separates the world that can be easily perceived and acted on from the world that cannot be easily perceived or acted on, but the left-right axis has few salient perceptual or behavioral asymmetries. This analysis predicts that, for the upright observer, things located along the head-feet axis should be fastest to retrieve, followed by things located on the front-back axis, followed by things located on the left-right axis. For the reclining observer, no body axis correlates with gravity, so accessibility depends entirely on the body axes. In this case, things located along the front-back axis should be fastest because of the forward bias of perception and action.

The spatial framework pattern of reaction times was compared to patterns predicted by two other theories in several dozen experiments. According to a theory based purely on the physical situation, the equiavailability model, no region of space has special status, so all directions should be equal. According to an account derived from theories of mental imagery (e.g., Kosslyn, 1980; Shepard & Podgorny, 1978), the mental transformation model, participants should imagine themselves in the scene. When a direction is probed, they should imagine themselves turning to face that direction to determine what object is there. Looking should take longer the greater the angle from forward. This model predicts that front should be fastest, followed by left, right, head, and feet, with back the slowest.

The spatial framework pattern of reaction times, derived from an analysis of perception and action, has been found in numerous variations (e.g., Bryant, Tversky & Franklin, 1992; Franklin, Tversky, & Coon, 1992; Tversky, Kim, & Cohen, 1999). Although the pattern of data does not fit the analog view of mental imagery, it does not fit a propositional account either (e.g., Pylyshyn, 1981). In particular, participants readily reorient under instructions that the observer turns to face a new object, but participants find it difficult to reorient under instructions that the room rotates so that the observer is facing a new object, even though formally, the two kinds of instructions require identical transformations (Tversky et al., 1999). Under normal conditions, people turn but environments do not, and those expectations affect updating mental worlds.

IMAGINARY ACTIONS IN
IMAGINARY WORLDS

The first investigations of the space around the body followed the example of storytellers and used prose to instill the worlds and changes in it. Later studies used models, diagrams, and real spaces to instill the worlds (Bryant & Tversky, 1999; Bryant, Tversky, & Lanca, 2001). Models induce observers to take the view of the central figure, a perspective embedded in the imaginary world. Diagrams induce observers to take a view from above, a perspective external to the imaginary world (Bryant & Tversky, 1999). One set of studies showed differences between locating objects from perception and from memory (Bryant, Tversky, & Lanca, 2001). When a scene is responded to from perception, the pattern of reaction times conforms to what might be termed the *physical transformation model*. Specifically, objects directly in front are fastest, those displaced by ninety degrees next – head, feet, left, and right – and objects behind are slowest. In this case, observers are turning to look at the probed locations to determine what is in the probed direction. However, once participants learn the environment, they cease to

look even though they could. Instead, they respond from memory, and their reaction times fit the spatial framework pattern; that is, responses to head and feet were fastest, followed by responses to front and back, and then responses to left and right.

The fact that responding from perception and responding from memory were different demonstrates that imagery is not simply internalized perception; rather, it is a construction, and sometimes a reconstruction of perception. The advantage of using spatial frameworks in memory rather than the particular views of perception is generality. The more abstract spatial framework representation allows for easy computation of many views as well as easy transformation between views.

Conceptions of the space around the body do not depend on the physical situation per se. Instead, as for the space of the body, conceptions of the space around the body derive from and are biased by enduring characteristics of perception and action of the human body in the world, the asymmetries of the body that affect how the body can act and perceive, and the asymmetries of the gravitational axis of the world, which also affect human action and perception. The next space to be considered, the space of navigation, is also a constructed mental space that is biased by perception and action.

Space of Navigation

The space we experience as we hike in the mountains or go from home to work or wander through a museum is the space of navigation. It is too large to be perceived from a single place, so it must be constructed from separate pieces. The pieces can be views from experience, they can be descriptions we have heard or read, or they can be maps we have studied. How are the different pieces and different modalities combined, the smaller spaces to form a large one? To put the pieces together requires a common reference frame and reference objects. These allow the separate pieces to be integrated, scaled, arranged. But the very factors that allow integration also produce distortions.

Consider first reference objects. Cities or landmarks or landmasses are located and remembered with respect to one another. North America is north of South America. Philadelphia is west of Rome. Grouping of landmarks follows the gestalt principle of grouping by proximity. However, when people remember landmarks or landmasses relative to one another, they remember them as more aligned than they actually were. As a consequence, a significant majority of observers chose a map in which North America is more directly north of South America than the true map in which South America barely overlaps North America (Tversky, 1981). Likewise, a significant majority of respondents think that Boston is east of Rio de Janeiro, though it is not. Landmasses oriented east-west are similarly distorted. A significant majority of observers chose a map in which Europe is located directly west of the United States rather than the true map, in which Europe is north of the United States. Likewise, a significant majority think that Philadelphia is north of Rome, though it is not. This error occurs for artificial maps as well as true ones, and it holds for blobs not viewed as maps. Alignment, then, is an inevitable consequence of grouping.

A similar error, termed *rotation*, arises when reference frames are used to organize elements within them, another prominent gestalt perceptual organizing principle. When students were asked to place a cutout of a map of South America in an NSEW frame, they placed South America upright. As it is, South American looks tilted; as an elongated shape, it generates its own set of axes, which are at odds with the geographic ones. Another example comes from the San Francisco Bay Area. The region runs west as it goes north. Yet, the overall conception is that the Bay Area runs from north to south, so residents are surprised to learn that Berkeley is west of Stanford, and Santa Cruz is east of Stanford.

Alignment and rotation are widespread; they occur for landmasses, for roads, and for cities; they also appear in memory for meaningless blobs, in children as well as adults. They reflect general perceptual organizing principles, with effects in memory for geography as well as other domains, such as graphs (e.g., Schiano & Tversky, 1992; Tversky & Schiano, 1989).

Other systematic errors in memory for the space of navigation help to characterize how that space is constructed. In natural spaces, some elements are naturally more prominent than others. In geographic space, these are landmarks: the Golden Gate Bridge in San Francisco, Times Square in Manhattan, the Eiffel Tower in Paris. Every city, every town, every campus, has them. Our lives, too, have temporal landmarks: family events, educational achievements, and the like. When asked to estimate distances from an ordinary building to a landmark, people give smaller distances than the distances from a landmark to an ordinary building (e.g., Sadalla, Burroughs, & Staplin, 1980). Thus, distances in the mind are not symmetrical! These asymmetries hold for metaphoric spaces as well as physical ones. For example, people think a son is more like his father than the father like his son (Tversky & Gati, 1978). Mental representations of abstract spaces, like mental representations of real spaces, have landmarks and prototypes.

When conceptual spaces get too large, the mind divides them into parts and subparts – so, too, for geographic spaces. Geographic spaces can be subdivided and grouped, by geographic, political, and other categories. People judge distances between entities within a group to be less than distances between entities situated in different groups (e.g., Hirtle & Jonides, 1985). Perspective also affects distance judgments, whether imagined or real. Students imagining themselves in San Francisco estimated the distance from San Francisco to Salt Lake City to be larger than those imagining themselves in New York City. Conversely, students imagining themselves in New York City estimated the distance from New York City to Pittsburgh to be greater than did students imagining themselves in San Francisco

(Holyoak & Mah, 1982). Of course, Steinberg had spoofed this distortion on the covers of the *New Yorker* long before. Both distortions due to grouping and distortions due to perspective have analogues in abstract thought, for example in judgments about in-group and out-group members (e.g., Quattrone, 1986).

These are not the only systematic errors in spatial judgments. The errors discussed so far could be called "perceptual errors," based on perceptual processing. However, there are errors from action or potential action as well. For example, routes that have more turns or landmarks are judged longer than routes with fewer turns or landmarks (Sadalla & Staplin, 1980a, 1980b). Trying to put together all these systematic distortions would not likely yield a cognitive map that is consistent and coherent. For this reason, a better metaphor for mental conceptions of large spaces is a cognitive collage (Tversky, 1993). Like collages, mental conceptions of space are constructed from fragments, from different perspectives, and from different modalities.

WHY ARE THERE SYSTEMATIC ERRORS?

At first thought, it is mystifying that the mind distorts the world. Further thought reveals that there are good reasons that it does so. Take, for example, the visual system. The world does not give us edges, corners, and contours, yet these are efficient for identifying the objects of importance. It is the nervous system that gives us edges, corners, and contours by sharpening and leveling – distorting – incoming information. For the space of navigation, what is important is integrating different views and different modalities into wholes that have some coherence. Integrating requires both extracting the entities that are important from all the views and modes and coordinating reference frames. This process has two consequences that lead to distortions: focusing on some information at the expense of other and integrating approximately or schematically, as the exact information is often missing or unnecessary (for a more detailed discus-

sion of these issues, see Tversky, 2003, 2005b).

TALKING ABOUT LARGE ENVIRONMENTS

Humans are talkative beings, and undoubtedly one of the early topics of conversation in the evolution of language was talking about space, telling others where to find food and shelter and where to avoid danger. Space is usually described from a perspective, as a perspective allows locating things relative to one another and a frame of reference. Spontaneous descriptions of large spaces take one of two perspectives or, interestingly, a combination of both (Taylor & Tversky, 1992, 1996). In a route perspective, speakers take the imagined point of view of a traveler in an environment and describe the locations of landmarks relative to the changing position of the traveler in terms of left, right, front, and back. In a survey perspective, speakers take a bird's-eye view of an environment, as if from a tree or mountaintop, and describe the locations of landmarks relative to one another in terms of north, south, east, and west. Each of these perspectives is situated; that is, each is a familiar way of viewing and interacting with an environment.

Significantly, survey and route perspectives have parallels in thinking about the landscape of time, yielding a bias familiar to academicians. When events are far in the future, we find room for them in the survey-like representation we use for the vast future, but when events are located in the near future, we think about them as routes from now to then, from here to there. Suddenly, the time and effort to get to that gorgeous spot remote in a mountain range looms large, especially against the other time-consuming events already scheduled (e.g., Trope & Liberman, 2003). More abstract parallels to route and survey perspectives abound. A good information-systems designer needs to plan the overall configuration of computers, servers, printers, and at the same time, take into account the set of possible procedures users are likely to need (Nickerson, Tversky, Corter, Zahner, & Rho, in press). Similarly, determining the organization of a manufacturing plant must include both the divisions of operation and the tasks to be performed. The survey perspective consists of wholes, parts, and subparts, and the route perspective of sequences within. More on sequences when we get to events.

Spatial Mental Transformations

In cognitive science talk, representations are static mappings of elements and relations in the world to elements and relations in the mind. Representations, though conceived to be static, can be used in mental actions. They can be mentally scanned (Kosslyn, 1980) or searched or, importantly, transformed. Mental transformations of or in mental representations again have situated and embodied origins (Shepard, 1984); that is, they reflect and derive from common perceptual experience. There are many (e.g., Tversky, 2005d), but two seem to be primary: imagining changes in objects, most notably, changes in orientation or mental rotation (Shepard & Cooper, 1982), and imagining changes to one's own orientation in space (e.g., Bryant & Tversky, 1999; Parsons, 1987; Wraga, Creem, & Proffitt, 2000; Zacks, Mires, Tversky, & Hazeltine, 2000). These two spatial mental transformations are independent, producing different patterns of reaction times and using different brain pathways (e.g., Bryant & Tversky, 1999; Parsons, 1987; Wraga et al., 2000; Zacks et al., 2000; Zacks, Vettel, & Michelon, 2003). In the course of their daily lives, people naturally change orientations in space themselves and naturally observe other objects changing orientation. These spatial transformations can be performed mentally and applied to representations of the concrete and the abstract, providing a spatial basis for imagination. Mental spatial transformations underlie a range of mental feats: figuring out a route from a map and enacting a route while navigating; constructing a laparoscopic surgical procedure; inventing acrobatics on ice, sea, or land; or designing the next great museum (see Shepard, 1978).

Situated Mental Spaces

Three spaces crucial to human interactions in the world have been discussed: the space of the body, the space around the body, and the space of navigation. There are other spaces and spatial reference frames, notably, the space around the jaw or the hand (e.g., Gross & Graziano, 1995). Each of these spaces subserves different perceptual-motor interactions, and conceptions of those spaces differ from physical measurements of the spaces in concordance with those interactions. For the space of the body, functional significance rather than size determines accessibility of body parts. For the space around the body, the axes of the body form a reference frame, in three dimensions, and the accessibility of axes depends on their significance in perception and action. The space of navigation is pieced together from different experiences by selecting common entities – landmarks – and a unifying frame of reference. The use of reference landmarks and reference frames lead to systematic errors in judgments of distance and direction. These spaces are used for thinking about other things, time, value, power, and a multitude of other abstract concepts, as revealed in language, gesture, and graphics. The use of space for general thought is especially evident in the spaces people create to serve as tools to augment their own cognition, spaces in the world that serve internal spaces in the mind. This discussion will be continued later, when we get to diagrams. But first we move from space to time, to the events that take place in time.

Action

PACKAGING LIFE INTO EVENTS
The world is never static. To make sense of the constant flux, the mind captures change in packets, called "events." Clues to those packets come from the ways we talk about them: go to work, eat dinner, see a movie. Thus, the continuous events that occur in time are segmented and categorized, much as the tremendous variety of things in the world are grouped and categorized (e.g.,

Rosch, 1978). For ordinary everyday events, like making a bed or doing the dishes, event packets are perceived as a sequence of hierarchical action-object couplets, culminating in achievements or accomplishments (for an analysis and review, see Zacks & Tversky, 2001). When asked to give play-by-play descriptions of films of everyday events like making a bed or doing the dishes, at coarse and fine levels, people provide a sequence of actions on objects that are hierarchically organized into goals and subgoals (Zacks, Tversky, & Iyer, 2001). The same occurs when people describe the units and subunits of generic events (Zacks et al., 2001) and of remembered events, like going to the doctor (Bower, Black, & Turner, 1979). The units of events are not actions, but action-object couplets; *put* is not a unit, but *put on the bottom sheet, put the dishes in the sink,* and *put the clothes in the washing machine* are units of making a bed, doing the dishes, and doing the laundry, respectively (e.g., Tversky, Zacks, & Hard, 2008). *Put* is not the same for *put on the bottom sheet* or *put the clothes in the dryer*. As sequences of action-object couplets, events are inherently situated, not just in the objects they entail but also in their characteristic actors and settings. The bed is made in the bedroom and the dishes are done in the kitchen, by household residents or by their helpers. Events are the stuff of our lives, and our understanding of them is situated in the appropriate settings, objects, and actors. Hierarchical organization of action serves as an action plan, a mental simulation of the action that embodies the action (cf. Gallese, 2005; Goldman, 2005).

ACTION UNDERSTANDING AND
PERSPECTIVE TAKING
Events performed by people, in contrast to natural events like hurricanes or earthquakes, are of special importance to people. We need to understand the actions and intentions of others to understand what they are doing, to react to what they are doing, and to perform those actions ourselves. Learning the action-object hierarchies that constitute events performed by people is

often a social process, which occurs from observing others perform actions. How might this happen? Recall the play-by-play descriptions of events like making a bed. They describe the actions of the actors and are from the perspective of the actor, not the perspective of the person who is viewing and describing the scene. Understanding the actions and inferring the intentions of others may begin with taking their perspective.

Neurophysiological evidence lends support to this possibility. There is ample evidence that watching others' actions and imagining one's own actions activate brain areas associated with action planning and performance (e.g., Cross, Hamilton, & Grafton, 2006; Decety & Grèzes, 2006; Koski, Iacoboni, Dubeau, Woods, & Mazziotta, 2003; Rizzolatti, Fadiga, Fogassi, & Gallese, 1999; Ruby & Decety, 2001). What is more, the motor activation appears to correspond to an anatomical mapping of the actor's body to the observer's body (Aziz-Zadeh, Maeda, Zaidel, Mazziotta, & Iacoboni, 2002). As Aziz-Zadeh et al. note, merely observing action seems to induce motor resonance or motor simulation on the part of the observer, a possible mechanism for action understanding and learning, one that effectively embodies observed behavior. Actively describing or imitating actions from the actor's perspective may promote action learning and understanding by enhancing these natural processes.

Shaping Communication: Gestures and Diagrams

Gestures: External Spaces

GESTURE IS EFFECTIVE IN
COMMUNICATION
The hands serve not just to perform actions but also to explain them. When people tell stories or explain things, they use their hands, especially when they relate how things are arranged in space or how to do something or how something works (e.g., Goldin-Meadow, 2003; McNeill, 2005). Of course, people gesture for many other reasons as well. Gestures appear to have

benefits both for those making the gestures and for those watching them. For performers of gestures, gestures serve to find words; when speakers sit on their hands, they are less fluent (Krauss, Chen, & Chawla, 1996; Krauss, Chen, & Gottesman, 2000). Children blind from birth gesture when describing a spatial layout, suggesting that gestures help to organize thought (Iverson & Goldin-Meadow, 1997). For viewers of gestures, gestures clarify meanings and facilitate comprehension (e.g., Alibali, Flevares, & Goldin-Meadow, 1997; Goldin-Meadow, 2003; Kelly & Church, 1998; McNeill, Cassell, & McCullough, 1994; Valenzeno, Alibali, & Klatzky, 2003). These many roles of gestures are a testament to the varieties of embodied cognition in thinking, in expressing thought, and in understanding thought.

GESTURES IN SPATIAL DESCRIPTIONS

Evidence for how gestures organize and express thought comes from a study in which participants were asked to describe environments they had learned from maps (Emmorey, Tversky, & Taylor, 2000), modeled on the previous work of Taylor and Tversky (1996). As before, some environments elicited primarily route descriptions; others, primarily survey descriptions; and others, mixed descriptions. The gestures corresponded to the description perspective, suggesting that both embodied gestures and symbolic language reflected the way speakers thought about the environments. Frequently, speakers used series of related gestures to create models of the environments. They virtually sketched the environments in the air, anchoring them with some places and indicating locations of other places relative to the anchors. The set of gestures, sometimes as long as fifteen gestures in a row, formed a coherent interrelated sequence.

GESTURES PLACE THINGS IN MEMORY

Remarkably, gestures occur in the absence of speech and in the absence of communication, strong evidence that they serve thought by embodying it. One activity people engage in throughout their lives is solving problems.

Participants were asked to solve a series of spatial problems, some easy and some difficult. After they solved them, they were asked to explain their solutions to a video camera so that someone watching the video would understand the solution (Kessell & Tversky, 2005). In explaining their solutions to the problems, nearly all participants gestured for all problems. Their gestures served to represent the problem, by using iconic gestures reflecting the spatial layout, and their gestures served to demonstrate the solutions to the problems – again, typically iconic gestures showing the transformations needed for solution.

More surprising was the finding that alone in a room, not speaking, many participants gestured when trying to solve certain problems. Only two of the problems elicited gestures in most participants. Those that elicited gestures were the problems with high demands on spatial working memory, keeping track of many rungs on a ladder or the locations and properties of six glasses. In these cases, the gestures represented the problems; they corresponded to the spatial layouts, vertical for the ladder and horizontal for the glasses, with the appropriate numbers for each. In a second parallel study, other participants were given paper and pencil when solving the problems. These participants used paper and pencil for exactly the same problems that had elicited gestures in participants without paper and pencil. Together, the findings suggest that gestures were used to off-load and organize spatial working memory when internal capacity was taxed. Using paper to off-load and organize working memory makes sense; it is permanent and can be referred to during problem solving. Using gestures to off-load working memory is more puzzling, as gestures are fleeting. Why might gestures facilitate working memory?

One possible explanation for why gestures are used to off-load working memory is that people remember where they put things. Or they remember better if they put the things somewhere than if someone else did. People remember routes when they navigate better than when they are taken somewhere. They remember actions better if they do them themselves (Engelkamp, 1998). The physical acts of placing or navigating appear to be intimately involved in spatial memory. Gesturing, putting, and placing, then, may invoke the same cognitive networks in the service of conceptual memory.

Thinking can be regarded as action, internalized. Indeed, we talk about thinking as actions: we frame our thoughts, we pull ideas together or take them apart; we buy ideas, we sell them, we build one idea on another. This simple example, placing imaginary objects to support memory of them, shows how thinking can involve the body acting in the world.

Diagrams: External Spaces

It seems that humans have always created artifacts. It is well known that many of these were intended to increase physical well-being, such as tools for harvesting and preparing food. But many are intended to increase mental well-being, such as to augment memory and facilitate information processing. Trail markers, tallies, pictographs, and maps are some of the cognitive tools created by cultures all over the globe. Often people do not have to create artifacts to augment cognition; they just co-opt what is there. Fingers get used for counting, and hands and feet for measuring.

Maps serve as a paradigm for a created cognitive tool. Maps have dozens of uses, not just to guide navigation but also to proclaim territory or to promote inferences about flows of populations, weather, or pollen. They use elements and spatial relations among elements on stone, clay, sand, or paper to convey elements and spatial relations in a larger world. But they do not just shrink the world, they omit much of the world and distort the world. Paths and landmarks are included that would not be visible at the scale of the map. Paths are straightened, turns are schematized to ninety degrees, distances are approximate. The reader will observe that these simplifications to external representations of space parallel the simplifications of internal representations of space. As noted, that may be one reason why they work; they include the information important to people and capture the way people think. That information in maps is frequently omitted and distorted often does not matter, as the environment supplements and disambiguates it.

Given that people think about abstract concepts spatially, as evident in language like *getting close* to someone, *feeling upbeat*, *arriving at* an insight, *entering* a new field, *wrapping one's head around* an idea, it seems surprising that external representations for abstract ideas were not common until the late eighteenth century (e.g., Beniger & Robyn, 1978; Carswell & Wickens, 1988; Tufte, 1983). Like maps, visualizations of the abstract use elements and spatial relations among them, but they use them metaphorically to represent abstract elements and relations. Part of their success is that they rely on human facility in understanding spatial information and making spatial inferences (e.g., Larkin & Simon, 1987; Tversky, 1993).

NATURAL CORRESPONDENCES
Spatial relations in graphics are readily produced and understood, even by preschool children. In one experiment, preschoolers, children, and adults were asked to arrange stickers on paper to express various spatial, temporal, quantitative, and preference concepts, for example, a TV show they loved, a TV show they were indifferent to, and a TV show they disliked (Tversky, Kugelmass, & Winter, 1991). Most of the youngest children arranged the stickers on a line, showing that they saw a dimension underlying the elements, and ordered them accordingly. For preference and quantity, they mapped more to up or left or right but almost never to down. That more goes up goes along with language and reflects the asymmetry of that axis in the world. Similarly, that more equally goes left and right reflects the symmetry of the horizontal axis. Preteen children also represented interval and ordinal relations among elements. These results – from children from a variety of language cultures – suggest that the correspondences of

proximity and direction in an abstract space to proximity and direction on paper are natural and spontaneous.

The use of elements on paper to represent elements in the world or the mind also seems to have natural correspondences. Early written languages provide examples, as they depicted meanings rather than recorded language as spoken (e.g., Gelb, 1963). Wherever possible, resemblance was used, but many concepts are difficult to depict. Then, figures of depictions, analogous to figures of speech, synecdoche (association represents element; e.g., *scales* for scales of justice) or metonymy (part of element represents element; e.g., horns of a sheep) are used (e.g., Tversky, 1995, 2001, 2005a). Diagrams and interfaces use similar techniques; think of icons in airport signs or on computers. Another readily comprehended kind of element is common in diagrams, schematic geometric forms like lines, arrows, and blobs (Tversky, Zacks, Lee, & Heiser, 2000). In quantitative graphs, for example, lines connect; they show that two (or more) variables share an underlying attribute but have different values. Bars contain and separate. The justification for using bars or lines relies on assumptions about the underlying data, lines for interval data and bars for categorical data. People's interpretation and production of bars and lines appears to derive from the natural graphic meanings of bars and lines. People, then, should readily interpret lines as trends and bars as discrete comparisons, and they do. What is more, they produce lines for trends and bars for discrete comparisons. For both interpretation and production, the graphic forms are stronger than the actual underlying dimensions (Zacks & Tversky, 1999). Arrows are asymmetrical lines and suggest asymmetrical relations. Arrows are frequently added to diagrams to suggest a variety of meanings: order, cause, motion, outcome, and more. When asked to interpret diagrams that do not have arrows of mechanical systems like pumps and brakes, people provide structural descriptions of the spatial arrangement of the parts. When asked to describe diagrams with arrows, people provide step-by-step causal relations (Heiser & Tversky, 2006).

USING MENTAL MAPS AND SKETCH MAPS

When asked to produce a map to aid a traveler to get from one place to another, people usually produce rudimentary maps (e.g., Tversky & Lee, 1998, 1999). Most of the detail is left out, and what is left in, typically, the paths that form the route, is distorted. Intersections are usually drawn at right angles and distances are approximate. Like mental maps of environments, sketch maps are distorted, and they are distorted in similar ways. Nevertheless, both mental maps and sketch maps serve their purpose; they help people find their destinations. How is that? Like mental maps, sketch maps are situated, used in context, in environments, and the environments disambiguate and correct (Tversky, 2003). If a turn is eighty or one hundred degrees instead of ninety, the traveler will turn the way the road goes. The traveler will turn upon reaching the next landmark, whatever the distance. All that is needed from the map is where to turn and which way, and in fact, that is the information included in verbal directions. Intersections and turns can be checked against the world. Actual navigation is even more deeply situated. After checking the landmarks and turns of either mental or paper maps against the world, successful navigation depends on coordinating eye and body to make the turns correctly.

Although these schematic elements – lines, arrows, blobs – have meanings that are readily interpreted in context, they have languagelike properties. Like words, they are categorical and can be combined to create many possible graphics, for example, route maps and networks. Context disambiguates them – a line in a graph has a different meaning from a line in a map. Context is necessary to disambiguate the words that parallel these forms. An occupational line and a train line are not likely to be confused in context, nor are mathematical and romantic relationships. Yet, unlike words, the meanings of these forms are readily available.

External spaces serve cognition, both individual and group, in a multitude of ways. They off-load the contents of memory, freeing working memory to manipulate external tokens instead of internal ones. They relieve working memory further by allowing externalization of intermediate products of mental manipulations. They promote organization and reorganization of the contents of memory. They can be viewed and manipulated by groups, thereby ensuring common understanding and facilitating collaboration. Because they are based on natural cognitive correspondences, external spaces both reflect and support human thought, concrete and abstract.

Situated Thought

We cannot get out of our bodies and we cannot get out of the world. We can do so only in our imaginations, but as we have seen, the imagination is constrained by our bodies and the world. Spatial thinking comes from and is shaped by perceiving the world and acting in it, be it through learning or through evolution. The embodied and situated cognitive structures and biases of thought about space and about action limit and bias abstract thought as well. Thought is grounded in the world and in the body. Our bodies not only sense but also participate in thought; we use our bodies to locate, to refer, to measure, to arrange and rearrange, to transform. Imagination is not limited by the body and the world; it is enabled by the body and the world. The representations and processes used to understand the spatial world and act in it are those that allow invention, creativity, and discovery.

Acknowledgments

I am grateful to the insightful comments of Pascale Michelon on an earlier draft of this chapter. Preparation of this chapter and/or of some of the research reported were supported by the following grants: NSF BNS 8002012; AFOSR 89-0076; the Edinburgh-Stanford Link through the Center for the Study of Language and Information at Stanford University; Office of Naval Research Grants NOOO14-PP-1-O649, N000140110717, and N000140210534, NSF REC-0440103; and the Stanford Regional Visualization and Analysis Center.

Some of the discussion has been reviewed elsewhere, and parts were reworked from Tversky (2005c).

References

Alibali, M. W., Flevares, L., & Goldin-Meadow, S. (1997). Assessing knowledge conveyed in gesture: Do teachers have the upper hand? *Journal of Educational Psychology, 89,* 183–193.

Andersen, E. S. (1978). Lexical universals of body-part terminology. In J. H. Greenberg (Ed.), *Universals of human language* (pp. 335–368). Stanford, CA: Stanford University Press.

Aziz-Zadeh, L., Maeda, F., Zaidel, E., Mazziotta, J., & Iacoboni, M. (2002). Lateralization in motor facilitation during action observation: A TMS study. *Experimental Brain Research, 144,* 127–131.

Beniger, J. R., & Robyn, D. L. (1978). Quantitative graphics in statistics. *American Statistician, 32,* 1–11.

Bower, G. H., Black, J. B., & Turner, T. J. (1979). Scripts in memory for text. *Cognitive Psychology, 11,* 179–220.

Brown, C. H. (1976). General principles of human anatomical partonomy and speculations on the growth of partonomic nomenclature. *American Ethnologist, 3,* 400–424.

Bryant, D. J., & Tversky, B. (1999). Mental representations of spatial relations from diagrams and models. *Journal of Experimental Psychology: Learning, Memory and Cognition, 25,* 137–156.

Bryant, D. J., Tversky, B., & Franklin, N. (1992). Internal and external spatial frameworks for representing described scenes. *Journal of Memory and Language, 31,* 74–98.

Bryant, D. J., Tversky, B., & Lanca, M. (2001). Retrieving spatial relations from observation and memory. In E. van der Zee & U. Nikanne (Eds.), *Conceptual structure and its interfaces with other modules of representation* (pp. 116–139). Oxford: Oxford University Press.

Carswell, C. M., & Wickens, C. D. (1988). *Comparative graphics: History and applications of perceptual integrality theory and the proximity compatibility hypothesis* (Tech. Rep.). Urbana: Institute of Aviation, University of Illinois at Urbana-Champaign.

Chatterjee, S. H., Freyd, J. J., & Shiffrar, M. (1996). Configural processing in the perception of apparent biological motion. *Journal of Experimental Psychology: Human Perception and Performance, 22,* 916–929.

Clark, H. H. (1973). Space, time, semantics, and the child. In T. E. Moore (Ed.), *Cognitive development and the acquisition of language* (pp. 27–63). New York: Academic Press.

Cross, E. S., Hamilton, A. F., & Grafton, S. T. (2006). Building a motor simulation de novo: Observation of dance by dancers. *Neuroimage, 31*(3), 1257–1267.

Decety, J., & Grèzes, J. (2006). The power of simulation: Imagining one's own and other's behavior. *Brain Research, 1079*, 4–14.

Emmorey, K., Tversky, B., & Taylor, H. A. (2000). Using space to describe space: Perspective in speech, sign, and gesture. *Journal of Spatial Cognition and Computation, 2*, 157–180.

Engelkamp, J. (1998). *Memory for actions.* Hove, UK: Psychology Press.

Franklin, N., & Tversky, B. (1990). Searching imagined environments. *Journal of Experimental Psychology: General, 119*, 63–76.

Franklin, N., Tversky, B., & Coon, V. (1992). Switching points of view in spatial mental models acquired from text. *Memory and Cognition, 20*, 507–518.

Gallese, V. (2005). "Being like me": Self-other identity, mirror neurons, and empathy. In S. Hurley & N. Chater (Eds.), *Perspectives on imitation: From neuroscience to social science* (Vol. 1, pp. 108–118). Cambridge, MA: MIT Press.

Gelb, I. (1963). *A study of writing* (2nd ed.). Chicago: University of Chicago Press.

Goldin-Meadow, S. (2003). *Hearing gesture: How our hands help us think.* Cambridge, MA: Belknap Press.

Goldman, A. (2005). Imitation, mindreading, and simulation. In S. Hurley & N. Chater (Eds.), *Perspectives on imitation: From neuroscience to social science* (Vol. 2, pp. 79–93). Cambridge, MA: MIT Press.

Goodnow, J. (1977). *Children's drawing.* London: Open Books.

Gross, C. G., & Graziano, M. S. A. (1995). Multiple representations of space in the brain. *Neuroscientist, 1*, 43–50.

Hegarty, M., Carpenter, P. A., & Just, M. A. (1990). Diagrams in the comprehension of scientific text. In R. Barr, M. L. Kamil, P. Mosenthal, & P. D. Pearson (Eds.), *Handbook of reading research.* New York: Longman.

Heiser, J., & Tversky, B. (2006). Arrows in comprehending and producing mechanical diagrams. *Cognitive Science, 30*, 581–592.

Hirtle, S., & Jonides, J. (1985). Hierarachies in cognitive maps. *Memory and Cognition, 13*, 208–217.

Hoffman, D. D., & Richards, W. A. (1984). Parts of recognition. *Cognition, 18*, 65–96.

Holyoak, K. J., & Mah, W. A. (1982). Cognitive reference points in judgements of symbolic magnitude. *Cognitive Psychology, 14*, 328–352.

Iverson, J., & Goldin-Meadow, S. (1997). What's communication got to do with it? Gesture in children blind from birth. *Developmental Psychology, 33*, 453–467.

Kellogg, R. (1969). *Analyzing children's art.* Palo Alto, CA: National Press.

Kelly, S. D., & Church, B. (1998). A comparison between children's and adults' ability to detect conceptual information conveyed through representational gestures. *Child Development, 69*, 85–93.

Kessell, A., & Tversky, B. (2005). Gestures for thinking and explaining. In B. G. Bara, L. W. Barsalou, & M. Bucciarelli (Eds.), *Proceedings of the Cognitive Science Society Meetings* (p. 2498). Mahwah, NJ: Lawrence Erlbaum.

Koski, L., Iacoboni, M., Dubeau, M.-C., Woods, R. P., & Mazziotta, J. C. (2003). Modulation of cortical activity during different imitative behaviours. *Journal of Neurophysiology, 89*, 460–471.

Kosslyn, S. M. (1980). *Image and mind.* Cambridge: Harvard University Press.

Krauss, R. M., Chen, Y., & Chawla, P. (1996). Nonverbal behavior and nonverbal communication: What do conversational hand gestures tell us? In M. P. Zanna (Ed.), *Advances in experimental social psychology* (pp. 389–450). San Diego, CA: Academic Press.

Krauss, R. M., Chen, Y., & Gottesman, R. (2000). Lexical gestures and lexical access: A process model. In D. McNeill (Ed.), *Language and gesture* (pp. 261–284). Cambridge: Cambridge University Press.

Lakoff, G., & Johnson, M. (1980). *Metaphors we live by.* Chicago: University of Chicago Press.

Larkin, J. H., & Simon, H. A. (1987). Why a diagram is (sometimes) worth ten thousand words. *Cognitive Science, 11*, 65–99.

McNeill, D. (2005). *Gesture and thought.* Chicago: University of Chicago Press.

McNeill, D., Cassell, J., & McCullough, K. E. (1994). Communicative effects of speech-mismatched gestures. *Research on Language and Social Interaction, 27*, 223–237.

Morrison, J. B., & Tversky, B. (2005). Bodies and their parts. *Memory and Cognition, 33*, 696–709.

Nickerson, J., Tversky, B., Corter, J., Zahner, D., & Rho, Y.-J. (in press). Diagrams as a tool in the design of information systems. In J. S. Gero & A. Goel (Eds.), *Design Computing and Cognition '08*. Dordrecht, The Netherlands: Springer.

Parsons, L. M. (1987). Imagined spatial transformation of one's body. *Journal of Experimental Psychology: General, 116,* 172–191.

Pylyshyn, Z. W. (1981) The imagery debate: Analogue media versus tacit knowledge. *Psychological Review, 88,* 16–45.

Quattrone, G. A. (1986). On the perception of a group's variability. In S. Worchel & W. Austin (Eds.), *The psychology of intergroup relations* (pp. 25–48). New York: Nelson-Hall.

Reed, C. L. (2002). Body schemas. In A. Meltzoff & W. Prinz (Eds.), *The imitative mind* (pp. 233–243). Cambridge: Cambridge University Press.

Reed, C. L., & Farah, M. J. (1995). The psychological reality of the body schema: A test with normal participants. *Journal of Experimental Psychology: Human Perception and Performance, 21,* 334–343.

Rizzolatti, G., Fadiga, L., Fogassi, L., & Gallese, V. (1999). Resonance behaviors and mirror neurons. *Archives Italiennes de Biologie, 137,* 85–100.

Rock, I. (1973). *Orientation and form.* New York: Academic Press.

Rosch, E. (1978). Principles of categorization. In E. Rosch & B. B. Lloyd (Eds.), *Cognition and categorization* (pp. 27–48). Hillsdale, NJ: Lawrence Erlbaum.

Ruby, P., & Decety, J. (2001). Effect of subjective perspective taking during simulation of action: A PET investigation of agency. *Nature Neuroscience, 4,* 546–550.

Sadalla, E. K., Burroughs, W. J., & Staplin, L. I. (1980). Reference points in spatial cognition. *Journal of Experimental Psychology: Human Learning and Memory, 5,* 516–528.

Sadalla, E. K., & Staplin, L. J. (1980a). An information storage model for distance cognition. *Environment and Behavior, 12,* 183–193.

Sadalla, E. K., & Staplin, L. J. (1980b). The perception of traversed distance: Intersections. *Environment and Behavior, 12,* 167–182.

Schiano, D., & Tversky, B. (1992). Structure and strategy in viewing simple graphs. *Memory and Cognition, 20,* 12–20.

Shepard, R. N. (1978). Externalization of mental images and the act of creation. In B. S. Randhawa & B. F. Coffman (Eds.), *Visual learning, thinking, and communication* (pp. 133–189). London: Academic Press.

Shepard, R. N. (1984). Ecological constraints on internal representations: Resonant kinematics of perceiving, imagining, thinking, and dreaming. *Psychological Review, 91,* 417–447.

Shepard, R. N., & Cooper, L. (1982). *Mental images and their transformation.* Cambridge, MA: MIT Press.

Shepard, R. N., & Podgorny, P. (1978). Cognitive processes that resemble perceptual processes. In W. K. Estes (Ed.), *Handbook of learning and cognitive processes* (Vol. 5, pp. 189–237). Hillsdale, NJ: Lawrence Erlbaum.

Shiffrar, M., & Freyd, J. J. (1993). Timing and apparent motion path choice with human body photographs. *Psychological Science, 4,* 379–384.

Talmy, L. (1983). How language structures space. In H. L. Pick, Jr. & L. P. Acredolo (Eds.), *Spatial orientation: Theory, research, and application* (pp. 225–282). New York: Plenum Press.

Taylor, H. A., & Tversky, B. (1992). Descriptions and depictions of environments. *Memory and Cognition, 20,* 483–496.

Taylor, H. A., & Tversky, B. (1996). Perspective in spatial descriptions. *Journal of Memory and Language, 35,* 371–391.

Trope, Y., & Liberman, N. (2003). Temporal construal. *Psychological Review, 110,* 403–421.

Tufte, E. R. (1983). *The visual display of quantitative information.* Cheshire, CT: Graphics Press.

Tversky, B. (1981). Distortions in memory for maps. *Cognitive Psychology, 13,* 407–433.

Tversky, B. (1989). Parts, partonomies, and taxonomies. *Developmental Psychology, 25,* 983–995.

Tversky, B. (1993). Cognitive maps, cognitive collages, and spatial mental models. In A. U. Frank & I. Campari (Eds.), *Spatial information theory: A theoretical basis for GIS* (pp. 14–24). Berlin: Springer-Verlag.

Tversky, B. (1995). Cognitive origins of graphic conventions. In F. T. Marchese (Ed.), *Understanding images* (pp. 29–53). New York: Springer-Verlag.

Tversky, B. (2000). Remembering space. In E. Tulving & F. I. M. Craik (Eds.), *Handbook of memory* (pp. 363–378). New York: Oxford University Press.

Tversky, B. (2001). Spatial schemas in depictions. In M. Gattis (Ed.), *Spatial schemas and abstract thought* (pp. 79–111). Cambridge, MA: MIT Press.

Tversky, B. (2003). Navigating by mind and by body. In C. Freksa, W. Brauer, C. Habel, & K.

F. Wender (Eds.), *Spatial cognition III: Routes and navigation, human memory and learning, spatial representation and spatial reasoning* (pp. 1–10). Berlin: Springer-Verlag.

Tversky, B. (2005a). Functional significance of visuospatial representations. In P. Shah & A. Miyake (Eds.), *Handbook of higher-level visuospatial thinking*. Cambridge: Cambridge University Press.

Tversky, B. (2005b). How to get around by mind and body: Spatial thought, spatial action. In A. Zilhao (Ed.), *Cognition, evolution, and rationality: A cognitive science for the twenty-first century*. London: Routledge.

Tversky, B. (2005c). La cognition spatiale: Incarnée et desincarnée. In A. Berthoz & R. Recht (Eds.), *Les espaces de l'homme* (pp. 161–184). Paris: Odile Jacob.

Tversky, B. (2005d). Visuospatial reasoning. In K. Holyoak & R. Morrison (Eds.), *Handbook of reasoning* (pp. 209–249). Cambridge: Cambridge University Press.

Tversky, B., & Gati, I. (1978). Studies of similarity. In E. Rosch & B. Lloyd (Eds.), *Cognition and categorization* (pp. 79–98). New York: Wiley.

Tversky, B., & Hemenway, K. (1983). Categories of scenes. *Cognitive Psychology*, 15, 121–149.

Tversky, B., & Hemenway, K. (1984). Objects, parts, and categories. *Journal of Experimental Psychology: General*, 113, 169–193.

Tversky, B., Kim, J., & Cohen, A. (1999). Mental models of spatial relations and transformations from language. In C. Habel & G. Rickheit (Eds.), *Mental models in discourse processing and reasoning* (pp. 239–258). Amsterdam: North-Holland.

Tversky, B., Kugelmass, S., & Winter, A. (1991). Cross-cultural and developmental trends in graphic productions. *Cognitive Psychology*, 23, 515–557.

Tversky, B., & Lee, P. U. (1998). How space structures language. In C. Freksa, C. Habel, & K. F. Wender (Eds.), *Spatial cognition: An interdisciplinary approach to representation and processing of spatial knowledge* (pp. 157–175). Berlin: Springer-Verlag.

Tversky, B., & Lee, P. U. (1999). Pictorial and verbal tools for conveying routes. In C. Freksa & D. M. Mark (Eds.), *Spatial information theory: Cognitive and computational foundations of geographic information science* (pp. 51–64). Berlin: Springer-Verlag.

Tversky, B., Morrison, J. B., & Zacks, J. (2002). On bodies and events. In A. Meltzoff & W.

Prinz (Eds.), *The imitative mind: Development, evolution and brain bases* (pp. 221–232). Cambridge: Cambridge University Press.

Tversky, B., & Schiano, D. (1989). Perceptual and conceptual factors in distortions in memory for maps and graphs. *Journal of Experimental Psychology: General*, 118, 387–398.

Tversky, B., Zacks, J. M., & Hard, B. M. (2008). The structure of experience. In T. Shipley & J. M. Zacks (Eds.), *Understanding events* (pp. 436–464). Oxford: Oxford University Press.

Tversky, B., Zacks, J., Lee, P. U., & Heiser, J. (2000). Lines, blobs, crosses, and arrows: Diagrammatic communication with schematic figures. In M. Anderson, P. Cheng, & V. Haarslev (Eds.), *Theory and application of diagrams* (pp. 221–230). Berlin: Springer-Verlag.

Tversky, B., Zacks, J. M., Morrison, J. B., & Hard, B. M. (in press). Talking about events. In E. Pederson, J. Bohnemeyer, & R. Tomlin (Eds.), *Event representation*. Cambridge: Cambridge University Press.

Valenzeno, L., Alibali, M. W., & Klatzky, R. (2003). Teachers' gestures facilitate students' learning: A lesson in symmetry. *Contemporary Educational Psychology*, 28, 187–204.

Varela, F. J., Thompson, E., & Rosch, E. (1991). *The embodied mind: Cognitive science and human experience*. Cambridge, MA: MIT Press.

Wraga, M., Creem, S. H., & Proffitt, D. R. (2000). Updating displays after imagined object and viewer rotations. *Journal of Experimental Psychology: Learning, Memory, and Cognition*, 26, 151–168.

Zacks, J. M., Mires, J., Tversky, B., & Hazeltine, E. (2000). Mental spatial transformations of objects and perspective. *Spatial Cognition and Computation*, 2, 315–332.

Zacks, J., & Tversky, B. (1999). Bars and lines: A study of graphic communication. *Memory and Cognition*, 27, 1073–1079.

Zacks, J. M., & Tversky, B. (2001). Event structure in perception and conception. *Psychological Bulletin*, 127, 3–21.

Zacks, J., Tversky, B., & Iyer, G. (2001). Perceiving, remembering, and communicating structure in events. *Journal of Experimental Psychology: General*, 130, 29–58.

Zacks, J. M., Vettel, J. M., & Michelon, P. (2003). Imagined viewer and object rotations dissociated with event-related fMRI. *Journal of Cognitive Neuroscience*, 15, 1002–1018.

CHAPTER 13

Remembering

John Sutton

1. Introduction: The Interdisciplinary Framework

The case of remembering poses a particular challenge to theories of situated cognition, and its successful treatment within this framework will require a more dramatic integration of levels, fields, and methods than has yet been achieved. The challenge arises from the fact that memory often takes us *out* of the current situation: in remembering episodes or experiences in my personal past, for example, I am mentally transported *away* from the social and physical setting in which I am currently embedded. Our ability to make psychological contact with events and experiences in the past was one motivation, in classical cognitive science and cognitive psychology, for postulating inner mental representations to hold information across the temporal gap. Theorists of situated cognition thus have to show how such an apparently representation-hungry and decoupled high-level cognitive process may nonetheless be fruitfully understood as embodied, contextualized, and distributed (cf. Clark, 2005a).

Critics of classical cognitive science often painted mainstream theories of memory as rigidly mechanistic and individualist, offering disparate phenomenological, Wittgensteinian, or direct realist alternatives (Ben-Zeev, 1986; Bursen, 1978; Casey, 1987; Krell, 1990; Malcolm, 1977; Sanders, 1985; Stern, 1991; ter Hark, 1995; Turvey & Shaw, 1979; Wilcox & Katz, 1981). Although the more recent work on memory in situated cognition and related (dynamical, distributed, enactive, and embodied) traditions described in this chapter has drawn substantially on these positive alternatives, the oppositional nature of the earlier debates has dissipated somewhat. Indeed the modern history of memory research across the disciplines undermines that easy stereotype of the cognitive sciences as monolithically logicist and internalist. Not only had key precursors of situated cognition long been points of reference in particular subdomains of memory theory, such as the developmental psychology of autobiographical memory (Vygotsky, 1930/1978); through independent internal movements within computational, cognitive, and social psychology alike over twenty-five years or more, situated or ecological approaches to memory have come themselves to occupy the mainstream.[1] Although their integration with traditional laboratory methods did not always come easily, the pluralism of contemporary memory studies is reasonably happy; ambitious recent syntheses deliberately triangulate robust data and constraints from distinct sources, incorporating as appropriate evidence from phenomenology; from neuroimaging and neuropsychology; and from cognitive, affective, developmental, social, and personality psychology all at once (Conway & Pleydell-Pearce, 2000; Siegel, 2001; Welzer & Markowitsch, 2005).

The sciences of memory have occasionally seemed somewhat isolated from broader shifts in cognitive science. But their more direct integration with the ideas discussed throughout this volume is now leading both to reevaluations of the relevance of other harbingers of the modern constructivist psychological and social sciences of memory, such as Bartlett (1932) and Halbwachs (1925/1992, 1950/1980), and to explicitly situated or distributed theories that see the vehicles of representation in memory, as well as the processes of remembering, as potentially spreading across world and body as well as the brain (Clancey, 1997, 1999; Donald, 1991; Rowlands, 1999; Sutton, 2003, 2004; Tribble, 2005; Wilson, 2004, 2005). This chapter offers a synoptic overview of situated work on memory and remembering, skating fast and light over vast and disparate literatures to sketch a positive synthesis of the field. It covers, in turn, relevant movements in cognitive psychology (section 2), developmental psychology (section 3), the social sciences and social philosophy (section 4), and distributed cognition (section 5). Conceptual tools from all of these fields are required to address the challenge of situating memory. The aim is an account of memory in general, or of the varieties and forms of memory in general, which can then be applied to diverse case studies across the disciplines to suggest just how in practice various coordinated contexts – neural, bodily, affective, technological, insti-

tutional, and so on – shape, constrain, and enable practices and activities of remembering. The case of memory should ideally fit David Kirsh's (2006) description of the general study of distributed cognition as "the study of the variety and subtlety of coordination . . . how the elements and components in a distributed system – people, tools, forms, equipment, maps and less obvious resources – can be coordinated well enough to allow the system to accomplish its tasks" (p. 258; cf. Wilson & Clark, this volume).[2]

2. Remembering as Constructive Activity and Interpersonal Skill

Remembering is an activity that takes place in and over time. Neither the form of that activity nor the detailed nature of what is remembered is straightforwardly or monocausally determined by any internally stored information. Inner memory traces – whatever they may be – are merely potential contributors to recollection, conspiring with current cues in rich contexts (Schacter, 1996, pp. 56–71; Tulving, 1983, pp. 12–14). But a focus on this occurrent activity, which is always situated in a range of contexts, does not on its own ground a situated approach to memory. Individualists, too, can acknowledge the existence of a range of contexts; so talk of (for example) the external or cultural or social context of remembering is not sufficient to give us a substantial situated view. Remembering itself, after all, might still be firmly contained within the bounds of the skull. On stronger situated theories, presumably, our understanding of the memory to which modifiers like *extended* or *distributed* are applied should itself be significantly revised (Wertsch, 1999). This means, further, that no neat division of labor between the cognitive and the social sciences of memory can be maintained, because the domain is not neatly sliced into distinct psychological and public aspects that may or may not interact (Sutton, 2004).

In "A Theory of Remembering," the central chapter of his great work *Remembering:*

A Study in Experimental and Social Psychology, Bartlett (1932) wrote:

> *Suppose I am making a stroke in a quick game, such as tennis or cricket.... When I make the stroke I do not, as a matter of fact, produce something absolutely new, and I never merely repeat something old. The stroke is literally manufactured out of the living visual and postural "schemata" of the moment and their interrelations. I may say, I may think that I reproduce exactly a series of text-book movements, but demonstrably I do not; just as, under other circumstances, I may say and think that I reproduce exactly some isolated event which I want to remember, and again demonstrably I do not. (pp. 201–202)*

For Bartlett, explicit remembering is a skill, with just the same peculiar features – combining the familiar and the unique – as complex embodied skills. There are a range of intriguing and relevant questions, which I cannot address here, about skill and habit, two key varieties of what psychologists label "procedural memory," and about how these forms of remembering relate to more explicit and consciously accessible memory (Sheets-Johnstone, 2003); but in this chapter, I describe situated accounts of the declarative forms of memory, with a focus on personal or recollective or autobiographical memory, which is both theoretically and personally important because of its emotional and moral significance and its role in temporally extended agency.[3] As background to the general consensus in situated cognitive psychology on constructivism, the most celebrated of Bartlett's theses, we examine the related ideas of remembering as skilled activity, and of the dynamic nature of the enduring states that ground that activity.

2.1. *Representations and Storage*

Situated approaches to memory not only depart from the internalism or methodological solipsism of the way internal representations were evoked in classical cognitive science but also, in general, reject the distinct idea that individual representations are independent from one another, stored at separate locations in some memory system. It is this localist picture of memory storage, which allows for no integration of enduring data with ongoing processing, that makes it difficult to update relevant background knowledge without explicit search (Copeland, 1993). This is why alternative models of memory were at the forefront of the revival of connectionism in the 1980s and have continued to play a central role in attempts to align neural network modeling with neuropsychology (Churchland & Sejnowski, 1992; Gluck & Myers, 2000).

Occurrent remembering in connectionist cognitive science is the temporary reactivation of a particular pattern or vector across the units of a network. This reconstruction is possible because of the conspiring influences of current input and the history of the network, as sedimented in the connection weights between units. So memory traces are not stored separately between experience and remembering but are piled together or "superposed" in the same set of weights. In fully distributed representation, the same resources or vehicles are thus used to carry many different contents (Clark, 1989; van Gelder, 1991). As McClelland and Rumelhart (1986) put it:

> *We see the traces laid down by the processing of each input as contributing to the composite, superimposed memory representation. Each time a stimulus is processed, it gives rise to a slightly different memory trace – either because the item itself is different or because it occurs in a different context that conditions its representation – the traces are not kept separate. Each trace contributes to the composite, but the characteristics of particular experiences tend nevertheless to be preserved, at least until they are overridden by canceling characteristics of other traces. Also, the traces of one stimulus pattern can coexist with the traces of other stimuli, within the same composite memory trace. (p. 193)*

Connectionist remembering is thus an inferential process, constructive not reproductive. Information survives only in dispositional form: "the data persist only implicitly by virtue of the effect they have on what the system knows" (Elman, 1993, p. 89). In this dynamic vision of representations, connectionism is clearly heir to Bartlett's (1932) vision:

> Though we may still talk of traces, there is no reason in the world for regarding these as made complete at one moment, stored up somewhere, and then re-excited at some much later moment. The traces that our evidence allows us to speak of are interest-determined, interest-carried traces. They live with our interests and with them they change. (pp. 211–212)

Neither this point that traces are plastic and malleable nor the more general constructivist movement in the cognitive psychology of memory directly entails a situated approach. But there is one natural link (Clark, 1997): stability over time in connectionist representational systems is maintained not through permanent storage, but through context-dependent reconstruction. Sometimes, then, remembering requires the interaction or coupling of complementary biological and external resources into temporarily extended cognitive systems. On this view, brains like ours need media, objects, and other people to function fully as minds. Seeing the brain as a leaky associative engine (Clark, 1993), its contents flickering and unstable rather than mirroring the world in full, forces attention to the diverse formats of external representations in the technological and social wild. If biological "engrams" are typically integrative and active in the way connectionism suggests, perhaps it is natural for creatures like us in using them to hook up with more enduring and transmissible "exograms," in Merlin Donald's coinage (1991, pp. 308–333). We compile memories (whether in thought or in public expression) on the fly, working them up or improvising them out of whatever materials we have: the vivid sensory detail that comes to mind in episodic fragments and the resources provided by external symbol systems, as well as the multiple influences of knowledge about the self and the world; of goals, motivations, and moods; and of the current interpersonal context. As the developmental psychologist Susan Engel (1999) argues, often "one creates the memory at the moment one needs it, rather than pulling out an intact item, image, or story" (p. 6). So memory's temporal cross-referencing does not run only between present recall and past experience, because remembering also has a raft of distinctive forward-looking or anticipatory features and functions.

2.2. Constructivism and Relational Remembering

A situated approach to memory, then, is one that treats this multifarious range of materials as potentially integral, complementary aspects of a cognitive system and its processes of remembering. Such an approach can thus fruitfully draw on the resources of personality and social psychology, as well as on cognitive psychology. Attention to social scaffolding and to technological mediations of memory is entirely compatible with an interest in individual differences in memory. Just because remembering is selective in this way, peculiarities of affective style or self-conception directly shape the way memory narratives condense, summarize, and edit past experiences for present purposes (McIlwain, 2006). Bartlett had explicitly argued that temperament, history, belief, and expectation should be incorporated within theories of memory when he adapted the term *schema* to refer to "an active organization of past reactions, or of past experiences" that act together "as constituents of living, momentary settings" (1932, p. 201; also pp. 308–314).[4] His interest was in the pervasive effects of preexisting beliefs and attitudes, or of an idiosyncratic personal history acting as a mass in filtering recall. But the constructivist consensus in the modern subdisciplines of psychology, which developed independently of connectionist computational modeling, has in some respects remained narrower in focus. Research on suggestibility and the effects of misinformation on memory, developed initially in the context of eyewitness testimony, was dramatically extended in the 1990s to the heart of personal memory (Hyman & Loftus, 1998; Loftus, 2003; Roediger, 1996) – "a variety of conditions exist," wrote Daniel Schacter (1995), "in which subjectively compelling memories are grossly inaccurate" (p. 22). Mainstream psychology of autobiographical memory has continued to treat the ongoing, interpersonally anchored revision and remolding of the remembered past as the ordinary means by which narratives of the self develop (Conway, Singer, & Tagini, 2004; Ross, 1989); these views are thus entirely compatible with situated cognition. But much work on "false memory" has focused on more malign forms of influence, on specific distortions or misleading additions inserted into the individual's mind by some external source.

This strand of constructivist memory theory tends thus to remain individualistic in orientation (cf. Campbell, 2004; Haaken, 1998). First, construction tends to be simply equated with distortion, thus neglecting the adaptability of memory's intrinsic dynamics, by which the very mechanisms that underlie generalization can in certain circumstances lead us astray (McClelland, 1995; Schacter, 1999). Second, influence is characterized as essentially or primarily negative, the relentless intrusion of the social into malleable individual memory. Questions about truth in memory do take on a new urgency within a constructivist framework, but the point need not be either that reliability is impossible or that interpersonal memory dynamics must bring error and confusion. Truth and related values like accuracy and fidelity in memory need be neither simple nor singular. In legal contexts, for example, concerns about contamination and conformity in witnesses' memories may be appropriate. But elsewhere, ordinary and successful remembering may be relational (Campbell, 2003), depending directly on the support and involvement of other people and on our abilities to create more or less enduring memory systems that transcend the capacities of the brain alone. One example comes from false memory research itself; after showing that misleading visual or verbal information, when presented in certain ways,

may be incorporated into many people's personal memories of childhood experiences, Strange, Gerrie, and Garry (2005) discuss further similar experiments in which subjects exposed to false information about their past were encouraged to discuss their memories with a sibling. Acknowledging that in real settings, "when confronted with a difficult to remember narrative about [their] childhood, people are likely to rely on others to verify their memories" (p. 241), these researchers found that after discussion with a sibling the proportion of false memories dropped dramatically.

Of course, such negotiations about the past do not always bring either agreement or truth; but the forthcoming examination of the development of autobiographical memory will suggest that we also learn to deal with disagreement about the past most directly and effectively through early memory-sharing practices. And in adult life, as Sue Campbell (2006) argues, our attempts to be faithful to the past are often supported and positively guided by listeners or by joint participants in shared memory activities. Both ordinary memory narratives and more public testimonial expressions of memory can be co-constructed without other people's role bringing corruption. Campbell argues, in particular, that locating appropriate emotion in remembering activities can be a significant component of recollective accuracy, where accuracy in understood in a context-dependent way; representational success in memory is rarely a simple matter of matching an isolated present item to a single past event (cf. Schechtman, 1994). Remembered events, after all, especially ones that matter, are themselves complex and structured. We often find ourselves striving for the needed affective shifts in relation to particular memories through renegotiating in company the meanings of the personal past. These commonplace ways of sharing memories, in co-constructing, jointly reevaluating, or just actively listening, bring obligations and accountability with them; and when the negotiations concern experiences that were themselves shared, the epistemic, affective, and mnemonic interdependence is magnified further.

So, one respect in which a thoroughly situated approach to memory can push the existing ecological focus on real-life or everyday memory phenomena further is in presenting constructive processes in remembering – and, more generally, memory's openness to various forms of influence – as more mundane or natural than inevitably dangerous. In the remaining sections, I try to merge these ideas about interpersonal memory dynamics with the postconnectionist picture of human beings as essentially incomplete machines, apt to incorporate what has – in the course of evolutionary, cultural, and developmental history – become apt for incorporation (cf. Clark, 2006).

3. Remembering as Social Interaction and Joint Attention to the Past

Children start talking about the past pretty much as soon as they start talking, but their initial references are fleeting and fragmentary, and the capacity to refer to specific events in the personal past develops only gradually. A situated approach to the development of autobiographical memory needs to characterize the explanatory target richly, and then seek to extend dynamical models from more basic domains to capture these high-level cognitive phenomena. The child's emerging ability to think about experiences at particular past times is more than the capacity to understand sequences of events or intervals between events and more than general knowledge of how things usually go. A sociocultural developmental theory must address multiply interactive developmental systems spanning the child's brain and local narrative environment. Nelson and Fivush (2004), building on a twenty-year tradition of social interactionist work, characterize the emergence of autobiographical memory as "the outcome of a social cultural cognitive *system*, wherein different components are being opened to experiences over time, wherein experiences vary over time and context, and wherein individual histories

determine how social and cognitive sources are combined in varying ways" (p. 487).

Robust experimental data in this tradition addresses the shaping of the child's developing memory by parental and cultural styles or models for the recounting of past events. In general, for example, the spontaneous later memory activity of children whose parents' talk about the past is more elaborate and rich, or more emotional, is itself more elaborative or emotional (Reese, Haden, & Fivush, 1993); and in general, both mothers and fathers talk more richly and more emotionally about the past with girls than with boys (Fivush, 1994). A range of cultural differences track these interactions, so that, for example, Caucasian American children's spontaneous memories highlight the self more, in general, than do those of Korean children (Mullen & Yi, 1995; cf. Leichtman, Wang, & Pillemer, 2003).

Some presentations of these results suggest that parental influence – in particular maternal reminiscence style – is the primary driving force behind the emergence of autobiographical memory; the structure and content of the child's early thought and talk about the past is provided to a large degree by adults, whose communicative actions construct the scaffolding for such early memories. The idea that the direction of influence is from social and narrative context to autobiographical memory is perhaps encouraged by some uses of the Vygotskian scaffolding metaphor.

But it seems likely that elaborative parental talk, commonly defined as adding details or richness about a particular aspect of a past event, is not as vital as the related but distinct feature of contingency in conversation; a contingent utterance is related in content to the conversational partner's prior utterance, whereas some elaborations may not be relevant to the specific conversational context and thus not genuinely dialogical (Petra, Benga, & Tincas, 2005). Here, a better metaphor is that of a spiral process, in which the child's changing competence in dialogue about the past itself in turn directly influences the parent's reminiscence style, encouraging the dynamic co-construction of richer narratives (Haden, Haine, & Fivush, 1997). On a thoroughly situated perspective, we should reconstruct the difference between scaffolding and spiral models not as a theoretical choice with only one right answer but as an empirical spectrum of possibilities. This requires a developmental systems framework in which the relative influence of multiple concurrent processes can vary across cases (cf. Griffiths & Stotz, 2000; Smith & Thelen, 2003). So, recent presentations of the social-interactionist theory address not only the roles of language and the local narrative environment but also the neural and psychological development of other memory systems, the development of a self-schema and of theory of mind, the emergence of a concept of the past, and the role of affective factors such as motivation and attachment security (Nelson & Fivush, 2004; Reese, 2002). Autobiographical memory development can thus be highly buffered in that different factors play different roles at different stages for different children. For example, children with weaker linguistic skills but stronger early self-recognition skills, Elaine Reese (2002) has shown, "enter the system through a less verbal and more autonomous route" (p. 252) than children who engage in highly elaborative conversations about the past. And when dealing with such highly history-dependent developmental processes, in which social and neural influences are "bidirectionally and fundamentally interactive at all levels of organization" (Bjorklund, 2004, p. 344), we would also expect the degree of significant individual variability that requires substantial longitudinal study (Harley & Reese, 1999; Reese, 2002).

In an exemplary cross-disciplinary collaboration, philosopher Christoph Hoerl and psychologist Teresa McCormack have investigated more precisely the role of the joint reminiscing activities studied in this social-interactionist tradition. Building on John Campbell's (1997) point that mature autobiographical memory requires us to coordinate and align egocentric and objective conceptions of time, Hoerl and McCormack suggest that children need to grasp that both the world and the self are causally connected over time. Their idea is that the memory sharing in which parents and children engage can best be understood as a peculiar form of joint attention, directed – unlike other forms of joint attention – at the past. To grasp "the causal significance of the order in which sequences of events unfold," the child needs to understand that "later events in the sequence can obliterate or change the effect of earlier ones," so that the state of the world and of the child's current feelings depends on this independently ordered history (Hoerl & McCormack, 2005, pp. 267–270).

Using a delayed video-feedback technique in which children are shown two games in different orders, Povinelli, Landry, Theall, Clark, and Castille (1999) demonstrated that three-year-olds could not use information about which of two events happened more recently to update their model of the world as a series of causally related events unfolds, but that with clear instructions, five-year-olds could do so. Building on these methods in ingenious experiments that examine not only temporal updating but also the ability to make temporal-causal inferences, McCormack and Hoerl (2005) have shown that children under age five and some five-year-olds who can successfully engage in simple updating of their knowledge base when they observe or infer the world being modified have serious difficulty in making these more sophisticated temporal-causal inferences in which they must grasp the objective sequence of events.

They suggest that this kind of temporal-causal reasoning is just what conversations about past events elicit or jointly generate, as parent and child together construct a temporally structured narrative that explains the influence of the past on the present. In joint reminiscence, a parent is often not merely modeling these narrative abilities but also directly exerting an influence on the child by encouraging the child to see that things are not now as they once were. The context is very often directly affective; the sore finger that caused the child's past sadness and pain is no longer sore, because since then

Daddy came and made it better (Hoerl & McCormack, 2005, p. 275, quoting Fivush, 1994, p. 149). The shared outlook on the past that emerges is thus also evaluative, and in turn grounds other ongoing collaborative activities; children then come to value memories of particular past events for themselves, "because the sharing of such memories is a way of establishing, maintaining, or negotiating a distinctively social relationship with others" (Hoerl & McCormack, 2005, p. 283).

So, this may be how the local narrative practices studied by the social interactionists, with all their cultural idiosyncrasies, themselves put the child in touch with an objective conception of time and causation. The practical engagement involved in jointly attending to past events and sharing memories helps the child understand that there can be different perspectives on the same once-occupied time; and thus such shared, co-constructed narratives shape the child's initial grasp of the causal connectedness of self and world. The acquisition of competence in these shared narratives is, inextricably, cognitive and social development at once.

4. Shared Remembering

4.1. *Halbwachs on Collective Memory*

Maurice Halbwachs is not often explicitly recognized as a forerunner of situated cognition, but in fact his conceptual contributions are as relevant as those of Bartlett or Vygotsky. In *The Social Frameworks of Memory* (1925) and the posthumous *The Collective Memory* (1950/1980), Halbwachs developed striking views about shared remembering and applied them in studies of family memory, religious memory, memory and place, and musicians' memory. Halbwachs's influence has been felt much less in the psychology of memory than in history and the social sciences (Hutton, 1994; Misztal, 2003; Olick & Robbins, 1998), where many have criticized the vagueness of invocations of collective memory and social memory in contemporary social theory (Berliner, 2005; Gedi &

Elam, 1996; Kansteiner, 2002; Klein, 2000). This situation exemplifies the ongoing and damaging lack of contact between the cognitive and the social sciences; in this case it is partly because the only English translation of Halbwachs's 1925 book simply omits most of the relevant material (the first four chapters, which cover 145 pages in the second French edition of 1952, are condensed into 13 pages in the 1992 translation), and partly because relevant ideas in situated or distributed cognition remain inaccessible to those social theorists who are keen to forge links with psychology (Bloch, 1998; Middleton & Brown, 2005; Olick, 1999; Winter & Sivan, 1999). The time is ripe for integrative work to close these gaps (Nelson, 2003; Rubin, 1995; Sutton, 2004; Wertsch, 2002; Wilson, 2005).

Halbwachs argues that what individuals retain of the past, if considered outside of their ordinary social context as (for example) in dreaming, is often incomplete or shrouded, based only on "the disordered play of corporal modifications" (1992, pp. 41–42; 1980, pp. 71–76). My memory traces are not "fully formed in the unconscious mind like so many printed pages of books that could be opened, even though they no longer are," a view Halbwachs attributes both to Freud and to his own teacher Bergson (1980, p. 75). In remembering and reconstructing the past, we normally draw not just on such episodic fragments as we hold on our own but also on the vast and uneven resources of our multiple social groups, material symbols, and social practices with which we have surrounded ourselves. This is so not only when actually remembering in company but also by way of the virtual groups we turn toward affectively when we revivify experiences; ways of thinking and feeling that did not originate with me stay with me as the influences of various groups and continue to animate the explicit memories I draw from my world (1980, p. 24; on the necessity of an affective community, see also pp. 30–33). I do have my own unique memories, as a result of my idiosyncratic history, but this is just a contingent fact about the complexity of the particular intersection of social groups and influences at which they lie (1980, pp. 44–49).

Robert Wilson (2005), arguing that Halbwachs anticipates "something like an extended mind view of memory" (pp. 229–231), suggests that slightly different theses are defended at different points in Halbwachs's works. On the one hand, "it is individuals as group members who remember" (Halbwachs, 1980, p. 48), but memory is always and constitutively socially manifested. On the other hand, "it is only natural that we consider the group in itself as having the capacity to remember" (Halbwachs, 1992, p. 54). Wilson sees some tension between these claims, characterizing the latter as an application to memory of a more general thesis about group-level cognition, which is also found in ideas about superorganisms and swarm intelligence in biology (Wilson, 2004, pp. 265–307). But Halbwachs himself saw the two claims as not just compatible but complementary: "One may say that the individual remembers by placing himself in the perspective of the group, but one may also affirm that the memory of the group realizes and manifests itself in individual memories" (1992, p. 40). Neither individual nor shared memory has ontological priority. Methodologically, as David Velleman (1997) argues for the case of shared intention, before we rule out the possibility of shared cognitive states on the ground that there are no group minds to have them, we should first offer independent characterizations of the cognitive states in question and investigate whether they can be held in common (cf. Clark, 1994; Gilbert, 1989, pp. 432–434).

4.2. The Plural Subject of Memories

Indeed it is far from clear that proponents of socially situated cognition in general need the idea of collective minds; mind is a much trickier concept than (for example) memory, intention, belief, or action, and is much less entrenched in ordinary usage and perhaps far more culturally and historically variable (MacDonald, 2003; Wierzbicka, 1992). What is arguably

required, though, to ground the stronger idea we found in Halbwachs that a group itself can remember is some alternative way of characterizing the kind of more or less transient, socially extended cognitive systems that can have distributed memories or intentions or beliefs, or can engage in genuinely joint action. This demand might be met by applying to memory the notions of mutual knowledge and of the plural subject developed in the field of social ontology, as a way of taking ordinary "We remember" statements seriously.

Some people who happen to have shared experiences clearly do not have a shared or collective memory; even if each of them separately retains information about the same event, and even though their distinct memories could in principle be aggregated, the social dimension of memory in this case is in an obvious sense accidental or superficial. In contrast, think of the way certain ordinary small groups – friends, partners, or a family, for example – may continue to revisit their shared experiences, when the events they remember together may have a distinct interpersonal and affective significance alongside their personal significance. Perhaps they reevaluate parts of their lives, in part, on the basis of – or just by way of – retelling and reinterpreting some of these earlier shared experiences. Occasionally, in a long-standing close network, significant renegotiation of relationships and plans may be partly enacted through this ongoing joint reinterpretation of the still-live shared past. Clearly, there are many intermediate cases; but it is only in the latter kind of case that the commonplace notion of a group being partly held together by, or identified with, some of its memories has a grip.

The sharing of memories in this stronger sense is a pervasive social phenomenon, built in to the interpersonal fabric of human life in significant ways. How should it be understood? The plural-subject analysis developed in other contexts by Margaret Gilbert (1989, 2003, 2004) may capture features of this kind of shared remembering that cannot be accounted for so easily in alternative theoretical models. For example, collective-memory phenomena could be treated as the aggregate of many individual memories. This kind of summative approach is exemplified, in the social sciences of memory, by survey-based studies of what and how the members of groups or generations remember about some set of events. Schwartz and Schuman (2005), for example, react against models that exclude the individual by surveying what many individual Americans of different generations remember about Abraham Lincoln. Whether examining memories of historical and public events or of more personal experiences, this collected memory approach – to use Olick's (1999) useful label – does not directly address the active interpersonal dynamics of memory sharing; it might be merely accidental that the aggregated individual memories converge to whatever extent they do.

So, a fuller account of genuinely shared memory must allow for it to be common knowledge among the members of the group that they all share the memories in question. In the strongest cases, this common knowledge must not itself be accidental but must result from and involve the members' open expressions of willingness to remember jointly and to remain jointly ready and committed to the shared remembering. By thus pooling their wills, the members of a group become for these purposes a plural subject, the subject of the "we remember" thoughts and claims. This kind of analysis, here very roughly adapted from Gilbert's (1989, pp. 154–167, 288–314) treatments of shared action and collective belief, could potentially cover both occurrent joint activities of remembering and the standing shared memories to which groups retain a joint commitment over time. It should also begin to explain the characteristic structure of obligations, commitments, and expectations that participation in a community of memory brings. This, of course, is compatible with the fact that there is always room for disagreement and renegotiation over the details and meaning of shared memories. And, further, the problematic but pervasive notions of collective and shared responsibility

and regret might be partly illuminated by such an analysis of shared memory, as there is plausibly some link between responsibility and memory (on the ethics of memory, see, e.g., Margalit, 2002).

4.3. *Collaborative Recall*

To this kind of conceptual analysis of shared memory phenomena, we can add the experimental dimension provided by psychological studies of collaborative recall. Some of this work shares the individualistic orientation of false memory research as mentioned previously, focusing for example on memory contagion and memory conformity in groups (Gabbert, Memon, & Allan, 2003; Roediger, Bergman, & Meade, 2001); but the methods developed in these paradigms do not inevitably rely on the assumption that external influence necessarily distorts individual memory. Studies of transactive memory, for example, treat the emergent and often implicit structures of memory organization in small groups, families, or couples as key components of shared expertise in successfully negotiating a complex shared environment (Moreland, Argote, & Krishnan, 1996; Wegner, Erber, & Raymond, 1991). And in collaborative recall paradigms, groups working together typically remember more than individuals recalling alone but less than the nominal pooled sum of the individual memories (Basden, Basden, & Henry, 2000; Weldon & Bellinger, 1997). The causes of this collaborative inhibition effect, in which individuals' retrieval strategies are somehow disrupted in the collaborative process, are far from clear, and little work in the area has dealt with emotional or autobiographical memories (Yaron-Antar & Nachson, 2006). Further investigations of the cognitive, social, and motivational parameters of group influence are needed, as of the impact of subtle differences in the mechanisms of collaboration and in the specific nature and history of the groups in question.

In one suggestive line of research, William Hirst and his colleagues (Hirst & Manier, 1996; Hirst, Manier, & Apetroaia, 1997; Hirst, Manier, & Cuc, 2003) examine the way in which specific group dynamics and processes can influence individual members' subsequent enduring memories. In the basic design, each individual first gives his or her memories of an event that the whole group has seen or lived through. After various delays, the group as a whole is then asked to recall what happened; after a further manipulable delay, each member again offers his or her own memory. Hirst is particularly interested in cases in which a dominant individual or narrator – such as one parent in a family group – has a disproportionate influence on the content (or emotional tone, or narrative structure) of both the group's consensual account (where one emerges) and members' subsequent individual recollections. Memory contents migrate in the process of shared remembering, so that sometimes each member's later recall incorporates, without his or her awareness, elements that were only offered by the dominant narrator in the group phase. Basic cognitive-affective processes and subtle situational factors operate together both in the group's production of a shared or social memory and in the effect of collaboration on subsequent individual memories.

5. Distributed Cognition and Exograms

Most socially distributed transactive memory systems are not, in fact, exclusively social in that the spread of resources drawn on in complex activities of remembering may include material, symbolic, technological, and cultural artifacts and objects as well as other people. It is not enough to see external resources or representational systems as merely adding supplementary storage capacity; again, the most trenchant individualist could accept this.

Again, we can draw on Halbwachs's direct anticipation of distributed cognition. In *The Collective Memory of Musicians*,[5] Halbwachs asks how classical musicians reliably remember how to play such an enormous array of pieces of music. He denies both that musical sounds are fixed in mem-

ory as specific auditory reminiscences and that our untrained natural memory for sounds is sufficient to explain the expert's competence. But because musicians have wholly assimilated the conventional system of musical notation, they do not need to conserve all relevant combinations distinctly in their brains. External representations can then be used to preserve the complex combinations: "the score in this case functions exactly as a material substitute for the brain" (1980, p. 162). In the long process of acquiring musical skills, musicians not only have learned how to read these external symbols but also have artificially remolded their onboard representational apparatus, and they come to rely on these new mechanisms in their musical habits and thinking whether or not they are actually using a score.

In our terms, Halbwachs is arguing that onboard biological memory is transformed rather than simply augmented. He imagines an alien neurophysiologist ignorant of human musical culture and notation. The alien might, Halbwachs suggests, come to understand the basic representational workings of the human auditory system as it responds to natural sound. But it could not make sense of the traces connected to musical characters. These culturally laden traces "reveal the action exerted on the human brain by . . . a system or colony of other human brains" (1980, p. 163), and the musical system with which they operate is shared across the entire musical world of a culture. So, for Halbwachs, in these entirely typical respects, the human brain "cannot be considered in isolation" (p. 164); or, as we might put it, the musical mind extends beyond the brain. The external symbol system of musical notation has been annexed, exploited, and assimilated "deep into our mental profiles" (Clark, 2003, p. 198; Wilson & Clark, this volume).[6]

5.1. *The Cognitive Life of Things*

So, where classical cognitivists projected stability in information storage onto our internal psychological economy, situated approaches to memory see it as an emergent product of organisms' meeting, within specific cognitive niches, with external symbol systems and other resources. As Clark (1997) puts it in his account of Hutchins's case study of expert navigation, "the computational power and expertise is spread across a *heterogeneous* assembly of brains, bodies, artifacts, and other external structures" (p. 77; Hutchins, 1995, 2006). The point is not that the external resources do the cognitive work on their own; it is no argument against a situated approach to emotion, for example, to complain that "the black tie I wear at the funeral isn't doing my grieving for me" (Harris, 2004, p. 729). Neither, after all, do brains tend to perform their cognitive functions in isolation.

Studies of such cases as the sketch pads without which artists cannot iteratively reimagine and successfully create an abstract artwork (van Leeuwen, Verstijnen, & Hekkert, 1999) can be characterized as investigations of "the cognitive life of things" (Sutton, 2002, extending Appadurai, 1986). In his initial discussion of the changes to human memory that resulted from the spread of external representations, Merlin Donald (1991, pp. 315–316) focused on typical differences between engrams and exograms; the latter, in general, last longer, have greater capacity, are more easily transmissible across media and context, and can be retrieved and manipulated by a wider variety of means. Hooking up with such systems of exograms in more or less transient networks for particular purposes, we can – collectively and individually – dramatically transform our cognitive profile and hold information more securely over time than our fragile biological memory allows.[7] But, of course, not all external representations need be permanent or endlessly reformattable. Some of the liveliest recent applications of situated cognition to the case of memory show that systems of exograms are not necessarily meant to be permanent or limitlessly transmissible, or turn out to be less stable in practice than in intention. Art historians and theorists (Forty, 1999; Klein, 1997; Kwint, 1999), cognitive archaeologists

(Knappett, 2005; Renfrew & Scarre, 1999), and sociologists of science (Bowker, 2005) offer rich studies of cases in which external resources are less passive and medium-independent than on Donald's basic scheme. So, as Clark (2002) writes, the urgent task for a science of biotechnological memory systems is to understand "the range and variety of types of cognitive scaffolding," by constructing "a taxonomy of different types of external prop, and . . . of how they help (and hinder) human performance" (p. 29; see also Susi, 2005).

In addition to this direct mediation of memory by the use of cognitive artifacts, however, humans also characteristically learn, in some circumstances, to drop the real external object and thereby create an inner surrogate for it. The requisite auxiliary stimuli are "emancipated from primary external forms" when we internally reconstruct the familiar active operations and means of recall (Vygotsky, 1930/1978, p. 45; cf. pp. 52–57). So, not all cognitive technologies must in fact be outside the skin. Among the many resources we use to think about the past are a range of internalized representations, symbol systems, and habits of thought, which we learn (historically and developmentally) to manage with both idiosyncratic and culturally specified strategies. We are not untouched by our ongoing interaction with different media and symbolic technologies; even language, as used cognitively, provides us with more memorable, context-resistant mental objects to carry around with us and take as objects of thought in their own right (Clark, 1997, p. 210; 2006). Lasting changes in our minds result from internalizing the mediating function of artifacts. For instance, we become capable of self-scaffolding, engaging in various forms of virtuoso artificial self-manipulation by way of words, tags, and maxims that can freeze, counteract, recalibrate, or buffer us against our ordinary cognitive-affective flow (Clark, 2005b; Hutchins, 2005).

So, it is one natural tendency of socialized brains like ours to co-opt cultural and moral, as well as linguistic, inner prostheses, altering our own cognitive machinery by exploiting and importing whatever tools and labels we can. Questions about the location of memory processes may no longer seem so important; rather, we are studying the transformation and propagation of representational states "across a set of malleable media," whether inside or outside the skin (Hutchins, 1995, p. 312; Latour, 1996, 1999). We can acknowledge that embodied organisms bring something specific to the interface, underpinning their enduring individual histories and idiosyncratic styles of planning and remembering, without assuming distinct inner and outer realms of engrams and exograms, the natural and the artificial, each with its own inevitable proprietary characteristics (Sutton, in press).

6. Conclusion

The challenge set by the nature of human memory to theories of situated cognition, as I mentioned at the outset of this chapter, is to see how social or material resources outside the brain could possibly be an integral or constitutive feature of memory states or processes, when the events or episodes remembered are long gone. We now have the elements of a response in place – as on many issues in inchoate research programs these are not so much arguments as sets of attitudes or possible ways of approaching difficult topics. We retain the invocation of representations while departing from classical cognitivism in two ways: by treating inner representations and traces as often incomplete, partial, and context-sensitive, to be reconstructed rather than reproduced, and by widening the representational realm outside the organismic boundary (Wilson, 2004). This leads to the expectation that mnemonic stability is often supported by heterogeneous external resources as well as, and in complementary interaction with, neural resources. I examined the social nature of human memory in its development, suggesting that joint attention to the past is integral to the cognitive shift by which children come to grasp the specificity

of particular past experiences. I offered an integrative picture of shared memory and social memory, triangulating a rereading of Halbwachs with a new social ontology of memory and a sketch of ongoing experimental investigations of collaborative recall. And finally I rehearsed some central ideas in the situated and distributed cognition movements about the role of material and technological artifacts in complex cognitive and mnemonic practices.

The last point here about the internalization of memory prostheses is crucial for the overall response to the challenge. The world may be "an outside memory" in the context of visual processing, in that the detail of the visual scene is all out there and potentially available to the viewer (Myin & O'Regan, this volume), but it would seem that the present world cannot function as an outside memory in support of memory itself, because the detail of the past simply is not always recoverable from the current situation. Even when there are interpersonal or material supports to remembering, they still need the embodied remembering agent to bring considerable history to bear in the memory process; and often, in any case, there simply are not any relevant external triggers or cues in the present environment.

But our assessment of the role of situations in driving and shaping memory need not be restricted to the role of contextual features that happen to be outside the skin: that might be a relatively superficial characteristic. In even the most abstruse and detached activities of autobiographical remembering, our memory processes still lean and operate on the internal wing of the vast, extended system of cultural and personal habits, hints, and patterns through which the inner representational regime has been sculpted and disciplined (cf. Clark, 2005b, p. 264). Again, adding a genuinely diachronic dimension to our picture of the neuroscience and psychology of memory means that we do not have to see the temporarily isolated brain as fundamentally or intrinsically alone, having to revert to some purely biological starting state whenever the trappings of culture are not around. For, again, in our unusual case, the biological brain is itself incomplete and always already permeated by structures and history that take it out of itself.

Acknowledgments

My warm thanks to the editors for their patience and support. I am also grateful for help with this material to Amanda Barnier, Pascal Boyer, Andy Clark, Ed Cooke, Christoph Hoerl, Doris McIlwain, Monte Pemberton, Lyn Tribble, and Rob Wilson.

Notes

1 In 1978, for example, Ulric Neisser could fairly lament, "If X is an interesting or socially significant aspect of memory, then psychologists have hardly ever studied X" (1978/2000, p. 4). But by the time of the second edition of *Memory Observed: Remembering in Natural Contexts*, Neisser and Hyman could afford understatement in noting that the study of everyday or real-world memory "has now become an influential and widely accepted research tradition" (2000, p. xiii; see also Neisser, 1997).

2 Situated approaches are potentially relevant to a number of further topics in the interdisciplinary study of memory, which I do not discuss in this chapter. As well as issues about memory systems, amnesia, and localization, I should particularly mention questions about reduction and interlevel relations in the sciences of memory, with which the integrative version of a situated approach to memory which I sketch here needs to engage (see, e.g., Craver, 2002).

3 However, one plausible lesson of the constructivist research in cognitive psychology described in this section is that the processes and contents of personal memory are thoroughly entangled with factual or semantic memory, the other central form of declarative memory. Indeed, some situated approaches threaten the idea of firm conceptual and psychological distinctions between these autobiographical and semantic memory systems, and between memory and other psychological capacities (Toth & Hunt, 1999).

4 There is ongoing controversy – both conceptual and empirical – over Bartlett's account of schemas and conventionalization (Brewer, 2000; Roediger et al., 2000); but the recent history of the schema concept is an intriguing illustration of the potential links between cognitive-connectionist computational theories of memory and more obviously situated approaches (Rumelhart, Smolensky, McClelland, & Hinton, 1986; Strauss & Quinn, 1997).

5 First published as a separate case study in 1939, translated in 1980, pp. 158–186.

6 For an intriguing historical study in distributed cognition, see Tribble (2005), which in impressive detail applies Hutchins's framework in *Cognition in the Wild* to a historical puzzle about how Shakespearean actors remembered a staggering number of plays without fixed scripts or extended rehearsal periods.

7 "Even such comparatively simple operations as tying a knot or marking a stick as a reminder change the psychological structure of the memory process. They extend the operation of memory beyond the biological dimensions of the human nervous system and permit it to incorporate artificial, or self-generated, stimuli, which we call *signs*" (Vygotsky, 1930/1978, p. 39).

References

Appadurai, A. (1986). Introduction: Commodities and the politics of value. In A. Appadurai (Ed.), *The social life of things: Commodities in cultural perspective* (pp. 3–63). Cambridge: Cambridge University Press.

Bartlett, F. C. (1932). *Remembering: A study in experimental and social psychology*. Cambridge: Cambridge University Press.

Basden, B. H., Basden, D. R., & Henry, S. (2000). Costs and benefits of collaborative remembering. *Applied Cognitive Psychology, 14*, 497–507.

Ben-Zeev, A. (1986). Two approaches to memory. *Philosophical Investigations, 9*, 288–301.

Berliner, D. (2005). The abuses of memory: Reflections on the memory boom in anthropology. *Anthropology Quarterly, 78*, 197–211.

Bjorklund, D. F. (2004). Introduction: Special issue on memory development in the new millennium. *Developmental Review, 24*, 343–346.

Bloch, M. (1998). *How we think they think: Anthropological approaches to cognition, memory, and literacy.* Boulder, CO: Westview Press.

Bowker, G. C. (2005). *Memory practices in the sciences.* Cambridge, MA: MIT Press.

Brewer, W. F. (2000). Bartlett's concept of the schema and its impact on theories of knowledge representation in contemporary cognitive psychology. In A. Saito (Ed.), *Bartlett, culture, and cognition* (pp. 69–89). London: Psychology Press.

Bursen, H. A. (1978). *Dismantling the memory machine.* Dordrecht, The Netherlands: D. Reidel.

Campbell, J. (1997). The structure of time in autobiographical memory. *European Journal of Philosophy, 5*, 105–118.

Campbell, S. (2003). *Relational remembering: Rethinking the memory wars.* Lanham, MD: Rowman & Littlefield.

Campbell, S. (2004). Models of memory and memory activities. In P. DesAutels & M. U. Walker (Eds.), *Moral psychology: Feminist ethics and political theory* (pp. 119–137). Lanham, MD: Rowman & Littlefield.

Campbell, S. (2006). Our faithfulness to the past: Reconstructing memory value. *Philosophical Psychology, 19*(3), 361–380.

Casey, E. S. (1987). *Remembering: A phenomenological study.* Bloomington: Indiana University Press.

Churchland, P. S., & Sejnowski, T. (1992). *The computational brain.* Cambridge, MA: MIT Press.

Clancey, W. J. (1997). *Situated cognition: On human knowledge and computer representations.* Cambridge: Cambridge University Press.

Clancey, W. J. (1999). *Conceptual coordination: How the mind orders experience in time.* Hillsdale, NJ: Lawrence Erlbaum.

Clark, A. (1989). *Microcognition: Philosophy, cognitive science and parallel distributed processing.* Cambridge, MA: MIT Press.

Clark, A. (1993). *Associative engines: Connectionism, concepts and representational change.* Cambridge, MA: MIT Press.

Clark, A. (1994). Beliefs and desires incorporated. *Journal of Philosophy, 91*, 404–425.

Clark, A. (1997). *Being there: Putting brain, body, and world together again.* Cambridge, MA: MIT Press.

Clark, A. (2002). Towards a science of the biotechnological mind. *International Journal of Cognition and Technology, 1*, 21–33.

Clark, A. (2003). *Natural-born cyborgs: Minds, technologies, and the future of human intelligence.* Oxford: Oxford University Press.

Clark, A. (2005a). Beyond the flesh: Some lessons from a mole cricket. *Artificial Life, 11*, 233–244.

Clark, A. (2005b). Word, niche and super-niche: How language makes minds matter more. *Theoria, 20*, 255–268.

Clark, A. (2006). Material symbols. *Philosophical Psychology, 19*(3), 291–307.

Conway, M. A., & Pleydell-Pearce, C. W. (2000). The construction of autobiographical memories in the self memory system. *Psychological Review, 107*, 261–288.

Conway, M. A., Singer, J. A., & Tagini, A. (2004). The self and autobiographical memory: Correspondence and coherence. *Social Cognition, 22*, 491–529.

Copeland, J. (1993). *Artificial intelligence: A philosophical introduction.* Oxford, UK: Blackwell.

Craver, C. F. (2002). Interlevel experiments and multilevel mechanisms in the neuroscience of memory. *Philosophy of Science, 69*(Suppl. 3), S83–S97.

Donald, M. (1991). *Origins of the modern mind: Three stages in the evolution of culture and cognition.* Cambridge, MA: Harvard University Press.

Elman, J. L. (1993). Learning and development in neural networks: The importance of starting small. *Cognition, 48*, 71–99.

Engel, S. (1999). *Context is everything: The nature of memory.* New York: W. H. Freeman.

Fivush, R. (1994). Constructing narrative, emotion, and self in parent-child conversations about the past. In U. Neisser & R. Fivush (Eds.), *The remembering self* (pp. 136–157). Cambridge: Cambridge University Press.

Forty, A. (1999). Introduction. In A. Forty & S. Kuchler (Eds.), *The art of forgetting* (pp. 1–18). Oxford, UK: Berg.

Gabbert, F., Memon, A., & Allan, K. (2003). Memory conformity: Can eyewitnesses influence each other's memories for an event? *Applied Cognitive Psychology, 17*, 533–544.

Gedi, N., & Elam, Y. (1996). Collective memory: What is it? *History and Memory, 8*, 30–50.

Gilbert, M. (1989). *On social facts.* London: Routledge.

Gilbert, M. (2003). The structure of the social atom: Joint commitment as the foundation of human social behavior. In F. F. Schmitt (Ed.), *Socializing metaphysics* (pp. 39–64). Lanham, MD: Rowman & Littlefield.

Gilbert, M. (2004). Collective epistemology. *Episteme*, 1, 95–107.

Gluck, M., & Myers, C. (2000). *Gateway to memory: An introduction to neural network modeling of the hippocampus and learning*. Cambridge, MA: MIT Press.

Griffiths, P. E., & Stotz, K. (2000). How the mind grows: A developmental perspective on the biology of cognition. *Synthese*, 122, 29–51.

Haaken, J. (1998). *Pillar of salt: Gender, memory, and the perils of looking back*. New Brunswick, NJ: Rutgers University Press.

Haden, C. A., Haine, R. A., & Fivush, R. (1997). Developing narrative structure in parent-child reminiscing across the preschool years. *Developmental Psychology*, 33, 295–307.

Halbwachs, M. (1992). The social frameworks of memory. In L. A. Coser (Ed.), *On collective memory* (pp. 35–189). Chicago: University of Chicago Press. (Original work published 1925)

Halbwachs, M. (1980). *The collective memory* (F. J. Ditter & V. Y. Ditter, Trans.). New York: Harper and Row. (Original work published 1950)

Harley, K., & Reese, E. (1999). Origins of autobiographical memory. *Developmental Psychology*, 35, 1338–1348.

Harris, R. 2004. Integrationism, language, mind and world. *Language Sciences*, 26, 727–739.

Hirst, W., & Manier, D. (1996). Remembering as communication: A family recounts its past. In D. C. Rubin (Ed.), *Remembering our past* (pp. 271–290). Cambridge: Cambridge University Press.

Hirst, W., Manier, D., & Apetroaia, I. (1997). The social construction of the remembered self: Family recounting. In J. Snodgrass & R. Thompson (Eds.), *The self across psychology* (pp. 163–188). New York: New York Academy of Sciences.

Hirst, W., Manier, D., & Cuc, A. (2003). The construction of a collective memory. In B. Kokinov & W. Hirst (Eds.), *Constructive memory* (pp. 111–116). Sofia: New Bulgarian University.

Hoerl, C., & McCormack, T. (2005). Joint reminiscing as joint attention to the past. In N. Eilan, C. Hoerl, T. McCormack, & J. Roessler (Eds.), *Joint attention, communication, and other minds: Issues in philosophy and psychology* (pp. 260–286). Oxford: Oxford University Press.

Hutchins, E. (1995). *Cognition in the wild*. Cambridge, MA: MIT Press.

Hutchins, E. (2005). Material anchors for conceptual blends. *Journal of Pragmatics*, 37, 1555–1577.

Hutchins, E. (2006, April). The cognitive life of things. The Cognitive Life of Things: Recasting the Boundaries of Mind symposium conducted at the meeting of the McDonald Institute for Archaeological Research, Cambridge, UK. Retrieved May 20, 2008, from http://liris.cnrs.fr/enaction/docs/documents 2006/ImaginingCogLifeThings.pdf.

Hutton, P. (1994). Sigmund Freud and Maurice Halbwachs: The problem of memory in historical psychology. *History Teacher*, 27, 145–158.

Hyman, I. E., & Loftus, E. F. (1998). Errors in autobiographical memory. *Clinical Psychology Review*, 18, 933–947.

Kansteiner, W. (2002). Finding meaning in memory: A methodological critique of collective memory studies. *History and Theory*, 41, 179–197.

Kirsh, D. (2006). Distributed cognition: A methodological note. *Pragmatics and Cognition*, 14(2), 249–262.

Klein, K. L. (2000). On the emergence of memory in historical discourse. *Representations*, 69, 127–150.

Klein, N. M. (1997). *The history of forgetting*. London: Verso Books.

Knappett, C. (2005). *Thinking through material culture: An interdisciplinary perspective*. Philadelphia: University of Pennsylvania Press.

Krell, D. F. (1990). *Of memory, reminiscence, and writing: On the verge*. Bloomington: Indiana University Press.

Kwint, M. (1999). Introduction: The physical past. In M. Kwint, C. Breward, & J. Aynsley (Eds.), *Material memories* (pp. 1–16). Oxford, UK: Berg.

Latour, B. (1996). Cogito ergo sumus! Or, psychology swept inside out by the fresh air of the upper deck: Review of Hutchins 1995. *Mind, Culture, and Activity*, 3, 54–63.

Latour, B. (1999). A collective of humans and nonhumans. In *Pandora's hope: Essays on the reality of science studies* (pp. 174–215). Cambridge, MA: Harvard University Press.

Leichtman, M., Wang, Q., & Pillemer, D. (2003). Cultural variations in interdependence and autobiographical memory: Lessons from Korea, China, India, and the United States. In R. Fivush & C. Haden (Eds.), *Autobiographical memory and the construction of a narrative self:*

developmental and cultural perspectives (pp.73–98). Hillsdale, NJ: Lawrence Erlbaum.

Loftus, E. F. (2003). Our changeable memories: Legal and practical implications. *Nature Reviews Neuroscience, 4*, 231–234.

MacDonald, P. S. (2003). *History of the concept of mind.* Aldershot, UK: Ashgate.

Malcolm, N. (1977). *Memory and mind.* Ithaca, NY: Cornell University Press.

Margalit, A. (2002). *The ethics of memory.* Cambridge, MA: Harvard University Press.

McClelland, J. L. (1995). Constructive memory and memory distortions: A parallel distributed processing approach. In D. L. Schacter (Ed.), *Memory distortion: How minds, brains, and societies reconstruct the past* (pp. 69–90). Cambridge, MA: Harvard University Press.

McClelland, J. L., & Rumelhart, D. E. (1986). A distributed model of human learning and memory. In J. L. McClelland & D. E. Rumelhart (Eds.), *Parallel distributed processing: Explorations in the microstructure of cognition* (Vol. 2, pp. 170–215). Cambridge, MA: MIT Press.

McCormack, T., & Hoerl, C. (2005). Children's reasoning about the causal significance of the temporal order of events. *Developmental Psychology, 41*, 54–63.

McIlwain, D. (2006). Already filtered: Affective immersion and personality differences in accessing present and past. *Philosophical Psychology, 19*(3), 381–389.

Middleton, D., & Brown, S. D. (2005). *The social psychology of experience: Studies in remembering and forgetting.* London: Sage.

Misztal, B. (2003). *Theories of social remembering.* Maidenhead, UK: Open University Press.

Moreland, R. L., Argote, L., & Krishnan, R. (1996). Socially shared cognition at work: Transactive memory and group performance. In J. L. Nye & A. M. Brower (Eds.), *What's social about social cognition? Research on socially shared cognition in small groups* (pp. 57–84). London: Sage.

Mullen, M. K., & Yi, S. (1995). The cultural context of talk about the past: Implications for the development of autobiographical memory. *Cognitive Development, 10*, 407–419.

Neisser, U. (1997). The ecological study of memory. *Philosophical Transactions of the Royal Society B: Biological Sciences, 352*, 1697–1701.

Neisser, U. (2000). Memory: What are the important questions? Reprinted in U. Neisser & I. E. Hyman, Jr. (Eds.), *Memory observed: Remembering in natural contexts* (2nd ed., pp. 3–18).

New York: Worth. (Original work published 1978)

Neisser, U., & Hyman, I. E., Jr. (2000). Preface. In *Memory observed: Remembering in natural contexts* (2nd ed., pp. xiii–xiv). New York: Worth.

Nelson, K. (2003). Self and social functions: Individual autobiographical memory and collective narrative. *Memory, 11*, 125–136.

Nelson, K., & Fivush, R. (2004). The emergence of autobiographical memory: A social cultural developmental theory. *Psychological Review, 111*, 486–511.

Olick, J. K. (1999). Collective memory: The two cultures. *Sociological Theory, 17*, 333–348.

Olick, J. K., & Robbins, J. (1998). Social memory studies: From "collective memory" to the historical sociology of mnemonic practices. *Annual Review of Sociology, 24*, 105–140.

Petra, L., Benga, O., & Tincas, I. (2005). A dynamic approach to the co-construction of autobiographical memory: Insights from dyadic conversations about the past. In *Proceedings of the 27th Annual Conference of the Cognitive Science Society* (pp. 1732–1738). Wheat Ridge, CO: Cognitive Science Society.

Povinelli, D. J., Landry, A. M., Theall, L. A., Clark, B. R., & Castille, C. M. (1999). Development of young children's understanding that the recent past is causally bound to the present. *Developmental Psychology, 35*, 1426–1439.

Reese, E. (2002). A model of the origins of autobiographical memory. In J. W. Fagen & H. Hayne (Eds.), *Progress in infancy research* (Vol. 2, pp. 215–260). Hillsdale, NJ: Lawrence Erlbaum.

Reese, E., Haden, C. A., & Fivush, R. (1993). Mother-child conversations about the past: Relationships of style and memory over time. *Cognitive Development, 8*, 403–430.

Renfrew, C., & Scarre, C. (Eds.). (1999). *Cognition and material culture: The archaeology of symbolic storage.* Cambridge, UK: MacDonald Institute for Archaeological Research.

Roediger, H. L. (1996). Memory illusions. *Journal of Memory and Language, 35*, 76–100.

Roediger, H. L., Bergman, E. T., & Meade, M. L. (2000). Repeated reproduction from memory. In Λ. Saito (Ed.), *Bartlett, culture, and cognition* (pp. 115–134). London: Psychology Press.

Roediger, H. L., Meade, M. L., & Bergman, E. T. (2001). Social contagion of memory. *Psychonomic Bulletin and Review, 8*, 365–371.

Ross, M. (1989). The relation of implicit theories to the construction of personal histories. *Psychological Review, 96,* 341–357.

Rowlands, M. (1999). *The body in mind: Understanding cognitive processes.* Cambridge: Cambridge University Press.

Rubin, D. C. (1995). *Memory in oral traditions: The cognitive psychology of epic, ballads, and counting-out rhymes.* Oxford: Oxford University Press.

Rumelhart, D. E., Smolensky, P., McClelland, J. L., & Hinton, G. E. (1986). Schemata and sequential thought processes in PDP models. In J. L. McClelland & D. E. Rumelhart (Eds.), *Parallel distributed processing* (Vol. 2, pp. 7–57). Cambridge, MA: MIT Press.

Sanders, J. T. (1985). Experience, memory, and intelligence. *Monist, 68,* 507–521.

Schacter, D. L. (1995). Memory distortion: History and current status. In D. L. Schacter (Ed.), *Memory distortion: How minds, brains, and societies reconstruct the past* (pp. 1–43). Cambridge, MA: Harvard University Press.

Schacter, D. L. (1996). *Searching for memory: The brain, the mind, and the past.* New York: Basic Books.

Schacter, D. L. (1999). The seven sins of memory. *American Psychologist, 54,* 182–203.

Schechtman, M. (1994). The truth about memory. *Philosophical Psychology, 7,* 3–18.

Schwartz, B., & Schuman, H. (2005). History, commemoration and belief: Abraham Lincoln in American memory, 1945–2001. *American Sociological Review, 70,* 183–203.

Sheets-Johnstone, M. (2003). Kinesthetic memory. *Theoria et Historia Scientiarum, 7,* 69–92.

Siegel, D. J. (2001). Memory: An overview, with emphasis on developmental, interpersonal, and neurobiological aspects. *Journal of the American Academy of Child and Adolescent Psychiatry, 40,* 997–1011.

Smith, L. B., & Thelen, E. (2003). Development as a dynamic system. *Trends in Cognitive Sciences, 7,* 343–348.

Stern, D. G. (1991). Models of memory: Wittgenstein and cognitive science. *Philosophical Psychology, 4,* 203–218.

Strange, D., Gerrie, M. P., & Garry, M. (2005). A few seemingly harmless routes to a false memory. *Cognitive Processing, 6,* 237–242.

Strauss, C., & Quinn, N. (1997). *A cognitive theory of cultural meaning.* Cambridge: Cambridge University Press.

Susi, T. (2005). In search of the holy grail: Understanding artefact mediation in social interactions. In *Proceedings of the 27th Annual Conference of the Cognitive Science Society* (pp. 2110–2115). Wheat Ridge, CO: Cognitive Science Society.

Sutton, J. (2002). Porous memory and the cognitive life of things. In D. Tofts, A. Jonson, & A. Cavallaro (Eds.), *Prefiguring cyberculture: An intellectual history* (pp. 130–141). Cambridge, MA & Sydney: MIT Press/Power Publications.

Sutton, J. (2003). Memory. In E. N. Zalta (Ed.), *The Stanford encyclopedia of philosophy.* Retrieved May 20, 2008, from http://plato.stanford.edu/archives/spr2003/entries/memory/.

Sutton, J. (2004). Representation, reduction, and interdisciplinarity in the sciences of memory. In H. Clapin, P. Staines, & P. Slezak (Eds.), *Representation in mind: New approaches to mental representation* (pp. 187–216). Amsterdam: Elsevier.

Sutton, J. (in press). Exograms and interdisciplinarity: History, the extended mind, and the civilizing process. In R. Menary (Ed.), *The extended mind.* Aldershot, UK: Ashgate.

ter Hark, M. (1995). Electric brain fields and memory traces: Wittgenstein and Gestalt psychology. *Philosophical Investigations, 18,* 113–138.

Toth, J. P., & Hunt, R. R. (1999). Not one versus many; but zero versus any: Structure and function in the context of the multiple memory systems debate. In J. K. Foster & M. Jelicic (Eds.), *Memory: Systems, process, or function?* (pp. 232–272). Oxford: Oxford University Press.

Tribble, E. (2005). Distributing cognition in the globe. *Shakespeare Quarterly, 56,* 135–155.

Tulving, E. (1983). *Elements of episodic memory.* Oxford: Oxford University Press.

Turvey, M. T., & Shaw, R. (1979). The primacy of perceiving: An ecological reformulation of perception for understanding memory. In L.-G. Nilsson (Ed.), *Perspectives on memory research* (pp. 167–222). Hillsdale, NJ: Lawrence Erlbaum.

van Gelder, T. (1991). What is the "D" in "PDP"? A survey of the concept of distribution. In W. Ramsey, S. P. Stich, & D. E. Rumelhart (Eds.), *Philosophy and connectionist theory* (pp. 33–59). Hillsdale, NJ: Lawrence Erlbaum.

van Leeuwen, C., Verstijnen, I., & Hekkert, P. (1999). Common unconscious dynamics underlie uncommon conscious effects: A case study in the interaction of perception and creation. In J. Jordan (Ed.), *Modeling consciousness across the disciplines* (pp. 179–218). Lanham, MD: University Press of America.

Velleman, D. (1997). How to share an intention. *Philosophy and Phenomenological Research, 57,* 29–50.

Vygotsky, L. S. (1978). *Mind in society: The development of higher psychological processes.* Cambridge, MA: Harvard University Press. (Original work published 1930)

Wegner, D. M., Erber, R., & Raymond, P. (1991). Transactive memory in close relationships. *Journal of Personality and Social Psychology, 61,* 923–929.

Weldon, M. S., & Bellinger, K. D. (1997). Collective memory: Collaborative and individual processes in remembering. *Journal of Experimental Psychology: Learning, Memory, and Cognition, 23,* 1160–1175.

Welzer, H., & Markowitsch, H. J. (2005). Towards a bio-psycho-social model of autobiographical memory. *Memory, 13,* 63–78.

Wertsch, J. V. (1999). Mediated action. In W. Bechtel & G. Graham (Eds.), *A companion to cognitive science* (pp. 518–525). Oxford, UK: Blackwell.

Wertsch, J. V. (2002). *Voices of collective remembering.* Cambridge: Cambridge University Press.

Wierzbicka, A. (1992). *Semantics, culture, and cognition: Universal human concepts in culture-specific configurations.* Oxford: Oxford University Press.

Wilcox, S., & Katz, S. (1981). A direct realist alternative to the traditional conception of memory. *Behaviorism, 9,* 227–239.

Wilson, R. A. (2004). *Boundaries of the mind.* Cambridge: Cambridge University Press.

Wilson, R. A. (2005). Collective memory, group minds, and the extended mind thesis. *Cognitive Processing, 6,* 227–236.

Winter, J., & Sivan, E. (1999). Setting the framework. In J. Winter & E. Sivan (Eds.), *War and remembrance in the twentieth century* (pp. 6–39). Cambridge: Cambridge University Press.

Yaron-Antar, A., & Nachson, I. (2006). Collaborative remembering of emotional events: The case of Rabin's assassination. *Memory, 14,* 46–56.

CHAPTER 14

Situating Concepts

Lawrence W. Barsalou

1. Conceptual Systems

A conceptual system represents an individual's knowledge about the world. Conceptual systems differ significantly from recording systems that capture holistic images (e.g., cameras, tape recorders). Rather than being a collection of holistic images, a conceptual system is a collection of category representations, with each category representing a different component of experience. Knowledge of these components includes categories for agents, objects, locations, times, events, actions, interoceptive states, relations, roles, and properties.[1]

The conceptual system supports the spectrum of cognitive activities. During on-line processing, as people achieve goals in physical settings, the conceptual system performs many important functions: (1) it supports perceptual processing via figure-ground segregation, anticipation, and filling in; (2) it predicts the entities and events likely to be present in the current situation, speeding up their processing; (3) it produces cate-

gorizations by mapping perceived entities and events to specific categories; and (4) it produces inferences based on categorization about the properties of perceived entities and events, their origin, what they are likely to do next, how to interact with them, and so forth.

The conceptual system also supports off-line processing during memory, language, and thought, as people represent entities and events not present. During memory processing, the conceptual system elaborates perceived entities and events at encoding, organizes them in storage, and produces reconstructive memory inferences about them at retrieval. During language comprehension, the conceptual system contributes to the interpretation of words, phrases, sentences, and texts, and to the generation of inferences that augment these interpretations. During thought, the conceptual system represents the objects, events, and mental states that constitute the content of reasoning, decision making, and problem solving.

1.1. *The Dominant Theory of the Conceptual System: Semantic Memory*

Although modern researchers have entertained many accounts of the conceptual system, the semantic memory view has dominated. This way of thinking about the conceptual system arises from Tulving's (1972) classic distinction between episodic and semantic memory. According to this distinction, episodic memory contains memories of specific episodes whose time and location can be remembered, along with other memory content. In contrast, semantic memory contains conceptual knowledge whose episodic origins have been lost. Many subsequent models of the conceptual system have instantiated the general construct of semantic memory, including feature set models (e.g., Hampton, 1979; Rosch & Mervis, 1975) and network models (e.g., Collins & Loftus, 1975; Collins & Quillian, 1969). E. E. Smith (1978) provides an integrative review of these early accounts. Since then, the central assumptions of semantic memory models continue to shape how researchers think about the conceptual system. Throughout cognitive science and cognitive neuroscience, researchers continue to incorporate various forms of the semantic memory view into their research.

From the perspective of the alternative view developed here, four critical assumptions underlie the semantic memory view (for further detail, see Barsalou, 2003b). First, semantic memory is a modular system, being autonomous relative to episodic memory, and relative to systems in the brain for perception, action, and interoception. From this perspective, the conceptual system does not share representation and processing mechanisms with these other brain systems but is an independent module that operates according to different principles.

Second, representations in semantic memory are amodal. Semantic memory representations are redescriptions or transductions of modality-specific representations into a new representation language that differs from representations in modality-specific systems (e.g., for vision, action, affect). Instead, these representations contain arbitrary symbols that stand in for modality-specific representations and for the entities in the world that produce them.

Third, semantic memory representations are decontextualized. In a typical theory, a category representation is a prototype (or definition) that extracts probable (or definitive) properties across exemplars. Idiosyncratic properties of exemplars and background situations are typically lost in the distillation process. Thus, the representation of *BIRD* might be a decontextualized prototype that includes *wings*, *feathers*, and *beak*, with idiosyncratic properties and background situations filtered out.[2] As a consequence, semantic memory representations often seem like encyclopedia entries that describe sets of category members generically.

Fourth, semantic memory representations are stable. When representing a given category, different people share roughly the same knowledge, and the same person uses the same knowledge on different occasions.

1.2. *Overview*

A different perspective on the conceptual system is adopted here. The following two sections present the theoretical assumptions of this approach. Section 2 proposes that simulations in the brain's modality-specific systems underlie conceptual processing. Section 3 proposes that these simulations are inherently situated, tailored to guide goal-directed action in particular situations. Section 4 reviews empirical evidence that conceptual representations are situated. Section 5 raises issues for future study.

2. Modality-Specific Simulations in Conceptual Processing

In this section, three subsections introduce the constructs of reenactment, simulator, and simulation, respectively. According to this account, the conceptual system shares mechanisms with modality-specific systems, such that the conceptual system is not modular. As a consequence, conceptual representations are at least partially modal, not completely amodal.

2.1. *Reenactments of Perception, Action, and Interoception*

Modal reenactments of perceptual, motor, and interoceptive states constitute the central mechanism of the theory presented here (for further detail, see Barsalou, 1999b, 2003a; Damasio, 1989). The reenactments that underlie knowledge are assumed to be approximately the same as the reenactments underlying mental imagery in working memory (e.g., Farah, 2000; Finke, 1989; Grèzes & Decety, 2001; Kosslyn, 1994; Zatorre, Halpern, Perry, Meyer, & Evans, 1996). The process of reenactment has two phases: (1) storing modality-specific states and (2) partially reenacting these states at later times. Each is addressed in turn.

2.1.1. STORING MODALITY-SPECIFIC STATES

When an entity or event is experienced, it activates feature detectors in the modality-specific systems that perceive and act on it. While processing a dog visually, for example, neurons in the visual system fire for edges and planar surfaces, whereas others fire for color, movement, and configural properties. The activations across this distributed, hierarchically organized system represent the entity visually (e.g., Zeki, 1993). Analogous activations in other sensory systems represent how the dog feels to the touch and how it sounds. Activations in the motor system execute actions while interacting with the dog. Other activations underlie the interoceptive states that arise during the interaction, such as activations in the amygdalae and orbitofrontal cortex that represent emotional reactions.

As feature representations become active in a modality, conjunctive neurons in association areas capture them for representational purposes on later occasions. A population of conjunctive neurons codes the pattern, with each neuron typically coding many different patterns (i.e., coarse coding; but see Quiroga, Reddy, Kreiman, Koch, & Fried, 2005). Damasio (1989) refers to these association areas as convergence zones and reviews evidence for their presence at multiple hierarchical levels in the brain (for further development of this account, see Simmons & Barsalou, 2003). Initially, convergence zones near a modality capture patterns that become active within it. Association areas near the visual system capture visual representations, whereas association areas near the auditory system capture auditory representations. Later, cross-modal association areas in the temporal, parietal, and frontal lobes integrate activations from different modalities to establish multimodal representations.

2.1.2. REENACTING MODALITY-SPECIFIC STATES

The architecture just presented has the ability to partially reenact the multimodal representations it captures. Once conjunctive neurons across association areas capture a collection of modality-specific features, they can later reactivate these features for representational purposes. To remember an experience with a dog, for example, conjunctive neurons partially reactivate the visual states active while perceiving it. To remember an action performed on the dog, conjunctive neurons partially reactivate the relevant motor states. The reenactment process never produces a complete reinstatement of the original experience. In addition, a wide variety of biases may enter in and distort it. Almost always, reenactments tend to be partial and somewhat biased. Most important, however, some semblance of the original state is reenacted. Amodal symbols are not deployed.[3]

Conscious experiences do not always accompany the reenactment process. Although conscious reenactment is typically assumed to accompany mental imagery, reenactments need not produce conscious mental images. Instead, the reenactments that underlie memory, conceptualization, comprehension, and reasoning may often be unconscious to a large extent (Barsalou, 1999b).

2.2. *Simulators and Simulations*

Barsalou (1999b, 2003a) proposed that a fully functional conceptual system can be built on reenactment mechanisms (for a brief review, see Barsalou, Simmons, Barbey, & Wilson, 2003b). As these articles illustrate, reenactment mechanisms can be used to implement the type-token distinction, categorical inference, productivity, propositions, abstract concepts, and a wide variety of basic cognitive processes, including working memory, short-term memory, language comprehension, and various forms of thought. Because these phenomena are not relevant here, they will not be addressed further.

The two central constructs of this approach are simulators and simulations. Whereas simulators integrate multimodal information across a category's instances, simulations represent specific conceptualizations of the category. Each construct is addressed in turn.

2.2.1. SIMULATORS
The properties of a category's members tend to be correlated (e.g., McRae, de Sa, & Seidenberg, 1997; Rosch & Mervis, 1975). As a result, interacting with different instances of the same category should activate similar neural patterns in feature systems (cf. Cree & McRae, 2003; Farah & McClelland, 1991; McCrae & Cree, 2002). In turn, similar populations of conjunctive neurons in association areas tuned to these particular conjunctions of features should tend to capture these similar patterns (Simmons & Barsalou, 2003). Across different category members, a multimodal representation of the category results, distributed across relevant feature systems and the association areas that integrate them. According to Barsalou (1999b) each of these distributed systems is a simulator that functions as a conceptual type, because it integrates the multimodal content of a category across its experience members. Later, when an instance of the category is perceived, the simulator becomes bound to it,

construing it as a category member and providing inferences based on previous members (Barsalou, 2003a). The simulator functions as a type that interprets the instance as a token in a type-token relation.

Consider the simulator for the category of *DOGS*. Across experiences with different dogs, visual information about dogs becomes integrated in the simulator, along with auditory information, somatosensory information, motor procedures, affective responses, and so forth. Over time, a distributed system develops throughout the brain's feature and association areas that accumulates conceptual content for the category.

2.2.2. SIMULATIONS
Once a simulator exists for a category, it reenacts subsets of its content as simulations. Not all of the content in a simulator becomes active at once. Instead, only a small subset becomes active to represent the category in a given situation (for further detail, see Barsalou, 1987, 1989, 1993). Thus, the *DOG* simulator might simulate a sleeping puppy on one occasion, whereas on others it might simulate a working sheepdog or a dog pulling its master along a sidewalk. Because a tremendous amount of experienced content for dogs resides in the *DOG* simulator, diverse subsets are simulated across different situations.

Simulations can serve many different cognitive functions (Barsalou, 1999b, 2003a). Simulations can represent a category's instances during memory, language, and thought. Simulations can produce inferences about a category's perceived instances, using the pattern completion procedure described later. Simulations can combine productively to construct infinitely many conceptual combinations. Simulations, together with simulators, can represent the classic truth-evaluable propositions that underlie interpretation and comprehension.

Simulations can also represent novel category instances not stored in a simulator from previous experience. For example, instances stored previously may merge together during retrieval to produce reconstruction and averaging effects. Remembering a previous dog seen just once might be distorted toward a similar dog seen many times. Additionally, deliberate efforts to combine simulations of conceptual components can produce simulations that do not correspond to an experienced category member. Someone could simulate a dog and then vary simulations of its color and patterning systematically to represent a wide variety of novel dogs never experienced.

2.2.3. TYPES OF SIMULATORS

A potentially infinite number of simulators can become established in the cognitive system. Simulators can develop for all aspects of experience, including agents, objects, properties, settings, events, actions, interoceptions, and so forth. In general, a simulator develops for any component of experience that attention selects repeatedly (Barsalou, 1999b, 2003a). For example, if attention focuses repeatedly on a type of object (e.g., *DOGS*), a simulator develops for it. Analogously, if attention focuses on a type of action (e.g., *SCRATCHING*) or on a type of interoception (e.g., *LOVE*), simulators also develop to represent them. The open-ended potential to establish simulators is consistent with Schyns, Goldstone, and Thibaut's (1998) proposal that the flexible use of selective attention creates new primitive properties that become relevant for categorization. Notably, these properties do not result from combining existing properties productively, but instead result from focusing attention on regions of perception for which no primitive property currently exists. Whenever the flexible and open-ended process of attention selects a component of experience repeatedly, a simulator develops for the component, representing it conceptually in a wide variety of cognitive processes.[4]

Another central issue is how simulators represent abstract concepts. According to Barsalou (1999b), simulators for abstract concepts are grounded in situations. Consider how a simulator might represent one everyday sense of *TRUTH*. Imagine that a speaker makes a claim about a situation, such as, "It's sunny outside." Further imagine

that a listener represents the claim (perhaps as a simulation), compares it to perception of the actual situation, and decides whether the claim interprets the situation accurately. If the simulated claim represents the perceived situation accurately, the claim is interpreted as true. Thus, *TRUTH* is grounded in a complex multimodal situation extended over time. According to this account, people simulate situations like these to represent abstract concepts and focus attention on relevant content within them. For *TRUTH*, people focus on the speaker's claim, their simulation of its meaning, their perception of the corresponding situation, their comparison of the simulated claim to the perceived situation, and their conclusion about whether the two match. Although much of the situation is backgrounded, it frames the focal content distributed across multimodal content in perception, action, and interoception.

Besides offering this simulation-based account of *TRUTH*, Barsalou (1999b) also offers accounts of *NEGATION* and *DISJUNCTION*, and suggests similar approaches for implementing mathematical and logical reasoning. In general, many abstract concepts, such as *FREEDOM* and *INVENTION*, can be viewed as grounded in complex simulations of multimodal situations, with simulated content about events, interoceptive states, and the relations between them being foregrounded.

Barsalou and Wiemer-Hastings (2005) and Wiemer-Hastings, Krug, and Xu (2001) offer preliminary support for this proposal. First, they show that the meanings of both abstract and concrete concepts are situated. In general, people appear to frame concepts in terms of situations, often producing broad situational content when asked to describe concepts. Just as people frame abstract concepts in situations, they similarly situate concrete concepts in situations, as when representing *HAMMER* in the context of its functional use. Second, these researchers show that subjects focus on aspects of the situation central to the meaning of specific concepts, describing these aspects more than less relevant ones. Whereas subjects focus on the physical aspects of situations when representing concrete concepts (e.g., objects, settings, simple actions), they focus on other aspects of situations for abstract concepts (e.g., events, interoceptions, the relations between them). Clearly, much further theory and research is necessary to develop this account of abstract concepts.

3. Situating Concepts

This section begins with an analogy: conceptual representations are situated because perceptions are situated. A second subsection suggests that concepts are situated because of evolutionary convenience and computational efficacy. A third section presents definitions for concepts, situations, and the relations between them. The final section presents the central construct of situated conceptualization.

3.1. *A Situational Analogy from Perception to Conception*

If simulation underlies conceptual processing, a potential implication for the representation of concepts follows: if a conceptual representation simulates a perceptual experience, it should simulate a situation, because situations provide the background of perceptual experiences. To see this analogy, consider the content of perception. At any given moment, people perceive the space around them, which may include agents, objects, and events. Their perceptual experience is multimodal, potentially containing visual, auditory, tactile, gustatory, olfactory, proprioceptive, and interoceptive information. Most important, when people focus attention on a particular entity or event in perception, they continue to perceive the background situation. The situation does not disappear, leaving the focal entity or event in a perceptual vacuum.

If perceptions take the form of situations, and if conceptual representations simulate perceptions, then conceptual representations should take the form of perceived situations. When people construct simula-

tions to represent a category, they should simulate the category in relevant perceptual situations, not in isolation. When people conceptualize DOG, for example, they should simulate not only a dog but also a more complete perceptual situation, including the surrounding space, along with any relevant agents, objects, events, actions, and interoceptions.

3.2. *Origins of Situated Concepts*

The situational analogy between perception and conception may reflect two origins: evolutionary convenience and optimizing prediction. Each is addressed in turn.

3.2.1. EVOLUTIONARY CONVENIENCE
As described earlier, the human conceptual system appears to be grounded in the brain's modality-specific systems. One reason for this relation between perception and cognition may be that evolution capitalized on existing brain mechanisms to implement conceptual systems rather than creating new mechanisms (e.g., Gould, 1991).

If so, the importance of situations in conception could simply reflect the importance of situations in perception, such that the presence of situations in conception is largely accidental and inconsequential. As described next, however, there is good reason to believe that situations play fundamentally important roles in optimizing cognitive processing. Rather than merely being an accident, situational representations make cognitive computation tractable.

3.2.2. OPTIMIZING PREDICTION
Researchers across multiple disciplines have argued that situating cognition greatly enhances cognitive processing. During language comprehension, a text can be incomprehensible if the relevant situation is not apparent (e.g., Bransford & Johnson, 1973). During conversation, shared situations help human speakers establish common ground (e.g., Clark, 1992); shared situations also help nonhuman communicators (e.g., Smith, 1977). Extensive evidence demonstrates that situation models underlie people's

representations of text meaning (e.g., Sanford & Garrod, 1981; Zwaan & Kaschak, this volume; Zwaan & Radvansky, 1998). In general, language comprehension appears to be a heavily situated process (Barsalou, 1999a). During problem solving and reasoning, drawing valid conclusions without the support of concrete situations is often difficult (e.g., Cheng & Holyoak, 1985; Gick & Holyoak, 1980; Johnson-Laird, 1983). In cognitive development, situations appear central to acquiring cognitive and social skills (e.g., Vygotsky, 1991). During social interaction, situations are central to predicting behavior (e.g., Mischel, 1968; Smith & Semin, 2004; Smith & Conrey, this volume). In linguistics, situations underlie the theory of construction grammar, with the content and relations of syntactic structures evolving out of the analogous structure in situations (e.g., Goldberg, 1995). In philosophy, situations motivated the theory of situation semantics, with logical inference being optimized in the context of specific situations (e.g., Akman, this volume; Barwise & Perry, 1983). In artificial intelligence, situating robotic cognition in physical environments greatly enhances practical intelligence (Brooks, 1991; Kirsh, 1991). At a broader level, general arguments about the centrality of situations in cognition have been presented by Clark (1997), Dunbar (1991), Glenberg (1997), Greeno (1998), Barsalou et al. (1993), and Barsalou (2003b).

Situations appear to enhance cognitive processing by optimizing prediction. Specifically, these benefits appear to result from increasing the breadth and specificity of inference. Situations broaden inference by extending processing beyond a focal object or event. When representing *TABLE*, for example, a conceptual system could simply infer the likely properties of a table per se. Such isolated inferences, however, omit broader situational information that may be highly useful for processing. If one wishes to find a table, for example, it is helpful to know locations that contain them. By representing tables conceptually in their respective situations, agents can draw immediate inferences about where to find them (e.g.,

kitchens, dining rooms, offices). Such inferences also provide important information about nearby objects and likely actions. Representing a table in a dining room, for example, is likely to also represent nearby chairs, which could be helpful while planning actions in the situation, such as sitting at the table to eat. As this example illustrates, situating an object concept produces a broad range of inferences useful to goal-directed pursuit.

Framing concepts with respect to situations also increases the specificity of inferences. Once the background situation for a focal object is known, specific inferences about the object's properties follow. For example, when one expects to find a chair in a dining room, the chair is likely to have four long legs, a relatively flat and rigid seat, and a relatively upright back. In general, knowing the situation produces a variety of specific inferences about everything found in the situation, along with specific relations between them. Drawing inferences about a particular chair and its relations to other setting objects depends on whether the chair is found in a dining room, living room, office, theater, jet, ski lift, and so on.

By organizing knowledge around situations, the cognitive system greatly simplifies the many tasks it faces. Rather than searching through everything in memory, the system need only focus on the knowledge and skills relevant for the current situation. Knowing the current situation makes it easier to recognize objects and events, to retrieve relevant knowledge and skills, to understand language, to solve problems, and to predict the actions of other agents. Clearly, entities and events can occur in unexpected situations. As the literature illustrates overwhelmingly, however, such occurrences challenge processing considerably. In contrast, when entities and events occur in their expected situations, processing is relatively easy and effective.[5]

3.3. *Definitions*

Now that the relation between concepts and situations has been introduced, each can be defined a little more carefully. As will be apparent, developing such definitions is critical, because a central question is whether situational content resides inside or outside concepts. As will be seen, the latter possibility is pursued.

3.3.1. CONCEPTS

It is first important to distinguish between concepts acquired from experience versus concepts established by means of productivity and reasoning. Of primary interest here are concepts acquired from experience. Nevertheless, it is possible for people to combine concepts acquired from experience to represent concepts that they have never experienced (e.g., *STRIPED WATERFALLS*), concepts that do not exist (e.g., *UNICORNS*), and concepts that are impossible (e.g., *SQUARE CIRCLES*). Barsalou (1999b, 2003a) proposes how simulation-based approaches can represent these latter concepts. Wu and Barsalou (2008) offer preliminary evidence.

Within the framework developed here, a concept acquired from experience is the accumulated information in memory extracted for a category via selective attention, where a category is a set of things perceived as the same type for one of many possible reasons. As described earlier, a multimodal simulator implements a concept, where a simulator is an organized body of knowledge that produces specific simulations of a category's instances. For example, the simulator for *CHAIR* might simulate a *DINING ROOM CHAIR*, a *LIVING ROOM RECLINER*, an *OFFICE SWIVEL CHAIR*, and so on. What links all these different conceptualizations of *CHAIR* together is the fact that a common simulator produces them. Although tremendous variation exists at the level of simulations, stability exists at the level of simulators, because a relatively discrete simulator represents a category.[6]

A central assumption is that the simulator for a category does not include background situations. Instead, the simulator represents only information abstracted from category exemplars per se. As described shortly, other simulators for settings, agents, events, and interoceptive states become linked to simulators for objects, thereby representing their background situations.

3.3.2. SITUATIONS

Within the framework developed here, a situation is a region of perceived space that surrounds a focal entity over a temporal duration, perceived from the subjective perspective of an agent. The space surrounding the entity may include various entities and events, and the agent's subjective perspective on the region may contain a variety of interoceptive states. For detailed accounts of situational content, see the coding schemes in Wu and Barsalou (2008), Cree and McRae (2003), and Barsalou and Wiemer-Hastings (2005).[7]

Within this framework, simulators for settings, events, mental states, and so forth combine to represent background situations (e.g., Barsalou, 2003b; Barsalou et al., 1993; Barsalou, Niedenthal, Barbey, & Ruppert, 2003a). When people represent someone working in an office chair, simulators for the setting (*OFFICE*), the action (*SITTING*), and the interoception (e.g., *THINKING*) might all contribute simulations to the overall representation of the background situation for this particular chair. When the exemplar of the category changes, so do the simulations that combine to represent its background situation. When people conceptualize sitting in a living room chair, for example, simulators for *LIVING ROOM* and *RELAXING* might contribute to the background situation, and the simulator for *SITTING* contributes a different simulation of sitting.

3.3.3. RELATIONS BETWEEN CONCEPTS AND SIMULATIONS

As these definitions illustrate, this approach assumes that information about concepts is abstracted. Nevertheless, this abstracted content remains tightly coupled with the background situations that framed it originally. As we shall see in the literature review to follow, these relations between concepts and situations constantly come into play during conceptual processing, thereby producing ubiquitous situation effects.

3.4. *Situated Conceptualizations*

Barsalou (2003b) contrasts two theoretical perspectives that researchers have taken on concepts (see also Barsalou, 1999a). Many researchers view concepts implicitly as detached databases, as in traditional semantic memory theories. According to this perspective, the properties and exemplars of a category are integrated during learning into a database of information about the category that is relatively detached from the goals and situations relevant to specific agents. These databases capture the statistical properties of a category and can be consulted when these statistical tendencies are of interest. In many such theories, but not all, it is often further assumed that a person uses the same general abstraction established for a category to represent it in different situations. For example, the same prototype or rule for *CHAIR* is used to represent a currently experienced chair, regardless of whether it is an office chair, living room chair, jet chair, or theater chair.

Alternatively, concepts can be viewed as agent-dependent instruction manuals. On a given occasion, a concept delivers a specialized package of inferences to guide an agent's interactions with a particular category instance in the current situation. Across different situations, the same concept delivers different packages of inferences, each tailored to current instances, goals, and other situational constraints. Because a single general description would be too vague to support all the relevant inferences in a particular situation, more specialized representations are constructed instead. From this perspective, a concept is neither a static database nor a single abstraction. Instead, it is an ability or competence to produce specialized category representations that support goal pursuit in the current setting, where each specialized representation is akin to an instruction manual for interacting with a particular category member.[8]

Barsalou (2003b) referred to a particular package of situation-specific inferences as a situated conceptualization. For example, the simulator for *DOG* can activate many different situated conceptualizations, each tailored to helping an agent interact with dogs in different contexts. No general description of the category exists, although attempts to construct ad hoc generalizations can occur online (Barsalou, 2003a). One conceptualization for *DOG* might support interacting with a timid puppy, whereas others might support interacting with a defensive guard dog, or with a dog that wants to chase a ball. From this perspective, the concept for *DOG* is not a detached statistical database of category information. Instead, the concept is the ability to construct a wide variety of situated conceptualizations that support goal achievement in diverse contexts.

3.4.1. MULTIMODAL SIMULATIONS IMPLEMENT SITUATED CONCEPTUALIZATIONS

Within the framework developed here, a complex simulation becomes active across modalities to implement a situated conceptualization (for further detail, see Barsalou, 2003b; Barsalou et al., 2003a). Consider a situated conceptualization for interacting with a dog that seeks petting. This conceptualization simulates how the dog appears perceptually. When dogs want petting, their bodies adopt particular shapes, they perform certain actions, and they produce distinctive sounds. All of this perceptual content can be represented as modal simulations in the situated conceptualization.

A situated conceptualization about a dog that seeks petting is also likely to simulate actions that the agent could take in the situation, such as petting the dog. Again, modal simulations can represent these aspects of the situated conceptualization, this time via simulations in the motor system.

A situated conceptualization about a dog that seeks petting is also likely to include simulations of interoceptive states. Because people experience particular internal states while petting dogs, the respective situated conceptualizations include simulations of motivations, goals, emotions, and so on.

Finally, a situated conceptualization for a dog that seeks petting is also likely to simulate a setting in which the event could take place. The event is not simulated in a vacuum. Thus, petting a dog might be simulated in a kitchen, yard, park, and so on. Again, such knowledge is represented with a simulation, this time as a reenactment of a particular setting.

In summary, a situated conceptualization is defined as typically simulating four basic types of situational content: (1) perceptions of relevant people and objects, (2) agentive actions and other bodily states, (3) interoceptive states, such as motivations, emotions, and cognitive operations, and (4) likely settings. Thus, a situated conceptualization is a multimodal simulation of a multicomponent situation, with each modality-specific component simulated in the respective brain areas. Barsalou (2005) conjectures that situated conceptualizations provide continuity of the conceptual system across species, on the basis of evidence for situated conceptualizations in monkeys (Gil-da-Costa et al., 2004), and the likely presence of them in other organisms.

Finally, a situated conceptualization places the conceptualizer directly in the respective situation, creating the experience of being there (Barsalou, 2002). By reenacting agentive actions and interoceptive states during the process of representing categories, situated conceptualizations create the experience of the conceptualizer being in the situation. The situation is not represented as detached and separate from the conceptualizer. The conceptualizer is in the representation.

3.4.2. ENTRENCHED SITUATED CONCEPTUALIZATIONS

Over the course of their lives, people experience many situations over and over again in their interactions with people, artifacts, social institutions, and so on. In the process, knowledge about these familiar situations becomes entrenched in memory, thereby supporting automated performance in them. Entrenched knowledge can also be extended analogically to interactions in novel situations that are similar to familiar situations (e.g., Andersen & Chen, 2002). Although entrenched knowledge may not always fit perfectly, it may often fit well enough to provide useful inferences.

Within the framework developed here, situated conceptualizations represent people's entrenched knowledge of repeated situations. As a situation is experienced repeatedly, multimodal knowledge accrues in the respective simulators for the relevant objects, people, actions, interoceptions, and settings. Specifically, the components of the situated conceptualization become entrenched in the respective simulators, as do associations between these components. Over time, the situated conceptualization becomes so well established in memory that it comes to mind automatically as a unit when the situation is detected. After petting a particular dog on many occasions, for example, the situated conceptualization that represents this situation becomes entrenched, such that minimal cuing activates it on later occasions.

Once situated conceptualizations become entrenched in memory, they play important roles throughout cognition. In perception, they support efficient processing of familiar scenes (e.g., Biederman, 1981). In memory, they produce reconstructive memory retrieval (e.g., Brewer & Treyens, 1981). In language, they produce situation models and diverse forms of inference (e.g., Zwaan & Radvansky, 1998). In reasoning, they provide background content that facilitates deduction (e.g., Johnson-Laird, 1983). In social cognition, they provide inferences about myriad aspects of interpersonal interaction (e.g., Barsalou et al., 2003a).

3.4.3. PATTERN-COMPLETION INFERENCES

Entrenched situated conceptualizations support these diverse forms of cognition via a pattern completion inference process. A situated conceptualization can be viewed as a pattern; namely, a complex configuration of multimodal components that represents the respective situation. When a component of this pattern matches something in a perceived situation (e.g., a person, a setting, an object), the pattern becomes active in memory, with the unobserved pattern components constituting inferences about what else could be present. Because the remaining components have occurred frequently with the perceived components in the past, inferring the remaining components is plausible. Thus, when a partially viewed situation activates a situated conceptualization, the conceptualization completes the pattern that the situation suggests. It is useful for the agent to anticipate what will happen next, so that optimal goals can be adopted and optimal actions taken. The agent attempts to draw inferences that go beyond the information given (e.g., Bruner, 1957).

Consider the example of seeing a particular dog. Imagine that the dog's face, fur, and bark initially match modality-specific simulations in one or more situated conceptualizations that have become entrenched in memory for *DOG*. Once one conceptualization comes to dominate the activation process, it provides inferences via pattern completion, such as actions that this particular dog is likely to take, responses that the agent typically makes, interoceptive states that typically result, and so forth. The unfolding of these pattern completion inferences – realized as simulations – produces useful prediction.

3.4.4. THE STATISTICAL CHARACTER OF INFERENCE

All aspects of the pattern completion inference process have a statistical character (e.g., Barsalou, 1987, 1989, 1993; Smith & Samuelson, 1997). Each simulator that contributes to a situated conceptualization is a dynamical system capable of producing infinite simulations (Barsalou, 1999b, 2003a, 2003b). In a given situation, each simulation constructed reflects the current state of the simulator, its current inputs, and its past history. An entrenched situated conceptualization is

essentially an attractor, that is, an associated collection of simulations that is easy to settle on because the associations linking them have become strong through frequent use. Infinitely many states near the attractor, however, offer different versions of the same conceptualization, each representing a different adaptation to the situation. Thus, the entrenched conceptualization for interacting with a dog that seeks petting is not a static representation, but rather the ability to produce many related simulations. On encountering the same situation on different occasions, the situated conceptualizations that guide processing vary dynamically, depending on a wide variety of factors that influence the contributing simulators.

As a consequence, the inferences that arise via pattern completion also vary dynamically. As the conceptualizations that represent a situation vary across occasions, the pattern completions that follow also vary. Somewhat different inferences result from completing somewhat different patterns.

4. Evidence for Situated Concepts

This section reviews evidence for the account of situated concepts just presented. Although evidence for the modality-specific nature of concepts is not presented, it is reviewed elsewhere (e.g., Barsalou, 2003b, 2008; Barsalou, Simmons, Barbey, & Wilson, 2003b; Martin, 2001; Thompson-Schill, 2003; see also Pecher & Zwaan, 2005). The review of situation effects here, however, assumes that multimodal simulations represent situated conceptualizations.

The first evidence reviewed for situation effects illustrates classic effects in memory and conceptualization. When concepts become active, accompanying representations of situations become active as well. In turn, situational representations dynamically affect the content of the concepts they frame. The second and third subsections review evidence for situated conceptualizations in cognitive psychology and social psychology, respectively. In each case, situated inferences about objects, people, settings, action, interoceptions, and perspectives become active to guide goal pursuit in specific situations. The fourth and final subsection reviews evidence for the central role of situations in representing abstract concepts. Although all concepts appear to be framed in relevant situations, abstract concepts appear to rely on them particularly heavily.

4.1. *Evidence for Situated Representation in Memory and Conceptualization*

Yeh and Barsalou (2006) review classic situation effects in memory and conceptual processing. In particular, the literature that they review supports two theses about the relations between concepts and situations.[9] According to thesis 1, situational information is linked to concepts, producing the following two consequences. When a concept becomes active, it activates associated situations. Conversely, when a situation becomes active, it activates associated concepts. Because tables are stored with dining rooms, activating the concept for *DINING ROOM* is likely to activate *TABLE*. Conversely, activating *TABLE* is likely to activate *DINING ROOM*. Thus, concepts tend to be processed not in a vacuum but in a situated manner.

According to thesis 2, a concept produces different conceptualizations in different situations, with each form relevant to the current situation. Thus, the concept *TABLE* may be represented as an attractive wooden table in a dining room or as a more functional but less attractive table in an office. Conversely, activating the concept of *DINING ROOM* tends to produce conceptualizations of *TABLE* that are attractive and wooden, whereas activating *OFFICE* tends to activate conceptualizations of *TABLE* that are more functional and less attractive. Most important, concepts are not represented as generic, highly abstracted data structures. Instead, their content is tailored to the current situation.

Thesis 2 could be implemented computationally in at least two ways. According to one view, all information for a concept is active in every situation. However, information that is relevant in the current situation is weighted more heavily than information that is not irrelevant. According to a second view, only a small subset of a concept's content is active in a given situation (Barsalou, 1987, 1989, 1993). Only a small subset is active for two reasons. First, because much of the possible content for a concept is likely to reside at low levels of accessibility in memory, it is unlikely that it all becomes active simultaneously. Second, if all of this information did become active at once, it would produce a computational nightmare. While processing an office chair, for example, activating information about living room chairs, jet chairs, and theater chairs would be distracting and potentially misleading. Although current evidence probably does not distinguish between these two accounts of how thesis 2 is implemented, the second account is probably more plausible. Regardless, both views are consistent with thesis 2, proposing that the information most functional for a concept varies across situations. Exactly how the functionally relevant content of a concept is implemented remains an important issue.

Yeh and Barsalou (2006) first review evidence from the episodic memory literature that supports theses 1 and 2. One might wonder why findings from episodic memory are relevant to situation effects on concepts. Because concepts enter centrally into memory during encoding, storage, and retrieval, however, episodic memory provides a window on conceptual processing. People do not simply store and retrieve surface stimuli, such as pictures and words, in the way that cameras and audio recorders do (Barsalou, 1999b). Instead, concepts become active at encoding as people process stimuli, such that the stored memory contains conceptual information as well as the actual information presented (e.g., Craik & Lockhart, 1972). Furthermore, concepts become active at retrieval, producing extensive effects of reconstructive memory (e.g., Bartlett, 1932). For these reasons, phenomena from the episodic memory literature provide a rich window onto situation effects in conceptual processing.

Consider an example for episodic memory of visual objects. In Mandler and Stein (1974), children viewed a pictured set of objects either arranged as in a real-world situation or arranged randomly. Several pieces of furniture, for example, might be shown arranged as in a living room, or they might be shown spatially scrambled. When the children later recalled the objects, they remembered more from the meaningfully arranged sets than from the randomly arranged ones. Consistent with thesis 1, viewing meaningfully organized objects activated scene schemata, which organized and elaborated the presented visual objects. As a result, the children were later able to remember the objects and their positions better than when they had not imagined situations for the scrambled scenes. As this finding, and many others like it, illustrates the episodic memory literature provides extensive support for thesis 1. As people encode stimuli into long-term memory, situational representations become active, such that situational information is stored in the resultant memory representation.

Much evidence from the episodic memory literature is also consistent with thesis 2, namely, the situation present at encoding – either actual or inferred – affects the content stored for the stimulus. Consider a classic experiment by Barclay, Bransford, Franks, McCarrell, and Nitsch (1974). Participants studied a critical word (e.g., "piano") in a sentence that stressed either its physical properties ("The man lifted the piano") or its musical properties ("The man tuned the piano"). At test, participants received a cue for recalling the critical word (e.g., "piano"). For some participants, the cue was related to the specific meaning of the critical word in the sentence (e.g., "heavy" for the sentence about moving a piano). For other participants, the cue was unrelated (e.g., "nice sound" from the sentence about moving a piano). Consistent with thesis 2, recall was better with related cues than with unrelated cues. When the cue activated the situation stored with the target word, the situation provided access to the episodic memory.

Yeh and Barsalou (2006) also review research that assesses the role of situations in conceptual processing more directly. In particular, they review situation effects in classic conceptual tasks, such as categorization, lexical decision, property verification, and property generation. As in episodic memory, people exhibit widespread situation effects that are consistent with theses 1 and 2. Because conceptual knowledge develops from episodic memories, these parallels are not surprising. Just as episodic memories exhibit a situated character, so does the conceptual knowledge that evolves out of them. During the abstraction of concepts from experience, concepts do not discard their situational histories.

Consider one example each from the visual object processing and language processing literatures. Classic work by Biederman (1972) found that people categorize a visually presented object faster in a coherent background scene than in a jumbled one, when the object's location in the display is cued beforehand. Consistent with thesis 1, the ability to process the object in a coherent scene facilitated object categorization. Recognizing the scene produced top-down activation to associated object categories that facilitated recognizing the target object. Conversely, when the ability to process the scene was compromised (i.e., in the jumbled scenes), categorization suffered because top-down support was not available.

Classic work by Miller and Isard (1963) similarly showed that the ability to identify spoken words was more accurate when the words belonged to a meaningful sentence than when the words belonged to an anomalous sentence. Again, when associations between focal categories and backgrounds situations remained intact, categorization benefited. Analogous to categorizing objects in coherent scenes, categorizing words in coherent sentences produced beneficial top-down support.

Many other findings from the visual-object and language-processing literatures further document the tight coupling between categories and background situations. Thus, theses 1 and 2 apply to diverse stimulus domains and diverse forms of processing performed on them. In general, concepts and situations are closely coupled, such that each activates the other, and situations dynamically affect the content represented for a concept on a particular occasion.

4.2. Evidence for Situated Conceptualizations from Cognitive Psychology

Barsalou (2003b) reviews evidence that supports the construct of situated conceptualization presented earlier, specifically, evidence showing that conceptualizations of categories often contain four types of situated information:

1. Properties of the focal category that are relevant in the current situation
2. Information about the background setting
3. Possible actions that the agent could take to achieve an associated goal
4. Possible interoceptive states that the agent might have while interacting with the category, including evaluations, emotions, cognitive operations, and so forth.

As described earlier, it is assumed that these four types of inferences are represented via neural simulations in the respective modality-specific systems. For example, contextually relevant object properties are simulated in the ventral stream, settings are simulated in parietal areas, actions are simulated in motor areas, and interoceptive states are simulated in areas that process emotion, reasoning, and so forth. Together, simulations of these four inference types produce the experience of being there conceptually (Barsalou, 2002). When a person processes a category, the concept that represents the category triggers a situated conceptualization, which represents the multimodal experience of what it would be like to process the category in the current situation.[10] Evidence

for the four types of inference that underlie situated conceptualization is reviewed in turn.

4.2.1. CONTEXTUALIZED CATEGORY INFERENCES

Evidence from multiple literatures shows that concepts do not produce the same representation in a situation invariant manner (e.g., Barsalou, 2003b; Yeh & Barsalou, 2006). Instead a concept produces one of many possible representations tailored to the current context. In on-line studies of sentence processing, context effects on lexical access are widespread (e.g., Barsalou, 1982; Kellas, Paul, Martin, & Simpson, 1991; Tabossi, 1988). For example, reading the word "basketball" does not normally activate the feature *floats* in most contexts. "Basketball" does activate *floats*, however, when a context makes it relevant, as when in need of a life preserver and a basketball is nearby. Similar inferences occur in memory (e.g., Barclay et al., 1974; Greenspan, 1986; Tulving & Thompson, 1973). As described earlier, when people read the word "piano" in a sentence about moving a piano, the property *heavy* is more active than the property *nice sound*, with the opposite occurring when people read about playing a piano.

In category learning, background knowledge about a situation constrains the properties of objects salient in them (e.g., Murphy, 2000). For example, if people are learning about a vehicle that is to be used for transportation in the Arctic, they acquire features relevant to the situation (e.g., *skis, insulation*), not features that are irrelevant (e.g., *tires, netting*).

In general, concepts are not represented in a vacuum, nor are they represented in a generic, abstract manner. Instead, concepts are contextualized such that they contain information relevant in the current situation.

4.2.2. SETTING INFERENCES

When the conceptual system represents a category, it typically situates the category in a background setting. The category is not represented in isolation. Again much work supports this conclusion (Barsalou, 2003b; Yeh & Barsalou, 2006). Numerous researchers have found that when people are asked to perform various tasks on individual concepts, information about background settings is activated implicitly. For example, Vallée-Tourangeau, Anthony, and Austin (1998) found that when people produce instances of categories, situations become active to guide the search process (see also Bucks, 1998; Walker & Kintsch, 1985). When participants produced instances of *FURNITURE*, for example, they imagined situations in which furniture is found (e.g., *LIVING ROOM*), scanned across the situations, and reported the category instances observed (e.g., *SOFA, TABLE*). Similarly, Wu and Barsalou (2008) found that when people are asked to generate the features of objects, they also describe background situations, which appear to be represented implicitly (see also Barsalou & Wiemer-Hastings, 2005). For example, when participants were asked to produce features of *APPLE*, they produced features about associated settings (e.g., kitchen), events (e.g., eating), and interoceptive states (e.g., enjoyable). Although the explicit instructions were to describe features of the target object, participants appeared to implicitly simulate a background situation, scan across it, and describe features encountered outside the object. As we saw earlier, much work on visual object processing similarly shows that representing objects activates background scenes (e.g., Biederman, 1981; Bar & Ullman, 1996; Intraub, Gottesman, & Bills, 1998; Mandler & Parker, 1976; Mandler & Stein, 1974; Murphy & Wisniewski, 1989). When an isolated object is perceived, a background scene is typically inferred immediately if one is not present. Bar (2004) reviews brain areas that underlie the representation of background settings.

4.2.3. ACTION INFERENCES

As we have seen, conceptual representations contain contextually relevant content and are framed against background settings. The findings in this subsection and the next show that the conceptual system represents agents in these settings, producing inferences about the actions they could take on situated objects and interoceptive states likely to occur, respectively. A variety of neuroimaging experiments show that the motor system becomes active when people process pictures of functional objects (e.g., Chao & Martin, 2000; Kellenbach, Brett, & Patterson, 2003) and when they process words for actions (e.g., Hauk, Johnsrude, & Pulvermüller, 2004). Martin (2001, 2007) reviews additional findings. For example, viewing a picture of a manipulable object (e.g., *HAMMER*) for a few seconds and naming it does not simply activate visual and linguistic areas, it also activates the grasping circuit in the brain, indicating that the brain is preparing for situated action with the object (Chao & Martin, 2000). Similarly, reading the word for a mouth action (e.g., "lick") or a foot action (e.g., "kick") activates the respective area of motor cortex for moving a foot or the face (Hauk et al., 2004). Again, representing a concept does not just activate an abstract semantic representation but instead induces preparation for situated action. In related behavioral research, Glenberg and Kaschak (2003) found that when people read sentences that describe actions ("You open a drawer"), they represented the meanings of these sentences as simulations in their motor systems.

Other research demonstrates that lesions in motor and somatosensory areas disrupt motor inferences (e.g., Adolphs, Damasio, Tranel, Cooper, & Damasio, 2000; Martin, 2001). For example, lesions in somatosensory cortex compromise the visual categorization of emotional expressions on faces (Adolphs et al., 2000). Although the task appears purely visual, the motor system immediately mimics the perceived expression in preparation for situated action, with feedback from the somatosensory system offering an important cue for the particular emotion being perceived. When somatosensory feedback is not available, categorization suffers. Much related work in social psychology similarly shows that the motor and somatosensory systems become active as people perceive social objects, in preparation for social interaction (e.g., Niedenthal, Brauer, Halberstadt, & Innes-Ker, 2001; Wallbott, 1991).

Developmental psychologists have also argued that the motor system is central to higher cognitive processes (e.g., Smith & Gasser, 2005; Smith, Thelen, Titzer, & McLin, 1999; Thelen, 2000). For example, the A-not-B, error in children's reasoning results, in part, from perseveration of action representations in the motor system.

Together all these findings demonstrate a close coupling between the motor and conceptual systems. When people conceptualize a category, they infer relevant actions that they could take on it. Barsalou et al. (2003a) review many further findings in social psychology that yield the same conclusion.

4.2.4. INTEROCEPTIVE AND PERSPECTIVE INFERENCES

People not only represent themselves in situated conceptualizations by simulating actions but further represent themselves in situated conceptualizations by simulating interoceptive states likely to arise, and by simulating subjective perspectives that they could take on settings. First consider interoceptions. Wu and Barsalou (2008) found that when participants are asked to generate the features of target objects, they also described interoceptions that they would be likely to have while interacting with these objects (see also Barsalou & Wiemer-Hastings, 2005). Specifically, participants often described emotions, evaluations, and cognitive operations relevant to interacting with a target object. Although the explicit instructions were to describe the object's features, participants appeared to implicitly simulate accompanying interoceptions from the background situation, which then leaked into their feature listings.

Another class of findings demonstrates that people simulate the subjective perspective that they would adopt on the situation that frames a target concept. Rather than represent the situation in a detached, objective manner, people represent it from a particular interoceptive perspective. For example, Spivey, Tyler, Richardson, and Young

(2000) found that participants simulated a particular perspective when hearing descriptions of settings (e.g., listening to a description of a skyscraper and then looking up as if they were there). Barsalou, Barbey, and Hase (2008) obtained a similar result as people produced features of concepts (e.g., describing features of BIRDS and looking up). Many other findings in the comprehension literature demonstrate similar effects (e.g., Anderson & Pichert, 1978; Black, Turner, & Bower, 1979).

4.2.5. BEING THERE CONCEPTUALLY

The findings reviewed in the previous four subsections support the conclusion that the conceptual system does not represent categories in an abstract, detached, generic manner. Instead, the conceptual system constructs situated conceptualizations dynamically, tailoring them to the current needs of situated action. Furthermore, the brain appears to implement these situated conceptualizations via simulations in the relevant modality-specific systems, such that experiences of being there with category members result. Together these packages of simulated inferences prepare agents for situated action. Because these inferences have similar representational forms as perceptions, actions, interoceptive states, and perspectives, they can be used to monitor and guide goal-directed performance as it unfolds in the current situation.

4.3. *Evidence for Situated Conceptualizations from Social Psychology*

Much further evidence for situated conceptualizations comes from decades of research that has documented the effects of bodily states on social cognition. On the basis of these findings, Barsalou et al. (2003a) concluded that people establish entrenched simulations of frequently experienced situations, where a given simulation includes (among many other things) a variety of bodily states, such as facial expressions, arm movements, and postures (see also

Niedenthal, Barsalou, Winkielman, Krauth-Gruber, & Ric, 2005). Barsalou et al. (2003a) proposed that these situated conceptualizations play a variety of important roles in processing social information.

4.3.1. SOCIAL INFORMATION PROCESSING PRODUCES EMBODIED STATES

Many experiments show that activating knowledge about a social concept generates associated bodily states. For example, Bargh, Chen, and Burrows (1996) activated various stereotypes by asking participants to process associated words. To activate the *ELDERLY* stereotype, for example, participants processed words for elderly properties like *gray*, *bingo*, and *Florida*, and were then asked them to use them in a sentence. Once the elderly stereotype became active, people walked more slowly to the elevator when they thought that the experiment was over, relative to when no stereotype was activated. In a related study, activating the elderly stereotype slowed the time to verify that letter strings are words (Dijksterhuis, Spears, & Lepanasse, 2001).

Other stereotypes produce analogous embodiments. Priming the *OBNOXIOUS-NESS* stereotype, for example, makes participants increasingly likely to interrupt a conversation (Bargh et al., 1996). Priming the *POLITICIAN* stereotype increases participants' long-windedness in writing an essay. As Dijksterhuis and Bargh's (2001) review of this literature demonstrates, activating a stereotype readily activates associated embodied states. As we will see in the next subsection, these embodiments have causal effects on social cognition, suggesting that they play central, not peripheral, roles (Barsalou et al., 2003a, provide further discussion on this issue).

Other social stimuli besides words for stereotypes also trigger embodied responses. As people view positive versus negative scenes, their facial musculature adopts positive or negative expressions, respectively (e.g., Cacioppo, Petty, Losch, & Kim, 1986). As participants view the faces of people from in-groups, their own faces adopt positive expressions; as participants view people

from out-groups, their faces adopt negative expressions (e.g., Vanman & Miller, 1993; Vanman, Paul, Ito, & Miller, 1997). Posture, too, is affected. When students receive a good grade, their posture tends to become erect; when they receive a poor grade, they tend to slump (Weisfeld & Beresford, 1982).

As these studies show, perceiving social stimuli triggers associated embodiments. Social stimuli do not simply activate amodal data structures that describe social situations and how to act in them. Instead, social stimuli activate simulations of these situations that include relevant embodied states.

4.3.2. EMBODIED STATES AFFECT SOCIAL INFORMATION PROCESSING

As we just saw in the previous subsection, processing social information produces accompanying embodiments as effects. In this subsection, we see that embodiments also function as potent causes in social situations. States of the face, head, arms, and torso all affect social cognition.

Much work has shown that when the face adopts a particular expression, it triggers associated emotions, which in turn color social processing (for a review, see Adelmann & Zajonc, 1989). In the typical experiment, participants are induced to adopt a facial expression under the guise of another task that obscures the nature of the expression and its hypothesized effects. Once the face is configured into a particular expression, it produces corresponding emotional states (e.g., Duclos et al., 1989). In turn, these emotions affect other tasks. Induced facial expressions, for example, affect the perceived funniness of a joke (Strack, Martin, & Stepper, 1988), or the perceived fame of a face (Strack & Neumann, 2000).

Inducing participants to perform various head movements also affects social processing. In one type of frequently performed experiment, participants were induced to either nod their heads forward and backward, or to shake their heads sideways, believing that they were trying to dislodge headphones from their heads while listening to music (e.g., Tom, Pettersen, Lau, Burton, & Cook, 1991; Wells & Petty, 1980).

Performing the nodding action led participants later to rate messages heard during this time as more compelling, and to judge products as more valuable, relative to performing the shaking action. Because nodding is associated with positive affect and shaking with negative affect, the different actions produced different affects, which in turn produced different judgments.

Inducing participants to perform arm actions also affects social cognition. An arm action that pulls an entity toward a person (approach behavior) produces more positive judgments than an arm action that pushes something away (avoidance behavior). For example, these different arm motions produce differential liking of novel visual figures (Cacioppo, Priester, & Bernston, 1993).

Finally, inducing postures also affects social processing. Adopting an upright posture produces positive affect and judgment, whereas adopting a slumping posture produces negative affect and judgment. For example, researchers have shown that posture affects participants' confidence in task performance (Riskind & Gotay, 1982) and how proud they are of it (Stepper & Strack, 1993).

As the results in this subsection illustrate, embodiment not only results from perceiving social stimuli but also causally affects subsequent social processing. When a particular bodily state is adopted, it activates situated conceptualizations that contain it. As these patterns become active, they trigger related emotional states that can then influence a variety of cognitive processes. In general, these conceptualizations prepare agents for situated social interaction.

4.4. Evidence for Situations in the Representation of Abstract Concepts

4.4.1. SITUATION AVAILABILITY

In a classic series of studies, Schwanenflugel, Shoben, and their colleagues showed that it is often difficult to retrieve situations for abstract concepts (for a review, see Schwanenflugel, 1991). For example, what is a situation in which TRUTH occurs? Although a jury trial in courtroom might come to mind eventually, it often takes awhile to retrieve a relevant situation. Conversely, situations seem to come to mind more easily for concrete concepts. For CHAIR, situations like dining rooms and offices come to mind rapidly.[11]

Schwanenflugel, Shoben, and their colleagues showed that the retrieval of situations affects the processing of both abstract and concrete concepts across a variety of cognitive tasks, including lexical decision, comprehension, and memory (e.g., Schwanenflugel, Harnishfeger, & Stowe, 1988; Schwanenflugel & Shoben, 1983; Schwanenflugel & Stowe, 1989; Wattenmaker & Shoben, 1987). Their findings led to two conclusions about processing words. First, the meanings of words are not established in isolation. A word's meaning is typically not a stand-alone representation that describes its associated category. Instead, words are typically understood against background situations. When a situation is not available, a concept is difficult to process. Many early studies on language comprehension reached the same conclusion (for reviews, see Bransford & Johnson, 1973; Bransford & McCarrell, 1974). Much recent work reaches this conclusion as well (e.g., Barsalou, 1999a; Clark, 1992; Clark, 1997). In general, situations provide essential information for representing and understanding concepts. Understanding the meaning of TABLE relies not only on properties of the physical object but also on the situations in which it is found (e.g., dining rooms) and the activities performed in them (e.g., eating). Knowledge about TABLE is inadequate if a person does not know how to interact with them in relevant situations.

A second conclusion also follows from the results of Schwanenflugel, Shoben, and their colleagues: retrieving situations for abstract concepts is generally more difficult than retrieving situations for concrete concepts. At least two factors may be responsible. First, abstract concepts may be linked to a wider variety of situations (Galbraith & Underwood, 1973). As a result of greater interference, retrieving a single situation for an abstract concept may be more difficult than retrieving one for a concrete concept. Second, when people process abstract concepts during everyday activities, a relevant situation may typically be in place already (Barsalou & Wiemer-Hastings, 2005). People may not usually entertain a concept like *TRUTH* unless a relevant situation has already been represented (or perceived) to which the concept applies. Consequently, the conceptual system becomes accustomed to retrieving information about abstract concepts with relevant situations already in place. Conversely, because it is relatively unusual to process abstract concepts in a situational vacuum, people draw blanks, at least initially, when receiving them out of context.

4.4.2. CONTRASTING THE CONTENT OF ABSTRACT AND CONCRETE CONCEPTS

It is widely assumed, at least implicitly, that abstract and concrete concepts have little in common. Alternatively, Barsalou and Wiemer-Hastings (2005) argued that concrete and abstract concepts share important similarities, captured in three hypotheses that they investigated empirically. According to hypothesis 1, abstract and concrete concepts share common situational content. According to hypothesis 2, however, abstract and concrete concepts differ in their focus within background situations, with concrete concepts focusing on objects and abstract concepts focusing on events and interoceptions. Finally, according to hypothesis 3, abstract concepts are more complex than concrete concepts, containing more content and being more distributed across situations.

Barsalou and Wiemer-Hastings (2005) reported evidence that supports these three hypotheses. Regarding hypothesis 1, abstract and concrete concepts shared extensive situational content. Both types of concepts activated information about events, settings, agents, objects, actions, and mental states. Indeed, the distributions of this content were remarkably similar. For both concept types, participants appeared to represent complete situations, which framed the focal content of interest. Consistent with

hypothesis 2, however, the distributions of content were not identical for abstract and concrete concepts. Whereas abstract concepts produced higher rates of information about interoceptions and events, concrete concepts produced higher rates of information for objects and settings. Although both concept types were represented in a situated manner, they highlighted different aspects of their background situations. Regarding hypothesis 3, abstract concepts appeared to be more complex and distributed across situations than concrete concepts, with abstract concepts organized around larger and deeper hierarchical structures.

Together, all these findings further implicate situations in conceptual processing. Both abstract and concrete concepts appear to be represented in a situated manner.

5. Further Issues

The findings reviewed here strongly suggest that conceptual processing is situated. Rather than processing concepts in a vacuum, people activate relevant background situations. Presumably the purpose of these situations is to prepare agents for situated action and to represent the focal category in a situationally appropriate manner. Although it seems clear that situations are implicated in conceptual processing, we have only begun to understand situational representations and their interactions with concepts. Several of many outstanding issues that remain are discussed briefly.

5.1. *Radial Categories*

One important problem is explaining how different conceptualizations of the same category become linked together. How do the various conceptualizations of *CHAIR*, for example, become integrated into a single category? One possibility is that they become integrated by analogy. When a perceived entity activates a structurally analogous conceptualization in memory, the two become linked (e.g., Brooks, 1978; Gentner & Markman, 1997; Holyoak & Thagard, 1989; Nosofsky, 1984). Perceiving an office chair, for example, may activate the conceptualization of a kitchen chair via their shared physical structure or via the common actions performed on it. As a result, the two conceptualizations become integrated in memory. As different kinds of chairs are increasingly encountered in different situations, their respective conceptualizations become related to similar conceptualizations, thereby forming linked chains. Although core properties could ultimately become established across the various conceptualizations of a concept, they need not be. When core properties do not develop, the linked chains of conceptualizations form a radial concept, with each conceptualization being closely related to at least one other (e.g., Lakoff, 1987; Malt, Sloman, Gennari, Shi, & Wang, 1999).

Essences could constitute another possible linking mechanism to integrate the different conceptualizations of a category. If all known conceptualizations of a category are believed to share a common essence, they become linked around the essence, even when their physical appearances differ (e.g., Gelman & Diesendruck, 1999). Depending on the category, the essence could reflect a real essence that actually exists across instances, or it could simply reflect the belief that an essence exists, even when one does not.

As these suggestions illustrate, the situated conceptualizations for a category could become linked in various ways. Following Barsalou (1999b, 2003b), the result is a simulator capable of producing many situated simulations of a category (see also Barsalou et al., 1993).

This claim does not simply reduce to the fact that a category has subordinates. The claim is significantly stronger. A category does not just take different subordinate forms. Instead, these different forms accommodate the constraints of different situations. Conceptualizations of CHAIRS, for example, take different forms because the constraints on having somewhere to sit vary from situation to situation. Furthermore, the key proposal is that conceptualizations are represented against background situations. They are not simply subordinates represented in isolation. Finally, the present framework extends well beyond subordinate categories. Consider CARS. The present framework predicts that a single subordinate, such as SEDAN, will be conceptualized in a variety of situations, such as driving a sedan, watching a sedan drive by, filling a sedan's gas tank, parking a sedan, and so forth. Instead of conceptualizing sedans as a subordinate in a generic, situation-independent manner, people conceptualize them differently in these various situations, focusing on different perspectives and properties in each. In these ways, the theoretical proposal here extends beyond the fact that categories have subordinates.

5.2. *Dimensions of Situations*

Creating a taxonomy of relevant phenomena often lays the groundwork for mechanistic models. In this spirit, Yeh and Barsalou (2006) developed a taxonomy of situation types. Specifically, they proposed that three factors – grain size, meaningfulness, and tangibility – can be used to construct a taxonomy of situations.

5.2.1. GRAIN SIZE

The situations that have been reported to affect conceptual processing range from large to small grain sizes. Toward one extreme, a situation can be an entire physical setting over an extended period of time, such as the classroom in which course material is learned over a one-hour period. Toward the other extreme, a situation can be the stimulus immediately adjacent to a target stimulus for a few moments, such as a context word that primes a target word momentarily.

Both spatial and temporal extent underlie grain size. Spatially, a situation can range from a large physical setting (e.g., a park) to a computer that presents a pictured scene, to an adjacent stimulus within a computer display (the object next to a target object in a pictured scene). Temporally, a situation can range from the entire learning phase of an experiment, to the serial presentation of several stimuli, to a trial that contains a single configuration of stimulus elements. Thus, a situation can vary from a large region of space over an extended period of time, down to a small region of space for a moment.

Typically, a given stimulus exists in a hierarchically organized set of situations across multiple grain sizes simultaneously. There is not just a single situation for a stimulus – typically there are many. Furthermore, it is difficult, if not impossible, to specify the potential space of situations exhaustively. A focal stimulus can potentially occur in an infinite number of situations and be viewed from an infinite number of perspectives. The situations that pervade cognition are open ended and difficult to enumerate. As Yeh and Barsalou (2006) show, situation effects at diverse grain sizes affect conceptual processing.

5.2.2. MEANINGFULNESS

The relation between a focal object and a situation can range from arbitrary co-occurrence to meaningful interdependence. In arbitrary co-occurrence, there is no explanation for why an object occurs in a situation and vice versa. Furthermore, predicting that the situation will contain the object is not possible. When participants learn random words in a particular classroom, for example, the relation between the words and the classroom is arbitrary. Knowing the situation does not explain or predict the focal elements of interest.

Alternatively, the relationship between an object and a situation can be meaningful and predictable. In these situations, the object and situation belong to a coherent system whose parts have strong dependencies between them. In a classroom that contains desks, chairs, and blackboards, for example, people can explain why these entities belong together, and they can predict one from perceiving the other.

As Yeh and Barsalou (2006) show, both arbitrary and meaningful situations produce situation effects. Even if an object only bears

an arbitrary relation to its situation, associations develop between the object and situation that produce these effects. Importantly, however, situation effects appear to be greater in meaningful situations, probably because stronger relations develop between situations and objects.

5.2.3. TANGIBILITY

Situations also vary in the extent to which they are physically present versus imagined. For any stimulus, a physical situation is always present. However, people also frequently imagine background situations for focal stimuli. While recalling a word list in a new room, for example, participants might imagine the original room in which the list was learned. As Yeh and Barsalou (2006) review, a focal stimulus often induces participants to imagine a background situation that is meaningfully related to the stimulus, especially when a meaningful situation is not provided. Participants might see a hat above a shirt, for example, and imagine that a nondepicted person is wearing them. Or a participant might see a picture of a bird with its wings extended and imagine it flying through the sky. Many situation effects result from imagined situations that target stimuli elicit.

5.3. *The Cumulative Nature of Situations*

As we just saw, situations appear to vary in grain size, meaningfulness, and tangibility. A potential implication is that people often perceive and imagine a complex set of hierarchically organized situations simultaneously for a given focal stimulus. At this time, we do not have accounts of what a hierarchically organized set of situations contains, or how it is constructed. What situations are present at what grain sizes? How do they originate? Are some always present in perception, perhaps because they reflect obligatory processing during perception? Are others created in an ad hoc manner as they become relevant to current goals?

A related issue concerns how all of the situations represented simultaneously at a given time become integrated to create the illusion of a single coherent situation. Also, how do situations at small grain sizes come and go while situations at large grain sizes remain relatively constant? These are just a few of the many fundamental issues associated with situated conceptualization that remain not just unresolved but unaddressed. Hopefully, issues such as these will receive significant attention in future research.

Acknowledgments

I am grateful to Phil Robbins and Eric Margolis for helpful comments on an earlier version of this chapter. This work was supported by National Science Foundation Grants SBR-9421326, SBR-9796200, and BCS-0212134 to Lawrence W. Barsalou. Address correspondence to Lawrence W. Barsalou, Department of Psychology, Emory University, Atlanta, GA 30322 (barsalou@emory.edu, http://userwww.service.emory.edu/~barsalou/).

Notes

1 *Interoception* will refer to the perception of internal states, including affects (e.g., calmness), emotions (e.g., happiness), motivations (e.g., hunger), pains (e.g., headache), cognitive states (e.g., belief), cognitive operations (e.g., comparison), and so forth. Interoception will not include somatosensory states, given their close coupling with the motor system.

2 Quotes will be used to indicate linguistic forms, and italics will be used to indicate conceptual representations. Within conceptual representations, uppercase italic font will indicate categories, whereas lowercase italic font will indicate properties of categories. Thus, *BIRD* indicates a category, whereas *feathers* indicates a property, with "bird" and "feathers" indicating the respective linguistic forms.

3 I do not mean to rule out the possibility of amodal symbols in the brain, although I am increasingly skeptical that they exist in classically postulated form. Perhaps a more likely possibility is that patterns of active neurons in association areas constitute amodal recodings of activations in modality-specific areas. Should such patterns exist, however,

they may not operate as stand-alone symbols but may primarily serve to activate modality-specific patterns that play central roles in the representation process. Furthermore, these patterns are likely to have modality-specific tunings, such that they are actually not amodal. Indeed, the fact that association areas often lie within modality-specific systems argues against their being completely amodal. For further discussion of these issues, see Damasio (1989) and Simmons and Barsalou (2003).

4 Why does selective attention focus on some components of experience but not others? Many factors influence this process, including genetics, language learning, cultural transmission, and goal pursuit. Explaining these mechanisms lies beyond the scope of this chapter. Furthermore, this is the classic problem of relevance (e.g., Murphy & Medin, 1985; Sperber & Wilson, 1986), and any theory of knowledge (not just this one) must address it.

5 The mechanism of situational constraint may also play a significant role in minimizing the frame problem, along with related problems associated with nonmonotonic reasoning.

6 Although this definition of concepts stresses empirical factors, genetic factors undoubtedly play central roles as well. There is no a priori reason, for example, why a simulator could not originate genetically. More plausibly, genetic factors probably play major roles in specifying the feature and association areas that underlie the empirical acquisition of simulators (e.g., Simmons & Barsalou, 2003). Furthermore, these genetic factors may reflect evolutionary history by anticipating features and conjunctions of features that are important for acquiring relatively constant categories in the environment, action, and interoception (cf. Caramazza & Shelton, 1998).

7 The definition of *situation* adopted here is designed to handle everyday situations that people encounter during daily activity. It does not attempt to cover more specialized situations that occur in technical and formal activities (e.g., mathematics). Situations are likely to be just as important in these other domains (e.g., Barwise & Perry, 1983; Chi, Feltovich, & Glaser, 198; Greeno, 1998). However, they are not pursued here.

8 As described later in the section on radial categories, this proposal about situated

conceptualizations is not equivalent to standard accounts of subordinate categories. Rather than simply represent a subordinate as an isolated category, the proposal here is that specific types of instances (including subordinates) are represented in background settings, such that a given subordinate might be represented separately in many possible situations in which it occurs regularly.

9 Yeh and Barsalou also propose a third thesis not discussed here, which states that the first two theses hold only when people perform conceptual processing and do not rely on superficial processing strategies, such as using familiarity to guide performance.

10 The expression "being there conceptually" could be understood as claiming that agents experience these situations consciously. The sense of being there conceptually intended here, however, is that neural systems ready themselves for perceptions, actions, and interoceptions likely to be relevant in the current situation. Although these neural systems may often produce conscious states, the focus remains on the neural processing that underlies consciousness.

11 In this literature, Schwanenflugel and other researchers refer to "situation availability" as "context availability." *Situation* is used here instead, because it has roughly the same meaning and is the central construct in this chapter.

References

Adelman, P. K., & Zajonc, R. B. (1989). Facial efference and the experience of emotion. *Annual Review of Psychology, 40*, 249–280.

Adolphs, R., Damasio, H., Tranel, D., Cooper, G., & Damasio, A. R. (2000). A role for somatosensory cortices in the visual recognition of emotion as revealed by three-dimensional lesion mapping. *Journal of Neuroscience, 20*, 2683–2690.

Andersen, S. M., & Chen, S. (2002). The relational self: An interpersonal social-cognitive theory. *Psychological Review, 109*, 619–645.

Anderson, R. C., & Pichert, J. W. (1978). Recall of previously unrecallable information following a shift in perspective. *Journal of Verbal Learning and Verbal Behavior, 17*, 1–12.

Bar, M. (2004). Visual objects in context. *Nature Reviews Neuroscience, 5*, 617–629.

Bar, M., & Ullman, S. (1996). Spatial context in recognition. *Perception, 25*, 343–352.

Barclay, J. R., Bransford, J. D., Franks, J. J., McCarrell, N. S., & Nitsch, K. (1974). Comprehension and semantic flexibility. *Journal of Verbal Learning and Verbal Behavior, 13*, 471–481.

Bargh, J. A., Chen, M., & Burrows, L. (1996). Automaticity of social behavior: Direct effects of trait construct and stereotype activation on action. *Journal of Personality and Social Psychology, 71*, 230–244.

Barsalou, L. W. (1982). Context-independent and context-dependent information in concepts. *Memory & Cognition, 10*, 82–93.

Barsalou, L. W. (1987). The instability of graded structure: Implications for the nature of concepts. In U. Neisser (Ed.), *Concepts and conceptual development: Ecological and intellectual factors in categorization* (pp. 101–140). Cambridge: Cambridge University Press.

Barsalou, L. W. (1989). Intraconcept similarity and its implications for interconcept similarity. In S. Vosniadou & A. Ortony (Eds.), *Similarity and analogical reasoning* (pp. 76–121). Cambridge: Cambridge University Press.

Barsalou, L. W. (1993). Flexibility, structure, and linguistic vagary in concepts: Manifestations of a compositional system of perceptual symbols. In A. F. Collins, S. E. Gathercole, M. A. Conway, & P. E. Morris (Eds.), *Theories of memory* (pp. 29–101). Hillsdale, NJ: Lawrence Erlbaum.

Barsalou, L. W. (1999a). Language comprehension: Archival memory or preparation for situated action? *Discourse Processes, 28*, 61–80.

Barsalou, L. W. (1999b). Perceptual symbol systems. *Behavioral and Brain Sciences, 22*, 577–660.

Barsalou, L. W. (2002). Being there conceptually: Simulating categories in preparation for situated action. In N. L. Stein, P. J. Bauer, & M. Rabinowitz (Eds.), *Representation, memory, and development: Essays in honor of Jean Mandler* (pp. 1–16). Mahwah, NJ: Lawrence Erlbaum.

Barsalou, L. W. (2003a). Abstraction in perceptual symbol systems. *Philosophical Transactions of the Royal Society of London: Biological Sciences, 358*, 1177–1187.

Barsalou, L. W. (2003b). Situated simulation in the human conceptual system. *Language and Cognitive Processes, 18*, 513–562.

Barsalou, L. W. (2005). Continuity of the conceptual system across species. *Trends in Cognitive Sciences, 9*, 309–311.

Barsalou, L.W. (2008). Grounded cognition. *Annual Review of Psychology, 59*, 617–645.

Barsalou, L. W., Barbey, A., & Hase, S. (2008). *Spontaneous body movements during property generation for concepts.* Manuscript in preparation.

Barsalou, L. W., Niedenthal, P. M., Barbey, A., & Ruppert, J. (2003a). Social embodiment. In B. Ross (Ed.), *The psychology of learning and motivation* (Vol. 43, pp. 43–92). San Diego, CA: Academic Press.

Barsalou, L. W., Simmons, W. K., Barbey, A. K., & Wilson, C. D. (2003b). Grounding conceptual knowledge in modality-specific systems. *Trends in Cognitive Sciences, 7*, 84–91.

Barsalou, L. W., & Wiemer-Hastings, K. (2005). Situating abstract concepts. In D. Pecher & R. Zwaan (Eds.), *Grounding cognition: The role of perception and action in memory, language, and thought* (pp. 129–163). New York: Cambridge University Press.

Barsalou, L. W., Yeh, W., Luka, B. J., Olseth, K. L., Mix, K. S., & Wu, L. L. (1993). Concepts and meaning. In K. Beals, G. Cooke, D. Kathman, S. Kita, K. E. McCullough, & D. Testen (Eds.), *Chicago Linguistic Society 29: Papers from the parasession on the correspondence of conceptual, semantic and grammatical representations* (pp. 23–61). Chicago: Chicago Linguistic Society.

Bartlett, F. C. (1932). *Remembering: A study in experimental and social psychology.* New York: Cambridge University Press.

Barwise, J., & Perry, J. (1983). *Situations and attitudes.* Cambridge, MA: MIT Press.

Biederman, I. (1972). Perceiving real-world scenes. *Science, 177*, 77–80.

Biederman, I. (1981). On the semantics of a glance at a scene. In M. Kubovy & J. R. Pomerantz (Eds.), *Perceptual organization* (pp. 213–253). Hillsdale, NJ: Lawrence Erlbaum.

Black, J. B., Turner, T. J., & Bower, G. H. (1979). Point of view in narrative comprehension, memory, and production. *Journal of Verbal Learning and Verbal Behavior, 18*, 187–198.

Bransford, J. D., & Johnson, M. K. (1973). Considerations of some problems of comprehension. In W. G. Chase (Ed.), *Visual information processing* (pp. 383–438). New York: Academic Press.

Bransford, J. D., & McCarrell, N. S. (1974). A sketch of a cognitive approach to comprehension: Some thoughts about understanding what it means to comprehend. In W. B. Weimer & D. S. Palermo (Eds.), *Cognition and the symbolic processes* (pp. 377–399). Hillsdale, NJ: Lawrence Erlbaum.

Brewer, W. F., & Treyens, J. C. (1981). Role of schemata in memory for places. *Cognitive Psychology, 13*, 207–230.

Brooks, L. R. (1978). Nonanalytic concept formation and memory for instances. In E. Rosch & B. B. Lloyd (Eds.), *Cognition and categorization* (pp. 169–211). Hillsdale, NJ: Lawrence Erlbaum.

Brooks, R. A. (1991). Intelligence without representation. *Artificial Intelligence, 47*, 139–159.

Bruner, J. S. (1957). Going beyond the information given. In J. S. Bruner, E. Brunswik, L. Festinger, F. Heider, K. F. Muenzinger, C. E. Osgood, & D. Rapaport (Eds.), *Contemporary approaches to cognition* (pp. 41–69). Cambridge, MA: Harvard University Press.

Bucks, R. S. (1998). *Intrusion errors in Alzheimer's disease.* Unpublished doctoral dissertation, University of Bristol.

Cacioppo, J. P., Petty, R. E., Losch, M. E., & Kim, H. S. (1986). Electromyographic activity over facial muscle regions can differentiate the valence and intensity of affective reactions. *Journal of Personality and Social Psychology, 50*, 260–268.

Cacioppo, J. T., Priester, J. R., & Bernston, G. G. (1993). Rudimentary determination of attitudes: II. Arm flexion and extension have differential effects on attitudes. *Journal of Personality and Social Psychology, 65*, 5–17.

Caramazza, A., & Shelton, J. R. (1998). Domain-specific knowledge systems in the brain: The animate-inanimate distinction. *Journal of Cognitive Neuroscience, 10*, 1–34.

Chao, L. L., & Martin, A. (2000). Representation of manipulable man-made objects in the dorsal stream. *Neuroimage, 12*, 478–484.

Cheng, P. W., & Holyoak, K. J. (1985). Pragmatic reasoning schemas. *Cognitive Psychology, 17*, 391–416.

Chi, M. T. H., Feltovich, P. J., & Glaser, R. (1981). Categorization and representation of physics problems by experts and novices. *Cognitive Science, 5*, 121–152.

Clark, A. (1997). *Being there: Putting brain, body, and world together again.* Cambridge, MA: MIT Press.

Clark, H. H. (1992). *Arenas of language use.* Chicago: University of Chicago Press.

Collins, A. M., & Loftus, E. F. (1975). A spreading activation theory of semantic processing. *Psychological Review*, 82, 407–428.

Collins, A. M., & Quillian, M. R. (1969). Retrieval time from semantic memory. *Journal of Verbal Learning and Verbal Behavior*, 8, 240–248.

Craik, F. I. M., & Lockhart, R. S. (1972). Levels of processing: A framework for memory research. *Journal of Verbal Learning and Verbal Behavior*, 11, 671–684.

Cree, G. S., & McRae, K. (2003). Analyzing the factors underlying the structure and computation of the meaning of chipmunk, cherry, chisel, cheese, and cello (and many other such concrete nouns). *Journal of Experimental Psychology: General*, 132, 163–201.

Damasio, A. R. (1989). Time-locked multiregional retroactivation: A systems-level proposal for the neural substrates of recall and recognition. *Cognition*, 33, 25–62.

Dijksterhuis, A., & Bargh, J. A. (2001). The perception-behavior expressway: Automatic effects of social perception on social behavior. In M. P. Zanna (Ed.), *Advances in experimental social psychology* (Vol. 23, pp. 1–40). San Diego, CA: Academic Press.

Dijksterhuis, A., Spears, R., & Lepanasse, V. (2001). Reflecting and deflecting stereotypes: Assimilation and contrast in automatic behavior. *Journal of Experimental Social Psychology*, 37, 286–299.

Duclos, S. E., Laird, J. D., Schneider, E., Sexter, M., Stern, L., & Van Lighten, O. (1989). Emotion-specific effects of facial expressions and postures on emotional experience. *Journal of Personality and Social Psychology*, 57, 100–108.

Dunbar, G. (1991). *The cognitive lexicon*. Tübingen, Germany: Gunter Narr Verlag.

Farah, M. J. (2000). The neural bases of mental imagery. In M. S. Gazzaniga (Ed.), *The cognitive neurosciences* (2nd ed., pp. 965–974). Cambridge, MA: MIT Press.

Farah, M. J., & McClelland, J. L. (1991). A computational model of semantic memory impairment: Modality specificity and emergent category specificity. *Journal of Experimental Psychology: General*, 120, 339–357.

Finke, R. A. (1989). *Principles of mental imagery*. Cambridge, MA: MIT Press.

Galbraith, R. C., & Underwood, B. J. (1973). Perceived frequency of concrete and abstract words. *Memory & Cognition*, 1, 56–60.

Gelman, S. A., & Diesendruck, G. (1999). What's in a concept? Context, variability, and psychological essentialism. In I. E. Siegel (Ed.), *Theoretical perspectives on the concept of representation* (pp. 87–111). Mahwah, NJ: Lawrence Erlbaum.

Gentner, D., & Markman, A. B. (1997). Structure mapping in analogy and similarity. *American Psychologist*, 52, 45–56.

Gick, M. L., & Holyoak, K. J. (1980). Analogical problem solving. *Cognitive Psychology*, 12, 306–355.

Gil-da-Costa, R., Braun, A., Lopes, M., Hauser, M. D., Carson, R. E., Herscovitch, P., et al. (2004). Toward an evolutionary perspective on conceptual representation: Species-specific calls activate visual and affective processing systems. *Proceedings of the National Academy of Sciences*, 101, 17516–17521.

Glenberg, A. M. (1997). What memory is for. *Behavioral and Brain Sciences*, 20, 1–55.

Glenberg, A. M., & Kaschak, M. P. (2004). Grounding language in action. *Psychonomic Bulletin & Review*, 9, 558–569.

Goldberg, A. E. (1995). *Constructions: A construction grammar approach to argument structure*. Chicago: University of Chicago Press.

Gould, S. J. (1991). Exaptation: A crucial tool for an evolutionary psychology. *Journal of Social Issues*, 47, 43–65.

Greeno, J. G. (1998). The situativity of knowing, learning, and research. *American Psychologist*, 53, 5–26.

Greenspan, S. L. (1986). Semantic flexibility and referential specificity of concrete nouns. *Journal of Memory and Language*, 25, 539–557.

Grèzes, J., & Decety, J. (2001). Functional anatomy of execution, mental simulation, observation, and verb generation of actions: A meta-analysis. *Human Brain Mapping*, 12, 1–19.

Hampton, J. A. (1979). Polymorphous concepts in semantic memory. *Journal of Verbal Learning and Verbal Behavior*, 18, 441–461.

Hauk, O., Johnsrude, I., & Pulvermüller, F. (2004). Somatotopic representation of action words in human motor and premotor cortex. *Neuron*, 41, 301–307.

Holyoak, K. J., & Thagard, P. R. (1989). Analogical mapping by constraint satisfaction. *Cognitive Science*, 13, 295–356.

Intraub, H., Gottesman, C. V., & Bills, A. J. (1998). Effects of perceiving and imagining scenes on memory for pictures. *Journal of Experimental Psychology: Learning, Memory, & Cognition*, 24, 186–201.

Johnson-Laird, P. N. (1983). *Mental models*. Cambridge, MA: Harvard University Press.

Kellas, G., Paul, S. T., Martin, M., & Simpson, G. B. (1991). Contextual feature activation and meaning access. In G. B. Simpson (Ed.), *Understanding word and sentence* (pp. 47–71). New York: Elsevier.

Kellenbach, M. L., Brett, M., & Patterson, K. (2003). Actions speak louder than functions: The importance of manipulability and action in tool representation. *Journal of Cognitive Neuroscience, 15*, 30–46.

Kirsh, D. (1991). Today the earwig, tomorrow man? *Artificial Intelligence, 47*, 161–184.

Kosslyn, S. M. (1994). *Image and brain*. Cambridge, MA: MIT Press.

Lakoff, G. (1987). *Women, fire, and dangerous things: What categories reveal about the mind*. Chicago: University of Chicago Press.

Malt, B. C., Sloman, S. A., Gennari, S., Shi, M., & Wang, Y. (1999). Knowing versus naming: Similarity and the linguistic categorization of artifacts. *Journal of Memory and Language, 40*, 230–262.

Mandler, J. M., & Parker, R. E. (1976). Memory for descriptive and spatial information in complex pictures. *Journal of Experimental Psychology: Human Learning, & Memory, 2*, 38–48.

Mandler, J. M., & Stein, N. (1974). Recall and recognition of pictures by children as a function of organization and distractor similarity. *Journal of Experimental Psychology, 102*, 657–669.

Martin, A. (2001). Functional neuroimaging of semantic memory. In R. Cabeza & A. Kingstone (Eds.), *Handbook of functional neuroimaging of cognition* (pp. 153–186). Cambridge, MA: MIT Press.

Martin, A. (2007). The representation of object concepts in the brain. *Annual Review of Psychology, 58*, 25–45.

McRae, K., & Cree, G. S. (2002). Factors underlying category-specific semantic deficits. In E. M. E. Forde & G. Humphreys (Eds.), *Category-specificity in mind and brain* (pp. 211–249). East Sussex, UK: Psychology Press.

McRae, K., de Sa, V. R., & Seidenberg, M. S. (1997). On the nature and scope of featural representations of word meaning. *Journal of Experimental Psychology: General, 126*, 99–130.

Miller, G. A., & Isard, S. D. (1963). Some perceptual consequences of linguistic rules. *Journal of Verbal Learning and Verbal Behavior, 2*, 217–228.

Mischel, W. (1968). *Personality and assessment*. New York: Wiley.

Murphy, G. L. (2000). Explanatory concepts. In R. A. Wilson & F. C. Keil (Eds.), *Explanation and cognition* (pp. 361–392). Cambridge, MA: MIT Press.

Murphy, G. L., & Medin, D. L. (1985). The role of theories in conceptual coherence. *Psychological Review, 92*, 289–316.

Murphy, G. L., & Wisniewski, E. (1989). Categorizing objects in isolation and in scenes: What a superordinate is good for. *Journal of Experimental Psychology: Learning, Memory, & Cognition, 15*, 572–586.

Niedenthal, P. M., Barsalou, L. W., Winkielman, P., Krauth-Gruber, S., & Ric, F. (2005). Embodiment in attitudes, social perception, and emotion. *Personality and Social Psychology Review, 9*(3), 184–211.

Niedenthal, P. M., Brauer, M., Halberstadt, J. B., & Innes-Ker, A. H. (2001). When did her smile drop? Facial mimicry and the influences of emotional state on the detection of change in emotional expression. *Cognition and Emotion, 15*, 853–864.

Nosofsky, R. M. (1984). Choice, similarity, and the context theory of classification. *Journal of Experimental Psychology: Learning, Memory, & Cognition, 10*, 104–114.

Pecher, D., & Zwaan, R. (Eds.). (2005). *Grounding cognition: The role of perception and action in memory, language, and thought*. New York: Cambridge University Press.

Quiroga, R. Q., Reddy, L., Kreimen, C., Koch, G., & Fried, I. (2005). Invariant visual representation by single neurons in the human brain. *Science, 435*, 1102–1107.

Riskind, J. H., & Gotay, C. C. (1982). Physical posture: Could it have regulatory or feedback effects on motication and emotion? *Motivation and Emotion, 6*, 273–298.

Rosch, E., & Mervis, C. B. (1975). Family resemblances: Studies in the internal structure of categories. *Cognitive Psychology, 7*, 573–605.

Sanford, A. J., & Garrod, S. C. (1981). *Understanding written language: Explanations of comprehension beyond the sentence*. Chichester, UK: Wiley.

Schwanenflugel, P. J. (1991). Why are abstract concepts hard to understand? In P. J. Schwanenflugel (Ed.), *The psychology of word meaning* (pp. 223–250). Mahwah, NJ: Lawrence Erlbaum.

Schwanenflugel, P. J., Harnishfeger, K. K., & Stowe, R. W. (1988). Context availability and lexical decisions for abstract and concrete words. *Journal of Memory & Language, 27,* 499–520.

Schwanenflugel, P. J., & Shoben, E. J. (1983). Differential context effects in the comprehension of abstract and concrete verbal materials. *Journal of Experimental Psychology: Learning, Memory, & Cognition, 9,* 82–102.

Schwanenflugel, P. J., & Stowe, R. W. (1989). Context availability and the processing of abstract and concrete words in sentences. *Reading Research Quarterly, 24,* 114–126.

Schyns, P. G., Goldstone, R. L., & Thibaut, J. P. (1998). The development of features in object concepts. *Behavioral and Brain Sciences, 21,* 1–54.

Simmons, K., & Barsalou, L. W. (2003). The similarity-in-topography principle: Reconciling theories of conceptual deficits. *Cognitive Neuropsychology, 20,* 451–486.

Smith, E. E. (1978). Theories of semantic memory. In W. K. Estes (Ed.), *Handbook of learning and cognitive processes* (Vol. 6, pp. 1–56). Hillsdale, NJ: Lawrence Erlbaum.

Smith, E. R., & Semin, G. R. (2004). Socially situated cognition: Cognition in its social context. *Advances in Experimental Social Psychology, 36,* 53–117.

Smith, L. B., & Gasser, M. (2005). The development of embodied cognition: Six lessons from babies. *Artificial Life, 11,* 13–30.

Smith, L. B., & Samuelson, L. K. (1997). Perceiving and remembering: Category stability, variability, and development. In K. Lamberts & D. Shanks (Eds.), *Knowledge, concepts, and categories* (pp. 161–196). London: Psychology Press.

Smith, L. B., Thelen, E., Titzer, R., & McLin, D. (1999). Knowing in the context of acting: The task dynamics of the A-not-B error. *Psychological Review, 106,* 235–260.

Smith, W. J. (1977). *The behavior of communicating.* Cambridge, MA: Harvard University Press.

Sperber, D., & Wilson, D. (1986). *Relevance: Communication and cognition.* Cambridge, MA: Blackwell.

Spivey, M., Tyler, M., Richardson, D., & Young, E. (2000). Eye movements during comprehension of spoken scene descriptions. In *Proceedings of the 22nd Annual Conference of the Cognitive Science Society* (pp. 487–492). Mahwah, NJ: Lawrence Erlbaum.

Stepper, S., & Strack, F. (1993). Proprioceptive determinants of emotional and nonemotional feelings. *Journal of Personality and Social Psychology, 64,* 211–220.

Strack, F., Martin, L. L., & Stepper, S. (1988). Inhibiting and facilitating conditions of the human smile: A nonobtrusive test of the facial feedback hypothesis. *Journal of Personality and Social Psychology, 54,* 768–777.

Strack, F., & Neumann, R. (2000). Furrowing the brow may undermine perceived fame: The role of facial feedback in judgments of celebrity. *Personality and Social Psychology Bulletin, 26,* 762–768.

Tabossi, P. (1988). Effects of context on the immediate interpretation of unambiguous nouns. *Journal of Experimental Psychology: Learning, Memory, & Cognition, 14,* 153–162.

Thelen, E. (2000). Grounded in the world: Developmental origins of the embodied mind. *Infancy, 1,* 3–30.

Thompson-Schill, S. L. (2003). Neuroimaging studies of semantic memory: Inferring "how" from "where." *Neuropsychologia, 41,* 280–292.

Tom, G., Pettersen, P., Lau, T., Burton, T., & Cook, J. (1991). The role of overt head movement in the formation of affect. *Basic and Applied Social Psychology, 12,* 281–289.

Tulving, E. (1972). Episodic and semantic memory. In E. Tulving & W. Donaldson (Eds.), *Organization and memory* (pp. 381–403). New York: Academic Press.

Tulving, E., & Thomson, D. M. (1973). Encoding specificity and retrieval processes in episodic memory. *Psychological Review, 80,* 352–373.

Vallée-Tourangeau, F., Anthony, S. H., & Austin, N. G. (1998). Strategies for generating multiple instances of common and ad hoc categories. *Memory, 6,* 555–592.

Vanman, E. J., & Miller, N. (1993). Applications of emotion theory and research to stereotyping and intergroup relations. In D. M. Mackie & D. L. Hamilton (Eds.), *Affect, cognition, and stereotyping: Interactive processes in group perception* (pp. 213–238). San Diego, CA: Academic Press.

Vanman, E. J., Paul, B. Y., Ito, T. A., & Miller, N. (1997). The modern face of prejudice and structural features that moderate the effect of cooperation on affect. *Journal of Personality and Social Psychology, 73,* 941–959.

Vygotsky, L. S. (1991). Genesis of the higher mental functions. In P. Light, S. Sheldon, & M. Woodhead (Eds.), *Learning to think: Child development in social context* (Vol. 2, pp. 32–41). London: Routledge.

Walker, W. H., & Kintsch, W. (1985). Automatic and strategic aspects of knowledge retrieval. *Cognitive Science, 9,* 261–283.

Wallbott, H. G. (1991). Recognition of emotion from facial expression via imitation? Some indirect evidence for an old theory. *British Journal of Social Psychology, 30,* 207–219.

Wattenmaker, W. D., & Shoben, E. J. (1987). Context and the recallability of concrete and abstract sentences. *Journal of Experimental Psychology: Learning, Memory, & Cognition, 13,* 140–150.

Wells, G. L., & Petty, R. E. (1980). The effects of overt head movements on persuasion: Compatibility and incompatibility of responses. *Basic and Applied Social Psychology, 1,* 219–230.

Wiemer-Hastings, K., Krug, J., & Xu, X. (2001). Imagery, context availability, contextual constraint, and abstractness. In *Proceedings of the 23rd Annual Conference of the Cognitive Science Society* (pp. 1134–1139). Mahwah, NJ: Lawrence Erlbaum.

Weisfeld, G. E., & Beresford, J. M. (1982). Erectness of posture as an indicator of dominance or success in humans. *Motivation and Emotion, 6,* 113–131.

Wu, L., & Barsalou, L. W. (2008). *Perceptual simulation in property generation.* Manuscript submitted for publication.

Yeh, W., & Barsalou, L. W. (2006). The situated character of concepts. *Journal of American Psychology, 119,* 349–384.

Zatorre, R. J., Halpern, A. R., Perry, D. W., Meyer, E., & Evans, A. C. (1996). Hearing in the mind's ear: A PET investigation of musical imagery and perception. *Journal of Cognitive Neuroscience, 8,* 29–46.

Zeki, S. (1993). *A vision of the brain.* Oxford, UK: Blackwell Scientific.

Zwaan, R. A., & Radvansky, G. A. (1998). Situation models in language comprehension and memory. *Psychological Bulletin, 123,* 162–185.

CHAPTER 15

Problem Solving and Situated Cognition

David Kirsh

Introduction

In the course of daily life we solve problems often enough that there is a special term to characterize the activity and the right to expect a scientific theory to explain its dynamics. The classical view in psychology is that to solve a problem a subject must frame it by creating an internal representation of the problem's structure, usually called a problem space. This space is an internally generable representation that is mathematically identical to a graph structure with nodes and links. The nodes can be annotated with useful information, and the whole representation can be distributed over internal and external structures such as symbolic notations on paper or diagrams. If the representation is distributed across internal and external structures the subject must be able to keep track of activity in the distributed structure. Problem solving proceeds as the subject works from an initial state in this mentally supported space, actively constructing possible solution paths, evaluating them and heuristically choosing the best. Control of this

exploratory process is not well understood, as it is not always systematic, but various heuristic search algorithms have been proposed and some experimental support has been provided for them.

Situated cognition, by contrast, does not have a theory of problem solving to compete with the classical view. It offers no computational, neuropsychological, or mathematical account of the internal processes underlying problem cognition. Nor does it explain the nature of the control of external processes related to problem solving. Partly this is a matter of definition. Problems are not regarded to be a distinct category for empirical and computational analysis because what counts as a problem varies from activity to activity. Problems do arise all the time, no matter what we are doing. But from a situated cognition perspective these problems should not be understood as abstractions with a formal structure that may be the same across different activities. Each problem is tied to a concrete setting and is resolved by reasoning in situation-specific ways, making use of the material and cultural resources locally available. What is called a problem, therefore, depends on the discourse of that activity, and so in a sense, is socially constructed. There is no natural kind called "problem" and no natural kind process called "problem solving" for psychologists to study. Problem solving is merely a form of reasoning that, like all reasoning, is deeply bound up with the activities and context in which it takes place. Accordingly, the situational approach highlights those aspects of problem solving that reveal how much the machinery of inference, computation, and representation is embedded in the social, cultural, and material aspects of situations.

This critical approach to problem solving is what I shall present first. In Part 1 I discuss the assumptions behind the classical psychological theory. In Part 2 I present the major objections raised by those believing that cognition must be understood in an embodied, interactive, and situated way, and not primarily as a cognitive process of searching through mental or abstract representations. There is a tendency in the situated cognition literature to be dismissive of the classical view without first acknowledging its flexibility and sophistication. Accordingly, I present the classical account in its best form in an effort to appreciate what parts may be useful in a more situated theory. In Part 3 I collect pieces from both accounts, situated and classical, to move on to sketch a more positive theory – or at least provide desiderata for such a theory – though only fragments of such a view can be presented here.

PART 1: THE CLASSICAL THEORY

1. Newell and Simon's Theory

In an extensive collection of papers and books, Herbert Simon, often with Allen Newell, presented a clear statement of the now-classical approach to problem solving (see, among others, Newell & Simon, 1972). Mindful that science regularly proceeds from idealization, Simon and Newell worked from the assumption that a theory based on how people solve well-defined problems can be stretched or augmented to

explain how people solve problems that are ill defined, which they recognized a large class of problems to be.

To develop their theory they presented subjects with a collection of games and puzzles with unique solutions or solution sets. Having a correct answer – a solution set – is the hallmark of a problem being well defined. Problems were posed in contexts in which the experimenter could be sure subjects had a clear understanding of what they had to solve. Games and puzzles were chosen because they are self-contained; it is assumed that no special knowledge outside of what is provided is needed to solve them. These sorts of problems have a strict definition of allowable actions (you move your pawn like this), the states these actions cause (the board enters this configuration), and a strict definition of when the game or puzzle has been solved, won, or successfully completed (opponent's king is captured). It was assumed that subjects who read the problem would be able to understand these elements and create their internal representation. Such problems are both well defined and knowledge lean, as "everything that the subject needs to know to perform the task is presented in the instructions" (VanLehn, 1989, p. 528). No special training or background knowledge is required.

2. Task Environment

In the classical theory, the terms *problem* and *task* are interchangeable. Newell and Simon introduced the expression *task environment* to designate an abstract structure that corresponds to a problem. It is called an environment because subjects who improve task performance are assumed to be adapting their behavior to some sort of environmental constraints, the fundamental structure of the problem. It is abstract because the same task environment can be instantiated in very different ways. In chess, for example, the task environment is the same whether the pieces are made of wood or silver or are displayed on a computer screen. Any differences arising because agents need to interact differently in different physical contexts are irrelevant. It does not matter whether an agent moves pieces by hand, by mouse movements, by requesting someone else to make the move for them, or by writing down symbols and sending a description of their move by mail. Issues associated with solving these movement or communication subtasks belong to a different problem.

A task environment, accordingly, delineates the core task. It specifies an underlying structure that determines the relevant effects of every relevant action that a given agent can perform. This has the effect that if two agents have different capacities for action they face different task environments. When four-legged creatures confront an obstacle, they face a different locomotion problem than two-legged creatures, and both problems are different from the locomotion problem the obstruction poses to a snake. Thus, two agents operating in the same physical environment, each facing the same objective – get from a to b – may face different task environments because of their different capacities. Their optimal path may be different. Moreover, of all the actions a creature or subject can perform, the only ones that count as task relevant are the ones that can, in principle, bring it closer to or farther from an environmental state meeting the goal condition. It is assumed that differences in expertise and intellectual ability affect search and reasoning rather than the definition of the task itself.

Task environments are theoretical projections that let researchers interpret problem-solving activity in concrete situations. They identify what counts as a move in a problem (for a given agent). As such, they impose a powerful filter over the way a researcher interprets subjects' actions. Scratching one's head during chess, for instance, is an action that would be interpreted by a researcher as irrelevant to the game. It not only would lie outside the task environment of chess construed as the set of possible chess moves but also would be treated as having no relevance to the game in any other way – an epiphe-nomenon. The same would apply to other things nonexperts do when they play, such as putting a finger on a piece, trying out possible actions on the board, using pencil and paper, talking to oneself, or consulting a book (if allowed at all). All are assumed irrelevant to task performance. They may occur while a subject is working on a problem, or while playing chess, but, according to the classical account, they are not literally part of problem-solving activity. This is obviously a point of dispute for situationalists, as many of these actions are regularly observed during play, and they may critically affect the success of an agent.

3. Problem Space

Task environments are differentiated from problem spaces, the representation subjects are assumed to mentally construct when they understand a task correctly. This problem-space representation might be distributed over external resources. It encodes the following:

- The current state of the problem. At the beginning this is the initial state.
- A representation of the goal state or condition – though this might be a procedure or test for recognizing when the goal has been reached, rather than a declarative statement of the goal.
- Constraints determining allowable moves and states, hence the nodes and allowable links of the space – these too may be specified implicitly in procedures for generating all and only legal moves rather than explicitly in declarative statements.
- Optionally, other representations that may prove useful in understanding problem states or calculating the effects of action.

Some of these other representations encode knowledge of problem-solving methods, heuristics, or metrics specific to the current task environment. Others encode

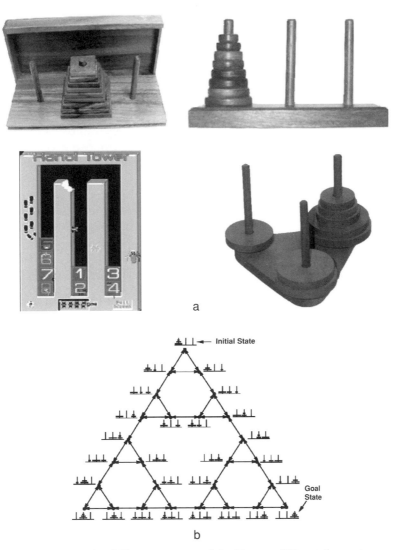

Figure 15.1. The different versions of the Tower of Hanoi shown in 15.1a share the same abstract task environment, shown in the graph structure displayed in 15.1b. All the versions have the same legal moves in an abstract sense, the goal of the game is the same, and the strategies for completion are the same. At a more microscopic level, moving heavy pieces in one game may require additional planning, but these extra moves and extra plans are not thought to be part of the game. Because the game is defined abstractly, any differences in the action repertoire of an agent are irrelevant. In other tasks we base our analysis of the task on the actions the agent can perform, so that more powerful agents may face different tasks than less powerful ones. Choice of level of abstraction is a theoretical decision.

methods, heuristics, and metrics that are domain independent, such as general methods of search, measures of when one is getting closer to a goal, and typical ways of overcoming impasses that arise in the solution-finding process.

4. Ill-Defined Problems

Puzzle and game cognition seems to fit this formal, knowledge-lean approach – at least in part. But Simon recognized that most of the problems we encounter in life are not well defined in this formal sense. Some have no unambiguously right answer, the result of applying an operational goal condition to possible solutions. This may be because there are many grades and forms of adequate answer, as is typical of problems arising in architecture, engineering, cooking, writing, and other creative or design-related work. Or it may be because the notion of what constitutes an adequate answer is not known in advance, and part of what a problem solver must learn in the course of working on a problem is what counts as a better answer. Still other problems have no fixed set of operators relevant to a problem space – no fixed set of choice points, fixed consequence function, fixed evaluation function, or well-defined constraints on feasible actions. Think of the problem a painter faces when confronting a blank canvas in a studio with all the paints, media, brushes, and tools he or she might ever want. Goals, operators, choice points, consequence, and evaluation functions are either undetermined by the very nature of the problem, or they have to be learned microgenetically, in the course of activity. The problem is largely being made up as it is being worked on (cf. Reitman, 1964).

Simon regarded the prevalence of ill-defined problems as a challenge to the classical theory but not an insurmountable one. Cognitive theories should start first with the clear, central cases of problems – which for Simon are well defined and knowledge lean – and then move outward to harder cases.

PART 2: CRITICISM OF THE CLASSICAL THEORY

1. Initial Summary of Objections

The ideas of task environment and problem space have a formal elegance that is seductive. They encourage treating problem solving as an area of psychology that can be studied using existing methods of mathematics and experimentation. But they can also justifiably be attacked from many sides, and not just because efforts to extend the theory to ill-defined problems have been mostly unsuccessful. Four objections that are congenial to a situated approach to cognition deserve close examination.

1.1. *Framing and Registration*

Framing and registration processes are integral to the problem-solving process and arguably the hardest part of it. The formal theory treats the heart of problem solving to be search. Indeed, this is the only part explained by the classical theory. But search in a problem space only makes sense after the hard work of framing has been done – after a problem has been well posed and put into a searchable graph structure. It is one thing to do this for games where the operations and objectives are typically told to us explicitly. It is another to do this for everyday problems, where we have to decide what is relevant and what is irrelevant. In artificial intelligence, a closely related problem of bounding the scope of what needs to be considered in planning, reasoning, and solving problems is called the "frame problem," and it remains an open question how people do this.

Moreover, what is the justification for treating the abstraction or framing part of problem solving to be separate and unconnected from the problem-solving part, which is assumed to be search? It may seem intuitive to see problem solving as having parts: recognize a problem in a concrete situation; abstract, frame, or bound the problem; find a solution; and reinterpret the solution in the concrete setting. It may seem intuitive that we can modularize these parts and study each component. But whether justified or not – and there are good reasons to challenge the modularization of steps – why accept that the locus of difficulty, the real challenge of problem solving, concerns the search part? Framing is notoriously hard, and so is registration.

To understand the registration problem, imagine yourself in a shopping mall, standing in front of a wall map, trying to find a path from your current location to a specific store. Which is harder: figuring out where you are relative to the map, assuming the map does not have an icon with a "You are here" label, or finding a path from *a* to *b* on the map? For most of us finding the path is the easy part. That is the part that is analogous to search in a problem space. It is far harder to figure out where you are and then translate the path you found back into action in the world. Those are the registration parts: connecting the abstract search space (whether internal or external) to the real world, and then reinterpreting the results of search, or some other action performed on an abstract representation, back into domain-specific terms.

Given the interactive nature of problem solving, the back-and-forth process of acting, observing the result, and then thinking of the next move, agents almost never do all their work in a problem space and then act in the world. They constantly translate moves in their abstract problem space into actions in their concrete context and back again. How subjects frame and interpret a problem therefore is essential to how they will proceed and how easy it is to translate between problem space and world. The more abstract a problem space, the more distant it is from the specifics of the current situation, and the harder this translation process is. Think of the distance between a recipe in a cookbook and its concrete execution by a cook in the kitchen. The recipe represents a solution to the problem of creating a certain dish given certain ingredients. But when cooks execute a recipe they go back and forth between the paper representation and their kitchen. Why can't they just remember the steps

and proceed without consulting and reconsulting the recipe? Plan and execution are connected in nonsimple ways. The interim effects of following a recipe alert a cook to details of the steps that need close attention. This interactive process of going back and forth, between world and representation (recipe), shows that there are two sides to the registration problem: encoding and decoding.

Registration and framing are related because in registering a problem one also has to find a way of tying concrete elements of a situation with a problem representation. Framing adds a further element: a bias on the knowledge that is relevant. When people think about something they see as problematic, they typically frame their difficulty in terms of their immediate understanding of their situation, an understanding that comes with preconceptions of what is relevant and potentially useful. This is often constraining. Problems of cooking, for instance, are framed in terms of ingredients, flame size, and pots and pans, rather than in terms of concepts in chemistry (e.g., reaction potential, catalyst) we may have learned in school and that are, in principle, relevant to understanding the cooking process. Expert chemists may bring such domain-external views to the cooking process. And expert mathematicians or expert modelers may bring the capacity to neatly formalize the concrete. But for the rest of us it is hard to get beyond the concrete to the abstract and general. If we could appreciate the abstract in the concrete, we would recognize analogies and be able to transfer learning from one domain to another more readily than we do. The reason we do not is because our understanding of problems is usually tied to the resources and tools at hand. We are hampered by the mindset appropriate to the setting in which our activity takes place.

Given the way problems arise in natural contexts, the burden of explanation ought to lie in psychology to show both that (a) people do have an abstract problem space representation of problems they solve, and (b) the hard part of problem solving is not to be found in the process of going back and forth between situational understanding and problem space understanding, but in search. This is the challenge which greater attention to the processes of framing and registration pose to the classical view. To my mind it has never been answered.

1.2. *Interactivity and Epistemic Activity*

Examination of actual problem solving in ecologically natural contexts as opposed to white-room environments reveals a host of interactions with resources and cultural elements that figure in the many phases of problem solving, such as understanding the problem, exploring its scope and constraints, getting a sense of options, and developing a metric for evaluating progress toward a solution. People generate a range of intermediate structures. In reducing problem solving to search in a problem space, the classical approach minimizes and misunderstands the complexity and centrality of local interaction.

There is much more going on during problem solving than searching in an abstracted problem space. Most of these actions-interactions lie outside the narrow definition of the problem. Although this echoes the first objection in stressing that problem solving is not reducible to search, it pushes that argument further by focusing on the nature of agent-environment interaction during problem solving. People do many more task-relevant things when problem solving than those allowed for in the strict definition of their task or problem. The notion of a task environment is far too narrow. These task-exogenous actions affect both the process and success of problem solving. Addressing this issue requires ethnographic attention to the real-world details of problem solving.

1.3. *Resources and Scaffolds*

Once focus shifts from puzzles to real problems arising in everyday environments, it is apparent that subjects have access to cultural products – tools, measuring devices,

graph paper, calculators, algorithms, tricks of the trade, free advice – that make their reasoning job easier. Even when no problem aids are lying around, the type of problem encountered is not a worst-case problem but a simpler version of a problem that only in its general form is hard to solve. It is well known that problems that are computationally complex when conceived in their general form invariably have many special forms that are quite easy to solve. Usually these are the ones people actually confront, and posing a problem in its more general form, as so often is done in the classical approach, makes the problem harder, encouraging cognitive scientists to propose solution methods that people do not have to follow.

It is not an accident that we encounter special cases. We live most of our life in constructed environments. Layers of artifacts saturate almost every place we go, and there are preexisting practices for doing things. These artifacts and practices have been designed, or have coevolved, to make us smarter, to make it easier for us to solve our problems and perform our habitual tasks. Everywhere there are scaffolds and other resources to simplify problem solving, including people to ask. Part of what we learn is how to use these resources and participate in the relevant practices. Approaching a problem as if it must be posed in its general form ignores the efficiencies and kludges that typify natural beings living in worlds scaffolded and designed for them. It supposes that our main problem-solving skills are tied to search, when in fact they may be more closely related to our ability to manage our artifacts, make effective use of scaffolds, and conform to practice. To focus on the 3 percent of problems only some of us solve risks misunderstanding the remaining 97 percent of problems we all solve.

1.4. *Knowledge Rich*

Most problems people face in daily life are not like knowledge-lean problems in which all relevant aspects of each problem can be given in a compact problem statement.

Naturally occurring problems rarely occur in a vacuum, where all an agent needs to know can be encapsulated in a few simple sentences. We typically bring more knowledge and expertise than formal accounts of problem solving discuss. Consider cooking, cleaning, shopping, gardening, the tasks confronted in offices that involve computer applications, or editing documents. In each case an intelligent novice performs less well than experienced participants. It might be that experience can be reduced to familiarity with search heuristics, domain metrics, and the like. But much surely has to do with knowing how to pose, view, dissolve, and work around problems, and knowing what is most effective in specific situations and how to coordinate the use of local resources – a deep knowledge of cases. Theories of knowledge-rich problem solving have become important in the literature since the 1980s. But even these studies place too little emphasis on the centrality of resources, scaffolds, interactivity, and cultural support. Almost none explain the process by which people understand problems.

In the next sections I will develop each argument further, calling attention to supporting articles in both the situated and classical literature where many of these concerns have been recognized but left unanswered.

2. Framing and Registration

2.1. *Framing*

The heart of the framing and encoding argument is that natural problems arise in concrete settings where agents are already operating in activity-specific provinces of meaning. It matters whether an agent is playing chess by mail or playing chess with a young child using Disney characters. The context affects the way the game is conceptualized and framed (e.g., chess for competition, chess for teaching beginners). This framing colors choice, evaluation, and local objectives, all factors involved in creating a problem space. In tasks that are less abstract than chess the setting and local resources

matter even more. They activate an interpretive framework that primes agents to look for and conceptualize features of their environment in activity-specific ways, biasing what they see as problematic and what they see as the natural or at-hand resources available to solve such problems. Problems, goals, operators, and representations are not abstract. They arise in concrete settings where agents have certain activities they have to perform. Features of these activity spaces affect the way the problem is represented and framed.

Lave (1988) and others (Rogoff & Lave, 1984) have explored the effects of context on problem conceptualization. In commenting on her well-known ethnography of mathematical activity in supermarkets, Lave wrote: "I have tried . . . to understand how mathematical activity in grocery stores involved being 'in' the 'store,' walking up and down 'aisles,' looking at 'shelves' full of cans, bottles, packages and jars of food, and other commodities" (Lave, 1996, p. 4). Each of these domain-specific terms has an impact on the way problems are conceptualized and posed.

To show that mathematical activity is not the same across settings, Lave looked at the techniques and methods shoppers in supermarkets use to solve some of their typical problems of choice, such as whether can A is a better buy than can B. She found that even though unit prices are printed on supermarket labels, shoppers rarely check them to decide what to buy. Instead they use less general strategies such as, "Product A would cost $10 for 10 oz., and product B is $9 for 10 oz., hence product B is the cheaper buy." Or faced with a choice between a 5 oz. packet costing $3.29 and a 6 oz. packet priced at $3.59, the shopper would argue, "If I take the larger packet, it will cost me 30 cents for an extra ounce. Is it worth it?"

Why do shoppers ignore unit price? It is clear that they are not indifferent to unit price because they usually use strategies that involve price comparison between specific items. But as retailers well know, the actual problem a shopper solves has many more variables. When people make a decision about what to take home they also consider where they will store the items, how long each item will last, how quickly it will be used, and the family's attitude to brand. Cans are hefted, labels are examined, and the factors that influence shoppers have been made sufficiently prominent by producers and retailers that shoppers can be certain to notice them. The effect is that reducing the problem of choice to comparing unit price strips the actual shopping problem of its complexity. Moreover, by placing competing brands side by side and placing related products nearby (spaghetti sauce near pasta), supermarkets provide a structure or organization for cognitive activity that biases they way shoppers think. Layout affects the way option sets are conceptualized (e.g., "I came in to buy spaghetti and decided to get linguini because I liked the look of the new Alfredo sauce"). This dynamic between product display and consumer framing of choice has coevolved.

In an earlier study, Carraher, Carraher, and Schliemann (1985) presented a related view. They found that Brazilian children selling goods in street markets invented special purpose procedures to add up prices and calculate change rather than use the more general pencil-and-paper methods they learned in school. They framed their problem in a domain-specific manner because the specialized cognitive artifacts they used to help them calculate were the ones built up in local practice and readily available in the situation.

For example, a girl who made money for the family as a street vendor, when asked the price of 10 coconuts selling at 35 cruzeiros per piece, did not use the add-o method for multiplying by 10, as she had been taught in school. She used the cost of three coconuts (105), which was a convenient group she regularly sold coconuts in, added to this the cost of two more of these threesomes (210), then added the cost of a single coconut (35) to the running total. She correctly reported the price of 10 coconuts as 350 cruzeiros. Street market children did less well at these

same problems in school, where they used the school-taught procedures. The authors noted that in the street, both children and older vendors used convenient groups for their additions, such as "three for 105," and that simple multiples of these groups, two or three of these three-for's were also very highly practiced so that, in effect, the vendors were substituting memory for summation or multiplication whenever they could. Predictably, school-taught procedures interfered with this type of situation-specific problem solving, and predictably, the street vendor kids performed better on the street than nonvendors with comparable education. Context and experience framed how the kids approached their problems and the resources and tools they deemed appropriate. Their activity in street environments was different than in classroom environments. Arguably, the cognitive resources in the street coevolved with the demands of street calculation.

In another study, this time by Scribner (1984), there is an account of how milkmen filled orders for different kinds of milk – white milk, chocolate milk, half-pints, quarts – by packing their delivery cases to make delivery more efficient and physically less effortful. This again is a numerical problem that was solved using contextualized knowledge.

Scribner noted that old-time milkmen used their delivery case itself as a thing to think with, and they filled orders faster and more accurately than students who filled orders using arithmetic calculations. The milkmen learned the numerical relations of various configurations of milk containers (one layer of half-pints is 16, two rows of quarts are 8, hence half as many as pints, and so forth) and used the compositional structure of layers and half layers, and so on, to fill cases with multiples of items without counting out each item. If they needed 35 half-pints to fill an order, they would know to fill two layers and then add three more on top. Deliverymen solved billing problems using a similar process of taking overlearned quantities or patterns, pulling them apart, and putting them back together. For instance, to figure out the cost of 98 half-pints a natural strategy was to take two times the case price (a case holds 48 half-pints and its price was memorized) and add the price of two half-pints. The patterns of milk cartons in the case are the elements of calculation. They became things to think with, patterns to decompose and recompose, to mentally manipulate. Again context and experience framed the way they saw their problems. The methods they developed were not universal, based on general algorithms for solving arithmetic problems; they were specialized and situation specific. And their deep familiarity with different situations showed in performance.

Cognitive scientists interested in learning theory have called the mathematical knowledge displayed here "intuitive" or "naive," to distinguish it from the formal knowledge taught in school (Hamberger, 1979). Intuitive knowledge is thought to be bound to the context in which the knower solves personally relevant problems.

The issue of who is right – the situationalist who looks at local resources as things to think with, or the formalist who frames the task more abstractly as a general type of problem, in these cases math problems that must be interpreted or applied to local conditions – lies at the heart of the situated challenge. Which problem are people trying to solve? If a subject thinks about a problem in concrete terms such as cans and shelves, and so has an internal conception and an external discourse that makes it seem as if the problem were about attributes of cans (e.g., their appearance, shape, volume, price, brand), why suppose he is deluded and is really talking about a basic number problem that happens to be couched in terms of cans? From his point of view, his problem is a naturally occurring one, quite unlike the contrived sentence problems presented in math class ("a bachelor comes to a supermarket with $15 looking for the best way to spend his money on pasta and beer. Spaghetti costs $1.75, fusilli cost $2.50, beer costs . . . "). From the formalist point of view, however, it is irrelevant that the numbers of interest refer to attributes of cans or bottles. Idiosyncrasies of the problem instance, such as what is near to what, or how information about price, volume, and so on, is displayed, do not matter. All that matters is the topological structure of the problem space, or the mathematical structure of the problem. And that may be the same whatever the labels are for nodes and links: can size, number of bottles, distances, or simply numbers.

Two findings discussed at length in the problem-solving literature – problem isomorphism and mental set – bear on this question of framing and abstraction. Both support the view that subjects are sensitive to surface attributes of a problem, so much so that two problems that are formally the same, or formally very similar, may be solved in such different ways and with such different speed-accuracy profiles that a process theory should treat them as different. Little is gained by seeing them as only different problem-space representations of the same task environment.

Take problem isomorphism first. Tic-tac-toe and the game of fifteen are superficially different versions of the same problem (see Figure 15.2). Legal moves and solutions in tic-tac-toe and legal moves and solutions in the game of fifteen can be put in one-to-one correspondence. From a formal point of view the problems, therefore, are isomorphic. They have the same mathematical structure. Yet subjects conceptualize them differently and their performance is different, as measured by their speed-accuracy profiles and the pattern of errors they generate. Predictably, subjects rarely transfer their expert methods for tic-tac-toe to the game of fifteen; they relearn them. Evidently, then, algorithms are sensitive to surface structure even if their success conditions are not.

What can be inferred? The obvious conclusion is that details of the problem context – the way it is presented and conceptualized, the richness of cues in the local environment – determine what subjects count as a solution and the resources they see as available to solve it. In the game of fifteen, if paper and pen are handy, for

Figure 15.2. The task environment of the game of fifteen and tic-tac-toe is isomorphic because there is a one-to-one correspondence between the legal permissible moves in tic-tac-toe and the game of fifteen. In the game of fifteen, players take turns choosing from a set of numbered tiles. The first player to collect three tiles that sum to fifteen wins. Because it is easy to see opportunities for three in a row visually, but harder to see opportunities for summing to fifteen, subjects can play tic-tac-toe faster and with fewer errors than in fifteen. Their skills in tic-tac-toe do not transfer and they have to relearn the tricks.

instance, subjects will often mark down sums and consequences of moves. How shall we view these paper actions? On the one hand, because actions on paper cannot improve the pragmatic position of a subject, paper and the actions it affords do not seem to be part of the problem context. On the other hand, for those who rely on paper to work out their next move, it is an important part of their problem-solving activity and makes a difference to their outcomes. In tic-tac-toe, scratch paper only gets in the way. Our visual system makes spotting consequences of moves easy. So in the game of fifteen versus tic-tac-toe, the resources, actions, and calculations relevant to a solution are, for many subjects, quite different. The formal state space of the two versions of the game is the same, but that space seems to abstract away from too many psychologically and activity-relevant details to explain the cognitive processes involved in problem solving. In fact, given such differences in problem-solving activity, why suppose the two even share an isomorphic task environment? The level of abstraction needed to view them in the same way seems too high. Because the purpose of a task-environment and problem-space approach is to provide us with constructs sufficient to explain psychological and behavioral activity, we need to find the right level of abstraction to capture generalizations. In these two cases, there seems too much difference in behavioral performance. Moreover, if our goal is a pro-

cess model of problem-solving cognition, we ought to attend to the way subjects distribute relevant states over environmental artifacts (scrap paper as well as the spatial layout of cards or the way the tic-tac-toe board is filled in), and how they work out game moves by performing epistemic actions (Kirsh & Maglio, 1995).

Our concern here is with the possibility of finding the right level of abstraction to characterize the psychological processes involved in solving problems, even well-defined ones, such as the game of fifteen. In the gestalt theory of problem solving, it is assumed that people see a problem as a meaningful question only against a background of assumptions. To a given subject something is foregrounded as problematic only against this backdrop of the unproblematic (Luchins, 1942). The possible lines of solution that subjects will consider, accordingly, are constrained by their mental set, which limits the information they attend to and the conjectures and resources they think are relevant. Sometimes the mental set a person brings to a task or situation is appropriate and helps in finding a solution. Sometimes it does not.

An example of ways of framing and mental set can prevent problem solving is found in insight problems, where to solve the problem subjects must break out of conventional thinking and try something nonstandard, a trick. Usually this trick involves breaking preconceptions about what is allowable

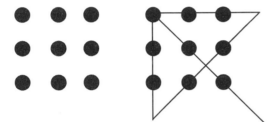

Figure 15.3. The nine-dot problem and its solution. The task is to connect all dots using four straight lines without lifting one's pen. Subjects frame the problem narrowly by assuming that lines must begin or end on dots and cannot extend beyond them. They incorrectly assume that all turning occurs on dots.

or what is the function of an available resource.

For instance, in the nine-dot problem, Maier (1930) told subjects to find a way to connect all the dots in a three-by-three matrix by using four straight lines, without lifting their pens or retracing any lines (see Figure 15.3). The problem is hard precisely because participants do not consider making non-dot turns (Kershaw, 2004). They rarely consider constructing lines that extend beyond the dots, and when they do they seldom consider making a turn in empty space, either between the dots or somewhere outside the matrix. The problem statement does not exclude these possible actions. But subjects frame the problem as if they consider these impermissible. Framing has prevented the subject from creating the right problem space, perhaps even from grasping the right task environment.

In separate work on mental set, in what is commonly regarded as the classical demonstration of set, Luchins (1942) presented subjects with water-jug problems in which they had to figure out how to get a certain amount of water (e.g., five cups), using any combination of three jugs: jug A holds eighteen cups, jug B holds forty-three cups, and jug C holds ten cups. They were free to dip their jugs into a well as many times as they like.

Luchins found that after subjects get the hang of the solution method and have more or less automatized it, they try to use that method on new problems and persevere in using it, even when there is a much better way to solve the new problems. This was seen as strong evidence for mental set because when other subjects were shown these alternative problems before the initial problem, they would soon learn the easy solution methods, suggesting that learning on one problem can interfere with learning and performance on another. Further support for the presence of mental set was found by Sternberg and Davidson (1983) and Gick and Holyoak (1980, 1983), who confirmed in new experiments that prior solution methods – prior set – worked against finding solutions to different problems, problems that subjects without that bias would be expected to solve.

The relevance of mental set for the situated approach is that how agents frame problems, what they see as possible actions, and good methods for success, depend on how they interpret their situation and their mindset in approaching a problem. To an experienced shopper, supermarket problems are their own sort of problem, quite unlike the general arithmetic problems learned in school. To the strongly mathematically inclined, however, supermarket problems are more likely seen as a special case of general arithmetic problems. Mathematicians see through the particulars of the shopping situation, grasping the more abstract mathematical problem. Their mental set is very different. And they worked hard to achieve that competence. To less mathematical reasoners, however, the supporting resources and scaffolds are so different and the tricks and visible cues are so different that, initially, at any rate, their whole mindset is different. The problem is different.

Even if one recognizes the abstract problem posed, the resources available still can strongly affect the method used to solve it. For instance, in math class at school students have pencil and paper. They write numbers down and rely on algorithms defined over the inscriptions they create. To multiply two numbers they line them up and use one of the multiplication algorithms. The same holds for division and determining ratios. Without pencil and paper, however, techniques and methods usually change. Even mathematicians might prefer to think with local artifacts if faced with a problem that is cumbersome to solve in their head.

The upshot is that though a task analysis may be important to determine the success conditions of different approaches, and indeed necessary to explain why they work, such analyses seem remote from a process theory. A psychological theory ought to explain the many phases and dynamics of the problem-solving process: how one sees a problem; why one sees it that way; and how one exploits resources, interacts with resources, and solves the problem in acceptable time. The bottom line, for the moment, is that how agents frame a problem, how they project meaning into a situation, determines the resources they see as relevant to its solution. If street vendors frame the "How much for ten of these?" problems in terms of today's price for three and today's price for one, then they prime a set of tools of thought distinct from those they learned in school. They do not look at the problem deeply. As work on transfer has shown, they stay on the surface, interpreting the problem in superficial ways.

2.2. Registration

As important as it is to extend the theory of problem solving to explain how problems are framed, this way of structuring problem solving still seems to locate the real part – the solving part – to take place after a task has been represented as a problem space; that heuristic search, in one form or another, is the driving force in problem solving, and that expertise is substantially about acquiring the right heuristics, metrics, and generalizations of cases as if framing is just a way of preparing for problem solving, not of solving it.

Two reasons to question this clean account are that first, creating a problem space may be a highly interactive process of framing, representing, exploring, reframing, and rerepresenting, so that reformulation is a key part of problem solving, and that framing, therefore, does not occur once and problem solving begins afterward; the two are often intertwined. Second, even when a subject is searching a problem space the search process is complicated by the need to continually anchor the search space in locally meaningful ways. Search itself is an interactive process that should not be reduced to internal symbol manipulation.

To appreciate these points, it is illuminating to contrast the concepts of registration and translation. In mapping a game of fifteen back into tic-tac-toe, we perform a translation. We similarly perform a translation when we map a word problem (Mary is two inches taller than Peter who is...) into a simple algebraic statement, or puzzles and games (nine dots, chess) into searchable graphs, or a problem in Euclidean geometry into a problem in analytic geometry using Cartesian coordinates. The value of the mapping is that the new representation offers another perspective with different methods and techniques, often simplifying problem solving. But the mapping process links two representations, or representational systems, and that is the key thing. Well-defined entities or relations in one representational system are mapped onto well-defined entities or relations in the other.

By contrast, when we orient and reorient a city or mall map to determine how the representations of buildings, pathways, and openings correspond with the buildings, pathways, and openings in the actual space, we are registering the map, not translating it, because we are trying to match up discrete representational elements in the two-dimensional map with nonrepresentational and often nondiscrete elements in the three-dimensional world, the arena where we perform physical actions. This means that much of problem-solving acumen, when registration is involved, may lie in knowing how to link representations (whether internal, external, or distributed over the two), with entities, attributes, and relations in the physical domain.

Examples of registration-heavy problems often arise when something goes wrong during practiced activity, when the normal method we use to get something done fails, and we are thrown into problem-solving mode to figure out how to recover. Cooking, cleaning, driving, shopping, assembly, and construction are all everyday domains where problems typically arise when there is a breakdown in normal activity. Much of what makes such problem solving hard is that the agent is not yet sure what to attend to: what events, structures, or processes to see as relevant. Every person has many frames for thinking about things, but which are the ones that fit the current situation?

Here is a trivial example, computer cases. Computer companies regularly devise new ways to open and close their cases and it can be surprisingly difficult to determine how to get inside a computer without first checking the manual. Problem solving consists of pushing or pulling on pieces, scrutinizing the case for telltale cues, for clear affordances or explicit indicators. It might be said that this activity is a form of external search. But more likely it is a form of registration: of trying to discover a pattern of cues that can be fit to a method we already know or to a mechanical frame that will make sense of the release mechanism. This is a form of registering because much of the reasoning involved in determining how to open the case is tied to exploring the affordances of the object and looking for ways to conceptualize or reconceptualize its different parts. In fact, in many everyday problems, the registration phase is more complex than the search phase.

In some instances, the phases of registration and search are virtually impossible to separate. We can rationally reconstruct problem solving so that there are distinct phases, but in fact the actual process is more interactive. This is especially true of wayfinding with a map. We can, if we like, describe map use sequentially: first, orient the map with immediate landmarks to establish a correspondence; second, determine current position; third, plot a route;

then, fourth, follow it. But discovering and following a route is typically interactive: look at the map, look at the surroundings, locate oneself, interpret map actions in physical terms, and repeatedly do this until the goal is in sight.

Navigational capacities depend on continually linking symbolic elements in the map to physical referents in the space. These referents serve as anchors tying the map down to the world so that a trajectory in the map can be interpreted in terms of visible structures in space. Thus, in a shopping mall we look for signs and arrows pointing to the food court or stores of interest to help us figure out where we are. We interactively make our way, often by working off the physical setting rather than the map. But when plotting a course we use all these cues to help us orient and make sense of the path we devised using the map. Subjects go back and forth between map and world. The reason this constant anchoring has not been a major issue is that in games such as chess, Tower of Hanoi, and tic-tac-toe, in math problems, and other verbally stated problems, interaction is focused on a spatially constrained representation, the chess board, the tower, the formulation of the problem. This sustains the illusion that problem solving is primarily a matter of controlling operators in an abstract representation.

The upshot is that in many naturally arising problems the locus of difficulty may lie as much in the registration process, the activity of selecting environmental anchors to tie mental or physical representations to the world, as it does in searching for paths in the representation itself.

3. Interactivity and Epistemic Actions

3.1. *People Solve Problems Interactively*

In most problem-solving situations people do not sit quietly until they have an answer and then announce it all at once. They do things along the way. If it is a word problem (John is half as tall as Mary . . .), they mutter, they write things down, and they check the question several times. If they are solving an assembly task (here are the parts of a bicycle, assemble it), they will typically feel the pieces, try out trial assemblies, and incrementally work toward a solution. Rarely does anyone work out a complete solution in their head and then single-mindedly execute it. People, like most other creatures, solve things interactively in the world.

The classical approach to problem solving failed to adequately accommodate this in-the-world and not just in-the-head inter-activity in two ways. First, the classical theory, in its strictest form, assumed that users completely search an internal representation of their problem before acting. Heuristics were proposed as a mechanism for reducing the complexity of this internal search so that solutions could actually be found. They were not meant to help a user figure out the next single action to perform; they were meant to help a user figure out a whole plan, an entire sequence of actions. This "Make a plan before you act" hypothesis was derived from Miller, Galanter, and Pribram (1960), and not surprisingly was repeatedly challenged in the planning literature, both in AI and in psychology.

The second way interactivity was mis-understood was that it was never seen as a force for reshaping either the search process or the problem space. Artificial intelligence theorists were quick to appreciate the value of incorporating sensing and perception into planning. But most AI planners incorrectly assumed that any actions that users perform in the world during problem solving are either

- External analogues of internal search – instances of searching in the world instead of in the head, or
- Stepwise execution of an incomplete plan – starting to implement a partial solution (or plan) before having the complete one in mind – then replanning in light of the resultant world state.

External interactivity was never (or rarely) seen as a mechanism for reducing the complexity of a problem, or as a mechanism for exploring the structure of a problem, or as a way of engaging other sorts of behaviors that might help subjects solve their problems. External activity was still related to search, one way or another. A theory of situated problem solving should give the principles of more interactive approaches.

3.2. *The Role of External Representations*

Although Simon and other exponents of the classical theory never accepted the centrality of interactivity, they took an important step forward when they began paying more attention to the role external representations play. Larken and Simon (1987) enlarged the orthodox account to allow problem states to be partially encoded internally and partially encoded externally. Accordingly, to solve a geometric or algebraic problem, subjects might rely on applying operators to external symbols, equations, illustrations of geometric figures, and so forth. Instead of representing the transformations of the equation $2x + 4y = 40$ in one's head, as in mental representations for $2(x + 2y) = 40$ followed by $x + 2y = 20$, Larken and Simon showed that it might be easier to generate such representational states in the world and track where one is both mentally and physically to decide what to do next.

The special value of external representations is obvious in visual problems, such as tic-tac-toe. Vision is a computational problem that terrestrial animals devote huge neural resources to solve. In tic-tac-toe, the computational cost of evaluating the consequences of a move can be borne by the visual system, which exploits parallel and highly efficient methods to project the outcomes of placements. This makes it easy to see that one or another move is pointless. For instance, in Figure 15.4a, given a visual display of the board, it is obvious where O must move to prevent immediate defeat. Choice can be made without serious consideration of other moves. Solving the same problem algebraically, as in the game of fifteen, or solving the same problem in one's head, especially more complex versions (see

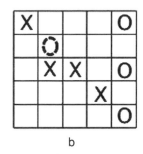

a   b

Figure 15.4. In harder versions of tic-tac-toe it is nearly impossible to determine the best moves without a visual representation of the board. Although the board state of 15.4a can be generated internally, and players can easily play without looking at the board, the cost of sustaining such states in mind increases with the complexity of the mental image or representation. In 15.4b, the five-by-five board is much less easy to keep in mind. To win it is necessary to get four in a row anywhere. As the structure of the problem increases and the complexity of the current state rises, vision pays off. The interactive nature of vision scales better with board complexity.

Figure 15.4b) is significantly harder. It is both cognitively easier and computationally simpler to use the external representation than an internal representation.

In treating problem solving as a process that may be partly in the mind and partly in the world, the classical view took a big step toward a more situated perspective. But the assumed value of external representations lay in the increased efficiency of applying visual operators and the stimulating role external representations can play in search. Using external representations was not seen as forcing a revision of the way problem solving unfolds. In particular, a concern with external representations did not lead to a discussion of other ways external resources figure in problem solving. Let us consider the role of external representations more closely.

Expanding the search space. In an elegant demonstration, Chambers and Riesberg (1985) showed that how people visually explore an external representation is often different from how they explore a mental image of the same thing (see Figure 15.5).

If you look at a Necker cube for half a minute or more your interpretation will almost certainly toggle, and the surfaces you see as front and back will swap places. That is, if you first see A as the front face and B as the back, then after a short while you will see B as the front and A as the back. This swapping of faces, this reinterpretation of the figure, does not occur in mental images. A mental image is an intentional object and as such must be sustained under an interpretation. If a mental image were conceptualized as an organized set of lines not yet interpreted as a cube, then new mental images might arise from thinking about the image. But if it is maintained as a unified object – a gestalt – it will not toggle unless deconstructed into constituent lines. People rarely deconstruct their mental images.

What if the same cognitive limitations apply to internal problem spaces? What if visual operators can explore parts of a search space more broadly than internal operators acting on mental representations of the same structure? This would suggest that certain problems might be solved only when they

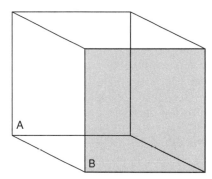

Figure 15.5. The Necker cube and other visually ambiguous structures have more than one interpretation, which subjects discover after a short while. When the cube is visually before them, they scan the edges, propagating constraints. But when the same image is imagined, the ambiguity of the figure goes undetected. It is grasped as a whole, without the need of "mental saccades" to test its integrity and sustain it.

are represented externally in figures or symbols. This would be a curious form of cognitive set.

In some of his work, Simon came close to making this point. In several coauthored articles he considered the role that auxiliary representations play in helping subjects solve algebraic word problems. He found that students used diagrams to detect additional assumptions about the problem situation that were not obvious from the initial algebraic encoding of word problems (Simon, 1979). Although such additional assumptions could in principle be discovered from the algebraic encoding alone, subjects found the cost of elaboration too great. Discovering such assumptions without diagrams requires far too much inference.

Given the interest in problem isomorphs at the time, proponents of the (revised) classical view did not regard the value of external representations as grounds for shifting the focus of problem-solving research away from heuristic search in problem spaces, to replace it with a study of how subjects interactively engage external resources. It was instead seen as further evidence that how subjects interpret problems affects their problem-solving behavior. It nicely fit the problem isomorph literature showing that surface representation strongly determines problem-solving trajectory.

In some respects it is surprising that the classical theory did not embrace interactivity at this point. The idea that it is useful, and at times necessary, to transform problems into different representational notations or representational systems is a truism in problem solving in math, and in science more generally. Every representational system makes it easy to represent certain facts or ideas and harder to represent others. What is explicit in one representation may be implicit in another (Kirsh, 1991, 2003). For example, in decimal notation it is trivial to determine that 100 is divisible by 10. But when 100 is represented in binary notation as 110010 it is no longer trivial. This holds whether we translate 10 into its binary equivalent, 101, or keep it in decimal notation. The

decimal notation is better than binary for certain operations, such as dividing by 10; the binary is simpler for other operations, such as dividing by 64. The proponents of the classical view certainly knew this and often discussed the importance of problem representation, but they never took the next step.

Their appreciation of the importance of diagrams, illustrations, and word formulations for problem-solving performance never led to a major departure from the problem-space, task-environment idea. Externalization was not seen as establishing a need to shift focus from problem spaces to affordances or to the cues and constraints of external structures. It never led to a revised concern for observing what people actually do, in an ethnographic sense, when they solve problems.

3.3. *Adding Structure to the Environment*

When we do look closely at the range of activities that people perform during the course of solving or attempting to solve problems, we find many things that do not neatly fit the model of search in an internal or external problem space.

For instance, in their account of subjects playing the computer game Pengo, Agre and Chapman (1987) discussed how a computer program, and by analogy humans, could exhibit planned behavior without search. Their program worked interactively. It used a set of simple rules to categorize the environment in a highly context-sensitive manner. The environment that *Pengi* – the name of the computerized penguin that Pengo players were attempting to control – consists of blue ice-blocks distributed in a random maze. Pengi starts in the center and the villains of the game, the sno-bees, set off from the corners. If Pengi is stung it dies, but it can defend itself by kicking an ice-block directly in front of a sno-bee thereby crushing it. If Pengi was chasing a bee, Agre and Chapman's system would classify the structural arrangement of the ice-blocks one way. If Pengi was running away from a bee, the system would classify the very same arrangement of ice-blocks another way. To achieve this difference in classification the system attached visual markers – visual memory projections or annotations – to certain parts of the situation. Thus, on two occasions, the same objective state might be classified in two ways depending on which of Pengi's goals were active, because the world would be visually annotated differently (see Figure 15.6).

Agre and Chapman then showed that with these visual markers the computer program was able to behave in a strategic manner using a few reactive rules. It was not necessary to search a problem space as long as the system could project additional representational structure onto the visible environment. The implication was that humans work this way, too. By performing certain types of visual actions, including actions that affected visual memory, humans are able to solve problems without search that are both complex and that on a priori grounds ought to require extensive search.

This tactic of adding structure, either material or mental, to the environment to simplify problem solving is surprisingly pervasive. People mentally enrich their situations in all manner of ways. To help improve recall there are strategies such as the method of loci, which involves associating memory items with spatial positions or well-known objects in one's environment. To improve performance in geometric problem solving, people project constructions, mental annotations (see Figure 15.7).

People have even more diverse ways of materially enriching their situations. They add reminders, perhaps with Post-it Notes, perhaps by rearranging the layout of books, papers, desktop icons, and so forth. They annotate in pen or colored pencil; they encode plan fragments in layouts; they keep recipes open; and of course they talk with one another, often asking for help or to force themselves to articulate their ideas, using their voice as an externalized thought. Indeed, it is widely accepted that the act of collecting one's thoughts to present a problem to another person is an effective method to identify and clarify givens, to articulate problem requirements, and to expose constraints on problem solutions or solution paths (Brown, Collins, & Duguid, 1989). Some of this facilitation, no doubt, occurs because different representations elevate different aspects of a problem. But some of it, as well, is due to the known value of talking out loud during problem solving (Behrend, Rosengren, & Perlmutter, 1989).

The thread common to all these different actions is that they reduce the complexity of the momentary computational problems that agents face. They help creatures with limited cognitive resources perform at a higher level.

Here is another, more prosaic example. In a card game, such as gin rummy, players tend to reorganize their hand as they play. Reorganizing a hand cannot change the value of current cards or the value of subsequent cards. Whether or not an ace of spades will be a good card to accept and the three of clubs a good card to throw away is unaffected by the way players lay out the cards in their hand. The objective problem state of the hand is invariant across rearrangement. Yet from a psychological perspective, rearrangements help players to notice possible continuations and to keep track of plans. Thus, the strategy *sort by suit then sort in ascending order across suit*, is an effective way to overcome cognitive set, or continuation blindness. This simple interactive procedure effectively highlights possible groupings. It is an epistemic activity. The knowledge dividend it pays exceeds its cost to an agent in terms of time and effort (Kirsh, 1995b).

3.4. Epistemic Actions

In a series of papers Kirsh (1995a, 1995b; Kirsh & Maglio, 1995) have argued that this sort of epistemic activity is far more prevalent than one might expect. Even in contexts where agents must respond very quickly it still may be worth their while to perform epistemic actions. For instance, in the arcade game Tetris, the problem facing players is to

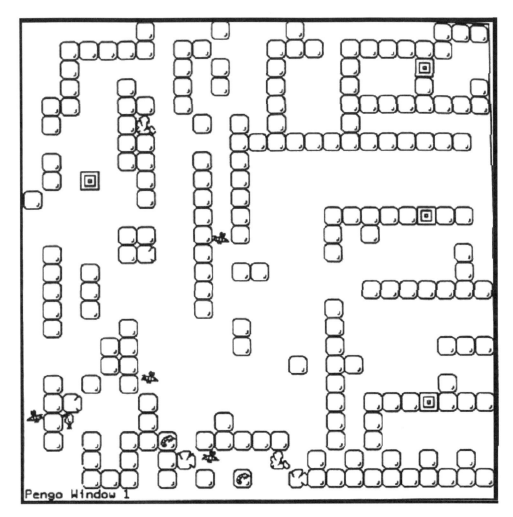

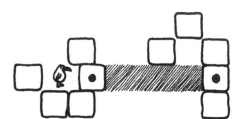

Figure 15.6. Here we see the game board of Pengo as a human sees it and a blowup of one section of a game where Pengi projects visual markers, indicated by dots, to allow it to act as if it has a rule "Kick the 'block-in-front-of-me' to the 'block-in-its-path.'" The dot markers serve as indexical elements that Pengi can project so that its current visual working memory has enough structure to drive the appropriate reactive or interactive rules it relies on to determine how to act. Some of these rules tell Pengi to add visual structure and others to physically act.

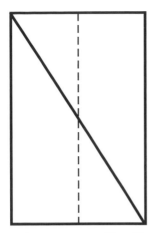

Figure 15.7. Humans can readily add mental structure to an illustration by projecting lines, bisecting angles, and generally adding mental annotations. In this example, an agent is shown a rectangle and asked to prove that a line that cuts a rectangle in half will also cut all diagonals of the rectangle in half. In those cases where subjects do not draw in the diagonal and bisector, they still can often find a solution by projecting first a diagonal and then a section line that bisects the rectangle. It is possible to add letters to projected points such as the intersection of the dotted bisection and the solid diagonal. This same capacity can be used in creative ways to add structure to other sorts of situations by envisioning the results of performing actions before performing them.

decide how to place small tetrazoidal shapes on a contour at the bottom of the board (see Figure 15.8). As the game speeds up, it becomes harder for players both to decide where to put the shapes and to manipulate them via a keyboard to put them into place.

What Kirsh and Maglio (1995) found was that players, even expert players, regularly performed actions that helped them to recognize pieces, verify the goodness of potential placements, and test plans (e.g., dropping a piece from high up on the board) despite there being a cost to their actions in terms of superfluous moves. Evidently the cost of moving a piece off its optimal trajectory was more than compensated for by the benefits of simplifying some aspect of the cognitive problem involved in identifying the piece and determining its best rest-

ing place. The novel feature of these epistemic actions is that their value depends crucially on when they are done. Because the game is fast paced, information becomes stale quickly. Twirling a "zoid" the moment it enters the board is a valuable action, but it is near useless to an expert 200 ms later. Twirling must be timed to deliver information exactly when it will be useful for an internal computation. From a purely problem-space perspective, where states and operators have a timeless validity, there is no room to explain these time-bound actions. Even though epistemic actions help agents to solve problems, and they can be understood as facilitating search by increasing the speed at which a correct problem representation can be created, they are not, on the classical view, part of problem solving, and they do not lie on a solution path. They help to discover solutions, but for some reason they are not part of the solution path.

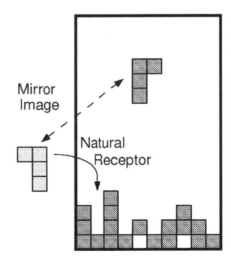

Figure 15.8. In Tetris the goal of play is to relentlessly fill gaps on the bottom layers so as to complete rows. The game ends when the board clogs up and no more pieces can enter. Because there are mirror pieces, and the choice of where to place a Tetris piece is strategic, players need many hours of practice to become expert. We found that players often perform unnecessary rotations to speed up their identification process, especially among pieces with mirror counterparts. (Kirsh & Maglio, 1995)

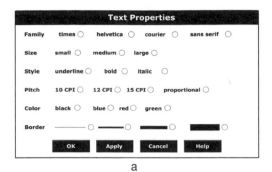 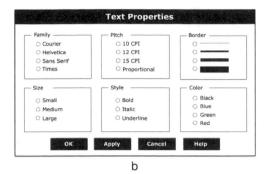

a   b

Figure 15.9. The consequence of thoughtful redesign is that tasks that were error prone and hard to manage become progressively easier. The two interfaces are small environments – tools, in a sense – that agents must thoughtfully use to complete a task. In this case the task is to set the font style of a region of text. By redoing the graphic layout, as in 15.9b, designers are able to lower the costs of planning what to do, monitoring what one is doing, and verifying that one has completed the task. If this task was treated as a problem to solve, the effect of redesign is that it is now easier, even though the task environment is the same.

The challenge epistemic actions pose to the classical approach, and to the psychological study of behavior more generally, is that without an analysis of the possible epistemic functions of an action it may be nearly impossible to identify the primary function of an action and so label it correctly. Actions that at first seem pragmatic, and so to an observer may seem to be an ordinary move, may not be intended by the player to be an ordinary move. Their objective may have been to change the momentary epistemic state of the player, not the physical state of the game. This important category of problem-solving activity lies outside the classical theory because the classical theory operates with a fixed set of actions and a fixed evaluation metric. Both action repertoire and metric are taken as objective features of the task environment and assumed insensitive to the momentary epistemic state of the agent.

4. Resources and Scaffolds

The classical theory also fails to accommodate the universality of cultural products that facilitate activity-specific reasoning. Environments in which people regularly act are laden with mental aids, so problem solving is more a matter of using those aids effectively. Supermarkets tend to display competitive items beside one another to help shoppers choose; large buildings tend to have signs and arrows showing what lies down a corridor because people need to find their way; microwaves and ovens have buttons and lights that suggest what their function is because people need to know what their options are; and most of our assembly tasks take place when we have diagrams and instructions. Wherever we go, we are sure to find artifacts to help us. Rarely do we face knowledge-lean problems like the Tower of Hanoi or desert-island problems. Our problems arise in socially organized activities in which our decisions and activity are supported.

There are several reasons why cultural products and artifacts saturate everyday environments. First, most of the environments we act in have been adapted to help us. Good designers intentionally modify environments to provide problem solvers with more and better scaffolds and resources, designs that make it easier to complete tasks (see Figure 15.9 and caption). And if designers are not the cause of redesign, it often happens anyway, as a side effect of previous agents leaving behind useful resources after having dealt with similar problems. Rarely are we the first to visit a problem.

A second reason resources and scaffolds almost always exist in our environments is that, as problem solvers, we ourselves construct intermediate structures that promote our own interactive cognition. As already mentioned, we create problem-aiding resources such as illustrations, piles, annotations, and notes that function like cognitive tools to help us to understand and explore questions and coordinate our inquiry. When we face problems, we typically have a host of basic resources at hand: tools such as pen, paper, calculators, and rulers; manipulables such as cans, cups, and chopping boards; cultural norms of gesture, style, language; and, of course, cultural resources and practices such as tricks for solving problems, techniques, algorithms, methods of illustration, note taking, and so on. When we attempt to solve a problem, we reach for these aids or call on tricks and techniques we have learned. Many of our solutions or intermediate steps toward solution take the form of actions on or with these materials. They seed the environment with useful elements (e.g., lemmas), they make it possible to see patterns or see continuations (e.g., the lines in tic-tac-toe), or they make it easier to follow rules (e.g., the lines in multiplication; see Figure 15.10).

A final source of resources and scaffolds is found in our neighbors or colleagues who are often willing to give us a helping hand, offering hints, suggestions, tools, and so on. In educational theory, the term *scaffolding* refers to the personalized problem-solving support that an expert provides a novice. *Help* is too simple a term to describe this support because a good teacher gives a student tools, methods or method fragments, and tricks about technique that the student is ready to absorb but that, taken on their own, do not provide an answer to the student's impasse. Scaffolds extend the reach of a student, but only if the student is in a position to make use of them. This was a key aspect of the way Vygotsky, the author

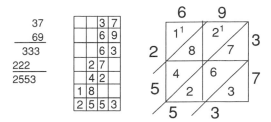

Figure 15.10. Multiplication problems are rarely solved in the head. Problem solvers reach for pen and paper, line up the numbers in a strict manner, and then produce intermediate products that are then relied on in their algorithm. Paper, pen, graph paper, and lines are all scaffolds that help agents to reduce error. In this figure we see three ways to multiply. The most noteworthy feature of these structures is the lines that guide the user. They are not elements of the algorithm. They are scaffolds indicating where the multiplicands end and the intermediate products of the problem solver are to be placed, and so on. They help agents stay in control, keep on track, monitor where they are, prevent error.

of the term, used it. In his view scaffolds are support structures in learners' immediate environment that might permit them to solve problems that are at the periphery of their problem-solving ability, problems that reside in what he called the "zone of proximal development." They are akin to hints. And intrinsic to this notion is the assumption that as soon as the student internalizes the requisite methods, norms, heuristics, and construction skills, scaffolding will be unnecessary and no longer found in the problem-solving situation. Workers put up scaffolds to help them reach parts of a building they cannot otherwise reach. But as soon as they have finished their job, they remove the scaffold. Training wheels are a classical example of scaffold in the learning literature. Other examples include the use of vowel markers in beginners' Hebrew that are omitted in normal Hebrew writing because context and knowledge make them redundant.

Outside of learning theory, the term *scaffold* is used to refer to the cultural resources – artifacts, representations, norms, policies, and practices – that saturate our everyday work environments and that remain even after we have internalized their function. They reflect the supports present in most work environments. The majority of our problem-solving abilities evolved in these resource-heavy environments; they rely on those resources being there.

Take the case of geometric problems. Students learn a variety of ways to solve such problems but most involve constructing illustrations. Part of a student's problem-solving competence consists in the ability to create apt illustrations and then to use them, not just to understand the problem but to work inside, annotating them, to solve the problem. In Figure 15.11, we see an example. Rather than tackle the problem algebraically, an easier approach is to modify the problem-solving environment so that it supports a range of different actions that the user finds easier to control and work with. As discussed earlier, these representations have a structure that makes the relevant attributes of the problem easier to manage.

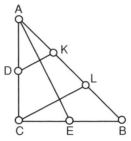

Figure 15.11. The written or formal statement of a geometric problem is almost impossible to understand without translating it first to a geometric diagram. In proving KL = BL, virtually all problem solvers use the figure as an arbitrary version of the problem that feeds intuitions. Students find it simpler to reason using the figure because it is easier to notice visual or geometric relations between properties in this problem than it is to notice algebraic relations. The validity of the proof depends on universal generalization: a proof method where one assumes an entity, an isosceles triangle of certain dimensions; one then proves a key statement about this triangle; and then one shows that nothing in the proof depended on having chosen this particular triangle as the example. The proof generalizes to all right-angled isosceles triangles.

> **Formal Problem.** ABC is an isosceles right-angled triangle with the right angle at C. Points D and E, equidistant from C, are chosen arbitrarily on AC and BC. Line segments from D and C are perpendicular to AE and meet the hypotenuse AB at K and L. Prove that KL = BL.

The presence of resources and scaffolds in an environment does not, in itself, challenge the view that people solve problems by searching through a problem space that is distributed over structures in the world and structures in the head. But it does call into question how to formulate the problem that people are solving. If the resources at hand change, or are different from situation to situation, why assume the problem is the same? Does a student who uses algebraic techniques solve the same geometric problem as his friend who uses an illustration? Do they operate in the same task environment? A task environment, after all, is defined with respect to operators too. How about a student who uses a pocket calculator to determine the square root of 1600 versus her friend, who calculates the value by hand: is it the same task environment? Tools, scaffolds, and resources seem to interact with tasks, usually changing them, often in ways that reduce their complexity.

5. Special-Case Solutions

A favorite pastime of situationalists is to enumerate instances in which resources in the environment have been put to creative use to transform the complexity of problem solving. No discussion of situated problem solving would be complete without mentioning the infamous example, "The intelligence is in the cottage cheese" (see Figure 15.12).

Although the method shown in Figure 15.12 is certainly simple, it is worth noting just how narrow it is. It is only because the daily allotment of cottage cheese is 3/4 of a cup, and tubs are exactly 1 cup (or because consumers have a measuring cup on hand), that it is possible to execute the algorithm and use the visual cues provided by the crisscrossing. This is a very special case. Weight watchers' dieticians might have allowed 7/16 of the daily portion of cottage cheese as the lunch portion. And they might have decided that the daily allotment was 3/5 of a cup.

But why would they? Problems and the environments in which they are solved are rarely independent. If for some reason 21/80 of a cup became important among a subset of consumers, how long would it be before manufacturers would change the tub size to make such calculations easy?

This highlights a key fact about situated problem solving: it is usually narrow, special-case-oriented, and shallow. The reason such approaches work is that most instances of naturally occurring problems, even problems that are theoretically hard, are confined to those versions of the problem that can be solved easily. The ones that resist simple methods are part of a small set of worst-case versions (technically known as the complexity core) that people rarely if ever encounter. On those improbable occasions where they do encounter an instance of this core, they usually do poorly.

Here is an example. The traveling salesman problem is computationally intractable in the general case. There exist some nasty problem instances – the worst cases, the complexity core – where the only way to determine an optimal tour among all the cities the salesman must visit is by checking every conceivable tour. Because a tour consists of visiting every destination exactly once, there are as many tours as sequences of destinations, and that is *n* factorial tours. For ten cities that means checking 10! or 3,628,800 tours.

Figure 15.12. To solve the problem of how much cottage cheese two-thirds of three-quarters of a cup is, a subject was observed to turn over a one-cup tub of cottage cheese, crisscross it to mark four quarters, remove one quarter, then take two of those three quarters, which is one-half. It would have been easy enough to multiply 2/3 by 3/4, but typical subjects require pencil and paper to do that and regard the task to be effortful and confusing. The cup-sized cottage cheese itself became a thing to think with.

Yet in practice, most of the problem instances a traveling salesman actually faces are not nasty. Indeed, depending on the road layout of a given sales region, it may be quite easy to compute an optimal tour (see Figure 15.13). Would a salesman well adapted to his specific region learn a slow general algorithm for solving the problem in all cases or a fast special algorithm that satisfactorily solves just his customary problems? Who would be better adapted to his task? And, if there happens to be one or two worst-case problems lurking in his sales region where his method gives him a suboptimal tour, the overall cost of traveling that imperfect tour one day a month is more than compensated by the benefits of having cheaply found optimal or near optimal tours the rest of the times he has gone out.

Findings in complexity theory justify this perspective. Hard problems are almost always easier if a second-best answer will be adequate much of the time. More precisely, a problem that is NP-complete (or worse) can usually be solved in polynomial time if it is acceptable to give a solution that is $1 - \delta$ from the perfect answer (Padadimitriou & Yannakakis, 1988).[1] The more tolerant one is about the precision of the answer – that is, the further from the perfect answer one can tolerate, the faster the algorithm. So if our traveling salesman does not require having the absolutely shortest path but will

Easy Tour   Hard Tour

Figure 15.13. Compare these two instances of the traveling salesperson problem. Why is the easy tour easy to compute and the hard tour hard? Because the easy tour lies on a convex hull. If we know this fact, then we can use a fast algorithm based on the truth of that assumption. If there is no convex hull, or if we have no reason to think that there is, then there is no fast algorithm to guarantee an optimal tour. In many cities, roads are laid out on a grid structure, which makes the determination of optimal tours more like easy than hard tours.

settle for one that he knows is close to the shortest, then he can have a quick, reliable method of finding that path. And the same benefits apply if he can tolerate a little uncertainty in his answer. Thus if he can accept being right at least 99 percent of the time, or more precisely, have confidence $1 - \varepsilon$ that his answer is optimal, then a fast algorithm exists (Karp, 1986). The reason such algorithms exist is that in all problems there is a large class of instances where there is structure in the problem that can be exploited. In Figure 15.13, the structures are apparent. In Figure 15.12, the cottage cheese case, the structure is the obvious relation between the numerator and denominator of the fractions $2/3 \times 3/4$, $1/2 \times 2/3$, $3/4 \times 4/5$, and so on. An agent does not have to know about this structure or understand it to rely on algorithms or heuristic methods that are valid in virtue of this structure. But an agent who is ignorant of the relevance of this structure will never know whether she is currently confronting an instance of the hard core or why her method sometimes fails.

The adequacy of special-case solutions suggests that, in general, agents operate with an understanding of their problems that is good enough for the cases they normally encounter. They conceptualize their context rather differently than formalists, who see the problem being solved as an instance

of a more general mathematical, logical, or planning problem. This raises a hard problem for formalists. How should the conceptualization people actually work with – the conceptualization that somehow figures in the problem space an agent creates – be matched against the real task environment associated with the problem in its more general form?

The answer to this question has deep implications for problem-solving methodology. As empiricists we ought to accept that it is an empirical question which of the many possible task environments that might fit a problem is the actual task environment that problem solvers must adapt to. It is not to be answered in ignorance of the frequency of the problem instances real problem solvers face. Presumably, it is misleading to choose too general a task environment if, in fact, problem solvers never face more than a small subset of the problem instances that fit the general task specification. That would be a bad framing of the problem.

For example, the task environment for the Tower of Hanoi, in most renderings of the task, is structurally the same whether it applies to towers made with thirty disks or to those made with three disks. From a mathematical point of view the task environment is the same because a recursive algorithm is used to generate the formal structure of the problem. Just as we treat multiplication of two thirty-digit numbers to be the same basic task as multiplication of two two-digit numbers, so it might seem natural to treat solving thirty-disk problems to be the same basic task as solving three-disk problems. Of course the actual problem space is much larger in the thirty-disk case than in the three-disk case because there are so many more combinations to consider. But why should that matter? If we think that subjects solve Tower of Hanoi problems with a recursive algorithm, it ought to be the same whether they face thirty disks or three.

Yet people who solve the three-disk problem often fail on larger problems, even ones as small as seven- or eight-disk problems. They usually have trouble keeping track of where they are in the problem; they have trouble maintaining current state. At some point they need a separate strategy to stay on course, and typically this is to use paper or some other way of encoding state. Can we pretend that this auxiliary strategy is not part of their problem-solving method for larger problems?

This raises the question: Do they face the same problem in both cases but use different methods because of memory and computational limits? Or do they face different problems because small and large versions of the Tower of Hanoi are actually different problems given the resources and methods subjects have? The answer depends on why we think it useful to invoke a task environment. The notion of a task environment was introduced to explain what rational agents adapt to as they get better at solving a problem. Namely, they adapt to the problem's structure, to the cues and constraints on paths to a solution. The paradox of large problems is that rational agents never do adapt. They cannot use the algorithms they use for smaller instances of the "same" problem, at least not in their head. And when they use paper, they perform many other actions related to managing their inscriptions that have nothing to do with the core algorithm. Why, then, maintain that the language of task environments is helpful? What does it predict? It does not predict the performance and pattern of errors that problem solvers display as the problem gets larger, because performance depends on the algorithms actually in use. All it can predict is how an ideally rational agent, unaffected by resource considerations, would behave.

If it is true that people do not use the same method in large and small versions of the Tower of Hanoi, why assume that they should use the same methods in other environments, such as shopping, assembly, selling, or navigation?

The upshot is that situated problem solving emphasizes that people solve problems in specific contexts. The methods they have learned are well adapted or efficient in those contexts but may be limited to special cases, not generalizable, and often idiosyncratic. Indeed, given the coevolution of settings

and methods of coping, we would expect that most problem solving in well-designed environments is computationally easy, with external supports that ensure it is so. No one has argued that situated problem solving is better than other methods. It is just more like the way we think. And that was the question at issue.

6. Knowledge-Rich Cognition

Experts know a lot about their domains. Even if they cannot articulate their knowledge, they have built up methods for achieving their goals, dealing with hassles and breakdowns, finding work-arounds, and more to make them effective at their tasks. That is why they are experts.

In regarding agents in their everyday contexts to be well adapted to their contexts of work and activity, we are treating them as rich in knowledge, as more or less experts in their commonsense world. They know how to get by using the material and symbolic resources supporting action. Perhaps the difference between situated cognition and problem-space cognition is the difference between knowledge-rich and knowledge-lean cognition.

An old distinction, still useful but potentially misleading, distinguishes declarative from procedural knowledge: knowledge of facts and explicit rules from the type of knowledge displayed in skills. Typical studies in knowledge-rich problem solving focus on the dense matrix of facts, procedures, heuristics, representational methods, and cases that experienced agents bring to their tasks. This is a mixture of declarative and procedural knowledge, though presumably some of the knowledge that experts have is related to knowing how to publicly use representations, to exploit their social networks, and to use tools – skills that seem to be more embodied than can be encapsulated in a set of procedures. Because most people become experts or near experts in dealing with their everyday environments – shopping, driving, socially conversing, preparing their meals, coping with familiar technology – they probably know enough about these domains to have effective problem-solving methods for handling the majority of problems they confront. For the few problems they cannot handle, they usually have work-arounds, such as calling friends for advice or knowing how to halt or abort a process, that let them prevent catastrophic failure.

On the classical account, a major source of the improved performance that experts display is to be explained in terms of improved search or improved representation of problems. They have better methods for generating candidate solutions and better metrics for evaluating how good those candidates are. It has also been observed that experts spend more time than novices in the early phases of problem solving, such as determining an appropriate representation of a problem. To cite one study (Lesgold, 1988), when a fund manager considers stocks to include and exclude from her portfolio, she is systematically reviewing a set of candidates. So we might start our interpretation of her problem solving with a problem space and operators. But before she makes her final decision she will have done many things, perhaps over several days, to uncover more information about stocks, and to get hints about what the Street thinks about each stock. Some of the things she might do include retrieving charts, extending and interpreting those charts, contacting analysts, reading their reports, examining the portfolios of her competitors, reading economic forecasts, and possibly even visiting companies.

This appreciation of the value of preparation reveals that when experts solve knowledge-rich problems they engage their environment in far more complex ways than just implementing operators. They interactively probe the world to help define and frame their problems. This suggests that deeper ethnographic studies of everyday problem solving may show a different style of activity than found in formal accounts of problem solving. Theories of knowledge-rich problem solving have become impor-

tant in the literature since the 1980s. But even these accounts place too little emphasis on the centrality of resources, scaffolds, interactivity, and cultural support. There is far more going on in solving a real-world problem than in searching a problem space.

PART 3: POSITIVE ACCOUNT – A FEW IDEAS

The view articulated so far is that problem solving is an interactive process in which subjects perceive, change, and create the cues, constraints, affordances, and larger-scale structures in the environment, such as diagrams, forms, scaffolds, and artifact ecologies that they work with as they make their way toward a solution. This looks like the basis for an alternative and positive theory of how people overcome problems in concrete settings. The positive element in situated cognition is this emphasis on agent-environment interaction. All that is missing from such a theory are the details!

How and when do people externalize inner state, modify the environment to generate conjectures, interactively frame their problems, cognize affordances and cues, and allocate control across internal and external resources? These are fundamental questions that must be answered by any positive account that attempts to locate problem solving in the interaction between internal representations or processes and external representations, structures, and processes. If problem solving emerges as a consequence of a tight coupling between inside and outside that is promoted and sustained by culture and the material elements of specific environments, then we need an account of the mechanisms involved in these couplings, and ultimately, of how culture, learning, and the structure of our artifacts figure in shaping that coupling.

It is beyond the goals of this article to present a positive theory, or even a sketch of one. I will discuss, however, four areas in which adherents of situated cognition, in my opinion, ought to be offering theories – areas in which a situationalist might constructively add value to the problem solving literature. My remarks should be seen more as suggestions or desiderata for a situated theory of problem solving than as an actual sketch of one. The four areas are as follows:

1. Hints
2. Affordances
3. Thinking with things
4. Self-cueing

It is important to appreciate that this positive approach is not meant to label other theories – more classical theories – as useless. Insight into problem solving can be found in the gestalt literature, in articles on clinical problem solving, in the study of learning and education, and also in the literature on task environments just criticized. What is offered here should be seen as an addition to those literatures, part of what one day might be a more integrated approach, though the proof that such as theory is viable will require the sort of dedication to ethnography, experimental research, and model building that has so far been lacking in situated cognition.

1. Sketch of a Theory of Hints

Hints come in all forms. They are a part of the natural history of problem solving. Here are a few examples drawn from the classroom. A teacher may tell or show a student how to use a special method or algorithm ("Here's a faster way to determine square root"), give advice on framing the problem ("First state the givens and thing to be shown, then eliminate irrelevant details and distracters"), or suggest useful strategies ("Generate as many lemmas as you can in order to fill your page with potentially useful things"). A fellow student may share illustrations or models, mention an analogous problem, give part of the answer, suggest a way of thinking or representing the problem, and so on. Is there a theory that might explain why a hint is a hint? Hints represent an

important element of the culture of problem solving (Kokinov, Hadjiilieva, & Yoveva, 1997).

A simple theory of hints might begin by defining a hint to be a verbal or nonverbal cue that acts like a heuristic bias on search. This would nicely fit the classical theory. Consider the hints people give in the game of I Spy – a child's game in which one player, the spy, gives clues about an object he or she observes and the other player(s) attempt to guess what the object is.

- "You're getting hotter" – metric information – your current guess is better than your last.
- "It's bigger than a loaf of bread" – constraint on candidate generation and an acceptable solution.
- "More over there" – gesture that biases the part of the search space to explore.
- "Try eliminating big categories of things first like 'Is it a living thing?'" – heuristics for efficiently pruning the space.
- "Don't ignore the color" – critical features to attend to that bias generation and evaluation.
- "Back up – abstract away from these sorts of details" – recharacterize the search space.

In thinking of hints in this way, we tie them to their role in both candidate generation and evaluation.

Situated cognition downplays search in a problem space as the determinant of problem-solving behavior. Psychological, social, cultural, and material factors are treated as more important. Nonetheless no approach to problem solving can overlook the importance of both candidate generation and evaluation. Ideas, possibilities, and possible ways of proceeding are always involved in problem solving, as is their evaluation as being fruitful, off the mark, or suggestive. Even in insight problems (Mayer, 1995), where discovering a solution requires breaking functional set – as when a subject suddenly realizes that an object can be used in a nonstandard way – it is still necessary to try out ideas of different ways of using objects. So there is always a component of generating candidate actions and testing their adequacy.

What drives the generation process? It depends on how easy it is to know that one is at a choice point and the set of actions available there. In knowledge-lean problems such as the Tower of Hanoi, there are a small number of possible moves at each step, and an agent knows what these are. The problem is discrete, candidate generation is easy, and state-space search is a good formalization of the problem, even though the agent's psychological task changes when the problem increases in size. In knowledge-lean problems the difficulty lies more in evaluation than in generation – in deciding whether a given option is a good one. Hints therefore ought to offer advice or heuristics for moving in a good direction. For instance, work toward clearing a peg completely; there are no short cuts.

In games like chess where there are many more possible actions at each choice point, a state space still captures the formal structure of the problem, because the agent knows perfectly well where the choice points are. Given how much knowledge is required for expertise it seems odd to call chess a knowledge-lean problem. In chess it is hard to see the downstream effects of action, because one's opponent is unpredictable. So it is hard to generate plausible chains of "If I do this, then you are likely to do that." The branching factor of the game is large and the space of possible continuations huge. This puts greater pressure on prudent candidate generation at each level of the search space. Accordingly, in chess, hints and suggestions often have to do with biasing generation. For instance, typical rules for opening are these: "Open with a center pawn." "Knights before bishops." "Don't move the same piece twice." "Always play to gain control of the center." Typical rules for middle game include these: "In cramped positions free yourself by exchanging." "Don't bring your king out with your opponent's queen on the board." And in the end game rules include these: "If you are only one pawn

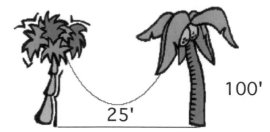

Figure 15.14. Try solving the flagpole problem. Why is it hard? It is not because we cannot think of a way to represent it. We can extract the givens, the solution condition, and constraints. Making an illustration is easy, as shown here. But is this a good illustration? If you have not solved the problem, here is a hint: work in from the extremes to see how the vertical drop changes as the separation between the trees increases or decreases. What kind of hint is this?

ahead, exchange pieces, not pawns." "Don't place your pawns on the same color squares as your bishop."[2]

In problems that do not count as knowledge-lean, or problems where it is not easy to determine when one is at a choice point and what the options are, the hardest step is often to figure out how to think about the problem, to pose it or frame it in a constructive way. Consider the problem in Figure 15.14. What should one do? Making an illustration is always a good idea, but which illustration, and how should it be annotated? The space of possible drawings and textual actions is huge. Moreover, once a sketch has been made there remains the question of how to proceed.

> **Flagpole problem** (Figure 15.14): Two palm trees are standing, each 100 feet tall. A 150-foot rope is strung from the top of one of the palm trees to the top of the other and hangs freely between them. The lowest point of the rope is 25 feet above the ground. How far apart are the two flagpoles? (Ornstein & Levine, 1993)

One reason some problems are hard is that people find it difficult to escape their familiar way of proceeding, another instance of mental set. Aspects of a problem may remind them of possible methods or method fragments, but if these seem unpromising, what is to be done? The difficulty hardly seems to lie in finding something to do. It lies in finding an interesting thing to do. Where do *interesting* ideas come from? Does staring at a problem help? Should the problem solver do things not directly connected with taking a step forward in the problem, such as doodling, reading more about related problems, talking to colleagues, brainstorming? How many candidate steps come from inside an agent's head and how many come from prompts from artifacts, group dynamics, and so forth?

Early experiments by Gestalt psychologists have shown the value of environmental cues, such as waving a stick or setting a string in motion (Maier, 1970), that call attention to an item that might figure in a solution. But a more theoretically motivated explanation of how these cues trigger candidate generation is needed. And, once subjects do have a new line of thought to pursue, where do they get their metrics on goodness, their ability to discriminate what is an interesting avenue to follow and what looks useless? How does the environment help?

A theory of situated problem solving should explain why hints are successful and the many ways our environments offer us hints on how to solve our problems. At a minimum there is a large body of relevant data to be found in hint-giving and hint-receiving behavior.

2. Affordances and Activity

A second element in a positive theory would explain how people discover candidate steps in a problem solution by interactively engaging their environment. In classical accounts, if a task environment is well defined there is a set of feasible actions specified at each choice point. An agent is assumed to recognize choice points and automatically generate feasible actions. In situations where problems have not been well framed, however, discovering moves to consider can be challenging. In Newell's theory, SOAR

(Laird, Newell, & Rosenbloom, 1987), failure to generate a feasible action creates an impasse and a new subproblem to be solved. An alternative suggestion by Greeno and colleagues (Greeno, Smith, & Moore, 1993; Greeno & Middle School Mathematics through Applications Project Group, 1998) is that problem solvers recognize possible moves by being attuned to affordances and constraints. If at first an agent does not see a possible action, she can interact with the environment and increase her chances of discovering it. This is a promising approach that deserves elaboration and study.

The inspiration for seeing problem solving emerging out of interaction with resources and environmental conditions is drawn from Gibson's (1966, 1977, 1979) theory of perception. Gibson regarded an affordance as a dispositional property like being graspable, pullable, or having a structure that can be walked on, sat on, picked up, thrown, climbed, and so on. These properties of objects and environments are what make it possible for an agent with particular abilities to perform actions: pulling X, walking on X, sitting on X, picking up X, throwing X, climbing over X. Agents with different abilities would encounter different affordances. For example, relative to a legless person, no environment, regardless of how flat it is, affords walking. The same applies to other actions and skills. Only relative to an action or activity repertoire does an environment have well-defined affordances.

Because affordances are objective features of an environment, there may be affordances present in a situation that are never perceived at the time. The affordances that are actually perceived depend on the cues available during activity. The more attuned a creature is to its environment, the more it picks up affordance-revealing cues and the more readily it accomplishes its tasks. So runs the theory according to Gibson.

Problem solving, Greeno and colleagues suggest, should likewise be seen as an active, dynamic encounter of possibilities and registering of affordances, constraints, and invariants. When engaged in a task, or when trying to solve a problem, skillful agents recognize affordances that are relevant to their immediate goals. A cook recognizes the affordances of the stove, the knobs, blenders, and ingredients. Because many of these affordances are representational (e.g., a dial) or rule based (e.g., it is a convention that pulling a lever forward increases rather than decreases the magnitude of whatever it controls), the world of affordances and constraints that a cook is sensitive to must include properties that are socially, culturally, and conventionally constructed. Thus linguistic structures as well as nonlinguistic ones can be affordances for Greeno. In his view, it is not relevant that linguistic and nonlinguistic affordances are learned differently or that they are grasped differently: that the way someone knows what depressing a button with the linguistic label "abort" will do is conceptual, whereas the way someone knows that a knife affords hefting or cutting is probably nonconceptual. Both types of possibilities for action are "seen" and qualify as affordances for Greeno.

This inclusiveness represents a major extension of the concept of affordance and constraints, as understood in ecological psychology, but if it can be made to work, it permits seeing problem solving to be the outcome of a more embodied encounter with cultural resources. Greeno and colleagues assume that people can perceive or register affordances for activities that are quite complex. For instance, they assume that the more familiar we are with tools, such as hammers, screwdrivers, chisels, knives, machine saws, and lawn mowers, the more we can see opportunities for using them. Carpenters can make hundreds of perceptual inferences about wood. And someone who mows his lawn every week can see when grass is ready for its next cutting or too dense for a given lawn mower. This is an important and useful extension but not without difficulties.

Because using tools invariably involves mastering practices, the affordances that tool users perceive must be complex.

Imagine the affordances, constraints, and invariants that a chef must pick up when preparing an egg sunny-side down. First a hard edge must be found for cracking the egg cleanly, then the egg itself must be held correctly when opened, the frying process must be monitored, and the egg shifted at the right time so that it does not stick. Flipping has its own complexities. Throughout the process a cook must be sensitive to the preconditions of actions, the indicators that things are going well or beginning to go awry, and the moment-by-moment dynamics of cooking. A sunny-side-down cooking trajectory, under normal conditions, is supposed to be an invariant for a competent cook. In the theory of attunement to affordances and constraints, all these cues, affordances, constraints, and invariants of normal practice are precisely the things that skilled agents are supposed to be attuned to.

In extending affordances to include the affordances that situations provide for tools (in the hands of competent users), Greeno and colleagues pushed the concept well beyond what can be perceived through normal perception – even ecological perception. Their theory goes even further, though, to include affordances for reasoning. Such things as marking up diagrams, working with illustrations, and manipulating symbolic representations are all actions that experienced agents can perform and that serve as steps in reasoning.

For instance, when a student of geometry sees an illustration as in Figure 15.15, it is assumed that she can recognize a host of affordances for construction. To someone who has learned to make triangular constructions it is natural to look at Figure 15.15b and imagine dropping perpendiculars, as in Figure 15.15c. With practice and a little prodding, most students realize that the area of Figure 15.15b is the same as the rectangle in Figure 15.15a, and both are base times height (b × h). The proof involves noting that the triangles in Figure 15.15c are congruent. If someone cut out the left-hand triangle, he could paste it on the right and produce a rectangle just like Figure 15.15a. It is possible to prod students to recognize and generalize

a b c d

Figure 15.15. For a student of geometry, 15.15b affords many different types of constructions, including dropping perpendiculars from vertices as in 15.15c, adding diagonals, bisecting, and so forth. These affordances for constructions can be projected mentally onto the figure or added by pencil or pen on the figure itself. Although there are an infinite number of constructions the figure affords, a geometer only considers those constructions that are part of the standard practices. For instance, in 15.15d a clever student might realize that the area of a trapezoid can be proved similar to the area of a rectangle by noticing that triangles constructed through the midsection of each vertical side are congruent and create a rectangle whose length is (top + bottom)/2.

this idea by giving them paper and scissors and the chance to cut and paste. When they perform this physical action a few times, or perform the construction on paper, they come to see an invariance preserved under a shearing transformation. Clever students who are able to prove the equality of area theorem more analytically may even be able to recognize opportunities for making less obvious constructions, as in Figure 15.15d, thereby generalizing further the equality of area theorem and recognizing the invariance under further transforms.

The idea that an experienced subject can become attuned to both affordances and relevant invariants is powerful but constitutes a theory of problem solving only if it offers predictions. This is a challenge for an attunement theory. It is not a lost cause but is certainly one that has yet to be met. Exactly when will a subject pick up affordances for construction and, given the vast number of such affordances, exactly which ones will she attend to? This last concern applies to all theories of affordances but is especially problematic for those that presume affordances for reasoning.

To see how serious this challenge is, consider Figure 15.16. The two shapes in Figure 15.16a are topologically invariant. There

is a stretching operation that transforms Figure 15.16a into Figure 15.16b. How many people see it? Because there are an infinite number of ways to stretch the figure, it requires an insightful mind to envisage the transform. Figure 15.16b gives one set of deformations that shows the equivalence. Yet how many people can see even the first transform from 1 to 2? A theory of affordance pickup must tell us who, when, and why some people can see this invariance and who, when, and why certain others cannot. It also must explain why the most useful affordances are the ones that come to mind.

Education researchers would love to provide a theory of attunement learning, though so far advances have been empirical rather than theoretical. For instance, Sayeki, Ueno, and Nagasaka (1991) found that students who were given a chance to play with a deck of cards as shown in Figure 15.17a, and then to chat about their activity, were soon able to recognize the invariance of the area in the figures shown in Figure 15.17b. Physical experience with the deck helped to imbue students with a strong sense of the transformations that preserve area. Presumably subjects who played with clay structures shaped into the structure shown in Figure 15.16a would similarly have an easier time following the constructions in Figure 15.16b.

Greeno and colleagues viewed this consequence of practice as support for their theory that problem solving is the result of attunement to affordances, constraints, and

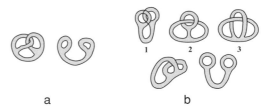

a b

Figure 15.16. All the figures shown in 15.16a and 15.16b are topologically the same: 15.16b is a sequence of transforms that is meant to prove the equivalence of figures in 15.16a. As with most proofs, not everyone is able to "see" the validity of each inferential step.

a   b

Figure 15.17. Students were shown a deck of cards as in 15.17a. The front face initially formed a square. As the deck was pushed around it became apparent that many four-sided and non-four-sided shapes could be constructed. The attribute common across all transformations is that the area of the front side always remains constant. The equivalence of the two images in 15.17b became obvious, intuitive, known in an embodied way.

invariance. Practice and engagement leads to improved attunement, which in turn leads to better solution exploration.

This is a rather different view than the classical account for two reasons. First, in the classical account, problem solving always involves search in a problem space. In the attunement account, problem solving involves evaluating perceived or registered affordances. This bypasses the need for a problem space where feasible actions are internally represented. Choice points are encountered rather than internally generated. And the choice points encountered depend on the actions actually taken by the agent – including mental projection actions. This means that the environment an agent encounters is partly co-constructed by its actions. As an agent begins to see things differently, especially ways it can project or construct, it partly creates new task affordances. Constructions support new projections and so on, though it must be said that there remains a need to triage or evaluate the many affordances registered and projected.

Second, in the attunement theory, transfer is the result of detecting similar affordances and constraints or invariances. Transfer is a direct consequence of being able to detect affordances and constraints, whether or not the agent has much grasp of the structure of a problem. Because similar affordances can be found in many situations, including those that pose very different problems, agents are more likely to try things

out before grasping deep analogies. An affordance detection approach would predict that problem solvers would be actively engaging their environment, both by projecting and by acting. In the classical theory, by contrast, the reason a subject is able to transfer problem-solving expertise from one problem to another is that the subject is able to detect deep structural similarities, and so methods found successful in the source domain are mapped over to the target domain. There is no deep need to interact with the problem environment.

If the theory of attunement were better specified, these advantages would be substantial. But the theory, as developed to date, falls short of details. How, for instance, does a subject choose which affordance to act on? There are infinitely many affordances available in any situation. This is particularly true once the notion of an affordance has been broadened to include the possibility of projecting structure or creating structure. In Figure 15.16a, for instance, there is no end of ways to deform the clay model. The challenge is to know which of the many ways to pursue.

In Greeno et al. (1998) it is suggested that dynamical system models may help here. It is easy to see why. If problem solving is a dynamic encounter with an affordance-rich environment, the language of attractors and repellors ought to be helpful in explaining why some affordances are perceived rather than others, or why some actions are pursued rather than others. Ecological psychologists have often advanced dynamical system accounts. But again, prior to a more complete account of the details, we can only wonder what controls this dynamic encounter. Discourse about basins of attraction and repulsion – the favorite terms in discussions of dynamical systems – sound remarkably like the discourse of gradient ascent: an action is selected if it yields a higher value. This is the method of hill climbing and is one of the cornerstone methods of problem-space search. Yet it is not enough. To explain much of the observed behavior of subjects on knowledge-lean problems, it has been found

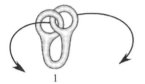

Figure 15.18. By adding annotations or other markings it is easier to envision the way this structure can be deformed. Such cues help to anchor projection and facilitate envisionment. It is a rich area for study.

necessary to introduce other weak methods such as difference reduction, depth-first search, breadth-first search, minimax search, abstraction, and others. Attunement theory owes us the details of how these sort of mechanisms of control can be implemented. If on the other hand dynamical systems are going to supplant the need for these additional control mechanisms, then we need to know more about how they will cope with the details of control that have seemed so useful in the classical theory.

There are further questions. Why are affordances and constraints sometimes visible and sometimes not? In Figure 15.16b, for example, it is hard for most people to see the legality of the transform between 1 and 2. But in Figure 15.18, with the simple addition of annotations, or hints, or material anchors, it is much easier. The details of an attunement model should explain the biases on affordance and constraint detection. It should tell us the types of detection errors that subjects make and why. It should tell us the biases we observe in human problem solving. And it should tell us the time course of affordance-constraint detection: why some are quickly seen and others are detected slowly. There is substantial opportunity for theory and experiment here. It may eventually pay off but it is clear there is much to be done.

3. Thinking with Things

How people use artifacts, resources, and tools as things to think with delineates a third class of phenomena that we would

expect a positive theory of situated problem solving to study and explain. In discussing how milkmen used their bottle cases to calculate efficient plans, we considered how overlearned patterns supported or embedded in artifacts – such as the regular pattern that forty-two bottles makes in a forty-eight-bottle milk case – could be used to help them solve specific planning and accounting problems. Experienced algebraicists use patterns in matrix representations to recognize properties of linear equations, and experienced milkmen use patterns of bottles, both present and imagined. These patterns figure in special-case solutions they have learned. The infamous weight watcher's example shows a similar trick: the physical form and size of cottage cheese when dumped from its carton can be used to support highly specific arithmetic operations that would be harder for most subjects to perform in their head. The idea of cutting a regular cylinder in half is so intuitive that for many people it is understood more directly than fractions. They can think with the parts the way they can think with symbols. C. S. Peirce (1931–1958) first mentioned this idea – that people use external objects to think with – in the late nineteenth century, when he said that chemists think as much with their test tubes as with pen and paper.

The notion that we use things to think with, that we distribute our thinking across internal and external representations or manipulables, is relatively uncontentious when the artifacts used are symbolic, such as written sentences, illustrations, numbers, or even gestures. Much ethnographic research has shown in detail how people use artifacts to encode information: how people represent information in external structures and then manipulate those external structures and read off the results. The same applies to gesture. People use body gestures to help them think in context, both when they think individually and when they think as a group or in a team. Gestures help them remember ideas, formulate thoughts, and not just supplement vocalization. A slightly different idea attaches to the use of artistic media. No one would deny that a sculptor is thinking or solving certain problems when using clay any more than someone would deny that an author is thinking or solving problems with the help of pen, paper, and written sentence. The medium has important properties that the artist or author is trying to exploit. Interaction is essential to the process. And though one might say that all the relevant cognition occurs inside the head of the human, the physical materials, scaffolds, tools, and structures are an important factor in the outcome. They help to structure the affordance landscape.

The question of how people think with things, how the determinants and dynamics of cognition depend on properties of artifacts and the context of action, is unquestionably at the heart of the theories of situated, distributed, and interactive cognition. But as with other tenets, it is in need of greater elaboration and empirical study. To date, the majority of studies have been confined to ethnographic examinations of particular cases. This is a necessary step given the importance of details. But little attention has been paid to the distinction between using objects to solve special-case problems – a method that reflects memorized techniques – and using objects or systems in more general ways as an intrinsic part of reasoning and problem solving. The distinction is important because if most instances of thinking with things are highly specific, if most are cases where dedicated tools are used to solve domain-specific problems, then too much of the rest of problem solving is left out and any hope of a more general theory of problem solving looks bleak. How much did we really learn about problem solving by observing weight watchers partition cottage cheese?

The theory situated cognition owes us is one that will explain how people harness physical objects to help them reason and solve problems. What characteristics must a thing to think with have if it is to be effective, easy to use, and handily learned?

Although a comprehensive theory would provide a principled taxonomy of the ways we can think with things, a tiny step toward this theory can be taken by looking at how people co-opt things to perform computations. Computation is about harnessing states, structures, or processes to generate rational outcomes. It is about using things to find answers. The most familiar forms of computation are digital, the manipulation of symbol strings, as in math, engineering, or computer science. But all sorts of nonsymbolic systems can be harnessed to perform computations. For instance, a slide rule is an analog mechanism for performing multiplication, addition, and a host of other mathematical operations. It does not have the precision of a calculator, or the range of functions of many other digital devices. But because it preserves key relationships – linear distance along each scale of the rule is proportional to the logarithm of the numbers marked on it – moving the slides in the correct way allows a user to perform multiplications. It can be used to simulate the outcome of digital multiplication because it preserves key relationships. It replaces symbol manipulation with manipulation of physical parts.

The same can be said, though less easily, for illustrations, sketches, and three-dimensional models. For instance, one of the most common ways we think with things is by using them as model fragments. A structure or process can be said to model or partly model another if it is easy to manipulate and examine the model and then read off implications about the target structure or process. An extreme example is seen in the architectural practice of building miniature three-dimensional models of buildings. The operations that architects perform on their small models are sufficiently similar to actions that inhabitants will perform on or in full-sized buildings that architects can try out on the model ways the full-sized building may be used. They can act on the model instead of the real object. This saves time, effort, and cost because mistakes have few consequences in models and simulations. This can even be done using two-dimensional diagrams, as shown by Murphy (2004), who recorded how architects reason about the uses of a building by bringing their bodies into interaction with their architectural drawings.

The formal part of a thinking-with-things theory should provide the analytic tools for evaluating why certain things can function successfully as things that can be thought with. Much of this work has already been done in other fields. For example, in math it is well understood that a powerful technique of reasoning is to map structures into different representational systems. Problems that may be hard to solve in one system, say, Euclidean geometry, may be easy to solve in analytic geometry. This mapping between representational systems may not seem to be a computation, but it is. It is a trick that is widely used. For instance, when sailors plot a course, they typically use more than one map. Every map represents the world under a projection that preserves some relations while distorting others. Mercator projections are good for plotting course but bad for estimating distance or area. Sailors overcome this problem by plotting their course in maps of different projection. They convert information from one map to another. The result is that they are able to track their location, distance, bearing, and speed more accurately and more quickly than they otherwise could (Hutchins, 1995). They think across maps. The result of using multiple maps is like using a fulcrum: it allows a weak user to do some heavy lifting because the maps or relation between the maps does much of the work.

An even more complicated way of using things to think with is found when people use the very thing they are interested in as its own model. For example, people solving tangrams seem to use the tangram pieces as things to think with. So do people when they assemble things without first reading the assembly manual. When Rod Brooks (1991a, 1991b) initially offered the expression "use the world as its own model," he meant that a robot would be better off sensing and reacting to the world itself than by simulating the effects of actions in an internal model of the world prior to selecting action.

If a robot were sufficiently tuned to the regularities of its environment and the tasks it needed to perform, it could be driven by a control system that would guarantee with high probability that the robot would eventually reach its goals, though not necessarily by the shortest path. If this sounds similar to the theory of attunement to affordances and constraints it is because it is the same theory though restricted here to problems such as trajectory planning, grasping, and physical manipulation, and without the requirement of mental projection.

Although such an approach may seem the antithesis of problem solving, it is a legitimate way of dealing with real-world problems – but only if certain conditions are met. Specifically:

- The world must be relatively benign. Moving toward goals can only rarely lead to disastrous downstream consequences (Kirsh, 1991, 1996).
- The world must be reversible. If you do not like your action, you can undo it and either return the world to the condition it was in before, or you can find a new path to any of the states you could reach before.

When can these conditions be counted on? Assembly tasks, math tasks, and puzzles, such as tangrams, support undoing without penalty. The Tower of Hanoi is another classic task supporting reversibility. And checkers, chess, and other competitive games usually have a form – correspondence chess, checkers – where subjects can search over possible moves directly on the board before deciding how to move. In other tasks, even if one cannot reverse the action, subjects can get a second chance to solve the problem. So as long as it takes no longer to try out an action in the world than trying it out in a model, there are advantages to acting directly in the world. First, subjects gain precision in the representation of the outcome because nothing is more precise than the real thing. Second, subjects gain practice in bringing things about, which can be of value where skill is required. Third, subjects save having to formulate a plan in their head, try it out in a model, and then execute the plan in the world. The execution phase is folded into the discovery phase.

But there are many other tasks where actions are not reversible and search in the world is a bad idea. In cooking, for example, as with many tasks, after an initial preparation phase when a recipe is selected and ingredients gathered, there is an execution phase where there is no turning back. There are many places where a plan can be modified or updated to deal with errors, setbacks, and unexpected outcomes. But in most tasks there are commitment points where it is inappropriate to do anything but the next move.

Most tractable analyses of thinking approach thought as a computational activity whether that computation is said to occur inside the head on internal representations, outside the head through the use of physical objects, or in the interaction between inside and outside. An even more profound approach to thought sees it as a mechanism for extending our perception, action, and regulation. This is a radical vision of how cognition is shaped through our interaction with artifacts.

The core idea in this more *enactive* theory of thought is that thinking is somehow tied up with the way we encounter and engage the world. A violinist encounters the world through his violin in a way that depends essentially on the violin. Violin problems are encountered only in violin playing and constituted in the interaction of player and instrument. The same applies to people who bicycle, whittle, manipulate cranes, or solve higher-math problems. The material instruments, representational languages, and sensorimotor extensions that artifacts provide offer new modes of experience and involvement with the world. The problems that arise are somehow essentially tied to those interactions and therefore cannot be properly analyzed until we understand what those who have those skills experience as problematic.

I personally think this is an exciting area of research. As with other areas this one is much in need of clarification and empirical exploration. Moreover, there is a danger that this activity-centric model makes thought so relativistic and hermeneutic that only violinists can understand other violinists, only sculptors can understand other sculptors, and so on. Although I believe such concerns can be answered, they highlight that there are philosophical and methodological problems as well as empirical ones that such an approach may face.

4. Self-Cueing and Metacognitive Control of Discovery

What controls search? In the classical theory the firing of productions, a form of associative memory, drives search. If a rule exists whose preconditions match patterns currently in working memory, then it is triggered, and unless other rules match current conditions and are therefore also triggered, that solitary rule fires and causes a change in working memory. Owing to this focus on what is in current working memory there is an inescapable *data-driven* bias to search, both on candidate generation and evaluation. Only a change in working memory can trigger new productions. Environmental state enters working memory through perception. A positive interactionist or situationist theory ought to provide an account of how we interact with our environments to overcome the lock that data-driven thinking has on our creativity. It must provide a theory of the dynamics driving the interactive exploration of a problem during the search for solution. One special line of inquiry looks at the way we self-cue, how we alter the cue structure of the environment to stimulate new ideas or candidate generation.

A nice example of how as data-driven creatures we self-cue to improve performance can be found in the way people play Scrabble (see Figure 15.19). The basic problem in Scrabble is to find the highest-value words that can be made from the letters

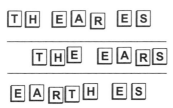

Figure 15.19. When people play Scrabble, they scan pieces on their tray, look for openings on the board, and search through a developing space of possible word and word fragments. Most people also periodically move the letters on their tray. Sometimes this is to hold their current candidate. But often it is to highlight high-frequency two- and three-letter combinations that figure in words.

on one's tray after placing them in a permissible position on the board. The challenge for a psychological theory is to explain how the external cues, comprised of the ordered letters on tray and board, mutually interact with a subject's internal lexical system. The challenge for an interactionist account is to show how subjects intentionally manage the arrangement of letters on their tray to improve performance.

In Maglio, Matlock, Raphaely, Chernicky, and Kirsh (1999), an experiment was performed to test the hypothesis that people who rearrange letters externally self-cue and consequently perform better than those who do not. The task was similar to Scrabble in that subjects were supposed to generate possible words from seven Scrabble letters. Unlike Scrabble, though, they just called out words as they recognized them; there were no constraints coming from the board or from values associated with letters. In the hands condition, participants could use their hands to manipulate the letters; in the no hands condition they could not. Results showed that more words were generated in the hands condition than in the no hands condition, and that moving tiles was more helpful in finding words that were more distant from the opening letter sequence.

Evidently, self-cueing helps beat the data-driven nature of cognition. We conjectured that the reason moving tiles is helpful is that when subjects rearrange tiles they are

in effect jumping to a new place in their internal lexical space. By lexical space we meant a system of discrete nodes consisting of letter sequences. How close one node is to another in this space is determined by such things as phonemic closeness (*bear* is close to *bare* and *air*), graphemic closeness (*bear* is close to *ear*), and perhaps others things such as semantic closeness (*bear* is close to *lair*). In our simulation we defined closeness as graphemic closeness alone. Thus two nodes are neighbors in or simplified model of internal lexical space if they can be reached by shifting or removing a few letters or adding a letter if there is an additional letter on the tray. Hence, *bear* is close to *bar, bare, bra* and if there is another *e* on the tray, then the word *beer* is also a graphemic neighbor. Letter sequences that do not form words, such as *bre ebra*, are also lexemic neighbors but less strongly attractive if they are infrequent sequences in English.

In discussing our findings we reasoned that although subjects can in principle apply as many mental transforms in lexemic space as they want and so, in both the no hands and hands condition, they can in principle move arbitrarily far from the letter layout on their physical tray. We expected that in practice subjects would tend to get stuck in the lexical neighborhood near to the groupings on their tray. This idea reiterates the data-driven nature of Scrabble.

The power of using one's hands comes from the difference in the constraints on physical movement and *mental movement*. A just-so story runs like this. The letters that subjects see exert a pull on their imagination much like an elastic band. The farther that subjects go in their lexemic space from the sequence on the tray the stronger the tension pulling them back. This tension is purely internal. In physical space, there is nothing preventing players from moving their tiles ever further from their first layout. It is easy to break the elastic-band effect. This means that a subject can jump to a new place in lexical space, and so activate a new basin of neighbors just by rearranging his or her tiles. The new arrangement will prime or cue a new set of lexical elements and make it more likely that new words will be discovered.

This approach to problem solving, if intentional, looks a lot like metacognition. It is reminiscent of the behavior of Ulysses (Elster, 1979), who recognized that he could not overcome the lure of the Sirens except by binding himself. To achieve his goal, given that he knew he would act inappropriately in the situation, he altered the situation. We do the same when we move our eyes. Given that our visual system is automatic and data driven, we cannot help but see what we look at. But we still can avert our eyes or direct them to other things. The decision to look elsewhere is often intentional, and when it is, it counts as metacognitive if it is based on reflectively exploiting the way our visual system works. The same applies to moving tiles in Scrabble and a host of problem-solving strategies we rely on in other domains. In math, for instance, we often copy onto a single page the lemmas we generated over many pages. This increases the chance of seeing patterns. In algebra, students soon learn that it helps to be neat because it is easier to see relations and patterns. Indeed, the strategy of rearranging the environment to stimulate new ideas when candidate generation slows down is pervasive. The principle relied on is self-cueing and metacognitive control. (For a more complete discussion of the role of metacognition in reasoning and learning, see Kirsh, 2004.)

The moral for research in problem solving should be clear: by studying more carefully how cues and affordance landscapes bias cognition, new interactive strategies will be discovered that show unanticipated ways subjects use the environment to shape their problem-solving cognition.

Final Discussion and Conclusion

By exposing how cognition is closely coupled to its social, material, and cultural context the situationalist approach has called attention to the deficiencies of the classi-cal theory of problem solving. It has forced us to reconsider the form an adequate theory should take. Is a general theory of problem solving possible? Is there enough resemblance between the actions that problem solvers take when solving or overcoming problems to hope to discover a general theory of the dynamics of problem solving, regardless of domain? I argued that such a theory must at least tell us for a given problem and situation how much of the control is to be found in internal processes, directed by such internal resources as problem-space representations and heuristic search, how much of the control is to be found in the setup or design of the environment influencing cognition through the affordances, cues, and constraints that a culture of activity has built up over time, and how much is to be found in the dynamic interaction between internal and external resources.

This is a tall order. It requires developing a set of supporting theories that explain how cues, constraints, and affordances affect how a subject thinks and acts. This point came up repeatedly: first when discussing the processes of registration, then when discussing interactivity and epistemic actions, scaffolds, and resources, and later when I discussed the direction a positive theory might take: explaining attunement to symbolic affordances and cues, explaining how subjects respond to hints, how they self-cue, and how they think with material things. A general theory of problem solving would have to pull all these supporting theories together to explain how subjects move back and forth among cues, scaffolds, visible attributes and the mental projections, structures, and problem spaces those subjects maintain on the inside. It would be an interactionist theory.

The situationalist approach, secondly, has exposed what is wrong with studying problem solving in constrained laboratory contexts, disconnected from the settings in which those mental and interactive processes originally developed. Subjects adapt to the world they live in. The internal costs of problem solving depend substantially on how experienced a subject is, whether the problem is presented to him or her in a familiar way, and how effectively he or she can exploit the surrounding resources, cues, affordances, and constraints. This concern with cognitive costs and benefits is consistent with the general theme of model building in cognitive science. But putting it into practice means paying closer attention to the details of natural contexts. This cannot be done without close ethnographic and micro-analytic study.

As a negative theory, situated cognition has been a success. But if approaches are judged by their positive theories, situated cognition has been a failure. All efforts at creating a substantive theory of problem solving have been underspecified or fragmentary. And it is too early to know whether the next dominant theory will bear a situationalist stamp.

Building on the critique presented in Part One and Part Two, I posed a set of questions and initial approaches that might indicate the direction situated research should pursue next. These include an analysis of hints and scaffolds, symbolic affordances and mental projection, thinking with things, self-cueing and metacognition, and an enactive theory of thought. Some of these studies are being undertaken outside of cognitive and computational psychology. They explore how people interactively populate situations with extra resources and how they exploit those resources to simplify reasoning. Some of these studies, however, are not yet being undertaken. The bottom line, it seems to me, is that it is not enough that we recognize the central insight of situated cognition – that the environment provides organization for cognitive activity, that the world enables and supports such activities – we must go further. We must explain how internal control processes work with these supports and organizational structures to regulate intelligent activity.

Acknowledgments

I am happy to thank the editors for their valuable suggestions and moral support during the writing of this chapter and for comments by Rick Alterman and Jim Greeno. Joachim Lyon carefully read the entire manuscript and gave thoughtful remarks throughout. Support for this work came in part from ONR Award # N00014-02-1-0457.

Notes

1 In computational complexity theory, problems are ranked according to the resources needed to solve their hardest instance, as measured by the number of steps and the amount of memory or scratch paper the best algorithm will use. For instance, solving a traveling salesman problem with two cities is trivial because there is only one combination of cities, one tour, to consider (A, B). But as the number of cities increases, the number of candidate tours that have to be written down and measured increases exponentially (as there are as many possible tours as sequences of all cities). It is the shape of this resource growth curve that determines the complexity class of a problem. A problem is said to be in the class of NP-complete if, in the worst case, the best algorithm would have to do the equivalent of checking every tour, and the test to determine whether one tour is better than another is itself not an NP-complete algorithm. There are infinitely many problems that are harder than NP-complete ones, and infinitely many problems that are easier. The easier ones have polynomial complexity.

2 Taken from "The Thirty Rules of Chess." Retrieved May 31, 2008, from http://www.chessdryad.com/education/sageadvice/thirty/index.htm.

References

Agre, P., & Chapman, D. (1987). Pengi: An implementation of a theory of activity. In *Proceedings of the Sixth National Conference on Artificial Intelligence* (pp. 268–272). Menlo Park, CA: AAAI Press.

Baker, B. S. (1994). Approximation algorithms for NP-complete problems on planar graphs. *Journal of the ACM, 41*(1), 153–180.

Behrend, D. A., Rosengren, K., & Perlmutter, M. (1989). Parent presence. *International*

Journal of Behavioral Development, 12(3), 305–320.

Brooks, R. A. (1991a). Intelligence without reason. In *Proceedings of the 1991 Joint Conference on Artificial Intelligence* (pp. 569–595). San Francisco, CA: Morgan Kaufmann.

Brooks, R. A. (1991b). Intelligence without representation. *Artificial Intelligence*, 47, 141–159.

Brown, J. S., Collins, A., & Duguid, P. (1989). Situated cognition and the culture of learning. *Educational Researcher*, 18, 32–42.

Carraher, T. N., Carraher, D. W., & Schliemann, A. D. (1985). Mathematics in the streets and in the schools. *British Journal of Developmental Psychology*, 3, 21–29.

Chambers, D., & Reisberg, D. (1985). Can mental images be ambiguous? *Journal of Experimental Psychology: Human Perception and Performance*, 11, 317–328.

Clark, A. (1997). *Being there: Putting brain, body, and world together again.* Cambridge, MA: MIT Press.

Devlin, A. S., & Bernstein, J. (1996). Interactive wayfinding: Use of cues by men and women. *Journal of Environmental Psychology*, 16, 23–39.

Elster, J. (1979). *Ulysses and the sirens.* Cambridge: Cambridge University Press.

Gibson, J. J. (1966). *The senses considered as perceptual systems.* Boston, MA: Houghton Mifflin.

Gibson, J. J. (1977). The theory of affordances. In R. E. Shaw & J. Bransford (Eds.), *Perceiving, acting, and knowing* (pp. 67–82). Hillsdale, NJ: Lawrence Erlbaum.

Gibson, J. J. (1979). *The ecological approach to visual perception.* Boston: Houghton Mifflin.

Gick, M., & Holyoak, K. (1980). Analogical problem solving. *Cognitive Psychology*, 12, 306–355.

Gick, M., & Holyoak, K. (1983). Scheme induction and analogical transfer. *Cognitive Psychology*, 15(1), 1–38.

Greeno, J. G., & Middle School Mathematics through Applications Project Group (1998). The situativity of knowing, learning, and research. *American Psychologist*, 53(1), 5–26.

Greeno, J. G., & Moore, J. L. (1993). Situativity and symbols: Response to Vera and Simon. *Cognitive Science*, 17, 49–60.

Greeno, J. G., Smith, D. R., & Moore, J. L. (1993). Transfer of situated learning. In D. K. Detterman & R. J. Sternberg (Eds.), *Transfer on trial: Intelligence, cognition, and instruction* (pp. 99–167). Norwood, NJ: Ablex.

Hamberger, J. (1979). *Music and cognitive research: Where do our questions come from? Where do our answers go?* (Working Paper Ser. No 2.). Cambridge: Massachusetts Institute of Technology, Division for Study and Research in Education.

Hutchins, E. (1995). *Cognition in the wild.* Cambridge, MA: MIT Press.

Hutchins, E., & Palen, L. (1997). Constructing meaning from space, gesture, and speech. In L. B. Resnick, R. Saljo, C. Pontecorvo, & B. Burge (Eds.), *Discourse, tools, and reasoning: Essays on situated cognition* (pp. 23–40). Heidelberg, Germany: Springer-Verlag.

Karp, R. M. (1986). Combinatorics, complexity, and randomness. *Communications of the ACM*, 29(2), 98–109.

Kershaw, T. C. (2004). Key actions in insight problems: Further evidence for the importance of non-dot turns in the nine-dot problem. In K. Forbus, D. Gentner, & T. Regier (Eds.), *Proceedings of the Twenty-Sixth Annual Conference of the Cognitive Science Society* (pp. 678–683). Mahwah, NJ: Lawrence Erlbaum.

Kirsh, D. (1991). When is information explicitly represented? In P. Hanson (Ed.), *Vancouver studies in cognitive science* (Vol. 1, pp. 340–365). New York: Oxford University Press.

Kirsh, D. (1995a). Complementary strategies: Why we use our hands when we think. In J. D. Moore & J. F. Lehman (Eds.), *Proceedings of the Seventeenth Annual Conference of the Cognitive Science Society* (pp. 212–217). Hillsdale, NJ: Lawrence Erlbaum.

Kirsh, D. (1995b). The intelligent use of space. *Artificial Intelligence*, 72(1–2), 31–68.

Kirsh, D. (1996). Today the earwig, tomorrow man? In M. Boden (Ed.), *Artificial life* (pp. 237–261). Oxford: Oxford University Press. (Reprinted from *Artificial Intelligence*, 47(3), 161–184.)

Kirsh, D. (2003). Implicit and explicit representation. In L. Nadel (Ed.), *Encyclopedia of cognitive science* (Vol. 2, pp. 478–481). London: Nature Publishing Group.

Kirsh, D. (2004). Metacognition, distributed cognition and visual design. In P. Gärdenfors & P. Johansson (Eds.), *Cognition, education and communication technology* (pp. 147–179). Hillsdale, NJ: Lawrence Erlbaum.

Kirsh, D., & Maglio, P. (1995). On distinguishing epistemic from pragmatic actions. *Cognitive Science*, 18, 513–549.

Kokinov, B., Hadjiilieva, K., & Yoveva, M. (1997). Is a hint always useful? In *Proceedings of the Nineteenth Annual Conference of the Cognitive Science Society*. Hillsdale, NJ: Lawrence Erlbaum.

Kotovsky, K., & Fallside, D. (1989). Representation and transfer in problem solving. In D. Klar & K. Kotovsky (Eds.), *Complex information processing* (pp. 69–108). Hillsdale, NJ: Lawrence Erlbaum.

Laird, J. E., Newell, A., & Rosenbloom, P. S. (1987). SOAR: An architecture for general intelligence. *Artificial Intelligence*, 33, 1–64.

Larkin, J. H., & Simon, H. A. (1987). Why a diagram is (sometimes) worth ten thousand words. *Cognitive Science*, 11, 65–99.

Lave, J. (1988). *Cognition in practice: Mind, mathematics and culture in everyday life*. Cambridge: Cambridge University Press.

Lave, J. (1996). The practice of learning. In S. Chailkin & J. Lave (Eds.), *Understanding practice: Perspectives on activity and context* (pp. 3–32). New York: Cambridge University Press.

Lesgold, A. M. (1988). Problem solving. In R. J. Sternberg & E. E. Smith (Eds.), *The psychology of human thought* (pp. 188–213). New York: Cambridge University Press.

Luchins, A. S. (1942). Mechanization in problem solving: The effect of Einstellung. *Psychological Monographs*, 54, 1–95.

Luchins, A. S., & Luchins, E. H. (1970). *Wertheimer's seminars revisited: Problem solving and thinking* (Vols. 1–3). Albany: State University of New York Press.

Maglio, P., Matlock, T., Raphaely, D., Chernicky, B., & Kirsh, D. (1999). Interactive skill in Scrabble. In *Proceedings of Twenty-First Annual Conference of the Cognitive Science Society*. (pp. 326–330). Mahwah, NJ: Lawrence Erlbaum.

Maier, N. R. F. (1930). Reasoning in humans: I. On direction. *Journal of Comparative Psychology*, 10, 115–143.

Maier, N. R. F. (1970). *Problem solving and creativity*. Belmont, CA: Brooks/Cole.

Mayer, R. E. (1995). The search for insight. In R. J. Sternberg & J. E. Davidson (Eds.), *The nature of insight* (pp. 3–32). New York: Cambridge University Press.

Miller, G. A., Galanter, E., & Pribram, K. H. (1960). *Plans and the structure of behavior*. New York: Holt, Rinehart & Winston.

Murphy, K. M. (2004). Imagination as joint activity: The case of architectural interaction. *Mind, Culture and Activity*, 11(4), 270–281.

Newell, A. (1990). *Unified theories of cognition*. Cambridge, MA: Harvard University Press.

Newell, A., & Simon, H. (1972). *Human problem solving*. Englewood Cliffs, NJ: Prentice Hall.

Norman, D. A. (1988). *The psychology of everyday things*. New York: Basic Books.

Ornstein, A. C., & Levine, D. U. (1993). *Foundations of education* (5th ed.). Boston: Houghton Mifflin.

Paige, J. M., & Simon, H. (1979). Cognitive process in solving algebra word problems. In H. A. Simon (Ed.), *Models of thought*. New Haven, CT: Yale University Press.

Papadimitriou, C., & Yannakakis, M. (1988). Optimization, approximation, and complexity classes. In *Proceedings of the Twentieth Annual ACM Symposium on Theory of Computing* (pp. 229–234). New York: ACM Press.

Peirce, C. S. (1931–1958). *The collected papers of Charles Sanders Peirce* (C. Hartshorne, P. Weiss [Vols. 1–6], & A. Burks [Vols. 7–8], Eds.). Cambridge, MA: Harvard University Press.

Pretz, J. E., Naples, A. J., & Sternberg, R. J. (2003). Recognizing, defining, and representing problems. In J. E. Davidson & R. J. Sternberg (Eds.), *The psychology of problem solving* (pp. 3–30). Cambridge: Cambridge University Press.

Reitman, W. R. (1964). Heuristic decision procedures, open constraints, and the structure of ill-defined problems. In M. W. Shelly & G. L. Bryan (Eds.), *Human judgments and optimality* (pp. 282–315). New York: John Wiley.

Rogoff, B., & Lave, J. (Eds.) (1984). *Everyday cognition: Its development in social context*. Cambridge, MA: Harvard University Press.

Sayeki, Y., Ueno, N., & Nagasaka, T. (1991). Mediation as a generative model for obtaining an area. *Learning and Instruction*, 1, 229–242.

Scribner, S. (1984). Studying working intelligence. In B. Rogoff & J. Lave (Eds.), *Everyday cognition: Its development in social context* (pp. 9–40). Cambridge, MA: Harvard University Press.

Scribner, S. (1986). Thinking in action: Some characteristics of practical thought. In R. J. Sternberg & R. K. Wagner (Eds.), *Practical intelligence: Nature and origins of competence in the everyday world* (pp. 13–30). Cambridge: Cambridge University Press.

Simon, H. A. (1969). *The sciences of the artificial.* Cambridge, MA: MIT Press.

Simon, H. A. (1979). *Models of thought* (Vol. 1). New Haven, CT: Yale University Press.

Simon, H. A., & Hayes, J. (1976). The understanding process: Process isomorphs. *Cognitive Psychology*, 8, 165–190.

Sternberg, R. J. (1997). *Thinking styles.* New York: Cambridge University Press.

Sternberg, R. J., & Davidson, J. E. (1983). Insight in the gifted. *Educational Psychologist*, 18, 51–57.

VanLehn, K. (1989). Problem solving and cognitive skill acquisition. In M. I. Posner (Ed.), *Foundations of cognitive science* (pp. 527–579). Cambridge, MA: MIT Press.

CHAPTER 16

The Dynamic Interactions between Situations and Decisions

Jerome R. Busemeyer, Ryan K. Jessup, and Eric Dimperio

The majority of judgment and decision-making research is based on laboratory experiments using very simple and artificial stimulus conditions. Eliciting preferences between simple gambles of the form, "Get $x with probability p, otherwise $y" is the primary basis on which rational principles of decision making are tested (Goldstein & Weber, 1995). The foundations of modern decision theories (see Luce, 2000) are built on findings from these simple gambling paradigms. These laboratory experiments are quite far removed from real-life decisions; nevertheless, many of the findings do generalize to real-world applications (Levin, Louviere, Schepanski, & Norman, 1983). However, new empirical phenomena and unique theoretical issues have surfaced by studying decision making in more natural environments. One of the goals of this chapter is to review these new findings and theoretical issues. A second goal is to examine more closely whether theories built from simple laboratory experiments are capable of addressing these new challenges.

1. Situated Decision Making

The term *situated cognition* may be unfamiliar to many decision researchers, but the ideas are not. Many decision researchers have considered, very seriously, the importance of using realistic environments for the study of decision making. Decision researchers have used terms such as *social judgment theory* or *decision analysis* or *naturalistic decision making*, which may be less familiar to cognitive scientists, to describe their explorations into work in the area of situated cognition.

Social judgment theory (see Hammond, Stewart, Brehmer, & Steinmann, 1975) is generally interested in understanding how experts form judgments based on cues provided by the environment. For example, in an experimental study of highway safety policies (Hammond, Hamm, Grassia, & Pearson, 1987), expert highway engineers were asked to predict accident rates for highways described by scenarios (e.g., videos). The scenarios were designed to manipulate ten cues that were identified as essential by the experts (e.g., highway size, traffic speed, traffic volume). Each scenario was constructed by sampling a combination of cue values for the ten cues. To estimate each expert's policy (i.e., the rule mapping cues to predictions), judgments were obtained from each expert using forty different highway scenarios. Statistical models (e.g., regressing the judgments on the cue values) were then used to estimate the expert's policy. From these analyses one can determine the importance weight of each cue for making a judgment.

Research in social judgment theory is based on Egon Brunswik's (1952) concepts of representative design and ecological validity. A representative design is achieved by sampling judgment situations by a method that preserves ecological validity; ecological validity holds when the sample correlations between cues and the criterion match the corresponding true correlations in the population. For example, highway size, traffic speed, and traffic volume are correlated with one another and correlated with accident rates in the real world, and these correlations should be reflected in sample scenarios presented to the experts. Students of Brunswik reject the use of experimental designs that create artificial and unnatural situations that break these correlations. For example, although the use of uncorrelated cues (e.g., factorial designs) would facilitate the statistical analysis of experts' policies, this artificial design violates the naturally occurring correlations among cues. According to Brunswik (and social judgment researchers; for a recent review, see Dhami, Hertwig, & Hoffrage, 2004), tampering with the naturally occurring environmental relations could destroy the phenomena under investigation. Instead, judgment situations should be sampled in a representative fashion so that the ecological validities of cues are maintained. In the preceding example of highway safety judgments, a representative sampling of situations was achieved by designing cue combinations that reproduced the true or natural intercorrelations and ecological validities of cues for the population of highways under study.

The discovery of general principles of human judgment is a primary objective of social judgment research. For example, in the highway-safety study, researchers may be interested in how the presentation format of the cues (abstract bar graphs versus concrete videos) generally affects the experts' policies. Experimental methods are still preferred over natural observation or field research for this purpose. However, the experiments are designed so that both the stimuli (situations to be judged) and participants (judges) are sampled in a way that represents the real-world population of situations and people.

Decision analysis is concerned with the development of prescriptive methods for improving difficult real-life decisions (Clemens, 1996; Keeney & Raiffa, 1976). A real-life example is a case in which an oil company had to select a site to drill for oil (see von Winterfeldt & Edwards, 1986). The basic principle is to divide and conquer – a complex decision is broken down into small manageable parts, judgments are made with respect to each part, and then these small parts are recombined to form an overall evaluation. Experts consult with decision analysts who help them form a representation of the problem in terms of decision trees (actions and events over time). Then probability estimates are elicited from the experts concerning the uncertain events on the branches of the decision tree. The consequences of the actions along the branches of the trees are decomposed into attributes, and each action is evaluated with respect to each attribute. For example, on the one hand, an oil site may have a large oil reserve, but on the other hand, it may be located in an environmentally protected region. Finally, a rational or optimal rule, called the "multiattribute expected utility rule," is used to combine the probabilities and values into a summary measure of utility.

Research in decision analysis is primarily concerned with the development and testing of methods for representing decision scenarios, tools for estimating probabilities, and techniques for eliciting value judgments. Decision-support systems serve as important external resources for decision makers – statistical analyses and computer simulations are used to help estimate event probabilities; computer analyses are used to provide instant feedback about expected utilities; and sophisticated human computer interfaces are used to help elicit judgments, facilitate group discussion, and communicate results.

The most difficult and controversial aspect of this research is assessing the quality of decisions produced by these methods (see Yates, Veinott, & Patalano, 2003). One cannot simply rely on the outcome of a single decision because of its probabilistic nature. A rational decision process may yield an unfortunate outcome by chance. For example, a carefully selected drilling site may nevertheless turn out to be a disaster because of an unpredictable environmental event (e.g., a hurricane). Many important decisions, such as selecting a drilling site, are made only once, which provides little opportunity to learn from experience. There are no absolute criteria for identifying a "correct" decision because the decisions depend on personal beliefs and subjective values. Assessing decision quality has been a long-standing problem in the evaluation of decision-analysis tools. Two minimal criteria for evaluating decision quality are consistency and robustness – the decision should not be affected by irrelevant changes in representation or by small adjustments caused by minor judgment errors (Kaplan, 1996).

Naturalistic decision making is a research methodology for understanding how actions are selected in dynamic, complex, real-life situations that involve high stakes, a high degree of uncertainty, and high time pressure (Zsambok & Klein, 1997). For example, in a study of emergency decisions, researchers followed thirty expert firefighting units to 126 emergency scenes and observed and recorded their activities; they also intensively interviewed the command and control decision makers immediately after the incidents (Klein, 1989). The findings from this field research indicated that traditional decision theory provided little

help in these types of decisions – they are much too complex and uncertain, and time is much too short to evaluate all the feasible actions.

Consequently, research on naturalistic decisions has uncovered some new views of decision making (Lipshitz, Klein, Orasanu, & Salas, 2001). First, situation assessment seems to be the most crucial component of the process for these types of decisions. Given a situational assessment, the next most important process is option generation. In many cases, following a situation assessment, the appropriate action is clear and immediate. In these cases, the decision seems fairly obvious, so that there is very little in the way of actual evaluation of alternative actions. This led Klein (1989) to propose what he calls the "recognition-primed decision model." According to this model, after completing a situation assessment and developing a mental model of the situation, the decision maker generates or retrieves an action that matches the assessed situation. Then this action is mentally simulated to determine its feasibility and the possibility of failure to achieve the goal. If the initially generated action is evaluated as acceptable (likely to succeed in achieving the goal), then the action is carried out without further deliberation or comparison with competing options. If it is not acceptable, then a second option is generated and evaluated for acceptability, and so forth. Thus, the options are evaluated serially one at a time and never directly compared. This contrasts sharply with traditional decision theory in which all options are carefully compared simultaneously, and the best option in a choice set is selected. In fact, the recognition-primed decision process is more closely related to Herb Simon's (1955) search and satisficing principles. It is also closely related to the "take the best" heuristic used by Gigerenzer and Todd (see Brighton & Todd's chapter in this volume).

Given the emphasis on real-life decisions, naturalistic decision making relies heavily on field research and interview methods, and these methods have raised some concerns (LeBoeuf & Shafir, 2001). One is that field research methods lack the control and measurement precision needed to rigorously test for decision biases. For example, much of naturalistic decision research is based on retrospective interviews, and basic research has shown that these retrospective reports (as distinct from on-line protocols) inaccurately reflect the basis of decisions (Ericsson & Simon, 1984; Nisbett & Wilson, 1977). This is because of possible hindsight biases (Fischoff & Slovic, 1978), as well as memory-recall failures and distortions (Loftus, 2003).

One of the distinct advantages of naturalistic decision making is also one of its greatest disadvantages. On the one hand, an intense focus on a specific yet complex situation generates a detailed description of that one real-life decision. On the other hand, this understanding is limited to that particular situation, and very little generalization to other decision situations is possible. In other words, the approach produces detailed descriptions but fails to produce general principles (Yates, 2004).

Dynamic decision-making tasks provide a good compromise between experimental control needed for basic research and simulation of real-life decisions (Edwards, 1962). For example, You (1989) studied a simulated health-management task in which subjects controlled their (simulated) patients' health using a (hypothetical) drug treatment. Participants chose a dosage level on each of fourteen (simulated) days on the basis of feedback from a patient's previous records (treatments and health states). Each simulated patient was actually programmed to respond according to a delayed second-order, linear-feedback system. The initially novice decision makers were given extensive training with a total of twenty simulated patients so that they develop some expertise for this particular task.

These types of laboratory tasks have some trade-offs that should be recognized. First, these tasks are artificially made to allow for experimental control and theoretical tractability, and they often end up oversimplifying the real-life tasks they simulate. Still, more complex tasks that provide greater realism have been designed without

giving up the benefits of the laboratory (e.g., Brehmer & Allard's [1991] fire-fighting simulation task, or flight simulators for training pilots). Second, the experimenter is giving up a certain degree of control so that stimulus events are influenced by the behavior of the subject. Thus, the design and analysis of such research would be better served if experimenters adapted a more cybernetic paradigm rather than the traditional stimulus-response paradigm (cf. Brehmer, 1992; Rapoport, 1975).

An important question that arises from this research is how to characterize the decision-making process for these complex dynamic tasks. One approach (Jagacinski & Hah, 1988; Jagacinski & Miller, 1978; Kirlik, Miller, & Jagacinski, 1993) is to estimate the decision maker's control policy by regressing the control decision (e.g., the drug treatment level) on the past decisions and past states of the system (past treatments and health levels). This provides an understanding of the importance of different kinds of information used to make control decisions in dynamic tasks. For example, You (1989) found that subjects' treatment decisions on each trial could be represented by a linear control model in which subjects made use of information about treatments and health states lagging back in time up to two previous (simulated) days.

Although human performers with extensive task training remain suboptimal in dynamic decision tasks (Sterman, 1994), most of the past studies reveal regular learning effects. Subjective policies may follow different paths but tend to evolve toward the optimal control policy over multiple trial blocks (Jagacinski & Hah, 1988; Jagacinski & Miller, 1978; You, 1989). Therefore, it is the particular learning processes that are more significant for explaining much of the variance in human performance on dynamic decision tasks (cf. Hogarth, 1981). At least three different approaches to learning to control dynamic systems have been developed. Anzai (1984) developed a production-rule model to describe how humans learn to navigate a simulated ship. An artificial neural-network model was developed to describe learning in a sugar-production task (Gibson, Fichman, & Plaut, 1997). An exemplar (instance base or case base) learning approach has been used in several dynamic control applications (Dienes & Fahey, 1995; Gilboa & Schmeidler, 1995; Gonzalez, Lerch, & Lebiere, 2003).

According to the exemplar learning approach, the decision maker matches the current state of the dynamic task with similar states that occurred in the past and recalls the outcomes of those past decisions. The action producing the best outcome in the past is then chosen for the current state. This is related to the idea of matching situations with actions in the recognition-primed decision model proposed by naturalistic decision researchers. So it seems that lessons learned from the laboratory using dynamic decision tasks converge on the same answers as those learned from studying naturalistic decision situations.

2. Alternate Approaches to Naturalistic Decisions: Sequential-Sampling Processes

Does the decision process really change so dramatically for naturalistic decisions as compared to laboratory decisions? Instead of looking for help from traditional decision theory, perhaps it would be better to look for help from cognitive psychology. Researchers from sensation (Smith, 1995), perception (Link & Heath, 1975), memory (Ratcliff, 1978), categorization (Ashby, 2000; Nosofsky & Palmeri, 1997), and decision making under uncertainty (Busemeyer & Townsend, 1993) have converged on the common idea that decisions are made by a sequential-sampling process: information and evaluations are sequentially sampled and accumulated over time in parallel for each possible course of action, and the process stops as soon as the strength for one action exceeds a threshold bound.

Sequential-sampling models of decision making originated in research on signal-detection types of decisions. For example, a radar operator may need to decide whether

a blip moving on the screen is an enemy or a friendly agent; or a radiologist may need to decide whether an image should be diagnosed as a harmless tumor or a cancerous node. In laboratory studies of signal detection, highly practiced individuals make decisions under uncertainty (e.g., low signal-to-noise ratio) within short deadlines (e.g., within a second) and real payoffs (e.g., lose $1.00 for each error). Although this situation clearly differs from real-life emergency decisions, the basic theoretical ideas may still be applicable.

The early versions of signal-detection theory (Green & Swets, 1966) were static and assumed that a decision was based on a fixed sample of information. These early models were effective for describing how hits (correctly responding signal) and false alarms (incorrectly responding signal) varied as a function of signal strength, prior probabilities, and payoffs. However, these early models failed to account for speed-accuracy trade-offs, as they provided no mechanism for predicting choice-response time. The subsequent development of sequential-sampling models (Luce, 1986; Vickers, 1979) provided a dynamic extension of signal-detection theory, which accounted not only for hit and false-alarm rates but also for choice-response time and the relation between speed and accuracy.

The sequential-sampling model of decision making is quite different from the recognition-primed decision model in two important ways. First, several courses of action are evaluated in a parallel competition over time for selection rather than serially. Second, situation assessment dynamically interacts with decision making. The assessment process does not run independently until completion; rather, it can terminate early or late during processing depending on the relative strengths of the competing alternatives. Let us analyze a real-life example to see how a sequential-sampling model of decision making differs from the recognition-primed decision model.

An experienced motorcyclist is riding cross-country on his motorcycle, cruising around eighty kilometers per hour down a two-lane state highway when he comes twenty-five meters behind a truck, loaded down with old car tires, traveling in the same direction. The highway is in poor condition, filled with potholes left by snowplows from the previous winter. The truck bumps into of one of these pits, causing a tire to somersault out of the truck and land flat on the road, directly in the motorcyclist's path. Thus, the motorcyclist faces an emergency situation, in which he very quickly generates three potential plans of action: (a) drive straight over the tire, (b) swerve to the side, and (c) slam on the brakes.[1]

Now, the standard operating procedure for most motorists in this situation is to slam on the breaks, but the motorcyclist notices that there was a line of cars following closely, and he could get hit from behind. He could also swerve to the side, but he noticed that the road had no shoulder, and an abrupt turn could topple the bike. The only remaining option under consideration is to drive straight over the tire, but his chain may get caught, causing the bike to flip over. These and many other thoughts and feelings race through his head during the brief second in which he must make a decision.

The basic ideas behind the sequential-sampling model for this example can be understood by considering Figure 16.1. The horizontal axis of the figure represents time, and the vertical axis represents the strength of preference. Each trajectory shows the preference strength for an action across time. The zero time point marks the onset of the decision process (i.e., the onset of the emergency situation). The top flat line represents the threshold bound (located at .70 in the figure; i.e., the strength of preference that an action needs to exceed to make a decision). Note that action C (slam on brakes) begins with a positive bias because this is the standard operating procedure for this type of emergency; actions A and B start at lower initial values because they are more unconventional.

As the deliberation process unfolds, evaluations start pouring into the decision maker's mind. In this example, evaluations

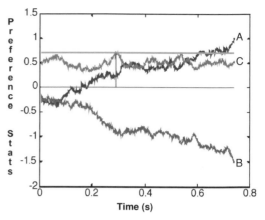

Figure 16.1. Example of the decision process for the motorcyclist's decision. Horizontal axis is time, and vertical axis is preference, and each trajectory represents an action. The top flat line is the threshold bound.

favoring action A (drive straight over) steadily overcome action C (slam on brakes), and action B (swerve) is driven systematically downward in preference. Before 250 ms, action C dominates the race; actions A and C strongly compete at 350 ms; but after 600 ms, action A overcomes action C. However, the threshold is set to a low criterion, allowing it to be reached for the first time by action C at 250 ms, and so action C is executed at this moment (for this example).

Notice that this description of the decision process is quite different from that given by the recognition-primed decision model. According to the latter, the rider would spend most of his time making a situation assessment and would not even consider actions until the situation-assessment process was complete. In contrast, the sequential-sampling model allows situation assessment to feed on-line into action evaluation. It can stop early if there is a sufficiently strong preference to warrant action, or it can continue longer if necessary to more clearly discriminate the competing options.

According to the recognition-primed model, once the situation was assessed, a single action that matches the situation is activated. The action that best matches this particular situation would be to slam on the brakes, which is the standard operating procedure for this kind of situation for most drivers. Only if the evaluation of the first action failed to exceed a threshold would another action be considered. Thus, actions are evaluated in a serial manner, and very likely only the first action is considered at all. This contrasts sharply with the sequential-sampling model in which all three actions are retrieved simultaneously, and all three dynamically compete over time in a race for the threshold bound to be selected.

The threshold bound has a crucial function in the sequential-sampling process. It determines the strength of preference required before making a decision. If this is set to a very low value, then very little strength is needed to make the decision. For example, if the threshold was set to 1.0 instead of .70, then action A would be selected a little after 750 ms. Setting the threshold to a high value requires more information to be processed and longer average decision times. Thus, the threshold is used to control speed-accuracy trade-offs. Short deadlines would require low thresholds to make quick decisions, but high stakes would push the threshold up higher to avoid making fast errors. Impulsive decision makers tend to use a low threshold and act with little thought, whereas careful decision makers tend to use a higher threshold and spend more time in thought before acting. In short, the threshold is a parameter used to control the average amount of time spent on making a decision.

A threshold parameter is also used in the recognition-primed model, but it serves a different purpose. Rather than controlling the length of time spent on situation assessment, it determines the likelihood of choosing the first action that matches the situation. If the threshold is very high, then the first action is likely to be passed up even if it is the best. If the threshold is very low, then the first action is likely to be chosen even if it is actually the worst. Thus, increasing the threshold does increase decision time, but it does not necessarily increase accuracy in the recognition-primed decision model.

Despite the differences mentioned between the two models, they can mimic each other under certain circumstances. Suppose one used the sequential-sampling process to make decisions. If there is a strong bias for the standard operating procedure for a given situation, and if the threshold bound is set very low under extreme time pressure, then the sequential-sampling model behaves very much like the recognition-primed decision model. For in this case, it is very likely that the sequential-sampling model will select the initially favored action for a particular situation.

There is a simple empirical test that can be performed to distinguish these two models. The sequential-sampling model predicts that the average amount of time required to make a decision depends not only on the action that is chosen but also on the nature of the action that was not chosen. If the discriminability is high (i.e., the incoming information strongly and consistently favors one action over another), then a decision will tend to be made very quickly; but if the discriminability is low (i.e., the incoming information inconsistently or weakly favors one action over another), then a decision will tend to be made more slowly. In short, average decision time is inversely related to discriminability between the competing actions. In contrast, the recognition prime model assumes that actions are evaluated serially, and the time required to evaluate a given action depends only on the comparison of this action with a threshold, and not on the strength of other possible competing actions. In laboratory experiments using signal-detection-type tasks, the evidence clearly indicates that decision time is inversely related to discriminability between competing options (see Luce, 1986; Vickers, 1979). However, this finding may be restricted to choices between a small number of competing options, and it may not be true for situations that provide a very large number of choices (e.g., choosing a move in chess; see Klein, 1989).

This brings us to ask, Under what conditions might one expect the sequential-sampling process versus a recognition-primed decision process to be used in naturalistic decisions? In the motorcyclist example, only a very small number of competing actions are immediately available, and there is a great deal of conflict among the competing actions. This is very likely to be a situation in which a sequential-sampling type of deliberation process is needed to separate out one option from a few strong competitors. However, consider for example searching through a very large set of possibilities, such as an escape route in an emergency with many possible exits. Here a serial search through options until one exceeds a threshold is a more likely description of the process. There is a growing literature examining stopping rules that individuals use to serially search through large option sets (e.g., see Bearden, Murphey, & Rapoport, 2005; for a review, see Diederich, 2003).

3. Decision-Field Theory

Figure 16.1 provides only a descriptive illustration of how a sequential-sampling decision process works. To get a clearer idea, we will provide a more formal specification of a theory, decision-field theory,[2] which was specifically designed for decision making under uncertainty with time stress (Busemeyer & Townsend, 1993; Roe, Busemeyer, & Townsend, 2001). However, we should mention that there are also other competing theories that provide alternate dynamic accounts of the decision-making process (see, e.g., Holyoak & Simon, 1999; Usher & McClelland, 2004).

Consider the motorcyclist's decision once again, and for simplicity, suppose that there are four possible outcomes that could result from each action: (c_1) a safe maneuver without damage or injury; (c_2) laying the motorcycle down and damaging the motorcycle but escaping with minor cuts and bruises; (c_3) crashing into another vehicle, damaging the motorcycle, and suffering serious injury; and (c_4) flipping the motorcycle over and getting killed. In the motorcyclist's opinion, driving straight over the tire (action A) is very risky, with high possibilities for the extreme consequences, c_1 and c_4. Swerving

(action B) is more likely to produce consequence c_2, and slamming on the brakes (action C) is more likely to produce consequence c_3. The affective evaluation of the jth consequence is symbolized as m_j, which is a real number that represents the decision maker's personal feelings about each consequence, such that a higher m_j is evaluated as a better consequence (clearly $m_1 > m_2 > m_3 > m_4$ in this example).

Figure 16.2 provides a connectionist interpretation of decision-field theory for this example. The affective evaluations shown on the far left are the inputs to this network. At any moment in time, the decision maker anticipates the consequences of each action, which produces a momentary evaluation, $U_i(t)$, for action i, shown as the first layer of nodes in Figure 16.2. This momentary evaluation is an attention weighted average of the affective evaluation of each consequence: $U_i(t) = \Sigma W_{ij}(t) \cdot m_j$. The attention weight, $W_{ij}(t)$ for consequence j produced by action i at time t, is assumed to fluctuate according to a stationary stochastic process. This reflects the idea that attention is shifting from moment to moment, causing changes in the anticipated consequences of each action across time. For example, at one moment in time the decision maker may believe he can successfully drive straight over the tire, but at the next moment he may change his mind and fear that the tire will get entangled with the motorcycle chain.

The momentary evaluation of each action is compared with other actions to form a valence for each action at each moment, $v_i(t) = U_i(t) - U(t)$, where $U(t)$ equals the average across all the momentary actions. The valence represents the momentary advantage or disadvantage of each action, and this is shown as the second layer of nodes in Figure 16.2. If the decision maker is being attracted to one action by a positive valence, then he or she must be repelled from other actions by negative valences, so that the total valence balances out to zero. All the actions cannot become attractive simultaneously.

Finally, the valences are the inputs to a dynamic system that integrates the valences

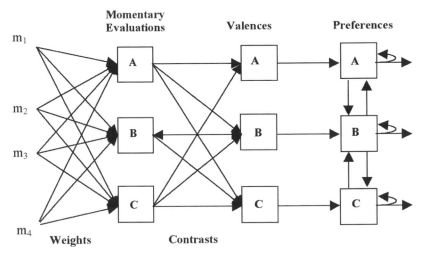

Figure 16.2. Connectionist interpretation of decision-field theory for the motorcyclist's example.

over time to generate the output preference states. The output preference state for action i at time t is symbolized as $P_i(t)$, which is represented by the last layer of nodes in Figure 16.2 (and plotted as the trajectories in Figure 16.1). The dynamic system is described by the following linear stochastic difference equation:

$$P_i(t + h) = \sum s_{ij} \cdot P_j(t) + v_i(t + h), \qquad (1)$$

where h is a small time step in the deliberation process. The positive self-feedback coefficient, $s_{ii} = s > 0$, controls the memory for past input valences for a preference state. The negative lateral feedback coefficients, $s_{ij} = s_{ji} < 0$ for $i \neq j$, produce competition among actions so that the strong inhibit the weak. The magnitudes of the lateral inhibitory coefficients are assumed to be an increasing function of the similarity between choice options. These lateral inhibitory coefficients are important for explaining context effects on preference, which are described later.

The initial state of preference, $P_i(0)$, represents the effect of past experience on the current decision. In the example shown in Figure 16.1, the option representing the standard operating procedure for a decision may start with a positive bias. The initial state can

also reflect the status quo or default option. It is generally assumed that the initial preference states sum to zero, so that positive initial biases must be offset by negative initial biases.

Are dynamic models of decision making, such as decision-field theory, radically different from the traditional expected utility model? To answer this question, it is informative to analyze the simple binary choice case in which the decision maker must choose between action A and action B (let us set $h = 1$ for simplification). In this simple case, Equation 1 implies the following:

$$[P_A(t + 1) - P_B(t + 1)] = \alpha[P_A(t) - P_B(t)] + [U_A(t + 1) - U_B(t + 1)], \qquad (2)$$

where $\alpha = (s_{11} - s_{21})$ and $0 < \alpha < 1$. The solution to this difference equation is

$$[P_A(t) - P_B(t)] = \alpha^{t+1}[P_A(0) - P_B(0)] + \sum_{\tau=1}^{t} \alpha^{t-\tau}[U_A(\tau) - U_B(\tau)]. \qquad (3)$$

The stochastic element $U_i(t)$ can be broken down into two parts: its expectation and its stochastic residual. The expectation of $U_i(t)$ is given by

$$u_i = E[U_i(t)] = E[\Sigma W_{ij}(t) \cdot m_j]$$
$$= \Sigma E[W_{ij}(t)] \cdot m_j = \Sigma W_{ij} \cdot m_j, \quad (4)$$

where $w_{ij} = E[W_{ij}(t)]$ is the mean attention weight or decision weight, as it is called in traditional decision theory. The last expression on the right-hand side of Equation 4 is the same formula that defines the weighted utility of an action according to modern decision theories (see, e.g., Tversky & Kahneman, 1992). Therefore we can define the residual as $\varepsilon_i(t) = [U_i(t) - u_i]$. Inserting $U_i(t) = [u_i + \varepsilon_i(t)]$ into Equation 3 produces

$$[P_A(t) - P_B(t)]$$
$$= \alpha^{t+1}[P_A(0) - P_B(0)] + \sum_{\tau=1}^{t} \alpha^{t-\tau}(u_A - u_B)$$
$$+ \sum_{\tau=1}^{t} \alpha^{t-\tau}[\varepsilon_A(\tau) - \varepsilon_B(\tau)],$$

which can be simplified as follows:

$$[P_A(t) - P_B(t)]$$
$$= \alpha^{t+1} bias + \left(\frac{1 - \alpha^{t+1}}{1 - \alpha}\right) \cdot (u_A - u_B)$$
$$+ error(t). \quad (5)$$

The bottom line, according to Equation 5, is that the difference in preference states evolves from an initial bias toward the difference in expected utilities over time (plus sampling error). Thus, there is a direct connection between the difference in expected utility and the difference in preference states of decision-field theory. Both models share a common set of parameters: the decision weights, w_{ij}, representing the belief that an action will produce a consequence, and the values, m_j, of the consequences. Decision-field theory also includes three new parameters: the initial bias $[P_A(0) - P_B(0)]$, the growth-rate parameter α, and the variance of the residual error. The variance of the residual is important for explaining the probabilistic nature of choice behavior

(Busemeyer & Townsend, 1993), the growth-rate parameter is important for explaining changes in strength of preference strength as a function of deliberation time (see Busemeyer, 1985), and the initial bias is important for producing reversals (for examples of bias under time pressure, see Diederich, 2003).

In summary, we examined a claim that naturalistic decisions required a completely new type of decision theory. Next, we argued that sequential-sampling theory, which assumes a dynamic interaction between situation assessment and decision processes, provides a viable explanation for many naturalistic decisions. Finally, we showed that sequential-sampling models, such as decision-field theory, can be viewed as dynamic extensions of the traditional decision theories. Therefore, sequential-sampling models provide a theoretical bridge between traditional decision theories and naturalistic decisions.

4. Situated Cognition in the Laboratory: Context-Dependent Preferences

Effects of choice context on preference are not limited to naturalistic situations. On the contrary, basic research with simple choice problems provides compelling evidence that our preferences are constructed in a highly context-dependent manner (Payne, Bettman, & Johnson, 1992). Consider the following experiment by Tversky and Kahneman (1991) that was designed to test a rational principle of choice called "independence from irrelevant alternatives." According to this principle, if option X is favored over option Y in the choice context that includes option R_x, then option X should also be preferred over option Y in the choice context that includes option R_y.

The basic ideas of the experiment are illustrated in Figure 16.3, where each letter shown in the figure represents a choice option described by two attributes; for example, consumer products that vary in price and quality. In this case, option X is low on price and quality, whereas option

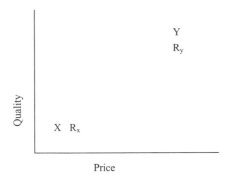

Figure 16.3. Illustration of stimuli used to produce reference-point effects. The horizontal axis represents price, the vertical axis represents quality, and each point represents a consumer product.

Y is high on price and quality. When presented with a straight binary choice between options X and Y, the options are (approximately) equally favored. The main theoretical question concerns the addition of a third option to the set, which is used to manipulate the choice context.

The critical context manipulation in this experiment was the introduction of a third option, called the "reference option," represented by either option R_x or option R_y. Under one condition, participants were asked to imagine that they currently owned the commodity R_x, and they were then given a choice of keeping R_x or trading it for either commodity X or commodity Y. From the reference point of R_x, option X has a small advantage on price and no disadvantage on quality, whereas Y has large advantages on quality and large disadvantages on price. Under these conditions, R_x was rarely chosen, and X was favored over Y. Under another condition, participants were asked to imagine that they owned option R_y, and they were then given a choice of keeping R_y or trading it for either X or Y. From the reference point of R_y, Y has a small advantage and no disadvantages, whereas X now has both large advantages and disadvantages. Under this condition, R_y was rarely chosen again, but now Y was favored over X.

In summary, even though the reference options, R_x and R_y, were rarely chosen, they nevertheless changed the choice context,

causing the preference order for X and Y to reverse across the two contexts. This preference reversal violates the rational principle of choice known as independence from irrelevant alternatives. This is just one example violation of this principle, but there are many others (see Roe et al., 2001; Tversky & Simonson, 1993).

What causes these context effects on preferences? Tversky and Kahneman (1991) interpreted this particular result in terms of a loss aversion effect: option X was favored when Y entailed large losses relative to the reference point R_x, but the opposite occurred when X entailed large losses relative to the reference point R_y. But this explanation leaves one to wonder about the mechanism that causes loss aversion.

Decision-field theory provides a dynamic mechanism for explaining the reference-point effect as well as many other context-dependent preference effects (see Busemeyer & Johnson, 2004; Roe et al., 2001). According to decision-field theory, these context effects are generated by the recurrent network shown as the third layer in Figure 16.2. We will skip the mathematical derivations here and simply present the conceptual ideas.

According to decision-field theory, these effects are contrast effects like edge enhancement effects that occur in the retina (alternatively, these effects can be conceptualized in the context of the lateral inhibition occurring within the striatum, part of the basal ganglia, during the process of action selection; see Frank, 2005; Wickens, 1997). The inferior reference option makes the closely related attractive option shine. First, consider the choice set that includes options X, Y, and R_x. Recall that according to decision-field theory, the lateral inhibitory links in the network depend on the similarity between options. Note that the reference point R_x is very similar to X, and so the lateral inhibitory link between these two is strong, whereas R_x is very dissimilar to Y, and so the lateral inhibitory link between these two is weak. Also note that R_x always experiences a disadvantage with respect to option X. This arrangement of options then produces the following dynamics: as processing time passes, option R_x is slowly driven down toward a negative preference state; this negative preference feeds back through a negative lateral inhibitory link to produce an enhancement or bolstering of option X. In other words, the relatively poor reference option, R_x, makes its close neighbor, option X, shine brighter. The distant option Y does not experience this enhancement because the lateral inhibitory link is too weak. Therefore the preference state for X gradually dominates Y. When the choice context is changed to include X, Y, and R_y, the same reasoning holds, but now option Y is bolstered by being close to a relatively poor reference R_y.

The preceding explanation for context-dependent preferences depends on a dynamic inhibitory mechanism that takes time to build up. Thus, decision-field theory predicts that these context effects should get stronger as deliberation time gets longer. In contrast, if these effects were caused by the use of simple heuristics to save time and effort, then the opposite is predicted – context effects should get larger with shorter deliberation times that force individuals to fall back on simple heuristic rules to save time. In fact, past research has found that the context effects increase with longer deliberation times, consistent with the predictions of a dynamic model and contrary to a heuristic choice model (see Dhar, Nowlis, & Sherman, 2000; Simonson, 1989).

5. Concluding Comments

The majority of decision research is based on simple laboratory experiments, and modern decision theories have been built on the basis of these findings. Recently, various groups of researchers have questioned the usefulness of these theories when applied to real-life situations. Three related programs of research have examined judgment or decision making through what could be called a "situated cognition" perspective. Social judgment theory focuses on expert judgments using environmentally provided cue-criterion relations. Decision analysis endeavors to provide people with optimized decision tools for real-life decisions in order to improve the quality of these decisions. Naturalistic decision making represents a paradigm in which descriptive models of dynamic, complex, high-uncertainty, high-stakes, and real-life decision situations are sought. Furthermore, in these complex, real-life situations there is not enough time or computational resources to systematically evaluate all the options. Consequently, naturalistic decision researchers claim that new theories and methods of research are needed.

In this chapter, we have attempted to address these concerns, specifically those of naturalistic decision researchers, through the use of dynamic, as opposed to static, tools. Rather than reject traditional decision theory and research when we enter naturalistic situations, we have tried to argue that a dynamic perspective (see Port & van Gelder, 1995; van Gelder, 1998) provides a foundation for building bridges between traditional decision theories and naturalistic decisions. Sequential-sampling models were developed from cognitive psychology to understand real-time cognitive processes observed in simple laboratory experiments. According to these models, decision makers make an online assessment of the situation that interacts with the evaluation of competing options over time; likewise, information accumulates in real time and decision times are influenced by a threshold for accrued information. We have argued that dynamic theories of decision making have the power to explain the basic findings from laboratory experiments, such as context-dependent preferences, as well as new phenomena that arise in the study of naturalistic decisions.

Notes

1   This incident happened to the first author, who decided to drive straight over the tire and survived to tell this story.

2   The name *decision-field theory* reflects the influence of Kurt Lewin's (1936) field theory of conflict.

References

Anzai, Y. (1984). Cognitive control of real-time event-driven systems. *Cognitive Science, 8,* 221–254.

Ashby, F. G. (2000). A stochastic version of general recognition theory. *Journal of Mathematical Psychology, 44,* 310–329.

Beardon, J. N., Murphey, R. O., Rapoport, A. (2005). A multiattribute extension of the secretary problem: Theory and experiments. *Journal of Mathematical Psychology, 49,* 410–422.

Brehmer, B. (1992). Dynamic decision making: Human control of complex systems. *Acta Psychologica, 81,* 211–241.

Brehmer, B., & Allard, R. (1991). Real-time dynamic decision making: Effects of task complexity and feedback delays. In J. Rasmussen, B. Brehmer, & J. Leplat (Eds.), *Distributed decision making: Cognitive models for cooperative work* (pp. 319–334). Chichester, UK: Wiley.

Brunswik, E. (1952). *The conceptual framework of psychology.* Chicago: University of Chicago Press.

Busemeyer, J. R. (1985). Decision making under uncertainty: A comparison of simple scalability, fixed sample, and sequential sampling models. *Journal of Experimental Psychology, 11,* 538–564.

Busemeyer, J. R., & Johnson, J. G. (2004). Computational models of decision making. In D. J. Koehler & N. Harvey (Eds.), *Blackwell handbook of judgment and decision making.* Oxford, UK: Blackwell.

Busemeyer, J. R., & Townsend, J. T. (1993). Decision field theory: A dynamic-cognitive approach to decision making in an uncertain environment. *Psychological Review, 100,* 432–459.

Clemens, R. (1996). *Making hard decisions: An introduction to decision analysis* (2nd ed.). Boston: PWS-Kent.

Dhami, M. K., Hertwig, R., & Hoffrage, U. (2004). The role of representative design in an ecological approach to cognition. *Psychological Bulletin, 130*(6), 959–988.

Dhar, R., Nowlis, S. M., & Sherman, S. J. (2000). Trying hard or hardly trying: An analysis of context effects in choice. *Journal of Consumer Psychology, 9,* 189–200.

Diederich, A. (2003). MDFT account of decision making under time pressure. *Psychonomic Bulletin and Review, 10*(1), 157–166.

Dienes, Z., & Fahey, R. (1995). Role of specific instances in controlling a dynamic system. *Journal of Experimental Psychology: Learning, Memory, & Cognition, 21,* 848–862.

Edwards, W. (1962). Dynamic decision theory and probabilistic information processing. *Human Factors, 4,* 59–73.

Ericsson, K. A., & Simon, H. A. (1984). *Protocol analysis: Verbal reports as data.* Cambridge, MA: MIT Press.

Fischoff, B., & Slovic, P. (1978). *A little learning: Confidence in multicue judgment tasks.* Eugene, OR: Decision Research.

Frank, M. J. (2005). Dynamic dopamine modulation in the basal ganglia: A neurocomputational account of cognitive deficits in medicated and nonmedicated Parkinsonism. *Journal of Cognitive Neuroscience, 17*(1), 51–72.

Gibson, F., Fichman, M., & Plaut, D. C. (1997). Learning in dynamic decision tasks: Computational model and empirical evidence. *Organizational Behavior and Human Performance, 71,* 1–35.

Gilboa, I., & Schmeidler, D. (1995). Case-based theory. *Quarterly Journal of Economics, 110,* 607–639.

Goldstein, W. M., & Weber, E. U. (1995). Content and discontent: Indications and implications of domain specificity in preferential decision making. In J. R. Busemeyer et al. (Eds.), *The psychology of learning and motivation: Decision making from a cognitive perspective* (Vol. 32, pp. 82–136). San Diego, CA: Academic Press.

Gonzalez, C., Lerch, J. F., & Lebiere, C. (2003). Instance-based learning in dynamic decision making. *Cognitive Science, 27,* 591–635.

Green, D. M., & Swets, J. A. (1966). *Signal detection theory and psychophysics.* Oxford, UK: Wiley.

Hammond, K. R., Hamm, R. M., Grassia, J., & Pearson, T. (1987). Direct comparison of the efficacy of intuitive and analytical cognition in expert judgment. *IEEE Transactions on Systems, Man, & Cybernetics, 17*(5), 753–770.

Hammond, K. R., Stewart, T. R., Brehmer, B., & Steinmann, D. O. (1975). Social judgment theory. In M. Kaplan & S. Schwartz (Eds.), *Human judgment and decision processes* (pp. 271–312). New York: Academic Press.

Hogarth, R. M. (1981). Beyond discrete biases: Functional and dysfunctional aspects of judgmental heuristics. *Psychological Bulletin, 90,* 197–217.

Holyoak, K. J., & Simon, D. (1999). Bidirectional reasoning in decision making by constraint satisfaction. *Journal of Experimental Psychology: General, 128*(1), 3–31.

Jagacinski, R. J., & Hah, S. (1988). Progression-regression effects in tracking repeated patterns. *Journal of Experimental Psychology: Human Perception and Performance, 14,* 77–88.

Jagacinski, R. J., & Miller, R. A. (1978). Describing the human operator's internal model of a dynamic system. *Human Factors, 20,* 425–433.

Kaplan, M. (1996). *Decision theory as philosophy.* Cambridge: Cambridge University Press.

Keeney, R. L., & Raiffa, H. (1976). *Decisions with multiple objectives: Preferences and value trade-offs.* New York: Wiley.

Kirlik, A., Miller, R. A., & Jagacinski, R. J. (1993). Supervisory control in a dynamic and uncertain environment: A process model of skilled human environment interaction. *IEEE Transactions on Systems, Man, and Cybernetics, 23,* 929–952.

Klein, G. A. (1989). Recognition primed decisions. In W. B. Rouse (Ed.), *Advances in man-machine systems research* (Vol. 5, pp. 47–92). Greenwich, CT: JAI Press.

LeBoeuf, R. A., & Shafir, E. (2001). Problems and methods in naturalistic decision-making research. *Journal of Behavioral Decision Making, 14*(5), 373–375.

Levin, I. P., Louviere, J. J., Schepanski, A. A., & Norman, K. L. (1983). External validity tests of laboratory studies of information integration. *Organizational Behavior & Human Performance, 31*(2), 173–193.

Lewin, K. (1936). *Principles of topological psychology.* New York: McGraw-Hill.

Link, S. W., & Heath, R. A. (1975). A sequential theory of psychological discrimination. *Psychometrika, 40,* 77–111.

Lipshitz, R., Klein, G., Orasanu, J., & Salas, E. (2001). Taking stock of naturalistic decision making. *Journal of Behavioral Decision Making, 14*(5), 331–352.

Loftus, E. F. (2003). Make-believe memories. *American Psychologist, 58*(11), 867–873.

Luce, R. D. (1986). *Response times: Their role in inferring elementary mental organization.* New York: Oxford University Press.

Luce, R. D. (2000). *Utility of gains and losses:*

Measurement-theoretical and experimental approaches. Mahwah, NJ: Lawrence Erlbaum.

Nisbett, R. E., & Wilson, T. D. (1977). Telling more than we can know: Verbal reports on mental processes. *Psychological Review, 84*(3), 231–259.

Nosofsky, R. M., & Palmeri, T. J. (1997). An exemplar-based random walk model of speeded classification. *Psychological Review, 104,* 226–300.

Payne, J. W., Bettman, J. R., & Johnson, E. J. (1992). Behavioral decision research: A constructive processing perspective. *Annual Review of Psychology, 43,* 87–131.

Port, R. F., & van Gelder, T. (Eds.). (1995). *Mind as motion: Explorations in the dynamics of cognition.* Cambridge, MA: MIT Press.

Rapoport, A. (1975). Research paradigms for studying dynamic decision behavior. In D. Wendt & C. Vlek (Eds.), *Utility, probability, and human decision making* (pp. 347–369). Dordrecht, The Netherlands: Reidel.

Ratcliff, R. (1978). A theory of memory retrieval. *Psychological Review, 85,* 59–108.

Roe, R. M., Busemeyer, J. R., & Townsend, J. T. (2001). Multi-alternative decision field theory: A dynamic connectionist model of decision-making. *Psychological Review, 108,* 370–392.

Simon, H. A. (1955). A behavioral model of rational choice. *Quarterly Journal of Economics, 69,* 99–118.

Simonson, I. (1989). Choice based on reasons: The case of attraction and compromise effects. *Journal of Consumer Research, 16,* 158–174.

Smith, P. L. (1995). Psychophysically principled models of visual simple reaction time. *Psychological Review, 102*(3), 567–593.

Sterman, J. D. (1994). Learning in and about complex systems. *System Dynamics Review, 10,* 291–330.

Tversky, A., & Kahneman, D. (1991). Loss aversion in riskless choice: A reference dependent model. *Quarterly Journal of Economics, 106,* 1039–1061.

Tversky, A., & Kahneman, D. (1992). Advances in prospect theory: Cumulative representations of uncertainty. *Journal of Risk and Uncertainty, 5,* 297–323.

Tversky, A., & Simonson, I. (1993). Context-dependent preferences. *Management Science, 39,* 1179–1189.

Usher, M., & McClelland, J. L. (2004). Loss aversion and inhibition in dynamical models of multialternative choice. *Psychological Review, 111*(3), 757–769.

van Gelder, T. (1998). The dynamical hypothesis in cognitive science. *Behavioral and Brain Sciences, 21,* 1–14.

Vickers, D. (1979). *Decision processes in visual perception.* New York: Academic Press.

von Winterfeldt, D., & Edwards, W. (1986). *Decision analysis and behavioral research.* Cambridge: Cambridge University Press.

Wickens, J. (1997). Basal ganglia: Structure and computations. *Network: Computation in Neural Systems, 8,* R77-R109.

Yates, J. F. (2004, March/April). "Let's just go with it.": The perils of decision neglect. *Ivey Business Journal.* Retrieved from http://www.iveybusinessjournal.com/article.asp?intArticle_id=472

Yates, J. F., Veinott, E. S., & Patalano, A. L. (2003). Hard decisions, bad decisions: On decision quality and decision aiding. In S. L. Schneider & J. L. Shanteau (Eds.), *Emerging perspectives in judgment and decision making research* (pp. 13–63). New York: Cambridge University Press.

You, G. (1989). *Disclosing the decision-maker's internal model and control policy in a dynamic decision task using a system control paradigm.* Unpublished master's thesis, Purdue University.

Zsambok, C. E., & Klein, G. (1997). *Naturalistic decision making: Expertise, research and applications.* Hillsdale, NJ: Lawrence Erlbaum.

CHAPTER 17

Situating Rationality

Ecologically Rational Decision Making with Simple Heuristics

Henry Brighton and Peter M. Todd

1. Introduction

Many within cognitive science believe that rational principles rooted in probability theory and logic provide valuable insight into the cognitive systems of humans and animals. More than this, some say that rational principles, such as Bayesianism, algorithmic information theory, and logic, not only provide elegant and formally well understood frameworks for thinking about cognition but also are the very principles governing thought itself, guiding inferences and decisions about the world (e.g., Chater & Vitányi, 2003; Feldman, 2003). It is not difficult to see why ascribing such principles to the cognitive system is a tempting and desirable goal: if correct, these principles would provide universal normative laws governing the cognitive system. Even faced with the diversity of tasks and environments handled by the cognitive system, a valid universal principle would have the advantage of providing a theoretical handle with which to grasp the range of cognition in a unified manner. In contrast, situated theories of cogni-

tion take the specific and concrete details of the interaction between mind and environment to matter significantly, so much so that seeking universal principles of rationality is seen as one of the primary wrong turns in the path of traditional approaches to understanding cognition (e.g., Smith, 1999).

Other approaches to cognition find similar fault with the search for universal mechanisms or all-powerful inferential machinery. The recently developed view of ecological rationality places a strong focus on the structural properties of environments, and takes a structure-specific, and, as we will show in this chapter, situated approach to the study of cognitive processes. Ecological rationality emerges when simple, cognitively plausible heuristic processes exploit specific environmental characteristics to make adaptive choices in particular circumstances (Gigerenzer, Todd, & ABC Research Group, 1999). Adaptive choices are those that help an organism function successfully in its environment. Rather than view the mind as a general-purpose processor endowed with the considerable computational resources demanded by classical notions of rational inference, we instead explore the possibility that the mind is more like a mixed bag of cognitive processes, each working within the limitations of the cognitive system, and each tuned to specific structures occurring in natural environments. We term this mixed bag of simple heuristics the *adaptive toolbox* (e.g., Gigerenzer & Selten, 2001). In section 3 we firm up this metaphor by providing examples of simple heuristics, and we discuss work that demonstrates, through computational modeling and experimental studies, that these heuristics are both plausible and often more effective than traditional models of inference.

In section 4 we address our main concern: situating rationality in such a way that the specific, concrete, engaged, and located nature of human cognition is given due significance. We argue that classical visions of rationality fail to consider the computational limitations of the cognitive system and the importance of the role of cognitive exploitation of environment structure. On this view, normative theories derived from classical notions of rationality prove limited in their ability to capture the specific nature of how the cognitive system interacts adaptively with the environment in inference and decision-making tasks. Although systems of logic, for example, can be tailored to specific tasks and environmental contexts (e.g., Stenning & van Lambalgen, 2004), the issue of how the cognitive system might plausibly process information to achieve logical consistency, and whether such a task is computationally feasible, remains unclear. In contrast, we argue that ecological rationality bounds rationality to the world by considering both ecological context and constraints on cognitive processing (Todd & Gigerenzer, 2003). This view of rationality is closely allied with the situated cognition movement, and in section 5 we clarify the ways in which ecological rationality can be understood in terms of the key dimensions of situated approaches proposed by Smith (1999).

2. Mind and Environment: The Terms of the Relationship

In what ways does the environment influence the contents of the mind? A wide range of possibilities exists. For some aspects of the cognitive system it could be that the environment plays an insignificant role in influencing the contents of the mind. The human language faculty, for instance, is thought by some researchers to be shaped not by the environment but by boundary conditions internal to the mind, in the sense that the linguistic system is an optimal solution for meeting the requirements of transforming thought between the conceptual-intentional system and the articulatory-motor system (Chomsky, 1995). According to this view, if we want to understand the language faculty, then it pays not to consider the environment at all, either over evolutionary or ontogenetic timescales. But for many aspects of the cognitive system we cannot ignore the important impact of the environment, and several possible forms of relationship between mind and environment need to be considered. Within psychology, the ecological approach to cognition seeks to understand the terms of such relationships. We begin by considering three metaphors (Todd & Gigerenzer, 2001) that aim to capture some key relationships.

2.1. *Three Kinds of Relationships*

To understand the contents of the mind, we should consider the environment in which it acts and in which it has evolved. This ecological, situated perspective has been promoted within cognitive psychology in particular by Roger Shepard's work (see, e.g., Shepard, 2001, and other papers in the special issue of *Behavioral and Brain Sciences* on Shepard's research and related efforts it has inspired), focusing on a particular vision of how the external world shapes our mental mechanisms. For Shepard (2001), much of perception and cognition is done with mirrors: key aspects of the environment are internalized in the brain "by natural selection specifically to provide a veridical representation of significant objects and events in the external world" (p. 2). In particular, Shepard considers how the cognitive system reflects features of the world, or laws, which support, for example, tracking the movement of objects in Euclidean space. These abstract principles are based "as much (or possibly more) in geometry, probability, and group theory, as in specific, physical facts about concrete, material objects" (Shepard, 2001, p. 601). Thus, the cognitive system possesses deeply internalized, abstract, and universal reflections of physical reality. Shepard's work can be viewed as ecological in that an understanding of mind is taken to be fundamentally dependent on identifying the important properties of the physical world. Yet this view also turns on the contentious issue of the mind representing properties of the world, albeit at a very abstract level. Without entering into arguments over the need for representations of any sort (for a discussion of the key issues, see, e.g., Brooks, 1991; Markman & Dietrich, 2000), we can still question whether assumed representations should be veridical, constructed to accurately reflect the world, or instead be useful in an adaptive sense. In short, whatever the functional role of such representations, this mirrorlike relationship characterizes those properties of mind that are present as a result of an internalization of universal laws governing physical environments.

A less exacting view of internalization can be seen in the work of Egon Brunswik (1955), who proposed a lens model that reconstructs a representation of a distal stimulus on the basis of the current proximal cues (whose availability could vary from one decision situation to the next) along with stored knowledge of the environmental relationships between those perceived cues and the stimulus. These relationships were later usually conceived of as correlations in the field of social judgment theory that followed from Brunswik's work (see Hammond & Stewart, 2001). For Brunswik, the mind models and projects the world more than reflects it (or, as he also put it, mind and world accommodate each other like husband and wife).

Herbert Simon (1990) expressed a still looser coupling between mind and environment: bounded rationality, he said, was shaped by a pair of scissors whose two blades are the characteristics of the task environment and the computational capabilities of the decision maker. Here, computational capabilities refer to sensory, neural, and other mental characteristics that may impose cognitive limitations on, for example, memory and processing. Crucially, these capabilities, when coupled with certain characteristics of the environment, can complement one another. Rather than the mind reflecting or projecting properties of the environment, Simon's scissors metaphor highlights a very different kind of relationship in which properties of mind are viewed as fitting properties of environments in an exploitative and complementary relationship. From this perspective, it is less clear how meaningfully one can characterize the relationship between mind and environment in terms of internalization or representation, as some properties of the mind can be only implicitly related to the environment rather than more directly, as suggested by metaphors of mirror images or projections. Considering this kind of exploitative relationship led Simon (1956) to consider, in the context of decision making, "how simple a set of choice mechanisms we can postulate and still obtain the gross features of observed adaptive choice behavior" (p. 129). This question highlights how an exploitative relationship between mind and environment has implications for the kind of cognitive machinery used by the mind: as Simon and others have since shown, simple, boundedly rational decision mechanisms coupled with the right environmental context can yield adaptive choice behavior that is typically attributed to more complex and information-hungry mechanisms.

2.2. *Appropriate Metaphors for Higher-Level Cognition*

We expect that the mind draws on mechanisms akin to all three tools, mirrors, lenses, and scissors, from its adaptive toolbox

(Gigerenzer & Todd, 1999). The question now becomes, Where can each be used, or where does each different view of situated cognition best apply? In perception, using Shepard's mirror or Brunswik's lens may often be the right way to look at things, but there are also examples in which these tools are inappropriate. Consider the problem of a fielder trying to catch a ball coming down in front of her. The final destination of the ball will be complexly determined by its initial velocity, its spin, the effects of wind all along its path, and other causal factors. But rather than perceive all these characteristics, reflect or model the world, and compute an interception point to aim at, the fielder can use a simple heuristic: fixate on the ball and adjust her speed while running toward it so that her angle of gaze – the angle between the ball and the ground from her eye – remains constant (McLeod & Dienes, 1996). By using this simple gaze heuristic, the fielder will catch the ball while running. No veridical representations or models of the world are needed – just a mechanism that fits to and exploits the relevant structure of the environment; namely, the single cue of gaze angle. How widely such scissors-like heuristics can be found in perception remains to be seen, but some (e.g., Ramachandran, 1990) expect that perception is a bag of tricks like this rather than a box of mirrors.

When we come to higher-order cognition and decision making, our main concern in this chapter, Simon's cutting perspective seems the most appropriate way to extend Shepard's and Brunswik's ecological views. Consider a simple decision rule that has been proposed as a model of human choice: the Take the Best heuristic (Gigerenzer & Goldstein, 1996). To choose between two options on the basis of several cues known about each option, this heuristic says to consider one cue at a time in order of the ecological validity of each (i.e., how often each cue makes correct decisions), and to stop this cue search with the first one that distinguishes between the options and make the final decision using only that cue (we will explain this heuristic in more detail later in the chapter). This "fast and frugal"

heuristic makes decisions about as well as multiple regression in many environments (Czerlinski, Gigerenzer, & Goldstein, 1999) but usually uses far less information (cues) in reaching a decision. It does not incorporate enough knowledge to reasonably be said to reflect the environment, nor even to model it in Brunswik's sense (because it only knows cue order, not exact validities), but it can certainly match and exploit environment structure: when cue importance is distributed in something like an exponentially decreasing manner (as is the case in some environments), Take the Best performs about as well on training data sets as multiple regression or any other linear decision rule (Martignon & Hoffrage, 1999) and generalizes to new data sets even better.

As another example, the QuickEst heuristic for estimating quantities (Hertwig, Hoffrage, & Martignon, 1999) is similarly designed to use only those cues necessary to reach a reasonable inference. QuickEst makes accurate estimates with a minimum of information when the criteria of the objects it operates on follow a J-shaped (power law) distribution, such as the sizes of cities or the number of publications per psychologist. Again this crucial aspect of environment structure is nowhere built into the decision mechanism, but by processing the most important cues in an appropriate order, QuickEst can exploit that structure to great advantage. Neither of these heuristics (which we will describe in more detail in the next section) embodies logical rationality – they do not even consider all the available information – but rather they demonstrate ecological rationality, making adaptive decisions by relying on the structure of the environment.

Why might it be that Simon's scissors could help us understand cognitive mechanisms more than Shepard's mirror? We (and others) suspect that humans often use simple decision-making mechanisms that are built on (and receive their inputs from) much more complex lower-level perceptual mechanisms. For instance, the recognition heuristic, an elementary mechanism for deciding between two options on the basis of which of them are merely recognized, simply uses the binary cue of recognized versus not recognized; however, the computational machinery involved in the lower-level assessment of whether a voice, or face, or name actually is recognized involves considerable complexity (Todd, 1999). If these decision heuristics achieve their simplicity in part by minimizing the amount of information they use, then they are less likely to reflect the external world and more likely to exploit just the important, useful aspects of it, as calculated and distilled by the perceptual system (which may well base its computations on a more reflective representation).

Thus, in extending the search for the imprint of the world on the mind from perception to higher-order cognition, we should probably look less for reflections and more for complementary pairings à la Simon's two scissors blades. This approach to studying environmentally situated decision mechanisms is just what we shall introduce in this chapter. While Simon studied bounded rationality, we use the term *ecological rationality* to emphasize the importance of the match between the structure of information in the environment and the structure of information processing in the mind. In the next section, we introduce the notion of the adaptive toolbox and describe how its contents can be studied, before expanding on some examples of its contents by describing simple ecologically rational decision heuristics. In section 4 we develop further the concept of ecological rationality by discussing how it contrasts with traditional notions of rationality, and why, in the context of the study of mind, ecological rationality is a more appropriate notion when considering aspects of high-level cognition. In section 5 we relate these discussions to the study of situated cognition by framing ecological rationality as a form of situated cognition.

3. The Adaptive Toolbox and Its Contents

It is certainly not the case that all of human behavior is ecologically rational, as defined here. For instance, people can (if given the luxury of sufficient time and training) use more general methods of reasoning according to traditional norms of rationality, such as the tools of logic or probability theory, to come to decisions with little concern for adapting their reasoning to the specific structure of the current task environment. Or people may use simple decision heuristics that try to exploit some features of the environment to allow for cognitive shortcuts, but in the wrong environment, so that biased decision making arises (as studied in the heuristics and biases research tradition; see, e.g., Kahneman, Slovic, & Tversky, 1982). But we propose that much of human decision making is ecologically rational, guided by typically simple decision heuristics that exploit the available structure of the environment to make good choices. Given the right environmental circumstances, these simple methods perform adequately for many tasks and sometimes better than more complex mechanisms. One consequence of this theory is that a single all-purpose decision-making system is no longer the appropriate unit of study, as different tasks call for different simple mechanisms. The idea of the adaptive toolbox leads us to consider a collection of simple mechanisms drawn on by the cognitive system. We view these mechanisms as structure specific rather than domain specific. In contrast to the concept of domain specificity, structure specificity is the ability of a process to deal effectively with informational structures found in environments that may or may not be encountered in multiple domains (e.g., a systematic correlation between recognition knowledge and some criterion of interest, which we discuss herein). These mechanisms are built from basic, cognitively primitive building blocks for information search, stopping the search, and making a decision based on the search's results. How heuristics are constructed using these building blocks, when and why one heuristic is used over another, and how and how well they work in different situations are all key issues confronting this research program. In this section, we give a taste of how these issues are addressed and discuss how this approach can be a productive route to understanding the cognitive system in terms of simple process models tuned to environment structures.

A number of steps are involved in studying the contents of the adaptive toolbox. First, after identifying a particular ecologically important decision domain, we must determine the structure of information available to people in that domain. As Shepard (2001) indicated, this involves discovering the "general properties that characterize the environments in which organisms with advanced visual and locomotor capabilities are likely to survive and reproduce" (p. 581) – these might include power laws governing scale invariance (Bak, 1996; Chater & Brown, 1999) or costs of time and energy in seeking information (Todd, 2001). Shepard (1987) considers only the longest-applying physical laws as stable parts of the environment, avoiding discussion of the biological and social realms that he feels have not been around as long and so will not have exerted as much pressure on our and other animals' evolved cognition. However, we have certainly evolved adaptive responses to these realms of challenges as well, and so we should extend the study of environmentally matched decision heuristics to biological and social domains (as is done within evolutionary psychology; e.g., Barkow, Cosmides, & Tooby, 1992; Buss, 2005). This means we should look for environmental-information regularities that may be internalized to guide our cognition when situated in different evolutionarily important domains, such as predator risk (e.g., Barrett, 2005), knowledge of infection and disease transmission (e.g., Rozin & Fallon, 1987), understanding genetic dynamics (e.g., kin selection; Hamilton, 1996), and social interactions of various types (e.g., on the dynamics of signaling between agents with conflicting interests, see Zahavi & Zahavi, 1997; on mate choice, social exchange, and dominance hierarchies, see Buss, 2005).

With these characteristic environment structures in mind as one half of Simon's scissors, we can look more effectively for the decision mechanisms that form the other matching half. This can involve a further set of steps, as follows:

1. Investigating, through simulation, candidate models of cognitive processes built from elementary processing abilities such as search and recognition; to achieve this, a model selection criterion is required (e.g., performance criteria such as predictive accuracy, frugality of information use). These yardsticks set the scene for comparisons with other models.

2. Identifying if and when these heuristics perform well in certain environments, and what the characteristics of these environments are, often using analytic methods. Is it possible to give precise environment-structure conditions for good or poor performance of the heuristics? Do these conditions match those of typical environments inhabited by humans?

3. With an understanding of how the model and the environment (or task) structure match, carrying out empirical studies to see if humans use these processes in appropriate situations.

The use of elementary processing abilities to guide the construction of candidate models reflects a commitment to bottom-up design. One consequence of this approach is that it leads to simple and testable models with few parameters and therefore makes for a more transparent relation between theory and data. Another consequence, which affects a core concern for the study of ecological rationality, is that the resultant cognitive models, by virtue of their simplicity and close reliance on fundamental processing abilities, are more likely to be cognitively plausible. This approach adopts the view that functioning cognitive models can be built with nontrivial consequences without needing to be monolithic, generally applicable, and computationally complex. In short, robust cognitive processing is achieved with simple and ecologically targeted mental heuristics. The concept of ecological rationality and the adaptive tool-box, in some respects, is close in spirit to Anderson's rational analysis, where a consideration of the structure of the environment constrains the development of cognitive models, and a focus on the plausibility of the cognitive models then steers future development (Anderson, 1990; Oaksford & Chater, 1998). However, rational analysis, in contrast to the approach explored here, places less of an emphasis on bottom-up design. One consequence of this difference is that the adaptive toolbox leads to a consideration of multiple simple models rather than fewer, more complex models.

What is in the adaptive toolbox? Several classes of simple heuristics for making different types of decisions in a variety of domains have been investigated (see, e.g., Gigerenzer et al., 1999; Kahneman et al., 1982; Payne, Bettman, & Johnson, 1993; Simon, 1990), including ignorance-based heuristics that make decisions based on a systematic lack of information, one-reason heuristics that make a choice as soon as a single reason is found on which to base that choice, elimination heuristics that whittle down a set of choices using as few pieces of information as possible until a single choice is determined, and satisficing heuristics that search through a sequence of options until a good-enough possibility is found. Other tools are also present, and more await discovery. Here we present three examples of the heuristic tools in the toolbox.

3.1. Paired Comparison Using the Recognition Heuristic

The capacity for recognition is common to many species. The most basic cognitive heuristic we will focus on exploits this capacity to make inductive inferences. Given the task of deciding which of two objects in the world scores higher on some criterion of interest, the recognition heuristic can provide a quick and robust decision procedure by exploiting a lack of knowledge. If one of the objects being considered is recognized and the other is not, then the recognition heuristic tells us to judge the

recognized object as scoring higher on the criterion. For example, given the names of two tennis players, the recognition heuristic simplifies the task of deciding which of these two tennis players is most likely to win the next Grand Slam tournament: if we only recognize one of the players and not the other, then the recognition heuristic tells us to pick the player we have heard of (Pachur & Biele, 2007). Similarly, given the task of choosing which of two cities has a higher population, the recognition heuristic tells us to pick the city we have heard of over the one we have not (Goldstein & Gigerenzer, 1999, 2002). Clearly, the appropriate use of this heuristic depends on (a) applicability, because to apply the recognition heuristic certain conditions must be met, and (b) validity, because the ability to apply the heuristic does not necessarily imply that it will lead to accurate inferences. Specifically, the recognition heuristic is applicable only when the decision maker has an intermediate amount of (recognition) knowledge, not complete knowledge or complete ignorance (which would render the recognition heuristic unusable). And this heuristic is only valid when the partial recognition knowledge is systematic; that is, correlated with the criterion on which the decision is being made – for example, given that winning tennis players are talked about in person and in media more than losing ones, more people will recognize the best players, meaning that recognition is correlated with past success, and hence, presumably, with future success as well. Both these conditions place restrictions on the kinds of environments in which the recognition heuristic will perform well, and defining such environments and determining how the heuristic operates in them are precisely the sorts of questions addressed and explored by the study of ecological rationality.

Using simple heuristics can also lead to surprising outcomes, which the ecological rationality framework can predict and explain. For example, when knowledge about and recognition of the objects in the environment (e.g., cities) is positively correlated with the criterion of interest (e.g., population), then the recognition heuristic can lead an individual with less knowledge to make more reliable decisions than a person with more knowledge. This less-is-more effect has been confirmed in simulations and demonstrated in experiments involving individuals (Goldstein & Gigerenzer, 1999, 2002) and groups of subjects (Reimer & Katsikopoulos, 2004). This example is striking because it shows how a simple mechanism built on a basic cognitive capacity, here recognition memory, when used in the right environmental setting, can enable the cognitive system to exploit environmental structure and subsequently make good decisions with little information or processing.

3.2. *Paired Comparisons Using Take the Best*

If only one object in a paired comparison task is recognized, then there is little choice but to apply the recognition heuristic. But when both objects are recognized, and knowledge of several cues about each object is available to aid the decision, then many possible decision processes exist. For example, the paired comparison task is a special case of the general task of learning to categorize from labeled examples, which is explored thoroughly in machine-learning research (Mitchell, 1997). In that field, a litany of potential processes exist, typically complex algorithms designed from an engineering perspective to approximate a general solution to the problem of learning from examples, which leads these methods to veer from considerations of cognitive plausibility. In contrast, the study of ecological rationality from the perspective of the adaptive toolbox takes the issues of cognitive plausibility and the specific nature of the task as fundamental. These emphases are reflected in a bottom-up approach in which simple processes are built from elementary building blocks chosen to match a particular task environment. In particular, as mentioned earlier, Gigerenzer and colleagues (1999) have explored the following types of building blocks for processing cues

representing features of objects encountered in the world:

1. Search rules, which define how information in the form of cues is searched for. For example, one possible search rule is to look through cues in an order that reflects how useful these cues have been in the past.
2. Stopping rules, which define when cue search is to be terminated. For example, given the task of comparing two objects in terms of their cue values, search can be terminated when a stopping criterion of different cue values for the two objects is met.
3. Decision rules, which define how the information found by the first two building blocks is used to make a decision. For example, given information about a cue that differs in value for two objects, the object with the higher cue value could be chosen.

Take the Best is a simple heuristic built from three such building blocks where (a) cues are searched in order of their ecological validity, (b) search stops at the first discriminating cue (i.e., the first cue that has a different value for each object, and hence discriminates between the two objects), and (c) the object selected is the one indicated by the discriminating cue. Ecological validity is a property of a cue, which indicates how frequently in the past the discriminating cue picked out the object with the higher criterion value. (Discrimination rate is another important property of cues, indicating how often a given cue discriminates between pairs of objects in some environment.) For example, Take the Best could decide which of two tennis players is more likely to win an upcoming competition by first considering the most valid cue, say, "Has this player won a Grand Slam competition in the past?" If this cue discriminates – that is, it is true for one player and not the other – then Take the Best will stop information search and select the previous-winning player over the other. If the first cue does not discriminate, then further cues are considered in order of ecological validity until one is found that does discriminate and is then used by itself to determine the decision.

Unlike many other models of decision making, which typically take all cues into consideration and combine them somehow to yield a decision, Take the Best is frugal in its use of information. The decision is made only on the basis of the first discriminating cue, and all other information is ignored. In this sense, Take the Best employs one-reason decision making. But does Take the Best suffer, in terms of performance, by ignoring so much of the available information? No – Take the Best often performs just as well as other less frugal and more computationally intensive models such as multiple linear regression, even though it uses only a fraction of the available information. But even more surprising is the fact that in a considerable number of decision environments examined so far, Take the Best can outperform rival models of decision making when generalizing to new decisions (Czerlinski et al., 1999). Furthermore, recent work demonstrates that Take the Best can even beat the key models of inductive inference used in machine-learning research on connectionist, rule-based, and exemplar-based approaches – as long as the environment has a particular information structure (Brighton, 2006; Chater, Oaksford, Nakisa, & Redington, 2003). Thus, this work has shown in principle that decision processes built from simple, cognitively plausible building blocks that use little processing and little information in ways that are matched to the task environments in which they are situated can outperform some of the most widely used and studied models of induction that take a domain-general, environment-agnostic approach.

But in practice, do people use such simple, fast-and-frugal heuristics to make decisions? A growing body of experimental and empirical work is demonstrating that people do use one-reason decision heuristics in appropriately structured environments, such as where cues act individually to signal the correct response (Rieskamp & Otto, 2005) or where information is costly or time consuming to acquire (Bröder, 2000; Bröder & Schiffer, 2003; Newell & Shanks, 2003; Rieskamp & Hoffrage, 1999). People also make socially and culturally influenced decisions based on a single reason through imitation (e.g., in food choice; Ariely & Levav, 2000), norm following, and employing protected values (e.g., moral codes that admit no compromise, such as never taking an action that results in human death; see Tanner & Medin, 2004).

3.3. Estimation Using QuickEst

Not all choices in life are presented to us as convenient pairs of options, of course. Often we must choose between several alternatives, such as which restaurant to go to or which habitat to settle in. In situations where each available cue dimension has fewer values than the number of available alternatives, one-reason decision making will usually not suffice, because a single cue will be unable to distinguish among all of the alternatives. For instance, knowing whether each of fifteen cities has a river is not enough information to decide which city is most habitable. But this does not doom the fast-and-frugal reasoner to a long process of cue search and combination in these situations. Again, a simple stopping rule can work to limit information search: seek cues (in an order specified by the search rule) only until enough is known to make a decision. But now a different type of decision rule is needed instead of relying on one reason. One way to select a single option from among multiple alternatives is to follow the simple principle of elimination (Tversky, 1972): successive cues are used to eliminate more and more alternatives and thereby reduce the set of remaining options, until a single option can be decided on.

The QuickEst heuristic (Hertwig et al., 1999) is designed to estimate the values of objects along some criterion while using as little information as possible. The estimates are constrained to map onto certain round numbers (e.g., when estimating city population sizes, QuickEst can return values of 100,000, 150,000, 200,000, 300,000, and other similarly round numbers), so this heuristic can be seen as choosing one value from several possibilities. The elimination-based estimation process operates like a coal sorter, in which chunks of coal of various sizes first roll over a small slit, through which the smallest pieces fall into a bin for fine-grained coal; the bigger pieces that remain then roll over a wider slit that captures medium-sized pieces of coal into a medium bin; and finally the biggest chunks roll into a large coal bin. In the case of QuickEst applied to city population estimates, the coal chunks are cities of different population sizes; the bins are the rounded-number size estimates; and the slots are cues associated with city size, ordered according to the average size of the cities without that cue (e.g., because most small cities do not have a professional sports team, this could be one of the first cues checked – i.e., one of the first slots that the cities roll past). To estimate a city's size, the QuickEst heuristic looks through the cues or features in order until it comes to the first one that the city does not possess, at which point it stops searching for any further information (e.g., if a city possesses the first several features in order but lacks a convention center, the city falls into that bin and search will stop on that cue). QuickEst then gives the rounded mean criterion value associated with the absence of that cue as its final estimate (e.g., the mean size of all entries in the bin for cities without an exposition site). Thus, in effect, QuickEst uses features that are present to eliminate all smaller criterion categories, and absent features to eliminate all larger criterion categories, so that only one criterion estimate remains. No cue combination is necessary, and no adjustment from further cues is possible.

QuickEst proves to be fast and frugal, as well as accurate, in environments characterized by a distribution of criterion values in which small values are common and big values are rare (a so-called J-shaped distribution, where the J is seen on its side). Such distributions characterize a variety of naturally occurring phenomena, including many formed by accretionary growth. This growth pattern applies to cities (Makse, Havlin, & Stanley, 1995), and indeed big cities are much less common than small ones. As a consequence, when applied to a data set of cities, QuickEst is able to estimate rapidly the small sizes that most of them have.

4. Rationality in the Real World: From the Classical to the Ecological

The heuristics introduced in the previous section are tools for making inductive inferences. Induction is the task of using the past to predict and make decisions about the future. Without being able to look into the future, we can never answer with certainty questions such as, say, which tennis player will next win Wimbledon. We instead have to make an inductive inference, a prediction about the future, based on observations and knowledge we have acquired in the past. Clearly, by using prior experience we can often make better than chance predictions about future events in the world. This would not be possible if the world were unstructured and behaved randomly. Fortunately, most environments we face are highly structured, so that principled decision making serves us well. But what principles should guide our decision making? Many theories take what we will term *classical rationality* as a source of answers. This is to say that for the task of reasoning under uncertainty, clear normative principles such as Bayesian inference and variants of Occam's razor based on algorithmic information theory tell us what the rational course of action is (e.g., Chater, 1999; Hutter, 2005; Pearl, 1988). Yet humans often deviate from the classically rational: we make errors in a sometimes-systematic fashion and appear to only partially adhere to normative ideals. This view of occasionally error-prone human behavior is most forcefully argued within the heuristics-and-biases tradition, which proposes that people rely on a limited number of heuristic principles that reduce the complex tasks of assessing probabilities and predicting values to simpler judgmental operations. In general, these heuristics are quite useful, but sometimes they lead to severe and systematic errors (Tversky, 1972, p. 1124).

In this section we develop and justify why the classical view of rationality, when adopted as a concept with which to understand human decision making and inference, fails to capture significant aspects of the inference task. We will contrast classical rationality with ecological rationality and argue that the latter offers a far more productive concept with which to understand human decision making, as it bounds rationality to the world rather than treats the two as fundamentally separate (Todd & Gigerenzer, 2003). Thus, the ecological approach differs significantly from both classical rationality and the heuristics-and-biases tradition, and it offers what we consider another way of thinking about rationality:

> There is a third way to look at inference, focusing on the psychological and ecological rather than on logic and probability theory. This view questions classical rationality as a universal norm and thereby questions the very definition of good reasoning on which both the Enlightenment and heuristics-and-biases views were built. (Gigerenzer & Goldstein, 1996, p. 651)

But in what sense does ecological rationality differ from classical rationality? The apparent strength of rational principles of inference stem from their generality and their formal justification by way of probability theory, and ultimately information theory (Li & Vitányi, 1997). For example, Occam's razor tells us to prefer simpler explanations over complex ones, and this principle proves productive when fitting a polynomial to a set of data points, choosing between scientific theories, or describing the behavior of human visual perception (Sober, 1975). That such principles hold across diverse tasks that are seemingly unrelated in their formulation, their physical characteristics, and importantly, the environmental context, is seen as evidence of their strength.

However, if our concern is the study of human and animal cognition, then there are good reasons to view these apparent strengths as weaknesses. Neither humans nor animals uniformly adhere to overarching principles because, as we will argue, such principles make cognitive demands that cannot always be met. Furthermore, the generality of rational principles is in large part due to abstractions away from specific aspects of the task. Sometimes specific considerations, such as response time, are significant and may outweigh more general considerations such as predictive accuracy. We suspect that no single and universal measurement can characterize what is functional for an organism for all tasks, and in this sense we should be weary of proposals that collapse the problem characterizing rational choice down to a single yardstick. The concept of ecological rationality accepts the deep problems that arise with universal and abstract principles of rationality and works with them.

First of all, an important distinction to consider is that rational principles of inference are normative vehicles for judging inductive inferences. As such, they are inert with respect to how, in processing terms, organisms should arrive at inferences. Herbert Simon (1990, chap. 2) made the distinction between substantive and procedural rationality. Although some formulations of rational behavior consider procedural rationality, rational theories of inductive inference are typically claims about substantive rationality. Substantive rational principles are yardsticks for judging inferences; they do not tell us, in mechanistic terms, how to arrive at inductive inferences. It is useful, therefore, to distinguish between the substantive problem of induction and the procedural problem of induction. This distinction is essential when we come to consider fundamental computational limits that make realizing rational norms in processing terms often intractable, if not provably uncomputable. Note that this problem – the dichotomy between what is rational and what is computationally achievable – extends beyond the particular details of the cognitive system. It is an issue for all computational processes carrying out inductive inferences. We mention the processing issue here because, if what is deemed rational is fundamentally unobtainable by organisms, then perhaps our motives for adopting such a concept of rationality should be questioned.

Another distinction we will draw contrasts the substantive problem of induction and the cognitive-ecological problem of induction. This distinction will lead us to consider how behaving rationally in the classical sense (the substantive problem) and behaving adaptively (a species-specific cognitive-ecological problem) are not necessarily the same endeavor. For instance, the inference suggested by the most probable prediction (and therefore the most rational one) may require expending considerable time, memory, and processing resources compared with an inference arrived at quickly and on the basis of a cognitively undemanding decision process requiring minimal information; moreover, the latter may be only marginally inferior in probabilistic terms. Adaptive behavior, that which fits the functional requirements of an organism, is unlikely to be characterized using probability theory and logic given that "people satisfice – look for good enough solutions – instead of hopelessly searching for the best" (Simon, 1990, p. 17). Put differently, the payoff function with which we measure the efficacy of a decision maker is not simply how accurate inferences are; it also must consider ecological factors that take into account the structure of the task, the criticality of response time, and factors contributing to cognitive effort. Now, in this section the question we ask is, Does one rationality fit all tasks?

4.1. *Living Up to Expectation: From Substantive to Procedural Rationality*

Substantive rationality refers to rational principles such as Bayesian inference or Occam's razor. Procedural rationality, in contrast, considers what can be accomplished when one takes into account the processing steps required to arrive at an inference. Once an inference has been made, the role of substantive rationality is clear: it provides a criterion with which to judge this inference

against others. By considering the problem of procedural rationality, we are taking one step toward situating the task of human decision making. Constraints on realization can transform the nature of the problem, or, as Herbert Simon (1990) put it: "at each step toward realism, the problem gradually changes from choosing the right course of action (substantive rationality) to finding a way of calculating, very approximately, where a good choice of action lies (procedural rationality)" (pp. 26–27). In stressing this difference between substantive and procedural rationality in this way, we do not want give the impression that substantive theories of rationality are wrong. The issue is how appropriately a given notion of rationality fits the question at hand. Simon's point, and the point we are developing here, is that, for the task of understanding cognition, procedural rationality is more appropriate than substantive rationality. Again, this does not imply that substantive theories of rationality, such as Bayesianism, are the wrong tool for studying cognition, but rather that such principles are inherently limited because they neglect the fact that organisms are constrained in their ability to process information.

Some tasks, because of their inherent difficulty, lack a clear notion of substantive rationality. For example, choosing which of two candidate moves in chess is most likely to lead to a win can, in the general case, be only an estimate. Unsurprisingly, this inherent difficulty makes the procedural problem of playing chess even harder. In other words, if we lack a clear formulation of rational choice in the first place, then we cannot expect that procedural solutions conform to this rational expectation. Although chess is a supremely unenlightening example of human inference that, at best, may tell us about the fringes of human cognition (Chomsky, 2000, p. 161), there are many other common human decisions that are similarly difficult – or impossible – to rationally analyze fully, such as deciding which of two potential mates to woo (Gigerenzer & Todd, 1999). Furthermore, there are tasks for which we do have a clear notion of substantive rationality, yet procedural rationality still forces us to rethink what is achievable from the perspective of the organism. This is the issue we will focus on.

Consider the modern formulation of Occam's razor: hypotheses that recode observations in such a way to minimize encoding length should be chosen over others (Grünwald, 2005; Hutter, 2005; Li & Vitányi, 1997; Rissanen, 1989). Such a formulation has been proposed as a unifying principle of the cognitive system (Chater & Vitányi, 2003; see also Feldman, 2003) and "suggests a possible (although of course partial) account of the remarkable success of the cognitive system in prediction, understanding, and acting in an uncertain and complex environment: that cognitive processes search for simplicity" (Chater, 1999, p. 283). Yet paradoxically, adherence to simplicity principles can be so complex in processing terms that it "will not be possible in general" (Chater, 1999, p. 283). As another example of the substantive-procedural gap, in both perception and action it is proposed that a "striking observation . . . is the myriad ways in which human observers act as optimal Bayesian observers" (Knill & Pouget, 2004, p. 712). Once again, however, it is acknowledged that, "owing to the complexity of the task, unconstrained Bayesian inference is not a viable solution for computation in the brain" (Knill & Pouget, 2004, p. 718). Here we see the struggle between the desire to find concise universal laws of rational behavior and the processing difficulties that accompany these principles. To see why this problem occurs, and how the concept of ecological rationality can help to clarify issues, we will consider the cognitive task of categorization. Categorization requires making inductive inferences, it is a ubiquitous ability of humans and other animals, and it offers a useful example for illustrating the dichotomy between procedural and substantive rationality.

For the categorization task, Bayesian inference and modern castings of Occam's razor provide well-defined and precise rational criteria with which to compare one potential category judgment against another. Given a series of observations, these criteria tell us, for any two candidate category explanations, which is the "best" category description. Stepping back from any specific solutions that the cognitive system may employ, it will prove useful to consider first the more general class of computational procedures for performing inductive inferences. Machine learning is the study of procedural solutions to inference problems (Mitchell, 1997), and therefore offers a useful source of insight into the relationship between substantive and procedural rationality (which is sometimes termed *approximate rationality* within artificial intelligence; see Russell & Norvig, 1995). Like economic and psychological research, artificial intelligence and, in particular, machine learning often appeal to classical notions of rational behavior (Goodie, Ortmann, Davis, Bullock, & Werner, 1999). For example, using algorithmic information theory to fix a universal (i.e., problem independent, parameterless, and rationally motivated by way of Occam's razor) prior probability distribution on the hypothesis space (Solomonoff, 1964), Bayesian-inspired models of inductive reasoning have led some to explore "a theory for rational agents acting optimally in any environment" (Hutter, 2005, p. 24). Unfortunately, when realized in procedural terms, such theories partly assume the "availability of unlimited computational resources" (Hutter, 2005, p. v). Even with extremely liberal constraints on resources, universally applicable laws of rationality, in processing terms, are difficult or even impossible to achieve.

In practice, machine-learning research places more conservative bounds on what is considered practical by often narrowing its interests to the class of computationally tractable algorithms. Computationally tractable algorithms are those that place computational demands on time and storage space resources that grow as polynomial function of the size of the problem (e.g., sorting a series of n numbers into ascending order is deemed tractable because it can be achieved by an algorithm requiring time and space polynomial in n). Under these constraints, a widespread realization, and arguably an axiom within machine learning, is that procedural adherence to rational expectation breaks down. One useful concept in thinking about ad hoc adherence to the rational ideal is inductive bias, which refers to any basis on which one explanation is chosen over another, beyond simple adherence to the observations (Gordon & Desjardins, 1995; Mitchell, 1997).[1] An appropriately formalized Occam's-razor principle is a bias, for example, but typically bias occurs as a result of restrictions on the representational power of the hypothesis space (the set of explanations the algorithm can consider) and how thoroughly the hypothesis space can be searched (the manner in which the search for the optimal hypothesis is approximated).

The important point here is that the inductive bias of an algorithm typically reflects concrete issues of realization such as the particular characteristics and assumptions imposed by the implementation of the algorithm (e.g., the nature of hypothesis space) rather than a rationally motivated normative bias, such as Occam's razor. Consequently, and as a result of tractability and computability constraints, the procedural problem of induction has a different character from that suggested by the rational problem. The combination of considering nontrivial tasks in conjunction with tractability constraints limits researchers to a vaguer adherence to rational expectations, where algorithms "should process the finite sample to obtain a hypothesis with good generalization ability under a reasonably large set of circumstances" (Kearns, 1999, p. 159). For machine learning, this breakdown in adherence to the rational, or optimal, outcome is simply a well-established fact. Algorithmic solutions are, to varying degrees, focused rather than general, and their performance is adequate rather than normative:

Induction is not unbridled or unconstrained. Indeed, decades of work in machine learning makes abundantly clear that there is no such thing as a general purpose learning algorithm that works equally well across domains. Induction may be the name of the game, but constraints are the rules that we play by. (Elman, 2003, from ms.)

Because uniform adherence to a normative criterion is taken as a goal, alleviating the discrepancy between this goal and what can be achieved in practice can partially be overcome through the selective choice of learning algorithms, dependent on the task structure. For example, given knowledge of the tasks for which some learning algorithm A performs better any other algorithm, then A could be chosen over all others when such a task is encountered. This problem is known as the selective superiority problem. It remains largely unexplored, and only limited practical progress has been made in addressing it (e.g., Kalousis, Gama, & Hilario, 2004). Unfortunately, for anything other than trivial tasks, machine learning tells us that there is a gap between substantive and procedural rationality. This gap exists because tractable algorithms tend to focus their performance on some problems at the expense of others. Crucially, most tasks are not trivial in the sense we mean here and require the expenditure of considerable computational effort to find good, let alone optimal, solutions. For example, the apparently trivial task of recognizing a face is extremely difficult from a computational standpoint: a full integration of the many facial properties that need to be considered is computationally intractable. In the study of artificial intelligence, which seeks engineering solutions for tasks like these, optimal solutions are almost always unobtainable (for discussion, see Reddy, 1988). Likewise, the study of cognition rarely reduces to the study of computationally trivial problems.

This brief discussion of machine learning provides us with some conceptual tools with which to consider the cognitive problem. The cognitive problem of induction is a particular instance of the procedural problem of achieving rationality, and one that is subject to hard biological/cognitive constraints rather than the more abstract notion of computational tractability encountered previously. As for machine learning's algorithmic rationality problem, the general human cognitive problem is also broken down into tasks with particular characteristics. For instance, tasks spanning low-level aspects of the visual system and high-level tasks such as concept learning and categorization are commonly viewed as inductive tasks (e.g., Chater & Vitányi, 2003; Sober, 1975). However, unlike a general constraint such as computational tractability, these cognitive tasks are likely to work within very different and more stringent constraints, such as the physical limitations of the underlying biological machinery; constraints imposed by other cognitive systems also using resources in the mind; and limits on attention, working memory, and the like. Thus, different cognitive tasks are likely to yield to processing solutions of different forms.

4.2. *Situating Decision Making: Confronting the Cognitive-Ecological Problem*

Processing makes demands on computational resources. Placing constraints on these resources limits the degree to which rational expectations can be met, and in particular, processes tend to be focused on some instances of the task with respect to their ability to adhere to the demands set by substantive rationality. Specific kinds of constraint impose specific kinds of focus and, as Simon argued (1990, 1996), a full consideration of cognitive limitations leads us to consider boundedly rational processes. On the one hand, constraints beyond those of an abstract computational nature would appear to limit even further the degree to which rational expectations are likely to be met, and, as a result, the human cognitive system needs to pull a neat trick if it is to measure up to the demands of rationality under these terms. On the other hand, we will argue that there are good reasons to view cognitive limitations not as barriers but as enablers of robust inference. Limitations can be viewed as adaptive constraints in the sense that they may lead an agent to exploit informa-

tional structures present in the environment (Hertwig & Todd, 2003; Todd, Billari, & Simão, 2005). In this sense, the cognitive system does pull a neat trick: its limitations can become enablers once we consider the ecological side of problem.

Until now we have focused on internal aspects of the organism. The previous section highlighted how, by coupling limitations in cognitive structure to environment structure, simple mechanisms can match or exceed the performance of more complex mechanisms. For instance, the simplicity of Take the Best can be interpreted as an inability to consider intercue correlations because Take the Best is restricted to acting on conditionally independent ecological cue measurements. For some environments, this inability actually acts as an enabler, as conditional information can be highly misleading and unstable. In fact, among twenty natural environments tested by Brighton (2005), over half reveal this property within the paired comparison task. In the same study, these characteristics of the environment posed serious problems for five classic machine-learning algorithms because they all carry out complex computations that consider conditional cue dependencies. As a result of their reliance on noisy cue relationships, they performed worse than Take the Best. Constraints that act as enablers illustrate how the adaptive-toolbox metaphor exploits the strengths of simplicity. This trick is worth considering in more depth.

For a specific task, the environment can be viewed as set of structures to be exploited by multiple simple processes. This perspective differs from the more traditional view, where a single task is often seen in terms of a single-process solution that is assumed to possess a general competence on a diverse range of environmental structures. Decomposing the problem space into structurally distinct subproblems, according to this view, is not the principle objective because we assume the competence of a single process to be sufficient for all relevant problems. For example, the paired comparison task addressed by the Take the Best heuristic can be viewed as a special case of the categorization task. Within this task, Take the Best is one process among several possible candidates tuned to particular instances of this problem. In contrast, both in machine learning and in psychological modeling, the categorization task is often viewed from the perspective of a single process, applied independently of the precise nature of the task environment. For example, PROBEX is presented as "a model of probabilistic inference and probability judgments based on generic knowledge" (Juslin & Persson, 2002, p. 563), yet such a claim cannot be sustained in any meaningful sense, as the inductive bias of PROBEX, like any other process, will lead to good performance on some instances of the problem at the expense of others. Such single-process approaches often neglect the structure of the environment, and therefore the models are general only in the sense that no clear understanding of their focus exists.

Simple heuristics can work extremely well because they are focused and tailor their inductive bias to match specific information structures in the environment. To support this view, our experiments show that in comparisons across twenty different natural environments, Take the Best more often than not outperforms all competitors drawn from a collection of neural networks, exemplar models, and decision-tree induction models (Brighton, 2006).

These simulation results strengthen the claim that, when faced with a varied set of environments, one approach toward achieving adaptive behavior is to rely on an adaptive toolbox, from which ecologically rational heuristics are selected contingent on the task and the ecological context. This notion of contingent application is the crucial difference between the adaptive-toolbox metaphor and the more widespread approach of focusing on a single general-purpose processing system. Thus, the performance of heuristics must always be considered conditional on the task, and in the study of adaptive behavior, understanding environmental context is just as important as understanding processing mechanisms. To be more precise, we say that a mechanism M is ecologically rational in environment

E in comparison to some other mechanism M' when M outperforms M' on some criterion, or currency, of comparison. There are two components to statements such as these. First, such statements are comparative rather than absolute: heuristics must be judged in comparison to other models. For example, Take the Best is ecologically rational compared to other models of inference (Brighton, 2006; Czerlinski et al., 1999), and the recognition heuristic is ecologically rational compared to those models that do not consider, and therefore cannot exploit, recognition information (Goldstein & Gigerenzer, 2002). Second, statements about the ecological rationality of a heuristic appeal to some criterion of comparison. For instance, models of inference are often compared using cross-validation, which considers the criterion of zero-one loss predictive accuracy (e.g., Browne, 2000), or using a criterion that measures the degree to which a heuristic compresses the observations (Grünwald, 2005).

For some, performance measures such as these call into question the concept of ecological rationality due to an ultimate appeal to rational criteria, which in the final analysis are used to justify and explain the performance of heuristics (Chater et al., 2003). But this argument misses a fundamental dimension of the concept of ecological rationality that we mentioned briefly at the start if this section. Given some criterion, the rational course of action is defined as the one that maximizes the criterion. Cross-validation tells us to prefer the model that yields the highest predictive accuracy, and Occam's razor tells us to prefer the model that compresses the observations most succinctly. Both these rational criteria consider only a single perspective, which we might dub "raw inductive performance," as they constitute perhaps the most basic and assumption-free rational criterion. For this reason their use is widespread in the comparison of machine-learning algorithms (Kearns, Mansour, Ng, & Ron, 1997) and between models of cognition (Pitt, Myung, & Zhang, 2002). However, these criteria ignore crucial aspects of the ecological problem. Mechanisms that blindly maximize the rational criteria may ignore marginally less predictive solutions that can be found using, for example, less information search and fewer processing steps. Thus, it is apparent that general and universal measures can abstract the problem away from significant factors influencing the adaptive function of the mechanism. Put differently, the appropriate payoff function with which to assess human decision making is likely to be both multidimensional and task specific. Rational criteria, because of their generality, necessarily sidestep this ecological aspect of the problem. Although rational criteria widely used to judge inductive performance are often also used to compare heuristics, their use in statements about ecological rationality is more a matter of practical factors than a reflection of conceptual necessity. For this reason, heuristics are often additionally compared using multiple criteria, such as cross-validation and frugality of information use (Czerlinski et al., 1999). Although substantive theories of rationality could, in principle, be elaborated to consider further costs and more complex payoff functions, issues of processing must, at some point, be considered. In the limit, such a refined notion of substantive rationality could become procedural rationality, the approach that we are advocating here. Thus, there are varying degrees of abstraction when formulating a rational theory, and ecological rationality is a form of rationality tailored to understanding cognitive processing in its ecological context.

4.3. *Ecological Rationality as a Form of Situated Cognition*

Ecological rationality depends on intelligent agents deploying their various decision strategies in particular situations, sensitive to the structure of the environment in which they are embedded. This sounds like cognition situated in specific settings – but can we say more precisely in what way the study of ecological rationality is related to the situated movement in cognitive science? In broad terms, and to varying degrees, situated-cognition approaches view "intelli-

gent human behavior as engaged, socially and materially embodied activity, arising within the specific concrete details of particular (natural) settings, rather than as an abstract, detached, general-purpose process of logical or formal ratiocination" (Smith, 1999, p. 769). As we argued in the previous section, the concept of ecological rationality is called for precisely because formal and generally applicable visions of rational behavior fail to consider significant aspects of human decision making. These aspects range from the algorithmic constraints on what can plausibly be achieved by the cognitive system to ecological considerations that affect the potential difference between adaptive (and ecologically rational) decisions and classically rational decisions. Thus, the concept of ecological rationality bears some of the hallmarks that characterize situated approaches.

At this point we lay down what we take to be some key characteristic features of situated approaches to studying cognition and how they apply to ecological rationality. The dimensions we consider are taken from Smith's (1999) characterization of situated approaches in terms of six key dimensions: located, concrete, engaged, specific, embodied, and social.

4.4. *Located*

The significance of being located arises when we adopt the view that "context-dependence is a central and enabling feature of human endeavor" (Smith, 1999, p. 769). Using Simon's metaphor of the scissors, context dependence is the environmental blade. In particular, Simon (1956) makes the point that "we might hope to discover, by a careful examination of some of the fundamental structural characteristics of the environment, some further clues as to the nature of the approximating mechanisms used in decision making" (p. 130). As we have shown, characteristics of the environment indeed represent a central and enabling feature when we consider their role in supporting cognitively simple heuristics. For example, some environmental contexts "enable" frugality in information use: in non-compensatory environments, where the best cues outweigh the combined strength of all other cues, there is no reason to consider any but the first discriminating cue found, which is just the strategy adopted by lexicographic decision strategies like Take the Best. It is the precise context that the environment presents that provides the traction enabling simple cognitive heuristics to perform so well. In these terms, location is everything when considering ecological rationality. Without the enabling aspects of each precise context, ecological rationality cannot get off the ground.

4.5. Concrete

The issue of concreteness refers to the view that "constraints of realization and circumstance are viewed as of the utmost importance" (Smith, 1999, p. 769). Constraints on realization, again using Simon's metaphor of the scissors, correspond to the cognitive blade. There are two degrees of concreteness we have considered. First, at a purely computational level, there are hard constraints on what can be achieved by computationally tractable processes (e.g., problems that cannot be solved in polynomial time). Second, moving from an abstract consideration of issues of computability to the more concrete issue of cognitive limitations, there are constraints arising from the cognitive system as a biologically realized computing device that further limit what can be achieved. The vagaries of the human memory system, for example, form a set of cognitive constraints that influence how information is processed. Yet constraints can also be important because they can enable some capabilities – continuing the memory example, the role of forgetting can be seen as an enabler for heuristic inference, as it affects the capacity for name recognition and therefore the ability to use the recognition heuristic (Schooler & Hertwig, 2005). In a nutshell, the details of the concrete realization of cognitive mechanisms matter because certain constraints enable the exploitation of context.

4.6. Engaged

The property of engagement considers how "ongoing interaction with the surrounding environment is recognized as primary" (Smith, 1999, p. 769). Because heuristics are specialized – tuned to specific environmental contexts – the adjustment of the decision mechanism contingent on the structure of the task environment demands that a decision maker consider the inference task as an ongoing rather than a static activity. Furthermore, because most of the heuristics in the adaptive toolbox involve search for information in the environment, these mechanisms are of necessity engaged in a process of environmental interaction. This can happen on a moment-to-moment basis, as when a consumer deciding which good to buy checks the packaging for information until he or she finds enough to make a choice, or when a fielder trying to catch a ball adjusts her running speed so as to maintain a constant gaze angle (McLeod & Dienes, 1996), or at longer time spans, as when a person encountering different decision tasks or environments must choose or adapt the decision mechanism he or she is using. Precisely how decision makers react to environments is the subject of ongoing research. For example, Todd and Dieckmann (2005) describe a process by which individuals may learn an order in which to use cues with Take the Best, and they show how this learned order itself influences the decisions made and the subsequent learning that an individual can perform. Strong path dependencies – a hallmark of an engaged process – emerge in the application of this learning mechanism as it is intertwined with ongoing decision making. Rieskamp and Otto (2005), in contrast, explore the changing use of particular fixed, simple heuristics in a reinforcement-learning scenario. Here, a balance between exploration and exploitation is struck by integrating feedback from the decision-making process, which in turn allows the agent to learn when to apply which strategy. This line of research is particularly promising, as there are potential connections with other psychological research into strategy selection (Erev & Barron, 2005; Gonzalez, Lerch, & Lebiere, 2003) and with attempts within machine learning to use human problem solving as inspiration for systems that learn to learn, where the relationship between multiple tasks is considered an enabling feature of human inductive performance (Thrun & Pratt, 1998).

4.7. Specific

Considerations of specificity refer to the fact that "what people do is seen as varying, dramatically, depending on contingent facts about their circumstances" (Smith, 1999, p. 769). For ecologically rational inference, the particular circumstances a decision maker faces are paramount. The discussion earlier of the importance of being located highlights how circumstance can act as an enabling feature in decision making. We take specificity to capture a slightly different set of contingencies of the tasks that people face, such as are evident from experimental studies of when people use heuristics. For example, circumstances in which subjects are required to act under time pressure show how the choice of decision strategy changes as a result, with subjects showing a strong tendency to prefer simple sequential, cue-based decision mechanisms (Edland, 1994; Payne et al., 1993). The costs of information search also have a strong bearing on which strategy is used. For instance, when subjects are required to search for information from memory, rather than on screen, they are far more likely to use fast-and-frugal decision strategies like Take the Best (Bröder & Shiffer, 2003). If subjects are required to estimate the values of associated with different choices, rather than simply make a choice, different decision strategies are, again, likely to be used (Westenberg & Koele, 1992). These studies not only highlight how subtleties in the specific nature of the task (in contrast to the statistical structure of the environment) can lead to quite different cognitive tools being used but also reveal that individual differences are often at play. Information processing, from the perspective of the adaptive toolbox, is highly dependent on both the specific nature of the task and the particularities of the individual cognitive system.

4.8. Embodied

The importance of embodiment refers to the fact that "material aspects of agents' bodies are taken to be both pragmatically and theoretically significant" (Smith, 1999, p. 769). In other words, the particular physical instantiation of the agent's body is taken to have a strong impact on how the problem is both conceived of and solved. The gaze heuristic for ball catching mentioned earlier, for example, is a process that relies on a particular morphology: an eye and a bipedal locomotion system. Embodiment is important, as an agent with a different morphological design may solve the problem of catching the ball using quite different processes: being equipped with wings and echolocation would open up entirely different ball-catching solutions. Ecological rationality has, to date, been studied in an embodied form mostly in the field of behavior-based robotics (e.g., Brooks, 1991; for a discussion, see Goodie et al., 1999), where simple heuristics are used to help physically embodied agents navigate through environments and solve different (usually rather simple) tasks. Despite these low-level investigations of embodied ecological rationality so far, we nevertheless take issues of embodiment to have significant impact on high-level cognition. In particular, these issues are important for considering the sensory and proprioceptive origins of the cues going into the decision process, as well as the bodily and motor-system consequences of the decisions being made.

4.9. Social

Being social means "being located in humanly constructed settings among human communities" (Smith, 1999, p. 769). In studying ecological rationality, we must acknowledge that a significant part of environment structure will often be made up of other individuals and the results of their actions, whether in choosing a mate (Todd et al., 2005), selecting a parking space (Hutchinson, Fanselow, & Todd, forthcoming), negotiating a fair division of resources (Takezawa, 2004), reaching a group decision (Reimer & Hoffrage, 2005; Reimer & Katsikopoulos, 2004), deciding how to communicate important information (Kürzenhäuser & Hoffrage, 2002), and many other situations. The social rationality called for in all of these cases is a special form of ecological rationality specifically dealing with social environments.

4.10. *Summary: The Role of Situatedness in High-Level Cognition*

It is clear that the concept of ecological rationality is closely allied and in strong agreement with the six defining characteristics of situated approaches to understanding cognition proposed by Smith (1999). However, it is worth pointing out that the approach we advocate here is conservative in comparison with other more radical situated positions. As the preceding sections have demonstrated, ecologically rational heuristics are uniformly described in terms of symbolic process models operating on representations. These processes draw on the classical notions of search, satisficing, and decision rules. In contrast to more radical positions, the concept of ecological rationality is agnostic with respect to, for example, issues of antirepresentationalism (Slezak, 1999; Varela, Thompson, & Rosch, 1991), dynamic systems theory (van Gelder, 1995), or more philosophical rethinkings of the nature of cognition (Winograd & Flores, 1996). These issues are certainly significant dimensions of some theories of situatedness, but we take the concept of ecological rationality to be orthogonal to, for example, what level and in what terms one describes processes (for a related discussion, see Vera & Simon, 1993). To be clear on this point, we could note that simple heuristics could be implemented just as well using connectionist networks or cognitive architectures such as ACT-R (Anderson & Lebeire, 1998; for an example, see Schooler & Hertwig, 2005),

but we do not see this as the key issue at stake in this discussion. In short, we should sound a note of caution. As Clancey (1997, p. 345) points out, it is often tempting and all too easy to present an either-or message. In our case, this would amount to claiming that existing principles of rationality are irrelevant to the study of human cognition. However, this is not the point we wish to make. When it comes to theorizing about situated cognition, we view ecological rationality as "adding new tools to cognitive science's tool kit" (Clark, 1997, p. 175) rather than replacing the existing ones (see also Vera & Simon, 1993).

Ecological rationality speaks to the relationship between mechanisms and environments and, in particular, how simple and cognitively plausible mechanisms that exploit the environment provide a productive basis on which to explore human decision making. Thus, the adaptive-toolbox vision of decision making has less to do with what Smith (1999) terms "situatedness with a vengeance" (p. 770) and more to do with recasting, rethinking, and adding to familiar concepts of cognition and situatedness. Mental representations, for instance, are not abandoned, but the fact that simple processing solutions exploit structure in the environment does suggest the possibility of a weaker reliance on internal models of the world. In Brooks's (1991) terms, we are sympathetic to the view that it is "better to use the world as its own model" (p. 139). Furthermore, in contrast to other frameworks with a focus on the relationship between rational principles and the role of the environment, such as Anderson's (1990) rational analysis (see also Oaksford & Chater, 1998), ecological rationality – realized through the adaptive toolbox – has a strong bottom-up orientation to model construction reminiscent of Brooks's subsumption architecture for behavior-based robotics (Brooks, 1991). In this sense, ecological rationality draws on concepts that are more often associated with situated approaches to lower-level aspects of cognition and demonstrates their productivity in studying higher-level aspects of human decision making and inference.

5. Conclusion

Ecological approaches to understanding the mind focus on the relationship between mind and environment. We have explored one form of this relationship, in which simple mental mechanisms can make adaptive decisions by exploiting the characteristics of environments. As such, the concept of ecological rationality proves closely tied with the key dimensions that characterize situated approaches to understanding the mind. To examine this connection, we began by considering three metaphors that have been used to characterize the relationship between mind and environment: mirrors, lenses, and scissors. Mirrors reflect fundamental features of the world such that aspects of mind are shaped by the external environment. Here, minds represent useful and ubiquitous properties of the world, and these properties help the mind to function in environments. A lens projects rather than reflects, and reconstructs a representation of a distal stimulus on the basis of the current proximal cues. Again, by projecting aspects of the environment into the mind, the environment can be acted on by processing this information. Scissors are different. The scissors metaphor captures a relationship in which properties of the environment are exploited by, rather than represented by, the capabilities of the agent. It is only in circumstances in which mind and environment fit together like the blades of a pair of scissors that this relationship works. We have argued that the scissors metaphor is often appropriate when considering high-level cognitive processing tasks such as decision making and inference. The concept of ecological rationality, realized using an adaptive toolbox of simple mechanisms, builds on this scissors metaphor.

Simple decision heuristics that exploit features of natural environments perform very well and sometimes better than more conventional and complex models of inference. Mechanisms such as these are termed *ecologically rational*, and we have argued that the concept of ecological rationality is far more productive than conventional notions of rationality when seeking to understand decision making and inference in humans. First of all, ecological rationality treats the cognitive task as both located and concrete in the sense that the particular structure making up the task environment can be exploited by the concrete limited structure of the processor. This relationship, the match between cognitive limitations and environment structure, is the core concept behind ecological rationality. Conventional notions of rationality consider neither aspect and instead seek universally applicable principles that are independent of both the capabilities of the actor and the structure of the task. Part of the motivation for considering ecological rationality, as we have discussed, is that the cognitive system needs to solve the procedural problem of arriving at inferences. This task is notoriously difficult, and we drew on machine-learning research to show how conventional notions of rationality cannot be universally adhered to. Faced with a fundamental dichotomy between procedural and classical visions of rationality, we question how appropriate these classical visions of rationality are when seeking to understand the cognitive system.

The approach of ecological rationality also turns on the engaged and specific nature of cognition. The use of simple heuristics changes over time and as a reaction to changes in the environment. Although few cognitive theories would deny such a state of affairs, this reactive aspect of cognition is far more pivotal when considering a toolbox of ecologically rational heuristics, because of their highly situation-specific nature. Ecological rationality also treats as highly significant the social and (to a lesser extent) embodied aspects of cognition. Humans inhabit environments constructed and occupied by other humans, and social heuristics exploit the structure of environments constructed by the behavior of other humans. Similarly, the concrete details of sensor and muscle morphology are likely to be significant in defining how simple heuristics exploit body-environment interactions.

Despite the widespread adoption of rational principles as normative laws governing the cognitive system, we have argued that there are solid grounds for questioning this assumption. Rather than being rooted in probability theory, information theory, and logic, the concept of ecological rationality provides an alternative vision of rationality rooted in the concrete constraints of the cognitive system and the structure of natural environments. Behaving in line with classical rational principles and behaving adaptively, as we have argued, are not necessarily the same endeavor. Ecological rationality, by taking a situated perspective, provides a vision of rationality bounded to the world in such a way that the limitations of the cognitive system and the specific context of cognition are viewed as significant and enabling features of adaptive cognition. If we are to understand the adaptive nature of high-level cognition, then the cognitive system needs to be viewed more as an ecologically rational bag of tricks and less in terms of a formally motivated calculating device adhering to general principles of classically rational inference.

Note

1 The use of the term *inductive bias* differs both from (a) the term *bias* in the heuristics and biases literature and (b) the term *estimation bias* in statistics (although inductive bias is connected to the latter; see Mitchell, 1997).

References

Anderson, J. R. (1990). *The adaptive character of thought*. Hillsdale, NJ: Lawrence Erlbaum.

Anderson, J. R., & Lebeire, C. (1998). *The atomic components of thought*. Mahwah, NJ: Lawrence Erlbaum.

Ariely, D., & Levav, J. (2000). Sequential choice in group settings: Taking the road less traveled and less enjoyed. *Journal of Consumer Research*, 27(3), 279–290.

Bak, P. (1996). *How nature works*. New York: Springer-Verlag.

Barkow, J. H., Cosmides, L., & Tooby, J. (Eds.). (1992). *The adapted mind: Evolutionary psychology and the generation of culture*. New York: Oxford University Press.

Barrett, H. C. (2005). Adaptations to predators and prey. In D. M. Buss (Ed.). *The handbook of evolutionary psychology* (pp. 200–223). Hoboken, NJ: Wiley.

Brighton, H. (2006). Robust inference with simple cognitive models. In C. Lebiere & B. Wray (Eds.), *Between a rock and a hard place: Cognitive science principles meet AI-hard problems* (pp. 17–22). Menlo Park, CA: AAAI Press.

Bröder, A. (2000). Assessing the empirical validity of the "Take The Best" heuristic as a model of human probabilistic inference. *Journal of Experimental Psychology: Learning, Memory, and Cognition*, 26, 1332–1346.

Bröder, A., & Schiffer, S. (2003). "Take The Best" versus simultaneous feature matching: Probabilistic inferences from memory and effects of representation format. *Journal of Experimental Psychology: General*, 132(2), 277–293.

Brooks, R. A. (1991). Intelligence without representation. *Artificial Intelligence*, 47, 139–160.

Browne, M. W. (2000). Cross-validation methods. *Journal of Mathematical Psychology*, 44, 108–132.

Brunswik, E. (1955). Representative design and probabilistic theory in a functional psychology. *Psychological Review*, 62, 193–217.

Buss, D. M. (Ed.). (2005). *The handbook of evolutionary psychology*. Hoboken, NJ: Wiley.

Chater, N. (1999). The search for simplicity: A fundamental cognitive principle? *Quarterly Journal of Experimental Psychology*, 52A(2), 273–302.

Chater, N., & Brown, G. D. A. (1999). Scale invariance as a unifying psychological principle. *Cognition*, 69, B17–B24.

Chater, N., Oaksford, M., Nakisa, R., & Redington, M. (2003). Fast, frugal and rational: How rational norms explain behavior. *Organizational Behavior and Human Decision Processes*, 90, 63–86.

Chater, N., & Vitányi, P. (2003). Simplicity: A unifying principle in cognitive science? *Trends in Cognitive Sciences*, 7, 19–22.

Chomsky, N. (1995). *The minimalist program*. Cambridge, MA: MIT Press.

Chomsky, N. (2000). *New horizons in the study of language and mind*. Cambridge: Cambridge University Press.

Clancey, W. J. (1997). *Situated cognition: On human knowledge and computer representations*. Cambridge: Cambridge University Press.

Clark, A. (1997). *Being there: Putting brain, body, and world together again*. Cambridge, MA: MIT Press.

Czerlinski, J., Gigerenzer, G., & Goldstein, D. G. (1999). How good are simple heuristics? In G. Gigerenzer, P. M. Todd, & the ABC Research Group (Eds.), *Simple heuristics that make us smart* (pp. 97–118). New York: Oxford University Press.

Edland, A. (1994). Time pressure and the applications of decision rules: Choices and judgements among multiattribute alternatives. *Scandinavian Journal of Psychology, 35,* 281–291.

Elman, J. L. (2003). Generalization from sparse input. In *Proceedings of the 38th Annual Meeting of the Chicago Linguistic Society*. Chicago: Chicago Linguistic Society.

Erev, I., & Barron, G. (2005). On adaptation, maximization, and reinforcement learning among cognitive strategies. *Psychological Review, 112*(4), 912–931.

Feldman, J. (2003). The simplicity principle in human concept learning. *Current Directions in Psychological Science, 12*(6), 227–232.

Gigerenzer, G., & Goldstein, D. G. (1996). Reasoning the fast and frugal way: Models of bounded rationality. *Psychological Review, 103,* 650–669.

Gigerenzer, G., & Selten, R. (Eds.). (2001). *Bounded rationality: The adaptive toolbox.* Cambridge, MA: MIT Press.

Gigerenzer, G., & Todd, P. M. (1999). Fast and frugal heuristics: The adaptive toolbox. In G. Gigerenzer, P. M. Todd, & the ABC Research Group (Eds.), *Simple heuristics that make us smart* (pp. 3–34). New York: Oxford University Press.

Gigerenzer, G., Todd, P. M., & the ABC Research Group (Eds.). (1999). *Simple heuristics that make us smart*. New York: Oxford University Press.

Goldstein, D. G., & Gigerenzer, G. (1999). The recognition heuristic: How ignorance makes us smart. In G. Gigerenzer, P. M. Todd, & the ABC Research Group (Eds.), *Simple heuristics that make us smart* (pp. 37–58). New York: Oxford University Press.

Goldstein, D. G., & Gigerenzer, G. (2002). Models of ecological rationality: The recognition heuristic. *Psychological Review, 109,* 75–90.

Gonzalez, C., Lerch, J. F., & Lebiere, C. (2003). Instance-based learning in dynamic decision making. *Cognitive Science, 27,* 591–635.

Goodie, A. S., Ortmann, A., Davis, J., Bullock, S., & Werner, G. M. (1999). Demons versus heuristics in artificial intelligence, behavioral ecology, and economics. In G. Gigerenzer, P. M. Todd, & the ABC Research Group (Eds.), *Simple heuristics that make us smart* (pp. 327–355). New York: Oxford University Press.

Gordon, D. F., & Desjardins, M. (1995). Evaluation and selection of biases in machine learning. *Machine Learning, 20,* 5–22.

Grünwald, P. (2005). Minimum description length tutorial. In P. Grünwald, I. J. Myung, & M. A. Pitt (Eds.), *Advances in minimum description length* (pp. 23–79). Cambridge, MA: MIT Press.

Hamilton, W. D. (1996). *Narrow roads of gene land: Evolution of social behaviour* (Vol. 1). Oxford: Oxford University Press.

Hammond, K. R., & Stewart, T. R. (Eds.). (2001). *The essential Brunswik: Beginnings, explications, applications*. New York: Oxford University Press.

Hertwig, R., Hoffrage, U., & Martignon, L. (1999). Quick estimation: Letting the environment do some of the work. In G. Gigerenzer, P. M. Todd, & the ABC Research Group (Eds.), *Simple heuristics that make us smart* (pp. 209–234). New York: Oxford University Press.

Hertwig, R., & Todd, P. M. (2003). More is not always better: The benefits of cognitive limits. In D. Hardman & L. Macchi (Eds.), *Thinking: Psychological perspectives on reasoning, judgment and decision making* (pp. 213–231). Chichester, UK: Wiley.

Hutchinson, J., Fanselow, C., & Todd, P. M. (forthcoming). *Car parking as a game between simple heuristics*. In P. M. Todd, G. Gigerenzer, & the ABC Research Group (Eds.), *Ecological Rationality: Intelligence in the World*. New York: Oxford University Press.

Hutter, M. (2005). *Universal artificial intelligence: Sequential decisions based on algorithmic probability*. Berlin: Springer.

Juslin, P., & Persson, M. (2002). PRObabilities from EXemplars (PROBEX): A "lazy" algorithm for probabalistic inference from generic knowledge. *Cognitive Science, 26*(5), 563–607.

Kahneman, D., Slovic, P., & Tversky, A. (Eds.). (1982). *Judgment under uncertainty: Heuristics and biases*. Cambridge: Cambridge University Press.

Kalousis, A., Gama, J., & Hilario, M. (2004). On data and algorithms: Understanding inductive performance. *Machine Learning, 54,* 275–312.

Kearns, M. (1999). Computational learning theory. In R. A. Wilson & F. C. Keil (Eds.), *The MIT encyclopedia of the cognitive sciences* (pp. 159–160). Cambridge, MA: MIT Press.

Kearns, M., Mansour, Y., Ng, A. Y., & Ron, D. (1997). An experimental and theoretical comparison of model selection methods. *Machine Learning, 27*, 7–50.

Knill, D. C., & Pouget, A. (2004). The Bayesian brain: The role of uncertainty in neural coding and computation. *Trends in Neurosciences, 27*(12), 712–719.

Kürzenhäuser, S., & Hoffrage, U. (2002). Teaching Bayesian reasoning: An evaluation of a classroom tutorial for medical students. *Medical Teacher, 24*(5), 516–521.

Li, M., & Vitányi, P. M. B. (1997). *An introduction to Kolmogorov complexity and its applications.* New York: Springer.

Makse, H. A., Havlin, B., & Stanley, H. E. (1995). Modeling urban growth patterns. *Nature, 377,* 608–612.

Markman, A. B., & Dietrich, E. (2000). Extending the classical view of representation. *Trends in Cognitive Sciences, 4*(12), 470–475.

Martignon, L., & Hoffrage, U. (1999). Why does one-reason decision making work? In G. Gigerenzer, P. M. Todd, & the ABC Research Group (Eds.), *Simple heuristics that make us smart* (pp. 119–140). New York: Oxford University Press.

McLeod, P., & Dienes, Z. (1996). Do fielders know where to go to catch the ball or only how to get there? *Journal of Experimental Psychology, 22*(3), 531–543.

Mitchell, T. M. (1997). *Machine learning.* New York: McGraw-Hill.

Newell, B. R., & Shanks, D. R. (2003). Take the best or look at the rest? Factors influencing "one-reason" decision-making. *Journal of Experimental Psychology: Learning, Memory, and Cognition, 29,* 53–65.

Oaksford, M., & Chater, N. (1998). *Rational models of cognition.* Oxford: Oxford University Press.

Pachur, T., & Biele, G. (2007). Forecasting by ignorance: The use and usefulness of recognition in lay predictions of sports events. *Acta Psychologica, 125*(1), 99–116.

Payne, J. W., Bettman, J. R., & Johnson, E. J. (1993). *The adaptive decision maker.* New York: Cambridge University Press.

Pearl, J. (1988). *Probabilistic reasoning in intelligent systems.* San Francisco: Morgan Kaufmann.

Pitt, M. A., Myung, I. J., & Zhang, S. (2002). Toward a method of selecting among computational models of cognition. *Psychological Review, 109*(3), 472–491.

Ramachandran, V. S. (1990). Interactions between motion, depth, color and form: The utilitarian theory of perception. In C. Blakemore (Ed.), *Vision: Coding and efficiency* (pp. 346–360). New York: Cambridge University Press.

Reddy, R. (1988). AAAI presidential address: Foundations and grand challenges of artificial intelligence. *AI Magazine, 9*(4), 9–21.

Reimer, T., & Hoffrage, U. (2005). Can simple group heuristics detect hidden profiles in randomly generated environments? *Swiss Journal of Psychology, 64*(1), 21–37.

Reimer, T., & Katsikopoulos, K. V. (2004). The use of recognition in group decision-making. *Cognitive Science, 28*(6), 1009–1029.

Rieskamp, J., & Hoffrage, U. (1999). When do people use simple heuristics and how can we tell? In G. Gigerenzer, P. M. Todd, & the ABC Research Group (Eds.), *Simple heuristics that make us smart* (pp. 141–167). New York: Oxford University Press.

Rieskamp, J., & Otto, P. (2005). *SSL: A theory of how people learn to select strategies.* Manuscript submitted for publication.

Rissanen, J. J. (1989). *Stochastic complexity and statistical inquiry.* Singapore: World Scientific.

Rozin, P., & Fallon, A. E. (1987). A perspective on disgust. *Psychological Review, 94*(1), 23–41.

Russell, S., & Norvig, P. (1995). *Artificial intelligence: A modern approach.* Englewood Cliffs, NJ: Prentice Hall.

Schooler, L. J., & Hertwig, R. (2005). How forgetting aids heuristic inference. *Psychological Review, 112,* 610–628.

Shepard, R. N. (1987). Towards a universal law of generalization for psychological science. *Science, 37*(4820), 1317–1323.

Shepard, R. N. (2001). Perceptual-cognitive universals as reflections of the world. *Behavioral and Brain Sciences, 24*(4), 581–601.

Simon, H. A. (1956). Rational choice and structure of the environment. *Psychological Review, 63,* 129–138.

Simon, H. A. (1990). Invariants of human behavior. *Annual Review of Psychology, 41,* 1–19.

Simon, H. A. (1996). *The sciences of the artificial* (3rd ed.). Cambridge, MA: MIT Press.

Slezak, P. (1999). Situated cognition: Empirical issue, "paradigm shift" or conceptual confusion? In J. Wiles & T. Dartnall (Eds.),

Perspectives on cognitive science (Vol. 2, pp. 69–98). Stamford, CT: Ablex.

Smith, B. C. (1999). Situatedness/embeddedness. In R. A. Wilson & F. C. Keil (Eds.), *The MIT encyclopedia of the cognitive sciences* (pp. 769–770). Cambridge, MA: MIT Press.

Sober, E. (1975). *Simplicity*. Oxford, UK: Clarendon Press.

Solomonoff, R. J. (1964). A formal theory of inductive inference, part 1 and part 2. *Information and Control*, 7(1–2), 224–254.

Stenning, K., & van Lambalgen, M. (2004). A little logic goes a long way: Basing experiment on semantic theory in the cognitive science of conditional reasoning. *Cognitive Science*, 28(4), 481–529.

Takezawa, M. (2004). *Developing a new framework of adaptive concession-making strategies: An approach to behavioral game theory from psychology*. Manuscript submitted for publication.

Tanner, C., & Medin, D.L. (2004). Protected values: No omission bias and no framing effects. *Psychonomic Bulletin and Review*, 11(1), 185–191.

Thrun, S., & Pratt, L. Y. (1998). *Learning to learn*. Boston: Kluwer Academic.

Todd, P. M. (1999). Simple inference heuristics versus complex decision machines. *Minds and Machines*, 9(4), 461–477.

Todd, P. M. (2001). Fast and frugal heuristics for environmentally bounded minds. In G. Gigerenzer & R. Selten (Eds.), *Bounded rationality: The adaptive toolbox* (pp. 51–70). Cambridge, MA: MIT Press.

Todd, P. M., Billari, F. C., & Simão, J. (2005). Aggregate age-at-marriage patterns from individual mate-search heuristics. *Demography*, 42(3), 559–574.

Todd, P. M., & Dieckmann, A. (2005). Heuristics for ordering cue search in decision making.

In L. K. Saul, Y. Weiss, & L. Bottou (Eds.), *Advances in neural information processing systems 17* (pp. 1393–1400). Cambridge, MA: MIT Press.

Todd, P. M., & Gigerenzer, G. (2001). Shepard's mirrors or Simon's scissors? Commentary on R. N. Shepard: Perceptual-cognitive universals as reflections of the world. *Behavioral and Brain Sciences*, 24(4), 704–705.

Todd, P. M., & Gigerenzer, G. (2003). Bounding rationality to the world. *Journal of Economic Psychology*, 24(2), 143–165.

Todd, P. M., Hertwig, R., & Hoffrage, U. (2005). The evolutionary psychology of cognition. In D. M. Buss (Ed.), *The handbook of evolutionary psychology* (pp. 776–802). Hoboken, NJ: Wiley.

Tversky, A. (1972). Elimination by aspects: A theory of choice. *Psychological Review*, 79(4), 281–299.

van Gelder, T. J. (1995). What might cognition be, if not computation? *Journal of Philosophy*, 91, 345–381.

Varela, F., Thompson, E., & Rosch, E. (1991). *The embodied mind: Cognitive science and human experience*. Cambridge, MA: MIT Press.

Vera, A. H., & Simon, H. A. (1993). Situated action: A symbolic interpretation. *Cognitive Science*, 17, 7–48.

Westenberg, M. R. M., & Koele, P. (1992). Response modes, decision processes and decision outcomes. *Acta Psychologica*, 80, 169–184.

Winograd, T., & Flores, F. (1996). *Understanding computers and cognition: A new foundation for design*. Norwood, NJ: Ablex.

Zahavi, A., & Zahavi, A. (1997). *The handicap principle: A missing piece of Darwin's puzzle*. Oxford, UK: Oxford University Press.

CHAPTER 18

Situativity and Learning

R. Keith Sawyer and James G. Greeno

1. Introduction

In the past two decades, education research has been transformed by cognitive science. Cognitive scientists have been interested in educational applications since the 1970s, when several artificial intelligence researchers began to develop intelligent tutoring systems (Bobrow & Collins, 1975; Sleeman & Brown, 1982; Wenger, 1987). The annual Carnegie Symposium in Cognition in 1974 provided a collection of early contributions on cognition and instruction (Klahr, 1976). In the 1980s, increasing numbers of cognitive scientists began to apply their research to learning. In 1987, John Seely Brown, David Kearns, and James Greeno cofounded the Institute for Research on Learning. In 1989, Roger Schank was recruited by Northwestern University to lead its new Institute for Learning Sciences. During this early period, the educational impact of cognitive science emphasized the internal mental processes of learning – this was consistent with the mentalist focus of early cognitive science, and with a belief among many educators that learning is an individual mental process.

The situative perspective emerged during the 1980s, when some social scientists began to analyze cognitive processes as aspects of interaction, and some cognitive scientists began to consider the social arrangements of learning as fundamental in determining what is learned. Lucy Suchman (1987) argued that the cognitive concept of action, a process governed by plans with adaptations to unanticipated aspects of situations, is inferior to an account in which "plans are resources for situated action, but do not in any strong sense determine its course" (p. 52). Suchman and others (e.g., Winograd & Flores, 1986) argued for a perspective in which "the organization of situated action is an emergent property of moment-by-moment interactions between actors, and between actors and the environments of their action" (1987, p. 179). Sylvia Scribner (1984), Jean Lave (Lave, 1988; Lave, Murtaugh, & de la Rocha, 1984), and Terezina Nunes, Annalucia Schliemann, and David Carraher (1993), analyzed problem

347

solving in everyday (i.e., nonlaboratory) settings and argued that solutions of problems involving mathematical reasoning were better understood as emerging from interactions between people and resources in the setting than as products of mental operations with and on symbolic representations. Another influential analysis of cognitive processes as aspects of social practice were Hutchins's (1995a) studies of reasoning and representational practices by navy ship-navigation teams, and of remembering by the system of people and technological resources in an airplane cockpit (1995b). Even color perception has been analyzed as a process embedded in social practices (Goodwin, 2000; Goodwin & Goodwin, 1996).

In the 1990s, researchers in the learning sciences founded a new disciplinary field, with international meetings and the *Journal of the Learning Sciences (JLS)*. The idea of situativity was adopted early on by some of these researchers. The term *situated cognition* was first used, in discussions of research on learning, by John Seely Brown, Allan Collins, and Paul Duguid (1989) and by Greeno (1989). Barbara Rogoff (1990) studied learning in family interactions and emphasized children's participation in activities. The term *situated learning* was introduced by Jean Lave and Etienne Wenger (1991), who argued that Brown et al.'s idea of cognitive apprenticeship should be replaced by a concept they called "legitimate peripheral participation," referring more generally to a learner's opportunities to participate meaningfully as a member of a community of practice rather than to a learner's social designation as an apprentice.

The situative perspective on learning brings together parts of cognitive science with parts of educational psychology, computer science, anthropology, sociology, information sciences, educational design studies, instructional design, and other fields. The approach we call "situative" has gone by many names, including *sociocultural psychology* (Rogoff, 1990; Wertsch, 1991), *activity theory* (Engeström, Miettinen, & Punamäki, 1999), and *distributed cognition* (Hutchins, 1995a). We consider that the core commitment of all of these is to analyze performance and transformations of activity systems that usually comprise multiple people and a variety of technological artifacts. Analyses can include studying how these aggregate performances and transformations correspond to and facilitate individual performance and learning, which are considered as participation and changes in participation in the activity system. The situative approach acknowledges that individual performance and learning can also be analyzed and explained in terms of individual mental structures. However, the situative perspective conceptualizes knowledge as distributed across people and artifacts, and the focus is on understanding activity and changes in activity systems in which knowledge is contributed and used in joint actions by the people and other resources that participate collaboratively.

A guiding principle of this new community is that learning is always situated. School learning is situated in a setting of a complex social organization that contain learners, teachers, curriculum materials, software tools, and the layout of the physical environment. Other learning is situated in a setting of an individual reading a book or just thinking. Although the adjective *situated* when applied to *learning* implies that there might be such a thing as nonsituated learning, learning scientists of the situative persuasion generally believe that all learning is situated. For this reason, we refer to a situative approach or situative perspective on learning rather than to situated learning or situated cognition.

Within traditional individualist cognitive science, the study of learning involves how mental structures change within the mind of the learner. Traditionally, cognitive scientists focus on the activities of individuals as they answer questions, solve problems, study texts, or respond to stimuli. Most often, they examine performance on experimental tasks or school assessments. Cognitive explanations are models of the processes that individuals use to construct store, retrieve, and modify patterns of information. Concepts and methods for analyzing these knowledge structures are the main focus of traditional individualist cognitive science.

The cognitivist study of problem solving is an example. Individual problem solvers are hypothesized to have constructed cognitive structures called "problem spaces" that represent the task, including objects of the problem, arrangements of the objects in different states, operators, goals, and strategies. Problem solving is understood as a process of searching in the problem space for a path from the initial state to the goal. In their activity, problem solvers construct additional structures of subgoals, evaluations of changes in the problem state, memories of past attempts, and so on (e.g., Newell & Simon, 1972).

Lave (1988) provided an analysis of reasoning and problem solving that contrasts with the standard cognitivist view. Her analyses support a conclusion that the problem space is not a stable information structure, as it is assumed to be to analyze problem solving as a search. She showed that reasoning by grocery shoppers was a process in which their decisions and the goals they eventually achieved were shaped jointly by their initial goals and preferences along with the objects and symbols in the aisles of the supermarket. This implies that the problem space is dynamically co-constructed by the problem solver in collaboration with material resources, sources of information, and (very often) other people in the situation. In another seminal analysis, Scribner (1984) showed that problem solving by workers in a dairy warehouse was a process in which their performance of placing the requested numbers of items in containers for delivery was jointly determined by the workers' reading of forms showing the numbers needed and the visible numbers of items and open spaces in containers in the situation.

The decisions made and the solutions produced in these two activity systems were generally optimal; that is, the shoppers generally chose products that had the best unit prices, and the dairy product loaders generally filled orders by moving the minimum number of items. When mathematical problems equivalent to those solved in these real-world systems are given to the participants in school-like tests, they generally perform poorly, as documented particularly by Nunes et al. (1993). One implication of this research is that it is meaningless to assess whether someone has learned a particular topic of mathematics without taking into account the kind of activity system in which the person's knowledge is to be evaluated.[1] For example, a paper-and-pencil test is a specific type of activity system, and a person's performance within that activity system is situated participation in a social practice, just as any other performance.

The claims and challenges of situative researchers were subjects of controversy in cognitive science. Alonzo Vera and Herbert Simon (1993) responded to the claim that behavior in complex settings requires a situative analysis, with examples such as fighting forest fires and highway driving that have been simulated or instantiated in computational systems, arguing that complex situations do not, in principle, require departing from a symbol-processing account. Several situative researchers responded to Vera and Simon (1993) in a special issue of *Cognitive Science*. Greeno and Joyce Moore's (1993) response focused on conceptualizations of symbols, noting that in situative analyses, symbols are assumed to be material or mental entities that are interpreted as having reference. In standard cognitive theory, according to the physical-symbol hypothesis, all of a person's activity is assumed to be mediated by symbolic representations. In the situative perspective, symbolic mediation is hypothesized to occur in some, but not all, activity.

Objections were also raised against the situative view by John Anderson, Lynne Reder, and Herbert Simon (1996), who disputed claims they attributed to the situative perspective, including the claim that if learning is situated it cannot transfer, and the claim that learning can be effective only if it occurs in groups. In response, Greeno (1997) argued that they were attacking a straw man: the situative perspective's commitment to analyzing learning at the level of activity systems does not preclude learning by individuals that transfers to other activity systems, nor effective learning by an individual in an activity system consisting of that individual with other resources (e.g., a textbook) and without other people participating.

Situative research provides an alternative to the mentalist idea that considers cognition as an internal mental process – one that may be influenced by the surrounding context but that is, at its root, internal. The situative approach shifts the focus: situated action within activity systems is central, with individuals and their actions considered constituents of the activity system. Analyses at the system level do not preclude analyses that focus on an individual participant, in which the other participants and resources are considered the context. Analyses at either the system level or the individual level can include hypotheses about information structures. At the system level, hypotheses are about shared information, the common ground that participants have and construct in their interaction. At the individual level, hypotheses are about what an individual knows, and what he or she perceives and understands in the activity setting. In the situative view, learning at an individual level involves transformation of the individual's participation in an activity system and occurs as part of a transformation of that activity system. Focusing on only individual learning, as traditional cognitive scientists do, requires an assumption that the cognitive processes of the activity system can be decomposed in such a way that specific elements can be associated with specific individual participants. But situative researchers have shown that activity systems differ in whether they are organized in ways that support such decomposition. The interactions of some activity systems, such as jazz or improvisational theater groups (Sawyer, 2003a, 2003b), are not decomposable in this way with our current methods of analysis, and for these activity systems, isolating the learning of any one individual would require more powerful analytical concepts and methods (see the discussion on complexity in section 7).

2. Settings of Learning and Learning Research

Traditionally (until the 1980s), there were two programs of research in the scientific study of learning. In one of the programs, in the purview of experimental psychology, research was conducted mainly in controlled laboratory settings, arranged to provide data to advance the theoretical programs of behaviorism and associationism. The other program, in educational research, was conducted mainly in classrooms, comparing different methods of teaching some topic in the curriculum. Scientists who conducted fundamental learning research in laboratories considered education research that was focused on what occurred within classrooms unsuitable for discovering fundamental concepts and principles of learning, because both the contents and situations of learning were too complex. These studies of learning in educational research were informed by general theoretical issues, such as the merits of discovery learning or the value of using concrete manipulative materials in mathematics, but the relation between experimental treatments and theories was not detailed enough to support substantive theoretical advances (Sowder, 1989).

The development of information-processing theory in cognitive science enabled formal analyses of subject-matter content of learning, and this research program was active beginning in the 1970s (e.g., Klahr, 1976). In this cognitivist perspective, learning is considered the acquisition of information structures that support improvement in tasks used in instruction. Empirical research used in developing and evaluating cognitive models of learning has mainly been done in laboratory studies in which participants engaged in tasks like those used in classroom instruction (e.g., Anderson, 1982; Kintsch, 1998). Concepts and principles developed and supported in this research have informed instructional systems, including curricula for reading (Palincsar & Brown, 1984), mathematics (Anderson, Boyle, Corbett, & Lewis, 1990; Carpenter & Fennema, 1992), and physics (diSessa

Table 18.1: Some Idealized Characteristics of Informal and Formal Education
(Adapted from Greenfield & Lave, 1982)

Informal Education	Formal Education
Embedded in daily life activities	Embedded in a context specialized for learning
Learners responsible for obtaining knowledge and skill, often in collaborative activity	Teacher responsible for imparting knowledge and skill, primarily to individuals
Personal; relatives are appropriate teachers	Impersonal; teachers should not be relatives
Little or no explicit pedagogy or curriculum	Explicit pedagogy and curriculum
Learning by observation and imitation	Learning by verbal interchange and questioning
Teaching by demonstration	Teaching by verbal presentation of general principles

& Minstrell, 1998; VanLehn et al., 2005), and these have been used and evaluated in school settings.

As researchers using the situative approach increasingly studied cognitive processes in settings of everyday activity, they took up studies of learning in a wide range of socially organized activities.

These studied included cross-cultural research by developmental psychologists and anthropologists, often in nonindustrial cultures where formal schooling was not universal. Of course, all cultures have learning environments within which to support learning by the young effectively; after all, formally institutionalized schooling is a relatively recent, modern invention. In the early stages of this program, researchers proposed a distinction between formal and informal learning environments in terms of some characteristics that seemed to contrast learning in school and learning in nonschool settings (see Table 18.1).

3. Considering Learning as Apprenticeship

In these early discussions, learning in apprenticeship was taken as a paradigmatic alternative to learning in school (e.g., Brown et al., 1989). In her study of a traditional tailor shop in Africa, Lave identified the central features of the productive form of apprenticeship she found in that setting (Lave & Wenger, 1991). First, apprenticeship empha-

sized specific procedures for accomplishing concrete tasks. Second, the procedures were used to accomplish meaningful real-world tasks, unlike formal schooling, where children learn knowledge that is not meaningful in the real world outside of school. Third, apprenticeship learning was embedded in a rich practical social context, unlike schooling, where the contexts for learning skills and knowledge are abstracted from their use in the nonschool world.

3.1. Cognitive Apprenticeship

Most of us think of very traditional trades when we hear the term *apprenticeship* – like shoemaking, silversmithing, or farming. John Seely Brown, Allan Collins, and their colleagues argued that the concept of apprenticeship had to be updated to make it relevant to modern subjects like reading, writing, and mathematics; they called this updated concept of apprenticeship "cognitive apprenticeship" (Brown et al., 1989; Collins, Brown, & Newman, 1989). It is cognitive because the focus is on cognitive skills and processes rather than physical ones. Traditional apprenticeship evolved to teach domains in which the process of carrying out a complex task can be observed, by both learner and expert, and the relationship between the task and the resulting product is relatively obvious. Because the apprentice's practice on the task is observable, the expert can comment on it, and they can work together to refine and correct the apprentice's performance. But with a lot of knowledge taught in schools, teachers cannot see the cognitive processes that are going on in students' heads, and it is difficult for them to comment on how the student is applying knowledge to problems and tasks. By the same token, students cannot see the cognitive problem-solving processes of their instructors; thus, they cannot learn through observation and imitation. Before apprenticeship methods can be applied to learn cognitive skills, the learning environment has to be changed to make these internal thought processes externally visible. Cognitive apprenticeship is designed to bring these cognitive processes into the open, where students can observe, enact, and practice them (Collins, 2006).

There are two additional differences between cognitive apprenticeship and traditional apprenticeship. First, because traditional apprenticeship is set in the workplace, the problems and tasks that are given to learners arise not from pedagogical concerns but from the demands of the workplace. Because the job selects the tasks for students to practice, traditional apprenticeship is limited in what it can teach. Cognitive apprenticeship differs from traditional apprenticeship in that the tasks and problems are chosen to illustrate the power of certain techniques and methods; to give students practice in applying these methods in diverse settings; and to increase the complexity of tasks slowly, so that component skills and models can be integrated.

Second, whereas traditional apprenticeship emphasizes teaching skills in the context of their use, cognitive apprenticeship emphasizes generalizing knowledge so that it can be used in many different settings. Cognitive apprenticeship extends practice to diverse settings and articulates the common principles, so that students learn how to apply their skills in varied contexts.

3.2. *Legitimate Peripheral Participation*

In retrospect, the concept of apprenticeship is less apt as an alternative to formally institutionalized schooling than was thought earlier. Even Lave's (Lave & Wenger, 1991) example of apprentice tailors is an imperfect fit to the then-prevalent characterization of informal learning shown in Table 18.1. Although the context of learning was a tailor shop, where the everyday work of manufacturing clothing was the main occupation, the activities of the apprentices were organized to support their learning; they did not simply absorb skills and knowledge incidentally from their presence in the tailor shop. Lave also reported that there was an explicit curriculum in which apprentices progressed from simpler to more complex tasks.

Lave and Wenger (1991) reviewed studies of apprenticeship learning, intending to identify major characteristics of this form of learning. They found that uses of the term *apprenticeship* in practice are very heterogeneous, and they concluded that it would be more appropriate to focus on a concept that refers to a central feature of apprenticeship that is productive for learning, such as the apprentice tailors that Lave studied (Lave & Wenger, 1991), but not present in many examples of apprenticeship and present in many learning arrangements that are not apprenticeship. They referred to this concept as "legitimate peripheral participation," which acknowledges that newcomers in a community of practice are not positioned to participate with full entitlements and accountability, but their participation can be organized so that they become more knowledgeable and skilled, changing along a trajectory toward full participation.

4. Considering Learning as Guided Participation

Although apprenticeship turned out not to be a useful organizing concept for learning research and design, aspects of productive versions of apprenticeship have been identified as productive characteristics of learning environments. In Lave's study (Lave & Wenger, 1991), apprentices learned these domain-specific methods through a combination of what Lave called observation, coaching, and practice. In this sequence of activities, the apprentice repeatedly observed the master and his or her assistants engaged in a complex task. The apprentice then attempted to execute some components of this task with coaching – guidance and help from the master. A key aspect of coaching was guided participation: the close responsive support that the master provided to help the novice complete an entire task, even before the novice had acquired every component skill. As the learner mastered more of the component skills, the master reduced his participation, providing fewer hints and less feedback to the learner. The master faded away completely when the apprentice had learned to smoothly execute the whole task. This concept of guided participation or scaffolding has been widely influential in the situative approach (Wood, Bruner, & Ross, 1976) and has frequently been connected to Vygotsky's concept of the zone of proximal development (Rogoff, 1990).

Rogoff (1990), who adopted the apprenticeship metaphor in her book *Apprenticeship in Thinking*, studied child-rearing practices among Guatemalan Mayans and found that much of their learning occurred through guided participation that shared many features with the apprenticeships studied by Lave. Her research revealed the importance of joint attention and intersubjectivity, and emphasized that learning involved a transformation in patterns of participation in an activity system.

These two research projects demonstrate key properties of learning that are found in every culture: learning occurs through situated social practices that have emerged in the culture to facilitate learning. Individual learning is almost impossible to understand apart from these situated social practices. Learning always occurs in historically unique social and cultural settings, with historically and culturally created social practices. Even formal classrooms are constructed social practices – they have emerged relatively recently in history, and they may not always exist in their current form.

In the situative approach, learning and development are reconceptualized as appropriation of tools and practices of the community rather than internalization of a body of facts and procedures (Wertsch, 1998). Practices are always situated – always stretched across multiple participants, working together with complex designed and technological artifacts. Learning as appropriation emphasizes that the individual is learning how to participate in the socially situated activity by appropriating the ability to perform a role within the system. The internal mental knowledge that may be required to support that participation is a question of secondary interest.

5. What Is Learned?

From the situative perspective, all socially organized activities provide opportunities for learning to occur, including learning that is different from what a teacher or designer might wish. In an ethnographic study of math lessons in a bilingual Spanish-English third-grade classroom, Lave and Hass (Lave, 1997) focused on eleven children in the upper math group for a three-week unit on multiplication and division. During the three weeks, the children gave no evidence of having adopted any of the specific strategies demonstrated by the teacher in her instruction, even though during group and individual work, the students worked hard on the math problems, and even though all eleven students turned in almost-perfect daily worksheets. But instead of using the procedures they were taught, they collaborated and invented new procedures that were easier. For example, they discovered that the multiplication table printed in the book could be used to solve division problems. However, essentially all of the problems were solved using counting and regrouping strategies, which were not presented in the lessons and were not supposed to be used. The children used their own invented procedures so as to produce the appearance of having used the teacher's procedures – by getting correct answers on the worksheets. After getting the correct answers using their own methods, they translated them into appropriate classroom form on the worksheets. Interviews with the teacher revealed that she was unaware of these interactive, collaboratively invented procedures.

The teacher and the textbook described in detail the procedures the children were supposed to use – but the children developed a different set of practices. They knew they had to get the right answer, but instead of learning the new procedure they learned how to draw on familiar known techniques. Even though they did not learn the material, they performed well on the tests and worksheets. Lave (1997) argues that rather than learning math, the children were learning how "to produce proper appearances of successful problem solving" (p. 31).

An individualist approach that relied only on tests and worksheets would not have revealed what was actually being learned in this classroom. The tests and the worksheets seemed to provide evidence that the intended learning was occurring. However, the situative approach – which analyzed the complex activity systems of the classroom, including the collaboration among the students and the ways they interacted with textbooks, tables, and worksheets – revealed that a different set of transformations was occurring.

The situative approach also provides a framework for research that studies the hidden curriculum – learning practices that are not explicitly taught, but that students need to know to participate effectively in learning activities. It is a mistake to think that school learning is decontextualized. Instead, school learning, like all learning, is situated activity. It is also a mistake to contrast school learning with everyday learning; school is the activity setting that students and teachers engage in every day (see Lave, 1997). Practices include patterns of discourse communication, such as those we discuss in the next section.

This perspective helps researchers to understand cultural differences in the goals of learning. From an individualist perspec-tive, learning is the continual accumulation of more and more knowledge – conceived of as representations that are possessed by the individual mind. From a situative perspective, learning is the gradual appropriation, through guided participation, of the ability to participate in culturally defined, socially situated activities and practices. And because every culture has its own unique set of practices, learning outcomes will be different within each culture. Thus, the situative approach contrasts with universalist developmental models traditionally associated with developmental psychology – for example, Piaget's four-stage model in which the pinnacle of development is formal, abstract thought.

6. The Key Role of Communication

Group learning always involves human communication, both verbal and nonverbal. To study group learning, situativity researchers use the methods of interaction analysis (Chi, 1997; Jordan & Henderson, 1995; Sawyer, 2006a). These methods evolved from several disciplinary strands, including ethnomethodology, discourse analysis, symbolic interactionism, and sociocultural psychology. This research focuses on how people talk to one another as they plan, evaluate, and coordinate their interactions with the material and technological systems in their environment. The goal is to identify patterns of interaction in which the people in the group coordinate their behaviors as they participate in their joint activity. Such patterns have been called "participation structures" (e.g., Erickson & Mohatt, 1982; Philips, 1972). Each culture and each group develops its own distinctive participation structures, and learning to become more effective in one's participation corresponds to achieving fuller participation in a community's practices (Lave & Wenger, 1991). For example, the participation structure of a traditional school classroom imposes specific roles on the teacher and the students, and provides a set of expected practices for each of those roles.

Students can talk only when given permission by the teacher, and even then the teacher determines the content of their talk. In contrast, the teacher has greater speaking rights; for example, he or she can interrupt a student if necessary, but students are rarely permitted to interrupt the teacher.

Interaction analysis studies the whole activity system, without yet having complete understanding of the individual components – particularly the individual human participants in the system. However, situativity researchers are interested in both group learning in activity systems and learning by individuals that advances their effectiveness in participation. The tension between the individual- and group-level approaches thus represents a general difficulty facing scientists who study complex systems: whether to proceed by reduction to study of the components or by holistic study of the entire system (Sawyer, 2005).

Interaction analysis has identified important patterns of conversational interaction – patterns of turn taking, opening and closing of topics, and mechanisms of repair in response to apparent misunderstanding have been reported and discussed (Sawyer, 2006a). Patterns of differential participation by different individuals can be analyzed; for example, in many classroom settings, students' contributions almost always respond directly to a question by the teacher (e.g., Bellack, Kliebard, Hyman, Frank, & Smith, 1966; Mehan, 1979); discourse in other classroom settings is arranged so that students also respond to one another's presentations and ideas (e.g., Cazden, 2001; O'Connor & Michaels, 1993).

Communication includes not only what is said but also how it is said and how it comes to be interpreted. In addition to characteristic participation structures, each culture has its own distinctive discursive practices. These practices include genre, style, catchphrases, wordplay, and joint routines. One of the speech genres most studied by education researchers is storytelling, or narrative; narrative scholars have discovered that different cultures often have very different discursive practices associated with storytelling. For example, literacy researchers are now examining how children learn to read by focusing on preliteracy or emergent literacy: how their informal interactions with parents and others prepare them for their first encounters with the printed word. One of the most important activities that families participate in collectively is telling stories. But this research is showing that children do not learn how to tell a story through explicit, formal instruction. Rather, they learn by engaging in joint storytelling interactions with their parents. At first, the parent may provide most of the detail, with the child filling in only occasionally; gradually, through a process of appropriation through guided participation, the child takes over increasing responsibility for telling the story. Through these complex activity systems, a storytelling duet (Falk, 1980), a child learns what a story is. (In fact, the narrative genre is subtly different in different cultures; there is no such thing as a universal narrative competence that all children uniformly develop toward. Michaels [1981] showed that even in the United States, European American and African American storytelling genres are substantially different – with negative impacts on students whose cultural background does not match that of the teacher. Again, the situative perspective provides a framework that allows us to better understand cultural differences in learning outcomes.)

7. The Emergence of Complex Social Mechanisms

The situative perspective within education is part of a broad recent trend in the social sciences, a trend that goes by many names but that is generally referred to as "complexity." The paradigm of complexity has primarily been applied to physical and biological systems, with the observation that theoretical analyses of some systems in terms of their components are so complex that an analysis in holistic terms provides a more satisfactory understanding than a reductionist analysis of the parts and then working back up from the parts in interaction to the whole system.

Many cognitive scientists have drawn on complexity concepts to analyze the human mind (e.g., Bechtel & Richardson, 1993). The brain is undeniably composed of individual neurons and their interactions, and understanding the brain can contribute to understanding mental processes. These facts have led several neuroscientists to pursue the usual reductionist approach in science: to understand the mind, first understand the behavior of individual neurons and collections of neurons, then understand the ways that neuronal structures interact, and then work upward to understand cognitive functions. However, many cognitive scientists and philosophers of mind are skeptical about the prospective reduction of analyses of mental states to analyses in terms of neurons and their interactions. And many who accept the possibility of eventual reduction still believe that the best way for current science to proceed is to continue analyses at both the neuronal and the mental levels.

The issues involved in the situative approach are analogous to these debates within the philosophy of mind, but moved up a level of analysis from the mind to the activity system. As in the philosophy of mind, there are reductionist scientists – the individualist cognitive scientists – who believe that study of activity systems should proceed by first analyzing individual mental states and processes of the people in the system, and then analyzing the people's interactions, thus working upward to an understanding of the entire activity system. Situativity researchers are analogous to the nonreductionist position in the philosophy of mind: activity systems may not be reducible to individual minds and their interactions, or at least the best scientific strategy for the field at this point in time is to include work at both the individual and the activity-system levels.

In this section, we list a few well-established characteristics of complex systems that have been identified by complexity scientists over the past two decades, especially by Bechtel and Richardson (1993).

These characteristics have been found in a variety of complex systems that have resisted reductionist explanation, from biological organisms to human minds to economic systems. To the extent that the activity systems associated with learning share these properties, their explanation is more likely to benefit from a situative approach (Sawyer, 2005).

8. Decomposition and Functional Localization

Bechtel and Richardson (1993) described the strategy of mechanistic explanation, which explains the behavior of a system in terms of the behaviors and interactions of the system's components. Mainly using examples from biology, they identified ways in which such explanations are similar and different.

All mechanistic explanations involve the behavior of some system and hypotheses about the system's decomposition into components. The hypotheses of a mechanistic explanation include a decomposition of functions, along with a decomposition into components and a functional analysis that hypothesizes ways that the behaviors of components and their interactions accomplish functions that, together, account for behaviors of the system as a whole.

Bechtel and Richardson's analyses show that mechanistic explanations differ in important ways. In some analyses, behavior of a system is explained as a simple aggregation of functions, each of which is accomplished by one of its components. According to such an analysis, the system is simply decomposable.

9. Decomposability

Simply decomposable systems are modular, with each component acting primarily according to its own intrinsic principles. Each component is influenced by the others only at well-defined input points; its function (its internal processing of those inputs) is not itself influenced by other components

(Simon, 1969). In such a system, the behavior of any part is intrinsically determined: it is possible to determine the component's properties in isolation from the other components, despite the fact that they interact. The organization of the entire system is critical for the function of the system as a whole. For example, one component's behavior may depend on products of other components. However, that organization does not provide constraints on the internal functioning of components.

Contemporary complexity theory has also argued that in functionally localizable systems, it is easier to reduce the analysis of the system to analysis of its components. A system is localizable if the functional decomposition of the system corresponds to its physical decomposition, and each property of the system can be identified with a single component or subsystem. If system functions or properties cannot be identified with components, but are instead distributed spatially within the system, that system is not functionally localized (Bechtel & Richardson, 1993, p. 24).

Some examples of explanations that hypothesize simple decompositions and functional localizations are production systems (e.g., Anderson, 1983; Newell, 1990). Each component of a production system is a production rule, composed of a condition and an action. Conditions test patterns in the database and actions add or change patterns in the database. On each cycle of its operation, the system tests the patterns of all the production rules, selects one that matches, and performs its actions. The behavior of each production rule depends on what other rules do, only in that they produce patterns that determine whether that production rule's condition is in the database.

There also are mechanistic explanations of what Bechtel and Richardson called "integrated systems," in which components behave very simply and functions are explained by hypotheses about the organization of the system; that is, by hypotheses about interactions between components. In an integrated system, the overall system organization is a significant influence on the function of any component; thus, component function is no longer intrinsically determined. Dependence of components on one another is often mutual and may even make it difficult to draw firm boundaries between components (Bechtel & Richardson, 1993, pp. 26–27). Functions that constitute the system's performance are not accomplished locally, by individual components or definable sets of components. Rather, their accomplishments are the result of interactivity in the system as a whole. Examples of integrated-system explanations include connectionist models of cognitive processes such as pattern recognition (e.g., Bechtel & Richardson, 1993; McClelland & Rumelhart, 1986). Each component of a connectionist system is a unit with the simple property of being more or less active. Connections between units transmit either activation or inhibition; that is, one unit causes either an increase or a decrease in the activity level of another unit, with the amount of the change depending on its current activity level. Running a connectionist model involves computing the activity levels of its units over many cycles, starting with some initial values, and with increased activation of some units because of an external event, such as the appearance of a stimulus. The collection of activation levels eventually converges to some configuration, and some configurations correspond to patterns. The system recognizes a pattern by settling into the configuration that corresponds to it. Unlike a production-system model, the function of recognizing a pattern by a connectionist network cannot be associated with a single unit or limited set of units. Instead, the configuration of activation for any recognizable pattern is achieved through the connections between units throughout the network.

Between the poles of simply decomposable systems and integrated systems, Bechtel and Richardson (1993) identified intermediate cases. Some explanations hypothesize nearly decomposable systems, with components whose behavior is mainly determined intrinsically, but with some nonnegligible interactions (cf. Simon, 1969). Other explanations hypothesize minimally decomposable systems, in which the behavior of the system and its components is mainly determined by interactions between components, but with some nonnegligible intrinsic characteristics of components.

10. Decomposability and Localizability of Activity Systems

A fundamental strategic issue for situative researchers is whether we should assume that explanations of behavior of activity systems characterize them as decomposable or nearly decomposable systems, or whether we should assume that explanations of activity systems turn out to require treating them as minimally decomposable or integrated systems.

The most obvious decomposition of an activity system treats its individual participants as components, along with other material and informational systems that contribute to the system's functioning. If an activity system is decomposable or nearly decomposable into those components, then progress toward a mechanistic explanation of its behavior can be made by studying the properties of individuals in the kinds of situations that the activity system encounters. For example, the large body of research on individuals solving problems has developed concepts and principles that account for many aspects of individual problem-solving performance and learning. If the problem-solving behavior of a group in an activity system is nearly decomposable into its individual components, we can expect that the concepts and principles developed by studying individual problem solving could provide the basis for explaining problem-solving performance and learning by the group. On the other hand, if the behavior of the group is minimally decomposable or integrated in solving problems, then principles of interaction between individuals are essential for explaining the group's performance and learning, and attempting to explain performance and learning by a group in terms of processes of individual problem solving could be counterproductive.

Those individualist scientists who would pursue the study of activity systems by focusing on individual minds are making a factoring assumption: the assumption that activity systems are decomposable and functionally localizable in the way Bechtel and Richardson (1993) described. However, studies by situativity researchers conclude that some activity systems are only minimally decomposable. This is the crux of the controversy between situativity theorists and individualist cognitive scientists; its resolution will ultimately rest on better understanding the nature of the composition of activity systems – a question that can only be addressed by studying the behavior of activity systems and evaluating the success of alternative explanatory accounts.

11. Functional Localizability

When individualist cognitive scientists analyze activity systems by focusing on one participant in the system, they typically assume functional localizability. For example, a complex team activity is easier to reduce to an individual-level analysis if each member of the team handles only one information-processing function in the context of the team. But when information functions are diffused and stretched across multiple members of the team, explaining even one activity system function requires explanations of multiple participants' mental structures and of their interactions over time.

In some activity systems, work is arranged so that the distribution of cognitive functions complies approximately with simple decomposition and functional localization. For example, Hutchins's (1995a) study of navy ship-navigation teams showed that in its normal operation, each team member had a single function in which he took an observation and reported it or received some information, performed a well-defined operation on it, and passed the results along. We expect that an explanation of this activity as a nearly decomposable and functionally localized system could be developed successfully. However, in an incident where there was a breakdown of the electrical system, the team's cognitive functioning became improvisational and distributed across several team members. When each component of team information processing was associated with a single individual, the factoring assumption would hold true and the activity system could potentially be understood by beginning with individual cognitive analysis and then working up to the team level. But when each step of information processing was diffused across multiple participants and accomplished by a process involving significant interaction, then the factoring assumption would not hold, and a valid information-processing analysis, such as the one Hutchins (1995a) provided, has to be done at the activity-system level.

12. Complex Communication among Units

In complexity theory, notions of emergence are based on interactions and relations among the component parts. For example, the criteria of nondecomposability and nonlocalizability are all defined in terms of the complex systemic relations among components. In many-bodied physics, the interactions are between molecules of a gas; in neuroscience, the interactions are synaptic transfer between neurons. Whether such a system is decomposable or functionally localizable is always determined by the nature of the interactions among units. Generally speaking, more simplistic interactions are more likely to result in reducible systems, because simplistic interactions are not capable of supporting the high information transfer among components required to support functional diffusion or nondecomposability. Consequently, several complexity theorists have suggested that the complexity of each interaction among components may be another variable contributing to emer-

gence (Sawyer, 2005). In contrast to the natural systems studied by most complexity theorists – gases or biological systems – the additional complexity of human language, with its complex symbolic interaction, is another characteristic that contributes to the irreducibility of activity systems.

In mechanical and biological systems, component relations are relatively well understood and well defined. Interactions between gas molecules in a container can be characterized using a few variables, such as mass, direction, and velocity. In contrast, human communication is qualitatively more complex for many reasons; for example, people are capable of metacommunicating about their ongoing interaction while it is under way, a property not found in the interactions of any other complex system. And the nature of peoples' interactions with technological artifacts is equally complex. The complex nature of interaction in activity systems makes them difficult to reduce to individual cognitive analysis.

13. Implications of Distributed Cognition for Decomposability and Functional Localization

Situativity researchers within education begin by observing that learning occurs in complex social situations, often with a wide variety of designed and technological artifacts (e.g., textbooks, lab equipment, tools of the trade, computer software). Most learning environments contain multiple individuals – particularly environments that are explicitly designed to facilitate learning, such as school classrooms or apprenticeship interactions. And even when an individual is apparently learning alone, that learning always requires interaction with complex designed artifacts that resulted from a historical and social process; for example, an individual may learn from reading a book in solitude, but that book was written and published through a complex and multistage organizational process, and the individual chose and acquired that particular book through another complex and social process. Although situativity researchers assume that all learning is situated – in the sense that even when an individual is alone, that solitude itself is socially constructed according to historically and culturally contingent norms – in empirical practice, they almost always study learning in groups, and typically in groups that are working with a variety of complex designed artifacts.

Hutchins (1995a) reported an influential study of group learning that we consider instructive regarding prospects for developing explanations of learning in activity systems. Hutchins analyzed a navigation team working on a navy ship. He found that the navigation task was cognitively distributed among the members of the team, in what he referred to as "distributed cognition." The official training manuals and training courses specified procedures for interaction and for how to use the complex technical devices on the bridge, but what actually happened on the navigation bridge very often diverged from the official, documented practice. In several cases, no one actually knew exactly how the entire system was operating, even though Hutchins was able to demonstrate that the system's emergent group practice was optimal.

Throughout his study, Hutchins examined how newcomers learned to participate in this complex activity system. But he also found that it was not only the newcomers who were learning; in some cases, the entire team was engaged in distributed learning. For example, in one very tense situation when the team's equipment broke down, which we mentioned earlier, the entire team had to collectively improvise and figure out a new way to distribute the cognitive task on the fly.

There was no official procedure for determining the ship's exact location when the equipment failed, and it turned out to be a complicated design problem to calculate the best way to distribute tasks among the group. The team had no time for complicated design; they had only minutes to reconfigure the group to handle the unex-

pected task. Instead of planning it first, the team improvised a response, one that turned out to be quite effective. Two team members evolved a new way to interact during the sixty-six location fixes that were taken during this tense time. When he analyzed his videotapes later, Hutchins found that the team had explored at least thirteen different organizational structures until, after about thirty fixes had been taken, an effective structure emerged. Hutchins (1995a) was so impressed that he began to think of the team as if it had its own brain: "the solution was clearly discovered by the organization itself before it was discovered by any of the participants" (p. 351).

Many learning environments are complex social systems that contain multiple people, some more knowledgeable than others; a wide range of physical and technological artifacts; and emergent and evolving cultural practices that bring together people and artifacts. These activity systems share properties with other complex systems that are not explained simply by intrinsic properties of their components: they are not simply decomposable or directly functionally localizable, at least according to current conceptual resources and methods, but possibly because activity systems may be inherently integral or minimally decomposable systems.[2] It is in this sense that learning environments are complex social systems, with emergent group properties that cannot be reduced to the mental structures of the individual participants without taking account of communicative and other interactions between the individuals.

The situative approach to learning analyzes learning environments as complex social systems. In keeping with the complexity project more generally, the situative approach resists reduction of learning environments to individual mental knowledge structures. The preferred method is to analyze the interactional mechanisms occurring within the learning system by using the methodologies of interaction analysis. Sawyer (2005) has argued that the key feature of collaborative groups that results in irreducible emergent properties is the complex communication enabled by human language.

The key to understanding learning in complex social groups is to analyze the processes of communication and to simultaneously analyze (1) how these processes give rise to emergent social properties, (2) to what extent those processes result in individual knowledge, and (3) to what extent that individual knowledge can be marshaled by the learner for use in a different complex social group (i.e., a different situation).

14. Explanations Differ Depending on Activities and Social Practices

Not all activity systems are alike, and the kind of explanation that can be developed for some activity systems may not be achievable for others. More specifically, we expect that aspects of a group's social practices – the regularities of the group's interactive behavior as it functions as an activity system – determine the degree of decomposability and functional localizability that can be assumed in explaining the group's activities. For example, an individual reading a page of printed text is an activity system that has been explained successfully with local functionality and simple decomposability. The physical text, after all, does not change in the process of its being read. This does not contradict our assertion that reading a text should be understood as an activity embedded in a social context, but while the person is alone, interacting with a text, the meanings that he or she attributes to the text are a function of the physical text and characteristics of the person. In contrast, we are confident that the activity system of a face-to-face conversation needs to be analyzed as a minimally decomposable system in which functions are achieved through joint action, not localized in the contributions of individual participants (Clark, 1996; Sawyer, 2005). Sawyer's (2003a, 2003b) studies of improvisational theater and jazz performance also provide clear cases requiring analyses as minimally decomposable and functionally nonlocalized systems. Intermediate cases, such

as interacting with a computer program, exchanging e-mail messages, conversing on the telephone, or performing scripted drama or scored music, need to be analyzed to determine the kinds of functional decomposition and localization that provide the most satisfactory explanations.

As learning scientists, we are especially concerned with the nature of explanations of activity in learning environments; that is, in activity systems that are organized deliberately for learning to occur. We expect that explanations of learning environments differ in the kinds of explanations that can be developed, depending on the social practices of their activity systems. For example, in classrooms that are organized didactically, with a teacher making extensive presentations, with discourse mainly consisting of initiation-response-evaluation (IRE) exchanges, and with most of the students' learning activity consisting of individual seatwork and homework, it seems plausible to expect successful explanations that characterize the activity as nearly decomposable and functionally localized systems. On the other hand, in classrooms that are organized primarily for collaborative learning activities with discourse patterns that include revoicing and other exchanges between students, we expect that successful explanations will require assuming minimal decomposability and achievement of functions by interaction rather than intrinsic properties of the individual teachers and students.

15. Bringing Together Individual Learning and Group Learning

Although situativity researchers emphasize that learning environments always contain complex activity systems, they nonetheless are interested in the learning associated with individual participants, as well as the learning that corresponds to transformations in the entire activity system. But unlike traditional cognitive psychology, individual cognition is considered in relation to transformations of the activity system. For example, in inquiry classrooms, students' understandings are shared as they formulate and evaluate questions, and propose and debate alternative meanings of concepts and explanations. Analyses can consider whether the actions of individual students contribute to the class's progress in achieving shared understanding, rather than simply being displays of the understandings they have already constructed cognitively in their prior interactions with textbooks, teachers, and computers.

Developing a situative explanation requires a simultaneous consideration of both the transformations of the entire activity system and of participants' knowledge structures that are used in the activity. These analyses often use many of the concepts that are standard in cognitive science; they differ in that they are based on records of conversation between participants (rather than laboratory experiments or think-aloud protocols). Situative studies bring cognitive science and interaction analysis together by providing analyses of interaction in activity systems and including hypotheses about structures of information used and constructed in the activity. These analyses include representing contributions of the material and technological tools and artifacts of the system. The goal is to understand cognition as the interaction among participants and tools in the context of an activity. For this reason, it is often said that the situative perspective studies distributed cognition: problem solving, planning, and reasoning are accomplished by a group of people, working together with complex technological artifacts and with external representations they generate during the task (e.g., diagrams, figures, models).

Thus, an analysis in the situative perspective can analyze three levels simultaneously: starting with the symbolic interaction among members of the group, working up toward an analysis of the emergent group properties that result, and working down toward an analysis of the thinking processes and knowledge structures perceived and constructed by one or more of the individuals participating in the group.

16. Example 1: A Study of Learning a Classroom Practice

To illustrate how learning scientists can study the learning of practices using the situative perspective, we describe two case studies. In this section, we summarize Hall and Rubin's (1998) analysis of how a new representational practice became established in a classroom (following Greeno, 1998). They documented how the practice originated in an individual's work, expanded through that student's small group, and then was broadcast to the class.

The teacher, Magdalene Lampert, developed innovative practice-oriented teaching methods and examined the processes of her teaching for several years. Lampert often had the students work in groups of four or five students to discuss challenging problems. Each student kept a journal in which he or she recorded problem solutions and explanations. Hall and Rubin (1998) analyzed videotaped records of several segments of class activity that illustrate Lampert's approach to teaching about distance, time, and speed of motion – all key concepts in elementary mathematics. They analyzed several incidents in the development and use of a kind of representational practice that they called a "journey line," which represents two quantities – time and distance – by marking units along the line that are labeled with distances above the line and times below the line. The journey-line representation was used by a student, Karim, to explain to another student, Ellie, why one of the problems should be solved using multiplication. Later, Lampert asked Karim to explain the representation to the class. After Karim's presentation, Lampert had Ellie explain the representation to the class, affirming that it was a resource to be used generally in the class's practice.

Hall and Rubin (1998) distinguished between three levels of activity: private activity (writing in the journal), local activity (small-group conversation), and public activity (presentations and discussions with the whole class). They identified several interactions in which the representational practice of the journey line played a key role – it functioned as a resource in the class's practices of problem solving and mutual sensemaking. Learning-sciences research often examines the role of representational forms as resources for collaborative sensemaking and reasoning. It also examines the ways that students talk about their developing understanding.

17. Example 2: A Study of Learning in a Scientific Work Environment

The second case study we describe was a study by Nersessian and her colleagues of how laboratory groups develop over time towards increasing understanding (Nersessian, 2005; Nersessian, Kurz-Milcke, Newstetter, & Davies, 2003). They found it productive to consider activity in the scientific laboratory they studied as an evolving distributed cognitive system. For example, Nersessian et al. (2003) gave a situative interpretation of several aspects of learning in a bioengineering lab that was trying to develop artificial blood vessels: the evolution of artifacts and methods, the evolution of relationships between individuals, and the evolution of relationships between individuals and artifacts.

Biomedical engineering is a new combination of disciplines in which new knowledge and practices are emerging continually, and the researchers are constantly learning during their problem-solving activities. The laboratory team included undergraduates, doctoral students, and postdocs, and all of these participants learned over time and transformed their participation in the activity system. Much of the equipment used in the laboratory is designed and built by the team, and the members of the team often modify the technological artifacts during their practice – such that not only the people but also the tools undergo change over time.

Nersessian et al. (2003) found that to understand how problems were solved in this laboratory, they had to expand the traditional cognitive science notions of problem space and mental representation to consider these distributed across the people and the technology in the laboratory – a defining feature of situative research. The problem space comprises models and artifacts together with a repertoire of activities in which simulative model-based reasoning plays a key role (Lehrer & Schauble, 2006). The problem-solving processes of the lab are distributed throughout the cognitive system, which comprises both the researchers and the cognitive artifacts that they use.

They used a mixed-method approach, combining cognitive analyses of the problems and models used by researchers with an ethnographic analysis of the situative activities and tools and how they are used in the ongoing activity of the laboratory. Their close ethnographic analysis allowed them to document temporary and transient arrangements of the activity system – the laboratory routines, the organization of the workspace, the cultural artifacts being used, and the social organization of the team members. Their cognitive analysis allowed them to document how people and their relationships changed over time – as they evaluated and revised problem definitions (often working closely with technological artifacts), as they revised models of phenomena, and as their concepts changed over time.

Because it is impossible to test artificial blood vessels in a live human body, modeling practices are critical to the work. The researchers have to design working models to use for experimentation. Each iteration of a model represents the lab's collective understanding of the properties and behaviors of the human body. For example, the flow loop is a device that emulates the shear stresses experienced by cells within the blood vessels. The flow loop originated in the research of the senior scientist and has been passed down through generations of researchers, enabling each to build on the research of others, as it is reengineered in the service of model-based reasoning. The flow loop is constructed so that the test fluid will create the same kinds of mechanical stresses as a real blood vessel. But because the model is a mechanical system, its design is subject to engineering constraints, and these often require simplification and idealization of the target biological systems being modeled. For example, in the body arterial wall, motion is a response to the pulsating blood flow, but in the flow-loop simulation, known as a *bioreactor*, the fluid does not actually flow; but it does model the pulsating changes in pressure experienced by the arterial wall.

In scientific laboratories, collaboration is often mediated by external representations such as these mechanical models, as well as diagrams and sketches. In this lab, devices are external representations of the collective knowledge of the group. Model-based reasoning is a distributed phenomenon, involving both the internal mental models that a researcher holds, as well as the shared external model manifested in devices and other models.

A situative analysis focuses on this distributed nature of cognition in the laboratory, treating it as a distributed process involving multiple people and the technological artifacts that they create and modify together. In the situative view of an activity system, learning is conceived of as transformations over time in the nature of the interactions among people and between people and their constructed artifacts. For example, when newcomers to the lab are first introduced to a device like the bioreactor, they assume that its design is fixed. As they begin to interact with these devices, they quickly learn the many problems: tubes leak, sutures do not keep, reservoirs overflow, pumps malfunction. The newcomers soon realize that everyone else, including the most experienced old-timer, is always struggling to get things to work, always revising and modifying the devices. The newcomer's learning is a process of coming to understand the contingent and changing nature of these devices – the newcomers build a relationship with the devices that Nersessian et al. (2003) called a "cognitive partnership."

18. Conclusion

Education research has contributed substantially to the situated cognition approach, beginning in the 1980s, when cognitive scientists first began to realize the situated nature of cognition and learning. Most of the seminal empirical studies that contributed to the emergence of the situated approach were conducted in learning environments. The situative approach has increased in influence in education research, from the late 1980s to the present. It is a core element of the new interdisciplinary field of the learning sciences (Sawyer, 2006b).

In this chapter we have written about the situative approach to learning rather than situated learning. Even if the researcher is a traditional cognitive psychologist, interested exclusively in how individual mental structures change during learning, that individual's learning will nonetheless be situated. The laboratory settings used by experimental cognitive psychologists are situations – complex activity systems – and the learning that occurs in such experiments is just as situated as a tailor's apprenticeship or a child's learning a first language.

Researchers taking a situative perspective generally accept that individuals do, in fact, learn in these situations; and that individual mental structures certainly change as part of this learning. The situative approach is complementary and compatible with traditional cognitive psychology, and both approaches contribute important pieces of the puzzle of how people learn. However, the situative approach changes the way we think about and use the findings of experimental psychology. It problematizes the decomposability assumption typically made by traditional psychologists and suggests that, before scientists can really understand what these experiments have taught us, we first have to analyze the experiment itself as a complex activity system – in other words, apply the situative approach to experimental settings.

The situative approach will continue to be central to the learning sciences, because this new interdisciplinary field is increasingly demonstrating that learning is most effective when students work collaboratively to solve authentic problems in rich, real-world tasks. In these new learning environments, it is extremely difficult to be misled into thinking that individual students learn in isolation – whereas in the traditional method of instructionist teaching, when students sat in rows at desks and were expected to internalize the teacher's pronouncements, one could more easily assume that learning was about internalizing the knowledge structures being explained by the teacher. A situative approach can make an important contribution to understanding how these new forms of learning take place and how we can design learning environments to be most effective.

Notes

1 An analogy with physics is instructive. Measurement of a moving object's velocity only makes sense if a frame of reference is specified. Assessment situations for assessing knowledge are akin to frames of reference for measuring properties of motion. Of course, the complexity of assessing what a person knows is much greater than the complexity of measuring how an object is moving, but the need to interpret findings of assessment in ways that take account of the frame of reference involved in the assessment is analogous.

2 The two of us differ in the strengths of our pessimism about the prospects of developing a reductionist or mechanistic explanation of cognitive processes in groups. In R. K. S.'s view, reduction of those activity systems that are highly integrated, even if one day possible in principle, might not add to the scientific knowledge of those systems that we had already acquired through analysis at the activity-system level and could require a vastly greater investment of resources (see Sawyer, 2005). In J. G. G.'s view, simple reduction of activity systems is out of reach now, given the theoretical resources that are available. However, future developments, such as better understanding how individuals are sensitive to one another's communicative intentions, could result in a theory (or

theories) that provides strong explanations of activity systems as nearly decomposable and localizable systems.

References

Anderson, J. R. (1982). Acquisition of cognitive skill. *Psychological Review, 89*, 396–406.

Anderson, J. R. (1983). *The architecture of cognition.* Cambridge, MA: Harvard University Press.

Anderson, J. R., Boyle, C. F., Corbett, A. T., & Lewis, M. W. (1990). Cognitive modeling and intelligent tutoring. *Artificial Intelligence, 42*, 7–50.

Anderson, J. R., Reder, L. M., & Simon, H. A. (1996). Situated learning and education. *Educational Researcher, 25*(4), 5–11.

Bechtel, W., & Richardson, R. C. (1993). *Discovering complexity: Decomposition and localization as strategies in scientific research.* Princeton, NJ: Princeton University Press.

Bellack, A. A., Kliebard, H. M., Hyman, R. T., Frank, L., & Smith, J. (1966). *The language of the classroom.* New York: Teacher's College Press.

Bobrow, D. G., & Collins, A. (1975). *Representation and understanding: Studies in cognitive science.* New York: Academic Press.

Brown, J. S., Collins, A., & Duguid, P. (1989). Situated cognition and the culture of learning. *Educational Researcher, 18*(1), 32–42.

Carpenter, T. P., & Fennema, E. (1992). Cognitively guided instruction: Building on the knowledge of students and teachers. *International Journal of Educational Research, 17*, 457–470.

Cazden, C. B. (2001). *Classroom discourse: The language of teaching and learning* (2nd ed.). Portsmouth, NH: Heinemann.

Chi, M. T. H. (1997). Quantifying qualitative analyses of verbal data: A practical guide. *Journal of the Learning Sciences, 6*(3), 271–315.

Clark, H. H. (1996). *Using language.* Cambridge: Cambridge University Press.

Collins, A. (2006). Cognitive apprenticeship. In R. K. Sawyer (Ed.), *The Cambridge handbook of the learning sciences* (pp. 47–60). New York: Cambridge University Press.

Collins, A., Brown, J. S., & Newman, S. E. (1989). Cognitive apprenticeship: Teaching the craft of reading, writing, and mathematics.

In L. B. Resnick (Ed.), *Knowing, learning, and instruction: Essays in honor of Robert Glaser* (pp. 453–494). Mahwah, NJ: Lawrence Erlbaum.

diSessa, A. A., & Minstrell, J. (1998). Cultivating conceptual change with benchmark lessons. In J. G. Greeno & S. V. Goldman (Eds.), *Thinking practices in mathematics and science learning* (pp. 155–187). Mahwah, NJ: Lawrence Erlbaum.

Engeström, Y., Miettinen, R., & Punamäki, R. (Eds.). (1999). *Perspectives on activity theory.* New York: Cambridge University Press.

Erickson, F., & Mohatt, G. (1982). Cultural organization of participation structures in two classrooms of Indian students. In G. Spindler (Ed.), *Doing the ethnography of schooling* (pp. 132–174). New York: Holt, Rinehart & Winston.

Falk, J. (1980). The conversational duet. In B. R. Caron (Ed.), *Proceedings of the Sixth Annual Meeting of the Berkeley Linguistics Society* (pp. 507–514). Berkeley: University of California, Berkeley.

Goodwin, C. (2000). Practices of color classification. *Mind, Culture, and Activity, 7,* 19–36.

Goodwin, C., & Goodwin, M. H. (1996). Seeing as situated activity: Formulating planes. In Y. Engeström & D. Middleton (Eds.), *Cognition and communication at work* (pp. 61–95). New York: Cambridge University Press.

Greenfield, P., & Lave, J. (1982). Cognitive aspects of informal education. In D. Wagner & H. Stevenson (Eds.), *Cultural perspectives on child development* (pp. 181–207). San Francisco: W. H. Freeman.

Greeno, J. G. (1989). Situations, mental models and generative knowledge. In D. Klahr & K. Kotovsky (Eds.), *Complex information processing: The impact of Herbert A. Simon* (pp. 285–318). Hillsdale, NJ: Lawrence Erlbaum.

Greeno, J. G. (1997). On claims that answer the wrong questions. *Educational Researcher, 26*(1), 5–17.

Greeno, J. G. (1998). The situativity of knowing, learning, and research. *American Psychologist, 53,* 5–26.

Greeno, J. G., & Moore, J. L. (1993). Situativity and symbols: Response to Vera and Simon. *Cognitive Science, 17,* 49–59.

Hall, R., & Rubin, A. (1998). There's five little notches in here: Dilemmas in teaching and learning the conventional structure of rate.

In J. G. Greeno & S. V. Goldman (Eds.), *Thinking practices in mathematics and science learning* (pp. 189–235). Mahwah, NJ: Lawrence Erlbaum.

Hutchins, E. (1995a). *Cognition in the wild.* Cambridge, MA: MIT Press.

Hutchins, E. (1995b). How a cockpit remembers its speeds. *Cognitive Science, 19,* 265–288.

Jordan, B., & Henderson, A. (1995). Interaction analysis: Foundations and practice. *Journal of the Learning Sciences, 4*(1), 39–103.

Kintsch, W. (1998). *Comprehension: A paradigm for cognition.* Cambridge: Cambridge University Press.

Klahr, D. (Ed.). (1976). *Cognition and instruction.* Mahwah, NJ: Lawrence Erlbaum.

Lave, J. (1988). *Cognition in practice: Mind, mathematics, and culture in everyday life.* New York: Cambridge University Press.

Lave, J. (1997). The culture of acquisition and the practice of understanding. In D. Kirshner & J. Whitson (Eds.), *Situated cognition: Social, semiotic, and psychological perspectives* (pp. 17–35). Mahwah, NJ: Lawrence Erlbaum.

Lave, J., Murtaugh, M., & de la Rocha, O. (1984). The dialectic of arithmetic in grocery shopping. In B. Rogoff & J. Lave (Eds.), *Everyday cognition: Its development in social context* (pp. 67–94). Cambridge, MA: Harvard University Press.

Lave, J., & Wenger, E. (1991). *Situated learning: Legitimate peripheral participation.* New York: Cambridge University Press.

Lehrer, R., & Schauble, L. (2006). Cultivating model-based reasoning in science education. In R. K. Sawyer (Ed.), *The Cambridge handbook of the learning sciences* (pp. 371–387). New York: Cambridge University Press.

McClelland, J., Rumelhart, D., & Parallel Distributed Research Group (Eds.). (1986). *Parallel distributed processing: Explorations in the microstructure of cognition.* Cambridge, MA: MIT Press/Bradford.

Mehan, H. (1979). *Learning lessons.* Cambridge, MA: Harvard University Press.

Michaels, S. (1981). "Sharing time": Children's narrative styles and differential access to literacy. *Language in Society, 10,* 423–442.

Nersessian, N. J. (2005). Interpreting scientific and engineering practices: Integrating the cognitive, social, and cultural dimensions. In M. Gorman, R. Tweney, D. Gooding, & A. Kincannon (Eds.), *Scientific and technological thinking* (pp. 17–56). Mahwah, NJ: Lawrence Erlbaum.

Nersessian, N. J., Kurz-Milcke, E., Newstetter, W. C., & Davies, J. (2003). Research laboratories as evolving distributed cognitive systems. *Proceedings of the Cognitive Science Society 25* (pp. 857–862). Hillsdale, NJ: Lawrence Erlbaum.

Newell, A. (1990). *Unified theories of cognition.* Cambridge, MA: Harvard University Press.

Newell, A., & Simon, H. A. (1972). *Human problem solving.* Englewood Cliffs, NJ: Prentice Hall.

Nunes, T., Schliemann, A. D., & Carraher, D. W. (1993). *Street mathematics and school mathematics.* New York: Cambridge University Press.

O'Connor, M. C., & Michaels, S. (1993). Aligning academic task and participation status through revoicing: Analysis of a classroom discourse strategy. *Anthropology and Education Quarterly, 24*(4), 318–335.

Palincsar, A. S., & Brown, A. L. (1984). Reciprocal teaching of comprehension-fostering and comprehension-monitoring activities. *Cognition and Instruction, 1,* 117–175.

Philips, S. U. (1972). Participant structures and communicative competence: Warm Springs children in community and classroom. In C. B. Cazden, V. P. John, & D. Hymes (Eds.), *Functions of language in the classroom* (pp. 370–394). New York: Teacher's College Press.

Rogoff, B. (1990). *Apprenticeship in thinking: Cognitive development in social context.* New York: Oxford University Press.

Sawyer, R. K. (2003a). *Group creativity: Music, theater, collaboration.* Mahwah, NJ: Lawrence Erlbaum.

Sawyer, R. K. (2003b). *Improvised dialogues: Emergence and creativity in conversation.* Westport, CT: Greenwood.

Sawyer, R. K. (2005). *Social emergence: Societies as complex systems.* New York: Cambridge University Press.

Sawyer, R. K. (2006a). Analyzing collaborative discourse. In R. K. Sawyer (Ed.), *The Cambridge handbook of the learning sciences* (pp. 187–204). New York: Cambridge University Press.

Sawyer, R. K. (Ed.). (2006b). *The Cambridge handbook of the learning sciences.* New York: Cambridge University Press.

Scribner, S. (1984). Studying working intelligence. In B. Rogoff & J. Lave (Eds.), *Everyday cognition: Its development in social context* (pp. 9–40). Cambridge, MA: Harvard University Press.

Simon, H. A. (1969). *The sciences of the artificial.* Cambridge, MA: MIT Press.

Sleeman, D., & Brown, J. S. (Eds.). (1982). *Intelligent tutoring systems.* New York: Academic Press.

Sowder, J. T. (1989). *Research agenda for mathematics education: Vol. 5. Setting a research agenda.* Reston, VA: National Council of Teachers of Mathematics.

Suchman, L. A. (1987). *Plans and situated actions: The problem of human-machine communication.* New York: Cambridge University Press.

VanLehn, K., Lynch, C., Schulze, K., Shapiro, J. A., Shelby, R., Taylor, L., et al. (2005). The Andes physics tutor: Five years of evaluations. In G. McCalla & C. K. Looi (Eds.), *Proceedings of the 12th International Conference of Artificial Intelligence and Education* (pp. 678–685). Amsterdam: IOS Press.

Vera, A. H., & Simon, H. A. (1993). Situated action: A symbolic interpretation. *Cognitive Science,* Special Issue: Situated Action, *17*(1), 7–48.

Wenger, E. (1987). *Artificial intelligence and tutoring systems: Computational and cognitive approaches to the communication of knowledge.* San Francisco: Morgan Kaufmann.

Wertsch, J. V. (1991). *Voices of the mind: A sociocultural approach to mediated action.* Cambridge, MA: Harvard University Press.

Wertsch, J. V. (1998). *Mind as action.* New York: Oxford University Press.

Winograd, T., & Flores, F. (1986). *Understanding computers and cognition.* Norwood, NJ: Ablex.

Wood, D., Bruner, J., & Ross, G. (1976). The role of tutoring in problem solving. *Journal of Child Psychology and Psychiatry, 17,* 89–100.

CHAPTER 19

Language in the Brain, Body, and World

Rolf A. Zwaan and Michael P. Kaschak

1. Introduction

Language is a uniquely human tool. It helps us situate ourselves in the world around us by directing our attention to people, objects, events, and possibilities for action. Language also situates us in worlds separate from our immediate environment. Through descriptions of real or imagined events, it serves to draw our attention to people, objects, events, and possibilities for action that are not present in the here and now. This situating of oneself in events outside of the here and now takes place through a process of mental simulation.

Mental simulation can be considered a vicarious experiencing of the events being described. Language is a sequence of stimuli that orchestrate the retrieval of experiential traces of people, places, objects, events, and actions. This retrieval occurs in part via a rapid, direct, and passive memory process similar to the resonance process described by Hintzman (1986). The experiential traces reflect the comprehenders' past experience with particular objects, actions, and events, as well as their previous experience with lan-

guage. For example, understanding a sentence about removing an apple pie from the oven would involve the retrieval of traces of motor experience (lifting the pie and feeling its weight) and perceptual experience (seeing and smelling the pie, feeling the heat coming out of the oven). The relevant memory retrieval occurs by probing the same sensorimotor processing mechanisms that would be involved if one were actually lifting, seeing, and smelling the pie (Barsalou, 1999). In a very literal sense, the comprehension of a sentence about removing the pie from the oven relies on much the same machinery that would be involved in actually carrying out the action. Understanding the sentence also involves the resonance of experiential traces of having heard, read, spoken, and written the words in the sentence.

A number of recent studies have pointed to the conclusion that the ability to mentally simulate actions (and their consequences) is crucial to our ability to plan and execute actions, and to understand the actions of others (e.g., Flanagan & Johansson, 2003; Wolpert, Doya, & Kawato, 2003). These data form the basis of our claims about the role of mental simulation in language comprehension. Just as we understand the actions of others by internally simulating their actions, we can understand the actions of people described in language through an internal simulation of their actions (e.g., Glenberg & Kaschak, 2002; Zwaan & Taylor, 2006). Thus, language comprehension is grounded in the same knowledge and processes that are used to support comprehension and conceptualization in many other domains (Barsalou, 1999, 2005).

The ability to experience situations vicariously is adaptive. It allows us to learn from (and empathize with) others' past experiences and to coordinate future actions. This provides the basis for anticipating future states within ourselves (or others) and in the environment. We call the process through which this anticipation arises "presonance." Presonance captures the idea that the quick-acting and passive memory retrieval posited in theories such as Hintzman's (1986) does more than simply bring forth past experiences; it also brings forth experiential memory traces that facilitate the processing of likely changes to the self or the environment. The ability to anticipate such changes to the self or the environment is crucial to the ability to plan and take action in the world (for a discussion of the role of trajectories of events in memory and memory retrieval, see Glenberg, 1997). For example, when we see a barking dog charge toward us, previous experience with similar situations tells us that the dog will continue its approach. Thus, we can prepare for this future state (approaching dog) by taking action to protect ourselves. It is important to stress that presonance should be viewed as an automatic and fast process and not as deliberative prediction.

In the context of language processing, presonance operates on many levels. Anticipating the next elements in the linguistic input – be they phonemes, words, or syntactic constructions – serves to facilitate the processing of those elements. Anticipating subsequent changes in the events being described (on a basic level, what is coming next in the story) can facilitate language comprehension (e.g., Hess, Foss, & Carroll, 1995). More broadly, knowledge about particular genres of language use allows comprehenders to anticipate the content and structure of a text, and thus tailor their reading strategies in appropriate ways (e.g., Zwaan, 1994). This anticipation is guided both by one's experience with real actions and events in the world and by one's previous experiences with language.

The claim that language processing involves the rapid use of information that points toward likely next states in the linguistic input is consistent with constraint-satisfaction views of language processing (e.g., Jurafsky, 1996; MacDonald, Pearlmutter, & Seidenberg, 1994; McRae, Spivey-Knowlton, & Tanenhaus, 1998). On this view, sentence processing proceeds by activating many possible interpretations for the sentence. These interpretations compete for activation on the basis of probabilistic information from the comprehender's experience with language. The likelihood of a particular word being used in a particular syntactic function (MacDonald et al., 1994), the likelihood of a particular syntactic structure being used (Jurafsky, 1996), the preceding context (e.g., Spivey & Tanenhaus, 1998; van Berkum, Brown, Zwitserlood, Kooijman, & Hagoort, 2005), and other such factors are simultaneously considered as the language-processing system works to develop the most likely interpretation of the sentence. When the language refers to elements of the here and now (rather than a displaced situation), additional factors (e.g., the affordances of the objects present in the environment; Chambers, Tanenhaus, & Magnuson, 2004) also exert an influence on on-line sentence comprehension (see Spivey & Richardson, this volume). There is now considerable evidence that these sources of information are used as soon as they are available to the language-comprehension system.

Closer to our notion of mental simulation, presonance may be based on a covert use of the language-production system (Pickering & Garrod, 2004; Townsend &

Bever, 2001). On the most basic level, there is evidence to suggest that our perception of speech sounds involves the activation (resonance) of the motor programs that would be used to produce those sounds ourselves (e.g., Porter & Lubker, 1980; for a brief review and discussion, see Fowler, 1996). The use of one's language-production system while processing language also takes place on higher levels of analysis. The general idea behind this premise is that comprehenders would continuously but subconsciously ask the question, What would I say or write here if I were the speaker or writer (for a discussion, see van Berkum et al., 2005)? This mimicry approach might be an effective mechanism of lexical and syntactic anticipation depending on the degree of common ground and common experience between the producer and the recipient of the message.

Language-based presonance is a largely automatic and effortless process in which the retrieval of experiential traces is triggered by the perception of linguistic structures. Activation of these traces allows the comprehender to vicariously experience the described situation. The depth of the vicarious experience is subject to the effectiveness of presonance, which is subject to a number of factors. As just noted, one major factor is the comprehender's own experience. Presonance is presumably greatest when the comprehender's experiential traces closely match those of the described situation. For example, a sentence about shifting a car from second gear into third gear will yield a more specific mental simulation in a person experienced in driving a stick-shift car than in a person who has only driven an automatic-shift car. Specifically, one might predict that the former would show activation in the motor area for the right leg, releasing the leg from the gas pedal, followed by activation of the left leg area, as this is used to push down the clutch right before the shift is made by a right-hand power grip of the shift stick and by subsequently moving the hand forward, away from the body. The expert might furthermore activate auditory and vestibular traces that typically accompany a stick shift. Instead of this sequence of sensorimotor activations, the automatic-shift driver might only activate an auditory representation of the sound associated with a stick shift.

Another major factor in the depth of one's vicarious experience is the comprehender's language comprehension skill. On the view outlined here, language comprehension skill reflects one's sensitivity to linguistic constructs, as reflected in the strength of the links between linguistic constructions – experiential traces themselves – and nonlinguistic experiential traces (Goldberg, 1995; Zwaan, 2004; Zwaan & Madden, 2004). Even if a comprehender has relevant experiential traces, if the reader fails to bring these to bear, the ensuing mental simulation will not be coherent. For example, in a second-language learner of English who has experience with shift sticks, the relevant experiential traces will not be activated if he or she does not know the meaning of *shifting gear* (i.e., has no links between *shifting gear* and the relevant experiential traces).

The notion that language processing involves perceptual and motor simulations of the described situation cannot be derived from traditional theories of comprehension. These theories conceptualize comprehension as the construction of a mental representation of the described situation, a situation model (van Dijk & Kintsch, 1983). Various studies have demonstrated that comprehenders are sensitive to aspects of the referential situation, as evidenced by reading times and the activation and deactivation of concepts (for reviews, see Zwaan & Radvansky, 1998; Zwaan & Rapp, 2006). One limitation of this earlier work is that it makes the (often-tacit) assumption that comprehension involves the activation and integration of abstract mental representations. This assumption derives from a basic tenet of the cognitive revolution; namely, that cognition can be studied as a system of abstract rules and representations, separated from the brain and the world. The idea that abstract rules and representations can form the basis of cognition has been called into question on the basis of what has been called the "symbol-grounding problem." Because abstract, arbitrary symbols and rules are not properly grounded in the world, they cannot form the basis of meaning (linguistic or otherwise; for discussion, see Glenberg, 1997; Harnad, 1990; Searle, 1980).

Contrary to this mind-as-computer view of cognition, the mental simulation view that we discuss in this chapter is based on the view that cognition is grounded in the systems of perception and action planning in one's own body (see also Spivey & Richardson, this volume). As a consequence, it should be possible to observe that the performance of cognitive tasks (e.g., comprehending language) involves the recruitment of one's systems of perception and action planning (as evidenced by priming and/or interference that arises between language processing on the one hand, and the performance of perceptual or motor tasks on the other hand). This prediction is now supported by a number of empirical observations involving psycholinguistic tasks. We review this literature, moving from the word level to the discourse level by means of the sentence level.

2. Experiential Traces at the Word Level

Central to the mental simulation view of language comprehension is the claim that individual words (linguistic constructs) are linked to sensorimotor memory traces that form the basis of the mental simulation. For example, when one processes the word *table*, the linguistic form resonates with perceptual traces (e.g., the shape, size, color, and other features of tables one has seen) and motor traces (e.g., actions that one has taken involving tables in the past) from one's experiences with tables. In the absence of a sharply defining context, the specific memory traces that contribute to the retrieval process will be varied and may vary across time (Barsalou, 2005). Thus, when one is talking about tables in general, there is a wide range of experiential traces that are relevant, and these will affect the retrieval

process. When one is talking about a specific table (e.g., your coffee table), the range of relevant experiential traces will be much smaller.

The link between word forms and sensorimotor memory traces reflects a process of grounding language in the surrounding environment that begins in the earliest stages of language acquisition. Much of the language that very young children hear is about the people, objects, and events that surround them (e.g., Tomasello, 2003). Caregivers use gestures and other paralinguistic devices to direct children's attention toward elements of the environment that are being discussed in an effort to ground new linguistic terms in the external world (Masur, 1997). Although the linking of linguistic forms to experiential memory traces is only a part of the important work that goes into language acquisition, it provides the basis for the child's growing ability to use language to describe the world around them and (later) worlds separate from the here and now.

2.1. *Perceptual Traces*

There is a great deal of evidence that reading or listening to isolated words activates perceptual representations. One experiment examined whether perceptual information, specifically the shape of objects, is activated during semantic processing (Zwaan & Yaxley, 2004). Subjects judged whether a target word was related to a prime word. Prime-target pairs that were not associated, but whose referents had similar shapes (e.g., *ladder-railroad*), yielded longer "no" responses than unassociated prime-target pairs, suggesting that shape information had been activated. A visual-field manipulation showed that, in right-handed subjects, this effect was localized in the left hemisphere. This finding is consistent with behavioral, brain imaging, and lesion data, which suggest that object shape at the category level is represented in the left hemisphere (for a detailed review, see Damasio, Tranel, Grabowskia, Adolphs, & Damasio, 2004).

In further support of the view that words activate perceptual representations, verifying the properties (denoted by adjectives) of objects (denoted by nouns) is faster when subsequent items remain in the same sensory modality. For example, verifying that a lemon is sour is faster after verifying that an apple is tart than after verifying that a lime is green, just as switching between modalities incurs processing costs in perceptual tasks (Pecher, Zeelenberg, & Barsalou, 2003). If words activate traces of perceptual experience, then exposure to words should lead to the activation of the neural substrates that are also active when their referents are perceived. Neuroimaging research has produced just such evidence (e.g., Martin & Chao, 2001).

2.2. *Motor Traces*

The processing of words denoting objects makes available the affordances (i.e., possibilities for interaction) of those objects (Tucker & Ellis, 2004). Subjects viewed a series of pictures and judged whether the objects in the pictures were natural or manmade. The judgment was made by producing a power grip or a precision grip. Participants responded more quickly to objects that would be used with a power grip when their judgment response required a power grip, and they responded more quickly to objects that would be used with a precision grip when the judgment response required a precision grip. In a subsequent experiment, Tucker and Ellis (2004) asked participants to perform the same task, except that they responded to the words that label each of the objects rather than a picture. As before, participants responded to the words more quickly when the grip they used in making the response matched the grip they would use in interacting with the object.

Converging evidence for the activation of motor information on the processing of words comes from recent work in neuroscience. Regions of the brain responsible for the production of actions are active during the comprehension of action words (Hauk, Johnsrude, & Pulvermüller, 2004;

for a review, see Pulvermüller, 1999). As expected on the mental simulation view, the patterns of activation that arise when processing words are somatotopically organized. The processing of words about hand actions, leg actions, and mouth actions activated different parts of the premotor cortex, each of which had been previously identified as responsible for executing hand, leg, and mouth actions.

2.3. *Other Traces*

The resituating power of words extends beyond the activation of perceptual and motor traces. For example, threat words, such as *destroy* and *mutilate*, presented as part of a modified Stroop task, have been shown to activate bilateral amygdala regions to a greater extent than do neutral control words, thus implicating subcortical structures in semantic processing (Isenberg et al., 1999). The amygdala's role in emotional processing is well documented (e.g., LeDoux, 1995). In addition, activation was found in sensory-evaluative and motor-planning areas, areas that are normally activated when the organism senses danger. This is all the more noteworthy given that the subjects' ostensive task was not comprehending words but naming the color in which they were shown.

3. Experiential Traces at the Sentence Level

As noted earlier, the experiential traces activated by individual words can be quite heterogeneous. Words may have several meanings, and traces relevant to each of these meanings are activated when the word is processed in the absence of a constraining context. For example, the word *nail* refers both to a body part (fingernail, toenail) and a metal fastener, and the processing of the word *nail* likely involves the activation of traces relevant to both senses of the word (at least initially). Sentences provide a constraining context that hones the retrieval of experiential traces for a given word (e.g.,

Tabossi, Colombo, & Job, 1987; Vu, Kellas, & Paul, 1998). Thus, in the sentence, "He used a hammer to drive the nail into the wall," the words *hammer* and *drive* create a particular context in which experiential traces relevant to *nail* will be retrieved. Under such conditions, the comprehender is likely to retrieve only those traces of *nail* that are relevant to the "metal fastener" sense of the word.

The preceding example highlights the fact that mental simulations evolve across time. As sensorimotor memory traces are retrieved, they produce a mental context that shapes the outcome of subsequent memory retrieval operations. For example, when one encounters the verb *throw*, many potential motor traces are activated. These traces are narrowed down when subsequent information in the sentence indicates which object is being thrown, where it is being thrown, and so on. In this sense, the construction of a mental simulation is akin to a constraint-satisfaction process.

3.1. *Perceptual Traces*

There is a growing body of evidence suggesting that perceptual information forms an important basis for the comprehension of sentences. In a series of studies, Zwaan and colleagues (Stanfield & Zwaan, 2001; Zwaan, Stanfield, & Yaxley, 2002) asked participants to perform a sentence-picture verification task. Participants would read sentences such as "John put the pencil in the cup." Subsequent to the sentence, participants saw a picture of a pencil and had to decide whether the object pictured appeared in the sentence (on critical trials, the answer was always "yes"). Participants respond to the picture more quickly when its orientation matched the orientation that the object would have in the situation described by the preceding sentence. For example, if the pencil was described as being in a cup, participants were faster to respond to a picture of a pencil oriented vertically than to respond to a picture of a pencil oriented horizontally. If the pencil was described as lying on a table, the opposite pattern was observed. Zwaan

and colleagues showed that language comprehenders represented both the orientation and the shape of the objects described in the sentence.

The preceding experiments show that static perceptual information is retrieved during language comprehension. More recent studies have shown that the perceptual simulations that arise during language processing have dynamic components as well. Zwaan, Madden, Yaxley, and Aveyard (2004) asked participants to read sentences about objects moving towards them ("The first baseman threw you the ball") or away from them ("You threw the first baseman the ball"). After each sentence, participants saw two images presented in rapid succession, and had to decide whether the images were the same. For example, the participants saw two dots presented in succession. On critical trials, the second dot was either slightly larger (simulating motion toward the participant) or slightly smaller (simulating motion away from the participant) than the first dot. The change was small enough that it was not reliably detected by the participants. Responses were faster when the direction of motion implied by the dots matched the direction of motion described in the sentence.

A more recent set of experiments has shown that the actual mechanisms involved in auditory and visual processing are engaged during language comprehension. Kaschak et al. (2005) asked participants to listen to sentences describing motion in one of four directions: toward ("The car approached you"), away ("The car left you in the dust"), up ("The rocket blasted off"), and down ("The confetti fell on the parade"). At the same time, participants viewed black-and-white stimuli depicting motion in either the same direction as that described in the sentence (e.g., viewing a *toward* percept while hearing a *toward* sentence) or in the opposite direction as that described in the sentence (e.g., viewing an *away* percept while hearing a *toward* sentence). Participants made sensibility judgments more quickly for the critical sentences when the direction of motion in the percept mismatched the direction of motion in the sentence. Kaschak et al. (2005) explained this pattern as the result of a competition for resources within the visual system. The *toward* percept is engaging the parts of the visual system that respond to *toward* motion, and thus it is difficult to use these parts of the visual system to simulate the *toward* motion described in the sentence. When the direction of motion in the percept and sentence mismatch, there is no such competition, and comprehension is more facile.

These findings have been extended to the auditory modality. Kaschak, Zwaan, Aveyard, and Yaxley (2006) asked participants to read sentences describing motion toward, away, up, or down while simultaneously listening to white noise manipulated to give the impression of motion in one of those four directions. As before, the direction of motion in the sound was either the same as the direction of motion in the sentence (toward-toward), or the opposite direction as that described in the sentence (toward-away). Again, responding was faster when the direction of motion in the percept mismatched the direction of motion in the sentence.

Interestingly, this pattern of data is reversed when the sentence and percept are presented in the same modality. The preceding experiments (in which responding was fastest in the mismatching conditions) all presented the linguistic input in a different modality than the percept. However, when participants processed auditorily presented sentences while also listening to the auditory motion stimuli, they responded more quickly when the direction of motion in the sentence matched the direction of motion in the percept. One explanation for this reversal in the pattern of response times is that presenting the sentences and percepts in a different modality allows both kinds of stimulus to be processed at the same time. This makes it possible to observe the competition for resources described previously. However, when the sentence and percept are presented in the same modality, the attentional demands of processing the sentence temporarily block the processing of

the percept (for discussion, see Lavie, 2005). Consequently, there is no competition for resources; instead, the direction of motion in the percept primes the comprehension of sentences describing motion in the same direction.

3.2. *Motor Traces*

The comprehension of sentences also involves the retrieval of motor traces. Klatzky, Pellegrino, McCloskey, and Doherty (1989) demonstrated that producing bodily postures (e.g., pinching the thumb and index finger together) facilitated the processing of sentences describing actions that required a similar body posture ("Aim a dart"). Thus, motor information can facilitate the comprehension of sentences. Glenberg and Kaschak (2002; see also Borreggine & Kaschak, 2006) showed that the converse is also true: processing sentences can facilitate motor responses. Participants read sentences describing an action that requires moving the arm toward the body ("Open the drawer") or away from the body ("Close the drawer"). The participants' task was to decide whether the sentences made sense. On critical trials, participants had to respond "yes" by making an arm motion either toward their body or away from their body. Half of the time the direction of the response matched the direction of motion in the sentence, and half of the time the direction of the response was the opposite of the direction of motion in the sentence. Participants responded more quickly when the direction of the "yes" response matched the direction of the action described by the sentence. Glenberg and Kaschak (2002) refer to this as the *action-sentence compatibility effect* (ACE).

Glenberg and Kaschak (2002) reported a reliable ACE across many kinds of sentences. Imperative sentences ("Open the door") and sentences about the transfer of concrete objects ("You gave Mike a pen") showed the ACE, as did sentences about abstract kinds of transfer ("You told Bill the story"). This latter finding suggests that the sensorimotor simulations underlie the comprehension not only of sentences about literal actions and events but also of sentences that involve abstraction.

The preceding studies used relatively coarse measures (e.g., whole sentence reading times) to assess the role of motor information in sentence processing. More recently, Zwaan and Taylor (2006) have begun investigating the motor resonance that occurs during on-line sentence processing. In one of their experiments they presented subjects with sentences such as "He / realized / that / the music / was / too loud / so he / turned down / the / volume." The sentences were presented in segments and subjects progressed through the sentence by turning a knob, with each five degrees of rotation producing a new segment. Half the subjects turned the knob clockwise and the other half counterclockwise. Zwaan and Taylor found that when the direction of rotation implied by the sentence (e.g., turning down the volume implies counterclockwise rotation) matched the rotation the subjects themselves were making to read the sentence, reading times were shorter than when the two directions mismatched. To our knowledge, this is the first experiment to report on-line effects of motor resonance in language comprehension.

An interesting aspect of Zwaan and Taylor's (2006) results is that motor resonance was constrained to the so-called target region in the sentence (i.e., the segment at which the rotation was being described). This was the verb region in all critical sentences. This finding has two important implications. First, motor resonance occurs immediately upon encountering the relevant word or phrase. Second, it is short lived. The immediacy of motor resonance is consistent with constraint-based models of sentence processing (MacDonald et al., 1994; McRae et al., 1998). The finding of motor resonance being short lived could be due to the nature of the sentences. The verb phrase is followed by a noun phrase, which shifts the focus away from the action toward its result. It is possible that this attentional shift is responsible for the limited duration of motor resonance (e.g., MacWhinney, 2005). We are currently investigating this issue.

Buccino et al. (2005) have provided further insight into the role of motor traces in sentence processing. Using a combination of transcranial magnetic stimulation (TMS) and behavioral measures of sentence processing, Buccino and colleagues report that the processing of sentences about action using a particular effector (e.g., the hand) interferes with making responses with that same effector. Thus, when a hand motion must be programmed while comprehending a sentence about hand motions, there appears to be a competition for resources that slows the execution of the hand motion. Although this matter needs to be investigated in more detail, it puts the ACE and related effects in a different perspective. Simulating a sentence about hand motions appears to interfere with the production of hand motions. However, the interference may be less when the motion described in the sentence is congruent with the motion that needs to be produced.

3.3. *Other Traces*

Glenberg, Havas, Becker, and Rinck (2005) have reported experiments suggesting that systems involved in emotional responses are engaged during language comprehension. In a series of experiments, Glenberg et al. (2005) used the Strack procedure (Strack, Martin, & Stepper, 1988) to induce a particular mood in their participants. This procedure involves either holding a pen in your teeth to force the face into a smiling posture or holding a pen in your lips to force the face into a frowning posture. While in these emotion-inducing postures, participants read sentences that were positive or negative in emotional valence. Glenberg et al. (2005) report that participants respond more quickly to sentences when the emotional valence of the sentence matches their induced mood.

4. Resituating at the Discourse Level

Although it is useful to study the processing of words and sentences presented in isolation, most language-comprehension situations involve connected discourse. There is very little research on discourse comprehension from an embodied perspective. Just as motor resonance has been demonstrated at the word and the sentence level, it has been shown to occur at the level of discourse. Spivey and Geng (2001) had subjects listen to stories describing events that involved vertical or horizontal motion. They surreptitiously tracked the subjects' eye movements and found that vertical events tended to be associated with vertical eye movements and horizontal movements with horizontal eye movements, as if the subjects were directly observing these events (for an in-depth discussion of eye movements, see Spivey & Richardson, this volume).

Just as comprehenders use eye movements to trace the actions described in a discourse, they also use gestures to keep track of discourse entities across time. McNeil (1998) has shown that, in cases where a conversation involves events that occur in different times and places, interlocutors use their gestures to indicate which events are being discussed. For example, events taking place in the present would be accompanied by gestures that are produced directly in front of the speaker's body, whereas events taking place in the past would be accompanied by gestures that are produced off to one side of the speaker's body. The spatial location of the gestures thus provides a reliable cue as to which set of events is being described in the current utterance. The gestures also facilitate transitions between talking about the past and present.

Another line of research has focused on cases in which the discourse structure deviates from everyday experience. If comprehenders process events conveyed though language the way they process actual events, then these deviations should bring about momentary disruptions of the comprehension process. For example, language allows us to deviate from the chronological and continuous flow of events we experience in real life. If we anticipate described events

the way we anticipate actual events, then violations of temporal continuity should negatively affect on-line language comprehension. This has indeed been shown to be the case; reading times for sentences that violate chronology and continuity are longer than reading times for sentences that do not (e.g., Mandler, 1986; Zwaan, 1996; for extensive reviews, see Zwaan, 2004; Zwaan & Radvansky, 1998). These findings can be interpreted as consistent with the notion of presonance. On the basis of their experience with actual events, comprehenders expect by default that linguistically mediated events occurred chronologically and contiguously. Because this expectation is violated, there is a momentary slowdown of the comprehension process. However, given its exposure to violations of this expectation in language, the comprehension system quickly gets back on track.

The mental simulation view of language comprehension also predicts that the contents of the comprehender's working memory should reflect the accessibility of objects and events in the real world given our human sensory, attentional, and action-related limitations. For example, when observing objects and events in the real world, objects that are occluded are not as available for processing as objects that are not occluded. This leads to the prediction that working memory should contain the following:

- Present objects rather than absent objects
- Present features rather than absent features
- Close objects rather than distant objects
- Ongoing events rather than past events
- Current goals rather than past goals
- Visible entities rather than occluded entities

Actions in the real world should also be affected by the information that is retrieved in the service of mentally simulating a referent world. Several predictions follow from this claim. These predictions principally follow from the idea that the performance of the perceptual and motor systems should be affected by the requirements of the mental simulation. Evidence that the processing of words affects perceptual processes was reported by Richardson, Spivey, Barsalou, and McRae (2003). Evidence that motor processes are affected by sentence comprehension has been reported by Glenberg and Kaschak (2002), Zwaan and Taylor (2006), and Buccino et al. (2005). Additionally, we expect that when not otherwise engaged in the actual situation (e.g., when one is reading or deliberately trying to maintain eye contact with someone), eye movements should reflect the vicarious experience of the referent situation.

The assumptions that are generally made in discourse comprehension research are that (a) information that is currently in working memory is more accessible (i.e., more highly activated) than information that is not, and (b) when probed, more accessible information will yield faster responses than less accessible information. Therefore, the presentation of probe words associated with the contents of working memory should facilitate responses. In accordance with this logic, various studies have demonstrated that the contents of working memory during comprehension reflect the nature of the described situation. Probe-word responses are faster when the probe refers to

- A present entity rather than an absent entity (Anderson, Garrod, & Sanford, 1983; Carreiras, Carriedo, Alonso, & Fernandez, 1997).
- A present rather than an absent feature (Kaup & Zwaan, 2003).
- A present object rather than a distant object (Glenberg, Meyer, & Lindem, 1987; Morrow, Bower, & Greenspan, 1989; Morrow, Greenspan, & Bower, 1987; Rinck & Bower, 2000).
- An ongoing event rather than a past event (Zwaan, 1996; Zwaan, Madden, & Whitten, 2000).
- A current goal rather than an accomplished one (Trabasso & Suh, 1993).

- A visible entity rather than an occluded one (Horton & Rapp, 2002).

As mentioned earlier, there is also evidence that comprehenders assume the spatial perspective of a protagonist in the story (Bower, Black, & Turner, 1979; Bryant, Tversky, & Franklin, 1992; Franklin & Tversky, 1990; Morrow & Clark, 1988; Rall & Harris, 2000).

5. Conclusions and Outlook

There is a good deal of evidence that language processing brings about the presonance of perceptual, motoric, and experiential traces in the comprehender. This evidence has been found at the word, sentence, and discourse levels. We argue that this evidence can be coherently explained by assuming that language comprehension is grounded in the same neural systems that are used to perceive, plan, and take action in the external world. In this way, the comprehension of language involves the vicarious experiencing of the people, objects, emotions, and events that are described in the text. More broadly, just as our ability to plan and take action in the world relies on the ability to anticipate likely changes that will occur in the environment, we argue that an essential part of the language comprehension process is the ability to anticipate what is coming next, both in the linguistic input and in the situations that are being described. This process of presonance is immediate and effortless. It allows us to resituate ourselves and vicariously experience (and learn from) events that have happened in situations other than the one we currently find ourselves in.

Whereas we find much promise in this general approach to language comprehension, significant research remains to be done on virtually all fronts. There is a relative dearth of research on how sensorimotor information is retrieved and used during online sentence comprehension. There has also been little work considering how known elements of perceptual or motoric processing systems can be integrated with an account that explains the moment-by-moment comprehension of sentences. Finally, very little effort has been put forth to determine how and when sensorimotor information might be retrieved and used during the comprehension of language in more naturalistic tasks (e.g., tasks in which reading does not involve twisting a knob or moving one's arm or viewing some sort of percept). These questions highlight the fact that we are only at the beginning of the process of building a sensorimotor account of language processing. As we look to the future, we see the development of a theory that firmly grounds the comprehension of language in our ability to plan and act and that views language not as something that is special and distinct from the rest of cognition but as something that is a natural extension of the cognitive processes needed to act successfully in the external world.

Acknowledgments

We thank Michael Spivey for helpful comments on a previous version of this chapter. Rolf Zwaan was supported by National Institutes of Health grant MH-63972. Both authors were supported by Grant No. BCS-0446637 from the National Science Foundation. Please address correspondence regarding this chapter to Rolf Zwaan, Department of Biological and Cognitive Psychology, Erasmus University, Rotterdam, The Netherlands, zwaan@fsw.eur.nl.

References

Anderson, A., Garrod, S. C., & Sanford, A. J. (1983). The accessibility of pronominal antecedents as a function of episode shifts in narrative text. *Quarterly Journal of Experimental Psychology*, 35A, 427–440.

Barsalou, L. W. (1999). Perceptual symbol systems. *Behavioral and Brain Sciences*, 22, 577–660.

Barsalou, L. W. (2005). Situated conceptualization. In H. Cohen & C. Lefebvre (Eds.), *Handbook of categorization in cognitive science* (pp. 619–650). St. Louis: Elsevier.

Borreggine, K. L., & Kaschak, M. P. (2006). The action-sentence compatibility effect: It's all in the timing. *Cognitive Science*, 30(6), 1097–1112.

Bower, G. H., Black, J. B., & Turner, T. J. (1979). Scripts in memory for text. *Cognitive Psychology*, 11, 177–220.

Bryant, D. J., Tversky, B., & Franklin, N. (1992). Internal and external spatial frameworks for representing described scenes. *Journal of Memory and Language*, 31, 74–98.

Buccino, G., Riggio, L., Mellia, G., Binkofski, F., Gallese, V., & Rizzolatti, G. (2005). Listening to action-related sentences modulates the activity of the motor system: A combined TMS and behavioral study. *Cognitive Brain Research*, 24, 355–363.

Carreiras, M., Carriedo, N., Alonso, M. A., & Fernandez, A. (1997). The role of verbal tense and verbal aspect in the foregrounding of information in reading. *Memory and Cognition*, 23, 438–446.

Chambers, C. G., Tanenhaus, M. K., & Magnuson, J. S. (2004). Actions and affordances in syntactic ambiguity resolution. *Journal of Experimental Psychology: Learning, Memory, and Cognition*, 30, 687–696.

Damasio, H., Tranel, D., Grabowskia, T., Adolphs, R., & Damasio, A. (2004). Neural systems behind word and concept retrieval. *Cognition*, 92, 179–229.

Flanagan, J. R., & Johansson, R. S. (2003). Action plans used in action observation. *Nature*, 424, 769–771.

Fowler, C. A. (1996). Listeners do hear sounds, not tongues. *Journal of the Acoustical Society of America*, 99, 1730–1741.

Franklin, N., & Tversky, B. (1990). Searching imagined environments. *Journal of Experimental Psychology: General*, 119, 63–76.

Glenberg, A. M. (1997). What memory is for. *Behavioral and Brain Sciences*, 20, 1–19.

Glenberg, A. M., & Kaschak, M. P. (2002). Grounding language in action. *Psychonomic Bulletin & Review*, 9, 558–565.

Glenberg, A. M., Havas, D., Becker, R., & Rinck, M. (2005). Grounding language in bodily states: The case for emotion. In R. A. Zwaan & D. Pecher (Eds.), *The grounding of cognition: The role of perception and action in memory, language, and thinking* (pp. 115–128). Cambridge: Cambridge University Press.

Glenberg, A. M., Meyer, M., & Lindem, K. (1987). Mental models contribute to foregrounding during text comprehension. *Journal of Memory and Language, 26,* 69–83.

Goldberg, A. E. (1995). *Constructions: A construction grammar approach to argument structure.* Chicago: University of Chicago Press.

Harnad, S. (1990). The symbol grounding problem. *Physica D, 42,* 335–346.

Hauk, O., Johnsrude, I., & Pulvermüller, F. (2004). Somatotopic representation of action words in the motor and premotor cortex. *Neuron, 41,* 301–307.

Hess, D. J., Foss, D. J., & Carroll, P. (1995). Effects of global and local context on lexical processing during language comprehension. *Journal of Experimental Psychology: General, 124,* 62–82.

Hintzman, D. L. (1986). "Schema-abstraction" in a multiple trace model. *Psychological Review, 93,* 411–428.

Horton, W. S., & Rapp, D. N. (2002). Occlusion and accessibility of information in narrative comprehension. *Psychonomic Bulletin & Review, 10,* 104–109.

Isenberg, N., Silbersweig, D., Engelien, A., Emmerich, K., Malavade, K., Benti, B., et al. (1999). Linguistic threat activates the human amygdala. *Proceedings of the National Academy of Sciences, 96,* 10456–10459.

Jurafsky, D. (1996). A probabilistic model of lexical and syntactic access and disambiguation. *Cognitive Science, 20,* 137–194.

Kaschak, M. P., Madden, C. J., Therriault, D. J., Yaxley, R. H., Aveyard, M., Blanchard, A. A., et al. (2005). Perception of motion affects language processing. *Cognition, 94,* B79–B89.

Kaschak, M. P., Zwaan, R. A., Aveyard, M., & Yaxley, R. H. (2006). Perception of auditory motion affects language processing. *Cognitive Science, 30*(4), 733–734.

Kaup, B., & Zwaan, R. A. (2003). Effects of negation and situational presence on the accessibility of text information. *Journal of Experimental Psychology: Learning, Memory, and Cognition, 23,* 439–446.

Klatzky, R. L., Pellegrino, J. W., McCloskey, B. P., & Doherty, S. (1989). Can you squeeze a tomato? The role of motor representations in semantic sensibility judgements. *Journal of Memory and Language, 28,* 56–77.

Lavie, N. (2005). Distracted and confused? Selective attention under load. *Trends in Cognitive Sciences, 9,* 75–82.

LeDoux, J. E. (1995). Emotion: Clues from the brain. *Annual Review of Psychology, 46,* 209–235.

MacDonald, M. C., Pearlmutter, N. J., & Seidenberg, M. S. (1994). Lexical nature of syntactic ambiguity resolution. *Psychological Review, 101,* 676–703.

MacWhinney, B. (2005). The emergence of grammar from perspective taking. In D. Pecher & R. A. Zwaan (Eds.), *Grounding cognition: The role of perception and action in memory, language, and thinking* (pp. 198–223). Cambridge: Cambridge University Press.

Mandler, J. M. (1986). On the comprehension of temporal order. *Language and Cognitive Processes, 1,* 309–320.

Martin, A., & Chao, L. L. (2001). Semantic memory and the brain: Structure and process. *Current Opinion in Neurobiology, 11,* 194–201.

Masur, E. F. (1997). Maternal labeling of novel and familiar objects: Implications for children's development of lexical constraints. *Journal of Child Language, 24,* 427–439.

McNeill, D. (1998). Speech and gesture integration. In J. M. Iverson & S. Goldin-Meadow (Eds.), *The nature and functions of gesture in children's communication: New directions for child development* (No. 9, pp. 11–27). San Francisco: Jossey-Bass.

McRae, K., Spivey-Knowlton, M. J., & Tanenhaus, M. K. (1998). Modeling the influence of thematic fit (and other constraints) in on-line sentence comprehension. *Journal of Memory and Language, 38,* 283–312.

Morrow, D. G., Bower, G. H., & Greenspan, S. L. (1989). Updating situation models during narrative comprehension. *Journal of Memory and Language, 28,* 292–312.

Morrow, D. G., & Clark, H. H. (1988). Interpreting words in spatial descriptions. *Language and Cognitive Processes, 3,* 275–291.

Morrow, D. G., Greenspan, S. E., & Bower, G. H. (1987). Accessibility and situation models in narrative comprehension. *Journal of Memory and Language, 26,* 165–187.

Pecher, D., Zeelenberg, R., & Barsalou, L. W. (2003). Verifying the properties of object concepts across different modalities produces switching costs. *Psychological Science, 14,* 119–129.

Pickering, M. J., & Garrod, S. (2004). Toward a mechanistic psychology of dialogue. *Behavioral and Brain Sciences*, 27, 169–226.

Porter, R., & Lubker, J. (1980). Rapid reproduction of vowel-vowel sequences: Evidence for a fast and direct acoustic-motoric linkage in speech. *Journal of Speech and Hearing Research*, 23, 593–602.

Pulvermüller, F. (1999). Words in the brain's language. *Behavioral and Brain Sciences*, 22, 253–336.

Rall, J., & Harris, P. L. (2000). In Cinderella's slippers? Story comprehension from the protagonist's point of view. *Developmental Psychology*, 36, 202–208.

Richardson, D. C., Spivey, M. J., Barsalou, L. W., & McRae, K. (2003). Spatial representations activated during real-time comprehension of verbs. *Cognitive Science*, 27, 767–780.

Rinck, M., & Bower, G. H. (2000). Temporal and spatial distance in situation models. *Memory and Cognition*, 28, 1310–1320.

Searle, J. R. (1980). Minds, brains, and programs. *Behavioral and Brain Sciences*, 3, 417–457.

Spivey, M. J., & Geng, J. J. (2001). Oculomotor mechanisms activated by imagery and memory: Eye movements to absent objects. *Psychological Research*, 65, 235–241.

Spivey, M. J., & Tanenhaus, M. K. (1998). Syntactic ambiguity resolution in discourse: Modeling the effects of referential context and lexical frequency. *Journal of Experimental Psychology: Learning, Memory, and Cognition*, 24, 1521–1543.

Stanfield, R. A., & Zwaan, R. A. (2001). The effect of implied orientation derived from verbal context on picture recognition. *Psychological Science*, 12(2), 153–156.

Strack, F., Martin, L., & Stepper, S. (1988). Inhibiting and facilitating conditions of the human smile: A nonobtrusive test of the facial feedback hypothesis. *Journal of Personality and Social Psychology*, 54, 768–777.

Tabossi, P., Colombo, L., & Job, R. (1987). Accessing lexical ambiguity: Effects of context and dominance. *Psychological Research*, 49, 161–167.

Tomasello, M. (2003). *Constructing a language: A usage-based theory of language acquisition*. Cambridge, MA: Harvard University Press.

Townsend, D. J., & Bever, T. G. (2001). *Sentence comprehension: The integration of habits and rules*. Cambridge, MA: MIT Press.

Trabasso, T., & Suh, S. (1993). Understanding text: Achieving explanatory coherence through on-line inferences and mental operations in working memory. *Discourse Processes*, 16, 3–34.

Tucker, M., & Ellis, R. (2004). Action priming by briefly presented objects. *Acta Psychologica*, 116, 185–203.

van Berkum, J. J. A., Brown, C. M., Zwitserlood, P., Kooijman, V., & Hagoort, P. (2005). Anticipating upcoming words in discourse: Evidence from ERPs and reading times. *Journal of Experimental Psychology: Learning, Memory, and Cognition*, 31, 443–467.

van Dijk, T. A., & Kintsch, W. (1983). *Strategies of discourse comprehension*. New York: Academic Press.

Vu, H., Kellas, G., & Paul, S. T. (1998). Sources of sentence constraint on lexical ambiguity resolution. *Memory and Cognition*, 26, 979–1001.

Wolpert, D. M., Doya, K., & Kawato, M. (2003). A unifying computational framework for motor control and social interaction. *Philosophical Transactions of the Royal Society*, 358, 593–602.

Zwaan, R. A. (1994). Effect of genre expectations on text comprehension. *Journal of Experimental Psychology: Learning, Memory, and Cognition*, 20, 920–933.

Zwaan, R. A. (1996). Processing narrative time shifts. *Journal of Experimental Psychology: Learning, Memory, and Cognition*, 22, 1196–1207.

Zwaan, R. A. (2004). The immersed experiencer: Toward an embodied theory of language comprehension. In B. H. Ross (Ed.), *The psychology of learning and motivation* (Vol. 44, pp. 35–62). New York: Academic Press.

Zwaan, R. A., & Madden, C. J. (2004). Updating situation models. *Journal of Experimental Psychology: Learning, Memory, and Cognition*, 30, 283–288.

Zwaan, R. A., Madden, C. J., & Whitten, S. N. (2000). The presence of an event in the narrated situation affects its activation. *Memory and Cognition*, 28, 1022–1028.

Zwaan, R. A., Madden, C. J., Yaxley, R. H., & Aveyard, M. E. (2004). Moving words: Dynamic mental representations in language comprehension. *Cognitive Science*, 28, 611–619.

Zwaan, R. A., & Radvansky, G. A. (1998). Situation models in language comprehension and memory. *Psychological Bulletin*, 123, 162–185.

Zwaan, R. A., & Rapp, D. N. (2006). Discourse comprehension. In M. A. Gernsbacher & M.

J. Traxler (Eds.), *Handbook of psycholinguistics* (2nd ed., pp. 725–764). San Diego, CA: Elsevier.

Zwaan, R. A., Stanfield, R. A., & Yaxley, R. H. (2002). Language comprehenders mentally represent the shapes of objects. *Psychological Science*, 13(2), 168–171.

Zwaan, R. A., & Taylor, L. (2006). Seeing, acting, understanding: Motor resonance in language comprehension. *Journal of Experimental Psychology: General*, 135, 1–11.

Zwaan R. A., & Yaxley, R. H. (2004). Lateralization of object-shape information in semantic processing. *Cognition*, 94, B35–B43.

CHAPTER 20

Language Processing Embodied and Embedded

Michael Spivey and Daniel Richardson

A language fractionated from all its referents is perhaps something, *but whatever it is, it is neither a language nor a model of a language.*

— *Robert Rosen*, Essays on Life Itself

1. Introduction

While driving in England recently, the second author was listening to a play on the radio. A Roman senator was telling another how Cicero had insulted him in court. In moments like those, it seems that language could not be less situated in the world. The senators were in Rome, not the English countryside; the events took place in the distant past; even within the play, the senator listening had not been in the courtroom or had ever met Cicero. Despite these many degrees of separation between the words of the Roman senator and the world of the radio listener, the play was perfectly understandable. Indeed, at one further degree of separation, you as a reader are perfectly able to understand what happened in the car.

The ability of language to convey information about objects, people, and ideas that have no immediate physical presence, or have never even existed before, would seem to mark it out as a prime example of a representation-hungry (Clark, 1997) cognitive task that is not situated in the world. Even if the mental representations underlying language are grounded in past perceptual or motor experiences of the world (Barsalou, 1999; Glenberg, 1997; Zwaan & Kaschak, this volume), this does not require that when it is spoken, an utterance has any deep connection to the environment in which it is heard, as the case of the radio play clearly demonstrates.

Such unembedded communication about objects and events that are not in the here and now is obviously possible, but it is not always successful. After all, how many times have you heard someone try to tell a funny story and end up saying, "I guess you had to be there." Being there is exactly what embedded language is about, and it is arguably our primary form of language use. It is somewhat ironic, of course, that we are using the medium of unidirectional scripted language to make our arguments, but in this chapter we will argue that, for the bulk of everyday language use by most people, language processing is inextricably embedded in the world. Production and comprehension display many of the hallmarks of situated cognition discussed in this volume and can often be understood best in terms of agents acting within a particular environment.

The situated and nonsituated aspects of language map onto a distinction made by Clark (1992) between two separate traditions within language research. The language-as-product tradition has lauded the nonsituated virtues of language: spoken language is an evanescent auditory signal, yet it can be used to refer to objects, people, and events that are not present. This tradition, which has dominated psycholinguistics, studies the processes by which listeners form internal linguistic representations. Experimentally, this tradition seeks to decontextualize linguistic stimuli where possible to isolate processes and representations. In contrast, the language-as-action tradition has characterized language use as a form of joint action that is embedded in the world. This tradition stems from the school of ordinary-language philosophy (Austin, 1962; Grice, 1989; Searle, 1969). Experimentally, this tradition has observed and analyzed the conversations of individuals in real-world social interactions and tasks.

In the past decade, attempts have been made to bridge these two traditions (see Trueswell & Tanenhaus, 2004). Following early work by Cooper (1974), eye-tracking technology has been used during task-oriented language use in rich contexts, following the language-as-action tradition, and has provided a fine-grained measurement of linguistic processing in the language-as-product tradition (e.g., Tanenhaus, Spivey-Knowlton, Eberhard, & Sedivy, 1995). We use the term *embedded language* to refer to this bridge between the language-as-product and language-as-action traditions. In this chapter, we will present evidence that the external world is involved in a wide range of linguistic processes, from parsing syntax

to encoding facts and understanding figurative phrases. In recent work, conversation appears as jointly situated cognition, in which conversants coordinate one another's visual attention around the external world. Our review of the literature suggests that fine-grained behavioral measures such as eye tracking convincingly demonstrate language use to be a prime example of situated cognition.

Embedded language processing involves complex situational variables imposing immediate influences on word recognition, syntactic parsing, and discourse comprehension. This means that language processing is an interdisciplinary activity in the brain, involving visual perception, auditory perception, motor processing, and reasoning, in addition to linguistic computations. Importantly, however, the purview of embedded language processing not only is coextensive with other internal cognitive processes but also extends beyond the language user's brain. That is, the very cognitive operations involved in embedded language processing are themselves coextensive among speaker, listener, and environment. We lay out these arguments at the computational level before offering empirical evidence at the behavioral level.

2. Computational Arguments

Language has been held up as the best case in the argument for cognitive modules that are isolated from one another and from external variables (Fodor, 1983). In contrast, situated cognition is about the inextricability of cognition from key situational variables in the environment. A particular mathematical distinction becomes especially important when discussing the separability of cognition from the environment, as well as the separability of individual cognitive processes from one another. Cognitive psychology's traditional information-processing approach (e.g., Neisser, 1967; Sternberg, 1969) relies heavily on an assumption of component-dominant dynamics, whereas a more continuous and interactive situated cognition approach (e.g., Greeno, 1998; Neisser, 1976) steers the mathematical description more toward interaction-dominant dynamics. In component-dominant dynamics, most of the important functional processes are carried out inside each subsystem (e.g., a language subsystem, a vision subsystem, a memory subsystem). And when those subsystems share information with one another, the transmission is extremely limited and constrained. The transmission process itself does not contribute significantly to the functional computational result. In contrast, interaction-dominant dynamics are when most of the important functional processes are carried out via the interactions between subsystems, not inside each of them. That is, each subsystem's behavior is substantially described by parameters external to it, and only partly described by its own internal state-transition parameters. In such a circumstance, the openness of these subsystems requires that the level of analysis be zoomed out a notch so that the larger system being described (which comprises those subsystems) is a bit more closed (not relying so much on parameters external to it), and therefore more scientifically analyzable. If internal mental processing is a sufficiently open system that proper analysis requires describing the larger system in which internal mental processing is embedded, then the appropriate level of analysis is the organism-environment dyad, not just the organism (Gibson, 1979; Turvey & Shaw, 1999).

When a system exhibits interaction-dominant dynamics, the traditional feed-forward linear-systems analysis borrowed from electrical engineering no longer suffices. That is, the popular divide-and-conquer scientific paradigm endorsed by the modularity framework is no longer valid for such a system. Instead, what is needed is a dynamical-systems framework that applies continuous mathematical descriptions to the functional interactions that emerge between subsystems (e.g., Kelso, 1995; Port & van Gelder, 1995; van Orden, Holden, & Turvey, 2003; Ward, 2002). The dynamical-systems framework, which is becoming increasingly popular in ecological psychology (Turvey & Carello, 1995; Turvey & Shaw, 1999), has the necessary explanatory tools for dealing with an account of cognition that is not limited to the individual organism's brain but also includes situational variables as part and parcel of cognition.

In what follows, we will review a variety of real-time experimental evidence from psycholinguistics that is gradually accruing support for rich interaction between cognitive subsystems as well as rich interaction between the biological substrate and the environmental substrate. These findings indicate that language processes rely heavily on situational variables at a very fine time scale, and therefore exhibit the kind of interaction-dominant dynamics that are more consistent with the developing situated cognition approach to psychology than with the traditional information-processing approach.

3. Spoken-Language Processing Embedded in a Situational Context

Put simply, language is not processed by language processors; it is processed by people. Much like J. J. Gibson's (1979) ecological psychology, where the level of analysis is the organism-cum-environment, a proper understanding of how language processing works requires attention to the perceptual-motor patterns that interface the organism with its environment (see Zwaan & Kaschak, this volume) and those environmental properties in which the language use is embedded. Without the many different environmental constraints that situate language processing – too often lumped together under the monolithic term *context* – language as we know it would not exist.

Eye movements are a particularly compelling example of how component-dominant dynamics do not provide a good description of how the brain and body interface with their environment and how interaction-dominant dynamics may provide a more appropriate description. Considerable evidence (e.g., Gold & Shadlen, 2000; Spivey & Dale, 2004; van der Heijden,

1996) supports the observation that the brain does not achieve a stable percept, then make an eye movement, then achieve another stable percept, then make another eye movement, and so forth. The eyes often move during the process of achieving a stable percept. As a result, before perception can finish settling into a unitary interpretation of its input, oculomotor output changes the perceptual input by placing new and different visual information on the foveas. For example, an initial eye fixation may cause certain dynamical perceptual processes to be set in motion, which then (before they become stable) cause a new eye movement, which then allows for different environmental properties to cause different dynamics in the perceptual process, which then cause yet another eye movement, and so forth. Thus, perception is simultaneously influenced by sensory input (caused by environment properties reflecting light onto the retinas) and by oculomotor output (caused by intermediate products of perception's own analog computations). Because eye movements tend to operate at a slightly finer time scale than does perceptual stabilization, the perception-action cycle in this case becomes a circular causal loop – for which distinguishing the chicken from the egg, so to speak, becomes moot. This kind of loop is called "impredicative" (Poincaré, 1906) because it comprises elements that can be defined only with reference to the larger system of which they are members (Rosen, 2000; Turvey, 2004). With impredicative systems, such as a continuously flowing perception-action loop, there can be no context-independent definition of each computational element, followed by a linear, feed-forward, componentwise integration of those elements. In this loop, perceptual and cognitive parameters, motor parameters, and environmental parameters are so causally intertwined with one another that the system can be adequately studied only as a whole: a mind situated in its environment.

As the time scale of eye movements brings into sharp relief this insight into the real-time situated character of cognition, it is natural that we first report on evidence for embedded language processing that comes from eye-tracking experiments. For a decade now, eye-tracking studies have been demonstrating the wide variety of ways in which the visual world is continuously accessed and integrated with spoken-language processing, at the level of word recognition (Allopenna, Magnuson, & Tanenhaus, 1998), reference resolution (Eberhard, Spivey-Knowlton, Sedivy, & Tanenhaus, 1995), syntactic processing (Tanenhaus et al., 1995), and thematic role assignment (Altmann & Kamide, 1999).

For example, even during the few hundred milliseconds it takes to hear a spoken word, situational constraints provided by the visual context can influence the activations of lexical representations that result from processing those first few phonemes. When sitting in front of a table with real objects (see Figure 20.1) and being instructed, "Pick up the candy," about one-third of the time participants initially fixate the candle for a couple hundred milliseconds before then fixating the candy to pick it up (Spivey-Knowlton, Tanenhaus, Eberhard, & Sedivy, 1998). They do this because that object's name shares several initial phonemes with *candy* (i.e., it is a cohort of the word; Marslen-Wilson, 1987). In a control condition, if you deliver the same spoken instruction with a visual display that does not contain a candle, participants quickly land their eyes on the candy and rarely fixate the other objects. (Similar results are found in the graded curvature of computer-mouse movements, with instructions like "Click the candle"; see Spivey, Grosjean, & Knoblich, 2005.) If you ask them whether they noticed having looked at the candle, they will deny having done so. Thus, in the right visual environments, eye movements can be used as an early strategy-proof measure of partially active representations that can be sampled without interrupting normal task performance.

To further strengthen this linking hypothesis between multiple lexical activations and the probability of fixating various objects, Allopenna et al. (1998) replicated

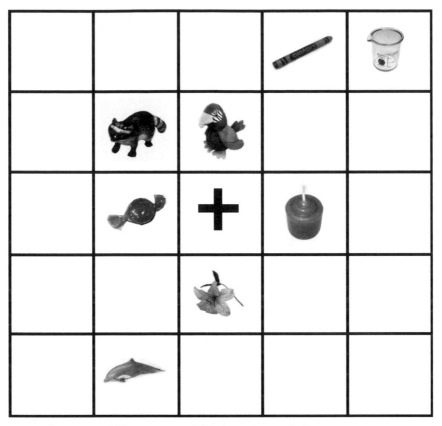

Figure 20.1. When instructed, "Pick up the candy," participants frequently look first at the (similar sounding) *candle*, and then quickly move their eyes to the candy to pick it up. At the time scale of the delivery of individual phonemes, linguistic and visual information is being integrated to drive saccadic eye movements (Tanenhaus et al., 1995) and continuous hand movements (Spivey et al., 2005).

the cohort effect, extended it to rhymes (looking at a *handle* when instructed, "Pick up the candle"), and demonstrated a close correspondence between the eye-movement data and the lexical activations of McClelland and Elman's (1986) TRACE model of spoken word recognition (see also Dahan, Magnuson, & Tanenhaus, 2001; Spivey et al., 2005). Similar eye-movement cohort effects have been observed in French (Dahan, Swingley, Tanenhaus, & Magnuson, 2000), in Russian (Marian & Spivey, 2003), and even across two languages (Ju & Luce, 2004; Spivey & Marian, 1999).

Notably, it is not just the mere visual copresence of an object during spoken-word recognition that influences the comprehension process, but more specifically how actionable the situational constraints allow that copresent object to be. For example, Chambers, Tanenhaus, Eberhard, Filip, and Carlson (2002) gave participants instructions like, "Put the cube inside the can," when there were two cans in the display. They found that situation-specific affordances (of one of the cans in the display being large enough to contain the cube and the other can being too small to contain the cube) immediately constrained the referential domain of "the can," such that participants looked only at the appropriately actionable object – despite the glaring

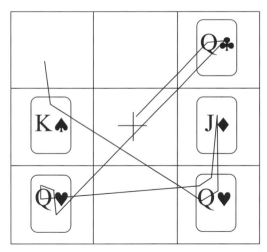

Figure 20.2. While listening to the instruction, "Put the queen of hearts that's below the jack of diamonds above the king of spades," participants concurrently make anticipatory fixations of various cards on the basis of partial input. See text for details.

referential ambiguity in the speech signal. Thus, speech input alone does not determine spoken-word recognition. The situational context, constrained by what relevant objects are visible and actionable, plays an immediate role in driving the processes that map phonemes onto lexical representations and lexical representations onto referential operations.

In fact, the temporal continuity with which the speech stream is integrated with visual and situational constraints can be systematically illustrated by tracking the comprehension of complex clause structures. Eberhard et al. (1995) gave participants instructions like, "Put the queen of hearts that's below the jack of diamonds above the king of spades." In Figure 20.2, a schematic example of a scan path shows the eye position starting at the central cross and jumping to the queen of clubs soon after hearing "queen." After hearing "of hearts," the eyes move down to the distracter queen of hearts and flit around there until hearing "that's below the jack of diamonds" causes them to fixate the target queen of hearts. After a quick check of that jack of diamonds, and once "king of spades" is heard, the eyes finally move up to the upper-left

corner of the display to begin planning the manual action. Thus, the eyes are linking referring expressions from the spoken linguistic input to their potential referents in the world about as quickly as they arrive.

Interestingly, when such prepositional-phrase structures contain syntactic ambiguities, the visual and situational context can be used immediately to resolve them. For example, if participants are presented with a display of real objects like that in Figure 20.3A, and instructed, "Put the spoon on the napkin in the bowl," they first look at the spoon and then frequently fixate the upper-right napkin, before finally fixating the bowl and carrying out the proper action (Spivey, Tanenhaus, Eberhard, & Sedivy, 2002; Tanenhaus et al., 1995). This suggests that participants are often initially parsing "on the napkin" as syntactically attached to the verb phrase (i.e., temporarily treating it as the goal for the spoon's "putting" event). The brief fixation of the irrelevant napkin is evidence of this incorrect parse because it does not happen in the control condition, where the spoken instruction is syntactically unambiguous (e.g., "Put the spoon that's on the napkin in the bowl"). The critical demonstration that visual and situational context can intervene during real-time syntactic processing comes from the condition where the same syntactically ambiguous instruction was delivered with the visual display in Figure 20.3B. In this context, participants hardly ever looked at the irrelevant goal (e.g., the other napkin). Because there are two spoons in this context, upon hearing "the spoon," the participant does not yet know which spoon is being referred to, and both spoons tend to get fixated briefly. Then, on hearing "on the napkin," the referential uncertainty introduced by having two potential spoons causes the comprehension process to parse "on the napkin" as syntactically attached to the noun phrase rather than to the verb phrase, thereby discriminating which spoon is being referred to (cf. Crain & Steedman, 1985). Thus, even syntactic processing (once thought to be the poster child of encapsulated modularity; cf. Frazier & Clifton, 1996)

A.

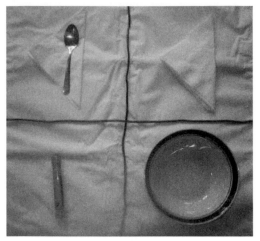

B.

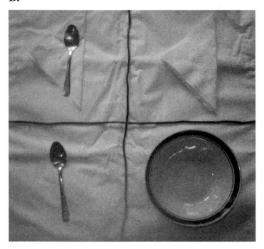

Figure 20.3. When instructed, "Put the spoon on the napkin in the bowl," participants often misparse the syntactic attachment of the initial prepositional phrase when there is only one visible referent for spoon (panel A), but not when there are two such referents (panel B).

is fluidly integrated in real time with the situated context in which language comprehension takes place.

Similar eye-movement evidence for the immediate use of situational context during syntactic parsing has been found with participants as young as eight years old (Trueswell, Sekerina, Hill, & Logrip, 1999). Moreover, Snedeker and Trueswell (2004) showed that

these situational constraints combine with the verb's frequency-based biases in argument structure (e.g., how strongly it prefers a prepositional phrase) to determine the likelihood of a misparse. Most important, for demonstrating the importance of situated context in language processing, the relative affordances of the objects being moved around play a crucial role in defining the situated constraints in which comprehension takes place. Chambers, Tanenhaus, and Magnuson (2004) gave participants instructions like, "Pour the egg in the bowl over the flour." When the second of the two referents (an egg in a glass) was compatible with the action (i.e., it was in liquid form and thus could be poured), the context functioned like the previous two-referent contexts and prevented the misparse associated with fixating the incorrect goal (an extra bowl that was empty). However, when that second egg was in shell form (and thus not able to be poured), participants immediately knew which egg was being referred to on hearing "pour the egg," and thereby fell into the trap of parsing "in the bowl" as a goal rather than a noun-phrase modifier.

Thus, as suggested by McRae, Ferretti, and Amyote (1997), individual verbs, such as *pour*, may activate rather complex sets of semantic features regarding the thematic roles (e.g., agents, patients, themes, goals) that are likely to participate in the event being described. For example, Altmann and Kamide (1999) presented participants with computer-screen displays containing pictures of a man, a woman, a newspaper, and a cake. As evidence of anticipations from a verb's thematic role preferences, when the spoken instruction was "The woman will read the newspaper," participants often fixated the newspaper shortly before hearing the word *newspaper* – immediately after hearing the word *read*, moreover, which is consistent with the notion of mental animation (Hegarty & Just, 1993; Matlock & Richardson, 2004). When Altmann (2004) showed the pictures and then took them away before presenting the sentence, he observed the same basic results, with participants fixating the appropriate blank regions that used to contain the relevant objects. This blank-screen paradigm illustrates how the external environment alone is not what imposes the situated constraints; rather, it is the time-dependent relationship between the environment and the internal mental representations that creates the situated character of language processing.

Even when two sentences describe identical referents in the world, aspects of figurative meaning are detectable in how a visual scene is inspected. When static referents in the visual scene are best understood by mentally animating them, eye movements can provide evidence of that mental animation (cf. Hegarty & Just, 1993; Rozenblit, Spivey, & Wojslawowicz, 2002). Matlock and Richardson (2004) contrasted literal descriptions of scenes ("The road is in the valley") with descriptions using fictive motion ("The road runs through the valley"). Fictive motion descriptions are a type of figurative language because they employ a verb of motion (*runs*) but no motion takes place. Norming results show that fictive and nonfictive spatial descriptions are equivalent in meaning. Participants heard one of these descriptions while looking at a schematic drawing of a scene. Matlock and Richardson (2004) found that participants spent more time fixating the path when it was described using fictive motion.

In that experiment, it is as if the eyes were acting out the subtle figurative spatial dynamics implied by the road "running" (cf. Matlock, 2004), and Richardson and Matlock (2007) demonstrated that such fictive motion descriptions affect eye movements specifically by evoking mental representations of motion. When participants heard information about terrain that would affect actual motion across the scene, it influenced how they viewed a picture if it was described with fictive motion. Looking times and eye movements scanning along the path increased during fictive motion descriptions when the terrain was first described as difficult ("The desert is hilly") as compared to easy ("The desert is flat"); there were no such effects for descriptions without fictive motion. It appears that some

form of dynamic visuospatial simulation is generated when comprehending fictive motion descriptions (Barsalou, 1999; Zwaan, 2004), and this simulation even incorporates information about terrain maneuverability.

A typical information-processing account might suppose that a linguistic figurative description is processed into a set of spatial relations, and if necessary, the result is later passed on for comparison with the output of a visual process. At odds with this view is the fact that traces of nonliteral content can be found in the earliest moments of visuomotor processing. Comprehension of figurative language can produce mental representations that are distinct from equivalent literal counterparts. These representations are immediately integrated with visual processing, such that various forms of dynamic spatial information can drive eye movements around a scene. In this way, even comprehension of nuances of figurative meaning appears to be embedded in the world.

3.1. *Semantic Memory*

We have seen that during language processing, the external world is interrogated continuously throughout the course of incremental linguistic input. This embedded nature can be seen at multiple time scales of language comprehension, even in the way that semantic information is encoded and recalled. In a series of experiments, Richardson and colleagues (Richardson & Kirkham, 2004; Richardson & Spivey, 2000) found that when listening to spoken information, relevant spatial locations are encoded and accessed with a saccade when relevant. These experiments can be seen as a linguistic case of situated cognition, related to epistemic actions (Kirsh & Maglio, 1994) and deictic pointers (Ballard, Hayhoe, Pook, & Rao, 1997).

Figure 20.4 shows a schematic of Richardson and Spivey's (2000) first experiment. Participants watched a video clip of a talking head delivering a short piece of information such as, "Shakespeare's first plays

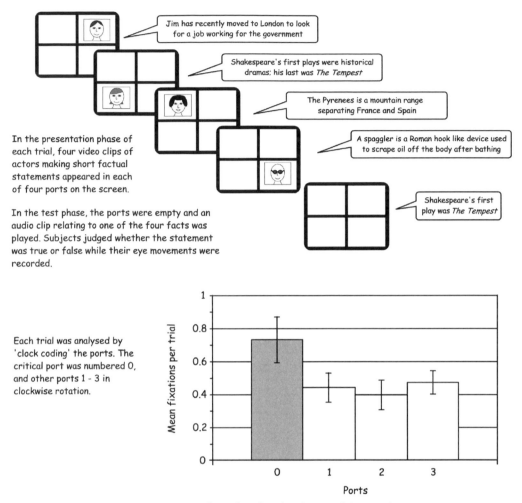

In the presentation phase of each trial, four video clips of actors making short factual statements appeared in each of four ports on the screen.

In the test phase, the ports were empty and an audio clip relating to one of the four facts was played. Subjects judged whether the statement was true or false while their eye movements were recorded.

Each trial was analysed by 'clock coding' the ports. The critical port was numbered 0, and other ports 1 - 3 in clockwise rotation.

Figure 20.4. Design and results of Richardson and Spivey (2000, experiment 1).

were romantic comedies. His last was *The Tempest*." These talking heads appeared in turn in each of four ports of a two-by-two grid. After presentation, the participants looked at a blank grid and heard a statement that related to one of the facts (e.g., "Shakespeare's last play was *The Tempest*"). They answered out loud whether it was true or false. As they answered, participants' eye movements were recorded. The port that had previously contained the talking head that conveyed the relevant information was termed the *critical port*. It was found that there were almost twice as many fixations to the critical port than to each of the other ports. This result was replicated when the video clips were replaced by four identical spinning crosses (Spivey & Richardson, 2000, experiment 2), when the ports moved to the center of the screen during presentation (Spivey & Richardson, 2000, experiment 5), and when the ports moved independently to different locations on the screen before the answer period (Richardson & Kirkham, 2004). Moreover, in all experiments, participants' accuracy in answering the factual question was not related to whether they looked at the critical port. Why, then, do participants continue to spatially index information – encoding location of an event and refixating that location when recalling its properties?

A first attempt to explain this spatial-indexing behavior might cite the phenomenon of context-dependent memory, in which memory is improved if the conditions that were present during encoding are reinstantiated during recall (e.g., Bradley, Cuthbert, & Lang, 1988; Godden & Baddeley, 1975; Winograd & Church, 1988). This explanation falls short on two counts, however. Memory was not improved in this paradigm, because looks to the critical port did not produce more correct answers. In several of the experiments, the conditions that were present during encoding were not reinstantiated during recall, because the ports were in different locations between presentation and test phases.

The more fitting explanation draws on the notion of external memory (Brooks, 1991; Clark, 1997; O'Regan, 1992). In everyday life (Simons & Levin, 1997) and carefully circumscribed experimental tasks (Ballard, Hayhoe, & Pelz, 1995; Hayhoe, Bensinger, & Ballard, 1998), it appears that participants do not encode many properties of the visual world. Instead, as and when information is needed, it is accessed from external memory via an eye movement. As every system of information storage needs a system of information retrieval, perhaps spatial indexing stores the addresses for a content-addressable memory that exists in the external environment rather than in the brain.

It could be argued that participants in the experiments of Richardson and Spivey (2000) and of Richardson and Kirkham (2004) were tacitly behaving as if the factual information they had heard could be accessed from external memory. When a fact was heard, participants associated the information with a port on the computer screen. As the information was needed during the question period, the association was activated and a saccade was launched to retrieve that information. Of course, in this case, there was no useful information there at all, and so accuracy in answering the question did not increase with fixations to the empty critical port.

This interpretation suggests that, in terms of their looking behavior, participants in the experiments of Richardson and Spivey (2000) and of Richardson and Kirkham (2004) were treating pieces of evanescent auditory semantic information as if they were stable physical objects in the world there to be reinspected whenever the need arose. Richardson and Kirkham (2004) found that despite the fragility of infants' spatial abilities around that age (Colombo, 2001; Gilmore & Johnson, 1997), infants as young as six months of age showed the same spatial-indexing behavior: they encoded the location of a toy that danced to a tune inside a port, tracked the location of the port as it moved, and refixated the port when the tune was heard again. These results suggest that the embedded nature of linguistic semantic memory has roots in early development.

3.2. Conversation

A stream of speech is processed by a listener, moment by moment, in reference to the external world. In this sense, language comprehension is embedded. But of course, in the main, language use is an interaction between people. What does the embedded nature of language entail for the interplay of comprehension and production that occurs during naturalistic conversation? The language-as-action tradition has long seen conversation as a form of joint action that is situated in the world (Clark, 1996). And recent technological advances have allowed the time course of conversation and linguistic processing to be studied in fine detail, and thus have formed a bridge to the language-as-product tradition (Trueswell & Tanenhaus, 2004).

In this section, we draw three broad conclusions from the current literature that speak to the embedded nature of conversation. First, participants in a conversation are aware of how the other is cognitively situated in the world. H. Clark (1996) describes this as knowledge of the common ground, and recent evidence supports his notion that linguistic processing is intimately affected by assumptions about an interlocutor's visual perspective, past experience, and beliefs.

Second, interlocutors actively manipulate the common ground for communicative purposes. Just as an individual may alter his or her environment during a situated cognitive task (Hutchins, 1995; Kirsh & Maglio, 1994), or two participants may anticipate one another's task constraints during joint action (cf. Knoblich & Jordan, 2003; Sebanz, Knoblich, & Prinz, 2003), so two conversants will use actions and gestures, concurrently with their speech, to coordinate their interaction and update the common ground. Last, the degree to which interlocutors are able to coordinate their visual attention moment by moment across a shared visual display is causally related to the success with which they communicate.

Listeners are certainly sensitive to some facts about a speaker. For example, Fitneva and Spivey (2004) showed that knowledge of the author of a spoken statement influences lexical ambiguity resolution. Although the word *case* is ambiguous between a court case and a container case, when a judge says the word, listeners immediately resolve it as meaning court case, and when a store owner says it, listeners immediately resolve it as a meaning a container case.

Metzing and Brennan (2003) showed that the identity of speakers is also important when parsing novel forms of reference known as *conceptual pacts* (Brennan & Clark, 1996). In their task, a participant and a confederate repeatedly referred to a novel object as, for example, the "shiny cylinder." This is an example of lexical entrainment (Garrod & Anderson, 1987). At a later stage the object was referred to again, either by the old or a new confederate, or by the old or a new name (e.g., the "silver pipe"). Although participants fixated the correct object equally fast regardless of which confederate used the old name, participants were relatively slow when the old confederate used the new name. This momentary confusion shows that speaker identity is linked to particular conceptual pacts and that listeners expect terms within common ground to be reliably used.

Initial results from other collaborative tasks, however, suggested that listeners do not extend very far into a consideration of the speaker's mental states (Keysar, Barr, Balin, & Paek, 1998). Keysar, Barr, Balin, and Brauner (2000) used a referential communication task (Krauss & Weinheimer, 1964) in which two people are seated on either side of an array of pigeonholes containing various objects and the director (a confederate) instructs the matcher to move objects. Some of the array is blocked so that the director cannot see some of the objects. Keysar et al. (2000) found that when the matchers hear, "Pick up the smallest candle," they fixate (and sometime pick up) the smallest candle they can see, even though that candle is occluded from the directors' view, and hence could not possibly be the intended referent. It was argued that during such a conversation, the matcher initially takes an egocentric interpretation of the director's instruction and can take into consideration only the director's knowledge state at the end of the process, as an error correction.

Later studies (Hanna, Tanenhaus, & Trueswell, 2003) argue that the Keysar et al. (2000) result misses the pervasive effect of common-ground information by swamping it with typicality effects. In short, when the matchers hear "the smallest candle," the object that is occluded from the speaker's perspective happens to be the most typical referent of the statement, and hence it attracts a higher proportion of fixations than a completely unrelated item. Using a similar design, Hanna et al. (2003) deconfounded these variables. In the key condition, the director instructs the matcher, "Put a triangle on top of the red one," when two red triangles are in view. One of these red triangles is not known to the speaker, however, and so could not be the intended referent. In this case, when the target and the competitor are identical, matchers make a higher proportion of fixations to the correct target from the very moment they hear the word *red*. Therefore, rather than act solely as a late source of error correction, common-ground information acts as a constraint (among many) on reference resolution at the earliest stages of linguistic processing (Hanna & Tanenhaus, 2004; see also Nadig & Sedivy, 2002).

In the matching studies discussed so far, common ground was investigated by manipulating whether a director had knowledge of the physical presence of a particular item. Conversants appear to keep track of changes in common ground brought about by linguistic manipulations as well. In an experiment by Brown-Schmidt, Campana, and Tanenhaus (2004), a speaker instructed a listener to move various blocks on a grid. Both were naive participants. Sometimes during this task, the speaker referred to "the red one" even though there were several red blocks in sight. The listener was able to fixate the correct block, however, because what the speaker had said previously had implicitly identified a smaller set of objects that included only one of the red blocks. In this way, linguistic context can circumscribe the referential domain.

Our second claim regarding the embedded nature of conversation is that participants not only are aware of how one another have situated their dialogue in the world but also actively manipulate that common ground as a coordinated joint activity that uses pointing, placing, and gestures (Clark, 1996, 2003; Clark & Brennan, 1991; Schober, 1993). For example, Bangerter (2004) examined how participants discussed pictures when they could or could not point. At long distances, where they would be ambiguous, there were fewer pointing gestures. At closer ranges, pointing increased and linguistic description of location decreased. In this way, pointing gestures were used opportunistically as part of a composite signal with speech.

Clark and Krych (2004) analyzed other forms of physical action that are employed to manipulate common ground. In their task, a director participant instructed a builder participant how to construct a Lego model. When the director could not see what the builder was doing, performance suffered. When the director was able to see the builder at work, this visual common ground was exploited and continually updated as a joint activity. For example, while the director was describing the next block to pick up, the builder might find it in a pile and exhibit it to the director, who would interrupt or alter his description midsentence to confirm whether it was the correct piece. Similarly, the builder would poise a block just above where he or she believed it should be attached to the model or turn the model to face the director so that the director simply had to acknowledge whether the move was correct. These gestures were precisely timed and coordinated with the director's speech. When a visual common ground is available, participants situate their dialog by engaging in complex joint activities that support and even supplant verbal communication (see also Brennan, 2004).

In a classic case of situated cognition, Kirsch and Maglio (1994) found that expert Tetris players would rotate shapes using a button press, as it was a faster way to view different orientations than using mental rotation. They termed this button press an *epistemic action* because participants take action in the world to manipulate knowledge rather than use purely mental operations. The external world was acted on to process information. Similarly, in situated communication, conversants take joint action in the world rather than use purely linguistic communication. In this way, the physical gestures and actions that conversants use can be thought of as joint epistemic actions.

But is it the case that these situated strategies and dynamic coordination of common ground are actually more efficient than unembedded one-way communication (as in reading or listening to the radio)? Research quantifying the degree of coordination between conversants' visual attention suggests that this is true. Richardson and Dale (2005) analyzed the statistical patterns of eye movements as a fine-grained index of how speakers and listeners deployed their attention within a visual common ground.

Rather than study speakers and listeners separately, and asking them to produce or comprehend short sentences, they tracked eye movements of both speakers and listeners who were engaged in a spontaneous, complex discourse. They quantified the temporal coupling (or entrainment) between conversants' eye movements and examined its relationship to the success of the discourse.

First, the speech and eye movements of one set of participants were recorded as they looked at pictures of six cast members of a TV sitcom (either *Friends* or *The Simpsons*). They spoke spontaneously about their favorite episode and characters, or described what had happened in a scene they had just watched. One-minute segments were chosen and used unedited, with all the deviations, hesitations, and repetitions of just a minute of normal speech. These segments were then played back to a separate set of participants. The listeners looked at the same visual display of the cast members, and their eye movements were recorded as they listened to the segments of speech. They then answered a series of comprehension questions about what was said by the speaker.

Listener and speaker eye movements were coded as to which of the six cast members (if any) was being fixated during every 33-ms time slice. Cross-recurrence analysis (Zbilut, Giuliani, & Webber, 1998; Zbilut & Webber, 1992) was used to quantify the degree to which the speaker and listener eye positions overlapped at successive time lags. This speaker × listener distribution of fixations could be compared to a speaker × randomized-listener distribution, which was produced by shuffling the temporal order of each listener's eye-movement sequence and then calculating the cross-recurrence with the speakers. This randomized series serves as a baseline of looking at chance at any given point in time, but with the same overall distribution of looks to each picture as the real listeners.

From the moment a speaker looks at a picture, and for the following six seconds, a listener was more likely than chance to be looking at that same picture. The breadth of this time frame suggests that speakers and listeners may keep track moment by moment of a subset of the depicted people who are relevant, just as listeners in Brown-Schmidt et al. (2004) were able to linguistically circumscribe the referential domain. Richardson and Dale (2005) found that the overlap between speaker and listener eye movements peaked at about 2000 ms. In other words, two seconds after the speaker looked at a cast member, the listener was most likely to be looking at the same cast member. The timing of this peak roughly corresponds to results in the speech production and comprehension literatures. Speakers will fixate objects 800 ms to 1000 ms (Griffin & Bock, 2000; Meyer, Sleiderink, & Levelt, 1998) before naming them, and listeners will typically take 500 ms to 1000 ms to fixate an object from the word's onset (Allopenna et al., 1998). These figures include cases of proper-noun production and comprehension, but this peak in overlap between speaker and listener eye movements was still present in the data when all names of the cast members, and associated speaker fixations, were removed from the analysis. (Of course, no such peak was observed in any of the speaker × randomized-listener analyses.) The coupling between speaker and listener eye movements was pervasive, suggesting that planning diverse types of speech will influence the speaker's eye movements, and a few seconds later, hearing them will influence the listener's eye movements.

Importantly, this entrainment of eye-movement patterns between speaker and listener was not merely an epiphenomenal by-product of the conversation process. It played a functional role in comprehension. When the overall proportion of cross-recurrence between individual speaker-listener pairs was quantified, the strength of the relationship between speaker and listener eye-movement patterns reliably predicted how many of the comprehension questions the listener answered correctly. This correlation was supported by a follow-up study that experimentally manipulated the relationship between speaker and

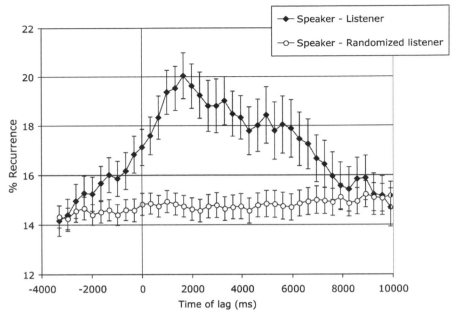

Figure 20.5. Average cross-recurrence of eye position at different time lags for forty-nine speaker-listener pairs (Richardson & Dale, 2005). See text for details.

listener eye movements. When a low-level perceptual cue made the eye movements of a listener more or less like the speaker's, the listener's performance on comprehension questions was correspondingly affected.

Despite the fact that conversants could not interact with each other in Richardson and Dale's (2005) experiments, their visual attention was coupled at the millisecond resolution of eye movements. Moreover, this coupling determined listeners' comprehension performance. Thus, cross-recurrence analysis shows that looking around the common ground in step with each other appears to drive the process of conversants' mutual understanding, and so provides a quantitative data visualization of the notion of embedded language and situated discourse.

4. Conclusion

Perhaps the case of a BBC radio play about Roman senators is actually a misleading place to start in an analysis of language. Perhaps cognitive psychology's long-standing preoccupation with circumstances of unidirectional unembedded language use, such as reading experiments and listening to decontextualized, prerecorded oration, was a misleading way to begin developing theories about language (cf. Spivey et al., 2002). The rarified ability to represent things that are not present or ideas not thought before, in the absence of immediate environmental support, might be better understood as the special peculiarity of language, not the core of its everyday function. For example, across developmental time, children take much longer to understand references to objects when they are absent, gaining competence in comprehension and then production throughout the second year of life (Huttenlocher & Smiley, 1987; Saylor, 2004; Swingley & Fernald, 2002). Interestingly, caregivers usually anchor their references to absent objects via objects that are present, asking, for example, "Where's Daddy?" and gesturing to his briefcase (Huttenlocher, 1974; Saylor & Baldwin, 2004). Similarly, one could speculate that across evolutionary time, language might well have first emerged situated in cooperative activities such as hunting and tool use (Barsalou, 1999; Corballis, 1992) rather than as a way to refer to abstract concepts and objects that were not present.

Regardless of the ontogeny and phylogeny of language, it is clear that the study of adult language use in naturalistic contexts reveals a rich interaction with the world. Language processing is not something that happens just in the individual brain of the speaker or the listener. In many circumstances, the proper analysis of language processing is at the level of the organisms and the environment in which they are situated. The phenomena that arise at such a level of analysis clearly exhibit interaction-dominant dynamics, rather than component-dominant dynamics, thus obviating the linear module-based analysis common to the information-processing framework. As part of the linguistic process of recognizing words or parsing syntax, participants make saccades to referents in the world that are phonetically, semantically, or pragmatically appropriate. In conversation, the degree to which a listener follows a speaker's gaze around the world is an indication of their understanding, and in face-to-face conversation, eye movements can serve as linguistic cues. Language comprehension could even be called "stubbornly situated" cognition, because several paradigms have found that participants look systematically at entirely blank regions of space (that used to contain the referents) during linguistic processing.

Although they are logically separable, the perspectives of embedded language and embodied language (see Zwaan & Kaschak, this volume) have an interesting synergy. For example, these ideas have been combined in the conversational robot Ripley (Roy, 2005; Roy & Mukherjee, 2004), which represents the meanings of objects by multimodal sensory expectations at certain locations (similar ideas have been developed in theories of perception; Noë, 2004; O'Regan & Noë, 2001). That is to say, for the robot, the meaning of the word *apple* is not merely a programmed list of conceptual features, but rather is composed of the sensorimotor experiences that it expects to be situated in the world on hearing the word *apple*. Perhaps, so with humans, our understanding of language is composed not of amodal logical symbols that are divorced from the real world, but instead of perceptual-motor simulations and of situated actions in the environment and with other language users.

Acknowledgments

We are grateful to Rolf Zwaan and the editors for helpful comments that improved the exposition, and to the two Sams for giving their fathers enough free time to write this chapter. Work on this chapter was supported by NIMH-R01-63961 to M. J. S.

References

Allopenna, P. D., Magnuson, J. S., & Tanenhaus, M. K. (1998). Tracking the time course of spoken word recognition using eye movements: Evidence for continuous mapping models. *Journal of Memory and Language, 38*(4), 419–439.

Altmann, G. T. M. (2004). Language-mediated eye movements in the absence of a visual world: The "blank screen paradigm." *Cognition, 93,* 79–87.

Altmann, G. T. M., & Kamide, Y. (1999). Incremental interpretation at verbs: Restricting the domain of subsequent reference. *Cognition, 73,* 247–264.

Austin, J. L. (1962). *How to do things with words.* Cambridge, MA: Harvard University Press.

Ballard, D., Hayhoe, M., & Pelz, J. (1995). Memory representations in natural tasks. *Journal of Cognitive Neuroscience, 7,* 66–80.

Ballard, D., Hayhoe, M., Pook, P., & Rao, R. (1997). Deictic codes for the embodiment of cognition. *Behavioral and Brain Sciences, 20,* 723–767.

Bangerter, A. (2004). Using pointing and describing to achieve joint focus of attention in dialogue. *Psychological Science, 15*(6), 415–419.

Barsalou, L. W. (1999). Language comprehension: Archival memory or preparation for situated action? *Discourse Processes, 28*(1), 61–80.

Bradley, M. M., Cuthbert, B. N., & Lang, P. J. (1988). Perceptually driven movements as contextual retrieval cues. *Bulletin of the Psychonomic Society, 26,* 541–553.

Brennan, S. (2004). How conversation is shaped by visual and spoken evidence. In J. Trueswell & M. Tanenhaus (Eds.), *Approaches to studying world-situated language use: Bridging the language-as-product and language-as-action traditions* (pp. 95–129). Cambridge, MA: MIT Press.

Brennan, S. E., & Clark, H. H. (1996). Conceptual pacts and lexical choice in conversation. *Journal of Experimental Psychology: Learning, Memory, & Cognition, 22*(6), 1482–1493.

Brooks, R. (1991). Intelligence without representation. *Artificial Intelligence, 47,* 139–159.

Brown-Schmidt, S., Campana, E., & Tanenhaus, M. K. (2004). Real-time reference resolution by naïve participants during a task-based unscripted conversation. In J. C. Trueswell & M. K. Tanenhaus (Eds.), *World-situated language processing: Bridging the language-as-product and language-as-action traditions* (pp. 153–172). Cambridge, MA: MIT Press.

Chambers, C. G., Tanenhaus, M. K., Eberhard, K. M., Filip, H., & Carlson, G. N. (2002). Circumscribing referential domains during real-time language comprehension. *Journal of Memory & Language, 47*(1), 30–49.

Chambers, C. G., Tanenhaus, M. K., & Magnuson, J. S. (2004). Actions and affordances in syntactic ambiguity resolution. *Journal of Experimental Psychology: Learning, Memory, & Cognition, 30*(3), 687–696.

Clark, A. (1997). *Being there: Putting brain, body, and world together again.* Cambridge, MA: MIT Press.

Clark, H. H. (1992). *Arenas of language use.* Chicago: University of Chicago Press.

Clark, H. H. (1996). *Using language.* Cambridge: Cambridge University Press.

Clark, H. H. (2003). Pointing and placing. In S. Kita (Ed.), *Pointing: Where language, culture, and cognition meet* (pp. 243–268). Mahwah, NJ: Lawrence Erlbaum.

Clark, H. H., & Brennan, S. E. (1991). Grounding in communication. In L. B. Resnick, J. M. Levine, & S. D. Teasley (Eds.), *Perspectives on socially shared cognition* (pp. 127–149). Washington, DC: American Psychological Association.

Clark, H. H., & Krych, M. A. (2004). Speaking while monitoring addressees for understanding. *Journal of Memory & Language, 50*(1), 62–81.

Colombo, J. (2001). The development of visual attention in infancy. *Annual Review of Psychology, 52,* 337–367.

Cooper, R. M. (1974). The control of eye fixation by the meaning of spoken language: A new methodology for the real-time investigation of speech perception, memory, and language processing. *Cognitive Psychology, 6*(1), 84–107.

Corballis, M. C. (1992). On the evolution of language and generativity. *Cognition, 44*(3), 197–226.

Crain, S., & Steedman, M. (1985). On not being led up the garden path. In D. Dowty, L. Karttunen, & A. Zwicky (Eds.), *Natural language parsing* (pp. 320–358). Cambridge: Cambridge University Press.

Dahan, D., Magnuson, J. S., & Tanenhaus, M. K. (2001). Time course of frequency effects in spoken-word recognition: Evidence from eye movements. *Cognitive Psychology, 42,* 317–367.

Dahan, D., Swingley, D., Tanenhaus, M. K., & Magnuson, J. S. (2000). Linguistic gender and spoken-word recognition in French. *Journal of Memory and Language, 42,* 465–480.

Eberhard, K., Spivey-Knowlton, M., Sedivy, J., & Tanenhaus, M. (1995). Eye movements as a window into real-time spoken language comprehension in natural contexts. *Journal of Psycholinguistic Research, 24,* 409–436.

Fitneva, S., & Spivey, M. (2004). Context and language processing: The effect of authorship. In J. Trueswell & M. Tanenhaus (Eds.), *World situated language use: Psycholinguistic, linguistic and computational perspectives on bridging the product and action traditions* (pp. 317–327). Cambridge, MA: MIT Press.

Fodor, J. A. (1983). *The modularity of mind.* Cambridge, MA: MIT Press.

Frazier, L., & Clifton, C. (1996). *Construal.* Cambridge, MA: MIT Press.

Garrod, S., & Anderson, A. (1987). Saying what you mean in dialogue: A study in conceptual and semantic co-ordination. *Cognition, 27,* 181–218.

Gibson, J. (1979). *The ecological approach to visual perception.* Boston: Houghton Mifflin.

Gilmore, R. O., & Johnson, M. H. (1997). Egocentric action in early infancy: Spatial frames of reference for saccades. *Psychological Science, 8,* 224–230.

Glenberg, A. (1997). What memory is for. *Behavioral and Brain Sciences, 20,* 1–55.

Godden, D. R., & Baddeley, A. D. (1975). Context-dependent memory in two natural environments: On land and underwater. *British Journal of Psychology, 66*(3), 325–331.

Gold, J., & Shadlen, M. (2000). Representation of a perceptual decision in developing oculomotor commands. *Nature, 404,* 390–394.

Greeno, J. (1998). The situativity of knowing, learning, and research. *American Psychologist, 53,* 5–26.

Grice, P. (1989). *Studies in the way of words.* Cambridge, MA: Harvard University Press.

Griffin, Z. M., & Bock, K. (2000). What the eyes say about speaking. *Psychological Science, 11*(4), 274–279.

Hanna, J. E., & Tanenhaus, M. K. (2004). Pragmatic effects on reference resolution in a collaborative task: Evidence from eye movements. *Cognitive Science, 28*(1), 105–115.

Hanna, J. E., Tanenhaus, M. K., & Trueswell, J. C. (2003). The effects of common ground and perspective on domains of referential interpretation. *Journal of Memory & Language, 49*(1), 43–61.

Hayhoe, M., Bensinger, D., & Ballard, D. (1998). Task constraints in visual working memory. *Vision Research, 38,* 125–137.

Hegarty, M., & Just, M. A. (1993). Constructing mental models of machines from text and diagrams. *Journal of Memory & Language, 32,* 717–742.

Hutchins, E. (1995). *Cognition in the wild.* Cambridge, MA: MIT Press.

Huttenlocher, J. (1974). The origins of language comprehension. In R. Solso (Ed.), *Theories in cognitive psychology: The Loyola symposium* (pp. 331–388). Potomac, MD: Erlbaum.

Huttenlocher, J., & Smiley, P. (1987). Early word meanings: The case of object names. *Cognitive Psychology, 19*(1), 63–89.

Ju, M., & Luce, P. (2004). Falling on sensitive ears: Constraints on bilingual lexical activation. *Psychological Science, 15,* 314–318.

Kelso, J. (1995). *Dynamic patterns: The self-organization of brain and behavior.* Cambridge, MA: MIT Press.

Keysar, B., Barr, D. J., Balin, J. A., & Brauner, J. S. (2000). Taking perspective in conversation: The role of mutual knowledge in comprehension. *Psychological Science, 11*(1), 32–38.

Keysar, B., Barr, D. J., Balin, J. A., & Paek, T. S. (1998). Definite reference and mutual knowledge: Process models of common ground in comprehension. *Journal of Memory & Language, 39*(1), 1–20.

Kirsh, D., & Maglio, P. (1994). On distinguishing epistemic from pragmatic action. *Cognitive Science, 18,* 513–549.

Knoblich, G., & Jordan, J. (2003). Action coordination in groups and individuals: Learning anticipatory control. *Journal of Experimental Psychology: Learning, Memory, & Cognition, 29,* 1006–1016.

Krauss, R. M., & Weinheimer, S. (1964). Changes in reference phrases as a function of frequency of usage in social interaction: A preliminary study. *Psychonomic Science, 1,* 113–114.

Marian, V., & Spivey, M. (2003). Competing activation in bilingual language processing: Within- and between-language competition. *Bilingualism: Language and Cognition, 6,* 97–115.

Marslen-Wilson, W. (1987). Functional parallelism in spoken word recognition. *Cognition, 25,* 71–102.

Matlock, T. (2004). Fictive motion as cognitive simulation. *Memory & Cognition, 32,* 1389–1400.

Matlock, T. M., & Richardson, D. C. (2004). Do eye movements go with fictive motion? In *Proceedings of the 26th Annual Meeting of the Cognitive Science Society* (pp. 909–914). Mahwah, NJ: Lawrence Erlbaum.

McClelland, J., & Elman, J. (1986). The TRACE model of speech perception. *Cognitive Psychology, 18,* 1–86.

McRae, K., Ferretti, T., & Amyote, L. (1997). Thematic roles as verb-specific concepts. *Language and Cognitive Processes, 12,* 137–176.

Metzing, C., & Brennan, S. E. (2003). When conceptual pacts are broken: Partner-specific effects on the comprehension of referring expressions. *Journal of Memory & Language, 49*(2), 201–213.

Meyer, A. S., Sleiderink, A. M., & Levelt, W. J. M. (1998). Viewing and naming objects: Eye movements during noun phrase production. *Cognition, 66*(2), B25–B33.

Nadig, A. S., & Sedivy, J. C. (2002). Evidence of perspective-taking constraints in children's on-line reference resolution. *Psychological Science, 13,* 329–336.

Neisser, U. (1967). *Cognitive psychology.* East Norwalk, CT: Appleton-Century-Crofts.

Neisser, U. (1976). *Cognition and reality: Principles and implications of cognitive psychology.* San Francisco: W. H. Freeman.

Noë, A. (2004). *Action in perception.* Cambridge, MA: MIT Press.

O'Regan, J. K. (1992). Solving the "real" mysteries of visual perception: The world as an outside memory. *Canadian Journal of Psychology, 46,* 461–488.

O'Regan, J. K., & Noë, A. (2001). A sensorimotor account of vision and visual consciousness. *Behavioral and Brain Sciences, 24,* 939–1031.

Poincaré, H. (1906). Les mathématiques et la logique. *Revue de Métaphysique et de Morale, 14,* 294–317. (Translated in W. Ewald (Ed.), 1996, *From Kant to Hilbert: A source book in the foundations of mathematics* (Vol. 2). Oxford: Oxford University Press.)

Port, R., & van Gelder, T. (Eds.). (1995). *Mind as motion: Explorations in the dynamics of cognition.* Cambridge, MA: MIT Press.

Richardson, D., & Dale, R. (2005). Looking to understand: The coupling between speakers' and listeners' eye movements and its relationship to discourse comprehension. *Cognitive Science, 29,* 39–54.

Richardson, D., & Kirkham, N. (2004). Multimodal events and moving locations: Eye movements of adults and 6-month-olds reveal dynamic spatial indexing. *Journal of Experimental Psychology: General, 133,* 46–62.

Richardson, D. C., & Matlock, T. M. (2007). The integration of figurative language and static depictions: An eye movement study of fictive motion. *Cognition, 102*(1), 129–138.

Richardson, D., & Spivey, M. (2000). Representation, space and *Hollywood Squares*: Looking at things that aren't there anymore. *Cognition, 76,* 269–295.

Rosen, R. (2000). *Essays on life itself.* New York: Columbia University Press.

Roy, D. (2005). Grounding words in perception and action: Computational insights. *Trends in Cognitive Sciences, 9,* 389–396.

Roy, D., & Mukherjee, N. (2004). Towards situated speech understanding: Visual context priming of language models. *Computer Speech and Language, 19,* 227–248.

Rozenblit, L., Spivey, M., & Wojslawowicz, J. (2002). Mechanical reasoning about gear-and-belt systems: Do eye movements predict performance? In M. Anderson, B. Meyer, & P. Olivier (Eds.), *Diagrammatic representation and reasoning* (pp. 223–240). Berlin: Springer-Verlag.

Saylor, M. M. (2004). Twelve- and sixteen-month-old infants recognize properties of mentioned absent things. *Developmental Science, 7*(5), 599–611.

Saylor, M. M., & Baldwin, D. A. (2004). Discussing those not present: Comprehension of references to absent caregivers. *Journal of Child Language, 31,* 537–560.

Schober, M. F. (1993). Spatial perspective-taking in conversation. *Cognition, 47*(1), 1–24.

Searle, J. (1969). *Speech acts: An essay in the philosophy of language.* New York: Cambridge University Press.

Sebanz, N., Knoblich, G., & Prinz, W. (2003). Representing others' actions: Just like one's own? *Cognition, 88,* B11–B21.

Simons, D. J., & Levin, D. (1997). Change blindness. *Trends in Cognitive Sciences, 1,* 261–267.

Snedeker, J., & Trueswell, J. (2004). The developing constraints on parsing decisions: The role of lexical-biases and referential scenes in child and adult sentence processing. *Cognitive Psychology, 49,* 238–299.

Spivey, M., & Dale, R. (2004). On the continuity of mind: Toward a dynamical account of cognition. In B. Ross (Ed.), *The psychology of learning and motivation* (Vol. 45, pp. 87–142). San Diego, CA: Elsevier.

Spivey, M., Grosjean, M., & Knoblich, G. (2005). Continuous attraction toward phonological competitors. *Proceedings of the National Academy of Sciences, 102,* 10393–10398.

Spivey, M., & Marian, V. (1999). Crosstalk between native and second languages: Partial activation of an irrelevant lexicon. *Psychological Science, 10,* 281–284.

Spivey, M., Tanenhaus, M., Eberhard, K., & Sedivy, J. (2002). Eye movements and spoken language comprehension: Effects of visual context on syntactic ambiguity resolution. *Cognitive Psychology, 45*(4), 447–481.

Spivey-Knowlton, M., Tanenhaus, M., Eberhard, K., Sedivy, J. (1998). Integration of visuospatial and linguistic information in real-time and real-space. In P. Olivier & K. Gapp (Eds.), *Representation and processing of spatial expressions* (pp. 201–214). Mahwah, NJ: Lawrence Erlbaum.

Sternberg, S. (1969). The discovery of processing stages: Extensions of Donders' method. *Acta Psychologica, 30,* 276–315.

Swingley, D., & Fernald, A. (2002). Recognition of words referring to present and absent objects by 24-month-olds. *Journal of Memory & Language, 46*(1), 39–56.

Tanenhaus, M. K., Spivey-Knowlton, M. J., Eberhard, K. M., & Sedivy, J. C. (1995). Integration of visual and linguistic information in spoken language comprehension. *Science*, 268(5217), 1632–1634.

Trueswell, J., Sekerina, I., Hill, N., & Logrip, M. (1999). The kindergarten-path effect: Studying on-line sentence processing in young children. *Cognition*, 73, 89–134.

Trueswell, J., & Tanenhaus, M. (Eds.). (2004). *Approaches to studying world-situated language use: Bridging the language-as-product and language-as-action traditions*. Cambridge, MA: MIT Press.

Turvey, M. T. (2004). Impredicativity, dynamics, and the perception-action divide. In V. K. Jirsa & J. A. S. Kelso (Eds.), *Coordination dynamics: Issues and trends* (Vol. 1, pp. 1–20). New York: Springer-Verlag.

Turvey, M., & Carello, C. (1995). Some dynamical themes in perception and action. In R. Port & T. van Gelder, *Mind as motion: Explorations in the dynamics of cognition* (pp. 373–401). Cambridge, MA: MIT Press.

Turvey, M., & Shaw, R. (1999). Ecological foundations of cognition: I. Symmetry and specificity of animal-environment systems. *Journal of Consciousness Studies*, 6, 111–123.

van der Heijden, A. (1996). Perception for selection, selection for action, and action for perception. *Visual Cognition*, 3, 357–361.

van Orden, G., Holden, J., & Turvey, M. (2003). Self-organization of cognitive performance. *Journal of Experimental Psychology: General*, 132, 331–350.

Ward, L. (2002). *Dynamical cognitive science*. Cambridge, MA: MIT Press.

Winograd, E., & Church, V. (1988). Role of spatial location in learning face-name associations. *Memory and Cognition*, 16(1), 1–7.

Zbilut, J. P., & Webber, C. L., Jr. (1992). Embeddings and delays as derived from quantification of recurrence plots. *Physics Letters A*, 171, 199–203.

Zbilut, J. P., Giuliani, A., & Webber, C. L., Jr. (1998). Detecting deterministic signals in exceptionally noisy environments using cross-recurrence quantification. *Physics Letters A*, 246, 122–128.

Zwaan, R. A. (2004). The immersed experiencer: Toward an embodied theory of language comprehension. In B. Ross (Ed.), *The psychology of learning and motivation* (Vol. 44, pp. 35–62). New York: Academic Press.

CHAPTER 21

Situated Semantics

Varol Akman

1. Situations and Context

What is it that we really want to convey
when we say "situated semantics"? We begin
with a brief digression and then proceed
toward the main concern of this chapter,
semantics.

Stage works in which the humor derives
from the situations the characters are placed
in (sitcoms) make one thing clear. Placed in
social situations, people construct the meaning of these situations in a subjective way.
This affects the way they behave in these
situations (e.g., the sort of roles they play
and the views they hold).[1] Following Mil-
ton Rokeach (1998), we define an attitude
as a relatively lasting organization of beliefs
around an object or situation preparing a
person to respond in some preferential manner. We care about attitudes because we
think that we can use them to predict behavior. This requires that social agents maintain
considerable uniformity to act in a certain
(more or less consistent) way in situations.
It was Erving Goffman's (2002) idea to look
behind situations to discover the structures
that implicitly govern them. These structures he called "frames." Where a situation
is given by its contents, a frame is described
by its components having a definite arrangement and stable relations (Gonos, 1977,
p. 860). Each of the forms of daily activities
scrutinized by Goffman has names (e.g., one
is at a birthday party or a fund-raiser). On
the other hand, situations are describable
but nameless (e.g., a shareholders' meeting
that ended in a fistfight; Goffman, 2002).

Situated semantics can be regarded as
an attempt at placing situational context

(context of situation) at the center of all discussions of meaning. The word *situation* (or more properly, *context of situation*) was used by John Rupert Firth to cover all the relevant circumstances in which a specific act of speech takes place. Also termed *extralinguistic context*, this referred to the entire situation in which an utterance is made (e.g., who is the speaker, who is the addressee, whether the delivery is formal or informal, the aim of utterance, the time of utterance, the location of utterance). In the analysis of a language, Firth (1957) thought, features recurring in individual utterances will be related to types of situation and to specific features in them.[2]

Blackburn (1994) offers a similar definition: "In linguistics, context is the parts of an utterance surrounding a unit and which may affect both its meaning and its grammatical contribution" (p. 80). He then adds that context also refers to "the wider situation, either of the speaker or of the surroundings, that may play a part in determining the significance of a saying." Angeles (1981) regards context as the totality of associations, preconceptions, and so forth that are closely related to a thing and influence one's perspectives, judgments, and knowledge of that thing. Accordingly, if something is seen in context (or put into context), it is considered with all the factors that are related to it rather than just being considered on its own, so that it can be properly understood.[3]

Clark and Carlson (1981) take context as information that is available to a person on a given occasion. Their intrinsic context (sometimes called the "common ground") refers to the totality of knowledge, beliefs, and suppositions that are shared by the speaker and the hearer.[4] Adopting a stance attributable to Leech (1981), we can say that "the specification of context has the effect of narrowing down the communicative possibilities of [a] message as it exists in abstraction from context" (p. 66). Thus, context has a disambiguating function,[5] for a so-called fleshing-out strategy – converting statements into decontextualized (eternal) sentences – cannot always be used. One seldom has full and precise information about the relevant circumstances.

Context has long been a salient issue in social studies of language; namely, how human beings employ language to build the social and cultural organizations that they inhabit. Lyons (1995) finds this inevitable: "In the construction of a satisfactory theory of context, the linguist's account of the interpretation of utterances must of necessity draw upon, and will in turn contribute to, the theories and findings of social sciences in general: notably of psychology, anthropology and sociology" (p. 292). Influenced by Firth, Goodwin and Duranti (1992) judge context as basic in ethnographical studies of language use. They claim that context "stands at the cutting edge of much contemporary research into the relationship between language, culture, and social organization, as well as into the study of how language is structured in the way it is" (p. 32).

2. Enter STASS

Situation theory is a theory of information content that takes context very seriously (Akman & Surav, 1996, 1997). Groundbreaking work on situation theory is due to the late Jon Barwise, noted logician, and John Perry, prominent philosopher of language. Barwise and Perry were the founders of Stanford University's Center for the Study of Language and Information (CSLI), which became almost synonymous with situation-theoretic research.[6]

The theory matured over the years. It was applied to a number of linguistic issues, resulting in what is commonly known as situation semantics. Situation semantics aims to construct a mathematically rigorous theory of meaning and the application of such a theory to natural language.[7] One is engaged in situation semantics if one is using situation-theoretic ideas – mathematical theories of information content – to study meaning in natural language. In fact, the two areas are not clearly separable, as the still-popular acronym STASS (situation theory and situation semantics) neatly shows.

Situation semantics is based on the following general observation: in evaluating a certain statement, one needs not only certain indices like times and worlds (of possible-world semantics). As Recanati (2004) notes:

> Why not also, for example, locations? If I say "It's raining," the location is unarticulated, but it is relevant qua feature of the circumstance of evaluation: what I say (or think) is true [if and only if] it's raining at the contextually provided location. Why not also consider the agent of the speech act (the speaker) or the thought act (the thinker) as (part of) the circumstance of evaluation, to handle cases in which the content to be evaluated is a property of agents which the speaker or thinker self-attributes? Why not extend [this approach] also to ordinary objects? If, talking about my car, the mechanic tells me "The carburetor is in good condition but there is a problem with the front wheels," my car is a crucial feature of the circumstance of evaluation. It is true (or false) of my car that the carburetor is in good condition, and so on. The same thing could have been said of another car, but as things turn out it is my car which figures in the [content] of the mechanic's utterance. (p. 122)

Situation semantics does not impose man-made assumptions on our conceptual scheme.[8] This makes it enticing for a newcomer to the realm of semantics. It is burdensome for someone to embrace, say, Montagovian intensions (Dowty, Wall, & Peters, 1981), but situations have a certain conceptual clarity. Actually, situation semantics is a fine exemplar of what a naturalized theory of semantics should be like.

In the history of natural language semantics, there was a period when it was considered *bon ton* to distinguish meticulously between formal semantics and pragmatics.[9] If you worked on the former, you counted as doing idealized – as opposed to ordinary – language philosophy. Two important desiderata – truth conditions and compositionality – were crucial to the meaning of a declarative sentence. Originating in the work of Donald Davidson, knowledge of meaning of a sentence coincides with knowledge of truth conditions (i.e., what the world is to be like if the sentence is true). (It is noted that actual knowledge of truth conditions is not required.) Compositionality fastidiously maneuvers to determine the meaning of the sentence in terms of the meanings of its constituents (Pietroski, 2003; Pulman, 1997).

The ordinary-language approach, on the other hand, studied the activity of saying things.[10] Thus, one has speech acts to analyze and as one could no more ignore irony, metaphor, implicature, and so on, one has to consider the so-called speaker's meaning. Communication succeeds as soon as the intentions (the m-intentions of Paul Herbert Grice) of the speaker are recognized by the hearer.

Idealized approaches to semantics underestimated the role played by context; they ignored factors such as intentions and circumstances of the individuals involved in the communicative process. (Or rather, they placed them in the pragmatics wastebasket.) But linguistic devices like indexicals, demonstratives, and tenses rely heavily on context for interpretation and are fundamental to the way language carries information. A sentence can be used over and over again in different situations to say different things (the so-called efficiency of language).[11] Its interpretation (i.e., the class of situations described by the sentence) is therefore subordinate to the situation in which the sentence is used. This context-providing situation (discourse situation) is the speech situation, including the speaker, the addressee, the time and place of the utterance, and the expression uttered. Because speakers are always in different situations, having different causal connections to the world and different information, the information conveyed by an utterance will be relative to its speaker and hearer (the so-called perspectival relativity of language). The insistence of situation semantics on contextual interpretation makes it compatible with speech-act theory and discourse pragmatics.

Situation theory starts with a fundamental observation: reality consists of situations. A situation is a rich object consisting of individuals having various properties and standing in a variety of relations. It is, in a sense, a small world. We always find ourselves in situations. J. J. Gibson (1979) famously argued that perception was regulated by response to properties in the visual world. He thus embraced the position that most thinking depends on suitable responses to environmental demands (Turvey & Carello, 1986). Deep down, the Barwise-Perry stance is also an ecological one.[12]

Although situations are commonsensical entities on the one hand, they can be quite problematical as soon as we start asking probing questions about their fundamental nature. Devlin (1991a, pp. 31–32) exemplifies this by imagining a dialogue between two participants (John and David) about a particular football game they have both seen. John and David can have an extended discussion about this game while maintaining informativeness and avoiding disorientation or puzzlement. How is that possible? Neither John nor David can enumerate every bit of information that this particular game situation supports. Actually, this would make their postgame discussion superfluous and not very enjoyable. Thus, the following query of Devlin (1991a) becomes vital:

[I]f you were to interrupt John and David in the middle of their conversation and ask them what they were talking about, they would reply "Last night's football game." Are we then to conclude that they were in fact talking about nothing; or that neither was really sure what it was they were discussing? (p. 32)

"Clearly not," Devlin replies, and mentions our inability to reduce situations to an amalgam of more familiar entities. Devlin considers the latter as one good explanation for people's disinclination to regard situations as bona fide objects. Devlin's question is in some sense relatively old. In discussions of vagueness in philosophy, vague objects have received considerable attention (Tye, 1990).

Consider a certain mountain. Keefe (2000) notes that

any sharp spatio-temporal boundaries drawn around the mountain would be arbitrarily placed, and would not reflect a natural boundary. So it may seem that [the mountain] has fuzzy boundaries, and so, given the common view that a vague object is an object with fuzzy, spatio-temporal boundaries, that it is a vague object. (p. 15)

It is not hard to generalize the approach briefly outlined above to situations of any kind. Although the description "last night's football game" does succeed in picking out a unique object, it is evident that that object (situation) has blurry spatiotemporal boundaries. Suppose John says, "The game was watched (in the stadium) by an even number of spectators." Because the woolly boundaries of the game situation, this should come out to be neither true nor false (hence indeterminate). Note that, in general, John and David would hardly ever argue about the truth of such statements. They are more likely to talk about matters regarding the Coke bottles thrown at the players or the colorful shirts worn by referees. In both of these cases, there can be little disagreement as to the truth value of the propositions under discussion.

Barwise and Perry were the first to formulate a full-fledged proposal about the use of situations for semantics, but it is worth mentioning that Austin (1979) saw the need for situations in his famous 1950 paper on truth. In this work, Austin makes key observations about statements. He notes that the making of a statement is a historic event: a speaker is uttering certain words (a sentence) to an audience with reference to a historic situation. Usually these words are used to talk about the world ("something other than the words"). This world exhibits similarities and dissimilarities; in an extremely chaotic or perfectly ordered world, there would be little to say. Austin then makes a fundamental distinction (1979, pp. 121–122) between descriptive and demonstrative conventions. The former correlate the words (sentences) with the types of situation, thing, or event present in the world. The latter correlate the words (statements) with the historical situations and so on present in the world. The truth of a statement then simply reduces to this: the historical state of affairs with which the statement is correlated by the demonstrative conventions is of a type with which the sentence used in making the statement is correlated by the descriptive conventions. As a simple illustration of the idea, take a signpost that reads "Checkpoint ahead." This says that there is checkpoint ahead (descriptive conventions). The word *ahead* probably means something like a couple of hundred yards. The sign makes a true statement if there is indeed a checkpoint ahead (at a reasonable distance). It would be making a false claim if one encounters no such checkpoint.

3. Ontology

Individuals, properties, relations, and spatiotemporal locations are basic constructs of situation theory. Individuals are conceived as invariants; having properties and standing in relations, they tend to persist in time and space.

Infons (Devlin, 1992) are discrete items of information. They are denoted as $<R,a_1,\ldots,a_n,p>$, where R is an n-place relation, $a_1,\ldots,a_n$ are objects appropriate for the respective argument places of R, and p is the polarity (o or 1). If $p = 1$ (respectively, o) then $a_1,\ldots,a_n$ stand (respectively, do not stand) in relation R.[13] A situation is a structured part of the reality that an agent manages to pick out. Situations are intensional objects. For this reason, abstract situations are proposed to be their counterparts amenable to mathematical manipulation. An abstract situation is defined as a set (Devlin, 1991c). Given a real situation s, the set $\{i|s \models i\}$, where i is an infon, is the corresponding abstract situation. Here, s is said to support an infon i (denoted as $s \models i$ above) just in case i is true of s.

A scheme of individuation – a way of carving the world into uniformities – is an essential aspect of situation theory. The

notions of individual, relation, and spatio-temporal location depend on this. In other words, the basic constituents of the theory are determined by the agent's schema of individuation. Formal representation of these uniformities yields types. Situation theory provides a collection of basic types for individuating or discriminating uniformities of the real world: situation, infon, individual, n-place relation, temporal location, spatial location, type, and parameter. (We choose not to count polarities as types.)

Parameters are generalizations over classes of nonparametric objects (e.g., individuals, spatial locations). Parameters can be associated with objects that, if they were to replace the parameters, would yield one of the objects in the class that parametric object abstracts over. Hence, allowing parameters in infons results in parametric infons. For example, $<see,\hat{g},Alice,1>$ and $<see,\hat{g},\hat{h},1>$ are parametric infons where $\hat{g}$ and $\hat{h}$ stand for individuals. These infons are parametric on the first, and the first and second, argument roles of the relation *see*, respectively. (Their meaning can be rendered as "someone sees Alice" and "someone sees someone," respectively.) Anchoring (binding) parameters of an infon to objects yields parameter-free infons. For example, given $<see,\hat{g},Alice,1>$, if $F(\hat{g}) = $ Bob, then we obtain the parameter-free infon $<see,Bob,Alice,1>$.

Given a situation s, a parameter $\hat{g}$, and a set of infons I (involving $\hat{g}$), one can define $[\hat{g}|s \models I]$ to denote the type of all objects for which the conditions imposed by I hold in s. This process of obtaining a type is type abstraction. Here $\hat{g}$ is the abstraction parameter and s is the grounding situation.

A situation s' is part of another situation s just in case for all infons i, $s' \models i \rightarrow s \models i$. This relation is antisymmetric, reflexive, and transitive, and consequently provides a partial ordering of situations.

Situations in which a constituent sequence is assigned both polarities are incoherent. For instance, a situation s is incoherent if $<has,Alice,A\clubsuit,o>$ and $<has,Alice,A\clubsuit,1>$ are both supported by s. Although there cannot be a real situation s validating this, the constituent sequence <has,Alice,A♣> may be assigned these polarities for spatiotemporally distinct situation types (say, s and s′).

Situation semantics makes simple assumptions about the way natural language works. Primary among them is the assumption that language is used to convey information about the world (the so-called external significance of language). Even when two sentences have the same interpretation (i.e., describe the same situation), they can carry different information.

Suppose Alice was eating ice cream yesterday. She is eating ice cream now. Both of these situations share the same constituent sequence <eat,Alice,ice cream>. These two events, occurring at different times, have the same situation type. Situation types can be more general. For example, a situation type in which someone is eating something at home contains the situation in which Alice is eating ice cream at home. If Alice is not present in the room where this chapter is being written, then "Alice is eating ice cream" is not part of the room situation s and hence gets no truth value in s. Thus, situation theory allows partiality.

To see this more clearly, imagine two games that are going on, one across town from the other. Alice is playing cards with Bob, and Carol is playing cards with David. Elwood, watching the former game, mistakes Alice for Carol, and mutters: "Carol has the ace of clubs." According to the classical theory, if Carol indeed has the ace, his claim would be true since "Carol" and "the ace of clubs" are used to pick, among all the things in the world, the unique objects satisfying the properties of being someone named Carol and being the ace of clubs, respectively. In contrast, situation semantics identifies these objects with respect to some limited situation – the resource situation exploited by Elwood. Elwood's claim would then be false even if Carol held the ace in the other game.

Partiality makes it possible to distinguish between logically equivalent statements. For example, the statements "Bob is angry" and "Bob is angry, and Bob is shouting or Bob is not shouting" are logically equivalent in the classical sense. In situation semantics, these two sentences will not have the same interpretation. A situation s describing the circumstance in which Bob is only angry will not contain anything about Bob's shouting (i.e., s will be silent on Bob's shouting). However, another situation s′ obtained as the union of two situations ("Bob is angry and Bob is shouting" plus "Bob is angry and Bob is not shouting") will contain something about Bob's shouting.

To recap, in Tarskian semantics, statements that are true in the same models convey the same information. Situation semantics takes the view that logically equivalent sentences need not have the same subject matter, for they need not describe situations involving the same objects and properties. The notion of partiality leads to a more fine-grained notion of information content and a stronger notion of logical consequence that does not lose track of the subject matter.

4. Constraints

Intelligent agents generally make their way in the world by being able to pick up certain information from a situation, process it, and react accordingly. Being in a situation, such an agent would have information about the situations it sees, hears about, believes in, and so on. Thus, on hearing Bob's utterance "A wolf is running toward you," Alice would have the information that her friend is addressing her with *you*. Moreover, by relying on the situation described by the utterance, she would know that there is a wolf fast approaching her. Alice would run away, having in possession the acquired knowledge that wolves are hazardous. She would activate this knowledge from the situation she finds herself in via a constraint – the link between wolves and their reputation as life-threatening creatures.

A network of abstract links between high-order uniformities (i.e., situation types) provides such information flow. The statement "Smoke means fire" expresses the lawlike relation that links situations where there is smoke to situations where there is a fire. If s is the type of smoky situations and f is the type of fire situations, then having been attuned to the constraint s▶f, an agent can pick up the information that there is a fire in a particular situation by observing that there is smoke.[14] Anchoring plays a major role in the working of constraints. Cognitively, if the preceding constraint holds, then it is a fact that if s is realized (i.e., there is a real situation s_o of type s), then so is f (i.e., there is a real situation f_o of type f). To invoke the constraint, we have to use an anchoring function that binds the location parameters to appropriate objects present in the grounding situation (i.e., we have to first find a place and time at which there is smoke).

It is possible to identify three forms of constraints. Necessary constraints are those by which one can define or name things (e.g., every dog is a mammal). Nomic constraints are patterns that are usually called natural laws (e.g., blocks fall unless they are supported). Conventional constraints are those arising out of the customs that hold within a community (e.g., the first day of the month is payday). These are neither nomic nor necessary (i.e., they can be violated). All types of constraints can be conditional or unconditional. Conditional constraints can be applied to situations that fulfill some condition, and unconditional constraints can be applied to all situations.[15]

5. Meaning

Meaningful expressions are used to convey information not only about the external world but also about our minds (the so-called mental significance of language). Clearly, language could not work if it did not have information significance – if it were not about matters in a public world. Returning to an earlier example, consider the sentence "A wolf is running toward you" uttered by Bob. It can give Alice information about two different situations. The first one is the situation that she is located in. The second one is Bob's belief situation. If Alice is certain that he is hallucinating, then she

cares about the second situation, not the first. Situation semantics differs from other approaches in that in attitude reports we do not describe our mind directly (by referring to states of mind, ideas, senses, thoughts, and whatnot) but indirectly (by referring to situations that are external). To appreciate this point, consider the sentence "The wolf is approaching." Understanding what situations this sentence describes is essential to grasping its meaning. One such concrete situation is the one Bob is currently facing. But there are countless other (potential) situations that can be described in the same way. In other words, on hearing this sentence in our mind's eye are evoked all those situations accurately described by it. Now take the sentence "Bob wants a big stick," expressing a certain wish of Bob. It may be possible to understand this by trying to imagine all those private (internal) mental states of Bob correctly described by it. However, it is much more meaningful (less baffling) to resort to public situations for an explanation. Thus, Bob wants to achieve (arrive at) a situation in which he is holding a big stick. This he normally does by looking around to find something like that or by (creatively) crafting one – say, by breaking a tree branch – when he is not able to locate one lying on the forest floor.

In situation semantics, propositions are conceived as situations, and propositional attitudes are characterized as relations to such situations. To believe that a particular wolf is dangerous is then to stand in a relationship to that wolf and the property of being dangerous. Several researchers concur that major difficulties threaten the situation-theoretic rendering of propositional attitudes. Davis (2003, pp. 351–352) cites what he calls Frege's and Russell's problems: "Frege's problem arises from the intensionality of propositional attitude contexts, the fact that substitution of coextensive terms in such contexts does not always produce equivalent statements. Someone can believe that Cary Grant is famous, for example, without believing that Archibald Leach is.[16] Russell's problem arises from the intentionality of propositional attitudes, the fact that people can think about nonexistent objects and have other propositional attitudes concerning them. Many children believe that Santa Claus brings presents at Christmas, even though Santa Claus does not exist."

Davis notes that common responses to the former problem typically dispose of the view that propositional attitudes are relations between individuals and situations. Rather, such attitudes are assumed to be relations connecting individuals, situations, and modes of presentation (i.e., ways of believing).[17]

In their thorough account of propositional attitude reports, McKay and Nelson (2005) make similar claims:

> Recall that one of the problems facing naive Russellianism was that
>
> Lois believes that Superman is stronger than Clark Kent.
>
> threatens to entail
>
> Lois believes that Superman is stronger than Superman.
>
> which in turn threatens to entail
>
> Lois believes that Superman is stronger than himself.
>
> Because the situation that Superman is stronger than Clark Kent just is the situation that Superman is stronger than himself, these are the same beliefs. The situation semanticist cannot appeal to the difference between the property of being taller than Superman and the property of being taller than oneself, as the neo-Russellian can, to distinguish the properties. This is because a difference in structure doesn't correspond, for the situation semanticist, to a difference in proposition. But then the situation semanticist, as opposed to the naive Russellian, is committed to the claim that Lois believes that Superman is stronger than himself. But surely that is irrational!

According to situation semantics, meanings of expressions reside in systematic relations between different types of situations. They can be identified with relations on discourse situations d, (speaker) connections c, the utterance situation u itself, and the described situation e. Some public facts

about u – such as its speaker and time of utterance – are determined by the discourse situations. The ties of the mental states of the speaker and the hearer with the world constitute c.

A discourse situation involves the expression uttered, its speaker, the spatiotemporal location of the utterance, and the addressee. Each of these defines a linguistic role: the role of the speaker, the role of the addressee, and so on. The utterance situation u constrains the world in a certain way, depending on how the roles for discourse situations, connections, and described situations are to be filled. For instance, an utterance of "I am trembling" defines a meaning relation:

d, c ǁ I am trembling ǁ e.

Given a discourse situation d, connections c, and a described situation e, this holds just in case that there is a location L and a speaker s such that s is speaking at L, and in e, s is trembling at L.

Besides discourse situations, the interpretation of an utterance depends on the speaker's connections with objects, properties, times and places, and on the speaker's ability to exploit information about one situation to obtain information about another. Therefore, context supports not only facts about speakers, addressees, and so on, but also facts about the relations of discourse participants to other contextually relevant situations such as resource situations. Resource situations are contextually available and provide entities for reference and quantification.

In interpreting the utterance of an expression S in context, there is a flow of information, partly from the linguistic form encoded in S and partly from contextual factors provided by the utterance situation u. These are combined to form a set of constraints on the described situation e. This situation is not uniquely determined; there may be others satisfying the constraints. The meaning of an utterance of S and hence its interpretation are influenced by other factors such as stress, modality, and intonation. However, the situation in which S is uttered and the situation e described by this utterance seem to play the most influential roles.

In the remainder of this chapter, we give two applications of situation semantics. The first application is situated inference. This application is presented after the following section, which introduces some background material. The second application is literary interpretation.

6. Oracles

Let G be a collection of parametric infons. G provides one with a framework for conversing about some part of the world (or the whole world). By anchoring the parameters in an infon belonging to G, an item of information is obtained.

Given an individual or a situation s, the G-oracle of s, denoted as $O(G,s)$, is the situation comprising that part of the world and the entire body of knowledge that concerns s. This is relative to a set of issues (i.e., it is understood to be meaningful within the framework provided by G). Thus, different sets will enable one to talk – and glean information – about different aspects of the world.[18]

Oracles were invented by Devlin (1991a):

Just as various kinds of number (e.g., complex numbers) 'exist' because we postulate their existence (in the mathematical realm), so too with oracles. As with different kinds of number system, oracles are intended to provide a theoretical construct that corresponds to a certain feature in the world being studied. In this case, the 'feature' concerned is the situation comprising precisely those objects and facts of relevance to a given individual or situation. (p. 48)

If we stick to the classical assumption that among the situations available there is a unique, maximal situation ω – in STASS, ω is commonly known as the world – then the following can be stated. For any G-infon i in which only objects that are the constituents of $O(G,s)$ occur, $O(G,s)\models i$ if and only if $\omega\models i$. One particularly natural way

to understand this is as follows. If the only kind of information available to an agent is that supplied by G, then $O(G,s)$ cannot be distinguished from ω.

As an illustration, consider the Jerry Fodor oracle $O(G, Fodor)$, for an appropriate G. Stretching back in time to include his granny, and forward in time to include his grandchildren, it will contain Fodor's birthplace, his favorite books (including *The House at Pooh Corner*, of course!), positions he has held, students he has taught, and so on. One key observation has to do with the extent of this oracle. Different people at different times may have access to different information about it. Ernie Lepore must surely know more about it than I do, for I never met Fodor but am familiar, to some degree, with his oeuvre. Fodor himself will know considerably more about it, though a biographer of this philosopher may unearth facts that could be news even to Fodor.

Various observations regarding oracles can be stated (Devlin, 1991b):

- Oracles are situations. This necessitates that an agent would have only partial information about a particular oracle.
- Oracles (ipso facto, situations) make little sense if one tries to specify them in terms of which infons they support. The right way to specify an oracle is in terms of a description that is less primitive.
- In natural language, a single word or phrase can bring into focus an entire oracle situation corresponding to an individual.
- The more information two agents share about an oracle, the more efficient is the communication between them.[19]

7. Situated Inference

As noted in the preceding section, a set of issues is a collection of parametric infons that provide us with an information-theoretic framework for discussing the world or some part of it. By anchoring the parameters in this set, we obtain an item of information. Clearly, using different sets of issues, we can talk about different aspects of the world. For example, when talking about Bob in the context of a colloquium in Hawaii (PHIL '05), we may include stuff like his being the organizer of the colloquium, things that happened to him around the time of the colloquium, the personal characteristics of Bob that help one recognize him, and so on. However, what happened to Bob when he was five years old is probably not included in the set of issues (unless his colloquium talk is about his experiences in his early youth).

For example, O(G,Bob) contains (this is a very brief list):

< organize,Bob,PHIL'05,1 >

< go,Bob,Hawaii,2005,1 >

< male,Bob,1 >

G is, in some sense, a template of information which determines what portion of O(G,Bob) is to be considered. O(Bob) may contain a large amount of information about the medical state of Bob, but if G does not discuss these issues, O(G,Bob) would not include such information.

Because we need a notion of relevance here, we consider Sperber and Wilson (1986), in which relevance is psychological relevance of a proposition to a context. Their assumption is that people have intuitions of relevance (i.e., they can consistently distinguish relevant from irrelevant information). A proposition is relevant to a context if it interacts in a certain way with the (context's) existing assumptions about the world (i.e., if it has some contextual effects that are accessible). These contextual effects include the following[20]:

1. Contextual implication: a new assumption can be used together with the existing rules to generate new assumptions.
2. Strengthening: a new assumption can strengthen some of the existing assumptions.
3. Contradicting or eliminating: a new assumption may change or eliminate some of the existing assumptions.

Sperber and Wilson talk about degrees of relevance. Clearly, one piece of information may be more relevant to a particular context. Their following definition does the job: "An assumption is relevant in a context to the extent that its contextual effects in this context are large. An assumption is relevant in a context to the extent that the effort required to process it in this context is small" (Sperber & Wilson, 1986, p. 125).[21] To estimate relevance, we can try to measure the relevance of i to G. Here, we use the criterion proposed by Sperber and Wilson; namely, maximum contextual effect and minimum processing effort.[22] We interpret the effects of i on G as contextual effects. An infon is relevant to a context if it has some contextual effects on the context with a small-sized anchoring. It is irrelevant to a context if either it has no contextual effect on the context or otherwise some contextual effects with a large-sized anchoring.

Let us consider a context that contains the regularity "Birds fly." We represent this as

$$b = [\hat{s}|\hat{s} \models <bird,\hat{y},1>]$$
$$f = [\hat{s}|\hat{s} \models <fly,\hat{y},1>]$$
$$b \blacktriangleright f$$

The infon $i = <bird,Tweety,1>$ is relevant to this context, as with the anchoring $F(\hat{y}) = $ Tweety we can conclude that Tweety flies. The size of anchoring is 1, and thus the processing effort is minimal.

Consider now the following dialogue between Carol and Bob:

Carol: Did you see the fight in the baseball game on Foo TV last night?
Bob: I always watch Foo TV.

Did Bob see the fight? We begin by noting that Carol's utterance carries the following presupposition: A baseball game was shown on Foo TV last night. Additionally, we are aware of the (commonsense) rule: If some event is broadcast on a TV channel and someone watches that channel, then he or she also sees the event. The encoded versions of the first three items of information are, respectively, <see,Bob,the fight,?>, <watch,Bob,Foo TV,1>, and <show,Foo TV, the baseball game,1>. The constraint suggested by the commonsense rule is b►e, where b = [ŝ|ŝ ⊨<show,ŵ,û,1>&ŝ ⊨ <watch, ŷ,ŵ,1>] and e = [ŝ|ŝ ⊨<see,ŷ,ŵ,1>]; using the anchoring F(ŷ) = Bob, F(ŵ) = Foo TV, and F(û) = the baseball game, we achieve a contextual effect (i.e., the invocation of the constraint) and conclude that Bob saw the fight (i.e., the polarity denoted with ? above is 1). (Clearly, the fight situation is a part of the game situation.) Notice that the size of the anchoring is 3 this time.

8. Interpretation

In his work on literary criticism, Barwise (1989a) suggests a mock equation (a constraint C) to relate the basic constituents of content:

$$C(R,S,c) = P.$$

Here, S is a sentence and c is the situation in which S is used. R is defined as the language conventions holding between an author and a reader (or better yet, his readership). P is the content of S (i.e., the intended meaning). We assume that the communication between an author and a reader is limited only to written text. Thus, it is not feasible to ask the author about his intention for writing S; that will have to be discovered by a reader. For many kinds of written material, P is a single intended meaning (attributable to a determinate author). However, in most literary works and especially in poetry, authors may aim, for assorted reasons, at more than one intended meaning. The richness of a literary work may be rooted in its being ambiguous or multifaceted. All the parameters in the previous constraint are at the writer's disposal. He or she can play with them, as long as the constraint is satisfied. (Obviously, if the writer experiments with R – a fitting example would be *Finnegans Wake* – he has less chance of being understood.) Thus, the reader of a literary text S is faced with one equation in three unknowns: R, c, and P. Usually, the solution is not unique. The task of literary interpretation is to use the available information about the unknowns (e.g., biographical material, information about the culture in which the writing took place, etc.) to circumscribe the range of their possible values.[23]

Let the right-hand side of Barwise's equation be a set of possible intended meanings. These are clear to the author – we presume – during the writing activity but may be cumbersome to discover later.[24] An author of fiction creates an artificial circumstance at first and builds his or her work around that. The author has something in mind and wants to share this with readers; the author has an intended meaning P. To achieve P, the author determines the elements of circumstance that fit best to his or her needs. Here, the author can choose to play with the rules of language. This is also the point where the author makes either implicit or explicit assumptions about the language conventions (Percy, 1975).

A reader, picking up the written material in his hand, normally reads it from beginning to the end. Therefore, ideas frequently descend on him as they are written (sequentially). And more often than not, a reader understands the text at first pass; the reader does not go through the text over and over again to bind variables, rewrite portions, reorder passages, make optimizations, and so on.

From the perspective of a reader, the author could have intended almost any meaning. This can be denoted with the cardinality of intention space being large. If a reader is familiar with the language conventions, we assume that he or she can read say, a book. Here, if the text is accessible, we can claim that the world the book presents can be built in the intention space of the reader. The reader may read sequentially, may skip pages or chapters, or may choose to browse. The intention space, with every element that is added, acquires new restrictions. The reader in turn begins to understand what the author is saying in the book.

Ambiguity comes in two kinds. The first is due to large intention spaces and the other to incompatible intentions. The former can be exemplified by the so-called open texts (Eco, 1979). In such texts, the openness stems from size: the intention space cannot be fully circumscribed in a reader's mind. The author does not write something to mean something definite in an open text. Rather, the author writes to keep his or her intention space large so that reader can consume only a portion of that. (And just what that portion might be is up to the reader.)

The second kind of ambiguity is in fact an incompatibility problem. In general, being a reader makes one divide the intention space into parts and discard irrelevant parts. The criterion to discard some part in favor of another seems to be the exact problem of understanding texts.

Authors must also assume some familiarity on the part of a reader with the concepts they write about, and this assumption lies between the borders of R and c. Because this kind of familiarity is usually counted among the language knowledge, there will not be a clear distinction between c and R in these cases. If the author is telling us about some planet and assumes that a reader knows the meaning of the word *planet*, does he or she assume something for R, as the author assumes the reader must know what a planet is? Or does the author assume something about c, that is, if the reader knows what a planet is, the reader must be able to infer some knowledge about the circumstances mentioned in the work?

To cope with this problem, we can accept R and c as mutually exclusive, and define c as the special part of circumstances that are used in the work and R as the remaining part of the language. This is a hard-and-fast solution but does not present us with a standard about separating c and R. (Thus, the assumptions underlying children's books and Shakespeare's plays are not the same.) To produce some standard about the separation of c and R, one must come up with explicit definitions. Definitions may be reader oriented and follow the rules in the mind of a generic reader (i.e., the model reader of Eco) or writer oriented and follow the rules of the author.

9. Brief Guide to the Literature

Two book-length treatments of STASS are Barwise and Perry (1983) and Devlin (1991a). Although somewhat dated, the former is packed with excellent semantic common sense.[25] The latter proposes a standard vocabulary and pays close attention to the foundations; it is the only modern introduction to STASS, together with the most recent (Devlin, n.d.). Devlin also wrote accounts of STASS, mostly oriented toward the layperson (cf. Devlin, 1998, 2001). Seligman and Moss (1997) is a survey of situation theory that is mathematically demanding; it also has a good bibliography of technical papers.

Various versions of situation theory have been applied to a number of linguistic issues arising in English (Stucky, 1989). Barwise (1986, 1987) has written especially important papers in that they study classical areas of semantics such as conditionals, quantifiers, and anaphora. The ideas emerging from research in situation semantics have also been combined with well-developed linguistic theories, leading to rigorous formalisms (Fenstad, Halvorsen, Langholm, & van Benthem, 1987).

Indexicals, demonstratives, referential uses of definite descriptions, deictic uses of pronouns, tense markers, and names all have technical treatments in situation semantics. Gawron and Peters (1990) focus on the semantics of pronominal anaphora and quantification. They argue that the ambiguities of sentences with pronouns can be resolved with an approach that represents anaphoric relations syntactically. They use a relational framework that considers anaphoric relations as relations between utterances in context. Cooper (1991, 1996) offers detailed studies of linguistic problems to which situation semantics has been applied with some success. Tin and Akman (1996) show how situation theory can be given a computational twist. They offer a prototype to study practical problems, including anaphora resolution. Devlin and Rosenberg (1996) explore applications of situation theory to human-computer interaction.

Three early conference proceedings specifically devoted to developments in STASS are Cooper, Mukai, and Perry (1990), Barwise, Gawron, Plotkin, and Tutiya (1991), and Aczel, Israel, Katagiri, and Peters (1993). Today it is possible to find situation-theoretic work dispersed in conferences on logic, language, and information. Thus, despite what Partee (2005) asserts in her intellectual autobiography, today STASS is alive and well.[26]

10. Conclusion

For an expression to have meaning, it should convey information. On the basis of this fundamental insight, situation semantics develops a theory of meaning that is based on relations between situations. In analyzing a speech act S, situation semantics looks at various situations (e.g., discourse situations, resource situations) that contribute to the meaning of S. Doing so makes it possible to describe the meaning of both expressions and mental states in terms of the information they carry about the external world.

Situation semantics provides a fundamental framework for realistic semantics. The ideas emerging from research into situation semantics have been combined with linguistic work and have led to numerous useful proposals. This chapter gave only a glimpse of this exciting activity. Interested readers should consult the literature for a deeper appraisal.

Acknowledgments

The author gratefully acknowledges the moral support of the editors and insightful comments of the referees. The improved readability of this chapter is due to the able efforts of Katherine Faydash. A compressed article (two thousand words) using material from this chapter appeared in K. Brown (Ed.), *Encyclopedia of Language and Linguistics* (2nd ed.), published by Elsevier in 2006.

Notes

1 William Isaac Thomas argued that so-called social reality is essentially the totality of these constructions. He thought that social situations never repeat themselves. Every situation would be more or less novel in that it would include new human activities differently put together.

2 Not surprisingly, the word *situated* has also been used in artificial intelligence. Humans, delivery robots, and automated factories are all systems that have an intelligent, ongoing interaction with environments that are dynamic and imperfectly predictable. Such systems are often called "situated agents" (Rosenschein & Kaelbling, 1995). Rosenschein and Kaelbling present a particular approach to the design of situated agents. The approach is based on situated-automata theory and permits designers to use high-level language constructs to describe the informational content of agents.

3 Conversely, if a remark, statement, and so on, is taken or quoted out of context, it is considered only on its own and the circumstances in which it was said are ignored. It, therefore, seems to mean something different from the meaning that was intended.

4 Manfred Pinkal says this about the potential size of a context:

> *Aside from the surrounding deictic coordinates, aside from the immediate linguistic co-text and accompanying gestural expressions at closer view, the following determinants can influence the attribution of sense: the entire frame of interaction, the individual biographies of the participants, the physical environment, the social embedding, the cultural and historical background, and – in addition to all these – facts and dates no matter how far removed in dimensions of time and space. Roughly speaking, 'context' can be the whole world in relation to an utterance act. (Asher & Simpson, 1994, p. 733)*

5 Leech (1981): "The effect of context is to attach a certain probability to each sense (the

complete ruling-out of a sense being the limiting case of nil probability)" (p. 67).

6   In the beginning, the development of situation theory was hampered by a lack of appropriate modeling tools. Later, the theory assembled its foundations from innovations coming from nonstandard set theory (for a clear account, see Barwise & Etchemendy, 1987). Barwise and Seligman (1997) further advanced the theory by introducing the idea of an information channel, which preserves information as it is transmitted through a system. Historically, this idea can be said to originate from Dretske's (1981) groundbreaking work on information content.

   Devlin (2004) gives a general appraisal of STASS. This work may be consulted to get a better feel of the historical developments that shaped STASS. Many of the papers cited by Devlin can be found in Barwise (1989b).

7   In the rest of this chapter, we will use "situated semantics" and "situation semantics" interchangeably.

8   Barwise and Perry (1983) thought that "notions like logical form, logical constant, proper name, quantifier, variable, quantifier scope, opaque or transparent contexts, de dicto and de re readings, sense and reference, intension and extension, meaning postulate, possible world, rigid designator, truth conditions and T-sentences, and tense operator are all technical or pseudo-technical notions introduced by philosophers and logicians" (pp. xi–xii).

9   When Alfred Tarski invented model-theoretic semantics for first-order logic, he in a way opened the road to the semantics of natural language. In the Tarskian approach, logical sentences are interpreted in terms of a model. Because of the nature of classical logic, this implies that sentences come out true or false in such a model. Richard Montague believed that the techniques of formal semantics, as applied to systems of logic, were also suitable to ordinary language. In Montague's theory, syntax of language is modeled via a grammar. Syntactic rules are then associated with semantic rules that deliver the interpretation of a sentence from the interpretations of its parts (Kamp & Reyle, 1993). The Montagovian approach is a three-stage process (the upcoming description is somewhat crude but not incorrect). First, language expressions are syntactically analyzed using a categorial grammar. Then the outcome of this analysis is massaged into expressions in a tensed intensional logic. Finally, the latter expressions are interpreted with respect to a model. The oft-cited problem with this approach is that the truth conditions of a sentence are relative – to an interpretation, a world, and a time (Lepore, 1982).

10   Newcomers to linguistics are frequently surprised that linguists regard language as a living organism and thus invariably prefer to study spoken language.

11   Ambiguity is another aspect of the efficiency of language. Some natural language expressions have more than one meaning. There are factors such as intonation, gesture, the place of an utterance, and so on, which may play key roles in the interpretation of an utterance. Instead of downgrading ambiguity as an impurity of natural languages, situation semantics tries to build a full-fledged theory of linguistic meaning.

12   Butterworth (1998):

> On the ecological view, perception is necessarily situated within the ecology since it consists in obtaining information from the active relation between the organism and a structured environment. Indeed, it is a process of perception that situates the organism in the environment. The evidence from infancy suggests that perception is a 'module' or component of the cognitive system that is antecedent to thought and language and that may contribute to the mastery of reasoning. (p. 29)

13   If R is an n-place relation and $a_1, \ldots, a_m$, $m \leq n$, are objects appropriate for the argument places R, and if the filling of these argument places is sufficient to satisfy the minimality conditions for R, then $<R, a_1, \ldots, a_m, p>$ is a well-defined infon. Minimality conditions for a particular relation are the collection of conditions that determine which particular groups of argument roles need to be filled to produce an infon. If $m < n$, the infon is said to be unsaturated; if $m = n$, it is saturated.

14   We are slightly abusing the notation here. In fact, $s \blacktriangleright f$ is shorthand for the factual, parameter-free infon $<involve, s, f, 1>$.

15   Consider a man meeting with a real-estate agent who is going to show him an apartment for rent. When they enter the building, he

smells gas and warns the agent, a smoker, not to light a cigarette. What happened? This scenario is taken from Hunt (1999):

> My brain contained an internal representation of the physical state of the room and the habits of my companion. Processes internal to the brain constructed a second brain state that depicted a potential explosion. For each brain state there was an interpretation in terms of correspondence between properties of the brain state and a property of the external world. Further brain processes operated on the first and second states to produce a third state that initiated the external warning to my companion. (p. 9)

We can restate the story in terms of situated cognition. When something is situated, it is put in a certain position or circumstances. Conversely, to situate something is to establish or indicate the place of it, or to put in a context. Thus, Hunt was placed in a particular circumstance where his thinking clearly depended on a specific response to the demands of the environment.

16 In making this claim, Davis (2003) offers the caveat that he is interpreting belief descriptions opaquely (rather than transparently).

17 Davis (2003, pp. 352–353) is also careful to point out that Frege's and Russell's problems still arise in classical possible-world semantics, where propositional attitudes are characterized as relations between individuals and sets of possible worlds (and where propositions are defined as world sets).

18 Using ⊨, a technical definition of oracles is possible. Let the term *G-infon* denote any infon that results from anchoring the parameters in an infon in G. Then O(G,s) is the minimal situation s such that s⊨i for any factual, parameter-free G-infon i that genuinely involves s.

19 This is crucial in the case of celebrities, as Crimmins (1992) observes: "Agents who are normal members of our society are almost certain to have notions of very famous individuals" (p. 92).

20 Here, context is a psychological construct that represents an individual's assumptions about the world at any given time and place and is supposed to include information of the following kinds:

Logical: the inference rules (according to Sperber and Wilson, these rules are deductive)
Encyclopedic: information about objects, properties, and events
Lexical: rules that allow us to interpret the natural language utterances and sentences.

21 The measurement of contextual effects and processing effort is difficult (Sperber & Wilson, 1986):

> The problems involved in measuring contextual effects and processing effort are, of course, by no means specific to relevance theory or to pragmatics. They affect psychology as a whole. However, for relevance theory these problems take on a more specific form. Within relevance theory, the problem is not so much to assess contextual effects and processing effort from the outside, but to describe how the mind assesses it own achievements and efforts from the inside, and decides as a result to pursue its efforts or relocate them in different directions. (p. 130)

22 Mental operations of humans are, in general, similar to what an anchoring function does: humans individuate relations and objects and fill the gaps in the relations with appropriate individuals, and reason over them. On the other hand, finding an appropriate anchoring function that creates the desired contextual effects might be difficult.

23 This approach can be generalized to coherent multisentence discourse. Allen (1995) explains:

> A discourse is coherent if you can easily determine how the sentences in the discourse are related to each other. A discourse consisting of unrelated sentences would be very unnatural. To understand a discourse, you must identify how each sentence relates to the others and to the discourse as a whole. It is this assumption of coherence that drives the interpretation process. (p. 465)

The idea is that each new sentence should be interpreted (as a minimum) in the context provided by the sentences neighboring it.

24 This applies even to an author himself. Many
    of us have suffered in those situations where
    we see a note we have scribbled a month ago
    and spend a lot of time just to recover our
    original intention in writing it.
25 Lindström (1991) offers a thorough critique of
    this book.
26 We thus find the following claim in Partee
    (2005) unnecessarily harsh:

> Barwise and Perry's work, on the other
> hand, while starting off from some very
> interesting ideas about "scenes" and "sit-
> uations" as ontologically important cat-
> egories to include in the foundations of
> semantics... suffered from... problems
> that made it become less attractive to
> many of us than it seemed like it was
> going to be.... Some scholars have con-
> tinued to develop Barwise and Perry's
> situation semantics, and certain of its
> ideas were readily borrowed into other
> approaches, but it soon became periph-
> eral as a wholesale theory.

References

Aczel, P., Israel, D., Katagiri, Y., & Peters, S.
    (Eds.). (1993). Situation theory and its appli-
    cations (Vol. 3). Stanford, CA: CSLI Publica-
    tions.

Akman, V., & Surav, M. (1996). Steps toward
    formalizing context. AI Magazine, 17, 55–
    72.

Akman, V., & Surav, M. (1997). The use of sit-
    uation theory in context modeling. Computa-
    tional Intelligence, 13, 427–438.

Allen, J. (1995). Natural language understanding.
    Redwood City, CA: Benjamin/Cummings.

Angeles, P. A. (1981). Dictionary of philosophy.
    New York: Harper & Row.

Asher, R. E., & Simpson, J. M. Y. (Eds.). (1994).
    The encyclopedia of languages and linguistics
    (Vol. 2). Oxford: Pergamon.

Austin, J. L. (1979). Truth. In J. O. Urmson &
    G. J. Warnock (Eds.), Philosophical papers
    (pp. 117–133). Oxford: Clarendon.

Barwise, J. (1986). Conditionals and conditional
    information. In E. C. Traugott, C. A. Fer-
    guson, & J. S. Reilly (Eds.), On conditionals
    (pp. 21–54). Cambridge: Cambridge Univer-
    sity Press.

Barwise, J. (1987). Noun phrases, generalized
    quantifiers, and anaphora. In P. Gärdenfors

(Ed.), Generalized quantifiers (pp. 1–29). Dor-
    drecht, The Netherlands: Reidel.

Barwise, J. (1989a). On the circumstantial relation
    between meaning and content. In J. Barwise,
    The situation in logic, CSLI Lecture Notes (No.
    17, pp. 59–77). Stanford, CA: CSLI Publica-
    tions.

Barwise, J. (1989b). The situation in logic. Stan-
    ford, CA: CSLI Publications.

Barwise, J., & Etchemendy, J. (1987). The liar:
    An essay on truth and circularity. New York:
    Oxford University Press.

Barwise, J., & Perry, J. (1983). Situations and atti-
    tudes. Cambridge, MA: MIT Press.

Barwise, J., & Seligman, J. (1997). Information
    flow: The logic of distributed systems. Cam-
    bridge: Cambridge University Press.

Barwise, J., Gawron, J. M., Plotkin, G., &
    Tutiya, S. (Eds.). (1991). Situation theory and
    its applications (Vol. 2). Stanford, CA: CSLI
    Publications.

Blackburn, S. (1994). The Oxford dictionary
    of philosophy. Oxford: Oxford University
    Press.

Butterworth, G. (1998). Context and cognition
    in models of cognitive growth. In A. C. Quel-
    has & F. Pereira (Eds.), Cognition and context
    [Special issue of Análise Psicológica] (pp. 27–
    44). Lisbon: Instituto Superior de Psicologia
    Aplicada.

Clark, H. H., & Carlson, T. B. (1981). Context
    for comprehension. In J. Long & A. Baddeley
    (Eds.), Attention and performance IX (pp. 313–
    330). Hillsdale, NJ: Lawrence Erlbaum.

Cooper, R. (1991). Three lectures on situation-
    theoretic grammar. In M. Filgueiras, L.
    Damas, N. Moreira, & A. P. Tomás (Eds.),
    Natural language processing (pp. 102–140).
    Berlin: Springer.

Cooper, R. (1996). The role of situations in
    generalized quantifiers. In S. Lappin (Ed.),
    The handbook of contemporary semantic theory
    (pp. 65–86). Cambridge, MA: Blackwell.

Cooper, R., Mukai, K., & Perry, J. (Eds.). (1990).
    Situation theory and its applications (Vol. 1).
    Stanford, CA: CSLI Publications.

Crimmins, M. (1992). Talk about beliefs. Cam-
    bridge, MA: MIT Press.

Davis, W. A. (2003). Meaning, expression and
    thought. Cambridge: Cambridge University
    Press.

Devlin, K. (n.d.). Situation theory and situation
    semantics. Retrieved March 28, 2008, from
    http://www.stanford.edu/~kdevlin/HHL_
    SituationTheory.pdf

Devlin, K. (1991a). *Logic and information*. New York: Cambridge University Press.

Devlin, K. (1991b). Oracles in situation semantics. In J. Barwise, J. M. Gawron, G. Plotkin, & S. Tutiya (Eds.), *Situation theory and its applications* (Vol. 2, pp. 41–49). Stanford, CA: CSLI Publications.

Devlin, K. (1991c). Situations as mathematical abstractions. In J. Barwise, J. M. Gawron, G. Plotkin, & S. Tutiya (Eds.), *Situation theory and its applications* (Vol. 2, pp. 25–39). Stanford, CA: CSLI Publications.

Devlin, K. (1992). Infons as mathematical objects. *Minds and Machines, 2*, 185–201.

Devlin, K. (1998). *Goodbye, Descartes: The end of logic and the search for a new cosmology of the mind*. New York: Wiley.

Devlin, K. (2001). *Infosense: Turning information into knowledge*. New York: W. H. Freeman.

Devlin, K. (2004). Jon Barwise's papers on natural language semantics. *Bulletin of Symbolic Logic, 10*, 54–85.

Devlin, K., & Rosenberg, D. (1996). *Language at work: Analyzing communication breakdown in the workplace to inform systems design*. Stanford, CA: CSLI Publications.

Dowty, D., Wall, R., & Peters, S. (1981). *Introduction to Montague semantics*. Dordrecht, The Netherlands: Reidel.

Dretske, F. (1981). *Knowledge and the flow of information*. Cambridge, MA: MIT Press.

Eco, U. (1979). *The role of the reader: Explorations in the semiotics of texts*. Bloomington: Indiana University Press.

Fenstad, J. E., Halvorsen, P.-K., Langholm, T., & van Benthem, J. (1987). *Situations, language, and logic*. Dordrecht, The Netherlands: Reidel.

Firth, J. R. (1957). *Papers in linguistics, 1934–1951*. London: Oxford University Press.

Gawron, J. M., & Peters, S. (1990). *Anaphora and quantification in situation semantics*. Stanford, CA: CSLI Publications.

Gibson, J. J. (1979). *The ecological approach to visual perception*. Boston: Houghton Mifflin.

Goffman, E. (2002). Definition of the situation. In C. Calhoun (Ed.), *Dictionary of the social sciences*. Oxford: Oxford University Press. Retrieved June 13, 2008, from http://www.oxfordreference.com/views/ENTRY.html?subview=Main&entry=t104.e425

Gonos, G. (1977). "Situation" versus "frame": The "interactionist" and the "structuralist" analyses of everyday life. *American Sociological Review, 42*, 854–867.

Goodwin, C., & Duranti, A. (1992). Rethinking context: An introduction. In A. Duranti & C. Goodwin (Eds.), *Rethinking context: Language as an interactive phenomenon* (pp. 1–42). New York: Cambridge University Press.

Hunt, E. (1999). What is a theory of thought? In R. J. Sternberg (Ed.), *The nature of cognition* (pp. 3–49). Cambridge, MA: MIT Press.

Kamp, H., & Reyle, U. (1993). *From discourse to logic: Introduction to model-theoretic semantics of natural language, formal logic, and discourse representation theory, Parts I and II*. Dordrecht, The Netherlands: Kluwer.

Keefe, R. (2000). *Theories of vagueness*. Cambridge: Cambridge University Press.

Leech, G. (1981). *Semantics: The study of meaning*. Harmondsworth, UK: Penguin.

Lepore, E. (1982). What model theoretic semantics cannot do. *Synthese, 54*, 167–187.

Lindström, S. (1991). Critical study: Situations and attitudes. *Noûs, 25*, 743–770.

Lyons, J. (1995). *Linguistic semantics: An introduction*. Cambridge: Cambridge University Press.

McKay, T., & Nelson, M. (2005). Propositional attitude reports. Retrieved March 28, 2008, from http://plato.stanford.edu/entries/prop-attitude-reports

Partee, B. H. (2005). Reflections of a formal semanticist as of Feb. 2005. Retrieved March 28, 2008, from http://people.umass.edu/partee/docs/BHP_Essay_Feb05.pdf

Percy, W. (1975). *The message in the bottle: How queer man is, how queer language is, and what one has to do with the other*. New York: Farrar, Straus & Giroux.

Pietroski, P. M. (2003). The character of natural language semantics. In A. Barber (Ed.), *Epistemology of language* (pp. 217–256). Oxford: Oxford University Press.

Pulman, S. G. (1997). Semantics. In R. Cole, J. Mariani, H. Uszkoreit, A. Zaenen, & V. Zue (Eds.), *Survey of the state of the art in human language technology* (pp. 105–111). Cambridge: Cambridge University Press.

Recanati, F. (2004). *Literal meaning*. Cambridge: Cambridge University Press.

Rokeach, M. (1998). Attitudes. In G. Marshall (Ed.), *A dictionary of sociology*. Oxford: Oxford University Press. Retrieved June 21, 2008, from http://www.oxfordreference.com/views/ENTRY.html?subview=Main&entry=t88.e116

Rosenschein, S. C., & Kaelbling, L. P. (1995). A situated view of representation and control. *Artificial Intelligence, 73*, 149–173.

Seligman, J., & Moss, L. S. (1997). Situation theory. In J. van Benthem & A. ter Meulen (Eds.), *Handbook of logic and language* (pp. 239–309). Amsterdam: Elsevier Science.

Sperber, D., & Wilson, D. (1986). *Relevance: Communication and cognition*. Cambridge, MA: Harvard University Press.

Stucky, S. (1989). The situated processing of situated language. *Linguistics and Philosophy*, 12, 347–357.

Tarski, A. (1944). The semantic conception of truth and the foundations of semantics. *Philosophy and Phenomenological Research*, 4, 341–376.

Tin, E., & Akman, V. (1996). Information-oriented computation with BABY-SIT. In J. Seligman & D. Westerståhl (Eds.), *Logic, language, and computation* (Vol. 1, pp. 19–34). Stanford, CA: CSLI Publications.

Turvey, M., & Carello, C. (1986). The equation of information and meaning from the perspectives of situation semantics and Gibson's ecological realism. *Linguistics and Philosophy*, 8, 81–90.

Tye, M. (1990). Vague objects. *Mind*, 99, 535–557.

CHAPTER 22

Is Consciousness Embodied?

Jesse Prinz

1. Introduction

Consciousness is trendy. It seems that more pages are published on consciousness these days than on any other subject in the philosophy of mind. Embodiment and situated cognition are also trendy. They mark a significant departure from orthodox theories, and are thus appealing to radicals and renegades. It is hardly surprising, then, that consciousness, embodiment, and situated cognition have coalesced (see, e.g., Cotterill, 1998; Hurley, 1998; Mandik, 1999; Noë, 2004; O'Regan & Noë, 2001; Thompson & Varela, 2001). Both topics are exciting, and being exciting is an additive property. An embodied or situated theory of consciousness is the philosophical equivalent of a blockbuster. But excitement is not always correlated with truth, and the embodied and situated approach to consciousness may be easier to sell than to prove.

In this chapter, I assess situated and embodied approaches to consciousness. This is neither an exculpation nor an execution, but an exploration. My verdict is tempered.

The radicalism of embodied and embedded approaches has been taken too far, but people who are prepared to dismiss these approaches may be missing out on a catalog of helpful resources. I do not think embodiment and situated cognition hold the basic key to explaining consciousness, but something in this ballpark may help us explain certain aspects of conscious experience. We should resist the most seductive theories but pay close attention to more modest ones. In general, I think the great promise of embodied and situated cognition will emerge as the excitement dies down. As with connectionism, the value of these approaches is harder to see if we focus on how radical they are. Radicalism may be good for politics, but it is bad for science. In science, I promote middle-of-the-road liberalism. After critically evaluating some radical theories, I will advance four moderate proposals that take embodiment seriously.

Before proceeding, it will be useful to offer some working definitions. The term *embodied* is most generically used to mean involving the body (compare discussion in

Gallagher, 2005). To say that a mental capacity is embodied can mean one of two things. It can mean that the capacity depends on the possession and use of a body, not just a brain. I exclude the brain, because the brain is part of the body, and all materialists (and some dualists) believe that mental capacities involve the brain. Some embodiment theorists think other parts of the body are important as well. Other embodiment theorists do not go quite this far. Instead, they say that embodied mental capacities are ones that depend on mental representations or processes that relate to the body (see, e.g., Glenberg & Kaschak, 2003). Such representations and processes come in two forms: there are representations and processes that represent or respond to the body, such as a perception of bodily movement, and there are representations and processes that affect the body, such as motor commands. We can call the first class "somatic" and the second class "enactive." On this use of the term *embodiment*, everyone agrees that, say, proprioceptive states of the central nervous system are embodied. The controversy concerns whether other forms of perception and cognition are embodied. For example, only an embodiment theorist would say that vision is embodied in any of the ways described here. To say that consciousness is embodied is to say that consciousness depends either on the existence of processes in the body outside the head or on somatic or enactive processes that may be inside the head.

Colloquially, the term *situated* means located somewhere. On this definition, all materialists and many dualists think that mental states and processes are situated. The thoughts you are currently having are in your brain, and your brain is in a specific geographical location. We could locate your thoughts if we affixed a GPS device to your cranium. Defenders of situated cognition mean something stronger, of course. They mean that being located in a physical environment makes an essential contribution to our mental capacities. Consciousness is situated if being conscious in the way that we are depends on whether and

where we are located. Someone who held this view might suppose that, if two people with the same internal state were in different environments, their conscious experiences would be different. Defenders of situated cognition, like defenders of radical embodiment, would deny that a brain in a vat has conscious states like our own; a brain in a vat has no body and does not interact with the environment in the way that we do.

I will now argue that many of the standard ways of defending these hypotheses about consciousness do not enjoy adequate support (see also Prinz, 2000a, 2006). After that, I will get more concessive. I think that certain aspects of consciousness may depend on systems involved in perceiving and controlling the body. The brand of embodiment I favor may not be as sexy as other varieties on the market, but I think the brand I favor may capture what is true and important about this trend in consciousness studies. I think defenders of more radical views have ultimately done a great service by drawing our attention to the relationship between experience and action, and understanding that relationship will prove essential for an adequate theory of consciousness.

2. Situated Experience

People who advocate situated cognition tend also to advocate embodiment. This is not surprising. If you think that the environment makes an important contribution to mental capacities, then you might be disposed to accept the idea that the body makes a contribution. For one thing, the body can be regarded as part of the environment of the mind or brain – it is just a very local part. And, for another thing, we need a body to explore the environment, and for fans of situated cognition, interactions between the environment and the body are often regarded as crucial for intelligent behavior. For example, catching a baseball involves moving one's body in a way that keeps the ball in the center of the visual field. Nevertheless, it is useful to discuss situated cognition and embodiment separately, because the proposals that have been advanced with respect to consciousness are dissociable. It is possible, for example, to think that consciousness is embodied in some sense without accepting strong versions of the hypothesis that consciousness is situated. In this section, I will focus on situated consciousness.

At the outset, it is important to distinguish three ways in which conscious experiences may be dependent on the external environment. One form of dependency is semantic. Externalists about mental content argue that content does not supervene on what is in the head (e.g., Fodor, 1994; Wilson, 2004). Intentional content, in particular, depends on relationships between mind and world, where those relationships are usually understood as causal, teleological, or informational. Some people think that the character of conscious experiences depends on their intentional content; this is one version of the view known as representationalism (e.g., Dretske, 1995; Lycan, 1996; Tye, 1995). If you are a representationalist and an externalist, then you are committed to the view that conscious experience depends on the external environment. But this is not the kind of dependency that proponents of situated cognition are after. Externalists think that the relevant environment is the world that an agent resides in, or perhaps some merely possible world. Proponents of situated cognition think that conscious states depend on the local environment currently surrounding and impinging upon the agent. This dependency usually is not construed as semantic.

The second kind of dependency is causal. The experiences you are having might be causally dependent on the environment you are in. On one formulation, this hypothesis is uncontroversial. The environment can causally stimulate our sensory receptors and bring about experiences. Proponents of situated cognition defend a much more intimate link. First, they tend to suppose that conscious states are causally coupled with the environment (e.g., Thompson & Varela, 2001). *Coupling* is a term from dynamical systems theory. Roughly, two systems are

causally coupled if the equations describing the dynamics of one include variables that quantify over states of the other, and conversely. Almost everyone agrees that mind and world are causally coupled. What proponents of situated consciousness add to this platitude is the claim that conscious experiences arise only when certain dynamical relations are instantiated; the dynamical processes are essential for consciousness. If one thinks that consciousness depends on the instantiation of certain dynamical systems, and those systems are coupled with the environment, then one might conclude that conscious experiences would not arise were it not for causal interactions with things in the environment.

Presented in this way, the situated view still locates consciousness in the head. The hypothesis is that consciousness depends on processes in the head that simply could not arise in the way that they do if it were not for steady causal interactions with the world. An even more radical suggestion is that consciousness has a constitutive dependency on the environment. One might think that consciousness supervenes on features of the environment along with internal states. On this view, conscious states are realized by dynamical systems that extend beyond the skin. Thus, we have two situated consciousness hypotheses: causal and constitutive. Both of these hypotheses come in stronger and weaker versions. On the stronger version, we could not have conscious states at all were it not for being hooked up to the environment in a particular way. On the weaker version, consciousness can arise without environmental hookups, but the character of conscious experience is different in such circumstances; environmental hookups affect the character of experience. As Block (2005) and Adams and Aizawa (this volume) point out, these views are sometimes conflated by defenders of situated consciousness.

I think we can reject the stronger versions of the situated approach outright. Conscious states arise when we are dreaming or hallucinating despite the fact that, in those cases, the contents do not reflect causal interactions with the external environment. Even more dramatically, people have rich conscious experiences when they are put in sensory-deprivation chambers, suspended in liquid with their eyes, ears, and chemical senses cut off (e.g., Feynman, 1997). People in sensory-deprivation chambers report visual hallucinations, and there is no reason to suppose that the content of those hallucinations is dictated by the environment they are in.

What about the weaker suggestion that the character of conscious experiences is affected by the environment? I think the causal version is perfectly plausible. Everyone agrees that the environment can influence our experiences. It may turn out that the specific character of an experience depends on how internal states unfold dynamically over time, and such unfolding can be influenced by the environment. The causal situated hypothesis is really controversial only on stronger versions. It is controversial to say that we could not be conscious at all if we were not hooked up to the environment in a specific way, but it is relatively uncontroversial to say that the character of the experiences we actually have results from how we are dynamically hooked up to the environment. I will leave this relatively uninteresting suggestion to one side. Much more contentious is the constitutive view. Proponents of situated consciousness like to suggest that, when we are not dreaming or hallucinating, our experiences are constituted by an interaction between internal states and the environment. (I use *constitution* broadly to cover relations of identity, realization, constituency, and so on.) Views of this kind have been defended by James (1904) and Noë and Thompson (2004), among others. Noë (2004) says it is one way to cash out the idea of direct perception: perception is not mediated by an internal representation that stands between mind and world, but rather is constituted by a mind-world interaction.

It is difficult to defend a view like this. Given that consciousness can arise in situations that are indifferent to the external world (hallucination in a sensory-

deprivation chamber), we have reason to think that consciousness does not have environmental substrates on some occasions. Why, then, should we think the environment is ever a substrate of experience? On the face of it, hallucinations provide reason to reject situated consciousness. If veridical perceptions are just like hallucinations, and hallucinations are independent of the environment, then veridical perceptions are probably independent as well. But defenders of situated consciousness reject the first premise. They argue that hallucinations are not like veridical perceptions. I think that is a very hard nut to chew. Many hallucinations may be unlike real experiences in various respects, but given the fact that hallucinatory experiences (including dreams, mirages, phantom limbs, and psychotic experiences) are frequently mistaken for reality, it seems overwhelmingly likely that there can be hallucinations that are qualitatively indistinguishable from veridical perceptions.

Let me offer here what I consider the best argument for a situated view of consciousness. It is loosely inspired by suggestions made by Alva Noë (2004) and, following Noë, I will focus on vision. The argument begins with a premise that is axiomatic for situated cognition enthusiasts: the world is its own best model (Brooks, 1991). Proponents of situated cognition argue that if we form internal representations of the world at all, they are sparsely detailed; we do not internally represent the external environment in all its rich splendor. There is no need to. If we need more information than we have currently encoded at any given moment, we can always consult the world. Our senses can sample the environment at any given moment. The environment is trivially a more accurate source of information about itself than any internal representations we happen to form, so we might as well save processing power and represent as little of it as possible. This is what fans of situated cognition like to say, but, when it comes to conscious experience, a puzzle immediately arises. Conscious experiences seem to be richly detailed; the visual field, for example, seems to have shapes and colors in every corner. Some people think this is an illusion. Dennett (1969), for example, says that it is an introspective trap caused by the fact that, whenever we try to examine a part of the visual field, we sample the corresponding part of the environment and retrieve the relevant details. But this explanation is slightly unsatisfying. When I am watching TV, I can, at any moment, flip the channels and see what is happening on every network, but I have no illusion that I am experiencing multiple channels at once. In response, defenders of the view that richness in an illusion might argue that saccades are faster than channel switching on a TV set, and the speed is what makes the image seem so rich. But I do not see why speed should make a difference here. If each visual instant were lacking in detail, then we should experience a flickering barrage of sparse images. A rapid sequence of sparse images should engender an experience of a unified image only if the brain integrates the successive snapshots into a single rich composite. If you still think the saccade story can explain why the visual field seems rich, then try to stare at the scene in front of you keeping your eyes fixed. Much of what you experience may be blurry (sharp focus is restricted to the fovea), but the visual field will still seem very rich. The richness of experience seems to reside in the present, not in any capacity I have to get more information a moment from now. That aspect of phenomenology needs to be explained. And here is where the situated cognition thesis arises. If conscious experience is not restricted to what is in my head but includes the environment around me, then the richness of experience is not an illusion. Experience really is rich, even though internal representations are sparse. It is rich because experience is partially composed by the world, and the world is rich. The idea that the world is literally a component of conscious experience may sound bizarre, but it has been proposed as a serious possibility. Noë and Thompson (2004) say, "The substrates of consciousness – in particular of visual perceptual consciousness – seem to cut across the brain-body-world divisions" (p. 26).

The argument that I just sketched for the conclusion that consciousness is partially constituted by the world rests on two assumptions. It rests on the assumption that experiences are rich and that internal representations are not. I will not take issue with the first assumption. Admittedly, experience seems sparse under certain circumstances. For example, if you try to count the serifs in this letter P you might briefly lose awareness of the surrounding letters (see the discussion of inattentional blindness herein). But experience is not always sparse. If you stare at this whole page rather than a single P, it will look like a rich field of clustered letters. You probably will not be able to read those letters (they are not all in focus, and it is hard to read multiple letters simultaneously), but you will experience them, lined up in neat rows spanning across your visual field. Under such circumstances, it is difficult to deny that experience seems rich. I am not suggesting that the visual field seems uniformly detailed. When staring at a scene, many objects may be out of focus or unidentified, but we still seem to experience a field that is filled rather than sparse. That is what I mean when I say that experience seems rich.

If richness is hard to challenge, what about the second premise in the argument for situated consciousness? Should we accept the claim that the richness of experience is not a consequence of rich internal representations? Alva Noë (2004) thinks that we must accept this claim. He thinks there is empirical evidence demonstrating that internal representations are not rich. In particular, he cites studies on change blindness. In these experiments, subjects are presented with two consecutive images that differ in some respect. For example, a pair of people in the first image might swap hats, a parrot might change color, a building might shrink in size, an aircraft engine might disappear, and so on. These large changes in the pictures often go unnoticed. Many subjects cannot see any difference between the two pictures. That suggests that they are not encoding every detail. Noë uses these findings to conclude that internal representations are sparse.

But Noë's conclusion does not hold up on scrutiny. Another hypothesis is that people encode pictures in very rich detail but do not store all those details from moment to moment (Simons & Levin, 1997). On this interpretation, subjects form internal representations that change when the pictures are swapped, but they do not keep track of these changes; there can be changing representations without representations of the fact that a change has taken place. There is strong evidence suggesting that this interpretation of change blindness is right; people form rich representations and simply do not store all the details in memory long enough to make comparisons from moment to moment. Consider priming studies. Silverman and Mack (2001) have shown that information that people fail to notice during change blindness experiments can prime information processing. For example, if you show subjects an array of letters and then change some, they will not always notice that some have changed. But the letters from the initial array that went unnoticed must be internally represented, because when subjects are given a subsequent test in which they need to complete a picture of a letter than has been distorted, the letters that they were shown in the change blindness task influence their responses. In a more recent study, Mitroff, Simons, and Levin (2004) showed subjects consecutive pairs of images depicting an array of objects. Subjects were often unable to tell when one of the objects had changed, but when asked to confirm which objects they had seen on a subsequent probe, they were well above chance in recalling the objects whose disappearance had gone unnoticed. This suggests that those objects were internally represented. On the sparse representation interpretation of change blindness, unnoticed features are not internally represented. The Silverman and Mack study and the Mitroff et al. study contradict this hypothesis. Unnoticed features must be represented because they cause priming, and they are available for cued recall. Noë himself acknowledges this when he notes that people in change blindness experiments are above chance at cued recall for objects whose disappearance they failed to notice. But this concession undermines the argument for situated consciousness. That argument was premised on the idea that the apparent richness of experience can be explained only by the richness of the environment, because internal representations are not sparse in detail. The studies just reviewed refute this premise by establishing that internal representations are rich. If so, then one can explain the apparent richness of experience without making the radical claim that the external world is a substrate of experience.

Other arguments for the view that conscious experiences are constituted, in part, by the environment can surely be imagined, but I do not think any argument for that conclusion will be convincing. Such an argument would need to show that there can be aspects of phenomenal experience that are not explained by events in the head. In this spirit, proponents of situated consciousness argue that there are no neural correlates of consciousness (Noë & Thompson, 2004). Without taking up this issue, let me just comment that the attempts to correlate consciousness experiences with brain states has been amazingly productive (Jack & Prinz, 2003; Koch, 2004; Metzinger, 2000). We can find brain states that encode the same information as conscious states and occur at the same time. We find line detectors in visual areas active when we see illusory contours, and we find motion detectors active when we see illusory motion. Neuroscience is still a young field, but every phenomenal feature that we investigate seems to have a systematic correlate. Of course, we do not know why neural events give rise to phenomenal qualities (the hard problem), but that mystery will not be solved by assuming that consciousness supervenes on items in the environment. The bottom line is that there is no serious reason at this time to suppose that the correlates of consciousness will include anything outside the head. Indeed, given how far we have come in neuroscience, it is hard to take that suggestion very seriously.

3. Radical Embodiment

When interpreted as a thesis about constitution, situated consciousness is a very radical hypothesis; it says that the environment is a component of our conscious experiences. To accept this is to give up a central plank of modern materialism – the supposition that consciousness supervenes on the brain. I have yet to encounter an argument that is nearly powerful enough to consider giving up the brain doctrine. The claim that consciousness is embodied is sometimes presented as a version of situated consciousness. Just as proponents of situated consciousness locate experience partially in the world, some proponents of embodied consciousness locate experience partially in the body (outside the brain). Some combine these views, suggesting that consciousness supervenes on interactions between body and world. The claim that consciousness extends into the body is only marginally more plausible than the claim that consciousness leaks out into the world. We have never found any cells outside the brain that are candidates as correlates for experience. Such cells would have to co-vary with conscious states in content and time course. Every component of the body that we can experience is represented in the brain, and when the corresponding brain areas are damaged experience is lost. Conversely, bodily experience can continue after the body is damaged, as in the case of phantom-limb pain. There is, in short, little reason to think the correlates of experience extend beyond the cranium.

Fortunately, one can defend the view that consciousness is embodied without abandoning the assumption that consciousness resides in the brain. As we saw in the introduction, the term *embodiment* sometimes refers to views according to which mental capacities involve internal states and processes that control or respond to the body. Put loosely, on one use of the term, a mental capacity is embodied if it depends on bodily

mental representations. (This characterization is loose, because some embodiment theorists reject the representational theory of mind. I address antirepresentationalism elsewhere; Prinz & Barsalou, 2000.) If mental representations are located in the brain, then this approach to embodiment does not carry exorbitant metaphysical costs. It is less extravagant than the constitution version of the situated approach and worth taking more seriously.

Embodied approaches are less metaphysically extravagant, but they are often radical in other respects. As Hurley (1998) puts it, she and other defenders of embodiment want to dispose of the "classical sandwich" model of the mind, which dominates in contemporary philosophy and cognitive science. In the classical sandwich model, the mind divides neatly into input systems, which receive sensory information; cognitive systems, which engaging in thinking; and output systems, which execute motor actions. On this approach, thinking is a proprietary class of capacities nestled between input and output systems and largely independent of both. I am skeptical of the classical sandwich myself, because I believe that thinking incorporates representations used for perception and motor control (Prinz, 2002). But Hurley and others want to go even further. They want to demolish the border between inputs and outputs. I believe that the senses and motor systems interact, but they are nevertheless distinct; they use different representational codes, follow different rules, can function independently, and often reside in different parts of the brain. Hurley and some other radical embodiment theorists believe either that there is no division between input and output systems (instead we have unified sensorimotor systems) or, to the extent that such a division exists, input systems causally depend on output systems to do any serious work. In other words, embodiment theorists like to defend either a constitution thesis or a strong causal thesis about perception and action; perceiving is either partially constituted by processes that are motoric in nature or causally depend on those processes for normal operation. I will not dwell on this distinction. Following O'Regan and Noë (2001), I will refer to all versions of this general approach as "the enactive view."

The enactive view should be distinguished from less controversial hypotheses about the relationship between inputs and outputs. Everyone agrees that there can be causal interactions between the two. For example, everyone agrees that when a person looks at a hammer, she might spontaneously generate a motor command consistent with grasping the hammer. In Gibson's terms, we can see what actions an object affords. But seeing affordances is understood, in orthodox views, as an associative process. Visual states bring motor responses to mind. Likewise, everyone agrees that motor states can have some impact on perception. To take a trivial example, shifting your eyes affects what you see. It is even likely that a merely imagined shift of gaze can affect visual perception by shifting the focus of visual attention. Thus, motor representations can cause changes in visual representations. Defenders of the enactive view have something more radical in mind. They suppose that motor representations are (causally or constitutionally) essential to perceiving; we would be blind, in some sense, without them.

Applied to consciousness, the enactive view holds that the conscious experiences caused by sensory encounters with the world depend on motor responses. For example, visual experience may depend on motor representations that control eye position. O'Regan and Noë (2001) say that seeing involves a skillful engagement with the world. More specifically, they say that everything that we can distinguish in perception affords different potential motor interactions, and that perceiving involves the registration of these sensorimotor contingencies. As I understand it, the idea is that we have various action-dispositions associated with the stimuli that we encounter, and each of these dispositions, if carried out, would alter the sensory inputs; sensorimotor dispositions constitute implicit knowledge of how stimuli would change if we were to move in some way. When a stimulus impinges on our senses, those dispositions become available as operative possibilities for action, and, as proponents of the enactive approach believe, this is a precondition for normal perceptual consciousness. To see normally, for example, we must know how a visible surface would change if we were to alter the position of our eyes or bodies. O'Regan and Noë are a little vague about whether we could see at all without picking up on sensorimotor contingencies, but they clearly think that ordinary experience, including the distinctive qualities of colors and the differences between the senses, requires motor dispositions. In his book Noë (2004) is more explicit; he seems to suggest that we would literally be blind without having dispositional motoric responses to visual inputs. That is a fascinating hypothesis. I think it is false, but it certainly is not obviously false.

To assess the enactive view, we need to get a bit clearer on what its defenders claim. I will distinguish three enactive hypotheses. All are compatible, but they are potentially dissociable, and they call on different evidence. The first enactive hypothesis is developmental. One might think that ordinary conscious perception cannot develop without the exercise of motor skills. The developmental hypothesis is compatible with the supposition that perceptual consciousness does not depend on motor responses later in life. In this respect, it is a more moderate hypothesis than the next two that I will consider. But should we think it is true?

The main item of evidence advanced in favor of the developmental enactive view is a study conducted in 1963 by Held and Hein (see Cotterill, 1998; Mandik, 1999; Noë, 2004). Held and Hein performed an experiment with two young kittens, reared in darkness. For three hours a day, the kittens were brought into an illuminated room and placed on either side of a harness, which allowed one kitten to walk around a room while the other hung suspended in a cradle. The second kitten was able to see the room as the other kitten roamed around, but it was not able to move on its own. After ten days in this apparatus, the kittens were freed and their vision was tested. Held and Hein found that vision in the active cat was normal, but vision in the passive cat was abnormal in three respects: it did not blink when objects loomed toward it, it had difficult guiding its paws visually, and it did not avoid visual cliffs. They concluded that physical interaction with the world is necessary for development of vision. Applied to consciousness, one might be tempted to conclude that visual consciousness will not develop in the absence of physical interaction.

The Held and Hein result is fascinating, but it cannot be used to support a strong version of the hypothesis that consciousness depends developmentally on action. First, the passive cat was not blind. It was able to move about successfully using vision; it just suffered from very specific behavioral deficits. Second, these deficits are unsurprising. The cat failed to assign motoric significance to its visual episodes. It did not understand that an object rapidly filling its visual field was looming toward it (perhaps the object just appeared to be growing); it had difficulty with visually coordinating its paws, because it did not have experience calibrating kinesthetic feedback with visual feedback; and it did not avoid visual cliffs, because experience may be needed to learn that surfaces that look a certain way are farther away. But, for all that, the passive cat's visual experiences may have been just like the active cat's visual experiences; the difference was that the passive cat did not assign the same action-related significance to those experiences. This is utterly unsurprising. Deprive a cat of action, and it will not learn what actions various visual experiences afford. Third, the passive cat attained normal visual abilities quickly after the experiment. Fourth, the experiment has not been replicated. Fifth, lessons from cats may not apply to us. Rivière and Lécuyer (2002) recently studied visuospatial abilities in young children who suffer from congenital motor atrophy. These children had no experience moving around in the world but their visual abilities were the same as healthy children.

These points raise serious doubts about the developmental embodied consciousness hypothesis. I am aware of no good evidence for the thesis that moving around one's environment is necessary for the development of conscious perception, and there seems to be plenty of evidence against that hypothesis. Radical inferences from the Held and Hein cat studies should be put to rest.

Let me turn to a second radical enactive view. Some enactive theorists imply that there can be no conscious perceptual experiences in the absence of internal states that register sensorimotor contingencies – the motor responses that the perceptual states afford. This would be a stunning fact if true, but why should we believe it? Defenders of enactive consciousness are sometimes a bit unclear about what evidence is supposed to support this necessity claim, but let me consider one argument. Noë (2004) is impressed by results from the study of prism lenses that either invert or shift the visual field. When people wear these lenses, the sensorimotor contingencies that they have mastered no longer apply. Normally, if an object appears in front of us when we stare straight ahead, we can grasp it by reaching straight forward. If we are wearing lenses that shift the visual field to the left, a forward reaching motion will miss the object. Over a period of time, people wearing the lenses adjust to the new contingencies, and they report being very disoriented when they first put the lenses on. Noë is struck by the reports of disorientation. As he describes it, people are temporarily blinded when they first wear the glasses. This is just what the enactive hypothesis under consideration would predict. When we realize that the expected contingencies are wrong, we need to dispense with them, and as we do so, perceptual experience should be dramatically affected or lost.

The trouble is that Noë's characterization of what happens when people wear inverting lenses is misleading. People do not experience blindness and, as long as they do not try to move, the visual world will remain unaffected (I get this from first-hand reports by Fred Dretske, who has tried the lenses). Disorientation arises when people try to physically interact with the objects they see. It is very disorienting to reach for an object and miss! I am even willing to grant that inverting lenses can alter perceptual response. For example, I would not be surprised if receptive fields in visual areas of the brain shift as one adapts to the lenses; we know that receptive fields change with shifts of attention (Moran & Desimone, 1985). But those changes do not support the enactive view. Everyone agrees that the senses interact and that events in one sense can alter another. For example, ventriloquists can cause us to shift the location of speech sounds in auditory space by making us watch the lips move on a dummy. In the McGurk effect, the visual appearance of moving lips actually alters the sound that we hear, and the effect is instantaneous (McGurk & MacDonald, 1976). Likewise, we should not be surprised if misalignments of vision and action cause changes in visual experience. Such causal effects fall far short of the hypothesis that motor responses are necessary for perceptual experience. By analogy, the fact that vision affects hearing does not entail that we cannot hear without seeing.

To establish that motor representations are necessary for conscious perceptual experience, it would be useful to show that damage to motor systems results in perceptual deficits. There is little evidence for this in the clinical literature. For example, patients with amyotrophic lateral sclerosis (Lou Gehrig's disease) suffer from a degeneration of premotor neurons. This profoundly disrupts motor response, but it leaves perceptual consciousness intact (Kandell, Schwartz, & Jessel, 2000). Likewise, paralysis of the ocular muscles, which control eye movements, does not prevent people having conscious visual experience. For example, Land, Furneaux, and Gilchrist (2002) describe an individual who has relatively normal vision despite the fact that she had lifelong congenital ocular fibrosis, which prevents her eyes from moving. People with paralyzed eyes often report double vision, because their eyes come out of alignment, but they can certainly see. This is the case even when the paralysis of the eyes results from the elimination or receptors in the nerves that control eye movement, as in myasthenia gravis (Cassell, Billig, & Randall, 1998). In addition, people with damage to parietal cortex can suffer from disruptions in visually guided action, saccade control, and the allocation of attention to multiple objects, but they are not blind (Milner & Goodale, 1995). In summary, I am aware of no insult to any brain system involved in motor control that results in blindness.

To deal with the clinical findings, enactive theorists might argue that the relevant motor responses are located in the visual pathway and other sensory systems, not in areas traditionally associated with motor control. I hope it goes without saying that responses of this kind are ad hoc. Damage to visual pathways does not cause motor deficits, and there is no theory-independent reason to say that motor dispositions are encoded therein. If one retreats to dispositions and anachronistic definitions of the motor areas in the brain, there is a danger that the enactive view will become unfalsifiable. Enactive theorists should identify and test precise predictions of their theories. They should tell us which motor systems are involved in vision, and they should predict that insult to those systems would have serious repercussions for visual experience.

Enactive theorists should also provide evidence for the claim that motor systems are necessarily active when we have conscious visual experience. They often emphasize the importance of eye-movements for experience, but there is little evidence for the claim that visual perception depends on saccades. We perceive both during and between saccades, and when we keep our eyes fixed, we do not become blind. Defenders of the enactive view might respond by saying that, under these circumstances, motor responses are available dispositionally. Perhaps they are right, but this must be established empirically, and it must also be established that if the dispositions were disrupted or eliminated, experience would change. Suppose you train yourself to saccade to the right when you see a certain shade of blue, and then, after firmly establishing that disposition, you retrain yourself to saccade to the left. Will the visual experience of that blue change after retraining? I doubt it. Is this a prediction of the theory? If not, why not?

Let me turn now to one final enactive hypothesis. Suppose the enactive theorists were to concede that motor responses are not necessary for perceptual consciousness. They might still argue that motor responses, when available, affect the character of perceptual experiences. Now, to avoid triviality, this hypothesis cannot just be a causal claim. As noted, everyone can agree that motor responses can causally affect perceptual responses. To advance a substantive proposal, enactive theorists might defend a version of the constitution thesis. They might claim that when motor responses are available, they are constituent parts of perceptual experiences. When we see something, on this proposal, the conscious visual experience is partially constituted by the fact that we are registering sensorimotor contingences. Put differently, the enactive theorists might say that the phenomenal character of perceptual states is comprised in part by the motor consequences of those states.

This thesis is usually taken to have two implications. The first has to do with distinguishing phenomenal experiences within a single sense modality. Enactive theorists suggest that two different experiences within the same modality differ in virtue of being associated with different motor responses. For example, the experience of seeing a curved line and a straight line afford different kinds of grasping, and, more controversially, the experience of two colors affords different movement of the eyes and pupil aperture. Noë (2004) argues for the latter thesis by suggesting that color constancy – our capacity to recognize a color as the same under very different luminance conditions – might be achieved by keeping track of the ocular affordances that each hue has under multiple conditions.

The second implication of the enactive constitution view has to do with our capacity to distinguish different senses (Noë, 2004; Hurley & Noë, 2003). The proposal implies that vision and hearing, for example, are phenomenally different in virtue of differences in sensorimotor contingencies. The two senses can register the same feature of the environment, but, because they have different implications for action, they feel different. One item of evidence used to defend this claim comes from Bach-y-Rita's (1972) research on prosthetic vision (Noë, 2004; Mandik, 1999). Bach-y-Rita developed an apparatus that converts visual information (acquired from video cameras affixed to a pair of eyeglasses) into tactile information by pressing tiny pins configured in the same pattern as the visual signal into the torso or tongue. People who wear this apparatus come to report that the tactile inputs have visual significance. For example, they can use the tactile inputs to avoid looming objects, grasp, and navigate between obstacles. On the enactive interpretation, the tactile information has come to have the motor contingencies normally associated with vision, and that results in the tactile sensations actually feeling as if they were visual (see also Dennett, 1991). In this way, sight can be restored to the blind.

I am not persuaded by these lines of evidence for the enactive view. First consider the claim that we distinguish different qualities within a sense modality by distinguishing sensorimotor contingencies. That seems intuitively wrong. If you see a stick in the water, it looks curved, but if you know it is a stick, you know that you can grasp it the same way you would grasp a straight object. Sticks in the water and out of the water look different, but they afford the same actions. The color case is even less plausible for the enactive view than the shape case. Suppose you compare the experience of staring at two uniformly colored and uniformly bright fields, one red and the other blue. It is obvious that these look different but unlikely that they afford different eye movements. Of course red and blue may afford different eye movements under other conditions, but that fact is irrelevant; the colors look different here and now. Conversely, imagine staring at a giant field of red first with your eyes to the left, and then to the right. Under these two conditions, the red looks the same, but the sensorimotor contingencies differ; in one case you are able to shift gaze back to the right, and in the other you are able to shift gaze back to the left. Differences in sensorimotor contingencies are neither necessary nor sufficient for differences in perceptual qualities.

The same conclusion follows for distinguishing between modalities. Enactive theorists would have us believe that people using the prosthetic vision device experience visual qualities. That does not seem to be the case. Instead, they just learn to use tactile properties as a distance sense. Over time, they may stop focusing on the surface of their bodies and direct attention outward, but they are not having visual experiences. The blind do not suddenly see. Touch functions like vision in this case, but it does not feel like vision. By comparison, imagine feeling the surface of a street using a walking stick. Like Bach-y-Rita's device, this turns touch into a distance sense, but it does not result in a visual experience. Seeing a street and feeling it with a cane are phenomenally different. Indeed, there are many cases in day-to-day life where different senses afford the same behavioral responses. Compare hearing something to the left and seeing something on the left. Both cases afford head shifting and alternations in auditory and visual attention. When we see something on the left, we look and listen; and when we hear something on the left, we do the same. Despite these similarities in sensorimotor contingencies, the experience of seeing is qualitatively different from that of hearing. The enactive account of how we distinguish between the senses seems to be false. It is also unnecessary. There are plenty of differences in how our perceptual systems represent the world; they use different rules and representations. There is no need to appeal to motor processes to explain how we differentiate the senses.

4. Moderate Embodiment

I have been raising doubts about the enactive approach to conscious experience. Ear-

lier, I also raised doubts about the situated approach. Those who have been tempted by these views tend to be radical. Some of them entertain the view that consciousness does not reside entirely inside the head. Some argue that conscious experience could not occur in the senses without the activation of motor representations. Some maintain that motor representations are constituent parts of our sensory experiences and an essential contributor to ordinary perceptual qualities, such as color experiences. These views are exciting, to be sure, but they do not enjoy much empirical support. We should resist gratuitous radicalism. But that does not mean we should reject embodied and situated approaches entirely. There may be aspects of conscious experience that will ultimately be explained by appeal to our nature as embodied and embedded agents. Some authors have been developing theories of perception that emphasize the influence of action systems without arguing for strong forms of dependency (e.g., Findley & Gilchrist, 2003; Matthen, 2005). I will not review this literature, but I will indicate four avenues for future exploration.

The first possibility that I want to consider is that embodiment contributes to self-consciousness (see Bermúdez, Marcel, & Eilan, 1995; Boyer, Robbins, & Jack, 2005; Gallagher, 2005; Jeannerod & Pacherie, 2004; Roessler & Eilan, 2003). There is a notion of the self that is bodily in nature. On one use of first-person concepts, I am my body. If you kick my body, you are kicking me. To have a conscious experience of the self includes awareness of the body. It includes awareness of actions, posture, and the internal patterns of bodily changes that we experience as emotions and moods. Arguably, a person lacking experience of a body would lack an important kind of self-consciousness. Such a person would experience the external world, but not a self. Of course, such a person could observe her own body through vision, but that would be like observing the body of another person; it would not be an experience of the body as a self. Such a person would experience the world from a specific vantage point, of course; the senses deliver information from a perspective. But perspectival does not entail personal. By analogy, a movie camera captures the world from a point of view, but that does not imbue the camera's image with a self-like quality. Cameras provide a view from somewhere, not necessarily a view from someone. Without body experiences, perception and perceptual memories might feel like self-less sequences of film.

The second possibility builds on the first. If perception of the body constitutes a form of self-consciousness, then it is also plausible that experiences of the body contribute to the sense of ownership that inheres in ordinary perceptual experience. When I perceive the world, the perceptual experiences that I have seem to be mine. Experiences have a subject. One tempting explanation is that the experience of ownership comes from the fact that my experiences occur in my body and I can initiate and experience bodily responses to what I perceive. If an object looms towards me, I duck. Such sensorimotor contingencies may link perception of the external world to perceptions of the embodied self in a way that makes the embodied self feel like a subject of experience. The phenomenology of ownership may consist in my felt reactions to the world I perceive.

These two proposals leave various issues unsettled. Can one have a conscious experience of oneself and of ownership without bodily experiences? Does the bodily component of self-consciousness involve both the experience of motor responses and the perception of bodily changes (motor and somatic components), or is just one of these components enough? These are questions for future research.

I want to move now to a third possible role for embodiment in conscious experience. Sense modalities are independent from each other; they process different information, have different phenomenal qualities, are vulnerable to selective deficits, and reside in different parts of the brain. Despite this profound division between the senses, conscious episodes seem unified. When I experience sight and sound simulta-

neously, it is not as if I had two separate streams of consciousness, like the two hemispheres in a split-brain patient. Both sensory streams are part of a single coherent experience. What allows for such phenomenal unity?

One popular answer is that the modalities are bound together by some neural process; perhaps they fire at the same rate (e.g., Crick & Koch, 1990; Singer & Gray, 1995). The physiological evidence for neural synchrony theories of binding is not very strong (Reilly, Busby, & Soto, 2003), but let's suppose that bound experiences do fire at the same rate. Would that explain the unity of experience? Decidedly not. After all, cells in your brain may fire at the same rate as cells in my brain, but there is no unified consciousness encompassing our two heads. Simultaneous firing is, at best, a computational marker that allows a system to integrate experiences in some other way (for other objections, see LaRock, 2006). Perhaps embodiment holds the key.

Here is a highly speculative proposal. Perhaps I experience unity in my senses because they are all available to a common locus of agency. Perhaps unity consists in my capacity to act on information in each of my senses. Notice that the two streams of consciousness in a person with a split brain both contribute to control of the same body, but they are not available to a common locus of agency. The information processing resources that use inputs from the right hemisphere to select behavioral responses cannot avail themselves of inputs from the left hemisphere, and conversely. Thus, there is no transhemispheric unity in the split-brain patient. For the rest of us, inputs from both hemispheres are unified, and that unity may derive from the fact that both hemispheres feed to the same action control centers. Unity across the senses may work in the same way. This is certainly an avenue worth exploring.

Let me turn now to a fourth and final avenue for future research. One of the most vexing questions in consciousness studies concerns the function of consciousness. What purpose does consciousness serve? I suspect that there is no special function of consciousness as such; an unconscious creature could do what we do. But there is undoubtedly a particular functional role played by the mental states that happen to be conscious in us. To identify that role, we can first determine which of our mental states are conscious and then see whether those states make any distinctive contribution to information processing. Toward this end, I will briefly sketch a theory of consciousness that I have defended more fully elsewhere (Prinz, 2000b, 2005, forthcoming).

The theory begins with a question about the locus of consciousness. Perceptual systems have many components, and these are organized hierarchically. Marr (1982) presented a general theory of how these hierarchies are organized, which is still widely accepted today; Marr got details wrong, but he correctly distinguished three levels of perceptual processing. Low-level perception extracts the local features that impinge on the surfaces of our sensory receptors. Typically, these features are sampled piecemeal and not bound into unified spatiotemporal wholes. Low-level vision delivers a constellation of edges, and low-level audition gives us individual tones. At an intermediate level these parts are bound together into more coherent representations. Edges become shapes and tones become melodies or word sounds. High-level perception produces categorical representations by extracting invariants from the intermediate level. An intermediate-level visual representation of a cow will present it from a particular vantage point; it will be a bound contour assembled from the edges detected at the low level. High-level visual representations extract away from the vantage point and produce a representation of the basic form of a cow that remains constant across a wide range of viewing positions. Marr calls this a structural description. In audition, categorical representation may abstract away from specific acoustic properties. For example, if two people say the word *cow* there will be differences in the sound captured at the intermediate level, but the high level may treat the two sounds as if they were

alike. In 1987, Jackendoff took this theory of perception as a point of departure and asked, Where in the hierarchy does consciousness arise? The obvious answer is that conscious arises at the intermediate level. We see whole objects, not constellations of edges, and we see them from a particular point of view. We hear words and melodies, not isolated tones, and we hear their specific acoustic properties, rather than categorical invariants.

I think Jackendoff is right about where in information processing consciousness is located, but his theory of consciousness is incomplete in a crucial respect. Mere activation of an intermediate-level representation is not sufficient for consciousness. After all, we can perceive things subliminally. Consciousness requires something more. I think the missing ingredient is attention. When attention systems are damaged, as in cases of unilateral neglect, consciousness of the unattended regions is lost (Bisiach, 1992). This suggests that attention is necessary for consciousness. Cases of subliminal perception may be explained by supposing that subliminal stimuli are presented too quickly to become objects of attention.

To directly test whether attention is necessary for consciousness, researchers give subjects tasks that demand a lot of attention, and they see what effect this has on consciousness. For example, Mack and Rock (1998) asked subjects to determine which of the two lines comprising a crosshair was longer. This is difficult to do, and while subjects were intensely examining the crosshair, they briefly flashed a word, a face, or a geometrical shape. Many subjects failed to notice the flashed object. Attention prevented them from seeing. Most, Scholl, Clifford, and Simons (2005) have shown that subjects can fail to notice an object that slowly moves across the center of a computer screen if they are attending to movements of other objects on the screen. This phenomenon is called "inattentional blindness." It differs from change blindness because in cases of change blindness we probably do experience the stimuli presented to us in rich detail, we just fail to keep track of how those stimuli change from one moment to the next. In inattentional blindness, we do not experience the unattended stimuli. Indeed, when attention is very narrowly focused, the visual field loses much of its richness, as if it contained only those objects that are currently being attended. Ordinary we are not engaged in tasks that require highly focused attention, so we allocate attention resources diffusely over the space in front of us, allowing us to experience many things simultaneously. One can think of the visual field as a phenomenally varied landscape, with some things vividly present in consciousness, other things less vivid, and still others not consciously processed at all. This variation seems to be determined by the varied allocation of attention. These observations suggest that consciousness arises only when we attend, and to the extent we attend. Combined with Jackendoff's hypothesis, we end up with what I call the AIR theory: conscious states are Attended Intermediate-level Representations.

The AIR theory allows us to address the question of function. First, we can ask, what purpose do intermediate-level representations serve? Obviously, they allow us to derive high-level representations. Note, however, that they serve this purpose even when they arise unconsciously. To understand what function consciousness serves, we need to ask why intermediate-level representations ever become targets of attention. This question can be addressed by reflecting on how attention works. Attention is essentially a tool for directing information access. When we attend, perceptual information gains access to working memory. The term *working memory* refers to systems that store information for a brief period of time. Working memory is not a passive storehouse, however. As the name implies, working memory works. It is where we make decisions (as opposed to responding automatically). So the question of what consciousness is for boils down to the question of why intermediate-level representations become available for decision making. Why do the centers of decision have special need

for representations that are viewpoint specific?

The natural answer to this question is that viewpoint-specific representations are extremely valuable for making decisions about action. Suppose you encounter a bear while hiking through the woods. You need to make a quick decision about what to do. To make that decision, it is extremely important to know several facts: Is the bear facing you or facing away? Is it close to you or in the distance? Is it staring at you or looking elsewhere? These questions can be answered by consulting visual information that is encoded at the intermediate level, but probably not encoded at the high level, which abstracts away from such details of vantage point. The best explanation for why working memory gains access to intermediate-level representations is that those representations are privileged with respect to deciding how to act.

Low-level representations are too fragmented to be especially useful for decision-making; in responding to the bear, we have to see it as a coherent object, not as a disconnected group of edges. High-level representations can be useful for decision making, but they facilitate decisions that are different in kind from the decisions that depend on the intermediate level. If you encounter a bear, it is important to know it is a bear; if it were a bush or a pony or your uncle Charlie, then there would be no need to flee. High-level representations are presumed to be the primary tools for making such categorical judgments. It is at the high level, then, that we establish category-related goals. If you see a bear, your goal might be to get away from it somehow. But that is an end, not a means. You cannot decide how to achieve your goal without knowing how you are situated. If the bear is close by, looking at you, and approaching from the right, then you should flee to the left. If the bear is far off or facing another direction, then you should freeze. Viewpoint-specific information is needed to determine how your goal can best be realized; it is information that provides a means to the end. It is in that respect that the intermediate level is tightly linked to action. If you have to decide what to do with your body, rather than just where you want to end up, then the intermediate level becomes crucial.

I will not develop this rough proposal here. I mention it to suggest that consciousness and action might be closely related after all. If I am right, consciousness arises when decision centers gain access to the representations that are especially useful for deciding how to act. Consciousness may not require motor responses, but it works in the service of such responses. This is a moral victory for the enactive approach, even if many authors currently exploring the relationship between consciousness and action are hoping to identify a more intimate link. Those authors want action to be somehow constitutive of consciousness. I want to suggest that consciousness is a precondition for deciding how to act, and the representations that become conscious are ideally suited for this purpose. It is a central function of consciousness to provide action systems with the information needed to make real-time decisions.

5. Conclusions

Situated and embodied approaches have a tendency to drift toward excessive radicalism. Practitioners argue that orthodox conceptions of the mind will be completely undermined once we recognize a place for body and world in mental life. I think we should resist such extremes. In issuing that warning, the bulk of this discussion has been critical, but that was not my ultimate purpose. I think the situated and embodied approach has much to offer. Rather than focus on debunking or defending radical claims, we should look for the ways in which an embodied orientation can lead to genuine insights about the nature of consciousness. I think this approach is leading to exciting and promising views which might have been neglected otherwise. Recent work on self-consciousness has focused on awareness of the acting body, and work on the unity and function of consciousness may move in the

same direction. If these forecasts are right, a complete theory of consciousness will be an embodied theory, in a moderate sense of the term. A complete theory will implicate systems that are involved in representing and controlling the body. The contributions of these systems are, I suspect, highly significant. They give us a sense of agency, ownership, and unity. These are pervasive aspects of conscious experience. Moreover, the mechanisms that give rise to consciousness may have evolved in the service of action. If so, consciousness is not about sensing; we can do that without consciousness. Nor is consciousness about making life more pleasant or more miserable; these are just side effects. Rather consciousness is about acting – it emerges through processes that make the world available to those systems that allow us to select behavioral means to our ends. In resisting radical situated and embodied theories, we must not lose sight of this fundamental fact.

Acknowledgments

Philip Robbins and Wayne Wright each gave me comments on an earlier draft of this chapter. Their editorial corrections, bibliographical guidance, thoughtful suggestions, and challenging questions led to numerous improvements throughout. I am extremely grateful.

References

Bach-y-Rita, P. (1972). *Brain mechanisms in sensory substitution*. New York: Academic Press.

Bermúdez, J., Marcel, A., & Eilan, N. (Eds.). (1995). *The body and the self*. Cambridge, MA: MIT Press.

Bisiach, E. (1992). Understanding consciousness: Clues from unilateral neglect and related disorders. In A. D. Milner & M. D. Rugg (Eds.), *The neuropsychology of consciousness* (pp. 113–139). London: Academic Press.

Block, N. (2005). Review of Alva Noë's *Action in Perception*. *Journal of Philosophy*, 102, 259–272.

Boyer, P., Robbins, P., & Jack, A. (1995). Varieties of self-systems worth having. *Consciousness and Cognition*, 14, 647–660.

Brooks, R. A. (1991). Intelligence without representation. *Artificial Intelligence, 47*, 139–159.

Cassel, G. H., Billig, M. D., & Randall, H. G. (1998). *The eye book: A complete guide to eye disorders and health*. Baltimore: Johns Hopkins University Press.

Cotterill, R. (1998). *Enchanted looms: Conscious networks in brains and computers*. Cambridge: Cambridge University Press.

Crick, F., & Koch, C. (1990). Towards a neurobiological theory of consciousness. *Seminars in Neurosciences, 2*, 263–275.

Dennett, D. (1969). *Content and consciousness*. London: Routledge & Kegan Paul.

Dennett, D. (1991). *Consciousness explained*. Boston: Little, Brown.

Dretske, F. (1995). *Naturalizing the mind*. Cambridge, MA: MIT Press.

Feynman, R. (1997). *Surely you're joking, Mr. Feynman! Adventures of a curious character*. New York: W. W. Norton.

Findlay, J. M., & Gilchrist, I. D. (2003). *Active vision*. Oxford: Oxford University Press.

Fodor, J. A. (1994). *The elm and the expert: Mentalese and its semantics*. Cambridge, MA: MIT Press.

Gallagher, S. (2005). *How the body shapes the mind*. New York: Oxford University Press.

Glenberg, A. M., & Kaschak, M. P. (2003). The body's contribution to language. In B. Ross (Ed.), *The psychology of learning and motivation* (Vol. 43, pp. 93–126). New York: Academic Press.

Held, R., & Hein, A. (1963). Movement-produced stimulation in the development of visually guided behavior. *Journal of Comparative and Physiological Psychology, 56*, 872–876.

Hurley, S. (1998). *Consciousness in action*. Cambridge, MA: Harvard University Press.

Hurley, S., & Noë, A. (2003). Neural plasticity and consciousness. *Biology and Philosophy, 18*, 131–168.

Jackendoff, R. (1987). *Consciousness and the computational mind*. Cambridge, MA: MIT Press.

Jack, A., & Prinz, J. (2003). Searching for a scientific experience. *Journal of Consciousness Studies, 11*, 51–56.

James, W. (1904). Does "consciousness" exist? *Journal of Philosophy, Psychology, and Scientific Methods, 1*, 477–491.

Jeannerod, M., & Pacherie, E. (2004). Agency, simulation and self-identification. *Mind & Language, 19*, 113–146.

Kandell, E. R., Schwartz, J. H., & Jessel, T. M. (2000). *Principles of neural science* (4th ed.). New York: McGraw-Hill.

Koch, C. (2004). *The quest for consciousness: A neurobiological approach*. Denver, CO: Roberts.

Land, M. F., Furneaux, S. M., & Gilchrist, I. D. (2002). The organization of visually mediated actions in a subject without eye movements. *Neurocase, 8*, 80–87.

LaRock, E. (2006). Why neural synchrony fails to explain the unity of visual consciousness. *Behavior and Philosophy, 34*, 39–58.

Lycan, W. (1996). *Consciousness and experience*. Cambridge, MA: MIT Press.

Mack, A., & Rock, I. (1998). *Inattentional blindness*. Cambridge, MA: MIT Press.

Mandik, P. (1999). Qualia, space, and control. *Philosophical Psychology, 12*, 47–60.

Marr, D. (1982). *Vision: A computational investigation into the human representation and processing of visual information*. New York: W. H. Freeman.

Matthen, M. (2005). *Seeing, doing, and knowing*. New York: Oxford University Press.

McGurk, H., & MacDonald, J. (1976). Hearing lips and seeing voices. *Nature, 264*, 746–748.

Metzinger, T. (Ed.). (2000). *Neural correlates of consciousness: Empirical and conceptual questions*. Cambridge, MA: MIT Press.

Milner, D., & Goodale, M. (1995). *The visual brain in action*. Oxford: Oxford University Press.

Mitroff, S. R., Simons, D. J., & Levin, D. T. (2004). Nothing compares two views: Change blindness can occur despite preserved access to the changed information. *Perception & Psychophysics, 66*, 1268–1281.

Moran, J., & Desimone, R. (1985). Selective attention gates visual processing in the extrastriate cortex. *Science, 229*, 782–784.

Most, S. B., Scholl, B. J., Clifford, E., & Simons, D. J. (2005). What you see is what you set: Sustained inattentional blindness and the capture of awareness. *Psychological Review, 112*, 217–242.

Noë, A. (2004). *Action in perception*. Cambridge, MA: MIT Press.

Noë, A., & Thompson, E. (2004). Are there neural correlates of consciousness? *Journal of Consciousness Studies, 11*, 3–28.

O'Regan, J. K., & Noë, A. (2001). A sensorimotor account of vision and visual consciousness. *Behavioural and Brain Sciences, 24*(5), 939–1011.

Prinz, J. (2000a). The ins and outs of consciousness. *Brain and Mind, 2*, 245–256.

Prinz, J. (2000b). A neurofunctional theory of visual consciousness. *Consciousness and Cognition, 9,* 243–259.

Prinz, J. (2002). *Furnishing the mind: Concepts and their perceptual basis.* Cambridge, MA: MIT Press.

Prinz, J. (2005). A neurofunctional theory of consciousness. In A. Brook & K. Akins (Eds.), *Cognition and the brain: The philosophy and neuroscience movement* (pp. 381–396). Cambridge: Cambridge University Press.

Prinz, J. (2006). Putting the brakes on enactive perception. *PSYCHE, 12*(1). Retrieved June 13, 2008, from http://psyche.cs.monash. edu.au/symposia/noe/Prinz.pdf

Prinz, J. (forthcoming). *The conscious brain.* New York: Oxford University Press.

Prinz, J., & Barsalou, L. (2000). Perceptual symbols and dynamic systems. In A. Markman & E. Dietrich (Eds.), *Cognitive dynamics.* Dordrecht, The Netherlands: Kluwer.

Reilly, R., Busby, R., & Soto, R. (2003). Three forms of binding and their neural substrates: Alternatives to temporal synchrony. In A. Cleeremans (Ed.), *The unity of consciousness: Binding, integration, and dissocia-*

tion (pp. 168–192). Oxford: Oxford University Press.

Rivière, J., & Lécuyer, R. (2002). Spatial cognition in young children with spinal muscular atrophy. *Developmental Neuropsychology, 21,* 273–283.

Roessler, J., & Eilan, N. (Eds.). (2003). *Agency and self-awareness.* Oxford: Oxford University Press.

Silverman, M., & Mack, A. (2001). Priming from change blindness [Abstract]. *Journal of Vision, 1,* 13a.

Simons, D. J., & Levin, D. T. (1997). Change blindness. *Trends in Cognitive Sciences, 1,* 261–267.

Singer, W., & Gray, C. (1995). Visual feature integration and the temporal correlation hypothesis. *Annual Review of Neuroscience, 18,* 555–586.

Thompson, E., & Varela, F. (2001). Radical embodiment: Neural dynamics and consciousness. *Trends in Cognitive Sciences, 5,* 418–425.

Tye, M. (1995). *Ten problems of consciousness.* Cambridge, MA: MIT Press.

Wilson, R. (2004). *Boundaries of the mind: The individual in the fragile sciences.* Cambridge: Cambridge University Press.

CHAPTER 23

Emotions in the Wild

The Situated Perspective on Emotion

Paul Griffiths and Andrea Scarantino

1. Introduction

Many theoretical traditions have contributed to the scientific elucidation of emotion, but philosophers facing the question, What is an emotion? have concentrated on two of these in particular.[1] Philosophical cognitivism is inspired by the appraisal tradition in psychology (e.g., Arnold, 1960, 1970; Scherer, 1999). The alternative neo-Jamesian approach is inspired by the somatic marker hypothesis in affective neuroscience (Damasio, 1996; Panksepp, 1998). Cognitivists identify emotions with representations of the stimulus situation, or evaluative judgments (Solomon, 1976, 1993). Neo-Jamesians identify emotions with states of bodily arousal, which are detected by the brain as affect (Prinz, 2004b). Both these views of emotion parallel the view of cognition that has been called into question by situated cognition research (Smith, 1999; Clark, 1997). In both theories, emotions are conceived as internal states or processes and the role of the environment is confined to providing stimuli and receiving actions. Thus, although Prinz advocates embodied emo-

tions (Prinz, 2004a), his contribution does not emphasize the role of the environment, assimilating emoting to perceiving actual or as-if changes of one's own body (Damasio, 1999). In a further parallel with traditional views of cognition, both cognitivists and neo-Jamesians focus on the contributions that emotions make to the organism's internal psychological economy. The primary function of emotions, on both accounts, is to provide the organism's decision-making systems with information about the significance of a stimulus situation.

This chapter describes a very different perspective on emotion, according to which emotions are the following:

1. Designed to function in a social context: an emotion is often an act of relationship reconfiguration brought about by delivering a social signal;

2. Forms of skillful engagement with the world that need not be mediated by conceptual thought;

3. Scaffolded by the environment, both synchronically, in the unfolding of a particular emotional performance, and

diachronically, in the acquisition of an emotional repertoire;

4. Dynamically coupled to an environment that both influences and is influenced by the unfolding of the emotion.

We draw heavily on transactional accounts of emotion proposed by some contemporary psychologists (Fridlund, 1994; Parkinson, 1995; Parkinson, Fischer, & Manstead, 2005; Russell & Fernández-Dols, 1997). Although these authors do not, to our knowledge, conceive of their work as a contribution to the situationist literature that is the focus of this volume, we contend that their proposals constitute a fairly exact, affective parallel to situationist ideas about cognition. The primary aim of this chapter is to demonstrate that a situated approach to emotion already exists and is backed by a substantial experimental literature. This body of theory and data could make a major contribution to fleshing out the general situationist perspective on the mind.

We emphasize that adopting the situationist perspective does not require denying the results produced by other theoretical traditions in psychology, such as the affect-program tradition, or even the heuristic value of alternative theoretical perspectives. Instead, the situated perspective shifts our theoretical focus to neglected phenomena and questions. The situated approach to emotion is at its most compelling when applied to exemplars like anger in a marital quarrel or embarrassment while delivering a song to an audience. These are cases in which the emotion has a temporal course of development and involves an ongoing exchange of emotional signals (e.g., facial actions, tones of voice). This switch in the focus of emotion theory parallels the way in which situated cognition research switches the focus of cognitive science from exemplars like theorem proving to engaged, real-time exemplars like navigation in a cluttered environment.

Finally, the situated perspective on emotion has some points in common with active-vision accounts of situated perception (Noë, 2004). In traditional models of emotional appraisal, the organism receives information from the environment and uses it to determine the emotional significance of the situation that confronts it. In contrast, the situated perspective envisages organisms probing their environment through initial emotional responses and monitoring the responses of other organisms to determine how the emotion will evolve (see section 5).

2. Social Situatedness

A situated perspective on the mind recognizes that it is designed to function in an environmental context and that aspects of the environment may be causal components of mental mechanisms (Clark & Chalmers, 1998). Research on situated cognition has often emphasized the reliable physical properties of the environment, properties that can be exploited to reduce cognitive load. In contrast, a situated perspective on emotion emphasizes the role of social context in the production and management of an emotion, and the reciprocal influence of emotion on the evolving social context. Behaviors that have traditionally been viewed as involuntary expressions of the organism's psychological state are instead viewed as signals designed to influence the behavior of other organisms, or as strategic moves in an ongoing transaction between organisms.[2]

One of the most important experimental paradigms for a situated perspective on emotion is the study of audience effects – differences in emotional response to a constant stimulus which reflect differences in the expected recipient(s) of the emotion. Among the most dramatic effects are those obtained for the production of the so-called Duchenne smile – the pattern of movement of mouth and eyes generally accepted as a pancultural expression of happiness (Ekman, 1972). Ten-pin bowlers are presumably happiest when they make a full strike and less happy when they knock down a few pins. However, bowlers rarely smile after making a full strike when facing away from their bowling companions and smile very often after knocking down a few pins when they face their companions (Kraut & Johnston, 1979). Spanish soccer fans show a similar pattern in their facial response to goals and issue Duchenne smiles only when facing one another (Fernández-Dols & Ruiz-Belda, 1997). Fernández-Dols and Ruiz-Belda also demonstrate that at the 1992 Barcelona Olympics, although gold medalists produced many signs of emotion during the medal ceremony, they produced Duchenne smiles almost exclusively when interacting with the audience and officials.

These results suggest that smiles are not outpourings of happiness that are merely witnessed by other people but affiliative gestures made by one person to another with respect to something good that has occurred. This fits the model of emotions as strategic moves in the context of a social transaction. Obviously, people do smile and produce other classical emotional expressions when they are alone, but studies suggest that they do so far less often than one might expect. Even such apparently reflexive displays as facial expressions produced in response to tastes and smells appear to be facilitated by an appropriate social setting, and the same appears to be the case for pain expressions (Russell, Bachorowski, & Fernández-Dols, 2003). Furthermore, it would be a mistake to conclude that audience effects are absent when a physical audience is absent. Solitary subjects who mentally picture taking part in a social interaction produce more emotional facial signals than subjects who focus on the emotional stimulus without an imagined audience. Fridlund (1994; Fridlund et al., 1990) has described this as implicit sociality and remarked that his experimental subjects display to the audience in their heads.

The sensitivity to social context manifested in audience effects can be implemented by very simple mental mechanisms, as is evident from the prevalence of audience effects in animals. This is important because it helps to explain how the emotions can be produced strategically without becoming mere pretences of emotion (see also Griffiths, 1997, chap. 6; 2004b). Male Golden Sebright chickens, for example, make a fuss when they find and consume a valuable morsel of food, but only if there are female chickens in the vicinity (Marler & Evans, 1997). There is, presumably, no point in demonstrating foraging ability to other males! Results like these suggest that the social situatedness of emotion is not a special human achievement mediated by conceptual thought but a fundamental aspect of emotion (see section 3).

Socially situated emotions have a strategic aspect neglected in cognitivist and neo-Jamesian accounts of emotion. Emotions have been seen as more or less accurate responses to how things are, but they are also, and perhaps primarily, more or less effective goal-oriented responses. For example, one study in which people were asked to describe situations in which they had become angry found that the prospect of obtaining compensation is a significant factor determining whether a loss elicits anger or sadness (Stein, Trabasso, & Liwag, 1993). This is puzzling if anger is merely a response to having been wronged, but makes good sense if anger is a strategy to obtain restitution.

Embarrassment is an emotion that wears its social situatedness on its face, as most theories of embarrassment acknowledge (Parkinson et al., 2005, pp. 188–192). The finding that observers evaluate people who behave in a socially inappropriate manner more favorably if they show embarrassment suggests that one function of embarrassment may be to indicate knowledge of a violated norm and acceptance of its validity (for more on embarrassment elicitors, see section 3). In a study in which subjects were asked to record a karaoke-style performance of a notoriously embarrassing love song, the singer's subsequent level of embarrassment was reduced if he or she was given reason to believe that the experimenter knew the subject was embarrassed by the performance (Leary, Landel, & Patton, 1996). The authors take this result to suggest that embarrassment functioned as a signal: the singer needed to convey to the audience that he or she had a low opinion of the song, thus confirming the singer's knowledge of, and desire to conform to, community standards.

Some emotional behavior simply cries out for a transactional analysis. Sulking is normally thought of as a manifestation of emotion, but traditional theories of emotion do little to illuminate it. This is perhaps why there has been so little research on a phenomenon of such obvious importance to human relationship dynamics. Sulking sabotages mutually rewarding social transactions and rejects attempts at reconciliation. Traditional appraisal theory can identify sulking as a manifestation of anger, but does nothing to explain the specifics of sulking, which must be handed off to a separate theory of emotion management or emotion coping. It is also implausible that all (or even most) people who sulk sincerely judge themselves to have been wronged, so an ancillary theory of self-deceit is needed as well. In contrast, viewing an emotion as a strategy of relationship reconfiguration (Parkinson, 1995, p. 295) provides a compelling perspective on sulking. Sulking is a behavioral strategy for seeking a better deal in a relationship – an emotional game of chicken in which transactions that benefit both parties are rejected until appropriate concessions are obtained. The question confronting an agent deciding whether to become upset in this way is not whether they have been slighted simpliciter, but whether taking what has happened as a slight and withdrawing cooperation will give them leverage. Once again, this strategic appraisal of the situation may be realized by a relatively simple mental mechanism.

The situated perspective on emotion can be seen as an attempt to refocus discussion on a new set of examples. Rather than taking the meeting between a man and a bear in a lonely wood as a paradigm of fear, attention is focused on displays of fear produced by a child when her caregiver is at hand. Rather than taking righteous anger at the injustices of the world to be the paradigm of anger, anger is studied in the context of its development in a marital confrontation. The aim of this refocusing is twofold: first, to illuminate the aspects of emotional life that are arguably most relevant to practical issues of emotion management; second, to reveal the social aspects of many other emotions that

are overlooked when they are assimilated to the traditional exemplar cases.

3. Nonconceptual Emotional Content

Most situationist literature opposes the idea that the primary medium of cognition is conceptual thought. Although not denying that conceptual thought exists, situationists see it as only the icing on the cognitive cake. Other forms of cognition explain most of the practical abilities of organisms to negotiate their environments (Smith, 1999; Cussins, 1992). In this section we explore a similar perspective on emotional content.

To be credited with conceptual thought, a creature must fulfill requirements of maximal inferential promiscuity with respect to its thought contents (Hurley, 2003). A popular way to state this requirement is Evans's (1982) generality constraint, according to which a mental state qualifies as a "thought that a is F" just in case it is possible for the subject to decompose that state into recombinable ingredients and form with such ingredients mental states of two sorts: states that predicate of "a" any property G the subject can conceive of, and states that predicate F of any object "b" the subject can conceive of. The ability to entertain the thought "a is F" is therefore "a joint exercise of two abilities" (Evans, 1982, p. 104), namely, the ability to have the concept of a particular object "a" and the ability to have the concept of a particular property F. These abilities underlie the higher-order ability to think productively and systematically, sensu Fodor (1975 and elsewhere).

Situationists argue that skillful activities such as navigating an environment or cooking a meal can be conducted without conceptual thought in this sense, and that these abilities are at least as important a part of cognition as abilities that require conceptual thought (Smith, 1999). In a similar fashion, the situated perspective on emotion views emotions as forms of skillful engagement with the world and resists the view that they either are or essentially involve conceptual thought. The ability to emote is not to be explained in terms of propositional attitudes and their use in practical and theoretical inferences. Instead, the contentfulness of emotions emerges from the fact that they enable dexterous interactions with the environment. Importantly, when ascribing this form of emotional content to an organism, we are entitled to use concepts not possessed by the organism having the emotion, a standard condition for labeling a form of mental content as nonconceptual (Bermúdez, 2003).[3]

Although there is no room here to elaborate on the specifics of nonconceptual emotional representation, what appears to be crucial is that it is an action-oriented form of representation (Griffiths, 2004b; Scarantino, 2005). Emotional content has a fundamentally pragmatic dimension, in the sense that the environment is represented in terms of what it affords to the emoter in the way of skillful engagement with it. To get a more vivid intuitive grip on this, imagine the world-as-perceived (*Umwelt*) of an antelope suddenly confronted by a lion. The dominant elements of the antelope's *Umwelt* are escape affordances (Scarantino, 2003), as all of its cognitive, perceptual, and motoric abilities are recruited to discover and execute an action sequence that evades the predator. This representation of the world in goal-oriented terms is required by the urgency of the situation, which demands selectively transforming inputs into opportunities for life-saving output rather than generating a multipurpose representation of the environment.

A situationist, action-oriented approach to emotional content is diametrically opposed to classic cognitivist theories of emotions, which take emotions to be evaluative judgments or combinations of beliefs and desires (Marks, 1982; Nussbaum, 2001; Solomon, 1993). Although this approach may give an accurate account of some forms of sophisticated human emotionality, it falls short as a general theory of emotions. In particular, the assumption that conceptual thought is essential for emotion prevents us from making sense of emotions in infants and animals. This not only is wildly counter-

intuitive (monkeys are never really afraid) but also deprives us of two of the most fruitful avenues for the study of emotions: comparative animal studies and the exploration of ontogenetic emotional development. It is also inconsistent with the phenomenon of affective primacy (Öhman, 1999), in which emotion systems display some of the properties of a Fodorian module (Fodor, 1983): they are fast, mandatory, cognitively impenetrable, and have limited central accessibility. The case of phobias is exemplary in this respect, as a phobic can reconcile the conceptual thought that the object of their phobia is completely harmless with utter terror toward it. The traditional cognitivist must assimilate phobias either to inconsistent beliefs or to self-deceit. In the case of fear at least, there is good scientific reason to believe that phobias result neither from logical error nor from self-deceit, but from the neural architecture of the emotion system. By means of ingenious lesion studies, LeDoux (1993) has demonstrated that fear can be elicited in a reflex-like fashion through a neural low road that projects along a subcortical pathway directly to the amygdala and bypasses the neocortex. Because full-blown conceptual thought is generally assumed to involve the neocortex, this appears to be strong evidence that conceptual thought is not essential for fear.[4]

The biggest hurdle for a situated perspective on emotions is constituted by the so-called higher cognitive emotions (for skepticism about this label, see section 6). Guilt, shame, resentment, envy, and embarrassment, for example, seem connected by their very definitions to a range of sophisticated conceptual abilities. This perspective is supported by the psychological literature on emotional appraisal. The influential account of Lazarus (1991) suggests that each emotion is caused by an appraisal whose content can be captured by a core relational theme. Guilt is caused by the appraisal that one has transgressed a moral imperative and shame by the appraisal that one has failed to live up to an ego ideal. These appear to be paradigmatically conceptual thoughts, which demand possession of concepts such as moral imperative, self, and ideal. Conventional appraisal theory thus seems to tie these emotions to conceptual thought. But this not only would imply that emotions like guilt, shame, and even anger cannot conceivably occur in children and animals, it would also be inconsistent with the apparent occurrence of emotions such as victim guilt (Parkinson et al., 2005, and see next paragraph) or shame generated by merely interacting with a higher-ranking member of the community (Fessler, 1999).[5] Confronted by these and other difficulties, appraisal theorists have come to accept that even such apparently conceptually complex appraisals as Lazarus's core relational themes can be made (1) without the information evaluated being available to other cognitive processes, (2) before perceptual processing of the stimulus has been completed, and (3) using only simple sensory cues to define the property that has to be identified. The resultant multilevel appraisal theories (Teasdale, 1999) suggest that the same content can be possessed at different levels of appraisal, a view consistent with the idea that some levels of appraisal involve nonconceptual content.

The situated perspective on emotions identifies emotions like guilt and shame in a way that leaves open the extent to which they involve conceptual thought. The question becomes whether the social transaction corresponding to the emotion can occur in the absence of the appropriate conceptual thoughts. Parkinson et al. (2005) offer us reasons to think that this is indeed the case for many higher cognitive emotions. They report a study by Kroon (1988) in which only 28 percent of experimental subjects reporting guilt experiences deemed themselves causally related to the event that provoked their guilt. Parkinson (1999) further supports the view that it is not necessary to engage in thoughts of moral transgression to feel guilty by documenting instances of guilt generated by unwarranted accusations from relevant others. These forms of guilt can be explained from a transactionalist perspective if guilt is a form of skillful social engagement aimed at reconciliation.

When someone we care about accuses us, even unjustly, a need to repair the relationship emerges. Guilt is often a good strategy to meet this need, because it conveys a message of sympathetic suffering and the intention to avoid future involvement in harmful events affecting the accuser.

The transactionalist perspective makes sense of many otherwise mysterious forms of higher cognitive emotion. For example, although embarrassment has usually been associated with the recognition of personal failure with respect to relatively unimportant norms of conduct, embarrassment can be elicited simply by being pointed at in public (Lewis, 2000) or being deservedly praised in public (Parrott & Smith, 1991). Parkinson et al. (2005) interpret this as evidence that embarrassment can be a simple response to public attention, which does not presuppose negative self-evaluation. Embarrassment can thus occur as a result of mere unwanted attention, which may or may not be the result of having committed a faux pas. From this perspective, embarrassment may be available to prelinguistic children. Reddy (2000) reports the combination of coy smiles and gaze aversion in two-month-old infants, which suggests the possibility that primitive forms of embarrassment may emerge much earlier than the cognitive capacities generally assumed to underlie them: "the dynamics of interpersonal interaction may produce emotion without the internal cognitive representation of those dynamics. All that is required is a basic perception of self in relation to others, which may well be present at a very early age" (Parkinson et al., 2005, p. 210). This idea will be enlarged upon in the next section.

4. Cultural Scaffolding

The concept of environmental scaffolding has been central to situated cognition research: intelligent behavior is guided and supported by the context in which it unfolds. The emphasis here is on the active contribution of the environment to the cognitive process (Clark & Chalmers, 1998).

To disregard the enabling properties of the environment is to lose sight of the fact that the causal structure underlying a great many cognitive achievements projects into the relational space between cognizer and environment.

A situated perspective on emotion recognizes that the environment plays an active role in structuring and enabling emotional engagements, which like cognitive engagements are scaffolded by their natural context of occurrence.[6] The environment scaffolds emotion in two ways. Synchronically, the environment supports particular emotional performances – particular episodes of, say, anger or sadness (see section 5). Diachronically, the environment supports the development of an emotional phenotype or repertoire of emotional abilities. Thus, the provision of confessionals in churches enables certain kinds of emotional performance (synchronic scaffolding), and the broader Catholic culture supports the development of the ability to engage in the emotional engagements of confession (diachronic scaffolding). Synchronic scaffolding has received more attention than diachronic scaffolding in the literature on situated cognition (but see Thelen & Smith, 1994). In contrast, there is more research on the diachronic, developmental role of affective culture than on its synchronic role. This is a by-product of the longstanding debate over nature versus nurture in emotion theory.

To appreciate the potential interest of the extensive body of research on emotional development, we need to diffuse the heated but ultimately sterile debate over nature and nurture. Situated perspectives on emotion have traditionally been aligned with social constructionism because of the simplistic view that evolved features of the mind must develop in ways that are insensitive to the social environment – they are programmed in the genes (e.g., Ratner, 1989). Fortunately, it is increasingly recognized that evolution does not construct genetic homunculi but developmental systems designed to function in a developmental context that, in a species like ours,

includes socialization and exposure to all those factors that make up a culture (Cosmides, Tooby, & Barkow, 1992). Hence a feature of the emotional phenotype may be both a (phylogenetic) product of evolution and an (ontogenetic) product of a rich context of socialization. A fully adequate resolution of the nature-versus-nurture debate, however, requires the additional recognition that the role of the developmental context is not restricted to activating alternative outcomes prefigured in a disjunctive genetic program (Griffiths, 1997; Griffiths & Stotz, 2000). Developmental systems are usually competent to produce viable phenotypes outside the specific parameter ranges in which they have historically operated. This may even be an important source of evolutionary novelty (Schlichting & Pigliucci, 1998; West-Eberhard, 2003).

In our view, an adequate perspective on the relationship between evolution and social construction must recognize (1) that the way developing humans respond to inputs from the social environment and the fact that the social environments provide those inputs may both be subject to evolutionary explanation, and (2) that the biological endowment of a healthy human infant determines a norm of reaction that includes a large range of emotional phenotypes, not all of which have been specifically selected for nor need to have occurred before in human history (for similar perspectives, see Bjorklund & Pellegrini, 2002; Parkinson, forthcoming). That said, we hope that we can go on to discuss the role of the environment in the genesis of emotions without being accused of ignoring biology.

Parkinson et al. (2005, p. 224) formulate a useful framework for the study of the environment's many roles. They discuss both how the development of an emotional repertoire is diachronically scaffolded by the cultural context in which an individual grows up and how specific emotional performances are synchronically scaffolded by the social and cultural context in which they occur. They explore the potential social influences on emotion under the two broad areas of ideational factors and material factors, offering an adaptation of Markus and Kitayama's (1994) model. Ideational factors include normative standards about when emotions should be experienced or expressed (e.g., American wedding guests are normatively required both to be happy for the couple and to convey their happiness), emotion scripts (shared internalized understandings of the standard unfolding of an emotional episode), and ethnotheories (culture-specific belief systems about the nature and value of emotions). Material factors include emotional capital (e.g., the emotional resources associated with having a specific social status, gender, etc.), venues in which certain emotional performances are favored (e.g., a confessional, a stadium, a temple), and a range of emotional technologies for the management of emotions, from prayer beads to Prozac.

Parkinson et al. (2005) draw on existing work on emotional development to construct a model of the development of a culturally situated emotional phenotype (pp. 235–248). They distinguish three main ontogenetic stages: primary intersubjectivity, secondary intersubjectivity, and cultural articulation.

Primary intersubjectivity emerges in the first few months of a child's life, when patterns of attraction and aversion are established with objects and relevant others, most prominently caregivers. One form of emotional engagement emerging at this stage involves struggling in response to a tight embrace (Camras, Campos, Oster, Miyake, & Bradshaw, 1992). Parkinson, Fischer, and Manstead identify this as the ontogenetically earliest form of anger, despite the fact that the concepts that make up the core relational theme of anger are not available at this point. This identification is made possible by thinking of anger as a type of social transaction rather than as a conceptual thought embodying a core relational theme (see section 3). The primary anger reaction in infants is developmentally continuous with episodes of adult anger in which the core relational theme is not instantiated, such as anger elicited by repeated failure to open a jammed door.

When the child is about one year old, Parkinson et al. (2005) envisage the emergence of secondary intersubjectivity, characterized by the recognition not only of people and objects but also of the relations existing between them. A classic example of emotional engagement emerging at this stage is social referencing. Infants learn to engage objects emotionally in light of the emotional responses other people have to them. For example, if toddlers observe a disgusted expression on their mother's face when they are handling a toy, they are less inclined to play with it (Hornik, Risenhoover, & Gunnar, 1987).

Finally, infants articulate their emotions with the help of their emerging conceptual resources (cultural articulation). Drawing on symbolic resources in the surrounding culture, most important those afforded by language, the child organizes its experience of emotional transactions in conceptual form.[7] It is at this stage that ideational factors, such as emotion scripts and display rules, and material factors, such as emotional capital and emotional technologies, have their greatest impact on emotional development.

It is in their understanding of cultural articulation that Parkinson et al. (2005) depart from traditional social constructionism. Articulation does not simply cause emotions to take on the form suggested by the local affective culture. While the articulated, concept-mediated emotion is a real component of the emotion system, it is superimposed on an existing emotional repertoire grounded in primary and secondary intersubjectivity: "We don't learn to get angry in the first place by following cultural rules, even if those rules are applied to our anger after the fact" (Parkinson et al., 2005, p. 247). The conceptual articulation of the emotion allows for the emergence of tensions between emotional engagements reflecting different ontogenetic stages (e.g., some episodes of anger may not fit normative rules for their appropriate elicitation, as in the case of the jammed door). In such cases the subject will often struggle to interpret a spontaneous emotional response so as to fit the cultural articulation of an appropriate emotion.

Parkinson et al.'s (2005) account of the ontogeny of emotion allows individuals raised in different affective cultures to develop different emotional phenotypes. This could happen in either of two ways. First, individuals do conform to a significant degree with the norms and scripts that they have internalized. Second, all sorts of cultural differences – physical child-care practices, common toys, and so forth – may affect emotional development. It is worth noting, however, that these latter influences need not necessarily increase the fit between emotion as experienced and emotion as articulated. It is perfectly conceivable that some element of the upbringing of children in an affective culture might make it harder for them to conform to its norms as adults than would otherwise be the case. In any case, even when cultural articulation has had its full effect on the development of the emotional repertoire, a gap remains that allows emotions to occur in the absence of the conceptual conditions taken to define them.

We now turn from the cultural scaffolding of emotional development (diachronic scaffolding) to the cultural scaffolding of emotional performances (synchronic scaffolding). For society to function smoothly, individuals must have the right emotions at the right times, and it is not left to individual psychological processes to ensure that this occurs. It is hardly necessary to describe the emotional technologies used to ensure that soldiers hate the enemy, feel loyalty to their unit, and are not overwhelmed by fear in combat. Parkinson et al. (2005) use the more cheerful example of the wedding ceremony, in which ritual, music, and setting scaffold participants' performances of their complementary affective roles. It is not left to chance to make a wedding a big day for all concerned. Such real-time socialization is an alternative to inducing conformity with local affective norms via diachronic socialization (Parkinson et al., 2005, p. 226).

Another real-time process inducing conformity to emotional norms is social appraisal, in which an individual's appraisal of a situation is linked to that of others. The most famous experiment on social appraisal (more precisely, social referencing) demonstrated that the willingness of infants to crawl over a visual cliff reflected whether their waiting mother produced a positive or negative facial expression (Sorce, Emde, Campos, & Klinnert, 1985). Similar processes occur in adults. A tactless remark can be shrugged off when the other members of a social gathering treat it as a nonevent, or when they laugh it off, whereas it may be appraised as a deadly insult if bystanders meet it with silence or with a sharp intake of breath. Such distributed appraisal provides an emotional correlate to distributed cognition (e.g., Hutchins, 1995).

Real-time socialization is perhaps the closest parallel in emotion research to the forms of scaffolding that have been the focus of much philosophical discussion of situationism, such as the notorious notebook of Clark and Chalmers (1998). In our view, too much attention has been devoted to whether such cognitive aids imply that cognition is literally spread out into the world. Similar claims have been made in the literature on the emotions, with emotions said to exist in the social space between transactants, and so forth, but we believe it would be a mistake to focus on these questions, which are largely semantic. The real interest of situationist accounts of emotion lies in their methodological prescriptions for future psychological study of the emotions. We will return to this theme in section 6.

5. Dynamic Coupling

A situated perspective on cognition includes the realization that cognition is dynamically shaped by the context in which a cognitive episode takes place. This context changes over time, sometimes as a consequence of the cognitive activity. Context dependence generates a system of reciprocal causation that classic approaches to the mind tend to neglect, as they abstract from the local properties of the environment (Smith,

1999). A situated perspective on emotion explores some of the same themes, focusing on the temporal dynamics of skillful emotional engagement, exploring the way in which the emotional episode shapes the context of its development and is in turn shaped by it. Because the context of emotional episodes is largely social, understanding the dynamic coupling between emoter and environment amounts to understanding how the unfolding of an emotion episode affects the behaviors of other organisms and is in turn shaped by their behavior. Emotion is a form of skillful engagement with the social environment that involves a dynamic process of negotiation mediated by reciprocal feedback between emoter and interactants. This feedback is provided by reciprocal emotional signals.

Researchers on situated cognition have been strongly influenced by the dynamical cognitive science approach featured in the collection *Mind as Motion* (Port & van Gelder, 1995). The dynamicist ideas presented here have a rather different pedigree, as they are primarily grounded in the study of relationship dynamics (Hinde, 1979, 1981). This large body of work on topics such as infant attachment and romantic relationships starts from the premise that relationships are not an immediate function of the properties that individuals bring to a relationship, but emerge as a result of specific interactions between those individuals and inputs from a changing environment.

The ethologist Robert Hinde (1985a, 1985b) was the first to articulate the idea that emotional behavior can be a form of negotiation. He noticed that several kinds of emotional expressions, in both humans and animals, are issued only when a recipient is there to be influenced by them, and that it is the responses of the recipient that determine the subsequent behavior of the individual exhibiting the initial emotional behavior rather than the presumed emotion expressed by that behavior. Hinde noted that birds often flee after having issued a threat expression. Indeed, the threat display may be a better predictor of flight than of attack. His interpretation was that

threat displays "were given when the bird was uncertain what to do" and that "which of the several possible responses it showed next depended on the behavior of the rival." Hence threat expressions should be understood as "signals in a process of negotiation between individuals" (Hinde, 1985a, p. 109).

Hinde cast doubt on the assumption that "emotional behavior is the outward expression of an emotional state, and that there is a one-to-one correspondence between them," an assumption he associated with Darwin (1872). He also noted that the assumption of a one-to-one correspondence between emotional states and emotional behaviors does not make evolutionary sense, as it may be adaptive for an organism to mislead others about its motivational state. Natural selection will often favor sending nonveridical or ambiguous messages, a point that has also impressed transactional psychologists (Fridlund, 1994, 1997). Hinde acknowledged, however, that signals do not always serve negotiating purposes. His conclusion was that we should expect emotional behaviors to lie on a continuum between expressing and negotiating:

> *Such considerations suggest the view that emotional behavior may lie along a continuum from behaviour that is more or less purely expressive to behaviours concerned primarily with a process of negotiation between individuals. . . . In animals, bird songs lie nearer the expressive end, threat postures nearer the negotiation end. In man, spontaneous and solitary laughter are primarily expressive, the ingratiating smile primarily negotiating. However most emotional expressions involve both. (Hinde, 1985b, p. 989)*

We consider this an important insight. Hinde's suggestion is that many emotional expressions have a nonarbitrary relation to the organism's motivational states, but at the same time are aimed to make a move in a negotiation whose outcome is open ended and crucially dependent on the recipient's responses.

The first thing that is left open by an expressive action is whether the emoter will manifest the action tendency associated with that emotion. This will depend on what affordances are available to the emoter in the local context in which the emotional episode unfolds. Notably, neither the available affordances nor the emoter's intention to act on a particular one of them are pre-ordained at the beginning of the episode, but instead are partially determined by the interactant's responses, which are in turn influenced by the ongoing emotional signals received. Consider, for example, an episode of anger in the context of a marital confrontation, and assume that an action tendency of retribution is associated with anger. There are many ways in which the retributive action tendency could be manifested: sulking, insulting, leaving the house, asking for a divorce, and so on. Conversely, the retributive tendency could be inhibited. Anger can be diffused by emotion management techniques or redirected at another object (e.g., the poverty that may be the external driver of marital discord), or the aroused state of either party could facilitate the emergence of another emotion (e.g., fear of losing one's partner). This flexibility is one of the trademark properties of a large class of emotions, which distinguishes them from reflexlike responses like startle, and perhaps affect programs, whose behavioral consequences are relatively indefeasible.

What determines how a particular episode of anger unfolds is a feedback mechanism that involves the reciprocal exchange of signals delivered by expressions and other behavior in the course of time. The currency of this communication includes fixed stares, loud and high-pitched tones, brisk gestures, a confrontational demeanor, tears, firm declarations, forceful movements, and their strategic opposites (e.g., amicable stares, low-pitched tones, smiles) that will determine if and how anger manifests.

This is where the metaphor of negotiation comes to full fruition, as the anger episode is not exhausted by the interactant's reception of a one-shot message, but is dynamically shaped by how the interactant responds to the initial message, by how the emoter responds to the interactant's response, and so on. This context dependence is entirely

lost if anger is understood only as a response to a certain class of stimulus situations, ignoring the temporal dynamics of its unfolding and the strategy of relationship reconfiguration it embodies.

An emotional expression may also be open ended in a more radical way: in some cases the identity of the initial emotion is shaped by the ongoing process of negotiation. We are accustomed to think of anger as brought about by the appraisal of being slighted, and this is certainly what happens in many cases of anger. But on occasion this appraisal is best understood as the outcome of negotiation in an episode that already has the marks of the emotional (e.g., physiological arousal, focused attention, an urgent tendency to realign one's role in the context of a relationship). What is left partially undetermined and in need of context-dependent disambiguation is what exact emotion one is experiencing. Many marital quarrels begin from small matters of contention, which engage the partners emotionally, but that general emotionality can develop into a variety of distinct emotions. This idea of emotional uncertainty echoes some of the dynamics of threat displays described by Hinde (1985a, 1985b). The bird's confrontation with a rival activates an emotional engagement that is open ended in the sense that at the beginning of the process of negotiation it is undetermined whether the bird is angry or afraid. The identity of the emotion will be shaped through time by the responses received to the threat display. The appraisal that type identifies the emotion does not occur at the beginning of the emotional episode but in the course of it, depending on whether the interaction affords the advantageous manifestation of one emotion rather than the other.

At first blush, a situated perspective on emotions is in tension with the affect-program conception of emotions in the Darwin-Tomkins-Ekman tradition (Darwin, 1872; Ekman, 1972; Tomkins, 1962). In this theoretical tradition, a low-level (modular) appraisal occurs on exposure to certain stimuli and is followed by a cascade of responses, including physiological, expressive, and behavioral ones, which follow the appraisal quickly and automatically. A specific expression is associated with each basic emotion and consequently carries veridical information about what emotion is unfolding. The apparent conflict between affect-program theory and a situated approach, however, can be at least partly defused by noticing that the two approaches operate on different temporal scales. The situated approach focuses on longer emotional episodes that may comprise the activation of affect programs as proper parts. For example, a young man who is suddenly poked in the back while standing in a line will automatically undergo affect program anger, manifested in a reflexlike fashion through forceful turning around, baring of the teeth, and an aggressive action tendency. But there is no obstacle to conceiving of this execution of the anger affect program as part of a longer episode, which includes what happens after the identity of the offender has been determined. It is at this stage that the idea of negotiation acquires explanatory purchase. If the offender is a good-looking young woman who profusely apologizes, the agonistic action tendency is likely to be promptly substituted by an affiliative action tendency. If the offender is another young male, however, a different dynamic emerges, which may lead to an exchange of anger displays and ultimately escalate into a physical fight.

Moreover, a situated approach is not committed to the view that all things we call emotions in ordinary language are social engagements with a negotiating dimension. What we have described are emotions lying toward the negotiating end of the continuum discussed by Hinde, and the vernacular emotion domain contains states and processes on which a situated approach sheds no light, as we discuss subsequently.

6. What Is the Value of the Situated Perspective on Emotion?

In this final section, we illustrate what we take to be the theoretical payoff of a sit-uated perspective and try to diffuse some possible misunderstandings. Let us begin with what we are not saying. We are not claiming that, because the social environment provides dynamic scaffolding for the unfolding of emotional episodes, an emotion literally extends into the environment. This sort of ontological claim may be interesting in principle, but we do not think that its possible heuristic value for the psychology of emotion is likely to be worth the fuss it causes. An extended-emotion thesis potentially confuses the claim that the environment makes a causal contribution to a mental process with the more ontologically demanding claim that it is a constituent part of it (see Adams & Aizawa, this volume). Therefore, until it proves impossible to phrase the substance of the situated perspective in any other way, we will remain neutral on the extended-emotion thesis.

There are other potentially interesting questions we wish to remain neutral about, because we do not think the value of the situated perspective on emotions hinges on how we answer them. For example, it may be debated what sort of externalism about emotions is supported by the data and theory we have presented, or whether group emotions arising through mutual social referencing challenge methodological individualism in the psychology of emotion. We leave it to others to take definitive positions on these issues.

It may forestall another misunderstanding if we state explicitly that the plausibility of the perspective we propose is not hostage to the success of the wider situationist program. The situated perspective on emotion is supported, in so far as it is currently supported, by experimental data and theoretical considerations about the emotions.

The real theoretical payoff of the situated perspective on emotions is methodological. By shifting theoretical focus from the intrapsychic to the interpersonal, from the unbidden to the strategic, from the short lived to the long lived, from the context independent to the context dependent, from the static to the dynamic, the situated perspective points the attention of the research community to aspects of emotions that have been unduly neglected and that may hold the key to understanding the nature and function of a large class of emotions. These aspects of emotion have not been entirely ignored, of course (e.g., Frijda, 1986, and elsewhere; Solomon, 1998), but we think they would have become more central if a broader perspective on the mind suitable to encourage them had been available. We believe that the situated approach can offer such a perspective: the aspects of emotion we have highlighted as worthy of theoretical exploration largely correspond to those the situationist movement has singled out as neglected in classical cognitive science.

We emphasize once again that the situationist perspective is not, in principle, incompatible with other existing theoretical approaches (e.g., neo-Jamesianism, affect-program theory). In part this is a matter of temporal scale of resolution, as outlined in section 5. More importantly, we believe, and have argued extensively in earlier work, that the plurality of states and processes that form the domain of emotion leave emotion theorists with no viable alternative to theoretical pluralism. Griffiths (1997, 2004a) has argued that it is unlikely that all the psychological states and processes that fall under the vernacular category of emotion are sufficiently similar to one another to allow a unified scientific psychology of the emotions. The psychological, neuroscientific, and biological theories that best explain any particular subset of emotions will not adequately explain all emotions. In a slogan, emotion is not a natural kind. Scarantino (2005) has argued that the scientific project of answering questions of the form, What is an emotion? or What is anger? is best understood as a project of explication. Explication involves offering a theoretically motivated precisification of an existing concept. Explications are not good or bad simpliciter but relative to the theoretical objectives that motivate them. Where there is more than one sensible theoretical objective, quarreling about which explication should replace the original concept is simply not to have understood the ground rules of the activity of explicating.

We have suggested that the situated perspective on emotions affords new theoretical leads for the explication of the so-called higher cognitive emotions (e.g., guilt, shame, embarrassment). Although these are the emotions involved in phenomena we are most eager to understand (e.g., morality, art, mental disorders, daily emotional management), they are also among the most complex and challenging of emotional states. Although one of us made extensive use of the phrase "higher cognitive emotions" in earlier work (Griffiths, 1997), we now regard it as potentially confusing (Griffiths, 2004a). First, it suggests that the occurrence of these emotions necessarily involves conceptual thought, a view we have strongly questioned. Second, it seems almost irresistible to align the distinction between basic emotions and higher cognitive emotions with a distinction between two sets of vernacular emotion categories – anger, disgust, and surprise being paradigmatically basic, and guilt, shame, and embarrassment being paradigmatically higher. We believe, however, that there is as much need for pluralism in the theoretical treatment of subordinate categories of emotion as there is in the treatment of the superordinate category of emotion: some instances of anger, disgust, or surprise may be adequately accounted for in the affect program framework, but others may require other theoretical perspectives, and the same holds for episodes of guilt, shame, or embarrassment. The situated perspective on emotion, and the transactional psychology on which we have drawn in describing it, is just one of these theoretical approaches, and it is meant to cut across the dichotomy between basic and higher cognitive emotions as generally understood.

In a nutshell, the situated perspective suggests that certain forms of emotion cannot be understood without expanding our field of view. By confining our attention to neural circuitry or conceptual thought alone, we risk focusing on the proverbial tail of the emotional elephant. Its trunk and body may lie further afield, in the social and cultural environment in which emotional episodes unfold and emotional phenotypes develop.

Acknowledgments

Authors' names are in alphabetical order. We thank Franco and Adriana Scarantino for their hospitality at Pinetina while this chapter was written. Griffiths's work was supported by an Australian Research Council Federation Fellowship. Edouard Machery provided useful feedback on an earlier draft.

Notes

1 For the breadth of current psychological research, see Dalgleish and Power, 1999; Ekman and Davidson, 1994; and Lewis and Haviland-Jones, 2000. Recent philosophical work on emotion is surveyed in Griffiths (2003) and collected in Solomon (2004).

2 The strategic role of the emotions has long been noticed by economists (Frank, 1988; Hirshleifer, 1987). Until recently, however, this recognition was not linked to a new account of the nature of emotions themselves (but see Ross & Dumouchel, 2004). Not surprisingly, behavioral ecologists have also been sensitive to the strategic role of emotions in social interaction (e.g., Fessler & Haley, 2003).

3 The nonconceptual content literature has so far focused primarily on nonconceptual perceptual states, nonconceptual subdoxastic states, and nonconceptual representational states of creatures without language (Bermudéz, 2003). We think emotional phenomena constitute a representational domain of their own, which embodies a yet-to-be-understood brand of nonconceptual content (Griffiths, 2004a, 2004b; Scarantino, 2005).

4 The view that emotions are evaluative judgments has been extensively criticized for these reasons. Its defenders have replied that judgment need not involve full-blown conceptual thought (Nussbaum, 2001, 2004). This risks collapsing cognitivism into the uncontroversial view that emotions are in some sense or other directed at the world (Scarantino, 2005).

5 Fessler (1999) reports that *malu*, the emotion most closely corresponding to Western

shame in the culture he studied, was frequently manifested under these circumstances.

6 The term *engagement* has been previously used to characterize emotions, for example by Parkinson (forthcoming) and by Solomon (2004). This similarity may be explained by the presence in Solomon's cognitivism of a social constructionist strand, related to Sartre's theory of emotions, which emphasizes the active side of emotions along broadly transactionalist lines.

7 There is an evident parallel here with Annette Karmiloff-Smith's (1992) theory of representational redescription.

References

Arnold, M. B. (1960). *Emotion and personality.* New York: Columbia University Press.

Arnold, M. B. (Ed.). (1970). *Feelings and emotions.* San Diego, CA: Academic Press.

Bermudéz, J. (2003). Nonconceptual mental content. In E. N. Zalta (Ed.), *Stanford encyclopedia of philosophy.* Accessed July 9, 2005, from http://plato.stanford.edu

Bjorklund, D. F., & Pellegrini, A. D. (2002). *The origins of human nature: Evolutionary developmental psychology.* Washington, DC: American Psychological Association.

Camras, L. A., Campos, J. J., Oster, H., Miyake, K., & Bradshaw, D. (1992). Japanese and American infants' responses to arm restraint. *Developmental Psychology, 28,* 578–583.

Clark, A. (1997). *Being there: Putting brain, body, and world together again.* Cambridge, MA: MIT Press.

Clark, A., & Chalmers, D. (1998). The extended mind. *Analysis, 58,* 7–19.

Cosmides, L., Tooby, J., & Barkow, J. H. (1992). Introduction: Evolutionary psychology and conceptual integration. In J. H. Barkow, L. Cosmides, & J. Tooby (Eds.), *The adapted mind: Evolutionary psychology and the generation of culture* (pp. 3–15). Oxford: Oxford University Press.

Cussins, A. (1992). Content, embodiment and objectivity: The theory of cognitive trails. *Mind, 101,* 651–688.

Dalgleish, T., & Power, M. J. (Eds.). (1999). *Handbook of cognition and emotion.* Chichester, UK: John Wiley.

Damasio, A. R. (1996). The somatic marker hypothesis and the possible functions of the prefrontal cortex. *Philosophical Transactions of the Royal Society of London B, 351*(1346), 1413–1420.

Damasio, A. R. (1999). *The feeling of what happens: Body and emotion in the making of consciousness.* New York: Harcourt Brace.

Darwin, C. (1872). *The expression of the emotions in man and animals.* New York: Philosophical Library.

Ekman, P. (1972). *Emotion in the human face.* New York: Pergamon Press.

Ekman, P., & Davidson, R. J. (Eds.). (1994). *The nature of emotion: Fundamental questions.* New York: Oxford University Press.

Evans, G. (1982). *The varieties of reference.* Oxford: Oxford University Press.

Fernández-Dols, J. M., & Ruiz-Belda, M.-A. (1997). Spontaneous facial behavior during intense emotional episodes: Artistic truth and optical truth. In J. A. Russell & J. M. Fernández-Dols (Eds.), *The psychology of facial expression* (pp. 255–294). Cambridge: Cambridge University Press.

Fessler, D. M. T. (1999). Toward an understanding of the universality of second-order emotions. In A. L. Hinton (Ed.), *Biocultural approaches to emotions* (pp. 74–116). Cambridge: Cambridge University Press.

Fessler, D. M. T., & Haley, K. J. (2003). The strategy of affect: Emotions in human cooperation. In P. Hammerstein (Ed.), *The genetic and cultural evolution of cooperation* (pp. 7–36). Cambridge, MA: MIT Press.

Fodor, J. A. (1975). *The language of thought.* New York: Crowell.

Fodor, J. A. (1983). *The modularity of mind: An essay in faculty psychology.* Cambridge, MA: Bradford Books/MIT Press.

Frank, R. H. (1988). *Passions within reason: The strategic role of the emotions.* New York: W. W. Norton.

Fridlund, A. J. (1994). *Human facial expression: An evolutionary view.* San Diego, CA: Academic Press.

Fridlund, A. J. (1997). The new ethology of human facial expressions. In J. A. Russell & J. M. Fernández-Dols (Eds.), *The psychology of facial expression* (pp. 103–129). Cambridge: Cambridge University Press.

Fridlund, A. J., Schaut, J. A., Sabini, J. P., Shenker, J. I., Hedlund, L. E., & Knauer, M. J. (1990). Audience effects on solitary faces during imagery: Displaying to the people in your head. *Journal of Nonverbal Behaviour, 14*(2), 113–137.

Frijda, N. H. (1986). *The emotions.* Cambridge: Cambridge University Press.

Griffiths, P. E. (1997). *What emotions really are: The problem of psychological categories.* Chicago: University of Chicago Press.

Griffiths, P. E. (2003). Emotions. In S. Stich & T. Warfield (Eds.), *The Blackwell guide to the philosophy of mind* (pp. 288–308). Oxford and New York: Blackwell.

Griffiths, P. E. (2004a). Is emotion a natural kind? In R. C. Solomon (Ed.), *Thinking about feeling: Contemporary philosophers on emotions* (pp. 233–249). Oxford: Oxford University Press.

Griffiths, P. E. (2004b). Towards a Machiavellian theory of emotional appraisal. In P. Cruse & D. Evans (Eds.), *Emotion, evolution, and rationality* (pp. 89–105). Oxford: Oxford University Press.

Griffiths, P. E., & Stotz, K. (2000). How the mind grows: A developmental perspective on the biology of cognition. *Synthese, 122*(1–2), 29–51.

Hinde, R. A. (1979). *Towards understanding relationships.* London: Academic Press.

Hinde, R. A. (1981). The bases of a science of interpersonal relationships. In S. W. Duck & R. Gilmour (Eds.), *Personal relationships 1: Studying personal relationships* (pp. 1–22). London: Academic Press.

Hinde, R. A. (1985a). Expression and negotiation. In G. Zivin (Ed.), *The development of expressive behavior* (pp. 103–116). New York: Academic Press.

Hinde, R. A. (1985b). Was "the expression of emotions" a misleading phrase? *Animal Behavior, 33*, 985–992.

Hirshleifer, J. (1987). On the emotions as guarantors of threats and promises. In J. Dupré (Ed.), *The latest on the best.* Cambridge, MA: Bradford Books/MIT Press.

Hornik, R., Risenhoover, N., & Gunnar, M. R. (1987). The effects of maternal positive, neutral and negative affective communications on infants' responses to new toys. *Child Development, 58*, 937–944.

Hurley, S. (2003). Animal actions in the space of reasons. *Mind and language, 18*(3), 231–256.

Hutchins, E. (1995). *Cognition in the wild.* Cambridge, MA: MIT Press.

Karmiloff-Smith, A. (1992). *Beyond modularity: A developmental perspective on cognitive science.* Cambridge, MA: MIT Press.

Kraut, R. E., & Johnston, R. E. (1979). Social and emotional messages of smiling: An ethological approach. *Journal of Personality and Social Psychology, 37*, 1539–1553.

Kroon, R. M. (1988). *Aanleidingen en structuur van schuld gevoel.* Unpublished master's thesis, University of Amsterdam, Amsterdam.

Lazarus, R. S. (1991). *Emotion and adaptation.* New York: Oxford University Press.

Leary, M. R., Landel, J. L., & Patton, K. M. (1996). The motivated expression of embarrassment following a self-presentational predicament. *Journal of Personality, 64*(3), 619–636.

LeDoux, J. E. (1993). Emotional networks in the brain. In M. Lewis & J. M. Haviland (Eds.), *Handbook of emotions* (pp. 109–118). New York: Guilford Press.

Lewis, M. (2000). The emergence of human emotions. In M. Lewis & J. M. Haviland-Jones (Eds.), *Handbook of emotions* (2nd ed., pp. 265–280). New York: Guilford Press.

Lewis, M., & Haviland-Jones, J. M. (Eds.). (2000). *Handbook of emotions* (2nd ed.). New York: Guilford Press.

Marks, J. (1982). A theory of emotions. *Philosophical Studies, 42*, 227–242.

Markus, H. R., & Kitayama, S. (1994). The cultural construction of self and emotion: Implications for self and behavior. In S. Kitayama & H. R. Markus (Eds.), *Emotion and culture: Empirical studies of mutual influence* (pp. 89–130). Washington, DC: American Psychological Association.

Marler, P., & Evans, C. (1997). Animal sounds and human faces: Do they have anything in common? In J. A. Russell & J. M. Fernández-Dols (Eds.), *The psychology of facial expression* (pp. 133–226). Cambridge: Cambridge University Press.

Noë, A. (2004). *Action in perception.* Cambridge, MA: MIT Press.

Nussbaum, M. C. (2001). *Upheavals of thought: The intelligence of emotions.* Cambridge: Cambridge University Press.

Nussbaum, M. C. (2004). Emotions as judgments of value and importance. In R. C. Solomon (Ed.), *Thinking about feeling: Contemporary philosophers on emotions* (pp. 183–199). Oxford: Oxford University Press.

Öhman, A. (1999). Distinguishing unconscious from conscious emotional processes: Methodological considerations and theoretical implications. In T. Dalgleish & M. J. Power (Eds.), *Handbook of emotion and cognition* (pp. 321–352). Chichester, UK: John Wiley.

Panksepp, J. (1998). *Affective neuroscience: The foundations of human and animal emotions.* Oxford: Oxford University Press.

Parkinson, B. (1995). *Ideas and realities of emotion.* London: Routledge.

Parkinson, B. (1999). Relations and dissociations between appraisal and emotion ratings of reasonable and unreasonable anger and guilt. *Cognition and Emotion, 13*, 347–385.

Parkinson, B. (forthcoming). *The heart of emotion.* Unpublished manuscript.

Parkinson, B., Fischer, A. H., & Manstead, A. S. R. (2005). *Emotions in social relations: Cultural, group, and interpersonal processes.* New York: Psychology Press.

Parrott, W. G., & Smith, S. F. (1991). Embarrassment: Actual vs. typical cases, classical vs. prototypical representations. *Cognition and Emotion, 5*, 467–488.

Port, R. F., & van Gelder, T. (Eds.). (1995). *Mind as motion: Explorations in the dynamics of cognition.* Cambridge, MA: MIT Press.

Prinz, J. (2004a). Embodied emotions. In R. C. Solomon (Ed.), *Thinking about feeling: Contemporary philosophers on emotions* (pp. 44–59). Oxford: Oxford University Press.

Prinz, J. (2004b). *Gut reactions: A perceptual theory of emotion.* Oxford: Oxford University Press.

Ratner, C. (1989). A social constructionist critique of the naturalistic theory of emotion. *Journal of Mind and Behavior, 10*(3), 211–230.

Reddy, V. (2000). Coyness in early infancy. *Developmental Science, 3*, 186–192.

Ross, D., & Dumouchel, P. (2004). Emotions as strategic signals. *Rationality and Society, 16*(3), 251–286.

Russell, J. A., Bachorowski, J.-A., & Fernández-Dols, J. M. (2003). Facial and vocal expressions of emotions. *Annual Review of Psychology, 54*, 349–359.

Russell, J. A., & Fernández-Dols, J. M. (1997). *The psychology of facial expression.* Cambridge: Cambridge University Press.

Scarantino, A. (2003). Affordances explained. *Philosophy of Science, 70*, 949–961.

Scarantino, A. (2005). *Explicating emotions.* Unpublished Ph.D. dissertation, University of Pittsburgh, Pittsburgh.

Scherer, K. R. (1999). Appraisal theory. In T. Dalgleish & M. J. Power (Eds.), *Handbook of emotion and cognition* (pp. 637–663). Chichester, UK: John Wiley.

Schlichting, C. D., & Pigliucci, M. (1998). *Phenotypic evolution: A reaction norm perspective.* Sunderland, MA: Sinauer.

Smith, B. C. (1999). Situatedness/embeddedness. In R. A. Wilson & F. C. Keil (Eds.), *The MIT encyclopedia of the cognitive sciences* (pp. 769–771). Cambridge, MA: MIT Press.

Solomon, R. C. (1976). *The passions*. New York: Doubleday.

Solomon, R. C. (1993). *The passions* (2nd ed.). New York: Hackett.

Solomon, R. C. (1998). The politics of emotion. In P. A. French & H. K. Wettstein (Eds.), *Midwest Studies in Philosophy*, 22, 1–20.

Solomon, R. C. (Ed.). (2004). *Thinking about feeling: Contemporary philosophers on emotions*. Oxford: Oxford University Press.

Sorce, J. F., Emde, R. N., Campos, J. J., & Klinnert, M. D. (1985). Maternal emotional signalling: Its effect on the visual cliff behaviour of 1 year olds. *Developmental Psychology*, 21, 195–200.

Stein, N. L., Trabasso, T., & Liwag, M. (1993). The representation and organization of emotional experience: Unfolding the emotion episode. In M. Lewis & J. M. Haviland (Eds.), *Handbook of emotions* (pp. 279–300). New York: Guilford Press.

Teasdale, J. D. (1999). Multi-level theories of cognition-emotion relations. In T. Dalgleish & M. J. Power (Eds.), *Handbook of cognition and emotion* (pp. 665–681). Chichester, UK: John Wiley.

Thelen, E., & Smith, L. (1994). *A dynamic systems approach to the development of cognition and action*. Cambridge, MA: MIT Press.

Tomkins, S. S. (1962). *Affect, imagery, and consciousness*. New York: Springer.

West-Eberhard, M. J. (2003). *Developmental plasticity and evolution*. Oxford: Oxford University Press.

CHAPTER 24

The Social Context of Cognition

Eliot R. Smith and Frederica R. Conrey

Cognition almost invariably occurs in the context of other people: the web of face-to-face encounters, personal relationships, and social group memberships that make us who we are. These social entities not only very frequently constitute the content of our thoughts and feelings but also fundamentally shape the processes underlying our cognition and behavior as well. To detail some of the evidence for this broad claim, this chapter describes the interface of situated cognition with social psychology. We make the case that these two fields focus on many of the same empirical and conceptual issues, though sometimes taking different perspectives. Following a brief section that introduces the field of social psychology, the main body of the chapter is organized under four broad principles that we believe capture major areas of overlap and common interest between situated cognition and social psychology.

1. What Is Social Psychology?

Social psychology is a discrete area of theory and research that represents one of the half dozen or so main subdisciplines of psychology (e.g., cognitive, clinical, personality, developmental, social, biological). As such, it has its own scientific journals, conferences, textbooks, traditions, and distinctive foci of interest. The conceptual focus of social psychology is the study of human behavior in its social context, or to put it slightly less concisely, the study of how people's thoughts, feelings, and actions are influenced by the actual or implied presence of other people. Some specific areas of research interest that fall within this definition include the following:

- *Social perception:* How people perceive other individuals, interpret their behaviors, and infer their intentions; the role of social group memberships and group stereotypes in this process; how people perceive themselves and the influence of the self-concept on thoughts, emotions, and social behavior.
- *Social influence:* How people's opinions and behavior are influenced by persuasive messages from others or by conformity processes; how social groups form

norms that in turn regulate group members' behaviors.

- *Social relationships:* How people form close relationships (friendships, romantic attachments) and how relationships affect thoughts, feelings, and behavior; how people cooperate with others in groups that interact to make decisions or perform concrete tasks; when and how people help others or aggress against them.

Social psychology has been greatly influenced by its disciplinary neighbor, cognitive psychology, both in its methodological preference for controlled laboratory experiments as the most highly valued research method and in the focus of most common theories. Social psychological theories for the most part (albeit with important exceptions) are theories about mental processes that underlie the types of social phenomena outlined previously, such as person perception, social influence, and relationship formation. Of course, mental processes relevant to social psychology include not only narrowly cognitive processes such as language comprehension, causal ascription, and problem solving, but also the emotional and motivational processes that loom large when people interact either in friendly or conflictual ways.

With these characteristic interests and approaches, social psychology frequently finds itself pulled in two opposing directions. On the one hand, social psychological theories have frequently been formulated as abstract, disembodied stories about autonomous mental processes, expressed as "boxologies" with little or no concern for adaptiveness in, or even interfaces with, real social environments. This is the very approach whose shortcomings, whether realistically portrayed or caricatured and exaggerated, are so frequently the starting point for rationales and justifications of the situated cognition approach. As an example, consider social psychological research on the effects of stereotypes on person perception. Theorists had long assumed that perception of members of social groups (e.g., women,

Asians) inevitably led to activation of mental representations of generally shared and well-learned stereotypes associated with those groups, just as perception of words naming common concepts automatically leads to activation of those concepts. The activation and application of a stereotype is considered an autonomous cognitive process involving the access and modification of mental representations, taking place within a perceiver who functions as an uninvolved information processor, never actually behaving in the world but simply reporting his or her judgments and opinions. This caricature represents an almost completely nonsituated picture of human cognition.

On the other hand, other forces pull social psychology in exactly the opposite direction, toward consideration of the situated nature of cognition and behavior. The very definition of social psychology states that its ultimate concern is with effects of the social situation or context on cognition and behavior. This focus has kept the field from going too far down the road of focusing on autonomous inner processes. The tendency to boxologize the mind has been tempered by a constant focus on the ways in which personal relationships, group memberships, and our self-perceptions constrain and facilitate our cognition. In its emphasis on flexible processing in a social context, social psychology parallels the situated cognition approach in its focus on cognition as the underpinning of adaptive behavior, and its acknowledgement that thought is produced by the interaction between the organism and its environment. Social psychology already embraces many of the central tenets of the situated cognition approach, so research in social psychology can inform the study of situated cognition more broadly. In the domain of stereotyping, for instance, recent research has demonstrated, in contrast to the earlier picture of autonomous and automatic processes, that stereotype activation depends on the perceiver's active goals and motives. When perceivers have specific reasons to want to know in depth about the other person (Fiske, Neuberg, Beattie, & Milberg, 1987), or when they are motivated to think well or ill of that person (Sinclair & Kunda, 1999), activated stereotypes can be profoundly altered or suppressed. Person perception can thus be viewed as socially adaptive (e.g., Gilbert, 1998) and a product of the motivational context. Stereotyping and other processes unfold in ways that facilitate ongoing social interaction, relationship maintenance, and the accomplishment of the perceiver's social goals in a given social context rather than in fixed and invariant style. This line of research demonstrates the movement in social psychology toward a model of human social cognition as both situated and adaptive, and suggests ways in which research on social cognition might inform our understanding of situated cognition more broadly.

As a way of organizing our description of theory and research within social psychology that pertains to situated cognition, we adopt four major principles advanced by Smith and Semin (2004). These are intended to capture four interrelated and partially overlapping themes that are common to social psychology and situated cognition. The principles are as follows: (1) Cognition is for the adaptive regulation of action, and mental representations are action oriented; (2) cognition is embodied, both constrained and facilitated by our sensorimotor abilities as well as our brains; (3) cognition and action are situated in the sense of being contingent on specific aspects of the agent's social environment; (4) cognition is distributed across brains and the environment and across social agents (e.g., when information is discussed and evaluated in groups). With regard to each of these themes, we briefly review and integrate relevant social psychological research.

2. Cognition Is Action Oriented

Situated cognition offers the key insight that cognition is for adaptive action. Our minds evolved for the on-line control of behavior under the demands of survival rather than for detached puzzle solving or abstract cogitation. This principle implies the existence of close connections among cognition, motivation, and action, connections that have been core topics of study in social psychology. We offer three examples.

1. *Motivation shapes cognition.* Cognition is generally not neutral and detached but biased by the individual's motives and goals. Consider a person's understanding of the meaning of traits (such as reliable, honest, or intelligent), which are basic components of our impressions of other people as well as ourselves. Research shows that our definitions of such traits are not objective and invariant but are shaped in self-serving ways by our own perceived standings on those traits (Dunning & Cohen, 1992). As a second example, consider a person who is a member of two social groups that are stereotyped in opposite ways, such as an African American (poor, unintelligent) and physician (affluent, intelligent). If such an individual delivers praise to a social perceiver, research shows that features of the positive stereotype are automatically activated, whereas the delivery of criticism triggers activation of the negative stereotype (Sinclair & Kunda, 1999). In other words, the motivation to believe praise and disparage criticism tunes and constrains stereotype activation. A third example: Crowe and Higgins (1997) demonstrated that people in a promotion focus, those pursuing achievement, commit more errors of commission than do people in a prevention focus, those pursuing security and responsibility. That is, promotion-focused people are more willing to commit errors of commission in pursuit of hits, and prevention-focused people are more willing to commit errors of omission. Finally, the fundamental human need to belong shapes our social cognition. People experiencing a heightened need to belong, as after a social rejection, tune their attention and cognition to process social information in the environment more carefully and thoroughly (Pickett, Gardner, & Knowles, 2004). These and numerous other examples of biases in cognition caused by the perceiver's motivational concerns effectively illustrate how social cognition serves the needs of adaptive action (Brewer, 1991;

Brewer & Harasty, 1996; Gollwitzer & Bargh, 1996; Higgins & Sorrentino, 1990; Sorrentino & Higgins, 1986).

2. *Time pressure shapes cognition.* Because cognition is for adaptive action, real-world pressures such as time constraints often impinge on cognitive processes. Social psychology has a strong tradition of dual-process models, which specify how and when we use heuristics and biases to achieve cognitive goals with a minimum of effort, and how and when we employ more effortful processing (for a review, see Smith & De-Coster, 2000). Carrying on a conversation, for example, is an instance of social cognition under time pressure – the pragmatic demands of the situation may limit one's ability to ponder as deeply as might be desired. It is important to recognize that, though heuristic processing has sometimes been portrayed as sloppy or intrinsically error prone, it is more fruitfully viewed as adaptive: yielding good-enough results that satisfy pragmatic constraints of real-life, action-demanding situations (Gigerenzer, Todd, & the ABC Research Group, 1999).

3. *Mental representations are action-oriented.* The situated cognition approach suggests that not only cognitive processing styles but also mental representations should be action oriented, tuned to the effective and efficient control of action. Social psychological research has supported this hypothesis as well. The attitude, a mental representation specifying a perceiver's positive or negative evaluation of an object or concept, has been considered perhaps the most characteristic and central construct of the field (Allport, 1954). Examples of attitudes include antipathy toward specific social groups (i.e., prejudice), liking for oneself (i.e., self-esteem), and liking or disliking for consumer products, social policies, or abstract ideas (e.g., tax cuts, abortion rights). Attitudes are fundamentally action-oriented representations: their main function is to tell the perceiver how to relate to or interact with the object – whether to approach or avoid it, praise or blame it, cherish or damage it. Research shows that when people encounter objects toward which they

have strong attitudes, the attitude is automatically activated to color the perception of the object and influence judgments and actions (Fazio, Sanbonmatsu, Powell, & Kardes, 1986).

Our impressions of other people are also action-oriented representations, containing information about how we behave toward or interact with those others (Baldwin, 1992; Carlston, 1994; Holmes, 2000). In fact, different people with whom the perceiver has the same type of relationship tend to be confused with one another in memory – to a greater extent even than different people who share important social characteristics such as age or race – indicating that mental representations of people are structured by the types of actions they call for rather than by their abstract traits or category memberships (Fiske & Haslam, 1996).

In summary, social psychologists have enthusiastically endorsed the notion that cognition is oriented toward adaptive action (Fiske, 1992), and much research has spelled out concrete implications of this principle in such areas as motivated biases in cognition, effects of time pressure on cognitive processes, and the action-oriented nature of attitudes and other mental representations.

3. Cognition Is Embodied

An emphasis on action as the goal of cognitive activity suggests the importance of the body – the vehicle of all action – as a constraint on cognition. Thus, a second major theme of situated cognition is that bodily states and sensorimotor representations play an important role in all cognition. This issue has been explored in at least two domains within social psychology.

1. *Sensorimotor aspects of mental representations.* Attitudes, mental representations involving evaluations of objects, have close connections to sensorimotor systems related to approach and avoidance. For instance, muscle movements involving approach and avoidance have been shown to influence evaluative judgments of novel objects (e.g., Cacioppo, Priester, & Berntson, 1993).

Muscle movements associated with pulling an object closer lead to more positive judgments, while those associated with pushing away lead to negative judgments. Other studies (Neumann & Strack, 2000) present words on a computer screen over a background of a rotating spiral pattern. Rotation in one direction gives an appearance that one is moving toward the screen, and rotation in the other direction generates the appearance of moving away. When the screen appears to be moving closer, people can classify positive words more quickly, and when the screen appears to be moving farther away, negative words receive faster responses. These and similar findings suggest that attitudes or evaluations are not just in the head but involve the perceiver's whole body, being linked to movement toward or away from objects in a real physical sense.

Going beyond attitudes, Schubert (2004) showed that making a fist influences people's automatic processing of words related to the concept of power, suggesting that even such a highly abstract concept involves motoric elements in its representation. Recent research by Livingston and Brewer (2002) as well as by Blair, Judd, Sadler, and Jenkins (2002) shows that stereotyping is not purely a matter of the application of abstract knowledge about the characteristics of various social groups but has strong perceptual elements as well. Stereotypes applied to a given person are affected by that person's continuously varying perceptual attributes (e.g., skin tone, facial features) as well as by his or her discrete category membership.

Finally, in a broad theoretical paper, Niedenthal, Barsalou, Winkielman, Krauth-Gruber, and Ric (2005) apply Barsalou's (1999) model of perceptual symbol systems, sensorimotor-based representations, to various types of representations studied in social psychology, including attitudes, social judgment, and emotions. The perceptual-symbol systems model proposes that knowledge is represented by perceptual simulators: mechanisms in the mind that simulate multiple variations on the perceptual experience associated with a cognitive object. For instance, the system stores information about the perceptual experience of a cat's purr, the feeling of its fur, the appearance of its movements, and so on, and can reproduce the core aspects of these experiences in the mind to afford categorization, imagination, planning, and so on. Barrett (2006) offers a more detailed and specific account of how embodied conceptual knowledge combines with affective states to produce the experience of emotion, also applying Barsalou's model.

2. *Perception-behavior links.* William James (1890) was among the first in psychology to study the ideomotor or perception-behavior link. Recent work in diverse areas of psychology and neuroscience, at both the neural (Rizzolatti & Arbib, 1998) and the behavioral (Dimberg, Thunberg, & Elmehed, 2000) levels, confirms that motor processes are integral to perception. Within social psychology, research suggests that subtle activation of a concept such as politeness through reading words related to that concept actually influences people's overt behavior, making them act more polite. In a similar way, exposure to the concept of the elderly causes people to walk more slowly – that is, to behave in a way that is consistent with stereotypes about that social group (Bargh, Chen, & Burrows, 1996). People naturally tend to imitate the expressive or incidental behaviors of other people when they interact with them, and this type of imitation generally leads to increased liking (Chartrand & Bargh, 1999). All these effects show that action-oriented representations of behaviors are recruited as we perceive other people. In other words, we use our bodies in the process of social perception.

4. Cognition Is Situated

Cognition has sometimes been understood as implemented by abstract, amodal informational processes that proceed within an organism, isolated from the larger context except for a narrow set of defined inputs and outputs. The situated cognition approach, of course, rejects this picture of autonomous, context-free inner processes in favor of a view of an organism as involved in intensive moment-to-moment interaction with its environment. As we discussed previously, the physical body plays an important role in constraining and affording social cognition, but other aspects of the immediate physical and psychological environment are also important. Again, social psychology, by definition, is concerned with the influence of the situation on cognition. However, a view of cognition as infinitely flexible and responsive to the situation lacks predictive power, unless we can identify those features of the environment that are most important in determining the course of cognition. Social psychology's perspective suggests that many of the most important features of the cognitive context are not physical but social. The immediate, interactive conversational context, our relationships with other individuals, and our broader memberships in social groups represent three levels of interpersonal context in which cognition and action are situated.

1. *Communicative context.* Because social interaction is so complex and so fundamental to our experience, the immediate context, whether we are physically alone or with others, is often a communicative context. As a result, some of the most pervasive and most impactful factors that shape our cognition are norms of communication. Extremely subtle situational cues, if they signal communicative relevance of different contents, have been found to influence behavior and cognition. In social psychology, one well-replicated finding is that people explain others' behavior in terms of the actors' inner personality characteristics, wants, or beliefs rather than in terms of the demands of social situations (Gilbert, 1998). This tendency has been viewed as automatic, fundamental, linked to the properties of abstract mental processes (Ross, 1977). Yet in one experiment, participants asked to provide causal explanations for a social event on a questionnaire headed "Institute for Personality Research" provided more personal and fewer situational explanations than did participants asked to explain the same phenomena for the "Institute for Social

Research" (Norenzayan & Schwarz, 1999). These participants provided explanations that were relevant in the specific social context: a communication with a particular type of researcher. The cooperative norms of communication (Grice, 1975) require a constantly evolving representation of the goals of the self and of the other people in the interaction. A smooth completion of the interaction relies on the participants' ability to attend to the context and to select and provide situationally appropriate contributions.

2. *Relational context.* Beyond general communicative norms, our relationships with specific individuals have important implications for how we process social information. Research on close relationships, for instance, reveals the somewhat unsurprising result that we tend to idealize our close others. People's perceptions of their partners' attributes are closer to the attributes they believe would be ideal than to their partners' actual attributes as indicated by the partner's own self-reports. This bias is socially adaptive: the more we idealize our partners – the more inaccurate we are in perceiving their characteristics – the more satisfied we are with our relationships (Murray, Holmes, & Griffin, 1996). We defend our relationships not only by thinking of our partners as better than they are but also by thinking of our alternatives as worse than they are. For example, students in committed heterosexual relationships rate opposite-sex targets as less attractive than do their single counterparts (Simpson, Gangestad, & Lerma, 1990).

Personal relationships regulate cognitive and behavioral processes in other ways as well. Just as owners come to resemble their dogs (Roy & Christenfeld, 2004), we come to resemble our partners psychologically. People tend to choose romantic partners and friends who are already similar to themselves (Luo & Klohnen, 2005), and they also tend to grow closer to their significant others in their attitudes (Davis & Rusbult, 2001). We are also much more likely to be persuaded by people we like than by people we dislike (Cialdini, 1993).

Although they have been intensively studied, romantic relationships are not the only relationships that influence cognition. In fact, all the people we interact with affect us in some way. Romantic relationships are generally positive and lasting, but more immediate and less positive relationships, such as power relationships, also influence cognition. White women assigned the role of superior in a group interaction with African American women exhibit more racial bias than do white women assigned to the subordinate role (Richeson & Ambady, 2003). Positions in the power hierarchy with respect to other individuals affect not only how we think of them but also how we act toward them. These findings illustrate how cognition and action are influenced not only by the physical context in which we perform them but also by the specific individuals with whom we perform them.

3. *Group context.* The point that our place in the social context is fundamental to our cognition is further emphasized by the extensive literature on effects of social group memberships. The social context is made up not only of our relationships with specific others but also the groups we identify with (Turner, Hogg, Oakes, Reicher, & Wetherell, 1987), termed *social identities*. Social groups establish norms, or standards for correct and appropriate beliefs, opinions, and behaviors. For example, it may be appropriate to talk about one's salary woes among a group of friends but not with coworkers. Other norms dictate that men and women ought to differ in their interest in sports or their emotional expressiveness. Such norms influence our behavior all the time, whether or not other members of the groups are physically present. When a social identity is activated by situational reminders of membership or by our own intentional thought, we tend to conform to that group's norms. For example, Baldwin, Carrell, and Lopez (1990) studied Roman Catholic college students and found that their attitudes and behaviors reported when a photo of the pope was visible on the wall were more consistent with their religious norms, compared to those of similar students who reported them when no photo was present. Our important group memberships, potentially activated by subtle situational cues, regulate our social attitudes and behavior.

Social identities serve as much more than guides to our own appropriate behavior, however. Because an identity is a group membership that we share with some people but not others, it divides the world into us and them, and shapes how we think about and behave toward other people. People on the "us" side of the line, fellow group members, become better liked (Mullen, Brown, & Smith, 1992). We make positive attributions for their behaviors (Pettigrew, 1979), and we treat them better – more fairly and altruistically (Turner et al., 1987). Furthermore, just as we tend to think like our significant relationship partners, we tend to think like members of our in-groups. We are more easily persuaded by in-group than by out-group members (Mackie, Worth, & Asuncion, 1990), and we share emotions (Smith, 1993) and attitudes (Norton, Monin, Cooper, & Hogg, 2003) with members of the in-group. We also assume that they are similar to us (Robbins & Krueger, 2005).

People on the "them" side, out-group members, are seen as homogenous (Judd & Park, 1988) and as quite different from us (Robbins & Krueger, 2005). They are also seen as competitors rather than cooperators and are likely to become the targets of discrimination (Brewer, 1979). Both being a member of an in-group (Tesser, 1988), and discriminating against an out-group can make us feel better about ourselves (Rubin & Hewstone, 1998). Thus, any activated social identity is an aspect of the social situation that can have profound consequences for how we think and behave, and how we treat the people we interact with. Importantly, other group members need not be physically present for our in-group identities to form an important, perhaps a fundamental, part of the social context in which our cognition and behavior are situated.

Cognition is situated; sometimes this is taken to mean that it is almost infinitely flexible and responsive to the physical and psychological context. This flexibility sometimes makes it difficult to predict exactly how the infinitely variable context will change how we think and behave. A social psychological perspective identifies precisely which features of the environment are particularly important (those that are relevant to immediate conversational contexts, ongoing interpersonal relationships, or social group memberships) and allows understanding of how those features shape cognition and action.

5. Cognition Is Distributed

Our final theme is that cognition is distributed: not contained within minds, but implemented by systems that link minds with aspects of the physical and social environment. In other words, cognition is often enabled by information-processing loops that pass through the outside world as well as the mind, via perceptual and motor processes. One familiar illustration of distributed cognition is the fact that most of us would have great difficulty multiplying two three-digit numbers in our heads, but do it with ease given a pencil and paper. As we manipulate symbols, these external resources become part of an overall cognitive system, functioning as memory storage, offering cues for what digits to process next, and so on.

Treatments of distributed cognition, like this example, have typically focused on how cognition is enabled and scaffolded by features of the physical environment. For example, Kirsch (1995) discussed ways in which we use space to facilitate cognitive performance, and Hutchins (1995b) focused on how pilots' perceptual systems and minds interact with the design and layout of cockpit instruments to track the speed of airplanes. Although some work arising from the situated cognition tradition has examined the way cognition is shared across teams (Hutchins, 1991), group interaction and decision making has been a central focus of research within social psychology. And in reality, while cognition can certainly be

distributed across objects and the physical environment, much of our distributed cognition is actually distributed across other people. Such a distribution occurs whenever people establish and maintain a socially shared system of meaning. Although this idea has taken many forms in social psychology (for a review, see Thompson & Fine, 1999), the idea that people use symbols such as language to facilitate interaction, and that meanings are dynamically constructed and shared in groups, have been driving forces in the study of group cognition in recent years.

1. Distributed cognition in groups. Modern societies rely on committees such as boards, juries, and management teams to do a great deal of their important thinking: making decisions, managing projects, and developing new ideas. This reliance reflects the idea that group cognition should always be more effective than individual cognition: members of a committee can correct one another's errors, recall relevant information that others cannot, and in general reach more adaptive final decisions. Yet research shows that group performance is frequently worse than that of an equal number of individuals working independently (Levine & Moreland, 1998). What properties of socially distributed cognition account for this pattern? Might distributed cognition offer advantages in any situation? In fact, the literature on group performance has demonstrated that individual minds and interacting groups display many similar properties.

One broad conclusion is that groups tend to show enhanced versions of the very same biases that affect individuals (Hinsz, Tindale, & Vollrath, 1997). Individuals tend to ignore base rate information, overrely on information about representativeness (Argote, Devadas, & Melone, 1990), and escalate commitment to an action once it has been chosen (Whyte, 1993), but all of these effects tend to be even stronger in groups than in individuals. Individuals also tend to demonstrate a confirmation bias in information processing: they particularly like and attend to information that is consistent with the information or opinions they already have (e.g., Frey, 1986).

Similarly, groups have a tendency to attend more to members whose opinions are consistent with the group's existing opinion. The impact of each member's opinion decreases as a function of the distance between that opinion and the average opinion of the group (Davis, 1996). Ultimately this process can lead to a destructive uniformity of opinions within the group, to the disregard of relevant evidence, possibly leading to what has been termed *groupthink* (Janis, 1997). The difference between group thinking and individual thinking, then, is generally a matter of degree. Rather than groups being able to correct individual biases, the general findings suggest that groups exaggerate those biases.

Gigone and Hastie (1997) offer a different perspective that also suggests groups and individuals can be thought of in fundamentally similar ways. In their model, individuals come to a group discussion with specific items of evidence or information relevant to a decision, and function as information integrators, combining the implications of those items to arrive at their individual opinions. In turn, group discussion of the issue allows the individual opinions to be integrated into the overall group decision. Gigone and Hastie (1997) do not find that group discussion adds any extra value or emergent quality to the group decision, besides the simple integration of individual opinions. Their studies show that the effects of informational items on the final group decisions are entirely mediated by the opinions of the individual members before any discussion took place. Like the research on biases discussed previously, this research suggests that there is little qualitative difference between individual and group-based cognition, with both functioning essentially as simple information integrators.

2. Distributed memory in groups. Despite the fact that cognition distributed across groups is not necessarily better or more accurate than individual cognition, there is no denying that we do distribute our cognition across other people all the time. Rather than remembering things for ourselves, many of us store information about who knows information or has skills that we might need. In effect, we keep much of our memory in other people's heads. Wegner (1986) called this phenomenon "transactive memory." Transactive memory has been demonstrated to have important consequences for group performance. For example, training groups together so that they form a robust transactive memory system tends to lead to better group performance, compared to training group members separately and then bringing them together (Moreland & Myaskovsky, 2000). Transactive memory thus represents one potential mechanism by which groups might be able to attain better performance than a similar number of isolated individuals, if its benefits outweigh the increased processing biases characteristic of group cognition.

Our understanding of group-level cognition obviously owes much to our knowledge of individual-level cognition. But the reverse is equally true: distributed cognition, or cognition in groups, has important implications for individual-level cognition. In humans, conscious thought shares important features with group discussion. First, it is mediated and structured by language and therefore is influenced by the socially shared meaning inherent in our linguistic structures. Second, intrapersonal thinking, like conversation, is temporally constrained; just as only one person in a group can express an idea at once, we can only explicitly think one thing at a time. Finally and most important, it has been argued that individual-level thought follows developmentally from interpersonal communication, which is prior and primary (Vygotsky, 1962/1986). Socially distributed cognition precedes conscious reasoning, so thinking (holding conversations with ourselves) owes much to our ability to have conversations with other people. From this perspective, it is less insightful to say that group cognition is like individual cognition than it is to observe that individual thinking is a lot like thinking in groups. Extending our understanding of how distributed cognition operates between people should inform our understanding of individual thought.

6. Conclusion

As we hope this chapter has made clear, the topics studied by social psychologists overlap to a considerable degree with those that have interested researchers in the situated cognition perspective. The four themes that organized the discussion in this chapter reflect major points of convergence and agreement between these two areas. The two areas also share historical roots. The fundamental ideas of the situated cognition movement go back in various forms to Dewey, Mead, and particularly William James and Frederick Bartlett. These same individuals are considered as important forebears of social psychology, precisely because of the similar concerns of that field with the social situation and its effects on cognition and behavior.

Nevertheless, despite this convergence of interests, it is striking how little interchange there has been between these two areas to date. For example, Edwin Hutchins (a cognitive anthropologist) insightfully described distributed cognition in a navigation team (1995a), but totally without citations to highly relevant work from social psychology on group processes, team performance, or transactive memory. Many similar examples exist of researchers from cognitive science, anthropology, or other disciplinary areas investigating topics such as those discussed in this chapter, evidently without realizing that extensive, highly applicable bodies of theory and empirical findings exist within social psychology. On the other side of the fence, social psychologists often continue to develop and apply abstract, disembodied, nonsituated information processing models, with little evident awareness of the powerful critiques of such models that have been offered within the situated cognition movement.

A few instances of productive interchange between these fields are beginning to emerge. Semin and Smith (2002) and Smith and Semin (2004) offered descriptions of the overlapping interests of the fields, and as noted previously, specific models deriving from situated cognition (e.g., Barsalou's model of simulators as mental representations) are currently being applied within social psychology (Barrett, 2006; Niedenthal et al., 2005). Increased interchange of this sort seems highly desirable in view of the two fields' similar substantive and conceptual concerns.

Social psychology may offer one insight above all others to readers interested in situated cognition. That is its emphasis on the social context of behavior – the fact that human behavior in general takes place in, and is adapted to, a rich and complex network of group memberships, personal relationships, social motives, and the socially constituted self. This view represents a valuable supplement to the typical focus on behavior as situated in the physical environment (e.g., Kirsh, 1995). Finally and more concretely, the bodies of empirical and theoretical work in social psychology reviewed in this chapter may be helpful in enriching researchers' thinking about the nature of situated cognition in general.

References

Allport, G. W. (1954). *The nature of prejudice*. Oxford, UK: Addison-Wesley.

Argote, L., Devadas, R., & Melone, N. (1990). The base-rate fallacy: Contrasting processes and outcomes of group and individual judgment. *Organizational Behavior and Human Decision Processes*, 46(2), 296–310.

Baldwin, M. W. (1992). Relational schemas and the processing of social information. *Psychological Bulletin*, 112(3), 461–484.

Baldwin, M. W., Carrell, S. E., & Lopez, D. F. (1990). Priming relationship schemas: My advisor and the pope are watching me from the back of my mind. *Journal of Experimental Social Psychology*, 26(5), 435–454.

Bargh, J. A., Chen, M., & Burrows, L. (1996). Automaticity of social behavior: Direct effects of trait construct and stereotype activation on action. *Journal of Personality and Social Psychology*, 71(2), 230–244.

Barrett, L. F. (2006). Solving the emotion paradox: Categorization and the experience of emotion. *Personality and Social Psychology Review*, 10, 20–46.

Barsalou, L. W. (1999). Perceptual symbol systems. *Behavioral and Brain Sciences*, 22, 577–600.

Blair, I. V., Judd, C. M., Sadler, M. S., & Jenkins, C. (2002). The role of Afrocentric features in person perception: Judging by features and categories. *Journal of Personality and Social Psychology*, 83(1), 5–25.

Brewer, M. B. (1979). In-group bias in the minimal intergroup situation: A cognitive-motivational analysis. *Psychological Bulletin*, 86(2), 307–324.

Brewer, M. B. (1991). The social self: On being the same and different at the same time. *Personality and Social Psychology Bulletin*, 17(5), 475–482.

Brewer, M. B., & Harasty, A. S. (1996). Seeing groups as entities: The role of perceiver motivation. In R. M. Sorrentino & E. T. Higgins (Eds.), *Handbook of motivation and cognition: The interpersonal context* (Vol. 3, pp. 347–370). New York: Guilford Press.

Cacioppo, J. T., Priester, J. R., & Berntson, G. G. (1993). Rudimentary determinants of attitudes: II. Arm flexion and extension have differential effects on attitudes. *Journal of Personality and Social Psychology*, 65(1), 5–17.

Carlston, D. E. (1994). Associated systems theory: A systematic approach to cognitive representations of persons. In R. S. J. Wyer (Ed.), *Associated systems theory: A systematic approach to cognitive representations of persons* (Vol. 7, pp. 1–78). Hillsdale, NJ: Lawrence Erlbaum.

Chartrand, T. L. & Bargh, J. A. (1999). The chameleon effect: The perception-behavior link and social interaction. *Journal of Personality and Social Psychology*, 76, 893–910.

Cialdini, R. B. (1993). *Influence: Science and practice* (3rd ed.). New York: HarperCollins College.

Crowe, E., & Higgins, E. T. (1997). Regulatory focus and strategic inclinations: Promotion and prevention in decision-making. *Organizational Behavior and Human Decision Processes*, 69, 117–132.

Davis, J. H. (1996). Small-group research and the Steiner questions: The once and future thing. In E. H. Witte & J. H. Davis (Eds.), *Understanding group behavior: Consensual action by small groups* (Vol. 1, pp. 3–12). Hillsdale, NJ: Lawrence Erlbaum.

Davis, J. L., & Rusbult, C. E. (2001). Attitude alignment in close relationships. *Journal of Personality and Social Psychology*, 81(1), 65–84.

Dimberg, U., Thunberg, M., & Elmehed, K. (2000). Unconscious facial reactions to emotional facial expressions. *Psychological Science*, 11(1), 86–89.

Dunning, D., & Cohen, G. L. (1992). Egocentric definitions of traits and abilities in social judgment. *Journal of Personality and Social Psychology*, 63(3), 341–355.

Fazio, R. H., Sanbonmatsu, D. M., Powell, M. C., & Kardes, F. R. (1986). On the automatic activation of attitudes. *Journal of Personality and Social Psychology*, 50(2), 229–238.

Fiske, A. P., & Haslam, N. (1996). Social cognition is thinking about relationships. *Current Directions in Psychological Science*, 5(5), 137–142.

Fiske, S. T. (1992). Thinking is for doing: Portraits of social cognition from daguerreotype to laserphoto. *Journal of Personality and Social Psychology*, 63(6), 877–889.

Fiske, S. T., Neuberg, S. L., Beattie, A. E., & Milberg, S. J. (1987). Category-based and attribute-based reactions to others: Some informational conditions of stereotyping and individuating processes. *Journal of Experimental Social Psychology*, 23(5), 399–427.

Frey, D. (1986). Recent research on selective exposure to information. *Advances in Experimental Social Psychology*, 19, 41–80.

Gigerenzer, G., Todd, P. M., & the ABC Research Group. (1999). *Simple heuristics that make us smart*. New York: Oxford University Press.

Gigone, D., & Hastie, R. (1997). The impact of information on small group choice. *Journal of Personality and Social Psychology*, 72, 132–140.

Gilbert, P. (1998). The evolved basis and adaptive functions of cognitive distortions. *British Journal of Medical Psychology*, 71(4), 447–463.

Gollwitzer, P. M., & Bargh, J. A. (Eds.). (1996). *The psychology of action: Linking cognition and motivation to behavior*. New York: Guilford Press.

Grice, H. P. (1975). Logic and conversation. In P. Cole & J. L. Morgan (Eds.), *Syntax and semantics* (Vol. 3, pp. 44–58). New York: Academic Press.

Higgins, E. T., & Sorrentino, R. M. (1990). *Handbook of motivation and cognition: Foundations of social behavior* (Vol. 2). New York: Guilford Press.

Hinsz, V. B., Tindale, R. S., & Vollrath, D. A. (1997). The emerging conceptualization of groups as information processes. *Psychological Bulletin*, 121, 43–64.

Holmes, J. (2000). Social relationships: The nature and function of relational schemas. *European Journal of Social Psychology*, 30, 447–497.

Hutchins, E. (1991). The social organization of distributed cognition. In L. B. Resnick & J. M. Levine (Eds.), *Perspectives on socially shared cognition* (pp. 283–307). Washington, DC: American Psychological Association.

Hutchins, E. (1995a). *Cognition in the wild*. Cambridge, MA: MIT Press.

Hutchins, E. (1995b). How a cockpit remembers its speeds. *Cognitive Science*, 19(3), 265–288.

James, W. (1890). *The principles of psychology*. Oxford, UK: Holt.

Janis, I. L. (1997). Groupthink. In R. P. Vecchio (Ed.), *Leadership: Understanding the dynamics of power and influence in organizations* (pp. 163–176). Notre Dame, IN: University of Notre Dame Press.

Judd, C. M., & Park, B. (1988). Out-group homogeneity: Judgments of variability at the individual and group levels. *Journal of Personality and Social Psychology*, 54(5), 778–788.

Kirsh, D. (1995). The intelligent use of space. *Artificial intelligence*, 73, 31–68.

Levine, J. M., & Moreland, R. L. (1998). Small groups. In D. T. Gilbert, S. T. Fiske, & G. Lindzey (Eds.), *Handbook of social psychology* (4th ed., Vol. 2, pp. 415–469). Boston: McGraw-Hill.

Livingston, R. W., & Brewer, M. B. (2002). What are we really priming? Cue-based versus category-based processing of facial stimuli. *Journal of Personality and Social Psychology*, 82(1), 5–18.

Luo, S., & Klohnen, E. (2005). Associative mating and marital quality in newlyweds: A couple-centered approach. *Journal of Personality and Social Psychology*, 88, 268–278.

Mackie, D. M., Worth, L. T., & Asuncion, A. G. (1990). The processing of persuasive in-group messages. *Journal of Personality and Social Psychology*, 58, 812–822.

Moreland, R. L., & Myaskovsky, L. (2000). Explaining the performance benefits of group training: Transactive memory or improved communication? *Organizational Behavior and Human Decision Processes*, 82, 117–133.

Mullen, B., Brown, R., & Smith, C. (1992). Ingroup bias as a function of salience, relevance, and status: An integration. *European Journal of Social Psychology*, 22(2), 103–122.

Murray, S. L., Holmes, J. G., & Griffin, D. W. (1996). The self-fulfilling nature of positive illusions in romantic relationships: Love is not blind, but prescient. *Journal of Personality and Social Psychology*, 71(6), 1155–1180.

Neumann, R., & Strack, F. (2000). Approach and avoidance: The influence of proprioceptive and exteroceptive cues on encoding of affective information. *Journal of Personality and Social Psychology*, 79(1), 39–48.

Niedenthal, P. M., Barsalou, L. W., Winkielman, P., Krauth-Gruber, S., & Ric, F. (2005). Embodiment in attitudes, social perception, and emotion. *Personality and Social Psychology Review*, 9, 184–211.

Norenzayan, A., & Schwarz, N. (1999). Telling what they want to know: Participants tailor causal attributions to researchers' interests. *European Journal of Social Psychology*, 29(8), 1011–1020.

Norton, M. I., Monin, B., Cooper, J., & Hogg, M. A. (2003). Vicarious dissonance: Attitude change from the inconsistency of others. *Journal of Personality and Social Psychology*, 85(1), 47–62.

Pettigrew, T. F. (1979). The ultimate attribution error: Extending Allport's cognitive analysis of prejudice. *Personality and Social Psychology Bulletin*, 5(4), 461–476.

Pickett, C. L., Gardner, W. L., & Knowles, M. (2004). Getting a cue: The need to belong and enhanced sensitivity to social cues. *Personality and Social Psychology Bulletin*, 30, 1095–1107.

Richeson, J. A., & Ambady, N. (2003). Effects of situational power on automatic racial prejudice. *Journal of Experimental Social Psychology*, 39(2), 177–183.

Rizzolatti, G., & Arbib, M. A. (1998). Language within our grasp. *Trends in Neurosciences*, 21(5), 188–194.

Robbins, J. M., & Krueger, J. (2005). Social projection to ingroups and outgroups: A review and meta-analysis. *Personality and Social Psychology Review*, 9, 32–47.

Ross, L. (1977). The intuitive psychologist and his shortcomings: Distortions in the attribution process. In L. Berkowitz (Ed.), *Advances in experimental social psychology* (Vol. 10, pp. 174–221). New York: Academic Press.

Roy, M. M., & Christenfeld, N. J. S. (2004). Do dogs resemble their owners? *Psychological Science*, 15(5), 361–363.

Rubin, M., & Hewstone, M. (1998). Social identity theory's self-esteem hypothesis: A review and some suggestions for clarification. *Personality and Social Psychology Review*, 2(1), 40–62.

Schubert, T. W. (2004). The power in your hand: Gender differences in bodily feedback from making a fist. *Personality and Social Psychology Bulletin*, 30(6), 757–769.

Semin, G. R., & Smith, E. R. (2002). Interfaces of social psychology with situated and embodied cognition. *Cognitive Systems Research*, 3, 385–396.

Simpson, J. A., Gangestad, S. W., & Lerma, M. (1990). Perception of physical attractiveness: Mechanisms involved in the maintenance of romantic relationships. *Journal of Personality and Social Psychology*, 59(6), 1192–1201.

Sinclair, L., & Kunda, Z. (1999). Reactions to a black professional: Motivated inhibition and activation of conflicting stereotypes. *Journal of Personality and Social Psychology*, 77(5), 885–904.

Smith, E. R. (1993). Social identity and social emotions: Toward new conceptualizations of prejudice. In D. M. Mackie & D. L. Hamilton (Eds.), *Affect, cognition, and stereotyping: Interactive processes in group perception* (pp. 297–315). San Diego, CA: Academic Press.

Smith, E. R., & DeCoster, J. (2000). Dual-process models in social and cognitive psychology: Conceptual integration and links to underlying memory systems. *Personality and Social Psychology Review*, 4(2), 108–131.

Smith, E. R., & Semin, G. R. (2004). Socially situated cognition: Cognition in its social context.

Advances in Experimental Social Psychology, 36, 53–117.

Sorrentino, R. M., & Higgins, E. T. (1986). *Handbook of motivation and cognition: Foundations of social behavior*. New York: Guilford Press.

Tesser, A. (1988). Toward a self-evaluation maintenance model of social behavior. In L. Berkowitz (Ed.), *Advances in experimental social psychology* (Vol. 21, pp. 181–227). San Diego, CA: Academic Press.

Thompson, L., & Fine, G. A. (1999). Socially shared cognition, affect, and behavior: A review and integration. *Personality and Social Psychology Review*, 3(4), 278–302.

Turner, J. C., Hogg, M. A., Oakes, P. J., Reicher, S. D., & Wetherell, M. S. (1987). *Rediscovering the social group: A self-categorization theory*. Cambridge, MA: Blackwell.

Vygotsky, L. (1986). *Language and thought*. Cambridge, MA: MIT Press. (Originally published 1962)

Wegner, D. M. (1986). Transactive memory: A contemporary analysis of the group mind. In B. Mullen & G. R. Goethals (Eds.), *Theories of group behavior* (pp. 185–208). New York: Springer-Verlag.

Whyte, G. (1993). Escalating commitment in individual and group decision making: A prospect theory approach. *Organizational Behavior and Human Decision Processes*, 54(3), 430–455.

CHAPTER 25

Cognition for Culture

Felix Warneken and Michael Tomasello

Organisms inherit their environments as much as they inherit their genes. Indeed, biological adaptations come into existence ontogenetically "expecting" a certain environment: fish are born with fins, expecting water; bats are born with sonar, expecting caves. Some organisms even modify their environments, and then their progenitors biologically adapt to the new environment (so-called niche construction; Odling-Smee, Laland, & Feldman, 2003). For example, ants have evolved various skills for living in the anthills that they (i.e., their forebears) have built.

Human beings are big-time niche constructors, of course, with the added twist that different groups of humans construct very different niches (a.k.a. cultures), and so the species as a whole cannot be adapted to a particular constructed environment ahead of time. The solution is flexible learning and cognitive skills that enable individuals to acquire information locally and to make decisions based on that information without micromanagement from Mother Nature. This typically requires a long period of immaturity so that the young can learn about and explore the environment while still under the protection of parents (Bruner, 1972). Within this general learning-life-history strategy, some species also develop skills of social learning that enable individuals to take advantage of the knowledge and skills of group mates when that is to their benefit as well (Boyd & Richerson, 1985). Humans rely on learning and social learning perhaps more than any other species, and this both enables their unique form of cultural organization and is an adaptation to it.

What all of this adds up to is an observation banal in behavioral biology but not sufficiently appreciated in cognitive psychology: it makes no sense to speak of cognitive skills independent of the environmental contexts within which they evolved and operate. With specific reference to humans, our proposal here is that most, if not all, of the unique features of human cognition evolved as adaptations to humans' unique form of cultural organization, that is, as adaptations to a self-constructed niche involving cooperative social practices with group mates and their material and symbolic artifacts. Clearly this is not all there is to human cognition, as many human skills evolved in the context of such things as foraging (e.g., skills of object recognition, manipulation, categorization, and quantification), and other human skills evolved in the context of competitive interactions with group mates over food, mates, and other resources (e.g., the understanding of goal-directed action). However, our argument is that humans have also evolved some unique cognitive skills for cooperating and communicating with others culturally. That is, humans are adapted for special kinds of cooperative and communicative interactions that require them to take multiple perspectives on things, and ultimately, through some kind of internalization process, to develop so-called perspectival cognitive representations – which are taken for granted in cognitive psychology but are actually unique in the animal kingdom (Tomasello, 1999).

In this chapter, we argue and provide evidence for this view of the evolution of the unique features of human cognition and culture. After a brief evolutionary introduction, we do this, first, by looking closely at the process of human cognitive development, especially in its early social and cultural aspects, and then by comparing human social-cognitive skills to those of our nearest primate relatives, the great apes, who share some but not all of our skills for navigating through a complex social world.

1. Primate and Human Social Cognition and Learning

Nonhuman primates are intensely competitive creatures, and so they have evolved uniquely complex social-cognitive skills for competing with group mates for food, mates, and other valued resources. Following Humphrey (1976), the social cognition of primates has been characterized by appellations such as primate politics (de Waal, 1982) and Machiavellian intelligence (Byrne & Whiten, 1988). This competitive orientation becomes especially clear when we look at experiments aimed at testing nonhuman primates' theory of mind.

Chimpanzees and other primates have failed all sorts of experiments testing their ability to determine the perceptions, intentions, and beliefs of others (for overviews, see Povinelli, Bering, & Giambrone, 2000; Tomasello & Call, 1997). For example, they did not seem to take the visual perception of others into account as they indiscriminately begged for food from humans who either could or could not see them (Povinelli & Eddy, 1996), and they did not understand a human's communicative intention to indicate the location of hidden food by looking and pointing at it (for an overview, see Call & Tomasello, 2005). Importantly, in all of these studies, the chimpanzees interacted with a cooperative experimenter who would provide (rather than hide) information and act for (rather than against) them. However, these cooperative situations might not come as naturally to them as they come to humans. Consequently, Hare (2001) proposed that the chimpanzee mind is especially adapted for competitive encounters and will thus demonstrate its peak performance in competitive rather than cooperative situations. Thus, when Hare and colleagues placed a dominant and a subordinate chimpanzee in competition over food – with some pieces of food visible to both individuals and some only to the subordinate – the subordinates were more likely to go for the food that was hidden from the dominant's view (Hare, Call, Agnetta, & Tomasello, 2000; Hare, Call, & Tomasello, 2001). Relatedly, chimpanzees also try to conceal their own approach to contested food by selecting paths on which the competitor cannot see or hear them when they steal the food (Hare, Call, & Tomasello, 2006; Melis, Call, & Tomasello, 2006). Thus, chimpanzees can interpret what others see and how that affects their intentional actions (see also Call, Hare, Carpenter, & Tomasello, 2004) but mainly in the context of competitive social interactions. Taken together, these and a number of other studies provide evidence that chimpanzees actually do understand important aspects of intentional action and perception (Tomasello, Call, & Hare, 2003; but for a different view, see Povinelli

& Vonk, 2003). The fact that the majority of situations eliciting these skills are competitive in nature reveals something fundamental about the chimpanzee mind; namely, that it is mainly adapted for competitive rather than for cooperative social interactions. Accordingly, Tomasello, Carpenter, Call, Behne, and Moll (2005) have proposed two distinct biological adaptations underlying human social-cultural cognition. The first concerns the understanding of intentional action and perception, a pathway that humans share to a large extent with chimpanzees and that evolved in the context of intraspecific competition. The second concerns the skills and motivations to share these psychological states with others, which very likely is unique to humans and evolved in the context of intensely cooperative social activities of a particular kind.

Our proposal is thus that the human primate has evolved – on top of its competitive skills and propensities – additional skills and motivations for interacting with others cooperatively. Specifically, humans engage with one another in cooperative activities characterized by *shared intentionality* (Bratman, 1992; Gilbert, 1989; Searle, 1990, 1995; Tuomela, 1995). Shared intentionality refers to activities in which participants have a shared goal and jointly coordinate their actions to pursue that goal (joint intentions) – and both represent the entire interaction cognitively. This cognitive representation reaches beyond an understanding of the intentions the other individual might have (she intends to do x by means of y) in that so-called we-intentions are formed. Specifically, in we-intentions the intentions of each participant include something of the intentions of the other (we intend to do x by means of me doing y_1 and you doing y_2). This embedded intentional structure characterizes simple activities such as lifting a heavy stone together, as well as complex activities such as building a house or playing a symphony. When people share intentions with one another repeatedly in particular social contexts, this results in habitual social practices and beliefs that create what Searle (1995) calls "social or institutional facts": such entities as marriage, money, and government, which are of course uniquely human and exist only through the shared practices and beliefs of a group.

The evolutionary processes for this unique adaptation are still unclear, but it is possible that premodern humans developed these skills of shared intentionality, which enabled more complex forms of cooperation, ultimately leading to the cultural organizations characteristic of modern humans. These cooperative motivations might have originated in nuclear families (Wrangham, Jones, Laden, Pilbeam, & Conklin-Brittain, 1999) and spread as selection pressures favored individuals possessing these skills because groups pooling their individual efforts outcompeted other groups (Richerson & Boyd, 2005; Sober & Wilson, 1998).

Ontogenetically, human children grow up in the midst of all of these cooperative activities. Their emerging understanding of shared intentionality enables them to participate in an increasing number of interactions involving joint attention, cooperative communication, the use of artifacts and symbols, as well as normative social practices (the way we "ought" to do it). This understanding cannot be taken for granted, and indeed there are some individuals who are not equipped biologically to learn to participate in cultural activities. These are individuals with autism. Children with autism grow up in essentially the same environment as other children, but because of their biological deficit, they cannot participate in the cultural and symbolic activities around them in the species-typical manner. The development of human cognitive skills thus depends both on a species-typical cultural environment and on biologically evolved skills for participating meaningfully in such an environment.

2. The Ontogeny of Cultural Cognition

Perhaps the best place to observe the unique aspects of human cognition is in human infants and young children, as their

species-typical cognitive skills are first beginning to emerge. Comparison to nonhuman
primates helps to identify what are indeed
the species-unique aspects.

Cooperative Activities in the Second Year of Life

Human children do not just go around pursuing their own individual goals; they also
are interested in and concerned for others.
Thus, starting at around their first birthdays, infants show concern for others in
distress and occasionally comfort them (for
an overview, see Eisenberg & Fabes, 1998).
In experimental studies, infants at eighteen months of age – and to some extent
even fourteen-month-olds – perform spontaneous acts of helping (Warneken &
Tomasello, 2006) by, for example, helping
an adult retrieve an out-of-reach object or
opening the doors of a cabinet for him or
her. To engage in these helpful acts, the
children had to both understand the other's
unachieved goal and be motivated to altruistically help her to achieve it. This shows that
young children can use their understanding
of intentional action not only to learn from
others (imitation) or to predict the other's
next move in a competitive situation (as
chimpanzees) but also to actually act altruistically for another person. Young, human-
raised chimpanzees may also in some situations be helpful to humans (Warneken &
Tomasello, 2006).

But whereas in helping it is sufficient simply to understand another individual's individual goal, truly cooperative activities are
based on shared intentionality, with partners
coordinating interdependent roles directed
at a shared goal. The first steps in this
direction are taken when infants at around
one year of age engage in ritualized games
such as peekaboo or rolling a ball back and
forth, which rely on scaffolding by an adult
(Gustafson, Green, & West, 1979; Ratner &
Bruner, 1978; Ross & Lollis, 1987). Infants
appear to understand that these social interactions involve interdependent actions, as in
one study they prompted their adult partner to continue the game when she stopped

participating (Ross & Lollis, 1987). Infants of
this age also are able to reverse roles with
an adult in a joint activity, demonstrating
their understanding of the different roles
involved (Carpenter, Tomasello, & Striano,
2005). In a set of more naturalistic observations, Bakeman and Adamson (1984) found
that already in the first half of the second
year, infants are active participants in joint
activities. In a longitudinal study, they identified a considerable increase of coordinated
joint engagements in free-play situations at
home from fifteen to eighteen months of
age. The category coordinated joint engagement denotes triadic interactions between
a child, an adult, and an external object
or event, in which the child not only follows the adult's lead but also actively directs
the adult's attention. This shows that even
before language acquisition has begun in
earnest, young children become increasingly
more active partners in joint activities in
which they conceive of their own and a partner's actions and attentions as directed at a
third object and each other.

However, in one-year-olds, coordinated
social actions remain restricted to rather ritualized games. When approaching the second year of life, children begin to generate
bouts of coordinated social actions also in
simple nonritualized contexts, as shown in
a series of studies by Eckerman and colleagues (for an overview, see Eckerman &
Peterman, 2001). They do this mainly by
what the authors called the "imitative pattern," as the partners imitate each other's
actions in a turn-taking sequence. In a study
by Warneken, Chen, and Tomasello (2006),
children at eighteen to twenty-four months
of age were able to cooperate with an adult
partner in both novel social games and
problem-solving tasks. For example, in one
task, the partners had to perform complementary roles like one person holding a container open so that the other could retrieve
the object from inside. Interestingly, when
the partner interrupted in the middle of the
activity (as in the study of Ross & Lollis,
1987), children of both age groups frequently
communicated to the partner in an attempt
to request his or her cooperation. All

children produced at least one such communicative attempt. This shows that the children understood their own and their partner's action as interconnected parts of a joint activity. On a generous interpretation, this can also be taken as evidence that they were trying to redirect the partner toward a shared goal, insisting on the commitment to support each other's actions in a cooperative activity.

Between eighteen and twenty-four months, children's behavioral skills in coordinating their actions with a partner in time and space improve remarkably, as shown by Eckerman (e.g., Eckerman, 1993) and Warneken et al. (2006). This also marks the phase during which children become able to solve problems cooperatively with same-aged peers. In a study by Brownell and Carriger (1990, 1991), children at eighteen months virtually always failed in problem-solving tasks with complementary roles where one child had to manipulate an apparatus so that the other could retrieve an object, but children at two years solved the tasks successfully over repeated trials. Thus, despite the small number of studies in this age group, we may tentatively conclude that in the first half of the second year of life, children already understand the basic joint intentional structure of cooperative activities in social games and problem solving, and their improving behavioral skills during the second half of the second year of life enable them to establish coordinated interactions in a wider array of contexts with different social partners.

Cooperative Communication in the Second Year of Life

Human communication is an inherently cooperative activity (Clark, 1996). When human beings converse with one another they are playing the complementary roles of speaker and listener, and each does his or her part toward the shared goal of the listener comprehending the speaker's communicative intention. The speaker cooperates by expressing his or her communicative intentions in ways that are potentially comprehensible by the listener, even clarifying (helping) when necessary; and the listener cooperates by making good-faith attempts to comprehend the speaker's communicative intention and ask for clarifications (help) where necessary. These two roles are actually directly embodied in the main conventional devices that human beings have created for the purpose of communication, linguistic symbols, which are bidirectional in the sense that both speaker and listener can switch roles in using the symbol to influence the other's behavior that they influence themselves (Mead, 1934).

To comprehend and produce such conventional communicative means, especially nonlinguistic ones such as pointing, interactants have to create some shared frame of reference (common ground, joint attentional frame) in which these means become meaningful in specific situations. A point by itself means nothing. For instance, if I point at a drawer, you will probably be confused, but if we both know together that you are looking for your glasses, you would immediately comprehend my meaning. You understand that my communicative intention is to change your intentional act of searching for the glasses by providing new information. Such comprehension depends not only on the ability to grasp the embedded structure of a communicative intention but also on the ability to understand the cooperative motive behind it – that you are doing this for me to help me find the object.

This cooperative structure becomes apparent already in the preverbal communicative exchanges in which infants start to participate shortly after their first birthday – in terms of both their comprehension and their production. On the comprehension side, infants begin to follow another person's gaze direction and pointing gestures, interpreting such cues as communicative means to inform them about objects and events in the world. For example, in one study Behne, Carpenter, and Tomasello (2005) played a hiding and finding game in which the experimenter hid a toy in one of two locations and then, addressing the infant through eye-contact, indicated the correct location by either gazing or pointing at it. Already at fourteen months of age, infants chose the correct location, indicating that they used the experimenter's communicative cues to find the toy. Importantly, this was not an automatic gaze- or point-following response, but rather resulted from an actual understanding of the communicative intentions behind it. Thus, when the adult produced similar surface behaviors, but without expressing the communicative intent to inform them (e.g., the index finger directed at the target, but only because the experimenter was looking at her wristwatch), infants searched randomly. The infant constructed with the adult a joint activity in which he or she represented that what we are doing together is playing a game in which I search for a toy and you help me find it – and so the looking and pointing is taken as a communicative means to inform me of the location.

On the production side, it is in the same age range when infants make their first nascent attempts to express their own communicative intentions in putatively simple gestures such as pointing. First of all, infants point imperatively with the goal of having an adult do something for them, like hand them an object. This has been described as a situation in which they use the other person as a tool that can make certain things happen (Bates, 1979; Bates, Camiaoni, & Volterra, 1975). Second, they point declaratively to influence others' attention. When they see something interesting happening, they often point this out to adults and seem to expect them to comment back: they do not seem satisfied when the adult attends only to the object or only to the infant, as they repeat their point under these circumstances (Liszkowski, Carpenter, Henning, Striano, & Tomasello, 2004). Thus, these declarative points are aimed at sharing attention and interest in external objects and events. Third, infants sometimes point to provide information for others. In a study by Liszkowski, Carpenter, Striano, and Tomasello (2006), an adult was using some kind of instrument, for example, a stapler, which got misplaced together

with a distracter object. When the adult wanted to resume his action (e.g., picked up his papers ready to staple), he discovered the stapler missing and looked quizzically around. Twelve- and eighteen-month-old infants pointed more often to the target than the distracter object, presumably to help the adult find what he needed. In sum, starting at one year of age, infants point for three main reasons: imperatively, with the goal of having the other do something for them; declaratively, to share attention to and interest in external objects and events; and informatively, in which their pointing is directed at helping others with their goal.

These acts of preverbal communication can be seen as ontogenetic forerunners to fully linguistic communication in that the basic structure of human communication is already in place. In comprehending and expressing communicative intentions, infants demonstrate an understanding of the complementary roles of recipient and informant of a communicative act. In performing either role, they can take the other person's role into account and can switch between them, at one time requiring information (see Behne et al., 2005) and at other times being the informant themselves (see Liszkowski et al., 2006). Linguistic communication adds in the perspectival component inherent in linguistic symbols as different choices for construing a situation.

In general, human infants begin quite early to participate in cooperative activities involving the sharing of psychological states with others (e.g., attention toward or information about aspects of the world). In some theories, these interactions then become internalized in a Vygotskian fashion: comprehension of the external social interaction leads to an internal cognitive representation. Our proposal is that social interactions involving shared intentionality lead specifically to what we have called "dialogic cognitive representations" (Tomasello et al., 2005; see also Fernyhough, 1996). In dialogic cognitive representations, each participant conceives the activity holistically, with the shared goal and both roles (including its perspective) in a single representational format. These representations then enable children's full participation in cultural (mediated) practices such as linguistic communication and other forms of symbolic interaction with an interpersonal structure.

3. Children and Chimpanzees: From Understanding to Sharing Intentions

Comparing the cognitive skills of human children and chimpanzees – one of two closest relatives – is instructive because it helps us to identify those aspects of human cognition that were already present in the common evolutionary ancestor of the two species from those aspects that developed only in the human lineage. Such a comparison might also enable us to identify the social cognitive prerequisites for participating in a human culture, including in the comparison here of chimpanzees that have been raised by humans in a human environment, including exposure to artifacts and language. Interaction with humans may lead chimpanzees to adopt some more human-like skills of social behavior than is typical for their wild conspecies (the so-called enculturation hypothesis; Call & Tomasello, 1996; Tomasello & Call, 2004).

For making our summary comparison, we will rely on data from three studies involving the same three human-raised chimpanzees between one and five years of age: Tomasello and Carpenter (2005), Warneken and Tomasello (2006), and Warneken et al. (2006). The tasks in these studies were generally modeled after experiments with human children and were focused on two dimensions of social cognition: (1) the basic understanding of goal-directed action and perception, and (2) the ability to participate in cooperative and communicative interactions involving shared intentionality.

Understanding of Goal-Directed Action and Perception

Perhaps the most fundamental skill of primate social cognition is the understanding of intentional action and perception. If organisms observe others repeatedly in the same situations, they can predict what they will do next on the basis of simple association and memory. But if they are to predict what others will do in novel situations, they must know what the others are trying to do (their goal) and what they can perceive in the world around them.

With regard to the understanding of goals, the critical test involves exposing subjects to a situation in which the environmental outcome produced by an actor's action does not match with his goal. For example, Meltzoff (1995) had young children observe an actor try but fail to put a ring on a hook. Eighteen-month-old infants attempted to bring about the desired but unobserved goal (ring on hook) rather than the undesired but observed end state (ring falling down) (twelve-month-olds do not do this [Bellagamba & Tomasello, 1999] but fifteen-month-olds do [Johnson, Booth, & O'Hearn, 2001]). In the study of Tomasello and Carpenter (2005), when the three young chimpanzees were tested with the same procedure with a set of several novel objects (including control conditions), they reproduced the intended acts rather than the failed attempts, indicating that they were actually able to interpret the demonstrator's actions in terms of his goals. The same three chimpanzees showed their understanding of goal-directed action also in a similar study in which they successfully reproduced actions an actor produced on purpose while basically ignoring those he produced by accident (signaled by the vocal marker "Whoops!"; for the original study with fourteen-month-old infants, see Carpenter, Akhtar, & Tomasello, 1998).

Beyond the realm of social learning, there is another context in which the understanding of unachieved goals is crucial: helping. To successfully help another person, one has to have not only an altruistic motivation but also an understanding of the goal that the other cannot achieve. To test this, the helping tasks developed for the human infant study were adapted for the three human-raised chimpanzees (Warneken & Tomasello, 2006). As it turned out, all three chimpanzees helped the human caregiver by handing her objects she was unsuccessfully reaching for – for example, after she had accidentally dropped them on the floor (and did not bring them when she had discarded them intentionally). However, the chimpanzees did not help in the other kinds of situations with more complex goals (e.g., completing the stacking of objects, opening a door for the other). These findings support the interpretation that chimpanzees are able to understand goal-directed action, at least when the goal is easy to discern, as in situations in which a person is reaching for an object.

Just to round out the picture, we should also report that several other studies also demonstrate that other chimpanzees can distinguish accidental from intentional actions and trying and failing from succeeding (see Call et al., 2004; Call & Tomasello, 1998; Uller, 2004). Taken together, these results demonstrate that chimpanzees understand important aspects of intentional action, and they even do this on some occasions outside of competitive situations – namely, when learning about the properties of new objects and when helping another person to achieve a goal.

With regard to visual perception, it is well known that many nonhuman primates follow the gaze direction of others to targets (Tomasello et al., 1998). As did the chimpanzees in the study of Tomasello, Hare, and Agnetta (1999), the three human-raised chimpanzees followed the gaze direction of a human to hidden locations behind barriers. When an experimenter was alternating gaze between the chimpanzee and an object that the chimpanzee could not see because the view was obstructed by some kind of opaque barrier, the chimpanzee locomoted behind the barrier to see what the experimenter was looking at. Thus, these three chimpanzees knew that others see things that they themselves cannot see, similarly to human infants at twelve months of age (Moll & Tomasello, 2004).

However, despite the understanding of what others can or cannot see, the same subjects did not seem to understand that others attend to specific aspects of things in their perceptual field. Studies with human infants have shown that from around twelve to fourteen months of age they know that others selectively attend to things that are new to them. For example, in a study by Moll, Koring, Carpenter, and Tomasello (2006), an adult looked at a single object and exclaimed excitedly, "Oh, wow, look at that!" When the object was old for the adult – both child and adult had played together with the object – the children inspected the side of the object or looked for something else in the room, possibly because they assumed that the adult could not refer in such an excited way to the object as a whole that she already knew quite well. On the other hand, when the object was new to the adult, the children did not display such searching behavior presumably because they thought the adult was excited about the new object as a whole. When the three chimpanzees were tested with essentially the same method, they inspected the object indiscriminately of whether it was new or old to the experimenter.

Overall, then, the three human-raised chimpanzees demonstrated an understanding of perception – they know what others see even when that differs from what they themselves see – but they did not understand that humans selectively attend to things depending on what is new to them. This failure might be because chimpanzees simply do not understand that humans get excited about new rather than old things. It is also possible, however, that human infants but not chimpanzees can distinguish between aspects of the world that they have and have not previously shared with others in episodes of joint attention (see Moll & Tomasello, 2004). Thus, their failure in this task might reflect their general lack of skills and motivation for joint attention (see the subsequent section).

Understanding Shared Intentionality

Chimpanzees in the wild do many things in small groups, including hunting for monkeys (Boesch & Boesch-Achermann, 2000).

In experimental studies, chimpanzees will work together, under some circumstances, to obtain food, demonstrating in the process an understanding that the partner is needed and selecting the partners that work best (Melis et al., 2006). These behaviors from the wild and the laboratory could all be called "cooperative," in the general sense of the term, but it is not clear whether they are underlain more specifically by shared goals and intentions; that is, by skills and motivations for shared intentionality.

Warneken et al. (2006) adapted the four cooperation tasks from their experiment with children to test the three human-raised chimpanzees on their skills to engage in cooperative activities with their human caregiver. The chimpanzees were able to solve problem-solving tasks with food as target object (e.g., by lifting a door so that the partner could retrieve it for them), but they showed no interest in social games with no external goal as such. Most important, when the partner interrupted the activity by not performing her role, the chimpanzees never once attempted to reengage her actions. The chimpanzees instead tried to solve the task alone or disengage from the task completely, which suggests that they did not conceive of the activity as one involving two roles directed at a shared goal. This stands in stark contrast to the human children at eighteen and twenty-four months of age, who reliably produced such reengagement attempts.

Similarly, the three chimpanzees did not show evidence for role-reversal in simple social games such as one person holding out a plate and the other placing an object on top (Tomasello & Carpenter, 2005). The chimpanzees performed either action but did not perform it in a manner that could be interpreted as an overt invitation to the partner to take her turn. In contrast, human children at eighteen months – occasionally already at twelve months – reverse roles spontaneously. When they start out with one role (e.g., placing the object on top), they switch to the other role of holding out the plate for the partner, with an expectant look to the other's face (Carpenter et al.,

2005). The interpretation here is that human children – but not chimpanzees – understand joint activities from a bird's-eye view in which the shared goal and both roles are part of one representational format, and so easily reversed if needed.

In terms of cooperative communication, it is very interesting that chimpanzees basically never point out things to one another, show things to one another, or instruct one another intentionally (Tomasello, 2006). Human infants do these things from around their first birthdays, demonstrating a strong motivation to share experience with others. Chimpanzees do, however, sometimes point to things they want for humans. Thus, Tomasello and Carpenter (2005) found that all three of their human-raised chimpanzees produced communicative gestures from early in life. However, all of the gestures by the three human-raised chimpanzees were imperatives for action, such as pointing to distant objects to have the human retrieve it for them. Similarly, all three chimpanzees used more proximal gestures such as giving a closed container to their caregiver when they could not open it themselves. By contrast, they never once produced a declarative gesture such as showing or pointing to share interest in an object or an event, behaviors that are very common in human infants from around twelve months of age.

With regard to comprehension of communicative gestures, there is no indication that the three chimpanzees understood that pointing can be used to inform others of things in the world. They were tested in a situation very similar to the hiding and finding situation by Behne et al. (2005) used with human infants. When a piece of food was placed under one of two opaque containers, they randomly chose either one of them, unable to use communicative cues by the experimenter who indicated the correct location by pointing at it, or, in a variation of this, placing a marker on top (for a review of other studies coming to the same conclusion, see Call & Tomasello, 2005). Thus, in contrast to one-year-old infants, the chimpanzees were unable to interpret the cooperative communicative gestures of others. One interpretation for this is, again, that they did not view the interaction as a cooperative activity in which the other expresses the communicative intention to inform them about something.

Interestingly, when the situation was framed as a competitive one, chimpanzees were suddenly successful. Hare and Tomasello (2004) tested mother-reared chimpanzees by directly comparing a competitive and a cooperative version of the task. When they saw a competitor (human or chimpanzee) unsuccessfully reaching for one of two containers with a hand gesture very similar to pointing, they were able to infer that this was the one containing food and chose accordingly when it was their turn. However, when a cooperative experimenter pointed to the correct container, the same subjects chose at random. Thus, they were able to read the competitor's intention to snatch the food but did not understand the communicative intention to inform them of the correct location. Once again, one proposal to account for this difference is that this communicative situation is fundamentally cooperative and therefore not mastered by the chimpanzees. Cooperative gestures involving sharing information become meaningful only under the premise that the subject views the gesture as part of a joint activity, in which the gesturer is sharing information with them. Thus, although chimpanzees are able to read the perception and goals of others, a critical skill in the context of competitive interactions, they seem evolutionarily less well prepared to participate in cooperative activities that are based on sharing attention and intentions with others.

4. Conclusion

From an evolutionary perspective, cognition is always situated. In the case of humans in particular, many cognitive skills are situated in individual activities of locomotion, perception of the physical and social worlds, manipulation of objects, and so forth. But others are situated in social interactions. Our proposal is that primates, in general, developed skills for understanding intentional action and perception in the context of competitive social interactions, and this enabled all kinds of new skills for predicting and manipulating the behavior of others.

In addition, human beings also developed some additional skills of social cognition to create and participate in highly cooperative social interactions involving shared intentionality. These species-unique social-cognitive skills enabled the creation, over historical time, of all kinds of very different cultural practices and artifacts in whose midst human children in different cultures develop ontogenetically today. Following Vygotsky, we can posit that the internalization of these interactions leads to some new forms of dialogic or perspectival cognitive representations. These new forms of cognitive representation are fundamentally social in nature, involving both shared and differentiated perspectives on a single set of entities, so that one and the same entity may be simultaneously construed in different ways, under different descriptions, for different purposes. Such perspectival cognitive representations are taken for granted in cognitive science – all theories of knowledge representation assume them as a matter of course – but in fact there is no evidence that any other species develops such representations (Tomasello, 1999). Our proposal is that perspectival cognitive representations are an ontogenetic product resulting from humans' unique biological adaptation for social interactions involving shared intentionality, and that other species do not have such representations because they are not adapted for such social interactions.

Thus, we see here the basic human cultural dialectic: biologically evolved skills for social interaction enable the creation of cultural artifacts and practices, which then structure the ontogeny of each new generation of children. Children internalize the use of these cultural artifacts and practices, and the social interactions in which they are mastered, resulting in the kinds of perspectival cognitive representations that distinguish human cognition from that of all other animal species. A full understanding of any aspect of human cognition thus requires an understanding of the ecological contexts – in this case the social and cultural contexts – within which it has evolved and developed.

References

Bakeman, R., & Adamson, L. B. (1984). Coordinating attention to people and objects in mother-infant and peer-infant interaction. *Child Development*, 55(4), 1278–1289.

Bates, E. (1979). *The emergence of symbols: Cognition and communication in infancy*. New York: Academic Press.

Bates, E., Camaioni, L., & Volterra, V. (1975). The acquisition of performatives prior to speech. *Merrill-Palmer Quarterly*, 21, 205–224.

Behne, T., Carpenter, M., & Tomasello, M. (2005). One-year-olds comprehend the communicative intentions behind gestures in a hiding game. *Developmental Science*, 8(6), 492–499.

Bellagamba, F., & Tomasello, M. (1999). Re-enacting intended acts: Comparing 12- and 18-month olds. *Infant Behavior & Development*, 22(2), 277–282.

Boesch, C., & Boesch-Achermann, H. (2000). *The chimpanzees of the Taï forest: Behavioural ecology and evolution*. Oxford: Oxford University Press.

Boyd, R., & Richerson, P. (1985). *Culture and the evolutionary process*. Chicago: University of Chicago Press.

Bratman, M. (1992). Shared cooperative activity. *Philosophical Review*, 101(2), 327–341.

Brownell, C. A., & Carriger, M. S. (1990). Changes in cooperation and self-other differentiation during the second year. *Child Development*, 61(4), 1164–1174.

Brownell, C. A., & Carriger, M. S. (1991). Collaborations among toddler peers: Individual contributions to social contexts. In L. B. Resnick, J. M. Levine, & S. D. Teasley (Eds.), *Perspectives on socially shared cognition* (pp. 365–383). Washington, DC: American Psychological Association.

Bruner, J. (1972). The nature and uses of immaturity. *American Psychologist*, 27, 687–708.

Byrne, R. W., & Whiten, A. (1988). *Machiavellian intelligence: Social expertise and the evolution of intellect in monkeys, apes, and humans*. New York: Oxford University Press.

Call, J., Hare, B., Carpenter, M., & Tomasello, M. (2004). Unwilling or unable: Chimpanzees' understanding of human intentional action. *Developmental Science*, 7, 488–498.

Call, J., & Tomasello, M. (1996). The effect of humans in the cognitive development of apes. In A. Russon, K. Bard, & S. Parker (Eds.), *Reaching into thought: The minds of the great apes* (pp. 371–403). Cambridge: Cambridge University Press.

Call, J., & Tomasello, M. (1998). Distinguishing intentional from accidental actions in orangutans (*Pongo pygmaeus*), chimpanzees (*Pan troglodytes*), and human children (*Homo sapiens*). *Journal of Comparative Psychology*, 112(2), 192–206.

Call, J., & Tomasello, M. (2005). What do chimpanzees know about seeing revisited: An explanation of the third kind. In N. Eilan, C. Hoerl, T. McCormack, & J. Roessler (Eds.), *Joint attention: Communication and other minds* (pp. 45–64). Oxford: Oxford University Press.

Carpenter, M., Akhtar, N., & Tomasello, M. (1998). Fourteen- through 18-month-old infants differentially imitate intentional and accidental actions. *Infant Behavior & Development*, 21(2), 315–330.

Carpenter, M., Tomasello, M., &, Striano, T. (2005). Role reversal imitation in typically-developing infants and children with autism. *Infancy*, 8, 253–278.

Clark, H. (1996). *Uses of language*. Cambridge: Cambridge University Press.

de Waal, F. B. M. (1982). *Chimpanzee politics: Power and sex among apes*. London: Jonathan Cape.

Eckerman, C. O. (1993). Toddlers' achievement of coordinated action with conspecifics: A dynamic systems perspective. In L. B. Smith & E. Thelen (Eds.), *A dynamic systems approach to development: Applications* (pp. 333–357). Cambridge, MA: MIT Press.

Eckerman, C. O., & Peterman, K. (2001). Peers and infant social/communicative development. In G. Bremner & A. Fogel (Eds.), *Blackwell handbook of infant development* (pp. 326–350). Malden, MA: Blackwell Publishers.

Eisenberg, N., & Fabes, R. A. (1998). Prosocial development. In W. Damon & N. Eisenberg (Eds.), *Handbook of child psychology: Social, emotional, and personality development*

(5th ed., Vol. 3, pp. 701–778). New York: John Wiley & Sons.

Fernyhough, C. (1996). The dialogic mind: A dialogic approach to the higher mental functions. *New Ideas in Psychology*, 14, 47–62.

Gilbert, M. (1989). *On social facts*. London: Routledge.

Gustafson, G. E., Green, J. A., & West, M. J. (1979). The infant's changing role in mother-infant games: The growth of social skills. *Infant Behavior & Development*, 2(4), 301–308.

Hare, B. (2001). Can competitive paradigms increase the validity of social cognitive experiments on primates? *Animal Cognition*, 4, 269–280.

Hare, B., Call, J., Agnetta, B., & Tomasello, M. (2000). Chimpanzees know what conspecifics do and do not see. *Animal Behavior*, 59, 771–785.

Hare, B., Call, J., & Tomasello, M. (2001). Do chimpanzees know what conspecifics know? *Animal Behavior*, 61, 139–151.

Hare, B., Call, J., & Tomasello, M. (2006). Chimpanzees deceive a human competitor by hiding. *Cognition*, 101(3), 495–514.

Hare, B., & Tomasello, M. (2004). Chimpanzees are more skillful in competitive than in cooperative cognitive tasks. *Animal Behavior*, 68, 571–581.

Humphrey, N. (1976). The social function of intellect. In P. Bateson & R. A. Hinde (Eds.), *Growing points in ethology* (pp. 303–321). Cambridge: Cambridge University Press.

Johnson, S. C., Booth, A., & O'Hearn, K. (2001). Inferring the goals of a nonhuman agent. *Cognitive Development*, 16, 637–656.

Liszkowski, U., Carpenter, M., Henning, A., Striano, T., & Tomasello, M. (2004). Twelve-month-olds point to share attention and interest. *Developmental Science*, 7, 297–307.

Liszkowski, U., Carpenter, M., Striano, T., & Tomasello, M. (2006). Twelve- and 18-month-olds point to provide information for others. *Journal of Cognition and Development*, 7, 173–187.

Mead, G. H. (1934). *Mind, self, and society*. Chicago: University of Chicago Press.

Melis, A. P., Call, J., & Tomasello, M. (2006). Chimpanzees (*Pan troglodytes*) conceal visual and auditory information from others. *Journal of Comparative Psychology*, 120(2), 154–162.

Melis, A. P., Hare, B., & Tomasello, M. (2006). Chimpanzees recruit the best collaborators. *Science*, 311(5765), 1297–1300.

Meltzoff, A. N. (1995). Understanding the intentions of others: Re-enactment of intended acts by 18-month-old children. *Developmental Psychology*, 31, 838–850.

Moll, H., Koring, C., Carpenter, M., & Tomasello, M. (2006). Infants determine what others attend to by pragmatics and exclusion. *Journal of Cognition and Development*, 7(3), 411–430.

Moll, H., & Tomasello, M. (2004). Twelve- and 18-month-old infants follow gaze to spaces behind barriers. *Developmental Science*, 7(1), F1–F9.

Odling-Smee, F. J., Laland, K. N., & Feldman, M. W. (2003). *Niche construction. The neglected process in evolution*. Princeton, NJ: Princeton University Press.

Povinelli, D. J., Bering, J., & Giambrone, S. (2000). Toward a science of other minds: Escaping the argument by analogy. *Cognitive Science*, 24, 509–541.

Povinelli, D. J., & Eddy, T. J. (1996). Chimpanzees: Joint visual attention. *Psychological Science*, 7, 129–135.

Povinelli, D. J., & Vonk, J. (2003). Chimpanzee minds: Suspiciously human? *Trends in Cognitive Sciences*, 7, 157–160.

Ratner, N., & Bruner, J. (1978). Games, social exchange and the acquisition of language. *Journal of Child Language*, 5(3), 391–401.

Richerson, P. J., & Boyd, R. (2005). *Not by genes alone: How culture transformed human evolution*. Chicago: University of Chicago Press.

Ross, H. S., & Lollis, S. P. (1987). Communication within infant social games. *Developmental Psychology*, 23(2), 241–248.

Searle, J. (1990). Collective intentions and actions. In P. Cohen, J. Morgan, & M. Pollack (Eds.), *Intentions in communication* (pp. 401–415). Cambridge, MA: MIT Press.

Searle, J. (1995). *The construction of social reality*. New York: Free Press.

Sober, E., & Wilson, D. S. (1998). *Unto others: The evolution and psychology of unselfish behavior*. Cambridge, MA: Harvard University Press.

Tomasello, M. (1999). *The cultural origins of human cognition*. Cambridge, MA: Harvard University Press.

Tomasello, M. (2006). Why don't apes point? In N. Enfield & S. Levinson (Eds.), *Roots of human sociality* (pp. 506–524). New York: Berg.

Tomasello, M., & Call, J. (1997). *Primate cognition*. New York: Oxford University Press.

Tomasello, M., & Call, J. (2004). The role of humans in the cognitive development of apes revisited. *Animal Cognition, 7*, 213–215.

Tomasello, M., Call, J., & Hare, B. (1998). Five primate species follow the visual gaze of conspecifics. *Animal Behavior, 55*(4), 1063–1069.

Tomasello, M., Call, J., & Hare, B. (2003). Chimpanzees understand psychological states: The question is which ones and to what extent. *Trends in Cognitive Sciences, 7*, 153–156.

Tomasello, M., & Carpenter, M. (2005). The emergence of social cognition in three young chimpanzees. *Monographs of the Society for Research in Child Development, 70*(1).

Tomasello, M., Carpenter, M., Call, J., Behne, T., & Moll, H. (2005). Understanding and sharing intentions: The ontogeny and phylogeny of cultural cognition. *Behavioral and Brain Sciences, 28*(5), 675–691.

Tomasello, M., Hare, B., & Agnetta, B. (1999). Chimpanzees, *Pan troglodytes*, follow gaze direction geometrically. *Animal Behavior, 58*(4), 769–777.

Tuomela, R. (1995). *The importance of us: A philosophical study of basic social notions.* Stanford, CA: Stanford University Press.

Uller, C. (2004). Disposition to recognize goals in infant chimpanzees. *Animal Cognition, 7,* 154–161.

Warneken, F., Chen, F., & Tomasello, M. (2006). Cooperative activities in young children and chimpanzees. *Child Development, 77*(3), 640–663.

Warneken, F., & Tomasello, M. (2006). Altruistic helping in human infants and young chimpanzees. *Science, 311*(5765), 1301–1303.

Warneken, F., & Tomasello, M. (2007). Helping and cooperation at 14 months of age. *Infancy, 11*(3), 271–294.

Wrangham, R. W., Jones, J. H., Laden, G., Pilbeam, D., & Conklin-Brittain, N. (1999). The raw and the stolen: Cooking and the ecology of human origins. *Current Anthropology, 40*(5), 567–594.

CHAPTER 26

Neuroethology

From Morphological Computation to Planning

Malcolm A. MacIver

Introduction

Neuroethology is a field devoted to understanding the nervous system through the broader contexts of evolution, natural history, ecology, and everyday behavior; in other words, it is the study of situated nervous systems. Its focus is on how neural systems subserve behaviors that an animal performs in its natural habitat, such as capturing prey and evading predators, finding a mate, and navigating through its domain. Often the nervous system is examined in animals that exhibit extraordinary specializations in behavior, such as sonar-emitting bats and fish that hunt by detecting changes in a weak, self-generated electric field, because such specializations result in specialized neural circuitry, making neuron-level analyses more tractable. These experimentally tractable animals are sometimes referred to as "model systems." People generally prefer to work with an established model system so that they can build on a body of knowledge that has already been gathered about the system.

As a combination of the laboratory science of neurobiology and the field observation science of ethology, neuroethology has significant challenges, including determining how much of the ecological context of an animal is necessary or practical to import into the laboratory (for a review, see Pfluger & Menzel, 1999). Once the animal and its reduced environment are in the laboratory, another problem to be solved is how to extract, from its continuous and highly irregular activity, a particular behavior to focus on. One way that this issue has been dealt with historically (Pfluger & Menzel, 1999) is through avoidance of learned behaviors in favor of highly stereotyped innate behaviors. More recently, neuroethology has embraced model systems for studying limited forms of learning, such as the zebra finch (Marler, 1991), which learns its song from a tutor only during the first thirty-five days of life. After this period, the song is "crystallized" and does not vary.

With a behavior identified and characterized, the next step is to uncover its putative neural basis. Here a new set of issues comes into play, centered on the technical difficulty of obtaining reliable recordings of the electrical activity of the animal's nervous system. Often this may not be feasible unless the animal is under anesthesia. Options include working on a "reduced prep," in which slices of brain, dissociated cells, or whole parts of the nervous system may be placed into a chamber where they can be perfused with oxygen, nutrients, or neuroactive drugs and stabilized for recording. A better approach, comparatively rare because of its technical difficulty, is implanting one or more permanent recording electrodes in the brain, mounted on a platform that is glued to the head with the signals sent out via cables or wirelessly; this technique is called "chronic recording." Such tools at best monitor the ongoing activity of one to hundreds of cells in networks that can consist of millions of cells (and only the electrical activity, at that). Larger-scale properties, spanning multiple networks, biomechanics, and behavior, are sometimes examined through the development of computer models of individual components that are then recombined *in computo* in simulation environments, an endeavor sometimes referred to as "computational neuroethology" (Chiel & Beer, 1997; Cliff, 1995). This then is the neuroethologist's modus operandi: find an animal offering certain experimental conveniences such as behavioral specializations, identify and quantify a behavior, and measure its neural correlates, if possible in the "awake, behaving animal," or if not, in some reduced preparation while delivering stimuli similar to those occurring during the identified behavior.

Neuroethology has several aspects that will be of interest to the situated cognition community. Because ethology is all about what goes on when an animal is embedded in its environment (consider the title of an important monograph of one of its founders: *The Animal in Its World* [Tinbergen, 1972]), and neurobiology is all about what goes on in the brain, often with only cursory attention to matters beyond the periphery of the head, how can the enterprise of neuroethology

work in the first instance? Even if you do not believe that the properties of interest in neuroethology relate to cognition, how the tension between the outside-the-body tendencies of ethology and the inside-the-head tendencies of neurophysiology plays out in neuroethology is alone instructive. That these aspects can be in tension needs further explanation; otherwise one might think that this is simply a matter of groups of scientists working on different parts of a big problem, where everyone recognizes that a division of labor is practical and necessary. Neurophysiological approaches often implicitly suggest that many, perhaps most, components of the nervous system can be understood without examining an animal's larger context, be it behavioral, biomechanical, or evolutionary. In contrast, neuroethologists believe that unless the larger context is understood – for example, by quantifying the profile of sensory signals that an animal is subject to in its habitat or by placing neural characters of related animals into phylogenetic trees ("neurocladistics") – many aspects of neural function will not be understood. Exemplifying this point, in several model systems neuroethologists have found that neural circuits involved in sensory processing exhibit very different response properties when they are subjected to naturalistic stimuli than to the nonnaturalistic stimuli more commonly used in neurobiology, because these are easier to generate and manipulate experimentally (see Sharpee et al., 2006, and references therein).

In view of these considerations, in the first part of the chapter I will discuss how the tension between the inward- and outward-looking approaches of neuroethology may be resolved through excising bits of the world and encapsulating them into virtual reality apparatuses in the laboratory. In the second part of the chapter I will argue that results from neuroethology do, in fact, relate to cognition. Here I will first detail results from studies of morphological computation that expose the computational role of shape and structure in animal bodies in adaptive behavior, and then I will describe some recent results concerning the neuroethology of prey-capture behavior that may give insight into the origin of the paradigmatically cognitive faculty of planning. I will argue that the evolution of sensing systems that enable animals to perceive their environment far beyond the bounds of where they are immediately moving, possessing a *buena vista*, if you will, is key to the origin of planning. I call this the Buena Vista Sensing Club hypothesis. Through planning, members of the Buena Vista Sensing Club are able to make better use of this space in the guidance of their behavior than their more reactive *mala vista* brethren.

1. Internalism, Externalism, and Virtual Worlds in Neuroethology

The methodological and philosophical basis of neuroethology takes the situatedness of organisms as a basic fact and works forward from there. Both traditional cognitive science and much of neurobiology differ in emphasis, focusing on what goes on in the head (Clark, 1997; Hutchins, 1995; Noë, 2004; Rowlands, 1999; Wilson, 1995). This craniocentric approach often goes by the label of "internalism." What is variously called "situated cognition," "embodied cognition" (Ballard, Hayhoe, Pook, & Rao, 1997; Haugeland, 1998), "distributed cognition," "sensorimotor accounts of perception" (O'Regan & Noë, 2001), "active externalism" (Clark & Chalmers, 1998), "enactive externalism" (Noë, 2004), and "wide computationalism" (Wilson, 1994) all share the view that the properties of interest can depend on the head plus body plus environment. I will refer to these different approaches as "externalism."

Although situatedness is basic to neuroethology, as alluded to in the introduction, it is true that its two contributing disciplines pull in different directions: ethology to externalism and neurobiology to internalism. How is this tension resolved in neuroethology? Consider investigations into the sensory systems of two popular model systems in neuroethology, both nocturnal animals that – like miners wearing headlamps – provide their own source of illumination for perceiving their dark environments: sonar-emitting bats and electric field–emitting fish (Figure 26.1a and 26.1c). For both model systems a substantial part of the sensory system exists in the interplay between generated signals and objects in the environment (Nelson & MacIver, 2006). Thus, a fundamental part of the literature is devoted to describing and analyzing how the self-generated signals propagate and interact with the environment – characterizing the sensory system as it operates outside of the body of these animals (on bats, see Boonman & Jones, 2002; Ghose & Moss, 2003; Hartley & Suthers, 1989; Miller & Surlykke, 2001; Parsons, Thorpe, & Dawson, 1997; Schnitzler, Moss, & Denzinger, 2003; on fish, see Assad, Rasnow, & Stoddard, 1999; Chen, House, Krahe, & Nelson, 2005; Rasnow, 1996; Rasnow & Bower, 1996). Recently, this work has been referred to as research into the sensory ecology of an animal (Barth & Schmid, 2001; Dusenbery, 1992). In these studies, the nervous system of the animal may hardly be mentioned.

Whereas the externalist tendencies of neuroethology have their most literal form in the context of this work on the active-sensing model systems of bats and weakly electric fish, the focus on the relevant aspects of the external world in behavior is pervasive in the discipline, from characterization of odor plumes for studies of moths (Murlis, Willis, & Carde, 2000) to reconstruction of what a fly sees while it is buzzing around in an open field (van Hateren, Kern, Schwerdtfeger, & Egelhaaf, 2005). As pointed out by James J. Gibson (1979, p. 57), the pioneer of ecological approaches to perception, mechanical signals in the environment (stress, strain, pressure, inertia, gravity, friction, drag) are no less important in understanding behavior than are sensory signals in the environment. Neuroethologists therefore have an increasing stake in investigating mechanical factors with respect to both the animal and the environment (e.g., Chiel & Beer, 1997; Dickinson, 1996; Full & Tu, 1991; MacIver, Fontaine, & Burdick, 2004).

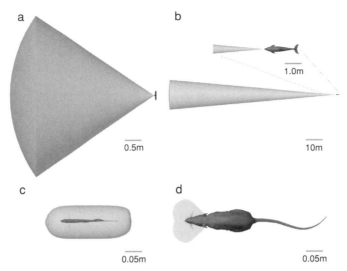

Figure 26.1. Sensory volumes of different active sensing animals. **a.** Bat echolocation beam; the illustrated range is the estimated detection range for small prey (mosquitoes) averaged across several bat species. **b.** Dolphin; the illustrated range is the estimated detection range for a prey-sized, water-filled sphere. **c.** Weakly electric fish; the illustrated range is the estimated detection range for small prey (water fleas). **d.** Rat whisker system. Reproduced with permission from Nelson and MacIver (2006).

In parallel with sensory ecology, I refer to this as an animal's "mechanical ecology."

Those with internalist leanings should not fear, however. First, there is the safe refuge of the cognitive; to take this refuge, the internalist would argue that what we are considering here are not cognitive properties in the first instance, whereas only the notion that cognition depends on the brain was at issue. I will return to this point later. Aside from this defense from the irrelevance of neuroethology, recall that the modus operandi of the neuroethologist is to eventually relate natural behaviors to neuronal structures. This is done by recording neural activity either in awake, behaving animals or, more often, in fixed and anesthetized, or otherwise drastically reduced, forms (e.g., brain slices). "Aha!" our internalist interlocutor will exclaim, "Now we get to the important business: what you are really interested in is what goes on in the brain; you're not stuffing recording electrodes into the environment, are you?" There is some sense to the internalist's intuition in this

case. My argument is not that the important properties of interest depend on the brain alone, which internalism would insist on (at least for cognitive properties). Instead, often the properties very definitely do depend on the brain plus body plus environment, but the elements of the causal chain that are most resistant to being understood are largely in the brain and body alone, in part for mundane technical reasons such as accessibility to measurement. Evidence for this claim is that, in some cases, we have the capability to mimic the animal's world in such a way that the animal does not know any better. I will present three examples of virtual worlds used in neuroethological research that exemplify this point (Figure 26.2) for studies of insects, fish, and mammals. These virtual worlds pass the embodiment Turing test – animals situated in them happily converse with the proxy as if it were the real deal.

The first example is from work at the Max Planck Center for Biological Cybernetics, in Tübingen, Germany, in the late 1960s.

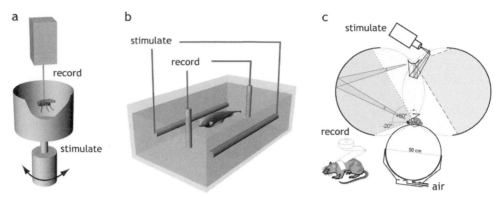

Figure 26.2. Three virtual worlds in neuroethology. **a.** Reichardt's closed-loop apparatus for the study of optomotor responses in house flies (Reichardt & Wenking, 1969). The fly is tethered on a rigid rod that senses the torques generated by the fly as it steers left or right and moves the surrounding visual panorama complementary to the motions that would naturally result from those torques. Modified from Reichardt and Poggio (1976). **b.** A closed-loop apparatus for the study of electromotor responses in weakly electric fish. The fish is held in the center of the tank either by mechanical constraint (not shown) or paralyzed by a drug and placed into a holder (not shown). Two graphite rods parallel to the fish deliver an electric field similar to what a nearby fish would emit. By bringing the frequency of the delivered field close to that of the fish in the tank (monitored via the vertical graphite rods), an electromotor behavior, the jamming-avoidance response, is triggered and sustained by following the fish's frequency changes. Similar to the apparatus in Watanabe and Takeda (1963). **c.** A closed-loop apparatus for studying the behavior of rats, based on Dahmen's (1980) similar device for insects and Götz and Gambke's (1968) servosphere. The ball is suspended by an air cushion. The animal walks while tethered to a force and torque sensor, whose signals are measured to alter the real time video projected onto the rat's visual surround. From Holscher et al. (2005) with permission.

During that time, Werner Reichardt used a preexisting system for recording the turning torque generated by flies that are flying while rigidly affixed to the end of a thin rod (Figure 26.2a). In his apparatus, the measured turning torque was transformed into a rotation of the surrounding visual panorama with an angular velocity proportional to the torque (Figure 26.2a; Reichardt & Poggio, 1976; Reichardt & Wenking, 1969), so that when the fly turned to the left or right, the surrounding visual scene changed appropriately. This approach has been heavily used in studies of fly behavior, from the neural basis of optomotor behaviors to learning and flight mechanics, as it enables precise control of the stimulus and quantification of behavior.

The second example involves the elicitation of an interesting electromotor behavior in weakly electric fish. These fish discharge their weak electric field at a particular frequency that is both species specific and individual specific. When two fish happen across each other in their native habitat while discharging within a few hertz of each other, they will shift their discharge frequencies (via a motor nucleus in the brain) to avoid jamming their electrolocation systems. To study this behavior, a fish is placed in a tank and fixed in place either mechanically or by paralysis, using a drug (Figure 26.2b).

The fish's electric field is recorded, and a field that is slightly higher or lower in frequency than its field is introduced into the tank, eliciting the jamming-avoidance response (Watanabe & Takeda, 1963). The approach used here is again closed loop, because any changes in output frequency by the fish are monitored and used to adjust the frequency of the jamming stimulus so that the behavior can be continuously elicited. Using this method combined with neurophysiology, the jamming avoidance response became the first vertebrate behavior whose complete neural circuit from sensory input to motor output was understood (Heiligenberg, 1991).

The third example, also originally developed in the late 1960s at the Max Planck Center, is from studies by Karl Götz and others: an insect would walk on a sphere that counterrotates in such a way that the animal is always in one place, again greatly simplifying the measurement of behavior with video and the delivery of controlled stimuli. The original version, called a "servosphere," tracked the animal's location and fed the movement back to two motors that rotated the sphere so that the animal stayed roughly at the apex of the sphere (Götz & Gambke, 1968; Kramer, 1975; Varjú, 1975). A more recent variation (Figure 26.2c) does not use motors but instead has the animal tethered above the apex of a hollow sphere that is suspended by an air cushion and rotated by the animal's own movements (Dahmen, 1980; Holscher, Schnee, Dahmen, Setia, & Mallot, 2005). It comes as no surprise that two of these three examples stem from an institute devoted to cybernetics. For more details on this tradition see Eliasmith (this volume).

One response to these examples would be that this proves the internalist's point – the world does not matter; all one needs is to synthesize and input the right kind of signals. However, Alva Noë (2004, p. 224) makes a convincing case that far from being a triumph of internalism, the success of virtual reality scenarios is precisely what an externalist should hope for: it demonstrates that the elicited behavior depends on the brain plus the given part of the world. Nevertheless, the externalist may be given pause by considering the success of virtual-reality systems in neuroethology. These demonstrate that we understand the relevant couplings to the external world in select cases in a sufficient – not to say complete – way, whereas we have a long way to go to understand the internal goings-on of the brain and body.

2. Is Neuroethology Relevant to Situated Cognition?

I had mentioned that one way a cognitively inclined person might assert that neuroethology is not relevant to cognition is by arguing that the processes under consideration are not cognitive. That is, given that many cognitive scientists hold that the extension of cognition itself outside of the usual human case is controversial (Wilson & Clark, this volume), how can results on the zoo of small animals that neuroethology studies provide insight into situated cognition? The difficulty of bridging these two domains is exemplified by the mismatch between the cognitive capacities we attribute to humans with those attributes of nonhuman animals that are sanctioned by neuroethology. The attributions of neuroethologists have a distinctly mechanistic flavor, such as "encodes stimulus amplitude with neuron spike rate" or "rotates head to zero azimuth to target by comparing the intensity of sounds between the ears" or, on a behavioral level, "advertises fitness to a potential mate by the complexity of the song." Cognitive faculties, such as remembering, planning, and deliberating, have their clearest form in conscious, occurrent thought processes in humans, and their presence in nonhuman animals is not often broached by neuroethologists.

Nonetheless, an attraction of externalist approaches such as situated cognition is their ecumenical approach to all kinds of phenomena that have been previously barred from the tent of cognition. According to Adams and Aizawa (this volume), this more open approach is confused and results from externalists (1) making the error of sliding from "x is causally coupled to a cognitive act" to "cognition is constituted by x," and (2) failing to clearly differentiate cognitive from noncognitive processes. An example they give of the first error is to make the jump from the fact that the reading of a thermostat is causally coupled to room temperature to the notion that the thermostat is constituted by the room-thermostat system. Similarly, they would argue, the fact that the cognitive act of long division with paper is causally coupled to the piece of paper is a fallacious basis for asserting that cognition is constituted by the human-paper system. However, unless one leaves cognition as an unanalyzed whole, it will have causally coupled subcomponents. Of these parts it would be correct, presumably, to make the move from causal coupling to constitution; in a case like this, the thermostat really would be constituted by the room-thermostat system. The key issue, therefore, is the proper characterization of what counts as cognition. Because this is poorly defined at present, I will take the strategy of considering causal proximity to cognition, in the hope that although we may not have a clear definition of cognition, we have some intuition about when we are closer to it or further away from it. We have clear intuition, for example, that the central processing unit in a computer is more proximal to a computation performed by the computer than is the table on which the computer is resting. Similarly, the most compelling examples of situated cognition are examples in which some bit of the world plays a central role: for example, the use of external objects such as maps during navigation (Hutchins, 1995), racks of letter tiles in Scrabble to remember words (Maglio, Matlock, Raphaely, Chernicky, & Kirsh, 1999), and paper and pen to manipulate numbers (Zhang & Wang, 2005). In these cases, one can reasonably argue that drawing the boundary of the cognitive at the skin is arbitrary (Clark & Chalmers, 1998).

With these considerations in mind (if not, perhaps, in the head), I will present results from neuroethology with a range of dependencies on the external world and causal proximities to the cognitive. I should state at the outset that this is not meant to be a representative set of results; most of neuroethology consists of detailing the operation of neuronal circuits that support natural behaviors, and these will not be discussed. Even the preceding virtual-world examples are not representative of neuroethology as a whole because the discipline has a strong bias toward sensory systems and sensory acquisition, with only a few active systems for the study of motor function apart from the ones presented, such as research into the neural network responsible for chewing in crustaceans. This bias may be in part due to there being too few closed-loop apparatuses like those described previously, all of which require a considerable amount of engineering expertise. For a more representative sampling of neuroethology, I refer the reader to Web sites of neuroethology courses (Hopkins, 2005; MacIver & Nelson, 1996), surveys (Barth & Schmid, 2001; Carew, 2000; Hughes, 1999; Land & Nilsson, 2002; Zupanc, 2004), and conference proceedings of the International Society of Neuroethology.

Under the rubric of morphological computation, I will give the example of how the ears of bats perform a signal processing function by dint of their convoluted shape, and how the geometry of the fly compound eye may allow for the efficient extraction of self-motion from the optic-flow field. These two examples concern how the earlier mentioned sensory ecology of an animal, the ambient set of behaviorally relevant signals in an animal's habitat, is interwoven with preneuronal signal processing. I then briefly discuss bilateral symmetry, a ubiquitous feature of animal body plans, and the passive walker, a robotic model of human walking that consists of only rigid links and joints and yet is able to walk with a human gait. Both are examples of how the mechanical ecology of an animal (the ambient inertia, stiffness and compliance, drag or contact friction, and so on, of the animal and its coupling to the habitat) is interwoven with locomotion and control of position.

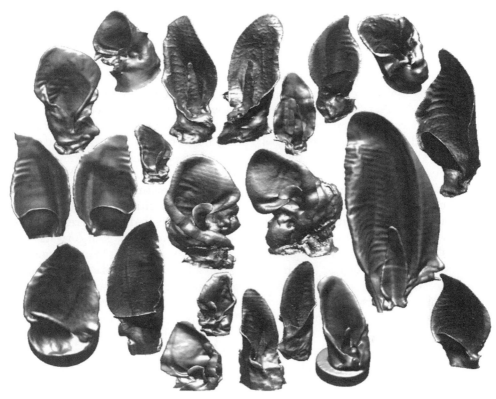

Figure 26.3. A potpourri of bat pinnae. Ear-shape data and rendering courtesy of Rolf Müeller. The pinna is the outer ear; the tragus is the small pointed flap of tissue coming up from the base of the pinna.

These two examples of morphological computation highlight the importance of transneuronal processes in sophisticated signal processing and mechanical capabilities. However, the capabilities at issue are distant from more familiar examples of cognition. Following the section on morphological computation, I try to partially close the gap by exploring how recent work on the neuroethology of prey capture may give insight into one potential origin of the paradigmatically cognitive faculty of planning. On the basis of this work, I will argue that the sensory transcendence of the space of immediate movement provides a core basis of planning, an idea that I call the Buena Vista Sensing Club hypothesis. Given prior discussions of the relationship between planning and consciousness (Bridgeman, 1992, 2003), the Buena Vista Sensing Club hypothesis may also be a useful step in articulating an empirical approach to the evolution of consciousness.

2.1. *Morphological Computation*

2.1.1. BAT EARS

Bats have been a staple model system of neuroethology since Galambos and Griffin (1940) first elucidated the role of self-generated acoustic emissions in their nocturnal hunting behavior. In the intervening years, a host of laboratories have investigated how bats are able to perform their high-precision, high-speed prey-capture maneuvers in total darkness by using acoustic pulses, emitted from either the nose or mouth. The bat is a very successful example of an active-sensing system (eight hundred echolocating species worldwide), in which an animal perceives the world via a self-generated signal source (Nelson & MacIver, 2006). From a signals perspective this is a remarkable feat, because all active-sensing animals must overcome spherical spreading (r^2) losses as a signal propagates away from them, as well as spherical spreading losses from the target back to the source, resulting in quartic attenuation of the signal with distance. Thus, to double their sensing range, active-sensing animals need to generate a signal at least sixteen times more powerful (Nelson & MacIver, 2006). As they hunt for prey, bats emit pulses of acoustic energy at frequencies of thirty kilohertz and above. The spectral composition of the signal varies greatly with species and habitat (Schnitzler et al., 2003). For example, bats that hunt in cluttered environments generate a call that has two components: a constant frequency (CF) portion followed by a downward frequency-modulated (FM) sweep. The CF portion of the call gives the bats better distance acuity, whereas the FM portion gives them multispectral cues concerning fine details of target shape and movement (Suga, 1990). During the final phase of a prey-capture sequence, called the "terminal buzz" phase, the bat rapidly increases the pulse rate (Ghose & Moss, 2003; Kalko, 1995) and switches exclusively to FM sweeps.

The bat is able to detect its horizontal angle (left-right bearing, or azimuth) to targets by analyzing both intensity and time differences in the sounds arriving at the two ears: if the target is to the left, the sound will arrive slightly earlier and with more intensity at the left ear than the right. However, an object's vertical position is not detectable in this manner. Instead, the intricate shapes of the bat's ear (pinnae) and tragi (Figure 26.3) provide cues to vertical elevation (Wotton, Haresign, & Simmons, 1995; Wotton & Simmons, 2000). Returning sonar cries follow different pathways through the pinna-tragus complex according to their angle of entry, inducing spectral cues that vary systematically with the elevation angle. The bat can then simply listen to these spectral cues to detect the elevation of the target. The con-

formation of skin and supporting tissue of the ear in the bat forms a computational device that solves a key problem in the localization of prey in three-dimensional space.

2.1.2 THE GEOMETRY OF THE FLY EYE
Movement through space creates a pattern of visual information called "optic flow." As you move forward through space, things to the side seem to move backward. The rate at which they move backward is a function of your distance to them, the horizontal angle, and your velocity: things looming directly ahead seem to hardly move at all. If you are rolling around the axis of forward motion, rather than translating (suppose you are flying in an ultralight airplane near the ground and a gust of wind hits so that one wing goes up and the other down), a different optic-flow pattern occurs. Flies detect self-motion to help stabilize flight, and neuroethological evidence is emerging that the geometry and wiring of the photoreceptors on the eye of the fly make computing optic flow a trivial problem (Egelhaaf et al., 2002). A key finding has been that the orientations of the rows of photoreceptors along which the optic flow is computed, a function of the eye's geometry, coincide with the preferred directions of the neuron that those sensors connect to (Figure 26.4). A neuron dedicated to detecting a rolling motion of the fly connects to a row of sensors, ommatidia, that lie parallel to the optic-flow pattern that occurs on the eye when the fly rolls. Activation of that neuron would then be a reliable indicator that the corresponding optic flow, and thus rolling self-motion, is occurring.

The examples of bat ears and fly eyes show how the physical configuration of the body performs a sophisticated computational role in the life of these animals. Other examples include spectral filtering through pigmented oil drops in the eyes of birds (Varela, Palacios, & Goldsmith, 1993), distinct filtering properties of ampullary versus tuberous electroreceptors in electric fish because of the presence of tightly packed skin cells in the lumen (Szabo, 1974), phonotaxis in crickets through resonance in their forelimbs (Michelsen, 1998;

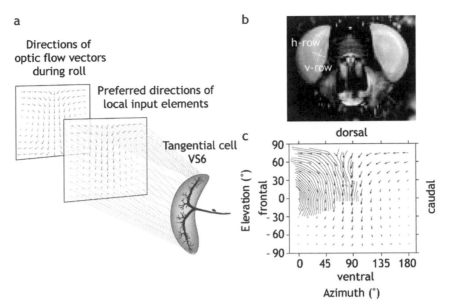

Figure 26.4. Computing optic flow through eye geometry.
a. Self-motion generates optic flow over the eyes. Arrows on the left plane represent the local motion vectors on the eye when the animal rolls around its longitudinal body axis. The local response properties of a neuronal tangential cell, the VS6 cell, are adapted to detect this particular self-rotation. It is assumed that with its large dendrite, this cell integrates signals from local input elements whose preferred directions (arrows on second-from-left plane) correspond to the direction of local motion vectors in roll-induced optic flow. **b.** Head of a female blowfly. White lines over the right eye indicate the course of ommatidial rows in the eye lattice. **c.** Organization of the receptive field of a VS6 cell. Orientation and length of arrows at different angular positions indicate the neuron's local preferred direction and motion sensitivity in the right visual hemisphere. 0° azimuth and 0° elevation corresponds to the point directly in front of the animal. Lines in the upper-left quadrant indicate the course of ommatidial rows, which are oriented vertically in the equatorial region of the eye (v-row). The direction of visual motion is thought to be analyzed mainly by interactions between ommatidia along the rows in the hexagonal eye lattice (cf. orientation of rows and arrows). In the dorsofrontal eye region, the course of the v-rows strongly shifts toward a horizontal orientation. This change in orientation is reflected by the change in local preferred directions of VS6 cells in corresponding regions of its receptive field. Text verbatim from Egelhaaf et al. (2002). Reproduced with permission.

Michelsen, Popov, & Lewis, 1994), and the role of cochlear micromechanics in hearing (Gummer, Hemmert, & Zenner, 1996; Russell & Kossl, 1999). In these cases, a significant amount of signal processing has been completed prior to entry of the signal into the nervous system. These examples show that key computations subserving adaptive behavior occur, in part, outside of the nervous system, a useful preliminary step toward the argument that cognition can depend on processes outside of the body. An important issue holding up acceptance of these points is how to relate the somewhat incommensurate form of analog computation apparent in these cases to the more mature notions of computation and algorithm complexity with digital representations (for an insightful discussion of the distinction between analog and digital, see Haugeland, 1981). This question, how computability over discrete spaces relates to computability over continuous spaces such as real numbers, has become a topic of interest over the past few years, and metrics such as the log of condition in the case of linear systems have been proposed (see reviews by Blum, 2004; Braverman & Cook, 2006).

2.1.3 BILATERAL SYMMETRY IN ANIMAL BODY PLANS

The bat and fly examples concern exploitation of structure in the sensory ecology of those animals. How do animals exploit structure in their mechanical ecology? A deep pattern connecting sensory processing and locomotion can be read in the bilateral symmetry of animals. All animals but sponges, jellyfish, comb jellies, and placozoans are bilaterally symmetrical. The bilaterian animal body plan, which appeared contemporaneously with the appearance of multicellular animals between 0.5 and 1.5 billion years ago, often includes high forward mobility along the midline axis (Grabowsky, 1994) and is closely coupled to cephalization, an adaptation that complements such mobility with a clustering of sensory organs around the anterior end of the organism. All vertebrates and most other highly mobile animals such as insects feature this neuromechanical complementarity. With this neuromechanical template (Full & Koditschek, 1999) came the active feeding behaviors and agile locomotion that correlate with the evolution of advanced nervous systems needed to control these behaviors (Conway, 1998; Dewel, 2000; Koob & Long, 2000; Northcutt, 2002; Paulin, 2005). I will return to these issues below when I discuss why the ability to sense objects distant from the body originated.

Consider what would happen during forward movement in a fluid were it not for symmetry around the midsagittal plane along which animals propel themselves: there would be an imbalance of drag forces

on the body, making the animal yaw (turn left or right) from the trajectory that is the shortest distance between two points. According to one theory of its origins, bilateral symmetry arose when a jellyfishlike ancestral form migrated from a midwater existence to crawling along the seafloor (Trochaea theory, Nielsen, 2001). Even when they are not moving on an aquatic or terrestrial surface, however, given their presence in volumes of water or air close to surfaces, all animals are more than two-dimensional creatures but not fully three-dimensional ones – even birds and fish typically move far less up and down than horizontally. As two-and-a-half-dimensional creatures, animals can exploit their bilaterally symmetrical sensory structures, such as ears, for control of horizontal bearing by simple comparisons between them, as in the bat (termed *tropotaxis*, and achieved by commissural fibers connecting bilaterally paired sensory nuclei in the brain; for more details, see Braitenberg, 1965, 1984; Hinde, 1970; MacIver et al., 2004). Thus, fundamental needs of efficient locomotion, and simple sensor-based control algorithms for the important decisions of leftward versus rightward movement via bilaterally paired sensory organs, appear to have been entrenched in the structure of animals since the dawn of their multicellular origins.

2.1.4 THE PASSIVE WALKER

Another observation concerning the importance of mechanical structure in subserving behavior comes from outside of neuroethology, in the field of robotics. Over the past several years, building on the work of McGeer (1992), Andy Ruina and others have been working on passive walkers. These robots, designed to be models of human bipedal walking, are able to walk with no energy other than the small amount imparted by an inclined plane, and nothing other than rigid links and joints. More recent versions use a very small amount of energy, similar to the amount used by humans, to walk on flat surfaces (Collins, Ruina, Tedrake, & Wisse, 2005). The implication of this work is that much of the efficiency

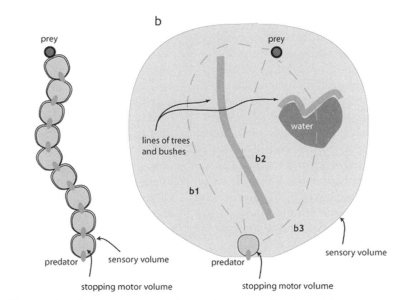

Figure 26.5. From reactivity with a *mala vista* to planning with a *buena vista*. Control and planning in prey-capture behavior as a function of the ratio between the sensory volume (SV) and the stopping motor volume (MV_{stop}) for two fictive animals: one (left) with the near unity ratio characteristic of many passive sensing animals that have poor acuity and active-sensing animals and another (right) with a large ratio to illustrate the rarer situation of long-range passive-sensing systems such as vision. **a.** With near-unity SV:MV_{stop} ratios, search proceeds in a raster-scan-like fashion through the environment. If a prey is close enough to be within one of these search tracks, it is detected and possibly captured. **b.** With large SV:MV_{stop} ratios, there is the possibility that multiple trajectories to a detected prey (dashed lines) can be assessed prior to action. After assessing multiple paths, one path is chosen (b1) that is longer than a path that may disclose the position of the predator to the prey too early (b2) or result in reaching an untraversable obstacle (b3).

of human movement may arise through having a skeletal structure and mass distribution that makes walking as energetically favorable to the body as swinging is to a pendulum. Such efficiency is enormously important: if we were as inefficient as the Honda bipedal robot Asimo, which requires at least ten times more energy per unit distance and weight (Collins et al., 2005), then with a full day's walking we would need to eat ten times more food than we typically eat. Further evidence of mechanical efficiency comes from computational studies using the technique of optimal control to find movements that minimize energy. These have derived commonly observed gaits in bipeds (Srinivasan & Ruina, 2006) and movements in fish (MacIver et al., 2004).

2.1.5 THE BONE-BRAIN CONTINUUM
A general pattern emerging from the work above is that regularities existing over disparate timescales in an animal's environment are absorbed by different systems of the body. The longest timescale regularities, such as the need for a balance of forces along the axis of travel to move in straight lines, are encapsulated at the level of structural tissues (bones, cartilage, chitin) in a bilaterally

symmetrical body plan. The maintenance costs of these tissues are the lowest of any body material. The shortest timescale regularities, such as the current state of self-motion, are encapsulated at both the structural level of sensor geometry and through energetically expensive neuronal processing, tissue which requires forty times more power per unit mass than bone (Martin & Fuhrman, 1955). The computations that an animal needs to move through space are spread across these systems. At this level of description, there is no basis for an invidious distinction between bone and brain.

2.2 *The Buena Vista Sensing Club*

The Buena Vista Sensing Club hypothesis suggests that the expansion of the range with which animals can monitor external space, relative to their usual velocity, has been one – perhaps the dominant – driving force for the evolution of the ability to plan. In most environments, distant goals cannot be effectively reached by single behaviors but instead require the sequencing of multiple behaviors. Although the sequencing could be purely reactive, it is clear that multiple approaches are possible when our perceptual world extends to a large expanse of heterogeneous space (Figure 26.5b); thus, at the very least, there is a basis for selection pressures that would lead to a capacity for evaluating multiple possible trajectories to a goal. The number of animals with the requisite sensory-mechanical balance conservatively includes cephalopods (squids, cuttlefish, octopus), raptors such as hawks and eagles, and many of the mammals. Before proceeding, I would like to address the question of why sensation jumped beyond the boundaries of animals in the first instance.

2.2.1 A BRIEF HISTORY OF TELECEPTIVE SENSATION

In his *Opticks*, Newton remarked, "Infinite space is the sensorium of the deity." In what ways is finite space the sensorium of lesser creatures? First, a bit of evolutionary background. Between 700 million years ago, the date of the earliest trace fossils of multicellu-

lar animals, and 1.6 billion years ago, the estimated time of the last common ancestor of plants and animals, all animals were unicellular and thus lacking a nervous system (Carroll, 2001; Meyerowitz, 2002). It seems likely that the nervous system is a solution to the problem of controlling the body when it is composed of more than a few cells (Nielsen, 2001), at which point diffusion breaks down as an effective communication system. Much of the nervous system is concerned with problems that arise from being mobile, and it appears that its evolution was greatly accelerated after animals discovered an appetite for eating other animals (Conway-Morris, 1998; Northcutt, 2002; Paulin, 2005). Consider the example of the tunicate, which has a mobile, bilaterally symmetrical larval stage, and a stationary (fixed to a substrate), asymmetrical adult phase: once it has reached its final resting spot, the tunicate digests much of its nervous system. Whether or not ignorance is bliss, for a sessile creature a brainless existence at least reduces the amount of grub it has to come by!

Let us consider the problem of sensory-signal-based movement guidance in some detail, because it appears central to the genesis of nervous systems. Our ancestors are unicellular animals for which, by dint of their small size, inertial forces on the body are dominated by drag forces (the ratio of these two is quantified by the Reynolds number). The simple consequence of this is that as soon as you stop generating forces to move, you will stop. Think of walking on normal ground versus skating on ice. In the former, as soon as you stop generating forces through your contact with the ground, you stop moving; in the latter, even after you stop pushing off the ice, you are still moving. In water, our ancestral environment, animals are in the viscous regime when they are below around a millimeter in size. As an animal grows larger, it enters the inertial regime, and now in the absence of active braking forces the animal will coast along through space for some time after cessation of force production. The relationship between control signals, such as those required to whip a flagellum to move forward, and the point in space that the animal needs to reach, perhaps some tasty bacterium, is not straightforward in the inertial regime. This is because the animal cannot simply halt motion at the point of contact with the bacterium but needs to perform state estimation to predict how soon before the bacterium is reached it will need to shut off the generation of force as a function of its current dynamics (Paulin, 2005). Contact sensors such as mechanoreceptors are not sufficient: you need a teleceptive sensory system – one that can detect targets some distance away from your body without contact. There are several of these, most obviously the visual system, but also auditory, chemosensory, electrosensory, and the mechanosensory lateral line, which detects flow disturbances in water at a distance. For a given object, the maximal distance at which it can be detected using one of these teleceptive systems – as one moves the object in all directions around the body – forms a surface we will refer to as the sensory volume (SV).

2.2.2 TELECEPTIVE SENSATION AND CONTROL

What determines how far away from the body, and in what directions, the sensory volume should extend to allow for effective control of the body in space? Consider the following scenario: you are driving along in the fog, able to only see a short distance in front of the car. Suddenly, a huge lumbering moose appears through the fog, standing in the roadway. You now have several options: step on the brakes, swerve, run into the moose, or some combination of these. Unfortunately, any action you take will be at least two hundred milliseconds after the moose-related sensory signals hit your retina, because of conduction and processing delays between the surface of your retina and the contraction of muscles in your lower or upper limbs. Now, if you see the moose three meters in front of the car, and you are going fifty kilometers per hour (fourteen meters per second), by the time you step on the brake, the moose is already going through your windshield. If we allow

about five hundred milliseconds for an evasive action such as braking or swerving to occur after you have initiated it (although actually it will be a function of, e.g., your velocity, mass, friction of the roadway-tire interface, braking power, speed of muscle contraction), that means you need to sense the moose around seven hundred milliseconds before contact, or ten or more meters away if you are going fifty kilometers per hour. In short, the neuromotor delay time plus the action time determine an effective horizon of reactivity; if you sense things inside of that horizon, you are powerless; if you sense things outside of the horizon, you will at least have time for the most basic of actions. This example gives a sense of the dynamic considerations involved in determining how far the sensory volume should extend in the direction of movement. As you extend your sensory volume beyond the horizon of reactivity, you allow for more than simple reactive control strategies, such as braking or swerving. With a *buena vista*, you can look far ahead and execute long-duration plans such as multiple lane changes prior to an exit. However, note that these considerations only apply to less predictable features of the space – a situation where, as Haugeland (1998) nicely puts it, "perception is cheap, representation expensive" (p. 219). In less dynamic contexts, such as long-range navigation, and where perception is costly, guiding movement through internalized spatial maps may be more effective. If, for example, that moose on the road in front of you is actually stuffed, and has been inconveniently installed in the center of the road, you could eventually learn to avoid it early on, on the basis of your recognition, say, that it is just past the hairpin turn before Crazy Bob's Taxidermy and Pedicure. This represents the internalization of space in a form that, other than issues of changes in the space and the need to localize your position in the space, may be interchangeable with sensation. I will return to this point to discuss reports that active-sensing animals possess highly accurate spatial maps.

Whereas we have the concept of sensing range for discussing how the sensory volume relates to control, there is no analogous concept for movement. In control theory, a discipline of engineering, where something can move over a given time span is called the "small-time reachable set," and I propose that this concept provides a usable motor system analogue to sensing range. To define it, we begin with a mechanical system characterized by a set of time-varying control inputs (e.g., for a car it could be rear-wheel rotational position and front-wheel steering angle). For this mechanical system one can estimate the small-time reachable set to be the region of space that the mechanical system can reach over a given time interval for all feasible control inputs (i.e., inputs that do not exceed the capacity of the system, such as a ninety-degree turning angle or acceleration beyond the power of the engine). The original work in this area concerns reachable sets of a kinematic car (e.g., Vendittelli, Laumond, & Nissoux, 1999), but more recent work treats the computation of reachable sets for continuous dynamical systems (Mitchell, Bayen, & Tomlin, 2005).

With the concept of the small-time reachable set, along with the notion of the sensory volume, I can address how the relative sizes of movement and sensing volumes relate to behavioral control. I will do this in the context of one popular model system for the study of sensory processing in animals, the weakly electric fish.

2.2.3 MOVEMENT AND SENSING SPACES IN WEAKLY ELECTRIC FISH

For studies of the weakly electric fish *Apteronotus albifrons*, the black-ghost knife fish, my colleagues and I have applied the concept of the small-time reachable set (hereafter termed the motor volume, MV) to determine the extent of the overlap between the motor volume and the sensory volume for detection and capture of prey (Snyder, Burdick, Nelson, & MacIver, 2007). As an object enters the weak electric field that the fish continually emits, distortions in the electric field are picked up by around fourteen thousand electroreceptors covering the entire body surface. These distortions

in the field are analyzed and used to direct subsequent behavior. Using the electric field and sensors as a teleceptive active-sensing system, the fish is able to hunt at night in the muddy rivers of the Amazon basin.

We quantified the three-dimensional shape and size of the electric fish's prey SV using a combination of behavioral and computational techniques that allowed us to estimate when the live prey could be detected (Snyder et al., 2007). The omnidirectional SV for prey is shown in Figure 26.6. The MV varies as a function of the time interval being examined, the fish's initial state, and the control inputs of the fish's musculoskeletal system over the time interval being considered. Because we do not have access to these control inputs, we estimated the MV empirically by analyzing motion capture data of these fish hunting for prey. The strategy we used was to look at all body displacements that occurred over a given time interval across multiple trials. We quantified the MV by placing a surface over the maximal displacements in all directions; thus, for each time interval, we obtained a particular MV. A fascinating and unexpected finding was that, similar to the SV, the MV is also omnidirectional, a testament to the remarkable morphology and maneuverability of these animals. Figure 26.6 shows the MV for three different time intervals, showing that it becomes larger and changes shape as the interval increases from over one hundred to seven hundred milliseconds.

We can now quantify how closely matched these two spaces are by coming up with a convenient measure of this match; we use the intersection of the two volumes divided by their union. When we examine this measure versus the time interval of movement, we find that the match is maximal at a time interval of about 432 milliseconds. The importance of this time interval is that it is close to the sum of the neuromotor delay and stopping times for the fish; it takes one hundred milliseconds for a detectable signal indicating prey to reach the brain and produce a behavioral reaction, and another two hundred milliseconds are required for

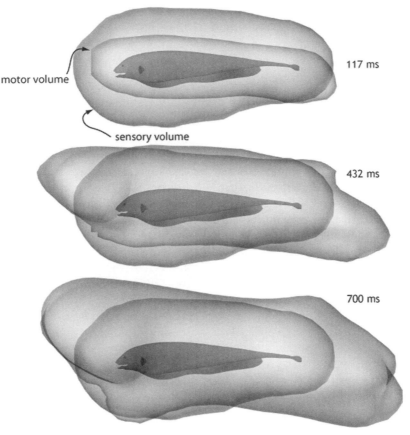

motor volume

117 ms

sensory volume

432 ms

700 ms

Figure 26.6. Sensory volume and motor volumes of a weakly electric fish. The prey SV (for a typical prey, the water flea *Daphnia magna*) and MVs of a weakly electric fish as a function of the indicated movement time. Adapted from Snyder et al., (2007).

the animal to come to a halt from standard hunting velocities and capture the prey. In other words, in an active-sensing animal, which has to invest metabolic energy to produce a sensing field, just enough energy is emitted for the animal to be able to detect the prey far enough out to stop. (Like many animals, these electric fish simplify the control problem of engulfing small prey by being nearly stationary at the point of ingestion.)

From an analysis of previously published data on bat prey capture we find evidence of a similar pattern: the echolocation SV (Figure 26.1a) is close to the MV at the sum of the neuromotor delay and the stopping time (Snyder et al., 2007). For convenience, I will refer to the particular MV associated

with coming to a stop as an animal's stopping motor volume (MV_{stop}).

When an animal needs to emit sixteen times more power to double its sensing range, we expect selection pressure against making the SV any larger than it needs to be. Here is where the great advantage of passive-sensing systems, such as vision, becomes apparent: now the only cost associated with having a longer sensing range is having a larger eyeball and associated visual signal processing circuitry (Brooke, Hanley, & Laughlin, 1999; Land & Nilsson, 2002). With the resolution of our high-acuity visual systems, about one-sixtieth of a degree under ideal conditions, we can resolve a thirty-centimeter-long rabbit at one kilometer – a distance that takes us more than ten minutes to walk at a good clip and about four minutes at a fast run. At night, and when our mechanical abilities are augmented by a vehicle, the relationship between our SV and MV_{stop} is not necessarily intuitive: we are strapping on a massive, fast mechanism that expands our MV_{stop}, while operating with low light levels, which shrinks our SV. The two factors combined with our considerable neuromotor latency result in surprisingly slow recommended night driving speeds from highway safety agencies (less than fifty kilometers per hour when using low-beam headlights; U.S. National Traffic Highway Safety Administration, 2004).

2.2.4 CONTROL AND PLANNING

How does this relate to control and planning? If the ratio of the SV to MV_{stop} is near one (Figure 26.5a), the set of behavioral options with respect to something just sensed is very small, limited to stopping, turning, and other behaviors that have simple relationships between sensory input and neuromotor output. We refer to these simple behaviors as "reactive" because there is only time for simple reflexive reactions. With simple mappings between inputs and movement, animals can embed control laws in parts of the nervous system like the spinal cord and hindbrain that feature minimal processing and conduction delays. As we increase the ratio of SV to MV_{stop}, an animal has the capacity to examine a larger space beyond that which it will immediately move several behavioral cycles into the future, where a behavioral cycle is the neuromotor delay time plus the time it takes to perform a simple action like stopping. The first consequence is that when targets of future behavior come into range, the animal has many options, and dynamics and neuromotor delays do not dominate potential response modes (Figure 26.5b). For example, an animal could sequence multiple behaviors to reach a goal, such as trotting over to a barrier, jumping over it, and then crouching under an obstruction. An animal with a low $SV:MV_{stop}$ ratio has little ability to evaluate different trajectories toward or away from the sensed object because of time and space constraints. With a large ratio, there will be multiple feasible trajectories to a distant goal. If these different trajectories vary in their likelihood of success, we would expect selection pressure to favor animals that are able to evaluate these different possibilities and then select the one most likely to lead to success.

Returning to the scene of Crazy Bob's Taxidermy and Pedicure, it is important to note that the preceding claims about control and planning are qualified by "with respect to something sensed." This is because we know that the ability to navigate through foraging areas far larger than the SV and return home is common among animals, whether they possess short- or long-range sensing systems. It appears that many animals develop a cognitive map of the larger territory over which they live, and they can index their position in this space either by using local landmarks or through path integration, where current position is estimated by updating some initially known position with each subsequent movement the animal makes (Hafting, Fyhn, Molden, Moser, & Moser, 2005). Provided that the features of interest in the space are not significantly altered between visits, it is quite conceivable that such animals could plan to revisit these features while relying only on path integration or on sensing of nearby landmarks.

In this way, a representation of space plus path integration or localization may be a good proxy for sensation. However, there are clear differences. Each unit of space contains potential harms and benefits for a typical animal. These fall into two categories: those items that are stable enough through time that their presence or absence can be internalized into an infrequently updated map of space, and those items that are not. In the former category are things such as environmental obstructions, the location of home, the level of the tide, where food has been cached for use during the winter, the location of flowering plants, and so forth.

Into the latter category is the present location of predators and prey and current weather conditions. Although there are clear advantages to being able to plan over stable features of the environment, planning over the SV is critical for predation and avoiding being preyed on. Because the shift to a mobile-predator lifestyle in the early Cambrian (more than five hundred million years ago) likely led to the innovation of the vertebrate head and related sensory structures from headless ancestors (Northcutt & Gans, 1983), any capacity that affects predatory ability has the potential to be a source of significant selection pressure on the nervous system of animals.

It is nonetheless interesting to consider some of the complex relationships among sensing range, rate at which the habitat changes over time, size of foraging area, animal speed, and accuracy of landmark-based guidance systems. For example, bats appear to prefer linear landmark features between roost and foraging area (Schnitzler et al., 2003). This preference probably facilitates their observed reduced reliance on echolocation along bat flyways (preferred paths from roost to hunting grounds), as well as allowing a cruder spatial map (e.g., less frequent location updates) than would be necessitated if the bat were to follow a more fractal landmark structure at their high flying speed. Active sensing animals in general seem to have particularly accurate spatial maps (on electric fish, see Cain, 1995; Cain, Gerin, & Moller, 1994; on rodents, see Hafting et al., 2005; O'Keefe & Burgess, 2005; on bats, see Schnitzler et al., 2003). Clearly, however, there are many different ways that space can be internalized. For example, internalization could be as rudimentary as following a trail of chemical laid down by a fellow traveler, such as occurs with ants, or as complicated as the hippocampus-dependent distributed spatial-cue binding found in mammals (Cohen & Eichenbaum, 1993).

A further difference between planning over sensed space and internalized space is that the latter may place significant demands on structures such as the hippocampal formation that appears to be central to spatial cognition (Cohen & Eichenbaum, 1993; O'Keefe & Nadel, 1978; Hafting et al., 2005). An example of this is the seasonal expansion and shrinking of related brain structures in food-caching birds (Krebs, Sherry, Healy, Perry, & Vaccarino, 1989; Sherry, Vaccarino, Buckenham, & Herz, 1989; Smulders, Sasson, & Devoogd, 1995). The shrinking and expansion of brain tissue with spatial memory load in these animals suggests that memory can be quite costly (Dukas, 1999). Quantification of this cost would allow us to assess the trade-off between maintaining a rapidly updated representation of space through sensation, with the associated costs of sensing (Laughlin, 2001), and a slowly updated representation that requires path integration or localization with the associated costs of spatial memory.

Ultimately, the tipping point between the effectiveness of single control laws versus planning (be it over internalized space or through sensing) may have to do with how densely occupied space is with behaviorally relevant contingencies, relative to movement speed and to the size of the MV_{stop}. This is similar to Levins's (1968) notion of environmental grain. Living in a very sparse environment and possessing long-range sensing systems, long reaction times, and a large amount of inertia (being massive and/or fast) is similar to living in a cluttered environment and having short-range sensing systems, short reaction times, and low inertia. The rain forest is not equivalent to a barren desert under equal sensory and movement conditions, but if the clutter of the rainforest contracts the SV or the desert increases speed, they could possess similar planning loads in this framework. In birds, it has been shown that flight speed increases with (body mass)$^{0.167}$, and visual resolution increases with (flight speed)$^{1.33}$, so larger birds with more inertia resolve objects at longer times to contact than do smaller birds (Brooke et al., 1999). In bats, prey detection range is matched to the wingbeat interval, which in turn has a power law relationship to body mass and flight speed (Holderied & von Helversen, 2003).

2.2.5 PUTTING *BUENA VISTA* TO THE TEST
To test the Buena Vista Sensing Club hypothesis, ideally we would start with behavioral correlates of planning in a wide range of animals and relate them to their sensory and motor capacities. Unfortunately, adequate behavioral data on planning behavior are not available. Quantitative data on the motor and sensing spaces of a vast array of animals other than more modern vertebrates are also lacking. Cognitive neuroscientists, however, have been investigating the neural locus of planning in humans for some time. Thus, in lieu of the missing behavioral data, we will consider some of this evidence.

In humans, cognitive neuroscience has shown that the prefrontal cortex is important for planning (Damasio, 1985). Within primates, we know that humans have nearly doubled the volume of Brodmann's area 10, a prefrontal cortical area considered important for planning, over the closest nonhuman primate (Semendeferi, Armstrong, Schleicher, Zilles, & van Hoesen, 2001), whereas human visual acuity is not significantly better than that of other primates (Ross, 2000). This may be an exception to the Buena Vista Sensing Club hypothesis. However, the ability to plan without the help of symbolic methods such as language may have reached saturation in early primates. It is possible that with language and other symbol systems, hominids took planning to a new level. Although language is thought to be a more recent innovation than is compatible with increased frontal lobe volume, given recent evidence concerning the auditory capacity of early hominids, language use may be quite ancient (Martinez et al., 2004). Symbolic approaches can effectively extend a perceptual system to encompass an indefinite amount of space for planning through the reports from fellow symbol users; one example of this is the bee's waggle dance, which allows individual bees to communicate the location and richness of a foraging patch far beyond the SV of bees at the hive. Given these considerations, comparing nonhuman primates, which as a group have larger eyes than other mammals (Ross, 2000), to other vertebrates may be more informative. Along these lines, it is known that mammals (which appear to make up the bulk of the members of the Buena Vista Sensing Club) have greatly increased the complexity of the forebrain over other vertebrates (Figure 26.7; Striedter, 2005).

One further point should be made to buttress the Buena Vista Sensing Club against complaints from members of the Mala Vista Sensing Club – all those animals with puny sensing ranges. They could argue that if anyone should have been pressured into having an ability to plan, it should have been them, because they would benefit even more from this ability than a Buena Vistite. There are three primary ways in which selection pressure to plan can be manifested. One is to evolve long-range sensing abilities, thus joining the Buena Vista Sensing Club. Another is through symbol use, such as language or waggle dances. The third is through an internal map plus path integration to determine where one is in that map, as discussed above. The first, joining the Buena Vista Sensing Club, is inapplicable, as we are addressing members of the Mala Vista Club. We will not consider the second, as symbolic approaches are rare. The third approach is possible, but we return to our previous point, that a capacity to plan over internalized space will not help with predation and avoiding being preyed on, both of which are significant sources of selection pressure on the nervous system. Whether other sources of selection pressure are sufficient to lead to planning is unclear. The presence of accurate spatial maps, and perhaps planning, in active-sensing animals would seem to suggest the answer is yes. However, two of the active-sensing modalities, echolocation and electrolocation, are in animals that have relatively recent, non-active-sensing ancestors. The ability to internalize large maps may be a holdover from long-range passive sensing habits and the exploitation of correspondingly large foraging areas – an echo of

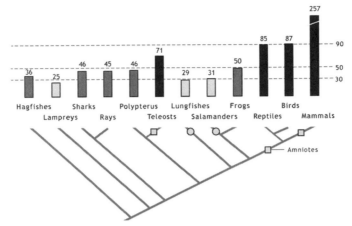

Figure 26.7. Toward a comparative biology of planning. Phylogenetic tree depicting the relationships of major vertebrate groups. Numbers across the top indicate the number of cell groups experts have described in the forebrains of representative species. The symbols indicate approximately where forebrain complexity is likely to have increased (squares) or decreased (circles). Modified with permission from Striedter (2005).

an ancestral condition when perception was cheaper.

3. Conclusion

I began with a précis of how neuroethology navigates the sometimes contested realm of its own externalist and internalist leanings. In excising a piece of the world with an animal and coupling these together in closed-loop apparatuses, neuroethology recognizes the unity of the external and internal in adaptive behavior. The virtual world examples also show that in some cases we understand the relevant external factors needed to elicit natural behaviors, whereas the neural and biomechanical underpinnings of these behaviors are still largely not understood; this in some measure supports an internalist bias in effort if not in philosophy.

As the first of two steps from neuroethology to situated cognition, I showed how present research on situated nervous systems within neuroethology is indicating the important computational role of non-neuronal sensory and mechanical structures in supporting adaptive behavior. Regularities in the world at multiple timescales

are encapsulated in the animal at a host of levels from structural tissues to neural responses, according to the temporal bandwidth of these regularities and associated energy trade-offs. For the second step, I elucidated how work on one model system in neuroethology, the weakly electric fish, may give insight into relationships among control, planning, and the ratio between the SV and MV_{stop}. I put forth the hypothesis that sensing beyond the MV_{stop} may be central to the evolution of planning. If true, the Buena Vista Sensing Club hypothesis naturalizes a formerly largely human faculty in a way that makes it approachable in more experimentally accessible animals.

Adams and Aizawa (this volume) raise the issue of the motivation for an externalist redefinition of cognition. As part of the effort to understand the intelligence of nonhuman animals, for neuroethologists the redefinition is driven by pragmatic needs. Craniocentrism simply does not work for understanding the kinds of quite sophisticated behaviors that neuroethologists are working on. As suggested by the three virtual-world examples, the instances of morphological computation, and the relationships among behavioral control, sensing, and mechanics I have discussed, they arise out of a tight interplay of body, brain, and environment, with deep ties to an animal's environment and evolutionary history.

I will end with some points about the implications of the Buena Vista Sensing Club hypothesis as it relates to extended mind issues and consciousness. In Clark and Chalmers's (1998) paper on the extended mind, they give the example of Otto the Alzheimer's patient and Inga – whose memory is unimpaired – determining the address of a museum. They argue that the address of the museum in Otto's address book, always with him, is functionally identical to Inga's (nonoccurrent) belief that the museum has some particular address. I would argue that the realm of readily interrogable space delivered by a long-range teleceptive sensory system can be equivalently thought of as an extended belief system; there as well, all potential subjects of perceptual fixation have the status of some type of belief in the extended cognitive system. The idea of the environment serving as an external memory story has been around since the 1970s, beginning with Dreyfus's work and later nicely encapsulated by Brooks in his "let the world be its own best model" (see Noë, 2004, p. 234, n14). Specific proposals as to how perceptual fixation via long-range sensing systems is important to cognition have been put forth by Dana Ballard and colleagues (Ballard et al., 1997). The need for members of the Buena Vista Sensing Club to manipulate this extended information space (LaValle, 2006) of beliefs to achieve distant goals would have gone quite beyond the capacity of reactive control strategies.

Bridgeman (1992) wrote, "Consciousness is the operation of the plan-executing mechanism, enabling behavior to be driven by plans rather than immediate environmental contingencies." Similar ideas were put forth by Humphrey (1992, p. 42). Consciousness, Prinz argues (this volume), is concerned with attention to intermediate-level representations that are useful for action. What I have presented here is a suggestion that planning, and perhaps therefore consciousness, was only necessary once perceptual systems delivered choices at such a distance that reactive (nonconscious) control schemes for action were no longer advantageous. The lead-up to consciousness could therefore have been a gift of space wrought by passive teleceptive sensation in a niche where such acuity paid fitness dividends. The need to sequence behaviors over this space would then have given rise to executive control structures in the brain, including working memory and attention, for carrying out these sequences, in a case study of how "it is not the animal's brain that organizes its world, but the evolutionary ecology of the animal that organizes its brain" (Reed, 1996, p. 69).

Neuroethology, with its comparative approach and close attention to evolutionary, ecological, behavioral, and neural aspects of animal life, may at first seem an unlikely contributor to the field of situated cognition. However, as I hope the preceding examples have suggested, it is well poised to push forward our understanding of how simple and direct behavioral responses to sensory input can give way to abilities we more readily recognize as cognitive.

Acknowledgments

I thank Andy Barto, Heather Eisthen, Kevin Lynch, Mark Nelson, and Rob Wilson for comments on earlier drafts, and Michael Dickinson, Mike Paulin, and Georg Striedter for useful discussions. Thanks to Rolf Müeller for images of bat pinnae from microcomputed tomography. This work was supported by National Science Foundation Grant No. IOB-0517683.

References

Assad, C., Rasnow, B., & Stoddard, P. K. (1999). Electric organ discharges and electric images during electrolocation. *Journal of Experimental Biology*, 202(10), 1185–1193.

Ballard, D. H., Hayhoe, M. M., Pook, P. K., & Rao, R. P. N. (1997). Deictic codes for the embodiment of cognition. *Behavioral and Brain Sciences*, 20, 723–767.

Barth, F. G., & Schmid, A. (Eds.). (2001). *Ecology of sensing*. Berlin: Springer.

Blum, L. (2004). Computing over the reals: Where Turing meets Newton. *Notices of the AMS, 51*(9), 1024–1034.

Boonman, A., & Jones, G. (2002). Intensity control during target approach in echolocating bats: Stereotypical sensori-motor behaviour in Daubenton's bats, *Myotis daubentonii*. *Journal of Experimental Biology, 205*(18), 2865–2874.

Braitenberg, V. (1965). Taxis, kinesis, and decussation. *Progress in Brain Research, 17*, 210–222.

Braitenberg, V. (1984). *Vehicles: Experiments in synthetic psychology*. Cambridge, MA: MIT Press.

Braverman, M., & Cook, S. (2006). Computing over the reals: Foundations for scientific computing. *Notices of the AMS, 53*(3), 318–329.

Bridgeman, B. (1992). On the evolution of consciousness and language. *Psycoloquy, 3*(15). http://www.cogsci.ecs.soton.ac.uk/cgi/psyc/newpsy?3.15, accessed May 17, 2008.

Bridgeman, B. (2003). *Psychology and evolution: The origins of mind*. Thousand Oaks, CA: Sage.

Brooke, M. D., Hanley, S., & Laughlin, S. B. (1999). The scaling of eye size with body mass in birds. *Proceedings of the Royal Society of London Series B, 266*(1417), 405–412.

Cain, P. (1995). Navigation in familiar environments by the weakly electric elephant-nose fish, *Gnathonemus petersii* L. (Mormyriformes, Teleostei). *Ethology, 99*(4), 332–349.

Cain, P., Gerin, W., & Moller, P. (1994). Short-range navigation of the weakly electric fish, *Gnathonemus petersii* L. (Mormyridae, Teleostei), in novel and familiar environments. *Ethology, 96*(1), 33–45.

Carew, T. J. (2000). *Behavioral neurobiology: The cellular organization of natural behavior*. Sunderland, MA: Sinauer.

Carroll, S. B. (2001). Chance and necessity: The evolution of morphological complexity and diversity. *Nature, 409*(6823), 1102–1109.

Chen, L., House, J. L., Krahe, R., & Nelson, M. E. (2005). Modeling signal and background components of electrosensory scenes. *Journal of Comparative Physiology A, 191*(4), 331–345.

Chiel, H. J., & Beer, R. D. (1997). The brain has a body: Adaptive behavior emerges from interactions of nervous system, body, and environment. *Trends in Neurosciences, 20*, 553–557.

Clark, A. (1997). *Being there: Putting brain, body, and world together again*. Cambridge, MA: MIT Press.

Clark, A., & Chalmers, D. (1998). The extended mind. *Analysis, 58*, 7–19.

Cliff, D. (1995). Neuroethology, computational. In M. A. Arbib (Ed.), *The handbook of brain theory and neural networks* (pp. 626–630). Cambridge, MA: MIT Press.

Cohen, N. J., & Eichenbaum, H. (1993). *Memory, amnesia, and the hippocampal system*. Cambridge, MA: MIT Press.

Collins, S., Ruina, A., Tedrake, R., & Wisse, M. (2005). Efficient bipedal robots based on passive-dynamic walkers. *Science, 307*(5712), 1082–1085.

Conway-Morris, S. (1998). *The crucible of creation: The Burgess Shale and the rise of animals*. Oxford: Oxford University Press.

Dahmen, H. J. (1980). A simple apparatus to investigate the orientation of walking insects. *Experientia, 36*(6), 685–687.

Damasio, A. R. (1985). The frontal lobes. In K. Heilman & E. Valenstein (Eds.), *Clinical neuropsychology* (pp. 339–375). Oxford: Oxford University Press.

Dewel, R. A. (2000). Colonial origin for Eumetazoa: Major morphological transitions and the origin of bilaterian complexity. *Journal of Morphology, 243*(1), 35–74.

Dickinson, M. H. (1996). Unsteady mechanisms of force generation in aquatic and aerial locomotion. *American Zoologist, 36*(6), 537–554.

Dukas, R. (1999). Costs of memory: Ideas and predictions. *Journal of Theoretical Biology, 197*(1), 41–50.

Dusenbery, D. B. (1992). *Sensory ecology: How organisms acquire and respond to information*. New York: W. H. Freeman.

Egelhaaf, M., Kern, R., Krapp, H. G., Kretzberg, J., Kurtz, R., & Warzecha, A. K. (2002). Neural encoding of behaviorally relevant visual-motion information in the fly. *Trends in Neurosciences, 25*(2), 96–102.

Full, R. J., & Koditschek, D. E. (1999). Templates and anchors: Neuromechanical hypotheses of legged locomotion on land. *Journal of Experimental Biology, 202*(23), 3325–3332.

Full, R. J., & Tu, M. S. (1991). Mechanics of a rapid running insect: 2-legged, 4-legged and 6-legged locomotion. *Journal of Experimental Biology, 156*, 215–231.

Galambos, R., & Griffin, D. R. (1940). The supersonic cries of bats. *Anatomical Record, 78*, 95.

Ghose, K., & Moss, C. F. (2003). The sonar beam pattern of a flying bat as it tracks tethered insects. *Journal of the Acoustical Society of America, 114*(2), 1120–1131.

Gibson, J. J. (1979). *The ecological approach to visual perception*. Mahwah, NJ: Lawrence Erlbaum.

Götz, K. G., & Gambke, C. (1968). Zum bewegungssehen des Mehlkäfers *Tenebrio molitor*. *Kybernetik*, 4, 225.

Grabowsky, G. L. (1994). Symmetry, locomotion, and the evolution of an anterior end: A lesson from sea-urchins. *Evolution*, 48(4), 1130–1146.

Gummer, A. W., Hemmert, W., & Zenner, H. P. (1996). Resonant tectorial membrane motion in the inner ear: Its crucial role in frequency tuning. *Proceedings of the National Academy of Sciences*, 93(16), 8727–8732.

Hafting, T., Fyhn, M., Molden, S., Moser, M. B., & Moser, E. I. (2005). Microstructure of a spatial map in the entorhinal cortex. *Nature*, 436(7052), 801–806.

Hartley, D. J., & Suthers, R. A. (1989). The sound emission pattern of the echolocating bat, *Eptesicus fuscus*. *Journal of the Acoustical Society of America*, 85(3), 1348–1351.

Haugeland, J. (1981). Analog and analog. *Philosophical Topics*, 12, 213–226.

Haugeland, J. (1998). Mind embodied and embedded. In J. Haugeland (Ed.), *Having thought: Essays in the metaphysics of mind* (pp. 207–238). Cambridge, MA: Harvard University Press.

Heiligenberg, W. (1991). *Neural nets in electric fish*. Cambridge, MA: MIT Press.

Hinde, R. A. (1970). Orientation. In *Animal behavior: A synthesis of ethology and comparative psychology* (pp. 146–192). New York: McGraw-Hill.

Holderied, M. W., & von Helversen, O. (2003). Echolocation range and wingbeat period match in aerial-hawking bats. *Proceedings of the Royal Society of London Series B*, 270(1530), 2293–2299.

Holscher, C., Schnee, A., Dahmen, H., Setia, L., & Mallot, H. A. (2005). Rats are able to navigate in virtual environments. *Journal of Experimental Biology*, 208(3), 561–569.

Hopkins, C. D. (2005). *Projects in neuroethology*. Retrieved September 18, 2005, from http://instruct1.cit.cornell.edu/courses/bionb424/

Hughes, H. C. (1999). *Sensory exotica: A world beyond human experience*. Cambridge, MA: MIT Press.

Humphrey, N. (1992). *A history of the mind*. New York: Simon & Schuster.

Hutchins, E. (1995). *Cognition in the wild*. Cambridge, MA: MIT Press.

Kalko, E. K. (1995). Insect pursuit, prey capture and echolocation in pipistrelle bats (*Microchiroptera*). *Animal Behavior*, 50, 861–880.

Koob, T. J., & Long, J. H. (2000). The vertebrate body axis: Evolution and mechanical function. *American Zoologist*, 40(1), 1–18.

Kramer, E. (1975). Orientation of the male silkmoth to the sex attractant bombykol. In D. A. Denton & J. P. Coghlan (Eds.), *Olfaction and taste* (Vol. 5, pp. 329–355). New York: Academic Press.

Krebs, J. R., Sherry, D. F., Healy, S. D., Perry, V. H., & Vaccarino, A. L. (1989). Hippocampal specialization of food-storing birds. *Proceedings of the National Academy of Sciences*, 86(4), 1388–1392.

Land, M. F., & Nilsson, D.-E. (2002). *Animal eyes*. New York: Oxford University Press.

Laughlin, S. B. (2001). The metabolic cost of information: A fundamental factor in visual ecology. In F. G. Barth & A. Schmid (Eds.), *Ecology of sensing* (pp. 169–185). Berlin: Springer.

LaValle, S. M. (2006). *Planning algorithms*. New York: Cambridge University Press.

Levins, R. (1968). *Evolution in changing environments: Some theoretical explorations*. Princeton, NJ: Princeton University Press.

MacIver, M. A., & Nelson, M. E. (1996). *Topics in neuroethology*. Retrieved October 17, 2005, from http://nelson.beckman.uiuc.edu/courses/neuroethol/

MacIver, M. A., Fontaine, E., & Burdick, J. W. (2004). Designing future underwater vehicles: Principles and mechanisms of the weakly electric fish. *IEEE Journal of Oceanic Engineering*, 29(3), 651–659.

Maglio, P., Matlock, T., Raphaely, D., Chernicky, B., & Kirsh, D. (1999). Interactive skill in Scrabble. In *Proceedings of the Twenty-first Annual Conference of the Cognitive Science Society*. Mahwah, NJ: Lawrence Erlbaum.

Marler, P. (1991). Song-learning behavior: The interface with neuroethology. *Trends in Neurosciences*, 14(5), 199–206.

Martin, A. W., & Fuhrman, F. A. (1955). The relationship between summated tissue respiration and metabolic rate in the mouse and the dog. *Physiological Zoology*, 28, 18–34.

Martinez, I., Rosa, M., Arsuaga, J. L., Jarabo, P., Quam, R., Lorenzo, C., et al. (2004). Auditory capacities in Middle Pleistocene humans from the Sierra de Atapuerca in Spain. *Proceedings of the National Academy of Sciences*, 101(27), 9976–9981.

McGeer, T. (1992). Principles of walking and running. In R. M. Alexander (Ed.), *Advances in comparative and environmental physiology 11: Mechanics of animal locomotion* (pp. 113–139). Berlin: Springer-Verlag.

Meyerowitz, E. M. (2002). Plants compared to animals: The broadest comparative study of development. *Science*, 295(5559), 1482–1485.

Michelsen, A. (1998). The tuned cricket. *News in Physiological Sciences*, 13(1), 32–38.

Michelsen, A., Popov, A. V., & Lewis, B. (1994). Physics of directional hearing in the cricket *Gryllus bimaculatus*. *Journal of Comparative Physiology A*, 175(2), 153–164.

Miller, L. A., & Surlykke, A. (2001). How some insects detect and avoid being eaten by bats: Tactics and countertactics of prey and predator. *Bioscience*, 51(7), 570–581.

Mitchell, I. M., Bayen, A. M., & Tomlin, C. J. (2005). A time-dependent Hamilton-Jacobi formulation of reachable sets for continuous dynamic games. *IEEE Transactions on Automatic Control*, 50(7), 947–957.

Murlis, J., Willis, M. A., & Carde, R. T. (2000). Spatial and temporal structures of pheromone plumes in fields and forests. *Physiological Entomology*, 25(3), 211–222.

Nelson, M. E., & MacIver, M. A. (2006). Sensory acquisition in active sensing systems. *Journal of Comparative Physiology A*, 192, 573–586.

Nielsen, C. (2001). *Animal evolution: Interrelationships of the living phyla* (2nd ed.). Oxford: Oxford University Press.

Noë, A. (2004). *Action in perception*. Cambridge, MA: MIT Press.

Northcutt, R. G. (2002). Understanding vertebrate brain evolution. *Integrative and Comparative Biology*, 42(4), 743–756.

Northcutt, R. G., & Gans, C. (1983). The genesis of neural crest and epidermal placodes: A reinterpretation of vertebrate origins. *Quarterly Review of Biology*, 58(1), 1–28.

O'Keefe, J., & Burgess, N. (2005). Dual phase and rate coding in hippocampal place cells: Theoretical significance and relationship to entorhinal grid cells. *Hippocampus*, 15, 853–866.

O'Keefe, J., & Nadel, L. (1978). *The hippocampus as a cognitive map*. New York: Oxford University Press.

O'Regan, J. K., & Noë, A. (2001). A sensorimotor account of vision and visual consciousness. *Behavioral and Brain Sciences*, 24(5), 977.

Parsons, S., Thorpe, C. W., & Dawson, S. M. (1997). Echolocation calls of the long-tailed bat: A quantitative analysis of types of calls. *Journal of Mammalogy*, 78(3), 964–976.

Paulin, M. G. (2005). Evolutionary origins and principles of distributed neural computation for state estimation and movement control in vertebrates. *Complexity*, 10(3), 56–65.

Pfluger, H. J., & Menzel, R. (1999). Neuroethology, its roots and future. *Journal of Comparative Physiology A*, 185(4), 389–392.

Rasnow, B. (1996). The effects of simple objects on the electric field of *Apteronotus*. *Journal of Comparative Physiology A*, 178(3), 397–411.

Rasnow, B., & Bower, J. M. (1996). The electric organ discharges of the gymnotiform fishes: I. *Apteronotus leptorhynchus*. *Journal of Comparative Physiology A*, 178(3), 383–396.

Reed, E. S. (1996). *Encountering the world: Toward an ecological psychology*. Oxford: Oxford University Press.

Reichardt, W., & Poggio, T. (1976). Visual control of orientation behavior in the fly. Part I. A quantitative analysis. *Quarterly Reviews of Biophysics*, 9(3), 311–375.

Reichardt, W., & Wenking, H. (1969). Optical detection and fixation of objects by fixed flying flies. *Naturwissenschaften*, 56(8), 424–425.

Ross, C. F. (2000). Into the light: The origin of Anthropoidea. *Annual Review of Anthropology*, 29, 147–194.

Rowlands, M. (1999). *The body in mind: Understanding cognitive processes*. Cambridge: Cambridge University Press.

Russell, I. J., & Kossl, M. (1999). Micromechanical responses to tones in the auditory fovea of the greater mustached bat's cochlea. *Journal of Neurophysiology*, 82(2), 676–686.

Schnitzler, H. U., Moss, C. F., & Denzinger, A. (2003). From spatial orientation to food acquisition in echolocating bats. *Trends in Ecology & Evolution*, 18(8), 386–394.

Semendeferi, K., Armstrong, E., Schleicher, A., Zilles, K., & van Hoesen, G. W. (2001). Prefrontal cortex in humans and apes: A comparative study of area 10. *American Journal of Physical Anthropology*, 114(3), 224–241.

Sharpee, T. O., Sugihara, H., Kurgansky, A. V., Rebrik, S. P., Stryker, M. P., & Miller, K. D. (2006). Adaptive filtering enhances information transmission in visual cortex. *Nature*, 439(7079), 936–942.

Sherry, D. F., Vaccarino, A. L., Buckenham, K., & Herz, R. S. (1989). The hippocampal complex of food-storing birds. *Brain, Behavior, and Evolution*, 34(5), 308–317.

Smulders, T. V., Sasson, A. D., & Devoogd, T. J. (1995). Seasonal variation in hippocampal volume in a food-storing bird, the black-capped chickadee. *Journal of Neurobiology, 27*(1), 15–25.

Snyder, J. B., Burdick, J. W., Nelson, M. E., & MacIver, M. A. (2007). Omnidirectional sensory and motor volumes in an electric fish. *PLoS Biology, 5*(11): e301 doi: 10.1371/journal.pbio.0050301.

Srinivasan, M., & Ruina, A. (2006). Computer optimization of a minimal biped model discovers walking and running. *Nature, 439*(7072), 72–75.

Striedter, G. F. (2005). *Principles of brain evolution*. Sunderland, MA: Sinauer.

Suga, N. (1990, June). Biosonar and neural computation in bats. *Scientific American*, 60–68.

Szabo, T. (1974). Anatomy of the specialized lateral line organs of electroreception. In A. Fessard (Ed.), *Electroreceptors and other specialized receptors in lower vertebrates: Handbook of sensory physiology* (Vol. 3, pp. 13–58). New York: Springer.

Tinbergen, N. (1972). *The animal in its world: Explorations of an ethologist, 1932–1972*. London: Allen & Unwin.

U.S. National Traffic Highway Safety Administration. (2004). *Driving at night can be deadly*. Retrieved September 19, 2005, from http://ntl.bts.gov/lib/000/200/251/deadly.pdf

van Hateren, J. H., Kern, R., Schwerdtfeger, G., & Egelhaaf, M. (2005). Function and coding in the blowfly H1 neuron during naturalistic optic flow. *Journal of Neuroscience, 25*(17), 4343–4352.

Varela, F. J., Palacios, A. G., & Goldsmith, T. H. (1993). Color vision of birds. In H. P. Zeigler & H. J. Bischof (Eds.), *Vision, brain, and behavior in birds* (pp. 77–98). Cambridge, MA: MIT Press.

Varjú, D. (1975). Stationary and dynamic responses during visual edge fixation by walking insects. *Nature, 255*(5506), 330–332.

Vendittelli, M., Laumond, J. P., & Nissoux, C. (1999). Obstacle distance for car-like robots. *IEEE Transactions on Robotics and Automation, 15*(4), 678–691.

Watanabe, A., & Takeda, K. (1963). The change of discharge frequency by A.C. stimulus in a weak electric fish. *Journal of Experimental Biology, 40*, 57–66.

Wilson, R. A. (1994). Wide computationalism. *Mind, 103*(411), 351–372.

Wilson, R. A. (1995). *Cartesian psychology and physical minds: Individualism and the sciences of the mind*. Cambridge: Cambridge University Press.

Wotton, J. M., & Simmons, J. A. (2000). Spectral cues and perception of the vertical position of targets by the big brown bat, *Eptesicus fuscus*. *Journal of the Acoustical Society of America, 107*(2), 1034–1041.

Wotton, J. M., Haresign, T., & Simmons, J. A. (1995). Spatially dependent acoustic cues generated by the external ear of the big brown bat, *Eptesicus fuscus*. *Journal of the Acoustical Society of America, 98*(3), 1423–1445.

Zhang, J., & Wang, H. (2005). The effect of external representations on numeric tasks. *Quarterly Journal of Experimental Psychology, 58A*(5), 817–838.

Zupanc, G. K. H. (2004). *Behavioral neurobiology: An integrative approach*. Oxford: Oxford University Press.

Index